D1252132

THEGREENGUIDE
Florida

South Beach, Miami, Photo: Visit Florida

MICHELIN

General Manager   Cynthia Clayton Ochterbeck

THEGREENGUIDE **FLORIDA**

Editorial Manager	Jonathan Gilbert
Editor	Cive Hebard
Principal Writer	Pamela Wright, Diane Bair, Paul Murphy
Production Manager	Natasha G. George
Cartography	Peter Wrenn
Photo Editor	Yoshimi Kanazawa
Photo Researcher	Claudia Tate
Proofreader	Nicky Gyopari
Interior Design	Chris Bell
Cover Design	Chris Bell, Christelle Le Déan
Layout	Michelin Apa Publications Ltd., John Heath
Cover Layout	Michelin Apa Publications Ltd.

Contact Us   The Green Guide
                                      Michelin Maps and Guides
                                      One Parkway South
                                      Greenville, SC 29615, USA
                                      www.michelintravel.com

                                      Michelin Maps and Guides
                                      Hannay House
                                      39 Clarendon Road
                                      Watford, Herts WD17 1JA, UK
                                      ✆01923 205240
                                      www.ViaMichelin.com
                                      travelpubsales@uk.michelin.com

Special Sales   For information regarding bulk sales,
                                      customized editions and premium sales,
                                      please contact our Customer Service
                                      Departments:
                                      USA   1-800-432-6277
                                      UK   01923 205240
                                      Canada 1-800-361-8236

Note to the reader Addresses, phone numbers, opening hours and prices published in this guide are accurate at the time of press. We welcome corrections and suggestions that may assist us in preparing the next edition. While every effort is made to ensure that all information printed in this guide is correct and up-to-date, Michelin Apa Publications Ltd. accepts no liability for any direct, indirect or consequential losses howsoever caused so far as such can be excluded by law.

HOW TO USE THIS GUIDE

PLANNING YOUR TRIP

The blue-tabbed PLANNING YOUR TRIP section gives you **ideas for your trip** and **practical information** to help you organize it. You'll find tours, practical information, a host of outdoor activities, a calendar of events, information on shopping, sightseeing, kids' activities and more.

INTRODUCTION

The orange-tabbed INTRODUCTION section explores Florida's **Nature** and geology. The **History** section spans from native settlement to the rise and impact of mass tourism. The **Art and Culture** section covers architecture, art, literature and music, while **The Region Today** delves into the modern state.

DISCOVERING

The green-tabbed DISCOVERING section features Principal Sights by region, featuring the most interesting local **Sights**, **Walking Tours**, nearby **Excursions**, and detailed **Driving Tours**. Admission prices shown are normally for a single adult.

ADDRESSES

We've selected the best hotels, restaurants, cafes, shops, nightlife and entertainment to fit all budgets. See the Legend on the cover flap for an explanation of the price categories. See the back of the guide for an index of hotels and restaurants.

Sidebars

Throughout the guide you will find blue, orange and green-colored text boxes with lively anecdotes, detailed history and background information.

😊 A Bit of Advice 😊

Green advice boxes found in this guide contain practical tips and handy information relevant to your visit or to a sight in the Discovering section.

STAR RATINGS★★★

Michelin has given star ratings for more than 100 years. If you're pressed for time, we recommend you visit the ★★★ or ★★ sights first:

★★★	**Highly recommended**
★★	**Recommended**
★	**Interesting**

MAPS

- 🗺 Regional Driving Tours map, Places to Stay map and Sights map.
- 🗺 Region maps.
- 🗺 Maps for major cities and villages.
- 🗺 Local tour maps.

All maps in this guide are oriented north, unless otherwise indicated by a directional arrow. The term "Local Map" refers to a map within the chapter or Tourism Region. A complete list of the maps found in the guide appears at the back of this book.

© Gino Santa Maria/Dreamstime.com

PLANNING YOUR TRIP

When and Where To Go 10
When to Go 10
Michelin Driving Tours 10
Useful Websites 10

What to See and Do 11
Outdoor Fun 11
Spectator Sports 17
Beaches........................ 20
Water Sports 21
Canoeing and Kayaking.......... 21
Scuba Diving and Snorkeling..... 22
Entertainment 22
Activities for Kids 23
Shopping 24
Books.......................... 26
Films 26

Calendar of Events 27

Know Before You Go 29
Florida Department of
Environmental Protection........ 29
Florida Association of RV Parks
& Campgrounds................. 29
Florida Department of
Transportation 29
Florida Sports Foundation 29
US Forest Service 29
Other Helpful Websites 29
Tourism Offices................. 29
International Visitors 29
Customs Regulations 30
Embassies and Consulates 30
Health 30

Disabled Travelers 31
Senior Citizens 31

Getting There 31
By Plane 31
By Train 31
By Car 32
By Bus 32

Getting Around 33
By Car 33
Rental Cars..................... 33
Recreational Vehicle (RV) Rentals . 33
Road Regulations................ 33
By Bus 34

Where to Stay and Eat 34

Basic Information 38

INTRODUCTION TO FLORIDA

© Alanrodriguez/Dreamstime.com

The Region Today 44
Economy........................ 44
People......................... 47
Recreation 48
Food and Wine 49

History 51
Prehistoric and Native Floridians . 51
First Spanish Period 52
British Period................... 53
Second Spanish Period 54
Early Settlement and the
Seminole Wars 55
Civil War and Reconstruction..... 56
20C Development 57

CONTENTS

Florida Today. 58
Time Line 59

Art 64
Visual Arts 64
Performing Arts 64
Film and Television 65
Folk Arts 65

Architecture 66

Literature 70

Nature 72
Geologic Foundations 72
Regional Landscapes 73
Climate 75
Water Resources. 77
Flora and Fauna 77

DISCOVERING FLORIDA

© John Anderson/Fotolia.com

The Everglades 82
Southern Everglades. 86
Northern Everglades. 91

The Keys 94
Key Largo 101
Islamorada to Marathon 102
Lower Keys. 104
Key West. 106

Nature Coast 124
Cedar Key 125
Crystal River. 126

North Central Florida 127
Gainesville 129
Ocala 132

Northeast Coast 134
Daytona Beach 136
Jacksonville 140
St. Augustine. 152

Orlando Area 165
Kissimmee 166
Orlando. 170
SeaWorld Orlando 180
Universal Orlando 184
Walt Disney World® Resort. 189

The Panhandle 208
Apalachicola 210
Emerald Coast. 212
Panama City Beach 214
Pensacola. 216
Tallahassee. 222

South Florida 236
Boca Raton. 238
Fort Lauderdale 242
Miami 248
Miami Beach 275
Palm Beach 284
West Palm Beach 289

Southwest Coast 293
Fort Myers 295
Naples. 299
Sanibel and Captiva Islands 302
Sarasota 306

Space Coast 321
Kennedy Space Center. 322
Cocoa. 327
Titusville. 328

Tampa Bay Area 330
Clearwater 331
St. Petersburg 334
Tampa 339
Tarpon Springs 349

Treasure Coast 351
Fort Pierce 353
Jupiter. 355

The Bahamas 356
New Providence Island. 357
Grand Bahama Island 367

Index. 370
Maps and Plans 381
Map Legend 382

Welcome to Florida

Everyone has an image of the Sunshine State: Cinderella Castle at Walt Disney World; the white sands of South Beach; 'gators and airboats in the 'glades; Sunset at Key West. Florida is one of the most colorful and exciting places on earth. But don't forget that just around the next corner are folksy backwoods, world-class art galleries and museums, pristine State Parks and centuries of history all waiting to be discovered.

THE EVERGLADES *(pp82–93)*

Florida's famed River of Grass is one of the state's last wilderness regions. Aside from the thrill of a noisy airboat ride and the occasional plop of an alligator ducking back into the water, all is peace and quiet here. There are few visitor attractions in this vast water prairie; mostly just trails and boardwalks for wildlife viewing.

THE KEYS *(pp94–123)*

This long line of coral islands falls lazily off the end of southern Florida. They begin at Key Largo, "Diving Capital of the World," progress through Islamorada, "Sport Fishing Capital of the World," and end in spectacular fashion at boho-gay-hip Key West, which if not "Party Capital of the World" is certainly the most buzzing place between Miami and Havana. In between, away from the main highway with its strip developments and resorts, are quiet Keys communities and pockets of nature, where little has changed in decades.

NATURE COAST *(pp124–126)*

The Nature Coast comprises the inside curve (aka Big Bend) area of the northwest coast. This is the "real Florida," that existed well before Disney's dreams and Miami's vices. Kick back on the porch at Cedar Key and swim with manatees in the Crystal River and you'll want to stay forever in this time capsule.

NORTH CENTRAL FLORIDA *(pp127–133)*

Best known for its huge Ocala Forest and Florida's most natural theme park, Silver Springs, North Central Florida is heaven for biking, fishing and canoeing enthusiasts.

NORTHEAST COAST *(pp134–164)*

Part of this shoreline is known as The First Coast, on account of its wealth of history. The highlight is the beautiful European-style old-world St Augustine. By contrast, Jacksonville boasts glittering skyscrapers and great beaches. Around the area are venerable ports and ancient forts to explore. Fernandina Beach is laidback and historic with a bohemian air, the very opposite of brash Daytona Beach, though away from the International Speedway and Strip, Daytona has a surprisingly mellow historical side.

ORLANDO AREA *(pp165–207)*

Needing no introduction, you'll always find something new to see and do in this ultimate man-made wonderland. The Disney parks continue to amuse and amaze, but Universal Orlando is a mighty strong contender for your thrill dollar, and when it really comes to splashing out, then it has to be SeaWorld. Yet there is more to Orlando than mega-theme parks: the city has some fine sights of its own, including delightful Winter Park.

THE PANHANDLE *(pp208–235)*

More good ol' southern than hip Floridian, this is where glades and palms are replaced by rolling hills and forests, swank malls give way to county stores, and catfish and grits take over on the menu from stone crabs and Key Lime Pie. The powder-white beaches here are every bit as good as down south and there's nearly as much historical legacy in Pensacola as in St Augustine. Panama City Beach is a full-on Daytona-style resort, while the countryside around boasts sink holes, state parks and *Gone With the Wind* plantations.

SOUTH FLORIDA *(pp236–292)*

Home to Florida's quintessential images, it is hard not to think of this region without visualizing speedboats, Art Deco hotels and flocks of pink flamingoes. Vibrant, multicultural Miami is Florida's adult resort par excellence; Palm Beach attracts an older, more monied set, while Fort Lauderdale has matured from its heady college spring break days into a fine all-round resort.

SOUTHWEST COAST *(pp293–320)*

This area is most famous for its talcum-soft white sand beaches, winning national (Dr. Beach) awards at Sarasota, and national acclaim at Sanibel Island ("America's Tahiti") for their shelling possibilities. The southwest is one of the state's most cultured quarters, boasting the fabulous John Ringling Museum plus high-end shopping, dining and the performing arts in Sarasota and Naples. Thomas Edison and Henry Ford used to winter here at Fort Myers, and their homes make for a fascinating museum.

SPACE COAST *(pp321–329)*

The epicenter of the US Space Program for more than 50 years, Kennedy Space Center is the only place in the US from which humans have been shot into space. This shrine to technology is set right in the heart of Old Florida amid some of the state's largest protected areas. Nearby Cocoa satisfies all the family with its Historic Village and surfing beach.

TAMPA BAY AREA *(pp330–350)*

With 361 days of sunshine per year and 28 miles of white-sand beaches (often voted best in the US) it is no wonder that the Pinellas Suncoast resorts—of which Clearwater is best known—are Florida's favorite west coast destination. St. Petersburg is becoming Florida's artsiest city and its Salvador Dalí collection alone is worth the trip. Tampa is most famous for Busch Gardens, the best theme park in the west, but offers lots more in terms of art, culture and, in its Ybor City enclave, lively Cuban nightlife.

TREASURE COAST *(pp351–356)*

The stretch of east coast between Jupiter and Melbourne has earned its name from the sunken booty that has been recovered from its offshore waters. Treasure Coast's real treasures these days are its wide open natural spaces and quiet, unspoiled barrier-island beaches.

THE BAHAMAS *(pp356–369)*

If you want even more sunshine—and an unmistakeable tropical vibe—the glorious Caribbean archipelago of the Bahamas lies just 55 miles off the southeast coast of Florida, a short cruise from Miami or Port Everglades.

Miami Beach
© Gino Santa Maria/Dreamstime.com

When and Where To Go

WHEN TO GO

In the Sunshine State most sights and attractions are open year-round, although peak seasons vary by region. High season in south Florida is during the **winter** (Oct–Apr) when many visitors escape colder climates. Daytime winter temperatures average 70°F/21°C, while in the Everglades and Keys daytime temperatures reach 73°F/23°C. North and central Florida enjoy the traditional four seasons: spring 67°F/19°C; summer 83°F/29°C; fall 69°F/21°C; and winter 55°F/14°C. January is usually the coldest month. Winter, when mosquitoes are tolerable and migratory birds are plentiful, is the best time to view wildlife in parks and reserves. Insect repellent is recommended year-round.

Although **summer** months are hot and humid throughout the state, sea breezes moderate temperatures along the coasts. Daytime temperatures average 88°F/31°C and do not vary much between the northern and southern regions. Daily afternoon showers are common between June and September.

The **hurricane season** is generally June to November, with the greatest activity occurring from August to October (*see Climate, Hurricanes*). Water temperatures are typically warm and pleasant year-round. Beaches are most crowded during school holidays, spring breaks and summer vacation periods. Reduced admissions to sights are generally available for senior citizens, students and children under 12.

Casual dress is accepted in most facilities. Better restaurants may request that men wear jackets, but rarely is a tie required. A hat will come in handy while standing in line, especially during the summer heat. A good sunscreen, even on a cloudy day, and sunglasses are recommended.

MICHELIN DRIVING TOURS

Refer to the Driving Tours Map on the inside back cover in order to make the most of Michelin's regional driving tours. The driving tour map in this guide includes tours of the **Atlantic Coast**; the **Florida Keys**; **Miami to Tampa**; **Tampa to Space Coast**; **North Central Florida and Orlando**; the **Nature Coast**; and the **Panhandle**.

USEFUL WEBSITES
VISIT FLORIDA

P.O. Box 1100, Tallahassee FL 32302.
℘850-488-5607 or 888-735-2872
www.visitflorida.com

AVERAGE DAILY TEMPERATURES

	January	April	July	October
Apalachicola	54°F/12°C	69°F/21°C	82°F/28°C	70°F/21°C
Gainesville	55°F/14°C	70°F/21°C	82°F/28°C	71°F/22°C
Jacksonville	53°F/12°C	69°F/21°C	82°F/28°C	70°F/21°C
Key West	69°F/21°C	78°F/26°C	84°F/29°C	80°F/27°C
Miami	68°F/20°C	76°F/24°C	83°F/29°C	78°F/26°C
Naples	65°F/19°C	73°F/23°C	82°F/28°C	77°F/25°C
Orlando	61°F/16°C	72°F/22°C	83°F/29°C	74°F/23°C
Pensacola	51°F/11°C	68°F/20°C	83°F/29°C	69°F/21°C
Sarasota	60°F/16°C	72°F/22°C	83°F/29°C	75°F/24°C
Tallahassee	51°F/10°C	68°F/20°C	82°F/28°C	68°F/20°C
Tampa	60°F/16°C	68°F/20°C	83°F/29°C	74°F/23°C

What to See and Do

OUTDOOR FUN
NATIONAL PARKS, SEASHORES AND MONUMENTS

Florida has three national parks, two national seashores, three national forests, two national monuments, two preserves, and more than 100 state parks.

Recreational activities available might include hiking, biking, fishing, swimming, snorkeling, boating, horseback riding and camping.

Parks are most frequently visited from Memorial Day to Labor Day, although in south Florida they are busiest during the dry season (Oct–Apr) when viewing of wildlife and migratory birds is best. Among Florida's national parks, entrance fees are charged only at Everglades National Park *($10/vehicle)*, Castillo de San Marcos National Monument *($5/person)* and the Fort Pickens section of Gulf Islands National Seashore *($8/vehicle)*. Prices are subject to change. All are at least partially accessible to people with disabilities.

Camping is permissible *(fees range from $10–$28)* at Everglades, Biscayne and Dry Tortugas national parks and Gulf Islands National Seashore *(for reservations: 877-444-677 7 in the US; 518-885-3639 internationally; www.recreation.gov)*.

Most visitor centers offer interpretive exhibits, slide presentations and maps. Picnic areas are provided at parks and seashores. In some cases, visitors can explore the surroundings on self-guided nature trails and participate in ranger-led hikes.

Boat rentals may be available. Most park beaches do not have lifeguards. Pets are welcome if kept on a leash but are not allowed in camping areas or on swimming beaches.

For detailed information, contact the individual park or visit the National Park Service website *(www.nps.gov)*.

Storm Safety Tips

- Take cover.
- Stay away from trees, metal objects, doors and windows.
- If riding in a vehicle, remain inside until the storm has passed.
- Avoid being in or near water.
- If in a boat, head for the nearest shore.
- Do not use electrical appliances, especially the telephone.

State and Local Parks

Visitors can choose from an ever-expanding state park system, including nature preserves and historic landmarks.

State parks are generally open year-round daily 8am–dusk. Visitor centers, museums and historic sites may have different opening hours. Entrance fees are usually $3.25–$5/vehicle (up to 8 people), $1/person when entering on foot or by bicycle. Camping fees vary according to season and location *(average $8–$19)*. To request a copy of the guide *Florida State Parks (free)*, contact the Department of Environmental Protection, Division of Recreation and Parks *(850-245-2157; www.floridastateparks.org)*. Copies are also available at official state welcome centers.

Local parks are generally open year-round daily 8am–dusk and are free-of-charge.

BIKING

Cycling is popular throughout the state, not least because of the flat terrain. The cooler months (Oct–May) are the best cycling "season" since summer temperatures and high humidity can make long rides a challenge. Bicycles are not allowed on highways, limited-access highways, expressways or some bridges. The most pleasant cycling conditions are north of I-4, in central Florida near Gainesville and Ocala, north in the Live Oak area, and on trails

11

😊 Biking Safety Tips 😊

- Obey all traffic laws and ride single file.
- The law requires cyclists under 16 to wear a helmet.
- Do not travel at night.
- Do not use electrical appliances, especially the telephone.

and greenways that link local and state parks and national forests. Beach areas from Fernandina Beach to Melbourne, and on Captiva and Sanibel Islands, offer pleasant riding paths. For more information, contact area tourist offices and local bike rental shops or the **Department of Environmental Protection**, Office of Greenways and Trails in Tallahassee (𝒫850-245-2052 or 877-822-5208; www.floridagreenwaysandtrails.com). The Office of Greenways and Trails publishes a great booklet, *Florida Bicycle Trails,* highlighting 29 paved and off-road **bike trails** from 2.6 to 183 miles long. The trails offer lots of scenic cycling, including wildlife-watching, historic rivers, pre-Civil War forts and natural springs. Order a free copy by calling 𝒫888-735-2872 or download it at www.dep.state.fl.us/gwt/PDF/biketrails_b_v6.pdf. Other sources for information: **State Bicycle Office**, Florida Department of Transportation in Tallahassee (𝒫850-487-1200; www.floridabicycle.org) and **Rails-to-Trails Conservancy** (𝒫850-942-2379; www.railtrails.org).

FISHING

Florida's rivers, lakes, ponds and wilderness waterways offer anglers some of the best fishing waters in the US. And you don't have to rent expensive boats to enjoy a day of fishing. Many coastal communities have public fishing piers where equipment can be rented from bait-and-tackle shops for a minimal fee. Fish camps along inland waterways offer boat and houseboat rentals and guided fishing trips for the whole family.

Saltwater – Miles of coastline on the Atlantic Ocean and Gulf of Mexico give the saltwater enthusiast the opportunity to catch more than 70 species of fish. Surf casting and bridge and pier fishing are popular pursuits. A variety of boat-charter services can accommodate every level of expertise and budget. Many marinas rent boats ranging from canoes to pontoon boats. Most backcountry channels in the Gulf are unmarked, so consider enlisting the services of a local, licensed guide who can lead you to the best fishing spots. For additional information on saltwater fishing, contact the Florida Fish and Wildlife Conservation Commission (𝒫850-488-4676; www.myfwc.com).

Freshwater – There are some 33 species of freshwater fish in Florida. For forecasts, fish identification, and boat ramp and fishing pier locations, visit www.FloridaFisheries.com. For freshwater **fishing regulations,** limits, and seasons, contact the Florida Fish and Wildlife Conservation Commission (🌙see above). Residents and nonresidents must have a **fishing license**; anglers are not required to have both freshwater and saltwater licenses, unless they are taking both freshwater and saltwater species. Licenses can usually be obtained at sporting-goods stores, marinas and some bait-and-tackle shops. To purchase a license, contact 𝒫888-347-4356 or www.myfwc.com. To receive a copy of *Florida Fishing & Boating Guidebook* (free), contact the **Florida Sports Foundation** (𝒫850-488-8347; www.flasports.com).

Deep-Sea Fishing – Many species can be found along the Florida Keys year-round, offering a great variety of offshore game fishing. Large "party boats" can take up to 20 people. Half-day trips are suitable for beginners, while full-day excursions are designed for the avid angler, allowing the captain to change locations, according to where the fish are biting. Most boats have a fishing license and knowledgeable crew. Prices range from $65–$260/person and up. Charter boats specializing in deep-sea sport fishing will appeal to the experienced fisherman who is looking to reel in "the big one"—sailfish, wahoo, tuna, kingfish and blue or white marlin. Charters are costly but include equipment, bait and fishing licenses.

GOLF

Ranked one of the nation's top golfing destinations, Florida boasts well over 1,200 golf courses, several designed by such legends as Jack Nicklaus and Arnold Palmer. Florida's balmy climate makes golf accessible year-round. Duffers can practice their driving and putting expertise at numerous public courses or watch professional golfers at one of the numerous tournaments that take place throughout the state. Many hotels and resorts include golf facilities, and some private courses allow nonmembers to play. Numerous courses offer golf clinics and private instruction. Make reservations well ahead of time; teeing off during midday means less-crowded fairways and lower humidity. Greens fees average $80 in winter, $50 in summer. The publication *Play Florida Golf Directory* is available *(free)* from Florida Sports Foundation (see p12).

Tee Times USA will make reservations *(free)* for tee times at more than 300 selected golf courses. Discount golf packages are available. Written confirmation and travel directions will be mailed, faxed or e-mailed. To request a brochure or to make reservations, contact Tee Times USA, PO Box 641, Flagler Beach FL 32136 (800-374-8633 or 386-439-0001; www.teetimesusa.com).

HIKING

The best time to hike is from late fall to early spring when temperatures are cooler, humidity is lower, and the insect population is at its lowest ebb. When hiking, stay on marked trails; taking shortcuts is dangerous and can cause erosion. Obtain up-to-date weather forecasts; a sudden storm can flood trails in swampy areas. If hiking alone, notify someone of your destination and anticipated return time.

The USDA Forest Service and the Florida Trail Assn. maintain the 1,400mi **Florida National Scenic Trail**, which extends from the Gulf Islands National Seashore in northwestern Florida to the Big Cypress National Preserve in southwestern Florida. All trails are marked; camping is limited. Some segments of the trail may be closed during hunting season. Before setting

Southern Dunes Golf Club

Visit Florida

13

Nature and Safety

Fauna Great and Small

A multitude of creatures share Florida's subtropical climate, including the not-so-beloved mosquitoes, chiggers, scorpions, lovebugs, fire ants, sand flies and cockroaches.

Mosquitoes are unavoidable, especially from June to September—the rainy months when humidity is high. In coastal areas mosquitoes are active year-round. Insect repellent is widely available; also consider wearing lightweight long-sleeved shirts and long pants. When camping, remember that smoke from a campfire is an effective mosquito deterrent.

You probably won't encounter **alligators;** they tend to avoid people unless provoked. However, stay clear of a mother guarding her young and do not swim in remote lakes, especially during gator mating season (mid-April). When hiking do not bring your dog; alligators have been known to attack dogs, especially small ones. Florida law prohibits the feeding or molesting of alligators.

😊 Visiting Public Lands 😊

Tips

♦ Enjoy the native vegetation, but please leave it untouched.
♦ Do not feed animals; they may become ill and die.
♦ Keep your distance from wildlife.
♦ Do not walk on sand dunes, but stay on boardwalks.
♦ Do not litter.
♦ Remember to pack out everything you pack in.
♦ Learn to recognize and avoid poisonwood, poison sumac, manchineel poison oak and poison ivy; contact may require medical attention.

Forty-four species of **snakes** inhabit the Florida landscape: the poisonous ones include several species of rattlesnakes and the coral snake. However, like most wildlife, snakes generally do not pose a threat to people unless provoked. Always wear appropriate footwear and look where you are walking.

Visitor Impact

When visiting a national wildlife refuge, state park or national forest, remember that while the disturbance of a single person may be small, the cumulative impact of a large number of visitors may be disastrous. "Take nothing but pictures; leave nothing but footprints" has been adopted as a slogan and is posted in many parks.

Hurricanes

The hurricane season typically runs from June to November with the greatest activity occuring from August to October. Hurricanes begin as tropical depressions and are classified as hurricanes once winds reach 74mph. The National Hurricane Center in Miami tracks all storms and issues advisories every six hours; stay tuned to radio and television. A hurricane **watch** is announced if hurricane conditions may threaten

😊 Hurricanes 😊

Precautionary Measures

♦ Check your car battery and fill up the gas tank.
♦ Make sure you have a battery-operated radio and extra batteries.
♦ Collect plenty of fresh water in containers and bathtubs.
♦ When staying in coastal areas, familiarize yourself with evacuation routes.
♦ Stay indoors once the hurricane has struck.
♦ Be aware of storm surges in coastal regions.
♦ Most importantly, never take a hurricane lightly, and follow instructions issued by local authorities.

an area within 36 hours; a hurricane **warning** is issued if sustained winds of at least 74mph are expected within 24 hours(🍃 See Climate, 'Hurricanes' in the INTRODUCTION).

Thunderstorms and Lightning

Storms occur almost daily in the summer in Florida *(Jun–Sept)* and can pass quickly. Peak lightning season is July to August. Some thunderstorms can be severe, featuring hail and dangerous lightning.

Beach and Water Safety

In the strong subtropical sun, visitors run the risk of sunburn, even in winter. Reflections from white sand and water increase the sun's intensity. Use sunglasses, wear a wide-brimmed hat and drink plenty of liquids. Apply sunscreen even on overcast days, since ultraviolet rays penetrate the cloud cover. Avoid strenuous exercise during midday.

Never swim alone and heed **red warning flags** that indicate dangerous conditions such as riptides. Warning flags are posted every mile along public beaches: blue means calm waters; yellow indicates choppy waters. Most public beaches employ lifeguards seasonally. Take care when swimming at an unguarded beach. Children should be supervised at all times. Scuba diving and snorkeling should never be undertaken alone. Attacks by **sharks,** though rare, have been on the increase along Florida shores recently. Be on the alert and heed instructions from lifeguards.

Stinging creatures such as jellyfish and sea urchins inhabit shallow waters. Although most jellyfish stings produce little more than an itchy skin rash, some can cause painful swelling. Treating the affected area with papain-type meat tenderizer will give relief. Stingrays and the Portuguese man-of-war jellyfish (though they look like jellyfish, they are in fact siphonophora) can inflict a more serious sting; seek medical treatment immediately. Occasionally, **red tides** occur off Florida's coast, caused by micro-organisms that release poisons into the water, discoloring it and creating a nauseating odor. The toxins have killed thousands of fish and can be irritating to people.

Boating

Check with local authorities about conditions before setting out on the water. If you rent a canoe or charter a small yacht, first familiarize yourself with the craft and obtain maps and the latest weather information. Most outfitters will offer some instruction before sending you out on your own. Always advise someone of your itinerary. **Life jackets** must be available for all paasengers; they should be worn by adults and *must* be worn by children under six years old.

Lifeguard stand, yellow warning flags

Visit Florida

Horseback riding, Columbia County

Visit Florida

out, check with the local managing authority or write to: US Forest Service, 325 John Knox Rd., Suite F100, Tallahassee FL 32303 (*850-942-9300*) or the Florida Trail Assn., 5415 S.W. 13th St., Gainesville FL 32608 (*877-HIKE-FLA or 352-378-8823; www. florida-trail.org*). Maps and trails may be downloaded from the website. Hiking and backpacking tips are included in the *Hiking Guide to the Florida Trail,* available from the association. For *A Guide to Your National Scenic Trail,* contact the US Forest Service *(above).*

HORSEBACK RIDING

Twenty-one of Florida's state parks and 15 state forests offer miles of unpaved roads and trails for horseback riding. State parks that provide overnight camping for riders and horses include Florida Caverns, Jonathan Dickinson, Little Manatee River, Lower Wekiva River, Myakka River, O'Leno, Rock Springs Run and Wekiva Springs. Call the park office to inquire about staging areas, camping facilities and trail conditions. Regulations require proof of a recent negative Coggins test for all horses entering park areas. Riders are required to stay on designated trails. The *Florida Horse Trail Directory,* with listings for 105 horse trails, is

available from the Florida Department of Agriculture, Room 416, Mayo Building, Tallahassee FL 32399-0800 (*850-488-4132;* download the brochure at *www.florida-agriculture. com*). Contact local chambers of commerce or the Florida Department of Environmental Protection *(see above)* for additional information. Horseback riding is allowed on several beaches. Check with local authorities before setting out.

HUNTING

Many different types of game await the sports hunter in Florida's forests, grasslands and vast swamps. Rifles and shotguns may be brought into Florida for hunting and sporting purposes (no permit required). Hunting is permitted in Big Cypress National Preserve, wildlife-management areas and most state and national forests. Whether fishing or hunting, sportsmen should be aware that native species of birds are protected by law, as are all endangered and threatened animals. For hunting **regulations,** bag limits, seasons and a copy of the *Florida Hunting Handbook (free),* contact Florida Fish and Wildlife Conservation Commission (*850-488-4676;* download the brochure at *www. myfwc.com/hunting).*

EXPEDITIONS AND CRUISES

Outdoor Adventures

Bird-watching tours in the Keys and Dry Tortugas are led by Victor Emanuel Nature Tours, Austin TX (℘800-328-8368; www.ventbird.com). Weekend and three-day **kayaking trips** to beautiful natural areas like the Everglades and 10,000 Islands are offered by Adventure Kayaking, Vero Beach, FL, (℘772-567-0522; www.paddleflorida.com). Some trips combine kayaking with camping; others include overnight stays in local lodgings.

Snorkel with manatees, and learn about Florida's gentle giants, with Birds Underwater Dive Center, in Kings Bay, Crystal River, 60mi north of Tampa (℘800-771-2763; www.birdsunderwater.com).

Cruises

A variety of cruise vacations catering to families and singles are available. Choose from a four-day sail to the Bahamas with ample time to explore the islands; a relaxing cruise to Mexico's Yucatan Peninsula or through the Panama Canal to Los Angeles; or a voyage to an island that includes educational lectures and on-shore excursions. Most cruise lines offer air/sea packages and discounts for early bookings.

Florida has seven ports that offer service year-round. The four largest are the Port of Miami, Port Everglades (Fort Lauderdale), Port Canaveral and Port Tampa. Major cruise lines departing from these ports include Carnival, Cunard, Holland America, Norwegian, Princess, Royal Caribbean. All ports provide parking facilities. For up-to-date information, check with individual cruise lines or contact the Cruise Lines International Association (℘754-224-2200; www.cruising.org) for a listing of travel agents that specialize in cruise vacations.

SPECTATOR SPORTS

For an overview of spectator sports available in Florida, see the Recreation section in the Introduction at the front of this guide. A comprehensive directory of Florida sports is available online at www.flasports.com.

MOTOR SPORTS

Daytona International Speedway is home to a number of racing events throughout the year including motorcycle and go-kart racing. Enthusiasts of automobile racing flock here from late January to mid-February when the Rolex 24 at Daytona sports car race and the world-famous **Daytona 500** stock car race take place. Held every spring, also

Daytona 500 stock car race

Visit Florida

in Daytona, Bike Week is a city-wide celebration of motorcycles. Gator-Nationals, the largest drag-racing contest on the Atlantic Seaboard, takes place each March in Gainesville.

RACING AND MORE

Most major cities have greyhound racing tracks close by. Winter brings the best horses and riders to south Florida. Horse lovers can experience the thrill of **thoroughbred racing** at four tracks in the Greater Miami area and at Tampa Bay Downs. For a listing of pari-mutuel (known as the Tote in some countries) betting establishments, visit www.myflorida. com. Pompano Park (*http://pompano-park.isleofcapricasinos.com*) hosts **harness racing** from October to June. West Palm Beach, Boca Raton and Vero Beach present **polo** matches from November to mid-April.
Jai alai facilities are located in Fort Lauderdale, Fort Pierce, Miami, Ocala and Orlando. For venues check local telephone directories or contact area tourist offices.

BASEBALL

In spring many of the country's major-league baseball (MLB) teams head for training camps in Florida. Warm-up practice starts in late February and "Grapefruit League" exhibition games are played daily through March. Practices are held between 10am–2pm and are free. Tickets for games range from $8–$24. Order tickets early by calling the stadium directly or the local Ticketmaster outlet. For a free schedule, write to Major League Baseball, 350 Park Ave., New York NY 10022. The *Spring Training* Yearbook (*$7*), published annually in late January, gives team histories, schedules, ticket details, directions and accommodations. To order, visit www.springtrainingmagazine. com. The *Spring Training Guide* is available free from the **Florida Sports Foundation** (*℘850-488-8347; www. flasports.com*).

Florida has two MLB representatives: **Tampa Bay Rays** (*http://tampabay. rays.mlb.com*) play at the Raymond James Stadium in Tampa. In 2007 they finished last in the American League East for the ninth time in their 10-season existence. The following season, 2008, however, saw a remarkable transformation; they won their first division title and proceeded to win the pennant. In 2009 the Rays finished a creditable third place.
Florida Marlins (*http://marlins.mlb. com*) play at the Sun Life Stadium in Miami. The team are set to move to a new ballpark in 2012 (in Little Havana, Miami) and will be renamed the Miami

Florida Marlins, Sun Life Stadium

© Greater Miami CVB

Marlins. The team has a proud history, winning the World Series in 1997 and 2003. In 2009 they achieved a bitter-sweet best non-playoff season.
The MLB season begins on the first Sunday in April and ends on the first Sunday in October.

AMERICAN FOOTBALL

Three Florida teams play in the top tier of, the National Football League (NFL). **Miami Dolphins** (*www.miamidolphins. com*) play their home games at the Sun Life Stadium, in Miami Gardens, 15 miles north of downtown. Their training facility is in Davie.
Tampa Bay Buccaneers (*www. buccaneers.com*), known to their fans as "the Bucs," play at the Raymond James Stadium. The most successful Florida team of recent years, from 1997 to 2007 they were consistent playoff contenders, and won the Super Bowl at the end of the 2002 season. Unfortunately they suffered a disappointing 2009 campaign.
Jacksonville Jaguars (*www.jaguars. com*) play and train at Jacksonville Municipal Stadium. The least successful of Florida's trio (and one of only four active NFL franchises never to have competed for the Super Bowl), there is continuing speculation that the Jaguars will be moved or sold. The NFL season begins in mid-September and ends with the Super Bowl held on the first week in February.

BASKETBALL

The state's two top NBA teams are the **Orlando Magic** (*www.nba.com/ magic*) and **Miami Heat**. "The Magic" play at the Amway Arena in 2009 was a fine season for the team, where they reached the NBA Finals but were beaten by the Los Angeles Lakers. Miami Heat (*www.nba.com/heat*), who won the NBA title in the 2005–2006 season, play at the American Airlines Arena.
The season begins in the first week of November and ends around the end of April though there is a break in between this period.

Florida Panthers, Bank Atlantic Center

© Michael Ludwig/Dreamstime.com

ICE HOCKEY

Although not as popular in the Sunshine State as in the colder northern states, Florida still boasts two National Hockey League (NHL) teams.
Tampa Bay Lightning (*http:// lightning.nhl.com*), nicknamed the Bolts, play their home games at the St. Pete Times Forum in Tampa. They won the Stanley Cup (league playoff) championship in 2004 but have performed poorly since 2007.
The **Florida Panthers** (*http://panthers. nhl.com*) are based in Sunrise, a suburb of Fort Lauderdale, and play their home games at the BankAtlantic Center.
They have a record of underachieving. and despite finishing the 2008–09 season with their second-best ever season, in 2009–10 they missed the playoffs for a 9th consecutive time. The NHL season is divided into an exhibition season (September), a regular season (from the first week in October through early to mid-April) and the Stanley Cup playoffs, from April to the beginning of June.

Sanibel Island
Visit Florida

BEACHES

Florida beaches are ranked among the finest in the world. The most authoritative list is that compiled by Stephen Leatherman ("Dr. Beach"), director of Florida International University's Laboratory for Coastal Research. The 2010 list included Siesta Beach in Sarasota, which took the No. 2 spot, and Cape Florida State Park in Key Biscayne (No. 10). Recent top beaches have included Fort De Soto and **Caladesi Island**.

Fortunately, for most of Florida, the Deepwater Horizon Oil disaster of 2010 only came as far the Alabama-Northwest Florida state line, with a clean-up effort mandated to eradicate long-term damage.

The waters along Florida beaches are generally warm compared to the rest of the US. Surf tends to be higher on the Atlantic coast—Cocoa Beach is where the Hang Ten crowd gather—with relatively little surf on the Gulf coast. Water temperature is also warmer on the Gulf coast than on the Atlantic coast.

Florida beach sand consistency in the northwest along Pensacola, and Panama City Beach is fine and very white. Clearwater Beach and the beaches of Sarasota also share this same fine and very white texture. Beaches along the Atlantic tend to shade towards light beige with a somewhat coarser texture. Daytona Beach is famous for its hard-packed sand suitable for driving motor vehicles. If you are looking for shells choose **Sanibel Island**.

If you want lively beaches with every amenity to hand, head for Miami, Key West, Panama City, Clearwater, Daytona Beach and Jacksonville—though also bear in mind that even the biggest resorts also include quiet uncommercialized beaches. The most pristine and least commercialized beaches of all are those managed by the Florida State Parks (SP) or designated as State Recreation Areas (SRA).

Caladesi Island
St. Petersburg/Clearwater Area CVB/Visit Florida

The following is a list of selected beaches that are the best of their kind. However, this is just a small selection and you may well find your very own stretch of paradise elsewhere!

THE PANHANDLE

Grayton Beach SP ; Henderson Beach SP; Perdido Key/Gulf Islands National Seashore; Panama City Beach; Pensacola Beach in Santa Rosa Island; St Andrews SP; St George Island SP; St Joseph Peninsula SP.

EAST COAST

Amelia Island SP; Anastasia SP; Daytona Beach; Flagler Beach SP; Fort Pierce Inlet SP; St. Augustine Beach; Sebastian Inlet SP; North Peninsula SP.

SOUTH FLORIDA AND THE KEYS

Bahia Honda SP; Bill Baggs Cape Florida SP; Crandon Park; Fort Lauderdale Beach; Haulover Beach; Hugh Taylor Birch SP; J. D. MacArthur SP, J. U. Lloyd Beach SP; Miami Beach.

GULF COAST

Coquina Beach; Clearwater Beach; Delnor-Wiggins SP; Gasparilla Island SP; Longboat Key; Lovers Key SRA; St Petersburg Beach; Sanibel Island beaches; Venice Beach.

WATER SPORTS

With hundreds of miles of prime coastline bordering the Atlantic and Gulf of Mexico, Florida is Water Sports Central, year-round. Inland lakes, rivers and springs create more opportunities to **swim**, paddle or simply enjoy the sound of the surf. Although Florida's Atlantic coast is not known for its large waves, **surfing** is popular along Sebastian Inlet south of Melbourne, and around Jacksonville, Flagler Beach and Miami. Surfboards and sailboards can be rented locally. Check water conditions with lifeguards or local authorities before setting out to surf or windsurf.

CANOEING AND KAYAKING

The Florida Canoe Trail system includes more than 1,000mi of scenic waterways. Canoe trails on rivers and creeks invite paddles to explore the slow-flowing waters of the Santa Fe River, glide through swampy areas along the upper Suwannee River, or camp on a secluded riverbank. For mor details download Florida Paddling Trails (www.dep.state.fl.us/gwt/PDF/ FL_Paddling_Trails.pdf), which also lists local outfitters and guides. You can also contact individual national parks, state parks or preserves for additional information on local canoe trails. The recently developed **Great Calusa Blueway** is a 100mi marked paddling trail that meanders the coastline of Lee County, from Charlotte Harbor to Bonita Springs on the Gulf of Mexico, past pristine islands and lush mangroves. Along the way are inns, camping areas and outfitters. For information, contact the Lee County Convention & Visitors Bureau (℘239-339-3500; www.fortmyers-sanibel.com) or visit www.greatclusablueway.com. Enjoy self-guided family paddle adventures on the Peace River that range from half-day canoe outings to overnight camping trips. For a brochure, contact Canoe Outpost (℘863-494-1215 or 800-268-0083; www.canoeoutpost. com). Canoe Outpost also offers trips

Canoeing

The law requires that each occupant wear a flotation device. Best carry an extra paddle to be on the safe side. Get a map of canoeing routes and keep abreast of weather conditions; also keep in mind that coastal rivers are affected by tides. Always avoid flooded rivers! Rivers in North Florida run high in spring and summer whereas in Central and South Florida rivers generally run high in summer and fall. Carry drinking water, and always advise someone of your plans.

on the Suwannee, Little Manatee, and Santa Fe rivers. Tampa's Hillsborough River offers a backcountry paddling experience within just a few miles of the city. To explore Tampa's 16,000-acre wilderness preserve at John Sargeant Memorial Wilderness Park, take a guided trip, or rent a kayak or canoe, from Canoe Escape (*813-986-2067; www.canoeescape.com*). To request a copy of the canoeing and kayaking directory that lists member outfitters, contact the Office of Greenways and Trails (*see above*). Flat-water wilderness canoeing can be experienced along the Wilderness Waterway in the Everglades. For canoeing in the Ten Thousand Islands area, contact North American Canoe Tours Everglades Rentals & Eco Adventures (*239-695-3299; www.evergladesadventures.com*).

SCUBA DIVING AND SNORKELING

The most popular areas are the Keys and south Florida, where dive shops offer trips. Most venues rent equipment and organize dive excursions. For more information visit www.fla-keys.com/diving.
A **Certified Diver's Card** is required to scuba dive. Certification courses are offered by most diving shops. Choose an instructor who is certified by the Professional Association of Dive Instructors (PADI) or the National Association of Underwater Instructors (NAUI). *See also Sports and Recreation.*

Scuba Diving, Fort Lauderdale
Visit Florida

Snorkelers and scuba divers can enjoy the living coral reef that lies off the Florida Keys.
To get close to the reef without an air tank, try **snuba,** a shallow water diving system that bridges the gap between snorkeling and scuba diving, which is safe and easy and does not require certification. Expeditions by Tilden's Scuba Centers (who offer scuba and snuba), based in Marathon and Duck Key, let you explore the reef connected to a 20ft breathing hose that is attached to an air tank secured to a raft on the surface (*888-728-2235 and 305-743-7255; www.tildensscubacenter.com*). For other snuba outfitters, visit www. snuba.com. Advance reservations are required for all dive and snorkel trips.
A few precautions: wear lightweight shoes to protect against sharp rocks; don't wear shiny objects that will attract fish; if you leave the boat, display a red-and-white "diver down" flag; and most importantly **never dive alone**. Seas are usually rougher in winter and can produce poor visibility on the reefs.

ENTERTAINMENT

Florida's sultry air is filled with the sound of music. Year-round, outdoor concerts—often free to the public—take place in local bandshells. Although you'll definitely encounter a fair share of Jimmy Buffett wannabes, you can often find good live jazz, folk music, country jazz, and bluegrass, even at the beach bars. If you're looking for international artists, Miami's new Carnival Center for the Performing Arts is a don't-miss venue. The Carnival Center is also home to the Florida Grand Opera, the Miami City Ballet, and the New World Symphony. The sophisticated little city of Sarasota is one of Florida's artiest enclaves, with several resident theater companies, the Sarasota Opera, and the Sarasota Film Society (sponsoring daily showings of foreign and art films). Sarasota's Van Wezel Performing Arts Hall hosts 200 or so performances

Incredible Hulk Coaster, Universal

Visit Florida

a year, including rock concerts and Broadway shows. Among Florida's major arts festivals are Miami Beach's Art Basel, a mammoth extravaganza of modern art featuring famous artists and promising unknowns (early Dec) and Melbourne's international art festival, celebrating the visual arts, theater, dance and music (Oct). Every July, Daytona Beach welcomes the London Symphony Orchestra to its Florida International Festival.

ACTIVITIES FOR KIDS 👥

In this guide, sights of particular interest to children are indicated with a 👥 symbol. Many sights and attractions offer reduced or free admission for children (usually under 12 years of age), as well as reduced rates for families. When booking accommodations, ask for family rates or discount vacation packages and check whether it offers organized children's programs. Restaurants frequently provide a children's menu. Theme parks are tops on most kid's wish lists. Florida is home to the biggies (Disney, Universal, Sea World), plus lots of quirky smaller attractions, like alligator farms. Many state parks and nature preserves sponsor activities for families. Miniature golf courses, with elaborate special effects like spewing volcanoes, have risen to an art form in Florida. Local festivals and fairs (👆 see Calendar of Events) can be fun events for youngsters.

Some (non-theme park) Activities for Kids 👥

♦ Take an airboat ride to look for gators at Myakka River State Park in Sarasota (📞941-361-6511; www.myakkariver.org/airboat.html).

♦ Attend a **spring training game** (👆 see Spectator Sports) and ask your favorite player to sign a baseball for you (have a ball and pen ready!).

♦ Tube down five stories or splash around in a wave pool at **Wet'n'Wild** in Orlando (📞407-351-1800; www.wetnwild.com).

♦ Commune with tiny sea dragons and toothsome sharks at the **Florida Aquarium** in Tampa(📞 813-273-4000; www.flaquarium.org).

♦ Learn to surf at Cocoa Beach, try **Ron Jon Surf Shop** (📞321-799-8888; www. ronjonsurfschool.com). Florida Surf Lessons offers surfing class and events at 15 Florida beaches (📞321-441-3926 or 888-672-4887; www.floridasurflessons.com).

♦ Take a trip to the moon (in a flight simulator!) at the **Museum of Discovery and Science** in Fort Lauderdale (📞 954-467-6637; www.mods.org).

SHOPPING

Florida is a shopper's paradise, with a huge range of goods caterng for all tastes and budgets from upscale boutiques to outlet malls and flea markets.Swimsuits, T-shirts, Disney-style merchandise and citrus-hued resort wear can be purchased in every large coastal city in Florida. For more details on shopping in the state visit www.visitflorida.com/shopping.

OUTLET MALLS

Sawgrass Mills at Fort Lauderdale is the daddy of them all, in fact the biggest in the world with over 400 stores. The following all boast over 100 stores: Orlando Premium Outlets, Orlando; Miromar Outlets in Estero, between Naples and Fort Myers; Lake Buena Vista Factory Stores, near Orlando and Prime Outlets (at several locations throughout the state).

CRAFTS AND SOUVENIRS

Handmade dolls, beaded belts and other **Native American crafts** are sold at the Miccosukee and Seminole reservations in the Everglades. **Seashells** are offered in countless souvenir shops, especially on Sanibel Island and along the southwest coast. The **Shell Factory** near Fort Myers boasts the largest commercial assortment of shells in the world.

Buy natural **sponges** from the Gulf of Mexico along the sponge docks in Tarpon Springs.

In historic Ybor City near Tampa, and in Little Havana, Miami, fine hand-rolled **cigars** make a prized gift for the connoisseur.

FARM PRODUCE

Agriculture is big business in the Sunshine State. Behold the bounty at local **farmers' markets**, held most Saturday mornings, and shop for produce, fresh fish, and flowers grown in nearby nurseries. Take some of Florida's sunshine with you when you buy oranges, grapefruit and other **citrus fruits**. **Mixon Fruit Farms** at Bradenton is a popular place, also offering grove tours. It is not uncommon to combine fruit and flea market shopping (see Antiques). Fruit can be shipped anywhere in the continental US, but do inquire about shipping costs as they can run higher than the merchandise.

ANTIQUES & FLEAMARKETS

The best selection can be found in North and Central Florida. Avonlea Antique Mall, near Jacksonville, offers the largest selection of fine antique furniture and house items in North Florida and South Georgia. The hamlets of Havana and Quincy near Tallahassee are known for their

Seashells for sale, Florida Keys

© Linda Bucklin/Dreamstime.com

The Mall at Millenia, Orlando

© Leabrooks Photography/Alamy

small-town charm and abundance of antiques, art galleries and shops selling collectibles. Also up north check out the the antique shops in the quaint old towns of Arcadia and Monticello.

In Central Florida, Micanopy's antique shops cluster along Cholokka Boulevard and Smiley's Antique Mall. The Munn Park Historic District in Lakeland features some 60 shops. Craft and antique shops line Fifth Ave. and Donnelly St. in Mt. Dora, south of Ocala. Waldo's Village, near Gainesville is also well worth a browse. Out on the coast, try Historic Cocoa Village. Ybor City boasts many antique shops, plus art galleries and studios. Check out **vintage clothing** stores in Sarasota, Ybor City, and Micanopy.

Antique car buffs flock to car shows in Daytona Beach that feature swap meets *(Mar & Nov)* offering vintage car parts and accessories.

Fleaworld on Highway 1792 between Sanford and Orlando claims to be America's largest fleamarket. More big ones are: Renninger's Antique Center and Farmer's & Flea Market at Mount Dora; the Super Flea and Farmers Market in Melbourne; the 1,000-booth Daytona Flea & Farmers Market; the Wagon Wheel Flea Market, located near St. Petersburg; Red Barn at Bradenton, Festival Flea Market at Pompano, near Fort Lauderdale.

A good site for checking out fleamarkets is www.pebblehaven. com/c/floridafleamarketassociation.

UPSCALE

Worth Avenue in Palm Beach attracts the monied set with its posh boutiques and trendy art galleries. Among Florida's glitziest shopping zones are Bal Harbour, Streets of Mayfair, Village of Merrick Park (Coral Gables) in Miami; St. Armands Circle in Sarasota; Galleria Mall *(www. galleriamall-fl.com)* and Las Olas Boulevard *(www.lasolasboulevard. com)* at Fort Lauderdale; The Mall at Millenia, Orlando; Park Avenue *(www.parkave-winterpark.com)* in Winter Park, just outside Orlando; Waterside Shops at Naples; St. Armands Circle Sarasota.

SPECIALTY

Surf dudes should make a beeline for Ron Jon's (various locations): the best one is at Cocoa Beach. For something different in Miami try the Lincoln Road Shopping District and for **Art Deco** gifts, call in at the Art Deco Welcome Center and Gift Shop *(1200 Ocean Drive)*. If you're in search of **Disney** merchandise, Downtown Disney Marketplace is the place to go for both the usual stuff and one-of-a-kind items. It includes the largest Disney character store in the world.

BOOKS
REFERENCE

The Everglades: River of Grass. Margery S. Douglas (1947; 1997).
> With her opening words, "There is no other Everglades in the world," Douglas drew public attention to the vast wilderness that developers were busily draining and damming. This led to President Harry Truman's decision to create a national park out of more than 2 million acres of land in the Everglades.

AUTOBIOGRAPHY

Cross Creek. Marjorie Kinnan Rawlings (1996). A classic tale that explores the odd assortment of characters living the rustic life in Cracker Country (Central Florida).

FICTION

The Yearling. Marjorie Kinnan Rawlings (1938). The Pulitzer Prize-winning story of a likeable family's wild, hard but ultimately satisfying pioneering life in inland Florida.

A Land Remembered. Patrick Smith (1998). This novel tells the tale of Central Florida, from pre-Civil War times through the 1960s, through the lives of three generations of the MacIvey family.

Skinny Dip. Carl Hiaasen (2004).
> Set in South Florida, Hiassen's comic novels feature a wacky line-up of oddball characters and situations.

NON-FICTION

Tales of Old Florida. Frank Oppel (1991).
> This collection of articles about the state of Florida from the turn of the century offers an entertaining trip back in time.

FILMS

The Yearling (dir. Clarence Brown, 1946).
> The film of the Pulitzer Prize-winning book (see above), starring Gregory Peck and Jane Wyman.

Creature from the Black Lagoon (dir. Jack Arnold, 1954).
> Florida stands in for the Amazon in this "man-in-a-rubber-suit" monster flick, in which an expedition team, searching for fossils, encounters a mysterious "gill man."

Where the Boys Are (dir. Henry Levin, 1960).
> Four Midwestern college co-eds set out to find love and adventure in Fort Lauderdale. This is the movie that put Fort Lauderdale on the map, and visitors still ask about it, 50 years later.

Body Heat (dir. Lawrence Kasdan, 1981).
> A South Florida heat wave is the perfect backdrop for this sizzling film noir starring William Hurt, Kathleen Turner, and scene-stealing newcomer Ted Danson.

Cocoon (dir. Ron Howard, 1985).
> A charming fable in which a group of Florida seniors are magically rejuvenated by aliens.

The Birdcage (dir. Mike Nichols, 1996).
> Robin Williams and Nathan Lane camp it up in this comedy about a gay cabaret owner and his drag companion who play it straight when they meet their uptight future in-laws. The title refers to a drag club on South Beach.

Scarface (dir. Brian De Palma, 1983).
> Al Pacino's performance as an ultra-violent foul-mouthed Cuban drug lord in Miami has (to the dismay of many) become something of a cult classic.

Calendar of Events

Listed below is a selection of Florida's most popular annual events; some dates may vary from year to year. For detailed information, contact local tourism offices (numbers listed under individual entries) or **Visit Florida** (*850-488-5607 or 888-735-2872; www.flausa.com*).

JANUARY
early-Jan: **FedEx Orange Bowl**
college football; Miami
Gator Bowl
www.gatorbowl.com; Jacksonville
Outback Bowl
www.outbackbowl.com; Tampa
Florida Citrus Bowl
www.fcsports.com; Orlando
6 Jan: **Festival of Epiphany**
Tarpon Springs
mid-Jan: **Art Deco Weekend**
www.mdpl.org; Miami Beach
late-Jan: **Rolex 24 at Daytona**
24-hour sports car race;
www.daytonainternational
speedway.com; Daytona Beach

FEBRUARY–MARCH
Feb: **Gasparilla Festival**, historic
pirate-themed festival; www.
gasparillapiratefest.com; Tampa
Florida State Fair, livestock, rides,
arts and crafts, entertainment;
www.floridastatefair.com; Tampa
Miami International Boat Show
www.miamiboatshow.com;
Miami Beach
Daytona 500, NASCAR/
stock car race; www.daytona
internationalspeedway.com;
Daytona Beach
Coconut Grove Arts Festival
www.coconutgroveartsfest.com;
Coconut Grove, Miami
Renaissance Festival, www.
discoverourfestival.com; Largo
International Kite Festival
Miami Beach
Feb–Mar: **Florida Strawberry
Festival**, www.flstrawberry
festival.com; Plant City
Bike Week, www.officialbike
week.com; Daytona Beach
Mar: **Carnaval Miami**,
www.carnavalmiami.com; Miami
Bike Week, www.officialbike
week.com; Daytona Beach
Spanish Night Watch, colonial
pageantry; St. Augustine

APRIL–MAY
Apr: **Springtime Tallahassee**,
festivals, parades, crafts;
www.springtimetallahassee.com
Festival of States, parades,
concerts, fireworks, crafts;
www.festivalofstates.com;
St. Petersburg

Gator Bowl, Jacksonville

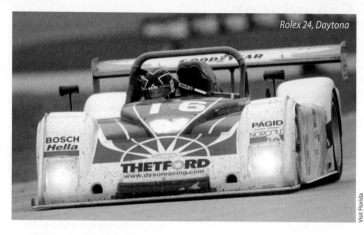

Rolex 24, Daytona

Visit Florida

MPS Group Championships
WTA women's tennis;
www.mpsgroupchamps.net;
Ponte Vedra Beach
Seven-Mile Bridge Run
marathon; www.southernmost
runners.com; Florida Keys
Fun 'N Sun Festival
parades, concerts, crafts;
www.clearwater-fl.com;
Clearwater
Apr–May: **SunFest**
www.sunfest.com; West Palm
Beach
**Isle of Eight Flags Shrimp
Festival**, www.shrimpfestival.com;
Fernandina Beach
**Daytona Beach International
Festival**, music; www.dbif.com
May: **Florida Folk Festival**,
www.floridafolkfestival.com;
Stephen Foster (SP),
White Springs
Jacksonville Jazz Festival
www.coj.net; Jacksonvile

JUNE
Jun: **Billy Bowlegs Festival**
pirate-themed festival;
www.fwbchamber.org;
Fort Walton Beach
Goombay Festival
www.goombayfestivalcoconut
grove.com; Coconut Grove,
Miami
Sarasota Music Festival
www.sarasotaorchestra.org

JULY
Jul: **Hemingway Days**
www.fla-keys.com; Key West

SEPTEMBER
Sept: **Destin Seafood Festival**
www.destinchamber.com

OCTOBER
Oct: **Clearwater Jazz Holiday**
www.clearwaterjazz.com
Guavaween
Latin-style Halloween;
www.cc-events.org/gw; Ybor City
John's Pass Seafood Festival
www.johnspass.com;
Madeira Beach
Fantasy Fest
gay and lesbian festival;
www.fantasyfest.net; Key West

NOVEMBER
Nov: **Florida Seafood Festival**
www.floridaseafoodfestival.com;
Apalachicola

DECEMBER
Dec: **Winterfest Boat Parade**
www.winterfestparade.com;
Fort Lauderdale
King Mango Strut
www.kingmangostrut.org;
Coconut Grove, Miami
Indian Arts Festival
www.miccosukee.com/festival;
Miccosukee Indian Village,
Everglades

Know Before You Go

FLORIDA DEPARTMENT OF ENVIRONMENTAL PROTECTION
Division of Recreation & Parks
3900 Commonwealth Blvd.
Tallahassee FL 32399-3000
℘850-245-2157
www.dep.state.fl.us./parks

Office of Fisheries Management
3900 Commonwealth Blvd.
Tallahassee FL 32399-3000
℘850-922-4340
www.myflorida.com

Office of Greenways and Trails
3900 Commonwealth Blvd.
Tallahassee FL 32399-2400
℘850-245-2052 or 877-822-5208
www.myflorida.com

FLORIDA ASSOCIATION OF RV PARKS & CAMPGROUNDS
1340 Vickers Rd.
Tallahassee FL 32303-3041
℘850-562-7151
www.floridacamping.com

FLORIDA DEPARTMENT OF TRANSPORTATION
605 Suwannee St., Tallahassee FL 32399
℘850-414-4100 or 866-374-3368
www.dot.state.fl.us

FLORIDA SPORTS FOUNDATION
2390 Kerry Forest Pkwy.
Tallahassee FL 32309
℘850-488-8347
www.flasports.com

US FOREST SERVICE
325 John Knox Rd.
Tallahassee FL 32303-4160
℘850-523-8500
www.fs.fed.us

OTHER HELPFUL WEBSITES
www.myflorida.com
State of Florida general information.

www.flheritage.com
State Office of Cultural and Historical Programs; information includes archeology and museum news; arts, and cultural resources.

www.floridastateparks.org
Information on features, fees and reservations at Florida's state parks.

www.see-florida.com
Attractions, lodgings, dining and recreation.

www.accuweather.com
Independent weather-forecasting service; excellent source of hurricane information.

TOURISM OFFICES
To request the *Florida Vacation Guide* (published annually) or a state map, contact **Visit Florida**, P.O. Box 1100, Tallahassee FL 32302 (℘850-488-5607 or 888-735-2872; www.visitflorida.com). You can also download brochures and guides www.visitflorida.com/guides. Local tourist offices (telephone numbers listed under each entry) provide information free of charge on accommodations, shopping, entertainment, festivals and recreation.

INTERNATIONAL VISITORS
ENTRY REQUIREMENTS
Citizens of countries participating in the Visa Waiver Pilot Program (VWPP) are not required to obtain a visa to enter the US for visits of fewer than 90 days if they have a machine-readable passport. Residents of visa-waiver countries must apply ahead for travel authorization online through the **ESTA program** (www.cbp.gov/esta). Travelers may apply any time ahead of their travel; at least three days before departure is strongly recommended. Citizens of non-participating countries must have a visitor's visa. Upon entry, non resident foreign visitors must present a valid passport and round-trip transportation ticket. Canadian citizens need a government-issued photo I.D., such as a driver's license,

plus proof of citizenship (such as a birth certificate) to enter the US. Naturalized Canadian citizens should carry their citizenship papers. Air travellers between the US. and Canada, Mexico, Central and South America, the Caribbean and Bermuda are also required to present a passport, Air NEXUS card or comparable documentation. All persons traveling between the US. and destinations listed above, by land or by sea (including ferry), may be required to present a valid passport or other documentation, as determined by the US. Department of Homeland Security. Inoculations are generally not required, but check with the US embassy or consulate before departing.

CUSTOMS REGULATIONS

All articles brought into the US must be declared at time of entry. **Items exempt** from customs regulations: personal effects; 150 milliliters (5 fl oz) of alcoholic beverage (providing visitor is at least 21 years old); 150 milliliters (5 fl oz) of perfume containing alcohol; 50 cigarettes and 10 cigars; and gifts (to persons in the US) that do not exceed $200 in value. **Prohibited items** include plant material, firearms and ammunition (if not intended for sporting purposes), and meat and poultry products. For other prohibited items, exemptions and information, contact the **US Customs Service,** 1300 Pennsylvania Ave. N.W., Washington DC 20229 (✆202-354-1000; www.cbp.gov).

EMBASSIES AND CONSULATES

In addition to the tourism offices throughout Florida (☙see individual entries), visitors from outside the US can obtain information in French, German, Japanese, Portuguese and Spanish from the web site of **Visit Florida** (www.flausa.com), or from the US embassy or consulate in their country of residence (partial listing below). For a complete list of American consulates and embassies abroad, visit the US State Department Bureau of Consular Affairs listing on the Internet at http://travel.state.gov. Many foreign countries have consular offices in Miami (for phone numbers, check the yellow pages of the telephone directory under Consulates).

BELGIUM

♦ **United States Embassy**
27, boulevard du Régent
1000 Brussels
✆02 508-2111
http://belgium.usembassy.gov

CANADA

♦ **American Embassy, Ottawa**
490 Sussex Drive
Ottawa, Ontario K1N 1G8
✆613-688-5335
http://canada.usembassy.gov

GERMANY

♦ **Embassy of the United States, Berlin**
Clayallee 170, 14191 Berlin
✆30 238 3050
http://germany.usembassy.gov

JAPAN

♦ **American Embassy**
10-5 Akasaka 1-Chome
Minato-ku Tokyo 107-8420
✆03-3224-5000
http://tokyo.usembassy.gov

SWITZERLAND

♦ **Embassy of the United States, Bern**
Sulgeneckstrasse 19, 3007 Bern
✆31 357 7011

UNITED KINGDOM

♦ **American Embassy, London**
24 Grosvenor Square
London W1A 1AE
✆207 499 9000

HEALTH

The US does not have a national health program that covers foreign nationals. Before departing, visitors from abroad should check their health-care insurance to determine if doctors' visits, medication and hospitalization in the US are covered. Prescription drugs should be properly identified, and accompanied by a copy of the prescription. Hotel staff can often make recommendations for doctors and other medical services. Companies offering travel insurance within the US include: **Access America** (℘800-284-8300; www.accessamerica.com), **Travelex** (℘800-228-9792; www.travelex-insurance.com), and **Travel Insured International** (℘800-243-3174; www.travelinsured.com).

DISABLED TRAVELERS

Many of the sights described in this guide are accessible to people with special needs. Sights marked with the symbol ♿ offer access for wheelchair users, but it is advisable to check beforehand by telephone.

Federal law requires that businesses, including hotels and restaurants, provide access for disabled people, devices for people who are hearing impaired, and designated parking spaces. Many public buses are equipped with wheelchair lifts and many hotels have rooms designed for disabled guests.

For further information, contact the **Society for the Advancement of Travel and Hospitality** (SATH), 347 Fifth Ave., Suite 610, New York NY 10016 (℘212-447-7284; www.sath.org). All **national parks** have facilities for disabled visitors. Free or discounted passes are available.

For details, contact the National Park Service, Office of Public Inquiries, P.O. Box 37127, Room 1013, Washington, DC, 20013-7127 (℘202-208-4747; www.nps.gov/pub_aff/access). For **state parks,** check with the **Florida Dept. of Environmental Protection,** Div. of Recreation & Parks, 3900 Commonwealth Blvd., Tallahassee FL 32399-3000 (℘850-245-2157; www.floridastateparks.org/accessforall). Passengers who will need assistance with **train** or **bus** travel should give advance notice to Amtrak (℘800-872-7245 or 800-523-6590 (TDD); www.amtrak.com) or Greyhound (℘800-752-4841(US only) or 800-345-3109 (TDD); www.greyhound.com). Reservations for adapted **rental cars** should be made well in advance with the rental company.

SENIOR CITIZENS

Many establishments offer discounts to those over age 62, including to members of the **American Association of Retired Persons** (AARP) (601 E St. N.W., Washington, DC, 20049; ℘888-687-2277; www.aarp.org)

Getting There

BY PLANE

Most US airlines offer direct and non-stop flights to Florida. For flight information, contact the airline directly. Twelve **international airports**—the largest are Miami, Orlando and Tampa International—offer services between Florida and Europe, Central and South America and the Caribbean. Smaller **regional airports** are usually accessible through commuter carriers. You might get a better airfare deal if you consider one of the smaller airports or **discount carriers**, such as AirTran, JetBlue and Southwest, who fly in and out of airports in Fort Lauderdale, Fort Myers and West Palm Beach, with more routes added frequently.

BY TRAIN

The **Amtrak rail network** offers various train travel packages that may combine rail, air and bus. Advance reservations are recommended. First-class, coach and sleeping cars are available; on some routes, **bi-level Superliner cars** with floor-to-ceiling windows give panoramic views. (⟁ See p31 for information on *passengers requiring special assistance.)* Canadian travelers should inquire with local travel agents regarding Amtrak/ VIARail connections.

The **USA RailPass** *(not available to US or Canadian citizens, or legal residents)* offers unlimited travel within Amtrak-designated regions at discounted rates: Passes are available in three travel durations and travel segments (15 days/8 segments, 30 days/12 segments, 45 days/18 segments) throughout the entire US. Daily service is provided on the **Silver Star** or **Silver Meteor** (New York–Miami, stopping at many other Florida stations en route). The **Sunset Limited** (Orlando–Los Angeles) used to make the transcontinental trip from Orlando to Los Angeles via New Orleans. Unfortunately, since the devastation brought about by Hurricane Katrina in 2005, the service between Orlando and New Orleans has been suspended indefinitely.

The **Auto Train** travels non-stop from Sanford, in central Florida, to Lorton, Virginia (17 miles from Washington, DC). It offers first-class sleeping accommodations, a full-service restaurant, floor-to-ceiling windows in the Sightseer Lounge and a movie presentation, all included in the ticket price *(leaves Lorton daily 4pm; arrives Sanford, Florida 9am)*. Only passengers with automobiles, vans, motorcycles, SUVs, small boats, jet-skis or other recreational vehicles are permitted on the train; no cars accepted after 3pm. Check restrictions when making reservations.

Amtrak and Continental Airlines offer an Air Rail travel program, though not within Florida. For information, contact Amtrak Vacations (&1-800-AMTRAK-2; www. amtrakvacations.com). Similarly, Amtrak has established a **Thruway Motorcoach** service partnerships with Greyhound throughout the country. Tickets must be purchased at Amtrak stations, travel agencies or by mail before boarding buses. For schedule and route information: &800-872-7245; www.amtrak.com.

BY CAR

Most car travelers enter the Sunshine State via one of two major north-to-south interstate highways: I-95, running along Florida's east coast, from just north of Jacksonville to Miami; and I-75, which enters the state north of Gainesville, and swings toward the west coast, ending in Fort Lauderdale. L-10 runs west to east across the Panhandle.

BY BUS

Greyhound offers access to most cities in Florida. The **Discovery Pass** allows unlimited travel anywhere for 7, 15, 30 or 60 days. Advance reservations recommended. For fares, schedules and routes: &800-231-2222; www.discoverypass.com.

Getting Around

BY CAR

Distances in Florida are relatively short; it only takes a couple of hours to travel between the east and west coasts (except in the northern part of the state). Even the stretch from the Panhandle to Miami can be driven in one day. Many towns are serviced by Amtrak. In some areas links are maintained with bus connections. Some of the more remote communities, especially along beaches, can only be reached by car. For information, contact **Florida Department of Transportation** (&850-414-4100; www.dot.state.fl.us). Florida has an extensive system of well-maintained major roads, some of which are designated limited-access highways that require a toll. Four major interstates traverse Florida: I-10 runs from Jacksonville to Pensacola; I-4 links Daytona Beach and Tampa; I-75 cuts southwest across the state from Georgia; and I-95 travels the length of Florida's east coast, ending at Miami. Welcome Centers on the interstates greet visitors with samples of free citrus juice and supply answers to your travel questions. Many rest areas have picnic tables; most are open 24 hours and are patrolled by security officers at night. Beware wildlife on roads in remote areas. Along highways and major urban thoroughfares, many gas stations stay open 24 hours.

Most self-service gas stations do not offer car repair, although many sell standard maintenance items. For free maps phone the tourist office for your destination (*see individual entries*) or contact Visit Florida (*see Tourism Offices*).

The **Florida Turnpike** (a toll road) branches off I-75 northwest of Orlando and slants southeastward across the state until it ends below Miami in Florida City *(around $22 for the entire distance)*. Toll booths are staffed, but for quick travel motorists should carry correct change. Call boxes placed at mile intervals allow travelers to phone for help. For further information: 800-749-7453.

RENTAL CARS

Most large rental companies have offices at (or near) major airports and downtown locations. Rentals typically include unlimited mileage. If a vehicle is returned at a different location from where it was rented, drop-off charges may be incurred. Reservations are accepted through a toll-free service with a major credit card. Minimum age for rental is 21. A surcharge *(min. $25/day)* for persons up to age 24 is applied to all rentals in Florida.

Be sure to check for proper insurance coverage, offered at extra charge. Liability is not automatically included in the terms of the lease. If you own a car and carry comprehensive car insurance for collision and liability, your personal auto insurance may cover a rental. Check your policy to be sure. Some credit cards offer CDW

Rental Company	Reservations
Alamo	800-327-9633 www.alamo.com
Avis	800-331-1212 www.avis.com
Budget	800-527-0700 www.budget.com
Dollar	800-800-4000 www.dollar.com
Enterprise	800-325-8007 www.enterprise.com
Hertz	800-654-3131 www.hertz.com
National	800-227-7368 www.nationalcar.com
Thrifty	800-331-4200 www.thrifty.com

(Toll-free numbers not accessible outside US.)

(collision damage waiver coverage). In addition to the national rental agencies, there are local companies that offer reasonable rentals (refer to yellow pages of local directories for phone numbers).

RECREATIONAL VEHICLE (RV) RENTALS

Motor-home rentals are offered from several locations in Florida. Some models accommodate up to eight people, and service can include free mileage and airport transfers. Make reservations 2–3 weeks in advance. In the summer months *(Jun–Aug)* and during holiday seasons, reservations should be made at least 4–6 weeks in advance.
Contact Cruise America RV Rentals: 480-464-7300 or 800-671-8042; www.cruiseamerica.com.

ROAD REGULATIONS

The maximum speed limit on interstate highways is 70mph, 60mph on state highways, unless otherwise posted. Speed limits are generally 30mph within city limits and residential areas. Right turns on red are allowed after coming to a complete stop, unless otherwise indicated. Florida law requires that

> ### 😊 Motoring Safety Tips 😊
>
> Don't stop if strangers flag your car down. If you carry a cell phone, dial FHP (*347) for the Florida Highway Patrol. Don't stop if your car is bumped from the rear; proceed to the nearest well-lit public area and contact the police. Ask at your hotel what parts of the city to avoid.

headlights must be turned on when driving in fog and rain. Authorities recommend keeping headlights on at dawn and dusk and when driving through smoke.

Seat belts must be worn by all front-seat occupants. Children under 6 must ride in crash-tested, federally approved child restraint devices (child safety seats are offered by most car-rental agencies; request these when making reservations). The law requires motorists in both directions to bring their vehicles to a complete stop when warning signals on a **school bus** are activated. Parking spaces identified by ♿ are reserved for handicapped persons only: anyone parking in these spaces without proper identification will be ticketed and/or their vehicle will be towed away. Drivers are required to have personal injury

protection and property liability insurance. Carry proof of insurance in the vehicle at all times.

Apart from local authorities, motor clubs (membership required) offer road assistance: **American Automobile Association** (AAA) (☎800-222-4357; www.aaa.com); **Shell Motorist Club** (☎800-355-7263).

IN CASE OF AN ACCIDENT

If you are involved in an accident resulting in personal injury or property damage, you must notify the local police and remain at the scene until dismissed. If blocking traffic, vehicles should be moved as soon as possible. In the case of property damage to an unattended vehicle, the driver must attempt to locate the owner or leave written notice in a conspicuous place of driver's name, address and car registration number.

BY BUS

Florida's largest cities all offer decent local bus services: it's usually inexpensive, and fairly easy to use. In some cities, like Orlando, the local bus line services hotel zones and major attractions, making the bus a real plus if you're visiting the theme parks and don't want to pay for parking.

Where to Stay and Eat

WHERE TO STAY

♿*Hotels and restaurants are described in the Address Books within the Discovering Florida section. For coin ranges, see the Legend on the cover flap.*

Although Florida is an all year-round destination, rates are lower **off-season**; i.e. in South Florida, May to October; in the Panhandle and northern coastal areas, December to February. In some hotels children under 18 stay free when sharing a room with their parents. Some small hotel and many motel

rooms include efficiency kitchens. All but the most basic accommodations are air-conditioned. Hotel taxes, which vary according to location, range from 6% to 12.5%, and are not included in rates quoted. The Official Florida Vacation Guide lists members of the Florida Hotel & Motel Assn. and is available from **Visit Florida** (♿*see Tourism Offices*). State-wide hotel information service: ☎850-488-5607; www.visitflorida.com.

TRADITIONAL LODGINGS
HOTELS/MOTELS

Accommodations range from luxury hotels (*$250 and up*) and superior hotels (*$150–$250*) to moderate

	☎/website		☎/website
Best Western	800-528-1234 www.bestwestern.com	**ITT Sheraton**	800-325-3535 www.sheraton.com
Clarion, Comfort & Quality Inns	800-228-5150 www.comfortinn.com	**Marriott**	800-228-9290 www.marriott.com
Crowne Plaza	800-227-6963 www.crowneplaza.com	**Omni**	800-843-6664 www.omnihotels.com
Days Inn	800-325-2525 www.daysinn.com	**Radisson**	800-333-3333 www.radisson.com
Hilton	800-445-8667 www.hilton.com	**Ramada**	800-228-2828 www.ramada.com
Holiday Inn	800-465-4329 www.holiday-inn.com	**Ritz-Carlton**	800-241-3333 www.ritzcarlton.com
Howard Johnson	800-446-4656 www.hojo.com	**Superior Small Lodging Assn.** 1809 Silver ValleyCt. Apopka FL 32712	407-880-1707
Hyatt	800-233-1234 www.hyatt.com	**Westin**	800-848-0016 www.westin.com
Inn Route PO Box 6187, Palm Harbor FL 34684	800-524-1880 www.florida-inns.com	*(Toll-free numbers may not be accessible outside of North America)*	

motels (*$80-$150*). Rates vary greatly according to season and location and tend to be higher during holidays and peak seasons. Many properties offer packages which might include meals, passes to local attractions, and organized trips. Some hotels include breakfast in the room rate. Advance reservations are recommended. Always advise the reservations clerk of late arrival; unless confirmed with a credit card, rooms may not be held after 5pm.
(🔖 *For major hotel and motel chains with locations throughout Florida see the table on p36.*)

BED-AND-BREAKFASTS AND COUNTRY INNS

Most B&Bs are privately owned and many are located in historic dwellings in residential sections of cities, or in small towns and rural areas. Amenities include complimentary breakfast ranging from simple continental fare to full home-cooking; some offer afternoon tea and the use of sitting rooms or garden areas where hosts and guests mingle. Most establishments are small and offer fewer than ten rooms. Private baths are not always available, and often there is no phone in individual rooms. Typically, smoking is prohibited. Make reservations well in advance, especially during holiday seasons, and be sure to ask about minimum stay, cancellation and refund policies. Most establishments accept major credit cards. Rates vary seasonally but range from $100 in low season to over $250 in high season for a double room per night. Rates are higher when amenities such as hot tubs, private entrances and ocean views are offered.

RESORTS AND SPAS

Many of the grand and famous South Florida resorts have been lavishly restored in recent years, combining modern amenities and luxuries with Old World trapping. On-site fine dining restaurants, indoor and outdoor swimming pools, tennis courts, fitness centers, 18-hole golf courses and even marinas have become standard features of large resort hotels. Destination spas offer a variety of programs from fitness, beauty and wellness to weight management, stress relief and outdoor adventure. Guests are pampered with mud baths, daily massages, state-of-the-art fitness and exercise programs, cooking classes and nutritional counseling.

Spas, most of which are fairly informal, offer luxurious facilities in beautiful settings that can include championship golf courses and tennis courts. Most offer packages for stays ranging from two to ten nights, which include health and fitness programs and spa treatments. Prices range from $1,000/week in summer to $4,000/week during the winter season, depending on choice of program. For more information contact Spa Finder, Inc., 91 Fifth Ave., New York NY 10003. **Reservation service**: ℘ 800-255-7727; www.spafinder.com.

OTHER ACCOMMODATIONS
CONDOMINIUMS

Furnished apartments or houses are more cost-effective than hotels for families with children. Amenities include separate living quarters, fully equipped kitchen with dining area, several bedrooms and bathrooms, and laundry facilities. Most condos provide televisions, basic linens and maid service. Depending on location, properties might include sports and recreational facilities, patios and beach access. Most require a minimum stay of three nights or one week, especially during peak season. When making reservations, ask about cancellation penalties and refund policies. Chambers of commerce and tourist offices have listings of local property management agencies that can assist with the selection. For vacation homes in Naples

and the Orlando area, contact **Florida Choice** (℘800-847-2731; www.floridachoice.com) and see their Vacation Home Rentals.

HOSTELS

Simple budget accommodations are offered at hostels in many resorts including Clearwater Beach, Florida City, Key West, Fort Lauderdale, Kissimmee, and Miami Beach. Dormitory-style rooms average around $15–$40/night. Private rooms are available at additional charge and amenities may include swimming pools, air-conditioning, common living room, laundry facilities, self-service kitchen and dining room. Blankets and pillows are provided; linens can be rented. Reservations are suggested. All hostels accept credit cards. For information and reservations, visit www.hostels.com.

CAMPING

Campsites are located in national parks, state parks, national forests, along beaches and in private campgrounds. Many campsites are located in central Florida near theme parks: most offer full utility hookups, lodges or cabins and recreational facilities. Florida's many rivers and lakes allow boat camping and usually include mooring facilities and marinas. Primitive (wilderness) camping is for the experienced camper only. Because there may be mosquitoes and other creatures present, plan to sleep well-protected in the outdoors. Make sure your tent is waterproof; sudden thunderstorms can soak through quickly. Advance reservations are recommended, especially during holidays and school vacations.

A variety of camping facilities, from full-facility camping to cabins, resort lodges, boat camping and primitive camping, await the outdoor enthusiast in Florida's national and state parks. Some facilities are available on a first-come, first-served basis, while others require advance reservations; permits are required for certain campsites. Reservations for campsites are accepted in advance; cabin rentals up to 11 months in advance. Rates vary according to season and facilities: cabins *($20–$130/day)*, campsites *($8–$31)*. For reservations *(generally only taken Mon–Fri 8am–5pm)* contact the park directly. For a free brochure listing all state park facilities, contact: **Florida Department of Environmental Protection**, Division of Recreation & Parks (*850-245-2157; www.floridastateparks.org*).

CAMPGROUNDS AND RECREATIONAL VEHICLE (RV) PARKS

The Florida Assn. of RV Parks & Campgrounds which lists member sites and offers details on hookups, laundry facilities, pools, playgrounds, sporting facilities, freeway access and shopping. You can view their directory *Camp Florida* online at http:// campflorida.com or order a free copy to be sent to you. Either request it online or call *850-562-7151*. Parks are family-oriented and open year-round. Most campgrounds offer daily, weekly or monthly occupancy for recreational vehicles. Prices range from $10–$60/night for campsites and average $20–$25/night for RVs.

Camping, St. Augustine

Visit Florida

Reservations are recommended, especially for longer stays and in popular resort areas, including the Keys. **KOA Kampgrounds** are located all across Florida; some resort properties offer pools, hot tubs, air-conditioned cabins, restaurants, boat ramps, deep-sea fishing and snorkeling. For a directory *($6, includes shipping)*, order online or write to KOA Kampgrounds, PO Box 30558, Billings MT 59114 (*888-562-0000; www.koa.com*).

WHERE TO EAT

Blessed with 1,200mi of coastline, Florida is famous for fresh seafood: whether you opt for mullet, stone crabs or blackened grouper, you'll find a huge variety on restaurant menus in many different types of establishment. Salmon won't be local, but grouper, mackerel, red snapper, pompano and yellowfin tuna were most likely caught in Florida waters. Look for stone crabs in season (mid-May through mid-October), and don't leave the Keys without sampling conch fritters or ceviche, preferably followed by a hefty slice of Key Lime Pie.

Thanks to Florida's melting pot of island cultures and influx of immigrants, "Floribbean" cuisine reigns in many restaurant kitchens, a tantalizing fusion of fresh Floridian fish and citrus, spiked with Caribbean and Latin flavors. Other menu items you're likely to encounter are gator tail (yes, it's actually alligator) and hearts of palm salad. In Miami, some of the best food can be found in Little Havana, where Cuban classics are the order of the day. Ybor City, Tampa, is another zone for Cuban fare. Miami is coming on strong as one of the country's top dining destinations, as the long waits for reservations at top tables will attest. Be sure to make advance bookings if there is a restaurant you covet. Also note, when the bill comes, that many restaurants have already added a gratuity to the bill, a practice familar to their Latin American and European guests.

Basic Information

BUSINESS HOURS

Most businesses operate Monday–Friday 9am–5pm. **Banks:** Monday–Thursday 9am–4:30pm, Friday until 5pm or 6pm; some banks in larger cities may be open Saturday morning. Most retail stores and specialty shops are open Monday–Saturday 10am–6pm (Thursday 9pm). Malls and **shopping centers** are usually open Monday–Saturday 10am–9pm, Sunday noon–6pm. Most **state and federal** government buildings (including city halls) are open Monday–Friday

January 1	New Year's Day
3rd Monday in January	Martin Luther King Jr.'s Birthday*
3rd Monday in February	Presidents' Day*
Last Monday in May	Memorial Day
July 4	Independence Day
1st Monday in September	Labor Day*
2nd Monday in October	Columbus Day*
November 11	Veterans Day*
4th Thursday in November	Thanksgiving Day
December 25	Christmas Day

8:30am–4:30pm. In general, **churches** are open daily, sometimes as early as 7am, until 5pm or 6pm, and later. Inquire at the church office to view the sanctuary, if permitted.

Most banks and government offices are closed on the holidays listed on the table on this page *(many retail stores and restaurants remain open on days indicated with *).*

DRIVING IN THE US

Visitors bearing valid driver's licenses issued by their country of residence are not required to obtain an International Driver's License to drive in the US. Drivers must carry vehicle registration and/or rental contract, and proof of automobile insurance at all times. Rental cars in the US are usually equipped with automatic transmission, and rental rates tend to be less expensive than overseas. Gasoline (petrol) is sold by the US gallon (= 3.8 liters, smaller than the imperial gallon = 4.54 liters). Most self-service gas stations do not offer car repair, although many sell standard maintenance items.

Road regulations in the US require that vehicles be driven on the right side of the road. Distances are posted in miles (1 mile=1.6 kilometers). Do not stop if strangers try to flag your car down.. Don't stop if your car is bumped from the rear; instead proceed to the nearest well-lit public area and contact the police.

Visit Florida

ELECTRICITY

Electrical current in the US is 120 volts AC, 60 Hz. Foreign-made appliances may need voltage transformers and North American flat-blade adapter plugs (available at specialty travel and electronics stores).

EMERGENCIES

In all major US cities dial **911** to telephone the police, ambulance or fire department. Another way to report an emergency is to dial **0** for the operator (*see also Telephones*).

LIQUOR LAWS

The legal minimum age for purchase and consumption of alcoholic beverages is 21; proof of age is normally required. Most restaurants/bars do not serve liquor prior to 1pm on Sunday. Liquor is sold in liquor stores only, while beer and wine is available at grocery stores. Consuming liquor in public places and carrying an open liquor container in a moving vehicle is illegal.

MAIL

Letters can be mailed from most hotels as well as from post offices. Stamps and packing material may be purchased at post offices, grocery stores and businesses offering postal and express shipping services located throughout the city (*see the Yellow Pages phone directory under "Mailing Services"*). Most post offices are open Monday–Friday 9am–5pm, some are also open Saturday 9am–noon.

MONEY

Most banks are members of the network of Automated Teller Machines (ATM), allowing visitors from around the world to withdraw cash using bank cards and major credit cards. ATMs can usually be found in airports, banks, grocery stores and shopping malls.

CREDIT CARDS AND TRAVELER'S CHECKS

Rental-car agencies and many hotels require credit cards. Most banks will cash brand-name traveler's checks and process cash advances on major credit cards with proper identification. Traveler's checks are accepted at most stores, restaurants and hotels. **American Express Co. Travel Service** has offices in Jacksonville, Miami and major Florida cities (*www.americanexpress.com*).

To report a lost or stolen **credit card**, call: American Express (*800-528-4800; www.americanexpress.com*); **Diners Club** (*800-346-3779; www.dinersclubus.com*); **Discover Card** (*800-347-2683; www.discovercard.com*); **MasterCard** (*800-627-8372; www.mastercard.com/us*) or the issuing bank; **Visa** (*800-VISA-911; http://usa.visa.com*).

CURRENCY EXCHANGE

For a small fee, the main offices of most national banks will exchange foreign currency; contact main or branch offices for information and locations. Some statewide banks (Bank of America, First Union and SunTrust) exchange foreign currency at their local offices.

Thomas Cook Currency Services operates exchange offices throughout Florida (*800-287-7362; www.thomascook.com*). Currency exchange offices are located at the international airports in Jacksonville, Miami, Orlando and Tampa.

SMOKING

Smoking is banned in most enclosed indoor workplaces, including restaurants. Exceptions include stand-alone bars, where food is merely incidental, and tobacco shops.

TAXES AND TIPS

Prices displayed or quoted in the US do not generally include **sales tax** (6% in Florida). Sales tax is added at the time of purchase and is not reimbursable (it can sometimes

EQUIVALENTS										
Degrees Fahrenheit	95°	86°	77°	68°	59°	50°	41°	32°	23°	14°
Degrees Celsius	35°	30°	25°	20°	15°	10°	5°	0°	-5°	-10°

1 inch = 2.54 centimeters	1 quart = 0.946 liter
1 foot = 30.48 centimeters	1 gallon= 3.785 liters
1 mile = 1.609 kilometers	1 pound= 0.454 kilograms

be avoided if purchased items are shipped to another country by the seller). The hotel occupancy tax (6%–12.5%) and tax rate for rental cars vary according to location; additional daily surcharges may be added as well. Some counties levy an additional local sales tax, and/or a 1%–5% tourist tax.

In the US it is customary to give a **tip** for services rendered by waiters/ waitresses, porters, hotel maids and taxi drivers. It is customary in restaurants to tip the server 15%–20% of the bill. (In popular tourist locations restaurants may automatically add a service charge; check your bill before you tip). At hotels, porters are generally given $1 per suitcase, housekeeping staff $1 per day. Taxi drivers are usually tipped 15% of the fare.

TELEPHONES

For emergencies (police, fire, ambulance), dial 911. Some public telephones accept credit cards, and all will accept long-distance calling cards. For **long-distance calls** in the US and Canada, dial 1 + area code (3 digits) + number (7 digits). To place a **local call,** dial the 7-digit number without 1 or the area code (unless the local calling area includes several area codes). To find a local number (within your area code), check the local telephone directory or dial **411** for information; to find a **long-distance** number, dial 1 + area code + 555-1212 (there is a charge for both services). For operator assistance or information, dial **0** for the local operator or **00** for the long-distance operator. To place an **international call,** dial 011 +

country code + area code + number. A list of country and city codes can be found in the beginning of local phone directories. To place a collect call (person receiving the call pays charges), dial **0** + area code + number and tell the operator you are calling collect. If it is an international call, ask for the overseas operator.

Most telephone numbers in this guide that start with **800** or **888** or **877** are toll-free (no charge) in the US and may not be accessible outside North America. Dial **1** before dialing a toll-free number. Most hotels add a surcharge for both local and long-distance calls. You can send, or have money transferred to you, via the Western Union system (℘800-325-6000; www.westernunion.com).

TEMPERATURE AND MEASUREMENT

In the US temperatures are measured in degrees Fahrenheit and measurements are expressed according to the US Customary System of weights and measures.

TIME ZONE

Most of Florida is on Eastern Standard Time (EST), 5hrs behind Greenwich Mean Time (GMT). The Panhandle region west of the Apalachicola River adheres to Central Standard Time (CST), 1hr behind EST. Daylight Saving Time (clocks are advanced 1hr) is in effect for most of the US from the second Sunday in March until the first Sunday in November. All the Bahamian islands are on Eastern Standard Time and observe Daylight Saving Time from March through November.

CONVERSION TABLES

Weights and Measures

1 kilogram (kg) 6.35 kilograms 0.45 kilograms	**2.2 pounds (lb)** 14 pounds 16 ounces (oz)	**2.2 pounds** 1 stone (st) 16 ounces	*To convert kilograms to pounds, multiply by 2.2*
1 metric ton (tn)	**1.1 tons**	**1.1 tons**	
1 litre (l) 3.79 litres 4.55 litres	**2.11 pints (pt)** 1 gallon (gal) 1.20 gallon	**1.76 pints** 0.83 gallon 1 gallon	*To convert litres to gallons, multiply by 0.26 (US) or 0.22 (UK)*
1 hectare (ha) **1 sq kilometre (km²)**	**2.47 acres** 0.38 sq. miles (sq mi)	**2.47 acres** 0.38 sq. miles	*To convert hectares to acres, multiply by 2.4*
1 centimetre (cm) **1 metre (m)**	**0.39 inches (in)** 3.28 feet (ft) or 39.37 inches or 1.09 yards (yd)	**0.39 inches**	*To convert metres to feet, multiply by 3.28; for kilometres to miles, multiply by 0.6*
1 kilometre (km)	**0.62 miles (mi)**	**0.62 miles**	

Clothing

Women					Men			
Shoes	35	4	2½		**Shoes**	40	7½	7
	36	5	3½			41	8½	8
	37	6	4½			42	9½	9
	38	7	5½			43	10½	10
	39	8	6½			44	11½	11
	40	9	7½			45	12½	12
	41	10	8½			46	13½	13
Dresses & suits	36	6	8		**Suits**	46	36	36
	38	8	10			48	38	38
	40	10	12			50	40	40
	42	12	14			52	42	42
	44	14	16			54	44	44
	46	16	18			56	46	48
Blouses & sweaters	36	6	30		**Shirts**	37	14½	14½
	38	8	32			38	15	15
	40	10	34			39	15½	15½
	42	12	36			40	15¾	15¾
	44	14	38			41	16	16
	46	16	40			42	16½	16½

Sizes often vary depending on the designer. These equivalents are given for guidance only.

Speed

KPH	10	30	50	70	80	90	100	110	120	130
MPH	6	19	31	43	50	56	62	68	75	81

Temperature

Celsius (°C)	0°	5°	10°	15°	20°	25°	30°	40°	60°	80°	100°
Fahrenheit (°F)	32°	41°	50°	59°	68°	77°	86°	104°	140°	176°	212°

To convert Celsius into Fahrenheit, multiply °C by 9, divide by 5, and add 32.
To convert Fahrenheit into Celsius, subtract 32 from °F, multiply by 5, and divide by 9.
NB: Conversion factors on this page are approximate.

Cà d'Zan, Sarasota Bay
© Alanrodriguez/Dreamstime.com

The Region Today

By the time Florida became part of the US in 1821, it already had a thriving plantation economy in the northern part of the state, where most of the people lived. After the Civil War, new and diverse industries sprang up: timber, citrus, shipping, cattle and cigar-making, helped establish Florida's importance in the national marketplace.

Once the railroads linked the state with the rest of the country in the late 19C, Florida's economy began to blossom. Speculative land sales rocketed in the 1920s, but ended just as suddenly several years later. The subsequent downturn in real estate activity, followed by the Depression, slowed the state's growth until after World War II. Since then Florida's population has expanded rapidly, with retirees and young families fueling a healthy economy that varies from high-tech electronics and finance to agriculture and fishing.

ECONOMY

Florida's **service** industries as a whole are projected to account for about 90 percent of new jobs created in the next decade. Leading this list are community and personal services such as health care and tourist-related enterprises. About 30 percent of the state's employees work in this sector, earning one-quarter of the gross revenues.

Economists forecast that with Florida's ageing population, **health care** will be one of the fastest growing industries in the next decade. The second biggest service industry, retail, generates over 10 percent of the state's revenue in some of the country's largest department stores, malls, car dealerships, service stations and grocery stores. Enlisting about 14 percent of all workers, **government** extends its hand into schools, hospitals and the military.

Another big wedge of the service pie belongs to **finance and real estate**. Real estate in particular has mushroomed with the state's population growth, and now employs more than double the national average. Although Miami has recently topped Jacksonville as the state's leading financial center, Jacksonville still reigns as the insurance king, with several major insurance company headquarters located there. Transportation and foreign trade round out the service sector, with the latter expected to be one of Florida's hottest industries in upcoming years.

Florida's 12 international **airports** make large-scale tourism possible, while **trucks** transport most of the state's industrial and agricultural products. Some 15 deepwater **ports** serve Florida's international clients, with Tampa doing the largest volume of business.

The **movie business** is a major industry in the US, with Florida ranking third for film production (after California and New York respectively) based on revenue generated. Unfortunately in the last few years, some of the leading players moved out of Florida, but in 2010 State government were looking at ways (such as legislation on tax credits) to lure back lapsed movie makers and to attract even more film-making talend to the Sunshine State.

Because of Florida's distance from major US cities, **manufacturing** has traditionally taken a back seat to tourism and other service industries. The space industry and associated high-technology products is the major exception to this rule, representing $4.5 billion of the state's economy. However, since the Space Shuttle program is to be retired from service by 2011 (finance for a successor is as yet unconfirmed), this amount will almost certainly decrease. Since the beginning of the space program in the late 1950s, **high-technology** products have become a staple of the state's economy. National firms have opened branches here for the manufacture of communications devices, x-ray equipment, semiconductors and other computer compo-

Centro Ybor, Tampa's shopping, dining and entertainment district

nents. The commercial and residential **construction industry** as a whole has fluctuated with speculation based on the availability of loans as well as the predicted need for new housing.

Florida engages in a sizable **food production** business that includes canned fruit juice, canned fruits and packaged vegetables.

NATURAL RESOURCES

Florida's waters hold more than 700 species of fish. The **commercial fishing** industry nets the state more than $200 million a year, led by catches of shrimp, lobster, crab and snapper. Other important local species include grouper, swordfish, tuna and mullet. Ten percent of the total US shrimp harvest comes from Florida, and the state's Gulf estuaries—particularly off Apalachicola and the Big Bend coast—produce about 6 percent of the US oyster catch. Unfortunately, overfishing, foreign competition and contamination have caused a recent decline in the shellfish haul, and Florida has made some attempts at aquaculture to provide a more reliable harvest.

Forests cover about half of Florida's total land area, or almost 16 million acres. The north part of the state is the most densely timbered—commercial forests occupy 75 percent of the northwest region. Since the early 19C, **forestry** has held a significant place in the state's economy. In the years before the Civil War, hardwoods were cut for lumber and pines were tapped for turpentine and rosin used in shipbuilding. By the 1920s the **turpentine industry** had already peaked, but pulp mills were on the rise. Between 1889 and 1933, more than one billion feet of board were sawed a year in Florida's great virgin forests before a division of forestry was established to manage this precious resource. Slash pine today ranks as the top commercial tree; common hardwoods include magnolia, black tupelo and oak. Among valued trees harvested almost to extinction are pecky cypress (a porous wood, resistant to termites and rotting) and Dade County pine, both popular local building materials during the early 20C.

Phosphate was discovered in the southwest part of the state in 1881. Florida now produces 80 percent of the country's phosphate—an essential ingredient in fertilizer. Florida also leads the nation in production of rutile and zircon, heavy minerals found in ancient beach deposits and used in ceramics, metals and chemicals. Found in greater quantities here than in any other state, **peat** is prized as a soil conditioner. Florida also boasts extensive amounts of **limestone** (its most prevalent mineral).

AGRICULTURE

Leading the southeastern US in farm sales, Florida produces a variety of fruits, vegetables and nursery plants that it transports fresh to northern markets in the winter and spring. **Citrus fruits**, first introduced to Florida around 1570, outpace all Florida's other agricultural products, with oranges claiming over three-quarters of the total citrus sales. Florida invariably leads the nation in orange and grapefruit production, and supplies 40 percent of the world's orange juice supply. Among Florida's many popular varieties of citrus are Valencia oranges (the world's most ubiquitous juice orange), Temple oranges, and Duncan grapefruit (the Duncan's white flesh is considered the most flavorful).

While it is the single biggest crop, citrus makes up only a third of the state's total crop sales. Florida stands as the nation's top producer of **sugarcane**. Sugar plantations of the late 18C and early 19C were largely destroyed during the Seminole Wars, but the industry held on until finally receiving a big boost when US trade relations with Cuba soured in 1961. Florida now produces nearly half the country's sugar, primarily in the area just south of Lake Okeechobee.

Within the US only California exceeds Florida in total production and value of **fresh vegetables**. Major local crops include tomatoes, sweet corn, green peppers, snap beans and cucumbers. The state's dairy and beef industries generate a quarter of its total farm income, making Florida the largest cattle state east of the Mississippi.

TOURISM

Visitors have been flocking to the Sunshine State to escape the cold winters of more northern climes since the late 19C when the railroads linked Florida's grand east coast resorts. With the widespread use of automobiles and the increase in small-scale tourist facilities, more people could afford an excursion to Florida. After World War II, the advent of indoor air-conditioning made south Florida a year-round destination. Now, nearly 85 million people visit the state annually, lured by clear subtropical seas, white-sand beaches and world-class tourist attractions. The opening of Walt Disney World in 1971 outside Orlando meant a greater distribution of tourists among the non-coastal areas; the Orlando area now attracts nearly 50 million tourists annually.

Visitors spend a total of $65 billion a year and generate work for 981,300 Floridians—about 12 percent of the state's jobs. Employing people in travel, restaurants, hotels, retail stores and recreational facilities, tourism continues to be the state's top economic resource. Winter remains the busiest tourist season, while spring lures vacationing college students to Daytona Beach and Panama City. Summertime brings auto-touring families to beaches and theme parks. Autumn sees the fewest visitors as it is traditionally hurricane season.

ECONOMIC OUTLOOK

The state's tourism industry has rebounded despite the economic downturn resulting from terrorist attacks on US soil on September 11, 2001. 2007 saw record numbers of visitors, a total of 84.5 million. By 2009, however, that had slipped back to just under 81 million. One sector of the economy that forecasters claim could outperform tourism in the next decade is **international trade**. Florida's proximity to Latin American and Caribbean markets, coupled with its international ports and modern airports give the state an edge in this burgeoning field; around, 40 percent of all US exports to Latin and South America pass through Florida.

As for regional growth, it is probable that Orlando will lead in population increase and housing construction, and Southeast Florida, the most populous region, will maintain a healthy economic climate. Smaller areas on the move include Naples, Fort Walton Beach, Panama City, Ocala, Fort Myers, Fort Pierce and Port St. Lucie.

PEOPLE

Four out of five Floridians are not native to the state: as a group, residents of Florida share the identity of "newcomer" more than anything else. Beyond this identity lies a hodgepodge of ethnicities, ages, origins and attitudes that sometimes sit uneasily side-by-side in this growing state. Yet, along with their status as newcomers, Floridians as a whole share a sense of hope. Some come here seeking new job opportunities, others political freedom; all come looking for a piece of the American good life—a place in the sun.

Florida's phenomenal growth has outstripped most of the rest of the country: in 1900 the state ranked 33rd in population; by 1960 it had risen to 10th. With more than 18.5 million people, it now ranks as the fourth-largest state in the nation. The population has redistributed itself as the south Florida wilderness has yielded to the dreams of pioneers and developers. In 1900 north Florida held 66 percent of the population, compared to 5 percent in south Florida. Today the north has shrunk to 20 percent, while the south carries 37 percent—with one-third of the entire state living on the 65mi strip from Miami to West Palm Beach known as the Gold Coast.

EARLY MINORITIES

One of the smallest ethnic groups, the **Seminoles** are themselves relatively new to Florida. They coalesced from various southeastern tribes and moved into Florida in the 18C to escape harassment by white settlers. Though most were relocated to Oklahoma in the mid-19C, about 2,000 Seminoles still live and maintain elements of their culture on reservations in and around the Everglades. The percentage of **African-Americans** decreased from 44 percent of the population in 1900 to about 13 percent in 1990. Numbers have since grown to some 2.3 million, or about 14 percent of Florida's population.

NORTH AND SOUTH

If some Floridians consider the label "Cracker" a slur, others proudly acknowledge it as an ethnic identity that extols the frontier virtues of independence and self-reliance. The term—which probably derived from the snapping noise of whips used by early Florida cowboys—refers loosely to descendants of native white Floridians who owned small farms or ranches in the north part of the state. Whereas the peninsula has funneled in Yankees from the northeast over the past 50 years, north Florida has retained the flavor and drawl of neighbors Georgia and Alabama. The north, with its large concentration of military retirees, takes conservative political stances, while the south, claiming a high number of Jews and Northeasterners, tends toward a more liberal outlook.

OLD AND NEW

Since the end of World War II, the elderly have pushed in from less hospitable climes, until Florida now claims a higher percentage of **seniors** than any other state. This group has made southwest Florida one of the fastest-growing areas in the country. Another large number of retirees, known as "snowbirds," migrate to Florida for the winter, then return home in the spring.

The most influential group of arrivals to Florida in recent times, **Hispanics**, have swirled up from Cuba, and other regions to the south, with the frequency of tropical storms ever since the Cuban revolution in 1959. From that time to this, more than 750,000 people from the Caribbean have moved to Florida, giving the state one of the largest populations of Hispanics in the country: almost three million, or nearly 20 percent of the state's population. About 72 percent live on the Gold Coast, imparting their lively language and customs to the Miami region.

OVER THE HILL

Florida's old-aged population explosion may see some relief as the Generation X group come of age, meaning fewer retirees in the Sunshine State. Along with slower growth and less crowding comes

47

a less robust economy. The Gold Coast area, already near capacity, has suffered in recent years from a high crime rate brought on, in part, by a heated mixture of diverse people jostling for the promised good life.

Other areas of Florida stand ready to usher in the next wave of arrivals, from wherever they may come, and residents and visitors alike will have the opportunity to witness a state once again in the process of redefining itself.

RECREATION

World-famous for over a century, Florida's glorious **beaches** continue to top the heap of the state's recreational venues. With their fine white sand, rolling dunes and gentle clear blue surf, these beaches attract hordes of sun-worshippers and swimmers. Sanibel Island and other Gulf Coast beaches offer **sea shelling** unparalleled anywhere in the country.

Over the past few years, 15 Florida beaches have been ranked among the top 20 in the nation by independent surveys. Variously rated for their beauty, water and air temperatures, sand softness, water clarity and solitude, beaches that have been awarded the highest marks include those at St. George Island, Grayton Beach, Caladesi Island and St. Joseph Peninsula state parks.

IN AND ON THE WATER

Water sports of all types abound along both coasts, with **surfing** concentrated on the Atlantic side and **sailing** and **windsurfing** on the calmer Gulf. Florida manufactures more pleasure boats than any other state in the country; many of them are used for **waterskiing** or for taking fishing parties out to cast for such deep-sea denizens as mackerel, marlin, bonefish, sailfish and tarpon. Inland, the state's numerous rivers, lakes and springs provide ample opportunity for freshwater **fishing** as well as **canoeing** through primeval swamplands. The Florida Canoe Trail system boasts more than 1000mi of designated routes along 36 rivers and waterways.

Snorkelers don fins and masks along both coasts to explore ancient wrecks and exotic fish. For sheer underwater beauty, **scuba divers** head to the coral reef that stretches off the shores of the Florida Keys. Divers also plunge into the mysterious underwater caves located in many of Florida's crystal-clear springs, where they encounter such creatures as American eels and blind crayfish.

BACK ON LAND

Florida has over 1,250 **golf courses**, more than any state in the union; most are open to the public. Another year-round sport, **tennis** is played through-

Canoeing, Lake Norris

Visit Florida

Tennis in Sarasota

Visit Florida

out the state; many hotels and resorts offer vacation packages that include tennis lessons with resident pros. A significant number of tourists escape to Florida to take advantage of its many **spas**, which promise rest for the weary and rejuvenation for the aged.

Backcountry in the Everglades and the Panhandle attracts **campers** to vast acreages of national and state parks. **Hiking** is becoming a more and more popular activity, with over 2,300mi of developed trails in the state. In the years ahead, state officials hope to link the **Florida National Scenic Trail** with the Appalachian Trail, thus extending the latter from Alabama and Georgia to the Everglades. The Florida trail currently crosses some 1,400mi through swampland, scrub and hardwood forest.

SPECTATOR SPORTS

Among the many spectator sports in the state, **jai alai** is perhaps the most uniquely Floridian. Originating in the Basque region of Spain and imported from Cuba, the world's fastest game is played on six *frontons* (176ft courts) throughout Florida, including America's oldest, the 1926 Miami Jai-Alai Fronton. Players hurl *pelotas* (balls) against curved walls at speeds of 170mph or more and catch them in *cestas* (baskets) attached to their arms. Betting is very popular.

Auto racing, which started on the beach near Daytona in 1902, continues on the Daytona International Speedway. Racing fans can also watch greyhound or horse track days throughout the state. Miami's Hialeah Park (est 1925) remains one of the most popular venues for horse racing in Florida.

Professional sports teams bring some of the country's top athletes to Florida. Since 1901 the state has been a favorite location for major league **baseball spring training camps**. Eighteen teams train here and hold exhibition games, while several minor league clubs provide summertime ballpark excitement.

FOOD AND WINE

Taking advantage of the bounty of its offshore waters, its year-round growing season and the influence of its Latin and Caribbean immigrants, the Sunshine State offers a crazy-quilt of cuisines that vary regionally from north to south. Whether your tastes run to "down-home" cooking or haute cuisine, you can find it in Florida.

CRACKER COOKING

Saltpork, cornmeal, molasses and turnip greens were staples in the diets of Florida's early settlers. Known as "Crackers" (*see p47*), these pioneers hunted squirrel, deer and raccoon to add to their tables. Freshwater fish, caught in local rivers and springs, was pan-fried. The ubiquitous Sabal palm was harvested for its edible bud, said to taste like raw cabbage. Called "swamp cabbage" by the settlers, this same delicacy is known today as "hearts of palm."

In the Panhandle and northeastern regions, dishes still echo the early style of cooking, replete with the southern accents of neighbors Georgia and Alabama. Steamed Apalachicola Bay oysters, broiled amberjack (a mild, flaky white fish), fried catfish or Gulf shrimp, hush puppies (small balls of deep-fried cornmeal dough) and grits (a bland gruel made from ground white corn) constitute typical northern fish-house fare. A menu in these restaurants might also include fried alligator and frog legs,

On the Wild Side: Florida's Exotic Fruits

South Florida's subtropical climate nurtures a plethora of little-known fruits from around the world. What follows is a sampling of Florida's exotic bounty.

Carambola – Each slice of the yellow-green, ridged carambola forms a star, thus its more popular moniker, star fruit. Hailing from East India, the crunchy carambola has a fresh, slightly acidic flavor that enhances desserts and salads.

Kumquat – Eaten raw, this Chinese quail-egg-size citrus fruit tastes tart and its rind bitter. Chefs recommend poaching kumquats in sugar syrup to render them more palatable.

Lychee – Another China native, resembling a small red ball with knobby skin, the lychee grew in Florida as early as 1886. Its honeyed, fragrant white flesh is often served for dessert in Chinese restaurants.

Mango – The dark oval fruit has been cultivated in tropical East Asia for over 6,000 years. Florida growers stagger ripening times so mango-lovers can enjoy this peachy treat for as long as five months a year.

Passion Fruit – Encased in a hard, bitter-tasting yellow or purple shell, the juicy edible pulp of the passion fruit is studded with tiny black seeds. This South American native caught on as a commercial fruit in the 1980s.

Plantain – This jumbo cousin of the banana originated in Africa. Rarely eaten raw, plantains—an essential ingredient in Cuban cuisine—are usually served fried, boiled or baked.

Sapodilla – Fans of the egg-shaped, brown-skinned sapodilla claim it tastes like a pear infused with maple syrup. This fruit grows wild in parts of Mexico and Central America.

Ugli Fruit – A cross between a tangerine and a grapefruit, the ugli is named for its unappealing thick yellow-green skin. Despite its appearance, this pear-shaped native of Jamaica boasts a sought-after, tart-sweet flavor.

as well as spicy Cajun creations such as the thick seafood stew called gumbo, and jambalaya, a hearty variety of meats and shellfish cooked with rice.

TROPICAL DELIGHTS

South Florida cooking takes its cues from the fresh vegetables, exotic fruits and the bountiful numbers of commercial fish harvested in the state. Here you can sample smoked mullet and freshly caught grouper (try it grilled or encrusted with macadamia nuts), pompano, snapper and mahi mahi—all often paired with tropical fruit salsas. Succulent stone crab claws, chewy conch fritters (made from the mollusk found inside Florida's once abundant state shell) and clawless spiny lobster constitute some of the state's unique shellfish dishes.

Although renowned for its citrus fruit—over 20 varieties are grown here—Flor-ida has added exotics such as passion fruit, papaya, mango and carambola to its expanding list of produce. In addition Florida claims the small, yellowish, bracingly tart key limes used in making **key lime pie**. A mixture of egg yolks, sweetened condensed milk and key lime juice in a graham-cracker crust, the state's famed dessert is traditionally topped with fluffy meringue.

Florida's ever-evolving cuisine is generously peppered with foreign flavors. Cubans have introduced plantains (a cousin to the banana), yuca (a mild-tasting root vegetable) and boniato (a nutty Cuban sweet potato) to grocery stores. Entrées on many restaurant menus will include dishes such as black beans and rice; *arroz con pollo* (chicken with yellow rice); and *ropa vieja* (Spanish for "old clothes"), shredded beef dressed with tomatoes, peppers, onions, garlic and white wine.

History

PREHISTORIC AND NATIVE FLORIDIANS

Prehistoric peoples probably inhabited the area of North America that now includes Florida as early as 10,000 BC. While it has long been thought that Ice Age nomads filtered southeast after crossing the Bering land bridge from Siberia into Alaska between 20,000 and 15,000 BC, there is now speculation that those who reached the Florida peninsula may have come instead from Central and South America through the Antilles. The earliest Indians here were hunter-gatherers whose diet included the meat of saber-toothed tigers, mastodons, bison and other Pleistocene animals. Divers in northern Florida rivers often discover fluted stone spearheads, known as Clovis or Suwannee points, used by prehistoric hunters.

The first semi-permanent settlements began to spring up along Florida's waterways around 5,000 BC. Evidence can be found in ancient **midden mounds** (trash heaps) of the shellfish that had become increasingly important to the Indians' diet. Agriculture, including the cultivation of squash, beans and corn introduced from South America or Mexico, began when the population became more sedentary around 1,000 BC.

Archaeologists have found some 14,000 **burial** mounds throughout the state (many lost to modern development). These mysterious mounds are thought to reflect the influence of the Hopewell cultures of Illinois and Ohio. The bodies of chiefs or religious leaders were found inside resting face-up toward the sun. Other important tribal figures were buried face-down above them. By the Christian era, some of the ceremonial sites had developed into large complexes comprising several individual mounds connected by an intricate system of canals and roadways.

By the time European explorers visited the Florida peninsula in the 16C, the native population numbered an estimated 100,000. There were six main groups: the **Timucua** (occupying northeast Florida as far south as present-day Cape Canaveral), the **Apalachee** (Panhandle), the **Ais** (central and southeast coast), the **Tequesta** (southeast coast), the **Tocobaga** (Tampa Bay area) and the **Calusa** (southwest region). Developing independently, each group maintained a separate culture with specific social orders and sophisticated religious and political institutions.

The northern Indians subsisted by farming, while those south of the Everglades generally hunted game and fished for seafood.

Reconstructed native Timucuan shelter of palm fronds, Fort Caroline National Historic Site on the St. Johns River, Florida

© North Wind Picture Archives/Alamy

51

Within 250 years of European colonization, intertribal wars, Spanish slave raids and European-imported diseases such as smallpox, influenza and measles, had decimated most of the Indian population. The few hundred remaining Timucua and Apalachee left Florida for Cuba with the Spanish in 1763. Today the only remaining traces of Florida's earliest native cultures are archaeological.

FIRST SPANISH PERIOD 1513–1763

European explorers and fortune hunters began making forays into the Caribbean and Florida Straits in the 15C. Soon after Christopher Columbus discovered Hispaniola in 1492, Italian-born cartographer **Giovanni Caboto** (also known as John Cabot), commissioned by England's King Henry VIII, ventured into the New World to chart his findings. Although there is no specific record of it, Cabot and his son Sebastian probably sighted the Florida peninsula in 1497 or 1498. At least three European maps made between 1502 and 1511 indicate that others soon followed. Accounts that early explorers encountered Spanish-speaking Indians on the Florida peninsula support the theory that Spanish slave hunters from the West Indies had been there as well.

In 1513 explorer **Juan Ponce de León**, awarded with a Spanish patent to colonize any lands he found, made the first recorded—and officially sanctioned—landfall. De León, who was looking for the island of Bimini, went ashore somewhere between present-day St. Augustine and the St. Johns River in early April. He gave the name La Florida to an area that covers most of the present-day Southeast, west to the Mississippi River and north into the Carolinas. When de León returned to the southwest coast in 1521, he was gravely wounded in an Indian attack; he then sailed to Cuba where he died within a few weeks. Subsequent Spanish colonization attempts also failed miserably. **Pánfilo de Narváez** set sail from Spain in 1527 with a patent to settle Florida—a reward from Emperor Charles V for de Narváez' service in the Spanish conquest of Cuba. In 1528 de Narváez landed in Tampa Bay, and with over half his cadre of 400 men, marched north by foot to Apalachee in search of gold, sending his ships up the coast to wait for him. When the men reached the coast, they found no ships so they set out for Mexico in several crude boats. De Narváez and all but 80 of his men subsequently met their end in a storm off the coast of Texas. Accomplished conquistador **Hernando de Soto**'s legendary three-year search (1539–41) for riches in the New World also proved disastrous. After trekking several thousand miles with his 600 men—throughout central and northern Florida and as far west as present-day Oklahoma—de Soto died from fever. The remaining dispirited fortune-hunters, some 300 survivors, eventually found their way back to Spain. Next to try his luck, wealthy Spanish viceroy **Tristán de Luna** followed de Soto in 1559. Plagued by storms, hunger and dissension among his soldiers, de Luna was forced to abandon his effort to establish a settlement at Pensacola Bay.

Finding plenty of trouble but none of the anticipated riches, Spain (already importing gold and silver from Mexico and Peru) temporarily lost interest in colonizing La Florida. The peninsula's strategic location on the Florida Straits, however, was vital to protecting the country's Caribbean trade routes from pirates. In 1562, a French expedition led by the ardent Calvinist **Jean Ribault** entered the St. Johns River in search of a site for a Huguenot colony. When Ribault's fledgling settlement completed building Fort Caroline near the river's mouth in 1565, an alarmed Spain moved to reclaim her hold.

Accordingly, later that year **Pedro Menéndez de Avilés** sailed into the Florida Straits and founded St. Augustine (to be the first permanent European settlement in Florida). He then massacred the French at Fort Caroline. At least one important legacy survives the French defeat: the published drawings and descriptions of the native population by French illustrator **Jacques Le**

Moyne remain one of the most detailed accounts of early Florida history.

THE MISSION CHAINS

Although Spain retained her power in Florida for the next two centuries, the region attracted few independent settlers outside the military and the Catholic Church. Besides two garrisons at Pensacola and St. Augustine, the Spanish presence consisted of about 100 missions. Begun in 1565, the first of two chains led north from St. Augustine along the coast of present-day Georgia and South Carolina. A second string, built from the early 1600s to 1704, stretched west across the Panhandle to the Apalachee Bay region. At its center stood powerful **San Luis de Talimali**, built in 1656 near present-day Tallahassee, which included a church, a convent for the friars, a cemetery and block houses, as well as an Apalachee Indian village and ball field. The missions functioned primarily as a strategic defensive system, designed to convert, centralize—and thus control—the Indians, who were coerced into labor and defense of the Spanish frontier. Ultimately the system failed, succumbing to both internal power struggles among the Franciscan friars and to external attack. By the early years of the 18C, most missions had been burned in raids—supported by defecting Indians—led by British soldiers from the English colony of South Carolina. Remaining structures, fashioned from perishable wooden frames roofed with palm thatch, quickly deteriorated, and soon all traces of the missions had disappeared.

BRITISH PERIOD
1763–1783

The 1763 **Treaty of Paris** ending the Seven Years War between England and France marked a decisive turning point in Florida history. Under the treaty's provisions, the Spanish colony was ceded to Britain in exchange for Havana, Cuba, which England had captured the previous year. Florida was then split into two parts. East Florida, with a capital at St. Augustine, included the peninsula and the Panhandle as far as the Apalachicola River. West Florida, with Pensacola as its capital, was bounded on the north by the present state line, and on the west by the Mississippi River. By British charter in 1764, Florida gained a section between the Mississippi and Chattahoochee rivers extending north to the present-day cities of Jackson, Mississippi, and Montgomery, Alabama.

In contrast to Spain, Britain attempted a self-supporting colony. Sugar, rice,

San Luis de Talimali

Visit Tallahassee

indigo and cotton plantations were established along the St. Johns River. Export subsidies and generous land grants drew Protestant settlers from Great Britain as well as Tory sympathizers who left Georgia and South Carolina after the Revolution. The new population also included a 1768 colony of some 2,000 Greeks, Italians and Minorcans at New Smyrna, about 75mi south of St. Augustine. By the 1720s, a number of different loosely organized Indian groups (later known as the Creek Confederacy), pushed by settlers out of Georgia, Alabama and South Carolina, had also begun to filter into northern Florida. From the Creeks, two main nations, the Hitchiti-speaking **Miccosukee** and the Muskogee-speaking **Seminoles**, emerged.

SECOND SPANISH PERIOD 1784–1821

British occupation of Florida was to last only 20 years. With Britain's forces engaged in Revolutionary War battles farther north, Spain (participating in the war indirectly as a French ally) took advantage of Florida's weakened defenses and recaptured Pensacola in 1781. Under the **Second Treaty of Paris** (1783) ending the Revolution, the remainder of Florida reverted to Spanish control—excluding the northern section added above the Panhandle in 1764. By about 1800, Seminole villages were scattered from Apalachicola east to the St. Johns River and from south Georgia down to the Caloosahatchee River. During the War of 1812, violence erupted repeatedly between white settlers and Indians, who were resented for harboring runaway slaves and controlling valuable land. In 1814, a battle with the Upper Creeks at Horseshoe Bend ended in Indian defeat and a treaty opening 20 million acres of Creek land to US settlement. From 1817 to 1818, Gen. Andrew Jackson led a special US command against the Seminoles, initiating a series of raids later known as the **First Seminole War** and attacking several Spanish settlements.

By this time it was clear that Spain could neither govern nor police its increasingly turbulent territory effectively. Its power thus diminished, Spain negotiated the **Adams-Onís Treaty** in 1819. This agreement transferred the land east of the Mississippi to the US and formalized the boundaries of present-day Florida, with the Panhandle terminating at the Perdido River. The treaty was ratified in 1821 and the two Floridas were handed over to General Jackson in Pensacola on 17 July.

Oldest Spanish School in the USA, St. Augustine

© Paul Brennan/Dreamstime.com

EARLY SETTLEMENT AND THE SEMINOLE WARS

In 1822 President James Monroe unified the two Floridas into a single territory with two counties: Escambia and St. Johns. Two years later, the first Territorial governor, William P. DuVal, named Tallahassee as the capital. In the new US Territory, the government recognized all land grants made before 1818, pending fulfillment of the original terms. Congress also granted the right of preemption to settlers, allowing squatters to remain if they purchased 80 acres of land at $1.25 an acre. With the area now open to settlers, tensions mounted over the Indian presence.

In the 1820s the US government attempted to contain the native population on a single tract of land in central Florida. When this effort failed, Jackson, now president, signed the **Indian Removal Act** in 1830, in hopes of resolving Indian conflicts once and for all by relocating eastern tribes to a designated area west of the Mississippi River. This law specified that the Indians must consent to moving, that they would be paid for their land and they would hold perpetual title to their new territories in the west. The Seminoles demonstrated the greatest resistance to this infamous forced exodus, known as the **Trail of Tears**. In 1832 a small group of Seminoles (unauthorized by their leaders) signed the **Treaty of Payne's Landing**, requiring the Indians to relinquish their land and relocate to a reservation in Arkansas (now Oklahoma). At the end of a three-year grace period, however, not a single Seminole had left.

US troops arrived in 1835 to enforce the treaty. In December Seminoles ambushed the command of Maj. Francis Dade near Bushnell, precipitating the **Second Seminole War**. The leader of the Seminole resistance was **Osceola**. Still remembered for his cunning and courage, this great man met a bitter end. In late 1837, he was tricked into entering a US army camp near St. Augustine. There under a flag of truce, he was imprisoned and transferred to Fort Moultrie in Charleston, South Carolina, where he died in 1838. The Seminole Wars ended in 1842, when at least 3,000 Indians and blacks were sent to Oklahoma. For every two Indians removed, one white soldier was killed; the cost to the federal government was $20 million. Eluding capture, several hundred Seminoles melted into the Everglades.

In 1845 Florida was admitted to the Union as the 27th state. Indian rights remained unresolved, as Floridians kept pressing the US government for total removal of the Seminoles from the state. Increasing incursions of the white man into Indian reservation land eventually led to the **Third Seminole War** of 1855–58, an inconclusive series of swamp skirmishes that ended with the surrender of Seminole chief Billy Bowlegs and never resulted in a formal treaty with the US government.

THE PLANTATION BELT

During early statehood, settlement remained primarily between the Suwannee and Apalachicola rivers in an area called Middle Florida, where pioneers and cattle drivers established small farms. The dark, sandy loam there also proved excellent for **cotton** cultivation and hundreds of plantations flourished by 1850, building a cotton economy comparable to that of antebellum Georgia. In 1834 the first railroad incorporated in Florida connected the cotton market of Tallahassee to the port of St. Marks. It was built for the express purpose of shipping cotton to textile mills in New England and overseas. Eventually, the plantation belt spread southeastward, encompassing Alachua and Marion counties by 1860. Aside from cotton, timber, turpentine and sugarcane, were common plantation products. Sugarcane plantations were concentrated along the St. Johns and Manatee rivers.

While plantation size varied from 1,000 to 5,000 acres, wealth was measured not by acreage but by the number of slaves one owned. "Planters" were defined as those who owned 20 or more slaves. The number of planters who owned 30 or more slaves doubled between 1850 and

1860. This elite group set the local political, economic and social tone.

THE STEAMBOAT AGE

The riverboat industry was critical to Florida's economic development and settlement. The first steamboat service was offered in 1827 on the Apalachicola River. This waterbody, along with the Chattahoochee and Flint rivers, formed an important cotton outlet. Lumber, then a major export, was also ferried via steamer. During the Second Seminole War, the government chartered 40 steamboats to transport troops and supplies. By 1848 service from Jacksonville connected Palatka and Enterprise on the St. Johns River, with the steamers came Florida's first winter tourists, a major portion of whom were northerners whose doctors had recommended a sunny clime to cure their ailments. Sick and healthy passengers alike slept in elegantly furnished staterooms and dined on fine food, while the exotic foliage, Spanish moss and alligators sighted on the banks of the dark, winding waterways, held the promised trappings of a wilderness adventure.

CIVIL WAR AND RECONSTRUCTION

A steady flow of settlers and the sound plantation economy increased Florida's population of 34,700 in 1830 to 140,400 in 1860. Almost half of them were "nonwhite." To protect its one-sided economy, which relied heavily on slave labor, the state seceded from the Union in 1861 and became an important supplier of beef, cotton and salt to the Confederacy. The major Civil War clash on Florida soil was the 1864 battle at Olustee near Lake City; there on February 20, Confederate troops drove back the Union soldiers and preserved supply lines to Georgia. A second important victory occurred the next year, when Tallahassee—the only southern capital to escape capture—was successfully defended in the Battle of Natural Bridge.

The war almost bankrupted the state, but reconstruction brought new investors from the north, ready to finance business, land speculation, transportation and tourism. Sharecroppers and tenant farmers, including freed blacks, took over the plantations. Cotton, timber and cattle sales helped boost the economy. In the late 1860s, some 6,000 Cubans immigrated to Florida at the start of Cuba's Ten Years' War of Independence (1868–78), establishing Key West as a major cigar-making center. Soon thereafter, the commercial sponge market, established in Key West in 1849, moved its hub north after new beds were discovered off Tarpon Springs in the 1870s. The commercial citrus industry increased and thrived until two terrible freezes in the winter of 1894–95 obliterated about 90 percent of the crop.

THE RAILROAD BOOM

Florida's late 19C growth was closely linked to its rapid railroad development, spurred by the state's 1881 sale of four million acres of swamp and overflow land in central Florida to Philadelphia entrepreneur **Hamilton Disston**. Most importantly, this sale provided funds to clear the titles of state-owned land from earlier railroad promotions and opened the way for subsidies and land grants to new railroad builders. The undisputed leaders in the field—and in Florida development—remain two of the most colorful figures in the state's history: railroad tycoons **Henry Bradley Plant** and **Henry Morrison Flagler**. Plant consolidated and expanded numerous existing short lines and extended track to Tampa in 1884 to create an important link to northern markets. The Plant system merged with the Atlantic Coast Line in 1902 to complete a network of about 2,250mi of track originating in Richmond, Virginia. Flagler concentrated on the **Florida East Coast Railway** (FEC), extending it from Jacksonville to St. Augustine in 1886 and subsequently to Palm Beach (1894), Miami (1896) and Key West (1912). As the railway system expanded to link Florida to the rail lines crossing the US, it also spurred the state's winter production of fruit and vegetables.

Extravagant hotels strategically placed at each new railhead, such as the sprawling Ponce de Leon in St. Augustine, the Royal Poinciana in Palm Beach (the dining room seated 1,600), and Miami's Royal Palm (with its circular six-hole golf course) became fashionable resort destinations for the northern social set in the late 19C.

20C DEVELOPMENT

The early 20C was Florida's gilded age, a brief period of glamor, extravagance and no income or inheritance tax. Millionaire industrialists luxuriated in fabulous villas, while movie stars arrived from Hollywood to make films in Jacksonville, then a leading motion-picture production center. The economy had benefited from the 1898 **Spanish-American War**, when embarkation camps for American troops were located in Tampa, Miami and Jacksonville. After the US won its bid to gain Cuban independence from Spain, many soldiers returned to Florida with their families. For the first time, good roads—the Florida Road Department was established in 1915—and the affordable Model T automobile, made vacations accessible to people who could not afford luxury hotels. Modest, family-operated motels and tourist courts sprouted on the Florida roadside. By the 1920s "tin-can tourist camps," filled with Tin Lizzies outfitted as campers, had appeared in every major Florida city.

Dozens of land speculators, including Carl Fisher in Miami Beach and George Merrick in Coral Gables, not only peddled Spanish bungalows, but also a new lifestyle and a rosy future in the "Empire of the Sun." From 1920–25, the state grew four times faster than any other. As real-estate agent and self-proclaimed conman Wilson Mizner (younger brother of architect Addison) assessed the situation: "Right up to January 1926, it was only necessary to point carelessly to a mudhole and tell a client that there was his future. He could not deny it, and even the salesman was in deadly fear that he spoke the truth."

Unfortunately, the bust was just as rapid as the boom. The real-estate crash came in 1926 on the heels of overspeculation and a destructive hurricane that beheaded palm trees, leveled cheaper construction and stopped new building in its tracks. A ruinous Mediterranean fruit fly invasion in 1929 devastated the citrus industry. The onset of the national Depression that same year only confirmed what Floridians already knew.

EFFECTS OF WORLD WAR II

Despite the lean years, Florida's population had grown to around two million by 1940. This number was supplemented by another three million tourists annually. World War II stimulated the economy with defense-related industry, road-building, and new and revitalized naval bases. After the war, servicemen who trained on the beaches of Daytona, Miami and St. Petersburg returned to find jobs or enroll in Florida colleges under the GI bill. The economy diversified. Frozen citrus juice concentrates became a major industry by 1950. The same year, the US inaugurated a long-range, missile-testing program at Cape Canaveral, followed by a new space satellite program eight years later.

After World War II, a strong Florida government made a concerted effort to bring corporate industry to the state. Millions of people began to vacation here as the two-week paid vacation became standard. To accommodate them, more new hotels appeared in Greater Miami between 1945 and 1954 than in all the other US states combined. In 1958 the first US domestic jet service, from New York to Miami, opened the way for more tourists. Highway travel increased, too, and with it small attractions—featuring everything from alligators to mermaids—mushroomed along the Florida roadside. These private businesses were the forerunners of corporate theme parks, including the Disney empire. Today, some 84 million visitors come to Florida each year.

During the same period, Florida hosted another growing population: foreign refugees. Most notably, the 1959 Cuban

Revolution sent waves of exiles into Dade County in that year and again in 1961. Between 1965 and 1973, a series of Cuban government-controlled airlifts—that came to be known as "Freedom Flights"—carried thousands more refugees to Florida. In 1980 the Cuban government again allowed emigration. This time, more than 125,000 residents of the port of Mariel, among them criminals released from Cuban prisons, landed on Miami's shores. The number of Cubans in Florida climbed to about 670,000 in 1990, infusing the state's culture with a strong Latin flavor.

FLORIDA TODAY

Only a few decades ago, Florida was seen as a region of infinite potential. "So many of Florida's resources are as yet undeveloped, so much wealth lies hidden in her soil, so great an area of wilderness beauty is yet to be discovered and appreciated," boasted a 1930 promotional booklet. Many would argue that during the next half-century, those same resources were not only overdeveloped, but exhausted. The boom cycles, transportation advancements and population influxes that define Florida history also brought the inevitable housing complexes, strip malls, high-rise beach developments and traffic jams—making it difficult to believe that the peninsula

Midtown Miami Condominium

© Nick Tzolov/iStockphoto.com

was a beckoning frontier as recently as the early 20C. The state's proximity to South America means that much of the illegal drug trade entering the US filters through Florida. Immigration remains a sensitive subject, as the influx of Cuban exiles, Haitians, Nicaraguans, Jamaicans, Vietnamese, Cambodians and many other groups continues. Another type of immigrant—northern retirees—has also made an indelible mark on the Florida landscape, boosting the economy yet crowding roads and towns.

Florida's resources still abound and in recent decades a trend toward preserving them has emerged. Begun in 1981, the award-winning planned town of Seaside on the Panhandle has become an international model of environmentally sensitive contextual design.

An effort to restore more natural water flow to the Everglades by removing man-made locks and spillways is reviving habitat for more than 60 threatened and endangered species, as well as providing flood control and a reliable water supply to Southern Florida. In 2008 the state bought 187,000 acres of land abutting the 'glades from the US Sugar Corporation, in order to help. The good news is that phosphorous concentrations in Everglades waters have been reduced to 12 parts per billion, compared to 170 parts per billion a decade ago, but much more remains to be done to restore America's River of Grass.

Unchecked urban sprawl has long been a Central Florida problem, affecting quality of life and economic performance. A 2005 national study by urban planners ranked Orlando among the worst sprawling communities nationwide, while two other Florida cities made the top 20 (Miami at No. 8 and Jacksonville at No. 20). Strip malls and condo complexes continue to sprout like weeds on undeveloped tracts of land, impacting the appeal of areas such as the Keys and other pockets of Old Florida. Maintaining a balance between tourism, growth, and preserving the character and environment of the state will continue to be a challenge to the administrators and governors of the Sunshine State.

TIME LINE

10,000-8,000 BC — First migration of prehistoric Indians to the Florida peninsula.

5000 BC — First semi-permanent Native American settlements in Florida.

1492 — Christopher Columbus lands in the region of the present-day Bahamas.

1513 — Spanish explorer **Juan Ponce de León** lands in the area of present-day St. Augustine and names the land *"La Florida."*

1521 — Ponce de León returns to the southwestern coast of the Florida peninsula and attempts to establish a colony.

1528 — Explorer **Pánfilo de Narváez** goes ashore at Tampa Bay and marches to Apalachee in search of gold.

1539–1541 — Conquistador **Hernando de Soto** explores the Florida interior, trekking north and west into the continent.

1559 — Spanish nobleman **Tristán de Luna** attempts to establish a settlement at Pensacola Bay.

1562 — French Protestant **Jean Ribault** explores the banks of the St. Johns River as a possible site for a Huguenot colony; led by René de Laudonnière, the colony is established in 1564.

1565 — **Pedro Menéndez de Avilés** founds San Augustine, the first permanent European settlement in America.

1565–1704 — Spain founds about 100 **missions** in two chains stretching north and west from St. Augustine.

1672 — Work begins on the **Castillo de San Marcos** at St. Augustine, the first stone fort built by the Spanish in Florida.

1702 — British colonel James Moore destroys St. Augustine but fails to capture the Castillo de San Marcos. Britain begins attacks on Spanish missions two years later.

1719 — French soldiers capture Pensacola but soon return the colony to Spain. France occupies the Gulf Coast west of Pensacola.

1720s — First migration of Creek groups—later called the Seminoles and **Miccosukee**—from Georgia into Florida.

1740 — The British military invades Florida from Georgia.

1763 — **Treaty of Paris** ends the Seven Years War (1756–63) between Britain and France. Britain gains Florida from Spain and splits the region into two provinces divided by the Apalachicola River.

1768 — Minorcan, Italian and Greek colonists establish a colony at New Smyrna.

1781 — Spanish recapture Pensacola from the British.

1783 — The **Second Treaty of Paris** ends the American Revolution. Florida returns to Spanish control.

1814 — Driven from their land in Alabama, homeless Creeks migrate to Florida, doubling the territory's Indian population.

1817–1818 — Gen. Andrew Jackson initiates a series of raids against the Seminoles, later known as the **First Seminole War**.

1818 — US gains Pensacola and pushes for Spanish withdrawal from the region.

1821 — Spain gains the Texas territory and relinquishes Florida to the US under the terms of the **Adams-Onís Treaty**. Jackson is elected the first governor of the two Florida colonies.

1822 — President James Monroe unifies East and West Florida into one territory and settlement begins. Jacksonville is founded.

1824 — Tallahassee is chosen as the state capital. Key West becomes a US naval station.

1827 — The first steamboat service is established on the Apalachicola River.

1830 — President Andrew Jackson signs the **Indian Removal Act** authorizing the relocation of eastern tribes to an area west of the Mississippi River.

1831 — First cigar factory is built in Key West.

1832 — US claims Seminole lands in Florida under the **Treaty of Payne's Landing**.

1834 — Florida's first railroad, the mule-drawn Tallahassee-St. Mark's line, is incorporated.

1835–1842 — US military forces and Florida Indians clash in the **Second Seminole War**. At least 3,000 Indians and blacks are relocated to Arkansas; the Kissimmee area is opened to white settlement.

1837 — Seminole leader **Osceola** is imprisoned under a flag of truce at a St. Augustine army base.

1838 — Osceola dies at age 34 in a South Carolina dungeon. First Constitutional Convention held in St. Joseph (Port St. Joe).

1841 — Yellow fever epidemic hits the Panhandle.

1845 — Florida becomes the 27th US state under President John Tyler. William D. Moseley is elected the first governor.

1849 — The first commercial sponge market opens in Key West.

1851 — Dr. John Gorrie patents the process of making ice artificially.

1855 — Under Florida's **Internal Improvement Act**, undeveloped Florida land is made available to investors.

1855–1858 — Billy Bowlegs—the last chief under whom all Seminoles were united— leads the Indian resistance in the **Third Seminole War**.

1860 — The first east-west Florida railroad, linking Cedar Key with Fernandina Beach, is completed.

1861 — Florida secedes from the Union.

1864 — Confederate troops win the **Battle of Olustee** near Lake City, Florida, preserving interior supply lines to Georgia.

1865 — Florida militia repulse Union forces at **Natural Bridge**, saving Tallahassee from capture.

1868 — New Florida constitution is adopted.

1875 — The city of Orlando is incorporated.

1881 — Philadelphia industrialist **Hamilton Disston** buys four million acres of land in central Florida and begins the first private land development in the state.

1883 — The first all-black high school is founded in Jacksonville.

1884 — **Henry Plant** completes a rail line into Tampa.

1885 — **Henry Flagler** begins building a rail line between Jacksonville and St. Augustine and establishes the Florida East Coast Railway.

1886 — Fire destroys the entire commercial district of Key West. Labor disputes cause the cigar industry to relocate from Key West to Tampa.

1894–1895 — Winter freezes destroy citrus crops in central and north Florida and force the

© Bettmann/Corbis

citrus industry to move south.

1896 — In April, Flagler extends railroad to Miami; three months later, the City of Miami is incorporated.

1898 — Embarkation camps for American troops are established in Tampa, Miami and Jacksonville during the **Spanish-American War**.

1901 — Fire destroys most of Jacksonville, gutting more than 2,000 buildings.

1906 — Drainage of the Everglades begins, spearheaded by Florida governor Napoleon Bonaparte Broward.

1912 — Flagler's **Overseas Railroad** from Homestead (near Miami) to Key West is completed.

1914 — First regularly scheduled commercial airline flight is made by pilot Tony Jannus between St. Petersburg and Tampa.

1917–1918 — World War I soldiers and aviators train in Florida.

1926 — Miami takes a direct hit from a deadly September hurricane.

1927 — Pan American Airways inaugurates commercial service with a flight from Key West to Havana, Cuba.

1928 — The Tamiami Trail (US-41) across the Everglades is opened.

1929 — A Mediterranean fruit-fly infestation destroys citrus crops in 20 central Florida counties.

1935 — A devastating Labor Day hurricane batters Key West, destroying the Overseas Railroad.

1941–1945 — Defense-related industry boosts the Florida economy during **World War II**.

1947 — University of Florida opens to female students. President Harry S. Truman dedicates **Everglades National Park**.

1950 — Frozen citrus concentrates become a major Florida business. US inaugurates long-range missile-testing program at Cape Canaveral.

1954 — The Sunshine Skyway bridge connects St. Petersburg with Manatee County to the south.

1955 — Florida legislature authorizes the construction of a turnpike to run the length of the state.

1958 — Newly formed National Aeronautics and Space Administration (NASA) begins operations at Cape Canaveral and launches first US satellite.

1959 — The first regularly scheduled domestic air flights begin between New York and Miami.

1959–1962 — Thousands of refugees flee Cuba for Florida to escape Fidel Castro's communist regime.

1961 — NASA launches the first American astronaut, Alan Shepard, into space from Cape Canaveral.

1962 — The first black students are admitted to undergraduate schools at Florida State University and the University of Florida.

1964 — Race riots break out in Jacksonville and St. Augustine.

1969 — On July 16, the first manned moon launch lifts off from Cape Kennedy.

1971 — Walt Disney World opens near Orlando.

1972 — Miami Beach hosts the Democratic and Republican national conventions.

1973 — Freedom flights from Cuba to Miami end after bringing over 250,000 refugees to the US.

1979 — The Miami Beach Art Deco district is designated a National Register Historic District.

1980 — Some 125,000 Cuban refugees land in Miami. Riots erupt in Miami after four white policemen are acquitted in the beating to death of a black man.

1981 — On April 12, the Kennedy Space Center launches the first space shuttle, *Columbia*.

1983 — A Christmas freeze strikes central Florida citrus groves; losses exceed $1 billion.

1986 — Space shuttle *Challenger* explodes shortly after take-off from Cape Canaveral, killing all seven crew members aboard.

1989 — Serial killer Theodore Bundy—who confessed to 31 murders in nine states—is executed in Florida's electric chair.

1990 — Senator Gwen Margolis, a Democrat from Miami Beach, is elected first

1992: Houses in Dade County wrecked from Hurricane Andrew

© Steve Starr/Corbis

woman president of the Florida Senate.

1992 — **Hurricane Andrew** smashes into Dade County on August 24, sending 80,000 citizens into shelters.

1993 — President Clinton names Janet Reno, State Attorney of Dade County, as US Attorney General. Nine foreign tourists are murdered in Florida within 12 months.

1994 — Florida Legislature passes the **Everglades Forever Act**, authorizing removal of agricultural pollutants from the area's waters.

1995 — Hurricane Opal wreaks havoc along the Panhandle coast in October.

1996 — Vice President Al Gore announces a comprehensive seven-year plan to restore the Everglades ecosystem in south Florida.

1998 — Environmental advocate **Marjory Stoneman Douglas**, champion of the Everglades, dies at the age of 108. Major grass fires ravage northeast Florida, forcing 70,000 residents to evacuate their homes.

2000 — The state holds the outcome of US presidential elections in the balance for six weeks as its ballots are painstakingly recounted. Florida's secretary of state reads the final tally, with George W. Bush receiving the majority of votes. The Supreme Court declares Bush the next president.

2001 — By summer's end, 24 of the 42 shark attacks worldwide occur off Florida's coast, several at New Smyrna Beach.

2002 — Katherine Harris, the state's former secretary of state (who certifed

President Bush's victory in the 2000 election), easily wins a seat in the House of Representatives. The President's brother, Jeb, is re-elected governor of Florida.

2003 — The 28th flight of the space shuttle *Columbia* ends in tragedy when the spacecraft disintegrates while re-entering the Earth's atmosphere. All seven astronauts on board die.

2004 — Hurricane Charlie makes landfall, with wind gusts topping 180mph in Punta Gorda, during one of Florida's deadliest hurricane seasons, causing $13 billion worth of damage. President George W. Bush announces that the Space Shuttle program will terminate in 2010.

2006 — The death of 14-year-old Martin Lee Anderson in a sheriff's boot camp in Panama City, leads to the elimination of military-style camps.

2007 — Charlie Crist inaugurated as 44th governor.

2008–2009 — After the collapse of several national mortgage lenders and the onset of the global financial crisis, Florida leads the nation in foreclosure rates, with deep and long-lasting effects on the real-estate market.

2010 — The BP Deepwater Horizon oil spill brings ecological and economic disaster to neighboring states but Florida escapes with minor pollution to some of the beaches of the northwest. Titusville and Space Coast communities fear some 30,000 jobs will go when the Space Shuttle program closes at the end of the year.

Art

VISUAL ARTS

A number of 19C painters visited Florida and captured its sun-drenched landscapes on canvas. Among them were Boston artist **William Morris Hunt** (1824–1879), who sought Florida's subtropical climate in 1873 as a balm for his jangled nerves; British painter **Thomas Moran** (1837–1926), who chose Fort George Island to illustrate an issue of *Scribner's Monthly;* **Martin Johnson Heade** (1819–1904), a Pennsylvanian from the Luminist school who favored Florida's salt marshes; and George Inness Jr. (1854–1926), who wintered and painted in Tarpon Springs.

Honoring those who have made significant contributions in the state, the Florida **Artists Hall of Fame** recognizes several nationally and internationally famous artists, including **Robert Rauschenberg**, a modern experimental painter who has lived off and on in Florida for many years. The abstract expressionist creations of **Hiram Williams**, a University of Florida faculty member, have earned him a national reputation. Also at the University of Florida, surrealist photographer **Jerry Uelsmann** has exerted a widespread influence on his field.

West Palm Beach's **Norton Museum of Art** and Winter Park's **Charles Hosmer Morse Museum of American Art** are among museums with fine collections of art by Floridians.

PERFORMING ARTS

Florida's performing arts have also blossomed in the last few decades. Since the founding of the **Greater Miami Opera** in 1941, six more companies have sprung up around the state. Florida now offers nearly 80 theater companies as well as more than 30 professional dance groups, including the **Miami City Ballet**, which has been performing classical and modern dance in south Florida since the mid-1970s.

Most of Florida's major cities have professional symphony orchestras, and numerous regional and university music ensembles present frequent concerts. The **Florida West Coast Symphony** performs for audiences in Bradenton and Sarasota. Florida's official teaching festival, the **Sarasota Music Festival** takes place every June, attracting talented young professionals from around the world. Young musicians (aged 21–30) also fill the ranks of the Miami Beach-based **New World Symphony**. Moving up the coast, the **Florida Philharmonic Orchestra** plays in Fort Lauderdale and

Fort George Island (1880), by Thomas Moran

© AAA Photostock/Alamy

Tarzan and the Amazons, (1945)

© Moviestore collection Ltd/Alamy

southeast Florida, while the **Jacksonville Symphony Orchestra** entertains music-lovers farther north.

Fueled by the success of singer **Gloria Estefan** and her producer-husband Emilio, Miami Beach has become the national capital for the Latin music boom. The Estefans' Sony Building in the Art Deco Historic District has full music- and video-production facilities. Another longtime Florida resident is singer-songwriter **Jimmy Buffett**, whose vagabond-sailor persona has beguiled an international following.

FILM AND TELEVISION

Famous for its theme parks that celebrate film and TV, Florida has carved out a solid niche for itself in the **movie industry**. After years of providing the jungle backdrop for such early films (1940s and 50s) as the Tarzan series and the *Creature from the Black Lagoon*, Florida welcomed Universal and Disney-MGM studios in the late 1980s. Operating as both theme parks and actual production facilities, these two Orlando operations add to the smaller studios in Miami to create an attractive milieu for filmmaking. Recent big-budget pictures filmed in Florida include *There's Something About Mary, Ocean's 11, The Truman Show* and *Miami Vice*. Over the years, the state has also hosted a number of television series, including *Flipper, Miami Vice, SeaQuest, CSI: Miami* and several Latin soap operas.

FOLK ARTS

Ethnic and regional **folk arts** are kept alive through numerous festivals, apprenticeships and grants. The annual Florida Folk Festival, held each May at the **Stephen Foster State Folk Culture Center** in White Springs, illustrates regional folklife through music, dancing and farm crafts. Namesake of the Folk Culture Center, Pennsylvania-born composer **Stephen Collins Foster** (1826–1864) immortalized Florida's Suwannee River in his 1851 song *Old Folks At Home*. In 1935 this folk tune was officially designated as the state song.

Ranking third (after New York and California) in state appropriations for the arts, Florida hands out $32 million every year in grants to artists, many of whom preserve the traditions of folklife maintained in the state's numerous ethnic groups. **Cubans** in Key West, Miami and Tampa's Ybor City make woodcarvings and *guayaberas*—shirts decorated with pleating and embroidery. Caribbean transplants continue a rich maritime craft tradition with handmade boats, sails and fishing gear. **Greeks**, who have maintained a vibrant presence in Tarpon Springs since the early 1900s, bring their own nautical arts to modern Florida, along with sponge diving, Greek folk dance, colorful embroidery and music. South Florida is home to tribes of **Seminole** and **Miccosukee** Indians, who still craft bracelets, bead necklaces, palmetto-fiber dolls, painted wood tomahawks, pine-needle and sweet-grass baskets, and dazzling calico clothing. The latter features colorful patchwork designs suggesting lightning, arrows, diamonds and other symbols. These Native American wares are plied in reservation gift shops and at arts fairs in the Everglades' Miccosukee Indian Village and Ah-Tha-Thi-Ki Museum.

Architecture

For a relatively young state, Florida claims a remarkably rich and diverse heritage of building traditions incorporating the practical, the outrageous, the witty and the bizarre in equal measure. A strong Mediterranean current has run through the architectural landscape here ever since 17C Spanish colonization. The tropical terrain and climate also influenced early design and continues to do so today as a new generation of architects begins to discover and re-invent the past.

NATIVE STRUCTURES

The traditional dwelling of the Miccosukee and Seminole tribes was the **chickee**, an open-air shelter framed with rot-resistant cypress poles and thatched with palmetto fronds. Well-adapted to the swampy glades where the tribes hid their camps, the practical structures featured a platform floor of split logs or sawn boards elevated about 3ft off the ground to provide protection from snakes, alligators and flood tides:

Seminole Chickee

R. Corbel/MICHELIN

compounds comprised several individual chickees for sleeping, cooking, communal eating and religious rites.

EARLY SPANISH BUILDING

Although Dominican and Franciscan friars were the true founders of Spanish colonial architecture in Florida, scant archaeological traces remain of some 100 wooden mission compounds established here beginning in 1565. The oldest extant Spanish-built edifice in Florida is the 1695 Castillo de San Marcos in St. Augustine. The massive structure of quarried **coquina** (native shellstone) is considered the best surviving example of a type of European fortress introduced after gunpowder was invented in the late Middle Ages. Most early Spanish colonial houses were simple one-storey, two-room palmetto-thatched shelters built of wood planks or coquina blocks and rough **tabby** plaster made of oyster shells and lime. Only the more substantial two-story 18C coquina structures have survived. Following Spanish tradition, the houses in Florida's two Spanish garrisons, St. Augustine and Pensacola, fronted directly onto the street and were part of private, walled compounds entered by a gate. Loggias, or galleries, captured cooling summer breezes and the low winter sun. The glass-paned double-hung windows (replacing earlier wood *rejas,* or open window grills), hipped roofs, dormers and clapboard upper stories seen on many 18C St. Augustine houses were probably introduced by the British during the 1763–83 occupation.

19TH CENTURY

The term "Cracker" is believed to have originated with the whip-cracking cattle drivers who began crossing into Florida in the early 19C (℮ see p46). The first so-called **Cracker houses** of the Panhandle and central Florida regions were log cabins of several standard types: **single-pen** (one room), **saddlebag** (two rooms and a central chimney) or **dogtrot** (two rooms and a central breezeway). Such structures were raised off the damp ground on blocks made of limestone, heart pine or rot-resistant cedar.

Florida's pioneer houses took on a number of interesting variations after the **balloon frame** (a system of framing a wooden building by nailing together lightweight wood studs) was invented in the 1830s and began to replace the more expensive and labor-intensive pegged-timber frame throughout the US. A typical balloon-frame Cracker house is the 1.5-story farmhouse, with vertical board-and-batten siding and a pitched roof (often of inexpensive sheet metal) sloping over a broad porch. The **four-square** Cracker house, named for the shape of its floor plan, incorporates a porch and hipped roof (four slopes), often vented with a rooftop cupola designed to draw warm air up and out of the interior. **Shotgun** houses served as cheap housing for laborers along the Gulf Coast in south Florida's early Bahamian settlements. This narrow one-room-wide structure with a long row of back-to-back rooms is thought to be an African form that evolved on Haitian sugar plantations. It was said that if a shotgun were fired through the front door, the load would pass straight through the line of rooms and out the back door.

Dogtrot Cracker Dwelling

R. Corbel/MICHELIN

Built from the 1830s to 1920s, the **Conch house** of Key West is named for the Bahamian islanders—colloquially known as "Conchs"—who settled in the Keys in the 19C. The earliest Conch houses were framed by ships' carpenters using a pegged-and-braced timber system borrowed from shipbuilding, but most of those remaining are balloon-frame structures. The one- or two-story clapboard Conch house is usually raised on stone or brick piers and topped by a peaked roof (shingled or tin) with the gable end facing front; louvered blinds at the doors and windows block the heat of the fierce tropical sun.

Gingerbread House, Key West

R. Corbel/MICHELIN

The first **plantation houses** built after Florida became a US Territory in 1821 were unpretentious two-story, wood-frame structures. In the antebellum years these were replaced by imposing **Greek Revival** mansions fronted by columned two-story porches. Dating from the late 19C, when many citrus and railroad fortunes were made, elaborate **Queen Anne** houses—featuring asymmetrical facades, turrets, ample verandas, recessed balconies, gingerbread trim, spindles, turned railings and decorated gables—may be found throughout the state. Look also for the charming white board-and-batten Carpenter Gothic churches from the same period, distinguished by their pointed-arch windows.

EARLY 20TH CENTURY

The building boom of the early 20C coincided with the rise of the **Mediterranean Revival** style, which borrowed loosely from medieval Moorish and

Don CeSar

Visit Florida

Spanish architecture. The style became popular after California featured a Spanish-style pavilion at the widely publicized California-Pacific Exposition in 1915. Although other period revivals were also fashionable at the time, the Mediterranean mode caught on especially well in California and Florida where Spanish roots were strong. Pastel-colored stucco walls, red-clay roof tiles, arcaded loggias, towers, arched windows and ornate wrought-iron detailing not only suited Florida's tropical landscape, but also "…express[ed] the spirit of a land dedicated to long, carefree vacations," as a 1925 issue of *House Beautiful* described it. The style became the unifying design theme for dozens of Florida's boom-era developments, including Carl Fisher's Miami Beach, George Merrick's model suburb Coral Gables, and Addison Mizner's 1,600-acre architectural playground, Boca Raton. Indeed, many society architects, among them Mizner, Carrère and Hastings, and Walter DeGarmo (Florida's first registered architect) made their names with commissions for the luxurious Mediterranean Revival villas that still dominate Florida's early seaside resorts.

RESORT HOTELS

Perhaps the most distinctive symbols of Florida's heyday are the great resort hotels of the pre-Depression era. The tradition of extravagant hospitality catering to affluent northerners started in the late 19C. The friendly rivalry of railroad magnates Henry Bradley Plant and Henry Morrison Flagler extended to gigantic (and often unprofitable) hotels located at each major railhead. The first was Flagler's 1888 Ponce de Leon Hotel in St. Augustine (now Flagler College), designed by Thomas Hastings (who was later a partner in the prestigious New York firm of Carrère and Hastings). Plant countered with the 500-room brick, minaret-crowned Tampa Bay Hotel in 1890. Subsequent hotels were built of less costly wood, and consequently most of these were later claimed by fire. Plant's multi-gabled, 600-room Belleview Hotel (now the Belleview Biltmore), which opened near Clearwater in 1897, may be the sole survivor.

A second wave of expensive resorts reached its peak in the 1920s. By this time, the **Mediterranean Revival** style was considered the apex of architectural design, and most of these enormous structures were built of masonry, adorned with decorative tiles, stone carvings, frescoes and woodwork. While many of the hotels fell into disrepair after the economic crash of 1926, a recent restoration movement has returned a few choice examples to their original luster. St. Petersburg boasts both the **Vinoy Park** (now the Renaissance Vinoy Resort), restored in 1992, and Henry Du Pont's **Don CeSar**, a five-story pink stucco confection with bell towers and red-clay roof tiles. Others include the majestic Coral Gables **Biltmore Hotel**, the Palm Beach **Breakers Hotel**, and Mizner's **Cloister Inn** in Boca Raton. Originally built as a 100-room hotel, the Cloister now forms the east wing of the Boca Raton Resort & Club.

MODERN MOVEMENTS

The first widely popular style in the US to purposely break with traditional historical revivals, **Art Deco** transformed hundreds of gas stations, diners, theaters, houses, hotels, motel courts and storefronts across the US into eye-catching streamlined designs between the late 1920s and the 1940s. An offshoot of the **International Style** with its simple forms and austere surfaces, Deco adopted the sleek lines, cubic massing and new materials of the technology-oriented modernist aesthetic that was emerging in Europe after World War I. Americans welcomed the fresh contemporary look of Art Deco buildings at a time when they were trying to bury memories of the recent war and Depression.

Rather than reject ornament, as pure modernists did, Florida's Deco designers embraced fanciful decoration wholeheartedly—in particular exotic motifs (palmettos, chevrons and ziggurats) inspired by ancient Egyptian, Aztec and Mayan design. A later phase of Art Deco, called **Streamline Moderne**, took on an even more futuristic look. Beginning in the 1930s, buildings were stripped of surface decoration and angular elevations were smoothed with rounded vers, horizontal bands ("speed lines") and porthole windows inspired by contemporary streamlined trains, planes and ocean liners. New mass-produced materials—steel, chrome, glass block and concrete block—made it possible to build quickly and cheaply. These

benefits proved a plus for developers of post-war boom towns like Miami Beach, which now possesses the largest and best-preserved concentration of Art Deco and Streamline Moderne buildings in the world.

By the 1950s Florida was better known for its glitzy resort architecture, most notably **Morris Lapidus**'s stupendous movie-set Miami Beach hotels, such as the Fontainebleau and the Eden Roc. More recently renowned modern architects have helped to make Florida's metropolitan skylines as sophisticated as any in the US. Downtown Miami boasts landmarks by I.M. Pei (International Place, 1985), Skidmore, Owings & Merrill (First Union Financial Center, 1984) and John Burgee and Philip Johnson (Miami-Dade Cultural Center, 1982). Florida's best-known architectural firm, Miami's **Arquitectonica**, features witty, brash designs incorporating both high-tech and historical references rendered in bold geometry and bright colors. Their work—described by critics as "beach blanket Bauhaus"—includes the exuberant Miracle Center Mall in Coral Gables as well as three extravagant luxury apartment towers erected during Miami's "Mondo-Condo" building boom of the early 1980s: the Palace, the 21-story Atlantis, and the Imperial.

The most notable example of the **New Urbanist** movement, which emphasizes human scale, historical references and the relationship of a building to its neighbors, is found in the Panhandle coast town of **Seaside**. Following the

Seaside

Gwen Cannon/MICHELIN

lead of developer Robert S. Davis, Miami architects Elizabeth Plater-Zyberk and Andres Duany created the master plan for this model beach community in 1981. Seaside observes traditional town-planning concepts by placing houses, shops and offices in close proximity to encourage a pedestrian community. The nostalgic pastel wood-frame buildings intentionally recall Florida's 19C Cracker houses and reflect a growing appreciation for the state's early vernacular architecture. Seaside has inspired other traditional developments, including Disney's Celebration, as well as sprawling suburban communities that borrow the style of New Urbanism (gabled roofs, front porches, clapboard siding), while ignoring its compact planning.

More recently, the development of Walt Disney World has added "entertainment architecture" to Florida's mélange of styles. Resembling larger-than-life cartoons, the **Dolphin and Swan hotels** (1990, Michael Graves) near Epcot illustrate the Disney sense of whimsy: each is crowned with a pair of its namesake animals. The literal symbolism combines the irony of post-Modernism with the elan of contemporary advertising. Also near Orlando, the **Team Disney** building (1991, Arata Isozaki) presents a riveting cluster of bright geometric shapes that create intriguing optical illusions. With the traditionally laid-out town of **Celebration** (1994), located south of Walt Disney World, the famed mega-entertainment giant joined the New Urbanist movement, offering traditional homestyles, technological sophistication and human-scale planning. Disney's Celebration has attracted notable architects Michael Graves, Philip Johnson, Cesar Pelli, Jaquelin Robertson and Robert A.M. Stern, and despite criticism of its restrictions, lack of diversity and high cost, has become the focus for the New Urbanist experiment nationwide.

Literature

Long after gaining statehood Florida remained largely an untamed frontier. The sense of mystery and raw natural beauty of the unfamiliar landscape lured both adventurers and romantics—writers among them—and have proved enduring themes in the region's literature.

EARLY VOICES

Naturalists were among the first visitors to chronicle Florida and its native inhabitants. Appointed "Royal Botanist of the Floridas" by King George III, **John Bartram** (1699–1777) traveled from Philadelphia into the tropical wilderness in 1765–66, documenting unknown species of flora and fauna in A Description of East Florida (1769). His son William Bartram followed with Travels Through North and South Carolina, Georgia, East and West Florida in 1791.

During the 19C, magazine fiction and travel stories constituted a major body of Florida writing. In the 1830s and 40s, the monthlies Knickerbocker and Graham's published Florida adventure tales by such popular figures as **Washington Irving** and **James Fenimore Cooper**. In 1897 **Stephen Crane** (1871–1900), author of The Red Badge of Courage (1896) and a brief resident of Jacksonville, wrote The Open Boat. This dramatic story was based on a shipwreck he survived off New Smyrna Beach on his way to Cuba to fight in the Spanish-American War.

Contemporary travel guides were pivotal in bringing settlers and tourists to Florida. Among the classics now coveted by collectors are Florida for Tourists, Invalids, and Settlers (1881) by George Barbour (a phenomenal best-seller in its day) and Florida: Its Scenery, Climate, and History (1875) by the acclaimed southern poet **Sydney Lanier** (1842–1881).

One of the many travelers who returned to Florida to live was author **Harriet Beecher Stowe** (1811–1896), who spent winters in Mandarin, just outside Jacksonville, from 1868 to 1884. Her widely read *Palmetto Leaves* (1873) celebrated the beauty of the St. Johns River and attracted hundreds of curious travelers to the area.

BLACK VOICES

Black writers have helped shape the state's literary tradition.

Jacksonville native **James Weldon Johnson** (1871–1938) was the author of several books, poems and songs. His works include *Autobiography of an Ex-Colored Man* (1912) and *Lift Every Voice and Sing*, which has been called the black national anthem.

Eatonville's master story-teller **Zora Neale Hurston** (1891–1960) is acclaimed for fiction and essays that celebrate black culture and bespeak the honest values of rural southern life: they include the autobiographical *Dust Tracks On A Road* (1942) and *Their Eyes Were Watching God* (1937), considered one of the first 20C black feminist novels.

20C

Remaining unspoiled well into the 20C, the rugged beauty of backwoods Florida captivated many northern writers, including **Marjorie Kinnan Rawlings** (1896–1953). Rawlings settled in the hamlet of Cross Creek in 1928, and shaped many of her novels and stories around characters and settings inspired by her rural surroundings. The 1938 classic *The Yearling*—the story of a young boy and his pet deer in the Big Scrub (now Ocala National Forest)—won a Pulitzer Prize in 1939. Other Florida-inspired Rawlings titles include *South Moon Under* (1933) and *Cross Creek* (1942).

A longtime resident of Coconut Grove, **Marjory Stoneman Douglas** (1890–1998) arrived in Miami in 1915 and became one of the state's first environmentalists. Her 1947 volume, *The Everglades: River of Grass,* remains an eloquent warning against the exploitation of this imperiled natural resource.

During the 1930s and 40s, novelist **Hervey Allen** (1889–1949) and America's then-Poet Laureate **Robert Frost** (1874–1963) taught at the University of Miami's Winter Institute of Literature.

CALL OF THE KEYS

Key West also proved a magnet for writers. **Wallace Stevens** (1879–1955), who frequented the island on his yearly travels south from Connecticut, touted the tropical lushness of South Florida in his poetry anthology, *Harmonium* (1923). **Ernest Hemingway**, Florida's favorite literary son, spent most of the 1930s in Key West. Among the many works he wrote there, *To Have and Have Not* (1937) evokes the dignity and despair of the Depression-era life in the then-hard-bitten fishing village. Cultivated during his Key West years, Hemingway's fascination with the physical and intellectual challenge of deep-sea fishing was later reflected in *The Old Man and the Sea* (1952). Poet **Elizabeth Bishop** (1911–1979) made Key West her home in the late 1930s and early 1940s.

Among the plays **Tennessee Williams** (1911–1983) wrote in his Duncan Street studio were *The Rose Tattoo* (1950) and *Night of the Iguana* (1961). Other well-known literary figures attracted to Key West include; Thornton Wilder, who penned *The Matchmaker* there in 1954; poet and playwright Archibald MacLeish; humorist S.J. Perelman; and poet Richard Wilbur. Contemporary Key West writers include Philip Caputo, Ralph Ellison and Thomas McGuane (whose 1978 novel *Panama* is set in Key West).

... AND BEYOND

Elsewhere in Florida, mystery writer and former Sarasota resident **John D. MacDonald** (1916–1986), author of *Condominium* (1977) and *The Lonely Silver Rain* (1985), used Florida's Gold Coast as the backdrop for the exploits of his fictional private eye, Travis McGee. Carl Hiassen, Gore Vidal and Alison Lurie number among the other novelists, short-story writers and essayists attracted to the Sunshine State, which continues to inspire literary themes ranging from ecological and social concerns to pure adventure.

Nature

Florida is surrounded by the sea: 1,197 miles of coastline give the Sunshine State the second largest coastal area in the US after Alaska. To the east lies the Atlantic Ocean, to the south, the Straits of Florida, and to the west, the Gulf of Mexico. On land, to the north and northwest, lie Georgia and Alabama, whose narrow corridor to the Gulf Coast reaches around Florida's extreme northwestern border along the Perdido River.

Thanks to the state's peninsular shape, no point is more than 80mi from salt water. Land elevations vary only slightly; the highest point above sea level, found in the Panhandle, is just 345ft. Ranking 22nd in land mass, the state comprises 59,988sq mi, of which 5,991sq mi is water. Florida has more lakes than any US state south of Wisconsin, with an estimated 30,000 lakes, including Lake Okeechobee, the nation's third-largest freshwater lake. Most of the lakes are natural, many the result of sinkholes.

Nearly a quarter of the nation's first-magnitude springs (those that discharge 64.6 million gallons or more of water per day) surface in Florida.

GEOLOGIC FOUNDATIONS

Lacking the telltale exposed strata of eroded mountain outcrops, Florida reveals its geology much less readily than other states. Early efforts at peering into the geological past were mainly a side benefit from deep well borings and other commercial explorations below the land surface. The evidence amassed by earth scientists over the years has helped sketch a composite portrait of what is probably the youngest region in the continental US—that is, the last to emerge from a primordial, subtropical sea only ten to 15 million years ago.

ORIGINS

During the late Paleozoic era, Florida was part of the supercontinent Pangea, a C-shaped, crustal conglomerate formed by the earth's colliding major landmasses some 280 million years ago. Straddling the equator, Pangea split along a north-south axis 130 million years later and began to break up into the modern continents of Eurasia, Africa, North and South America, Antarctica and Australia. The Atlantic Ocean was born as the larger continental plates drifted away from the sea's mid-ocean ridge.

Precambrian Florida was one of the many terranes, or smaller crustal pieces, set afloat among the larger continents. Tracking northwards, it was grafted onto the much larger North American plate at a time when a chain of volcanic islands erupted off the mainland and arced into what are now the Bahamas.

Over time balmy shallow seas covered this bedrock. While dinosaurs roamed the great landmass to the north, silts and clays washed down from the Appalachian Mountains and fanned out into extensive submarine deltas along Florida's northern shore. To the south, marine shells mixed with microscopic carbonate fragments accumulated in a massive layer of limestone and dolomite. In places 13,000ft to 18,000ft thick, these sedimentary rocks cover much of the Florida Plateau from the Gulf escarpment to the Atlantic Ocean.

During the late Oligocene, the plateau broke the surface of the sea. Florida's land area grew to up to twice its present-day size as Ice Age glaciers locked up more and more of the earth's water. During the early Pleistocene, this part of the continent became a haven for mammoths, mastodons, saber-toothed tigers, sloths and other large mammals retreating overland from the frozen north.

THE FLORIDA PLATEAU TODAY

As the continental ice sheets melted and refroze, the sea level rose and fell several times, etching successive terraces into ancient shorelines that are still visible today. Though much the same size, the plateau now lies half submerged, its edges defining the continental shelf which surrounds Florida at some 300ft below the sea. Deepwater harbors on the Gulf side result from a pronounced westward dip of the plateau that continues to this day: the plateau's surface rises about 6ft at Miami, and it tilts downward about 30ft at Pensacola.

REGIONAL LANDSCAPES

For the most part a flat terrain with sandy and clay soils, Florida holds within its boundaries an astonishing diversity of landscapes, each exhibiting its own distinct characteristics. From hardwood forests to freshwater marshes, from coastal dunes and barrier islands to tropical coral reefs, the Sunshine State is home to a stunning collection of natural environments.

NORTHERN HIGHLANDS

Encompassing much of the Panhandle between the Alabama state line and the Withlacoochee River, this hilly area of forests and rivers unrolls as a 250mi-long and 30mi-wide band from west to east. Florida's natural apex—at 345ft, not even as high as some of the state's urban skyscrapers—stands 25mi north of De Funiak Springs in Walton County near the Alabama border. Encased by scrub and high pine as well as temperate hardwood forests, Florida's principal rivers course through this sparsely populated, largely rural region, which is home to the state's largest springs.

Ranging from the Perdido River to the Apalachicola River, the **Western Highlands** form a south-sloping complex dissected by narrow stream valleys with steep bluffs. An open overstorey of longleaf pines and deciduous oaks above a ground cover of perennial grasses characterizes the vegetation of this region. Fire plays a crucial role in the lifecycle of regional plants like the longleaf pine, whose seed germination is fostered by lightning-sparked blazes, which in turn enhance pine forest regeneration.

The **Marianna Lowlands** may have been the first area of Florida to emerge from the sea. The area encompasses

Sinkholes

In 1981 a 300ft-wide sink opened up in Winter Park, engulfing six vehicles, a house and parts of two streets. This was the largest sink on record in Florida, measuring 100ft deep. Between 400 and 4,000 new sinkholes develop in Florida every year, most less than 20ft wide. It's no wonder that sinkhole insurance has become a popular financial instrument in the state.

most of the upstream drainage basins of the Chipola and Choctawhatchee rivers. Composed of Eocene sedimentary rocks, the rolling landscape wedged into this corner of the Inland Panhandle features numerous springs, scattered limestone outcrops, and countless sinkholes, lakes and ponds.

One of the state's unusual geographical features, **sinkholes**, occur when the limestone foundation erodes under topsoil, leaving a bowl-shaped depression in the earth. Whereas a solution sinkhole forms gradually, a sinkhole collapse happens suddenly when an underground cavern caves in. Sinks often result from either drought or heavy rain, both of which can weaken the underlying limestone structure; many become basins for swamps, ponds or lakes.

Just to the east of the Marianna Lowlands, the **Tallahassee Hills** stretch 100mi from the Apalachicola River to the Withlacoochee River. This region of gentle rises and forested valleys slopes upward to form a 300ft-high plateau west of Tallahassee near the Georgia border. Its fertile clay soils nourish hardwood forests (cypress, live oak, magnolia and hickory) more extensive than those found anywhere else in the state.

One of Florida's most remarkable geological formations can be found on the western border: the **Apalachicola River Bluffs**, a series of steep bluffs and ravines, line the eastern shore of the Apalachicola River in Gadsden and Liberty counties. Parts of this river system, which rose in the Appalachian

Mountains during the early Cenozoic era, have been above sea level for as long as 24 million years.

Forests along these bluffs shelter the native Torreya trees: now near extinction, *Torreya taxiflora* is preserved in Torreya State Park.

CENTRAL HIGHLANDS

The green spine of Florida runs down the middle of the peninsula from the southernmost reaches of the Okefenokee Swamp (the swamp dips across the Georgia border into northeast Florida) for 250mi to Lake Okeechobee.

Though the northern section bulges to 60mi in width, the region tapers to a point in the south, where it converges with the Everglades and the Coastal Lowlands. Characterized by longitudinal ridges and upland plains and valleys, this region boasts thousands of lakes.

The world's heaviest concentration of **citrus trees** flourishes along a 100mi-long ridge (1mi to 25mi wide and 240ft high) from Leesburg to Sebring. Acclaimed science writer John McPhee noted that "The Ridge is the Florida Divide, the peninsular watershed, and, to hear Floridians describe it, the world's most stupendous mountain range after the Himalayas and the Andes..." This infamous ridge reaches its pinnacle at 302ft Mount Sugarloaf.

Northern reaches of the Central Highlands also claim a high concentration of natural **springs**. The combination of warm climate, heavy humidity, abundant decayed vegetation and a thick limestone bedrock, makes north Florida ideal terrain for spring formation. Bubbling up from the Floridan Aquifer, these clear pools provide soothing, therapeutic waters for thousands of visitors each year. South of Lake Okeechobee, the limestone peters out as do the springs.

COASTAL LOWLANDS

Harboring nearly all the state's major commercial, industrial and resort areas, the flat, low-lying areas rimming the peninsula spread inland as much as 60mi in some places and include the Florida Keys and the Everglades. Dominated by pastureland and extensive farming, the region's interior contrasts sharply with its glittering margins, where the state's environment-based tourism and recreational activities are focused.

Florida's fine quartz and calcium carbonate (shell fragments) sand makes dazzling white beaches. The oldest, finest—and purest quartz—sand, washed over the eons to a powdery texture, can be found on Florida's west coast near Sarasota and along the Panhandle coast.

Blessed with a gentle climate and warm Gulf and Atlantic waters, the state's

Everglades National Park

Visit Florida

coastal areas encompass a variety of natural environments. **Estuaries**, the most productive marine habitat in Florida, line nearly the entire coast where fresh water mingles with salt water. These shallow-water communities are vital for the development of a tremendous number of marine organisms. Another nursery for fish and shellfish, **mangrove swamps** edge the southeast and southwest coasts. More than 200 different types of fish and 180 bird species find habitat here, as do the endangered American crocodile and Florida manatee. Wind-blown **dunes** and their backdrop of **maritime forest** harbor sea oats and 22 other native plant species, as well as hosts of shorebirds.

Along both the Atlantic and Gulf coasts, strings of narrow, elongated sandy spits form protective **barrier islands** sheltering the mainland's many inlets, bays and estuaries. In addition to the periodic damage caused by hurricanes and violent winter storms, their ecological survival is severely tested by coastal development.

THE EVERGLADES

Considered a separate ecosystem, the broad expanse of the Everglades is covered by a shallow, slow-moving river that flows southward from Lake Okeechobee to the Florida Bay. Freshwater marshes, saw grass prairies, swamps and hardwood hammocks cover this depression.

The youngest part of Florida, the area south of Lake Okeechobee emerged from the sea upon built-up layers of live coral clinging to submerged oolitic limestone. With the eventual formation of sand dunes that sealed out the ocean, a new freshwater basin filled with marine plant life and eventually became the peat- and boglands that served as the forerunner to the Everglades—a territory unlike any other in the world. Scattered along the southern end of the Everglades, small rocky hammocks—designated as **South Florida Rockland**—give rare shelter to pines and broad-leaved tropical plants among barren limestone outcrops.

TROPICAL CORAL REEFS

Vital to Florida's economy, **coral reefs** extend in a 150mi-long curve from near Miami to the Dry Tortugas, 69mi west of Key West. Commercial and recreational fishing industries depend on the reef ecosystems, as do diving and snorkeling enthusiasts. Found nowhere else in the continental US, these spectacular underwater worlds are composed of calcified limestone secreted by invertebrate coral polyps: the formations began some 7,000 years ago. Colorful fans, coral branches and plumes on the reef create intricate forests inhabited by diverse communities of tropical fish, sponges, spiny lobsters and other exotic sea creatures, making the Keys one of the world's most popular diving destinations.

BALANCING ACT

With one of the fastest growing populations in the country, Florida faces the likelihood of ever-greater loss of its wildlife, native vegetation and natural resources. Coral reefs and other marine environments contend with oil drilling and contamination; wetlands are lost to drainage, filling and development; and upland forests and flatwoods are reduced by logging and conversion to citrus groves. In response, state and private organizations have begun to buy more and more land to be set aside for conservation and recreation. Public awareness of the importance of these environments has also helped strike a balance between nature and mankind. Programs like the state-funded Preservation 2000, which commands a $300 million annual budget for purchasing environmentally sensitive land, offer Florida a fighting chance of preserving for future residents and visitors a few wild landscapes washed by balmy breezes and timeless subtropical seas.

CLIMATE

Considered by many its most important natural resource, Florida's climate generally remains pleasant from January to December, drawing tourists year-round. Conditions vary from tropical in the Keys and subtropical in the central region to temperate in the Panhandle. Positioned at a more southerly latitude than any US state except Hawaii, Florida claims the country's highest average year-round temperatures, with Key West ranking as the hottest city in the nation at an average of 77.4°F. The warm Gulf Stream, which flows around the Florida Straits and north up the Atlantic coast from the tropics, tempers the prevailing easterly wind that blows over the peninsula.

More than half the average annual rainfall (52in) falls between the beginning of June and the end of September (the month when most hurricanes occur). These hot, humid summers bring hordes of mosquitoes to the forests and marshes. Winter, the main tourist season, enjoys mild and relatively dry weather—especially in central and south Florida. The Panhandle suffers a more continental winter, with a higher frequency of freezing temperatures. Snowfall is almost nonexistent, though several inches—a dusting of which reached as far south as Miami Beach—were recorded in the north part of the state in 1977.

The combination of moist air and sun-heated land and water surfaces in Florida provides ideal conditions for the formation of **thunderstorms**. In fact, the state experiences more thunderstorms than anywhere in the world except East Africa. On summer days, hot air rises over the peninsula. When it meets with damp air from the Gulf and the Atlantic, converging airstreams force air upward, where it condenses into towering thunderheads. Parts of south Florida have more than 90 storms a year; Fort Myers leads the state with an annual average of 100 days with lightning.

HURRICANES

Florida lies in the path of intense tropical cyclones spawned in the Atlantic, the Caribbean and the Gulf of Mexico. Most common in August and September when weak low-pressure systems develop over warm water, hurricanes can measure upwards of 500mi in diameter and contain winds of up to 200mph (a tropical depression officially becomes a hurricane once its winds reach a speed of 74mph). These doughnut-shaped storms commonly churn across the Atlantic coast between Cape Canaveral and the Keys (a corridor popularly known as "hurricane alley"), though in recent decades the Panhandle has received a significant share of these storms as well.

An average of one hurricane a year, usually of low or moderate intensity, strikes Florida. Several devastating storms have hit in this century: a hurricane in 1926 scored a direct hit on Miami, causing the worst city damage in the city's history; two years later, another storm took some 2,000 lives when floodwaters breached levees around Lake Okeechobee; the Labor Day hurricane of 1935—holding the record for the highest sustained winds and storm tide—struck the Keys and ripped into the Gulf, killing more than 400 people. More recently, Hurricane Andrew mowed an 8mi swath across south Miami-Dade County in 1992, leaving in its wake 85 dead, 10,000 injured, and $30 billion in damage. An unprecedented four hurricanes – Charley, Frances, Ivan and Jeanne – hit Florida in 2004.

An estimated one in five homes in the state were damaged by hurricanes in August and September of that year, and 117 people lost their lives in the storms. Charley, the strongest and costliest, was a category 4 storm when it made landfall in Florida, causing approximately $14 billion in damage. On the positive side, Florida's epic storms invigorate its natural environment. High winds often distribute plant seeds over a wide expanse. The combination of winds and heavy rains stirs up sediments and nutrients

Nature's Dynamo

An average hurricane drops more than 2.4 trillion gallons of rain during each day of its existence and releases enough energy in one day to supply electricity for the entire population of the US for six months.

on the bottoms of bays and backwaters. When hurricanes level forests and other protective ground cover, sun-loving plants and small animals quickly exploit the newly available niches, regenerating the cycle of life.

WATER RESOURCES

Floridians have one of the highest per capita rates of water use in the country, thanks to the seemingly inexhaustible reserves of the **Floridan Aquifer**, the state's largest and only artesian aquifer (characterized by water that is forced up through cracks in nonporous rock by hydrostatic pressure). Called "Florida's rain barrel," the Floridan underlies the entire state and varies in depth up to 2,000ft in the areas surrounding Jacksonville and Orlando. Along with the shallower **Biscayne Aquifer**, which serves southeast Florida, the Floridan provides nearly 90 percent of the state's water for drinking, recreation, irrigation and waste disposal. These layers of porous limestone serve as underground reservoirs that give Florida more groundwater than any other state. Water levels are replenished by an abundant annual rainfall—the greatest amount falling in the extreme northwest and southeast corners of the state.

One of the largest sources of surface water in the state, **Lake Okeechobee** (Seminole for "big water") supplies south Florida's cities and farms, as well as the Everglades. At 700sq mi it ranks as the state's largest lake. After Okeechobee inundated nearby farming communities as a result of hurricanes in 1926 and 1928, the US Army Corps of Engineers began taming the lake with a new system of canals, dikes, pumping stations and spillways.

Now its waters can be manipulated to control flooding of surrounding fields and towns. With an ever-increasing population in south Florida, Lake Okeechobee today lies at the heart of many complex land-use controversies, which pit environmentalists against the area's farmers.

Sabal Palm

R. Corbel/MICHELIN

FLORA AND FAUNA

Dubbed by Ponce de León "Isle of Flowers" (for the Spanish *Pascua florida* Eastertime feast), Florida boasts an abundance of lush vegetation. Early botanists catalogued over 3,000 types of indigenous flowering plants, from tiny orchids to showy magnolias. Thousands of tropical and subtropical plants have been added to this total over the years. Positioned between 24°30′N and 30°N latitude—the same latitude as Egypt—Florida juts southward from the temperate zone into warm tropical seas. This location produces a unique inversion: temperate-zone plants bloom in winter and the tropical varieties flower in summer. Furthermore, Florida's regional climatic variations contribute to the great diversity of native botanical species found in the state, from the high pine forests of the northwest to the saw grass marshes of the Everglades. The state's vegetation is generally distributed among seven habitats—hammocks, pinelands, flatwoods, scrublands, swamps, savannas and salt marshes. Together they contain about half the tree species north of Mexico.

HAMMOCKS AND FLATWOODS

Occurring in the north and central regions, **hardwood hammocks** are raised islands of hardwoods and broad-leaved shrubs surrounded by prairie or pine forest. They harbor fertile soil that nourishes oaks, hickories, beeches, magnolias, cabbage palms and others, often swathed in Spanish moss or vines of rattan or wild grape. From the tree farms of slash and loblolly to the wild-growing longleaf of the uplands and the scrub pine of flat sandy areas, the state's many species of pine constitute Florida's most common tree.

Flatwoods containing boggy soil are found all over Florida and contain a number of blooms, including 64 kinds of terrestrial **orchids**. Found in the central peninsula and along the coastal dunes, **scrublands** are characterized by thick stands of evergreen live oaks, saw palmetto and blackjack. Much of this land has been converted to vast groves of oranges and grapefruit. The savannas (grasslands) in central Florida support a variety of marine grasses, including turtle, eel and manatee grasses.

A PROFUSION OF PALMS

Symbol of a luxuriant lifestyle, the **palm** proliferates in Florida, which claims several hundred species—more than any other state. The cabbage or **Sabal palm**, one of only 15 native palms, is Florida's official state tree and flourishes throughout the state; early settlers harvested its crunchy edible bud, which was said to taste like cabbage. Among other notable natives, the tall royal palm graces many prominent boulevards and the low-lying

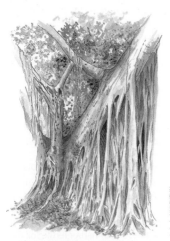

Aerial Roots of Weeping Banyan

R. Corbel/MICHELIN

palmetto forms dense thickets in the flatlands, varying in color from light green to grayish blue. The coconut palm grew lavishly in south Florida until an outbreak of lethal yellowing disease in the 1970s, when more than five million palms around Miami were destroyed. Many of the coconut palms were replaced by the hybrid Maypan and the coconut-bearing Malayan Dwarf.

THE MARVELOUS MANGROVE

The only known trees that can survive in salt water, mangroves have received much attention in recent decades, rising in status from developers' nuisance to coastal guardian. **Red mangroves** *(Rhizophora mangle)* thrive in the tidal zones; **black mangroves** *(Avicennia germinans)*, distinguished by short fingerlike aerating branches called pneumatophores that project above the soil, are found slightly more inland. **White mangroves** *(Laguncularia racemosa)* generally grow at the highest elevations. All have the ability to withstand the salt water of wind spray and high tide. Their cagelike root systems can stabilize a shoreline better than a seawall, as well as providing sanctuary for hundreds of species of fish. The most well known of the three Florida varieties, the red mangrove, grows near the water on reddish aerial roots that absorb oxygen and fresh water and filter out salt. (Indians dubbed the red mangroves "walking trees," because the aboveground roots look like legs wading out into the water.)

NATIVES AND EXOTICS

Among the 350 different types of trees found in Florida are the thick, coppery **gumbo-limbo** and the **manchineel**, one of the continent's most poisonous plants. Manchineel trees grow in swamps and produce a sap so toxic that even water dripping from their leaves can irritate the skin. A type of ficus native to the Sunshine State, the **strangler fig** wraps around its host (often a Sabal palm) and eventually kills it. The deciduous **bald cypress**, commonly found in Florida swamps, is named for its leafless winter appearance. A fig tree native to East India, the distinctive **banyan** tree is recognizable by its numerous trunks that appear like vertical bars of a prison cell. The tree's branches send out shoots that grow down to the soil and root to create additional trunks; the world's third largest banyan can be seen in the grounds of the Edison Ford Winter Estates.

Over the years many **exotic plants** have been introduced to Florida threatening the survival of many native species. Parks and conservation areas have implemented programs to rid their locales of such imported exotics.

Florida's gentle winters and warm sunshine support some 100 species of mammals and more than 400 species and subspecies of birds. While the increasing human population continues to reduce available territory for wildlife, a conservation movement has arisen to protect Florida's wildlife habitat.

At the coast you are likely to see bottle-nosed **dolphins**—a perennial favorite with visitors and residents—frolicking offshore. These sleek mammals frequent the shallow waters of the Gulf of Mexico as well as the Atlantic.

Perhaps the most easily observed animals, dozens of species of water birds make permanent or part-time homes in Florida. Of the species more likely to be found in Florida than anywhere else, the long-necked **anhinga** is known for its skill in spearing fish with its beak. Bird-watchers may also add **roseate spoonbills** to their must-see lists; sometimes mistaken for flamingos, spoonbills are also pink but much shorter than flamingoes with flat, spoon-shaped beaks. They flock over the wildlife refuges on Sanibel and Merritt islands. Another rare find, the **purple gallinule** frequents marshy waterways in the Everglades. This small bird is recognizable by its bright purple and blue feathers. The **brown pelican** makes a graceful sight skimming along the Atlantic and Gulf coasts. However the pelicans' prevalence in Florida is misleading: outside the state they are rare, their numbers diminished by pesticides.

Great Egret among Cypress Trees
© National Park Service

Florida provides haven to more than 67 species of threatened or endangered animals. Prominent on the endangered list are the reclusive **Florida panther**; the West Indian **manatee**; the diminutive **Key deer**; the **wood stork**, a wading bird once prevalent in mangrove and cypress swamps; and the **Florida sandhill crane**, another long-legged wader. The five kinds of **sea turtles** that nest in Florida are all either endangered or threatened; and the **American crocodile**, nearly extinct in the US, lives only in southern Florida.

While the high number of endangered species are worrying, Florida has actually made progress in slowing, and sometimes reversing, the decline of some species. Once hunted almost to extinction, **alligators** (which help control populations of snakes and small mammals) have enjoyed a renaissance in Florida and now number more than a million.

Florida Panther
© National Park Service

Everglades National Park
©John Anderson/Fotolia.com

DISCOVERING FLORIDA

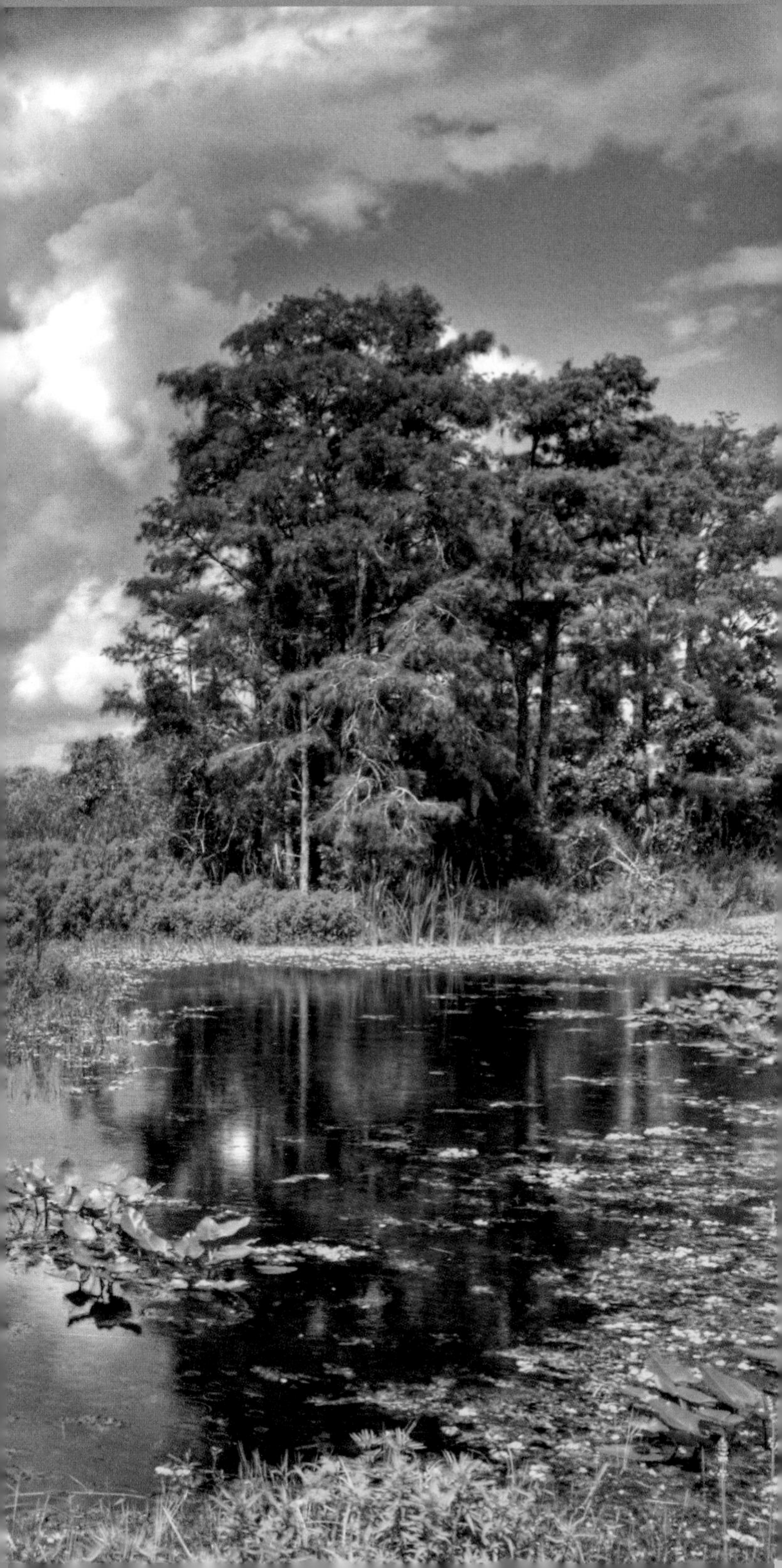

THE EVERGLADES

Renowned throughout the world, the vast "river of grass" known as the Everglades covers the southern end of the Florida peninsula in a subtropical wetland. It is home to hosts of rare birds, mammals and reptiles.

The 50mi-wide sheet of moving water stretching from Lake Okeechobee to the Florida Bay began to form during the last Ice Age, when a shallow tropical sea intermittently covered the area, creating the limestone bedrock that now underlies it. Waters draining from the Kissimmee Basin to the north gradually inundated the land. This slow-moving river—averaging 6in in depth and losing only 2in of elevation for every mile it slopes down toward the Gulf of Mexico—gives rise to diverse ecosystems: coastal and saw grass prairies, mangrove swamps, tree islands, pinelands, hardwood hammocks and coastal estuaries. All of these communities depend upon the seasonal rhythm of the flow of water feeding them. Heavy rains nourish the area during the wet season, from May to October, while the landscape becomes increasingly parched during the dry winter months.

Highlights

1 Cycling or taking the Tram Tour at **Shark Valley** (p85)

2 Spying alligators and other critters at the **Anhinga Trail** (p87)

3 Cruising the canals and Florida Bay at **Flamingo** (p90)

4 Canoeing the backcountry in the **Ten Thousand Islands** (p92)

5 Exploring the eerily beautiful forest at **Big Cypress Bend** (p93)

Calusa Indians

Calusa Indians were the first known people to inhabit what they called Pa-hay-okee, or "Grassy Waters." Archaeological evidence indicates that the Calusa lived in these coastal areas for as long as 2,000 years, disappearing from southern Florida only after the arrival of the Spanish in the 16C.

Small bands of Miccosukee and Seminoles took refuge in the Glades in the mid-19C, to escape the Seminole Wars and to avoid being sent west to reservations by the federal government. The remaining Indians developed a subsistence culture here and were virtually the area's sole inhabitants until the late 19C. At that time a few intrepid white settlers braved the heat and mosquitoes to settle along the coastal periphery of the Everglades.

Animals and plants in the Everglades today belong to a complex, inter-dependent cycle of water, fire, grasses and soils that has been interrupted in recent decades by the human manipulation of water flow. During floods too much water is channeled into the Everglades from urban and agricultural areas to the north; during droughts not enough water is allowed to flow south to the Gulf. Recent legislation seeks to address the increasingly complicated demands of this unique ecosystem in the dawn of a new century.

Ecosystem in Jeopardy – The timeless rhythm of the Everglades was seriously compromised in the early 20C, when **Napoleon Broward,** a Florida gubernatorial candidate, proposed draining the soggy area to provide water for agriculture and land for urban development. Broward won the election and, in the following decades, water was diverted from the Glades through some 1,400mi of man-made canals that drain the Everglades' water for farmland and suburban drinking water.

Though early grassroots conservationists protested against the desecration, their efforts generally proved ineffective. However, in 1916 the first Everglades preserve—the roughly 2,000-acre **Royal Palm State Park**—was established, thanks in large part to the efforts of the Florida Federation of Women's Clubs. Even so, development rolled on. In 1928 the **Tamiami Trail** (US-41), so called because it connects Tampa to Miami, was completed, cutting through the heart of the Everglades

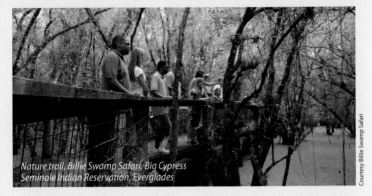
Nature trail, Billie Swamp Safari, Big Cypress Seminole Indian Reservation, Everglades

Courtesy Billie Swamp Safari

and blocking the water's southerly flow. Today these "grassy waters" lie mostly in private hands.

Preserving Pa-hay-okee – The establishment of the park in 1947 stemmed the tide of development that threatened to destroy this fragile ecosystem. About the same time, *The Everglades: River of Grass* appeared. This popular work by late Florida journalist **Marjory Stoneman Douglas** explained the need to protect the Glades, while extolling the beauty of "their vast glittering openness... the racing free saltness and sweetness of their massive winds, under the dazzling blue heights of space." Douglas remained in the forefront of the ongoing fight to preserve the Everglades and return their natural flow of water until her death in 1998 at the age of 108. Since the park's establishment, its boundaries have been increased several times, most recently with the 1989 **East Everglades Expansion Act,** which added an additional 107,600 acres to the park.

A Balancing Act

Now the third-largest national park in the continental US after Death Valley and Yellowstone, the area still suffers from its proximity to major farming and urban centers that introduce toxins—such as the 200 annual tons of phosphates from agricultural fertilizers and pesticides—into this wilderness. The Everglades ecosystem also has natural enemies. Exotic plants—like the fire-resistant Australian Melaleuca tree, one acre of which sucks up the area's precious water at a rate of 2,100gal per hour—that have been introduced into the Glades threaten to overtake native vegetation, thus upsetting the delicate ecological balance.

Florida's legislature began removing agricultural and other pollutants from the area's waters following the passage of the **Everglades Forever Act** in 1994; two years later, the federal government announced a comprehensive seven-year plan to restore the Everglades ecosystem. Construction projects to re-establish water flow are ongoing. The decline in fresh water flowing through the Everglades has damaged the fragile environment in Florida Bay, along the park's southern rim, fouling once-pristine sea grass flats and crippling the area's delicate ecosystem. Federal restoration plans for the Everglades are designed to help the bay as well. Balancing human needs against natural ones continues to be problematic, but fortunately policymakers now acknowledge Douglas' contention that "there are no other Everglades in the World." In December 2009, the Army Corps of Engineers began constructing a mile-long (1.6 km) bridge to replace the Tamiami Trail and thus increase water flow.

The region also faces Mother Nature. Hurricanes Katrina and Wilma visited the Everglades in 2005, sending trees to the ground and flooding the landscape. Wilma battered the Ten Thousand Islands with 125mph winds and a 17ft storm surge. Chokoloskee Island and Flamingo were hit especially hard, with many businesses closed.

THE EVERGLADES

GETTING THERE

BY AIR – Miami International Airport (MIA): Closest commercial airport, 34mi north of Homestead (*℘305-876-7000; www.miami-airport.com*). Shuttle service to Homestead: **Super Shuttle** (*24hr service; one-way around $45 per passenger, for reservations: ℘305-871-2000; www.supershuttle.com*). Major rental car agencies are located at the airport.

BY CAR – There are two entrances to **Everglades National Park**: to reach the southern end at Flamingo, take Route 9336 east then south from Florida City. US-41 (Tamiami Trail) borders the northern part of the park. Shark Valley entrance is accessible from US-41.

BY BUS – Daily between Miami and Cutler Ridge, near Homestead. Greyhound bus station (located at a gas station next to McDonald's, 10801 Caribbean Blvd., Cutler Ridge (*℘800-231-2222; www.greyhound.com*).

VISITOR INFORMATION

Park Headquarters, 40001 State Rd. 9336, Homestead FL 33034 (*℘305-242-7700; www.nps.gov/ever*). The park is open daily year-round. Entrance fee is $10/vehicle, valid at both park entrances for seven days. ⛺&. **Ernest F. Coe Visitor Center**: 11mi southwest of Homestead on Rte. 9336 (*open year-round daily 8am–5pm; ℘305-242-7700*). Additional visitor centers: **Royal Palm** on US-41 (*open year-round daily 8am–4pm; ℘305-242-7700*); **Flamingo** at terminus of Rte. 9336 (*open Dec–Apr 7:30am–5pm; rest of the year daily 9am–5pm; ℘941-695-2945*); **Shark Valley** on US-41 (*open year-round daily 8:30am–5:15pm; $10/vehicle; ℘305-221-8776*) and **Gulf Coast** in Everglades City (*open year-round daily 7:30am–5pm; ℘239-695-3311*). Rangers lead wildlife walks, canoe trips and evening programs Dec–Apr; for schedules check the park newspaper or visitor centers.

The **Everglades Area Chamber of Commerce** (*℘239-695-3172; www. evergladeschamber.net*) and **Tropical Everglades Visitor Assn** (*160 Hwy. 1, Florida City, FL 33934; ℘305-245-9180 or 800-388-9669; www.tropicaleverglades. com*) provide information on local lodging, gas stations and recreation.

WHEN TO GO

The best time to visit is definitely in **winter** during the dry season (Nov–mid-Apr*)*, when daytime temperatures range from 60°–80°F, mosquitoes are tolerable, and wildlife is easier to spot. The busiest week is 25 Dec–1 Jan. Make lodging and tour reservations several months in advance.

In **summer** (May–Oct) the Park is, unsurprisingly less crowded (by humans at least) as temperatures often soar to 95°F and the hot, humid weather brings clouds of mosquitoes and other biting insects. Insect repellent is recommended year-round.

Sawgrass in the Everglades

© National Park Service

ADDRESSES

🛏 STAY

Everglades City, Homestead and Florida City offer hotels, motels, campgrounds and RV parks. For posher options head for Naples or Miami.

$–$$$ Ivey House – *107 Camellia Street, Everglades City. ☎239-695-3299. www.iveyhouse.com.* This 1928 house, beautifully turned out with a pool, courtyard and native plants, is run by the owners of NACT Everglades Rentals & Eco Adventures who offer guests 20 percent off rentals and tours. Lodgings include a B&B with shared baths and a guest house; rates from $60–$200.

$$ Everglades Spa & Lodge – *201 Broadway W. Everglades City. ☎239-695-3151. www.bedbreakfasthome.com/banksoftheeverglades.* This former bank is now a comfy B&B with a (quite separate) day spa which offers massages, facials, clay baths etc. Rates from $110–$135.

$ Redland Hotel – *5 S. Flagler Ave., Homestead. ☎305-246-1904 or 800-595-1904. www.redlandhotel.com.* Built in 1904 this characterful place has also served as a mercantile store, and post office. It includes a pub and Internet cafe on site but is close to downtown.

TOURS

Boat captains narrate tours along the mangrove coast at both Flamingo and the Gulf Coast (visit *www.nps.gov/ever/planyourvisit* for details), and **Shark Valley tram tours** offers two-hour guided road tours, narrated by park naturalists, along a 15mi loop in the heart of the "River of Grass."
Tours depart from the park's Shark Valley Visitor Center *(late Dec–Apr hourly, 9am–4pm; May–late Dec 9:30am, 11am, 1pm, 3pm; ☎305-221-8455; www.sharkvalleytramtours.com).*
Shark Valley Tram Tours also rents **bicycles**. Touring the 15mi paved Shark Valley Loop Rd typically takes 2–3 hours. Bikes are available daily on a first-come, first-served basis from 8:30am–4pm (last rental at 3pm); $7.75 per hour.

🏃 SPORTS AND RECREATION

Camping at Long Pine Key and Flamingo *($16/camp site; available by reservation mid-Nov–mid-April; rest of year, first-come, first-served; ☎305-242-7873 (Long Pine Key) or 239-695-0124 (Flamingo); www.nps.gov/ever/planyourvisit).*
The **Back Country** is accessible by boat, canoe and on foot only. A permit *($10–$30)*, obtainable at the visitor centers, is required for all overnight trips.
A Florida **fishing** license, available at local bait and tackle shops, is required for fresh- and saltwater fishing.
Seven **canoe** trails thread the southern park region. Rental canoes are available at Flamingo Marina *(☎239-695-3101).*
Canoe the Wilderness Waterway with **North American Canoe Tours** *(Oct–Apr day trip $124/person, two-person minimum; night paddle $124/person).*
Crystal Seas offers three- and six-hour sea kayak tours *(Dec–Apr reservations required; ☎877-SEAS-877; www.crystalseas.com).*
Several **hiking** trails fan out from Flamingo; contact park headquarters for trail information. At Royal Palm Visitor Center, hike the Anhinga Trail.

😊 A Bit of Advice 😊

Everglades Advice and Regulations

- Water-skiing is prohibited.
- Firearms and hunting are prohibited. Smoking on trails is not permitted.
- No pets on trails.
- All vehicles must stay on designated roads; off-road vehicles prohibited.
- Reduce speed in wildlife areas.
- Campfires permitted in fire rings in campground areas only.
- Do not disturb or feed wildlife.
- When hiking, advise someone of your itinerary.
- Owing to abundant wildlife in freshwater ponds and poor underwater visibility, swimming is not encouraged.
- Beware sudden weather changes that can lead to heavy thunderstorms, especially if you are boating.
- Always wear a sunscreen and protective clothing.

Southern Everglades

A solitary highway cuts through the southern section of the park, from Florida City, east to the end of the road, west, at Flamingo. En route a series of trails and visitor centers will acquaint you with the quintessential 'glades.

- **Michelin Map:** p90.
- **Info:** ℰ305-242-7700; www.nps.gov/ever.
- **Don't Miss:** A tour boat ride or canoe paddle through the park's pristine waterways.
- **Timing:** Allow three days to get a good sense of this amazing environment.
- **Kids:** Spotting a 'gator on the Anhinga Trail.

🚗 DRIVING TOUR

76mi round-trip within park

While you can see the highlights in a day, to best experience and understand the Everglades you must spend some time hiking its trails and boating on its waters. Sights in the southern part of the national park are organized as a driving tour, going from north to south.

From Miami, take Florida's Turnpike (I-75) south until it dead-ends at Florida City. Turn right on Rte. 1 south to Palm Dr. (Rte. 9336).
Follow Rte. 9336 about 1.5mi and turn left on 192nd Ave. Continue 2mi to 376th St. S.W. Turn right and follow the road 5.6mi to park entrance.
Route 9336 then continues 38mi to its terminus in Flamingo.

Ernest F. Coe Visitor Center

On the right just before the park entrance. ⏱*Park open year-round daily 8am–5pm. Visitor center open year-round daily 8am–5pm.* ♿ 🚗*$10/vehicle for a 7-day pass.* ♿ 🅿 ℰ*305-242-7700. www.nps.gov/ever.*

The Coe Visitor Center, named for one of the park's early champions, was dedicated in 1996 to replace a previous visitor center destroyed by Hurricane Andrew. Its hipped metal roof and wood siding enable it to blend inconspicuously into the natural environment. Exhibits and films educate visitors not only on the Everglades, but also on the environmental crises confronting the greater South Florida ecosystem. An information desk provides details on recreational activities within the national park; administrative offices are in an adjoining building.

Whitewater Bay, Southern Everglades

© PhotoDisc.Inc

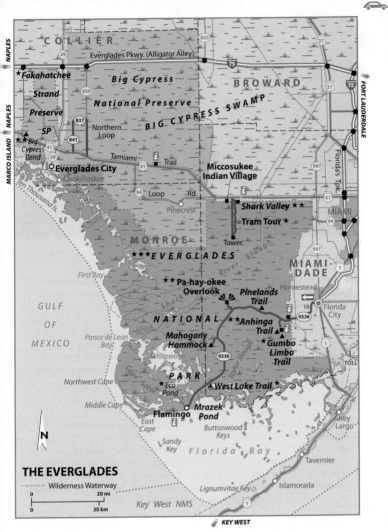

THE EVERGLADES

--- Wilderness Waterway

| 0 | 20 mi |
| 0 | 30 km |

Continue 2mi on Rte. 9336 and turn left at the sign for Royal Palm Visitor Center and the Gumbo Limbo and Anhinga trails.

Anhinga Trail★★

0.5mi. Begins at rear of visitor center. Ranger-led walks and lectures are held here several times daily (first-come, first-served).

One of the park's most popular areas, this trail begins as a wide paved path, which follows a portion of the Old Ingraham Highway. A boardwalk then leads across Taylor Slough (pronounced "slew"), a shallow, slow-moving river that channels through a marsh dense with willow thickets and punctuated by a palm hammock.

Alligators, turtles and myriad birds congregate here, particularly in the dry winter months.

Gumbo Limbo Trail★

0.4mi. This trail weaves through the luxuriant vegetation of historic **Paradise Key Hammock**, the area that formed the original **Royal Palm State Park.** A typical tropical island of hardwood trees, Paradise Key supports a rich variety of

Anhinga , Everglades National Park

© Michael Braun Photography/iStockphoto.com

A Haven for Wildlife

One of the major wetlands left on this continent, the Everglades supports some 600 species of animals, including 350 types of birds, 60 species of mosquitoes and 26 kinds of snakes, some of which are found nowhere else in the world. The southern Everglades, in fact, is the only place in the world where you'll find both alligators and crocodiles. Birds provide the greatest spectacle in the park, with herons, egrets, ibis, cranes and other waterbirds almost always within sight. Bald eagles and ospreys nest here, and white pelicans (the largest birds on the continent, with a wingspan of 9ft) winter here. The following creatures number among those that make their home in the Glades.

American Alligator *(Alligator mississippiensis)* – Once a species with a poor prognosis for survival, the alligator has made a strong comeback and is routinely seen gliding silently through freshwater channels and marshes. Reaching lengths of up to 16ft, male alligators rank as the largest reptiles on the continent. Mating occurs in the spring, after which the female will build a nest and deposit up to 80 eggs. Incubation requires between 9 and 10 weeks. For these cold-blooded reptiles, the sex of the hatchlings is determined by the temperature at which the egg incubates: temperatures below 87°F will produce females; temperatures above 89°F will yield males. The young are black with yellow bands; adults are black. Efficient predators, gators also contribute to the survival of other animals. As the dry season approaches, the reptiles dig out "gator holes," depressions that fill with underground water and help sustain many kinds of animals during the dry months.

American Crocodile *(Crocodylus acutus)* – Cousin to the alligator, the endangered American crocodile has been reduced to a few hundred animals, concentrated in the salty mangrove inlets in the southern part of Everglades National Park and in Crocodile Lake National Wildlife Refuge on the northern end of Key Largo. Crocodiles can be distinguished from alligators by their lighter gray-green coloring, long pointed snout, and the lower incisors that protrude from either side of their jaw when their mouth is closed. On land, these reptiles move with an agile swaying motion, enabling them to reach speeds of 15mph. Generally considered more aggressive than the alligator, American crocs tend to avoid humans, unless molested or protecting their young.

Anhinga *(Anhinga anhinga)* – This long-necked denizen of the Everglades has become its symbol, often spotted in trees with its black wings outstretched.

Lacking the oil covering that other birds have on their wings, the anhinga must air dry its wings in order to fly again after it has emerged from a feeding foray. To obtain food, the anhinga dives underwater and spears fish with its pointed bill. When swimming, only the bird's sinuous neck is exposed above the water; thus it is sometimes called the "snakebird."

Florida Panther *(Felis concolor coryl)* – Experts believe that only 50-70 of these big tawny-brown cats—designated Florida's state animal—still roam the state's wetlands, the only habitat left for them in the eastern US. The panther's birthrate of two to four kittens every other spring has been diminished by infertility caused by mercury-contaminated prey. Once widespread, these members of the cougar family have been squeezed down to the tip of the peninsula, mostly into the protected lands of Big Cypress Swamp and Everglades National Park. Secretive and difficult to spot, adults stand about 2ft high and weigh between 60 and 130 pounds.

Snail Kite *(Rostrhamus sociabilis plumbeus)* – This small, shy, gray-brown hawk survives exclusively on Pomacea, or apple, snails. With its curved beak, it extracts the snail from its shell. While snail kites are common in some parts of Central and South America, in North America these endangered birds are found only in central and southern Florida. Draining the Everglades has killed the kite's main source of food; it is estimated that fewer than 1300 snail kites remain in Florida.

Roseate Spoonbill *(Ajaia ajaja)* – This brightest of the Everglades denizens can be seen foraging in the shallows in Florida Bay, where over 200 breeding pairs nest on Sandy Key, Tern Key and Joe Key, plus other islands, from November through March. They also visit Mrazek Pond for a short period during winter, when dropping water levels force their food to concentrate there. A major period of decline for the spoonbill occurred in the early 1800s when the wings of this beautiful creature were made into fans, a "regular article of trade" in St. Augustine, according to John Audubon. The hat trade also took a heavy toll on the spoonbill in the late 1800s. The establishment of the Everglades National Park in 1947, however, seemed to have a positive affect on south Florida's spoonbill population, which began reusing nesting sites that hadn't been occupied since the late 1800s. Like flamingoes, with which they are sometimes confused while in flight, their pink coloration comes from a red pigment, related to Vitamin A, found in crustaceans that they eat.

American Alligator, Everglades National Park

© Paul Giamou/iStockphoto.com

ferns, lianas, orchids, royal palms and, of course, gumbo-limbo trees. The latter is known in Florida as the "tourist tree" because its red, peeling bark resembles sunburned skin.

 Return to Rte. 9336 and continue 4.4mi.

Pinelands Trail

0.3mi. A paved trail here circles through a rocky, drier landscape that supports one of the few existing forests of **Florida slash pine,** also known as Dade County pine. Highly prized for its durability, slash pine was extensively logged earlier in the 20C. That logging, and the suppression of forest fires, which allow the fire-resistant pine to compete with hardwoods, has led to the demise of the pine forests that once covered much of southern Florida.

Only a total of 20,000 acres of slash pine remain, making this species the continent's most endangered member of the pine family.

 Continue 6.3mi to the turn-off for Pa-hay-okee Overlook.

Pa-hay-okee Overlook★★

This elevated platform provides a sweeping **view**★★ of the Everglades' seemingly endless saw grass prairie, interrupted only by sporadic islands of trees. Saw grass *(Cladium jamaicense)*, part of the sedge family, is by far the most dominant flora in the Everglades. Though its long blades are razor-sharp, its soft roots are edible.

 Return to Rte. 9336 and drive 7mi; turn right at sign for Mahogany Hammock.

Mahogany Hammock

0.3mi. Tunneling through a lush display of ferns and mahogany trees, the boardwalk trail passes the largest known mahogany tree in the country. Unfortunately, this landmark was damaged by Hurricane Donna in 1960 and again by Hurricane Andrew in 1992.

 Return to Rte. 9336 and continue 11.3mi; turn right to parking area for West Lake.

West Lake Trail★

0.3mi. Follow the boardwalk here along the edge of West Lake across a watery mangrove swamp. The dense concentration of mangroves, with their complex tangle of roots and branches, typifies Florida's coastal areas, where fresh water and salt water mix. Three types of mangroves grow in the Everglades: red, distinguished by their reddish arcing roots; black, whose bases are surrounded by spiky breathing tubes called pneumatophores; and white, generally found on drier ground.

 Continue 3.6mi.

Mrazek Pond

Right by the road, this watering hole is popular with birders. At dawn and dusk, grebes, herons, egrets, ibis and roseate spoonbills congregate here to feast on fish and shellfish.

 Continue 3.5 mi to Flamingo.

Flamingo

Located at the southern terminus of Rte. 9336 (38mi from park entrance).

This small outpost overlooking Florida Bay serves as the visitor hub in the southern Everglades, providing the only food and camping facilities in this part of the park. The **visitor center** (*open Dec–Apr daily 7:30am–5pm; rest of the year daily 9am–5pm;* △✕⅙ P 𝒫*941-695-2945)* houses a small display area with natural history exhibits. The adjacent marina serves as the boarding point for **boat cruises**★★ that tour the backcountry canals and the open waters of Florida Bay.

Man-made **Eco Pond**★ *(0.9mi west of visitor center; bring binoculars)* is a bird-watcher's paradise, particularly at dawn and dusk when flocks of waterfowl and wading birds gather to feed. The **observation platform** provides an excellent vantage point.

Northern Everglades

Completed in 1928, the Tamiami Trail (US-41) cuts across the Everglades, linking Miami with Naples on the west coast. Along this strip is swampland and saw-grass prairie. The main entrance into the national park along this route is at Shark Valley.

🚹 **Michelin Map:** p90.

🅸 **Info:** ℘305-242-7700; www.nps.gov/ever.

☺ **Don't Miss:**
The entertaining Tram Tour for an insight into the Everglades' natural history.

👫 **Kids:** Gator wrestling at the Miccosukee Indian Village.

Shark Valley (Park Entrance)★★

30mi west of Miami, entrance on south side of US-41. ◐*Park open year-round daily 8:30am–5:15pm.* ⊛*$10/vehicle for a 7-day pass.* ♿🅿℘*305-221-8776. www.nps.gov/ever. Maps and detailed park information available at kiosk adjacent to the parking lot.*

Named for the shallow, slow-flowing slough that empties into the brackish—and shark-infested—Shark River to the southwest, Shark Valley is actually a basin that lies a few feet lower than the rest of the Everglades. The waters that drain this valley flow into the Gulf of Mexico.

Tram Tour★

Ticket booth adjacent to parking lot. Tours depart from parking lot late Dec–May daily 9am–4pm. Rest of the year daily 9:30am, 11am, 1pm, 3pm. 2hr-round trip. Commentary. Reservations suggested. ⊛*$17.25.* ♿🅿*($10). Shark Valley Tram Tours* ℘*305-221-8455, www.sharkvalley tramtours.com. Bring drinking water on tram. Bicycle rentals available.*

The 15mi loop road here—part of which was constructed by early oil prospectors—cuts through open fields of grassy wetland. The easiest way to traverse this route is via the park's open-air trams. Along the way, park naturalists point out some of the local denizens: snail kites, egrets, herons, alligators and gar fish, to name a few. Halfway round, the tram stops at an **observation tower** to view the expansive landscape.

👫 Miccosukee Indian Village

0.5mi west of Shark Valley entrance, on south side of US-41. ◐*Open year-round daily 9am–5pm.* ⊛*$10 (includes optional guided tour). Airboat rides (30min)* ⊛*$10.* ✕♿🅿℘*305-223-8380. www.miccosukeetribe.com.*

Since the mid 19C Miccosukee Indians have inhabited the Everglades. Originally a part of the Creek Confederation, this tribe shares some similarities with the Seminoles but remains a distinct group with its own language and traditions. Now numbering some 500 people, the Miccosukee are concentrated in the northern Everglades, where they maintain a residential enclave and attempt to preserve their native culture.

Miccosukee Indian Village, a commercial venture, re-creates a traditional settlement of chickees—palm-thatched,

Observation tower, Shark Valley

© Zoran Ivanovich/iStockphoto.com

Rap on Reptiles

The sluggish-looking alligator can sprint at speeds up to 15mph for distances of 50 yards. They have been clocked swimming at speeds of 14 knots, or 16mph. Alligators' jaws can crush their prey with 3,000 pounds of pressure per square inch! There are six types of poisonous snakes in Florida: pygmy rattlesnake (*Sistrurus miliarius barbouri*); eastern diamondback rattlesnake (*Crotalus adamanteus*); canebrake rattler (*Crotalus horridus articaudatus*); coral snake (*Micrurus fulvius*); Florida cottonmouth, a.k.a. water moccasin (*Agkistrodon piscivorus conanti*); and southern copperhead (*Agkistrodon contortrix contortrix*). Rattlesnakes and other pit vipers grow new fangs on the average of one set every three months. The small dark lizards you see everywhere in Florida are Cuban brown anoles (*Anolis sagrei sagrei*), a species introduced into the state from the West Indies. Its lesser-seen relative, the green anole (*Anolis carolinensis*), is a Florida native.

open-sided structures once used as shelters. Natives demonstrate crafts such as beadwork and the bright patchwork for which the Miccosukee are renowned. A **museum** displays reproductions of traditional clothing, tools and baskets, as well as historic photographs. In the village's **alligator arena,** wrestlers demonstrate the bare-handed way in which Miccosukee hunters once captured alligators, which were tied up and kept alive until the Indians were ready to eat them *(11am, 12:30pm, 1:30pm, 3pm, 4:30pm)*.

Airboat rides (just outside the National Park border), including the chance to see an authentic, hammock-style Indian Camp that has been owned by the same Miccosukee family for over 100 years, are another attraction.

Everglades City

4mi south of US-41 on Rte. 29.
⊙*Gulf Coast Visitor Center (Everglades National Park information) open year-round daily 7:30am–5pm.* P ℘*941-695-3311. www.nps.gov/ever.*
Established in the 1920s as a headquarters for the building of the Tamiami Trail, Everglades City is now the gateway to the northwestern Everglades.
The town's most famous institution is the **Rod and Gun Club** *(200 Waterside Dr, ℘239-695-2101; www.evergladesrodandgun.com)*. Serving as a fishing and hunting club since the late 19C, this structure was originally the residence of one of the area's first settlers, W.S.

Allen. The rambling white-frame Victorian, with its rich interior paneling, gained world renown in the 1930s as one of the most exclusive sports clubs in the nation. Then owned by **Barron Collier,** the land speculator largely responsible for the building of the Tamiami Trail, the club played host to a number of dignitaries. It now operates as an inn and restaurant.

Cruises of the Ten Thousand Islands★★

Cruises depart from the ranger station on Rte. 29.
⊙ *From US-41, take Rte. 29 south 4mi to traffic circle; stay on Rte. 29—3/4 turn around circle—and continue 0.5mi to Everglades National Park Gulf Coast Visitor Center on right.*
⊙*Open year-round daily 9am–5pm. Round-trip 1hr 30min. Commentary.* ⊙*$26.50. Everglades National Park Boat Tours* ✕ ♿ P ℘*239-695-2591.*
Park-sponsored tours offer a look at the marine world of **Chokoloskee Bay**. Countless small islets here are covered collectively with one of the largest mangrove forests in the world.
During the cruise you may see dolphins, manatees and numerous waterbirds, including ospreys, herons, roseate spoonbills, and perhaps even nesting bald eagles.
There is also a mangrove wilderness tour, exploring swampy areas of the park, on a six-passenger vessel. Tours last 1hr 45 min; ⊙*$35/person.*

Historic Smallwood Store

360 Mamie St.

From Everglades City, continue south on Rte. 29 about 3mi onto Chokoloskee Island; turn right on Smallwood Dr. and left on Mamie St.; follow Mamie to end.

Open Dec–Apr daily 10am–5pm, rest of the year Fri–Tues 10am–4pm.

Closed major holidays. $3. 239-695-2989. www.florida-everglades.com/chokol/smallw.htm.

From 1906 to 1982, this weathered wooden bayfront structure was a trading post and general store. Named for "Ted" Smallwood, the Collier County pioneer who founded it, the store now functions as a museum. It displays original turn-of-the-century wares and recalls the atmosphere of an earlier era.

Wilderness Waterway

A paradise for boaters and canoeists, this watery inland course twists 99mi through protected rivers and bays, from Flamingo to Everglades City. Markers designate the waterway, and campsites (some furnished with chickee shelters) punctuate the route. *National Park Service permits are required for overnight camping; course takes 6–8hrs by motorboat and 8–10 days by canoe. Pick up permit (no more than 24hrs before start of trip) and maps at the ranger station in Flamingo. 239-695-2945 or Gulf Coast Visitor Center (in Everglades City) 239-695-3311.*

Big Cypress National Preserve

Accessible from US-41 and I-75.

Open daily year-round. 239-695-1201. www.nps.gov/bicy.

Contiguous to the northern Everglades, the 729,000-acre preserve protects a portion of the 2,400sq mi **Big Cypress Swamp,** a rich variegated wetland covered with forests of bald cypress trees. Few giant cypress still stand, having been heavily logged early in the 20C, and much of the terrain is now covered with dwarf cypress and sawgrass prairie. In the 1960s, developers hatched plans to drain the vast swamp and build on its lands. In 1974, however, the government—recognizing that this area was a critical link in south Florida's

wetlands wilderness—established a 500,000-acre preserve. A major habitat for much of the same wildlife found in the Everglades, Big Cypress is particularly favored by dwindling numbers of the endangered Florida panther. About 30–35 of the big cats are thought to live in the park; all told, about 80–100 panthers exist in the state. Big Cypress Reserve is also a habitat for black bears; campers beware!

The **Oasis Visitor Center** *(19 mi west of Shark Valley on US-41;* open year-round daily 8:30am–4:30pm; *closed Dec 25;* 941-695-1201) shows a 15-min film on the geology, flora and fauna of Big Cypress. Stroll along the boardwalk for views of alligators. Behind the center, the **Florida National Scenic Trail** leads 21mi into the heart of the preserve.

A 26mi loop road *(Rte. 94 from Forty Mile Bend to Monroe Station)* circles through haunting cypress swamps in the southern part of the preserve—look for alligators, soft-shell turtles and raptors.

An unpaved **northern loop** *(16.5 mi)* begins at Route 839 and travels through wide-open saw grass prairie *(follow Turner River Rd./Rte. 839 north 7.3mi; turn left on Rte. 837 to Birdon Rd./Rte. 841, which leads back to US-41).*

Fakahatchee Strand Preserve State Park★

Big Cypress Bend trail parking located 7mi west of Rte. 29; park sign on right. *Open year-round daily dawn–dusk.* *239-695-4593. www.floridastate parks.org. Bring mosquito repellent.*

Adjacent to Big Cypress National Preserve, this "Amazon of North America." comprises a 20mi-long swamp forest, between 3 and 5 miles wide, containing a dense, exotic mix of vegetation. Its flora includes the largest stand of native **royal palm** in the US, as well as the greatest concentration and diversity of **orchids** (31 threatened and endangered species); 15 species of bromeliads; and a variety of epiphytes, or air plants. A boardwalk *(1 mi round-trip)* at **Big Cypress Bend**★★ leads through eerily beautiful virgin cypress forest, ending at a swamp frequented by alligators.

THE KEYS

Curving southwest 220mi from Biscayne Bay to the Dry Tortugas, the thousand-some islands and islets that compose the Florida Keys form a narrow archipelago separating the waters of the Atlantic from Florida Bay and, farther south, the Gulf of Mexico. Not far from the bustle of Miami some 50 miles north, the Keys maintain a laid-back atmosphere throughout, though the character of the individual islands varies. The upper and middle Keys serve as a jumping-off point for sportfishermen, divers, snorkelers and wildlife enthusiasts interested in the wealth of marine life on the offshore coral reef. The lower Keys are dominated by the town of Key West, a distinctive and internationally renowned destination.

Highlights

1 Getting under the water at **John Pennekamp State Park** (p101)

2 Enjoying the sea views from **Seven Mile Bridge** (p103)

3 Getting sand between your toes at **Bahia Honda** beach (p104)

4 Visiting the **Ernest Hemingway Home and Museum** (p120)

5 Enjoying **Key West Old Town**, by day and by night (p111)

A Bit of History

With the exception of the northernmost sand islands, the Keys consist of the remains of coral reefs that began forming as early as 10 to 15 million years ago, when the area was covered by a shallow sea. Until the 20C, most of these "chaotic fragments of coral reef, limestone, and mangrove swamps," supported only a small, scattered population of Indians and, later, indomitable fishermen and farmers. In the 1800s the islands were a less than hospitable place because of the plague of mosquitoes that blackened the sides of homes. In these early days, boats were the only means of transportation among the Keys.

In 1904, railroad magnate **Henry Flagler** launched plans to extend his railway south from Miami to Key West. Although the construction of "Flagler's Folly," as the **Overseas Railroad** was popularly known, was thwarted from the beginning by hurricanes, Flagler persisted; in 1912 the first train pulled into Key West. For 23 years Flagler's railroad provided transportation to the Keys, but disaster struck in September 1935, when a killer hurricane destroyed the line. Flagler's successors at the Florida East Coast Railway decided not to rebuild the line as it had never been a money-maker.

In 1938 the **Overseas Highway** was completed along the former railroad bed. Crossing 43 bridge/causeways (only one of them over land), this southernmost stretch of US-1 offers Atlantic views to the east and Florida Bay's aquamarine waters to the west.

Overseas Highway

©PhotoDisc

GETTING THERE

BY AIR – **Key West International Airport** (*305-296-5439; www.keywest internationalairport.com*) is serviced by most domestic airlines, including SeaCoast Airlines *(www.seacoastairlines. com)* who fly from St Petersburg/ Clearwater Airport. Rental car agencies are located at and near the airport. International flights connect through Miami International Airport.

BY BOAT – **The Intracoastal Waterway** Key West Express operates ferries between Key West and Marco Island seasonally (*Dec–mid-April*), and between Key West and Fort Myers year- round. Trip from Marco Island takes 3hrs, Fort Myers 3.5hrs. Round-trip rates are $119 and $145 respectively (*888-539-2628; www.seakeywest.com*).

BY CAR – Small green mile-marker **(MM)** posts, sometimes difficult to spot, are used to delineate locations of sites along US-1 (Overseas Highway) giving distances from Key West. The **Mile-Marker system** begins in Florida City (MM 127), on the mainland, and crosses a causeway to Key Largo (MM 110), reaching its terminus in Key West (MM 0). Much of the route is two-lane, and traffic can be heavy, particularly in the high season and on weekends. Allow 3hrs for the drive. The best places along US-1 to find lodging, restaurants and other amenities (marinas, recreational facilities) are: Key Largo (MM 110-87), Islamorada (MM 86-66), Marathon (MM 65-40), Big Pine Key (MM 39-9) and Key West (MM 0).

BY BUS – Greyhound **bus** makes scheduled stops in the Keys (*800-231-2222; www.greyhound.com*). A number of **shuttle** services offer transport to the Keys, including Keys Shuttle, operating from Miami International and Fort Lauderdale airports (*888-765-9997 or 305 289-9997; www.keysshuttle.com*).

WHEN TO GO

December through April is considered high season; afternoon temperatures range from 73°F to 79°F. The rest of the year they run 75°F to 85°F;

annual average temperature is 77.4°F. Rainfall is considerably less than on the mainland and falls in brief thunderstorms during summer afternoons. March is the pinnacle of Spring Break, when hordes of young people descend on the Keys and Key West in particular. Travelers are likely to encounter crowds in Key West, especially on Duval Street.

FESTIVALS

There is a festival of some kind every week in the Keys. Here are three that may be worth planning your trip around; all take place in Key West.

October: **Fantasy Fest**. A Mardi Gras for gays and lesbians. www. fantasyfest.net. April: **Conch Republic Independence Celebrations** (*see p109*). Around July 21: **Hemingway Days** - A celebration of the hellraising author (*see p116*).

VISITOR INFORMATION

FLORIDA KEYS VISITOR INFORMATION (*www.fla-keys.com; 800-FLA-KEYS*).

Key Largo Chamber of Commerce, MM 106, 105950 Overseas Hwy., Key Largo 33037 *(open 9am–6pm daily; 305-451-1414 or 800-822-1088; www.fla-keys.com/keylargo*).

Islamorada Chamber of Commerce, MM 83.2, PO Box 915, Islamorada FL 33036 *(Mon–Fri 9am–5pm, Sat, 9am–4pm, Sun 9am–3pm; 305-664-4503 or 800-322-5397; www.islamoradachamber.com*).

Marathon Chamber of Commerce, MM 53.5, 12222 Overseas Hwy., Marathon 33050 *(9am–5pm daily; 305-743-5417 or 800-262-7284; www.floridakeysmarathon.com*).

Lower Keys Chamber of Commerce, MM 31, PO Box 430511, Big Pine Key 33043 *(Mon–Fri 9am–5pm, Sat 9am–3pm; 305-872-2411; www.lowerkeyschamber.com*).

Greater Key West Chamber of Commerce, 510 Greene Street, First Floor, Key West, FL 33040 *(Mon–Fri 8:30am–6:30pm, Sat-Sun 9am–5pm; 305-294-2587 or 800-527-8539; www.keywestchamber.org*).

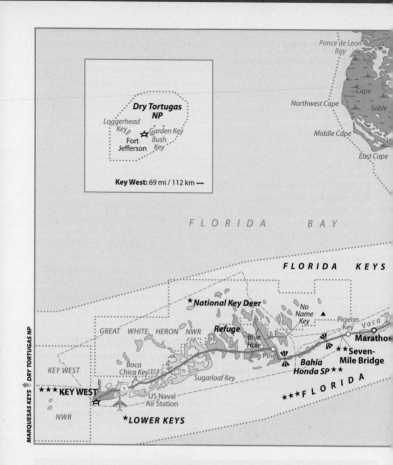

Preserving the Reef

The coral reef that lies off Key Largo forms part of the **Florida Reef**★★★ tract, the largest living coral reef system in North America and third-largest barrier reef in the world (after Australia's Great Barrier Reef and the Belize Barrier Reef). The reef protects almost 200 miles of coastline from south of Miami to the Dry Tortugas. Descending to depths of nearly 80ft, it consists of calcium carbonate (limestone) secreted over thousands of years by colonies of small, soft-bodied coral polyps. This fragile ecosystem, including coral reefs, sea-grass meadows and mangrove forests, is protected by the **Florida Keys National Marine Sanctuary,** which protects the waters surrounding the Keys from Biscayne National Park to the Dry Tortugas, encompassing the former Key Largo National Marine Sanctuary as well.

In order to remain healthy, coral requires water of a certain salinity, temperature and clarity. Over the years, pollution, overharvesting and careless use have adversely affected the Florida Reef. A comprehensive management plan and water-quality protection program developed for the Keys sanctuary is attempting to reverse the destructive trend and restore this national treasure to full health. The effort extends all the way "upstream" to the Everglades, which a massive federal and state program is attempting to revive. Water from the Everglades flows south into Florida Bay—also an endangered environment—through the narrow channels to the reefs that depend on the purity of this flow.

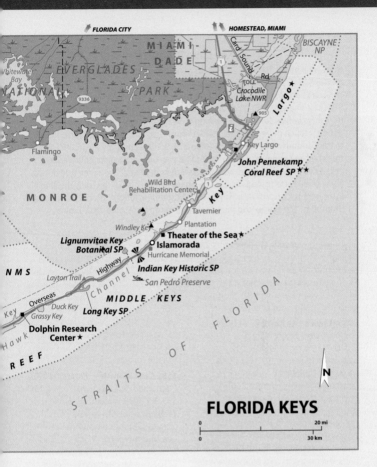

FLORIDA CITY

HOMESTEAD, MIAMI

MIAMI-DADE

BISCAYNE NP

Everglades

Whitewater Bay

NATIONAL

PARK

9336

Card Sound

TOLL

Crocodile Lake NWR

Rd.

905

Largo

Flamingo

Key Largo

MONROE

Wild Bird Rehabilitation Center

John Pennekamp Coral Reef SP ★★

Key

Tavernier

Plantation

Windley Key

Theater of the Sea ★

Lignumvitae Key Botanical SP

Islamorada

Hurricane Memorial

NMS

Highway

Indian Key Historic SP

San Pedro Preserve

Layton Trail

Channel

MIDDLE KEYS

FLORIDA

Overseas

Duck Key

Grassy Key

Long Key SP

Key

Dolphin Research Center ★

Hawk

REEF

STRAITS

OF

FLORIDA

N

FLORIDA KEYS

0   20 mi

0   30 km

ADDRESSES

🏠 STAY

Area visitors' guides including lodging directories are available (free) from area Chambers of Commerce.

Reservation services: Welcome Center of Florida Keys (𝄢305-296-4444 or 800-284-4482); **Apartment and condo rentals** are available through Vacation Rentals Key West (𝄢800 797-8787; www.vacationrentalskeywest.com).

Camping and **RV parks** are located throughout the Keys and offer full hookups, and in some cases beaches, freshwater pools, marinas and rental boats. There are KOA Kampgrounds at Fiesta Key (𝄢305-664-4922) and Sugarloaf Key (𝄢305-745-3549; www. koa.com). The three state parks in the Keys—John Pennekamp SP (𝄢305-451-1202; www.pennekamppark.com),

Long Key SP (𝄢305-664-4815; www. floridastateparks.org/longkey) and Bahia Honda SP (𝄢305-872-2353; www.florida stateparks.org/bahiahonda)—also offer dozens of campsites, but reservations are essential well in advance.

A different way of staying in the Keys is to rent a **houseboat** from Houseboat Vacations, Islamorada (3 days from $1,112, 7 days from $1,950 fully equipped; 𝄢305-664-4009; www.floridakeys. com/houseboats).

$$$$ Cheeca Lodge & Spa – Mile Marker 82, Overseas Hwy., Islamorada. ✕🚫🅿🏊 𝄢305-664-4651 or 800-327-2888. www.cheeca.com. 203 rooms. Colonial Bahamian elegance permeates the grounds of this deluxe resort, favored by former president George H. W. Bush as a base for his bonefishing excursions. Broad lawns and a 9-hole golf course surround the stucco-and-

Key Lime Products

See map pp 96–7. MM 95.2, Overseas Hwy. (bay side) in Key Largo. 305-853-0378 or 800-870-1780. www.keylimeproducts.com.

This roadside Key Largo shop carries just about everything imaginable made from key limes, including admirably tart iced smoothies that are perfect refreshers before continuing the long drive north out of the Keys. Key limes are good for much more than their namesake pies or blended drinks. Introduced to the Caribbean by Christopher Columbus on his second voyage in 1493, lime trees became endemic in the West Indies, evolving into a distinctive variety called Key Lime in the Keys. Most backyards in the Keys have a lime tree or two, and a small cottage industry has sprung up to make use of the fruit. The lime's astringent juice is a principal ingredient in soothing lotions, bracing soaps and shampoos, and sauces and marinades that range from savory to stinging.

tile buildings, creating the ambience of an estate. Tennis courts, two pools and a saltwater lagoon entice adult guests, as do sailboarding and other water activities; extensive children's programs keep the young ones occupied.

$$$$ Hawk's Cay Resort – *61 Hawk's Cay Blvd., Duck Key. 305-743-7000 or 800-432-2242. www.hawkscay.com. 193 rooms, 295 villas.* This Caribbean-style, 60-acre family resort offers every imaginable tropical activity, including swimming with dolphins. The complex includes a spa and five pools; the saltwater lagoon boasts its own small beach. Two and three-story buildings house the guest units, decorated in cool blue and white to echo the view of the Atlantic Ocean from their balconies. On-site dining options range from a coffee bar in the lobby to The Terrace open-air dining room and classic American Indies Grill.

$$$$ Jules' Undersea Lodge – *51 Shoreland Dr., Key Largo. 305-451-2353. www.jul.com. 1 unit (maximum 6 people).* You have to don scuba gear (but you don't have to be an expert diver) to reach your room at this unique property near John Pennekamp Coral Reef State Park. Situated 30ft below the surface of a little lagoon, 100ft from shore, Jules' advertises itself as the world's first undersea lodge. Guest accommodations are tiny but offer TV, microwave and air-conditioning.

$$$$ Kona Kai Resort – *Mile Marker 97.8.97802 Overseas Hwy., Key Largo. 305-852-7200 or 800-365-7829. www.konakairesort.com. 13 rooms and suites.* Set in a small, lushly landscaped compound, this resort, gallery and botanic gardens includes single-story stucco cottages, well off the highway, facing westward, and overlooking Florida Bay and its spectacular sunsets. All suites feature ceiling fans, DVDs and compact kitchens. Relax in the secluded pool or hot tub, sheltered by dense tropical foliage.

$$$$ Casa Morada – *136 Madeira Rd, Islamorada. 305-664-0044 or 888-881-3030. www.casamorada.com. 16 suites.* A spa-like serenity sets this all-suites boutique hotel apart from its neighbors. Blooming orchids, bright artwork and terrazzo floors give the property a Mediterranean-meets-Caribbean vibe. The three female hoteliers who run the property get all the small details right, down to the hidden bench by the waterfall (a perfect spot for reading) and lounge chairs perched at the water's edge.

$$ Largo Lodge – *Mile Marker 101.7, 101740 Overseas Hwy., Key Largo. 305-451-0424. www.largolodge.com. 7 cottages.* Equipped with kitchens, screened porches and living rooms, Largo Lodge's rustic cottages are spacious, comfortable and economical. A private beach and boat dock offer access to the Gulf of Mexico; the no-children (under 16) policy enhances the serenity. Reserve months in advance for winter weekends.

SPORTS AND RECREATION

Visitors can enjoy many activities including sailing, snorkeling, fishing, scuba diving and boating. **Diving** and snorkeling are first-rate on the Keys, thanks to good visibility, a great variety of sea life and corals, shipwrecks to explore, and amazing dive sites such as Looe Key Reef. Dive shops rent equipment and offer day trips and package deals as well as instruction. Diving in the Keys is best March–July.

Ocean Divers, MM 100, Key Largo (☎305-451-1113; www.oceandivers.com).

Sea Dwellers Dive Shop, MM 100, Key Largo (☎305-451-3640 or 800-451-3640; www.seadwellers.com).

Halls Diving Center, MM 48, Marathon (☎305-743-5929 or 800-331-4255; www.hallsdiving.com).

Strike Zone Charters, MM 29.5, Big Pine Key (☎305-872-9863 or 800-654-9560; www.strikezonecharter.com).

Looe Key Reef Resort, MM 275, Ramrod Key (☎305-872-2215 or 877-816-3483; www.divelakeys.com).

Snorkel Cruise: Theater of the Sea, MM 84.5; Islamorada offers an "Adventure and Snorkel Cruise" *(year-round daily 8:30am and 1pm; round-trip 4hrs; purchase tickets in advance; $69 including gear rental; ☎305-664-2431; www.theaterofthesea.com).*

Kayaking – Paddlers can explore pristine mangroves and remote islands that the casual traveler will never see. Outfitters are starting to crop up all over the Keys as this sport continues to explode. To explore the **backcountry**—Key West National Wildlife Refuge and the Great White Heron National Wildlife Refuge—visitors should engage a reputable guide, like Captain Bill Keogh of Big Pine Kayak Adventures. MM 30, No Name Key *(rentals, transportation and guided tours: ☎305-872-7474; www.keyskayaktours.com).*

Area **golf** courses: **Key West Golf Club**, MM 5 *(☎305-294-5232; www.key westgolf.com);* **Key Colony Beach**, MM 53.5, Marathon *(www.keycolony beach.net).*

Dolphin Encounter Sites – Visitors participate in a short marine orientation seminar, followed by a swim *(20–30min)* with Atlantic bottlenose dolphins. Participants must be at least 8 years old (5 years old if with parent in the water),

be good swimmers in deep water and be experienced in the use of mask and fins. Reserve well in advance. Prices range from $135–$189/person.

Dolphin Research Center (☎ see p103).

Theater of the Sea (☎ see p102).

SPORTFISHING TOURNAMENTS

General sportfishing information *(☎888-FISH-KEYS; www.fla-keys.com).*

late March – **Islamorada All-Tackle Spring Bonefish Tournament** *(☎305-852-1694)*

April – **World Sailfish Championship, Key West** *(☎305-395-3474 or 866-482-7529)*

late Apr–early May – **Tarponian Tournament, Marathon** *(☎215-542-1492)*

May – **Marathon International Tarpon Tournament** *(☎305-743-6139)*

late June – **Gold Cup Tarpon Tournament, Islamorada** *(☎305-664-2444)*

late Sept – **Marathon International Bonefishing Tournament** *(☎305-743-7368)*

Nov – **Islamorada Sailfish Tournament** *(☎305-852-2102)*

Sportfishing, Islamorada

Visit Florida

The Upper Keys ★★

The Upper Keys, the northernmost islands in the group, are made up of Key Largo, Islamorada (eye-la-mo-rarda) and Marathon.

Key Largo proclaims itself "Dive Capital of the World" with many superb dive sites, though little else of interest to landlubbers.

Islamorada is comprised of six islands including Plantation Key, Windley Key, Upper Matecumbe Key, Lower Matecumbe Key and the offshore islands of Indian Key and Lignumvitae Key. They say that every other salty dog that you meet in Key West is called "Cap'n" but with a fleet of perhaps the most highly-skilled recreational fishing captains in the state (and probably beyond), Islamorada's reputation as the Sport Fishing Capital of the World is well earned. Indeed, this might be the only place on Earth where it is possible to catch a sailfish in the morning, and then venture into the backcountry in pursuit of bonefish, permit, tarpon, snook and redfish in just inches of water. Islamorada isn't just for anglers, however. At Long Key State Park, there are lush, tropical nature trails; Windley Key Fossil Reef Geological State Park features an old quarry dug by Henry Flagler's railroad workers; and Indian Key Historic State Park and Lignumvitae Key Botanical State Park also offer visitors a glimpse into Florida's unique island history dating back to the early 1800s.

Located mainly on Vaca, Fat Deer and Grassy Key, Marathon is a 10-mile-long family-oriented island community rooted in a heritage of fishing, and reflects the old-Keys lifestyle that residents, snowbirds and visitors enjoy so much.

Scuba Diving, Key Largo

© Bob Care/Florida Keys News Bureau

Indian Key Historic State Park

© Photoshot

Key Largo★

Called *Cayo Largo,* or "Long Island," by 16C Spanish explorers, Key Largo is the first and largest—26 miles long but only one mile at its widest point —of the Florida Keys. Its real beauty is to be found along its shoreline and underneath its crystal blue waters. Immediately to the east lies the vast windswept Atlantic Ocean; to the west, the calm shallow Florida Bay serves as a nursery for birds and marine life.

SIGHTS (AND THE MOVIES)

Key Largo entered the consciousness of the nation following the eponymous 1948 Humphrey Bogart movie. Yet it was almost entirely shot in Hollywood—the **Caribbean Club Bar** (MM 104) is the only actual Keys location—and Key Largo, on land at least, is something of a disappointment to most visitors. As a token gesture to its Hollywood-Bogart success *The African Queen* is here, at the marina of the Holiday Inn at MM 100.

John Pennekamp Coral Reef State Park★★

MM 102.5. ⏱*Open year-round daily 8am–dusk.* ⊜*$8/vehicle plus 50c per person.* △*(reservations suggested)* ✖⌖🅿 ✆*850-245-2157. www.floridastateparks.org, www.pennekamppark.com.*
Stretching along Key Largo's coastline and reaching 3mi offshore, America's first underwater park was created in 1960. Some 96 percent of it lies beneath the waves, encompassing a dazzling kaleidoscope of vivid coral and sea creatures. Informative displays (including a floor-to-ceiling aquarium) relating to the reef and its marine life in the **visitor center** (⏱*open year-round daily 9am–5pm*) provide an excellent introduction to the undersea world offshore. One hundred and fifty species of tropical fish feed here, including angelfish, parrot fish, triggerfish and snapper. Sea fans, whips, plumes and sponges cling to the coral. Snorkeling tours are possible though you'll need a good pair of lungs, or tanks

▶ **Population:** 11, 886.
🖊 **Michelin Map:** pp 96–97.
ℹ **Info:** ✆305-451-1414 or 800-822-1088; www.fla-keys.com/keylargo.
▶ **Location:** Key Largo is 56mi south of Miami International Airport.
🅿 **Parking:** Parking is readily available in Key Largo.
👁 **Don't Miss:** John Pennekamp Coral Reef State Park, an underwater aquatic reserve boasting 40 species of coral and more than 650 varieties of fish.
🕐 **Timing:** Plan the length of your visit depending upon how much time you want to spend underwater. If you're not avid snorkelers or divers, plan a day at the park and a meal at the Fish House, MM 102.4, one of the best restaurants on the Keys.
👥 **Kids:** A glass-bottom boat trip to the reef is a great way to peek underwater without snorkeling.

and a respirator, to see the iconic **Statue of Christ of the Abyss**, an 8ft 6in, 4,000-pound bronze sculpture of Christ that stands in 25ft of water.

Statue of Christ of the Abyss

© Stephen Frink/Florida Keys News Bureau

Islamorada to Marathon

Sportfishing enthusiasts favor these islands—especially Islamorada—casting their rods for such deep-sea trophies as sailfish, tarpon, marlin and shark. Below MM 80, US-1 crosses a series of viaducts, causeways and bridges connecting myriad individual islands. Sweeping views★★★ of the Atlantic Ocean and Florida Bay fan out on either side of the road. Development returns with the roadside shopping plazas, motels and eateries in Marathon. Just past Marathon at the south end of Vaca Key, Seven-Mile Bridge spans the distance to the Lower Keys.

SIGHTS
👤👤 Theater of the Sea★

Windley Key, MM 84.5. ◷*Open year-round daily 9:30am–4pm (open 10:30am Dec 25). Reservations required for special programs.* ◉*$26.95; child (3–10 yrs) $19.45.* ♿🅿 ☎*305-664-2431. www.theaterofthesea.com.*

What this lushly landscaped 17-acre marine park (est. 1945) lacks in high-tech gloss, it makes up for in a friendly, personal approach. Open-air pools house

- 👤 **Michelin Map:** pp 96–7.
- ℹ **Info:** ☎305-664-4503 or 305-743-5417; www.fla-keys.com.
- ◖ **Location:** The stretch from Windley Key to Long Key is generally considered part of the Upper Keys (along with Key Largo and Tavernier), while the Middle Keys continue from Conch Key to the end of Seven-Mile Bridge.
- 🅿 **Parking:** Parking is fairly easy to come by here.
- ◈ **Don't Miss:** Islamorada for serious fishing. Tell them about the one that got away at the classic, weatherbeaten 7 Mile Grill, and catch a sunset, drink and meal at Lorelei.
- ◷ **Timing:** How long you spend here probably depends on your love of fishing, or interacting with dolphins.
- 👤👤 **Kids:** The animal shows at Theater of the Sea are lively, and just the right length for small fry.

Dolphin Research Center

© Bob Krist/Florida Keys News Bureau

Where are the Beaches?

Outsiders picture the Keys as a tropical paradise of white strands of sand, breeze-tossed palms and languid waters. Beach lovers should beware however. The beaches that do exist are fairly scant, and even these are often not ideal for swimming, given their very shallow depths and windy waters. The explanation is topographical: the waters surrounding the Keys, both Gulf and Atlantic, are almost invariably shallow, and bounded by reefs on the Atlantic side. The reefs block the currents that bring large quantities of sand to the high shore and scour the near-shore bottom, creating the typical ocean beach found world-wide. Most of the major resort complexes have "made" their own beaches, often by manufacturing saltwater lagoons on their property, or sometimes by dredging near-shore waters.

There are a few public beaches where visitors can enjoy water deep enough to swim. **Anne's Beach,** right along US-1 at MM 73 on Lower Matecumbe Key, offers clean sand and a series of swimming holes at the south end of the beach. **Sombrero Beach** in Marathon has clean water and sand and a pleasant park that is largely uncrowded. **Bahia Honda State Park,** MM 36.8, is well-known for the best beach in the Keys—famed enough to draw long lines of cars on weekends and holidays.

sharks, rays, sea turtles and fish. Regularly scheduled shows feature dolphins, parrots and sea lions.

🐬Continuous guided tours focus on animal behavior and environmental issues. The park also offers (extra cost) swim-with-the-dolphins and snorkeling excursions.

Long Key State Park

Long Key, MM 67.5. 🛆 🅿 🖉 *305-664-4815. www.floridastateparks.org.*
This 965-acre park touches both ocean and bay waters and offers paddling (rental kayaks), snorkeling, fishing and camping. The **Golden Orb Trail** *(1mi)* offers great views of a mangrove creek and lagoon where waterbirds congregate.

🐬 Dolphin Research Center★

Grassy Key, MM 59. 🕐*Open year-round daily 9am–4:30pm.* 🕐*Closed major holidays.* 🎫*$19.50.* ♿ 🅿 🖉*305-289-1121. www.dolphins.org.*
Not-for-profit research takes place at the DRC, where visitors watch trainers work with several groups of dolphins. Guides explain dolphin behavior, dolphins demonstrate their amazing abilities and guests have the chance to swim with them (♿*see p99*). This facility has been used in the filming of several dolphin movies, including *Flipper.* In fact the film's creator, Milton Santini, is also the man behind the DRC.

Crane Point Museums and Nature Point★

MM 50 in Marathon. 🕐*Open year-round Mon–Sat 9am–5pm, Sun noon –5pm.* 🕐*Closed major holidays.* 🎫*$12.* 🅿 🖉*305-743-9100. www.cranepoint.net.*
Trails wind through 63 acres of tropical forest connecting a **Museum, Children's Activities Center, Adderly House** (a Bahamian Conch house built 1903, made of Bahamian tabby) and **Marathon Wild Bird Center.** Displays in the museum highlight local flora and fauna, marine life on the coral reef and collections of native tree snails and butterflies.

Seven-Mile Bridge★★

MM 47-40, Knight Key to Little Duck Key. This engineering masterpiece ranks as the longest segmental bridge in the world with 288 135ft-long sections linking the Middle and Lower Keys. Completed in 1982 to replace Flagler's concrete and steel marvel, the new span is both wider and higher than the Old Seven-Mile Bridge, providing a 65ft clearance for vessels to pass underneath. Its heights afford expansive **views**★★ of the open ocean.

Lower Keys★

Scrub and slash pine characterize this handful of wooded islands extending from MM 45 to the outskirts of Key West at MM 5. Their low, wet land and surrounding waters provide refuge for a variety of wildlife, including the great white heron and the diminutive Key deer. For sun worshipers, Bahia Honda boasts one of the few sand beaches in the Keys; for those who prefer to be underwater, the unusually clear waters of the reef at **Looe Key**, part of the Florida Keys National Marine Sanctuary *(7 mi offshore in the Atlantic)*, are a diver's paradise.

🕙 **Michelin Map:** p96.
ℹ️ **Info:** ☎305-872-2411; www.fla-keys.com/ lower keys.
▶️ **Location:** The Lower Keys run from Mile Marker 37 to Mile Marker 9.
🅿️ **Parking:** Bahia Honda Park fills up quickly on weekends, and they close the gate when the lots are filled.
🕙 **Timing:** Relax here for a day or two before (or after) experiencing the crazy scene on Key West.

SIGHTS

The Lower Keys is mostly a quiet, natural place in which to kick back, enjoy the nature trails, maybe kayak a little and commune with nature. However, the facilities of Islamorada and the wilder pleasures of Key West are all within striking distance.

Bahia Honda State Park★★

Bahia Honda Key, MM 36.8. ⛺🅿️♿$8 *per vehicle, plus 50c per person.* ☎305-872-2353. www.floridastateparks.org/ bahiahonda.

Named by the Spanish for its "Deep Bay," Bahia Honda Key encompasses one of the largest stretches of sand **beach**♿☆☆ in the Keys. This popular park covers 524 acres and includes a lagoon, mangrove forest and a tropical hardwood hammock. Stroll through the **Silver Palm Trail** *(.25mi)*, where you'll glimpse West Indian specimens, such as yellow satinwood and Jamaica morning glory.

At the southern tip you can walk out on a segment of the original **Bahia Honda Bridge,** erected for Flagler's railroad and later remodeled for the Overseas Highway. From its vantage point, high over the ocean, stretch **views★** of stately palms swaying above tranquil turquoise water. Campsites on the beach (and cabins on the bay side) offer great views; reserve well in advance.

Swimming is popular in the Atlantic Ocean and Florida Bay, and for those who want to go further afield, kayaks can be hired per hour or half day to explore the waters around the park. Shore activities include cycling.

National Key Deer Refuge★

MM 30.5, on Big Pine Key.
▶️ *Turn right onto Key Deer Blvd. (Rte. 940) and follow it .3mi to the refuge office in Big Pine Key Plaza on the right.*
The refuge is 3mi west on Key Deer Blvd. Stay alert for deer crossing the road.
🕙*Open year-round daily dawn–dusk.* ♿🅿️ ☎305-872-2239. www.fws.gov/ nationalkeydeer.

This National Wildlife Refuge was established in 1954 to protect Key deer *(🕙see opposite)*. Two trails within the refuge provide good opportunities for deer sightings, particularly at dawn and dusk (feeding time). At **Blue Hole** *(west side of Key Deer Blvd., 1.25mi north of intersection with Watson Blvd.)*, look for deer drinking in this old rock quarry now filled with water. The pond is also home to alligators, turtles and sunfish. The **Jack C. Watson Wildlife Trail** *(continue 0.3mi north on Key Blvd.)* weaves half a mile through a thicket of slash pines and palms, a favorite Key deer habitat.

Key Deer

Key Deer

The unique Key deer (Odocoileus virginianus clavium) is found only in the lower Florida Keys. Smallest of all North American deer, the members of this subspecies of Virginia white-tailed deer measure about 2ft high at the shoulder and weigh from 50 to 100 pounds. How the deer came to occupy the Keys is unknown, but it is believed that they migrated here from the mainland thousands of years ago. Uncontrolled hunting and land development reduced the number of deer to less than 50 in the 1940s. Since the establishment of the national refuge, the population has grown. Today some 600 Key deer inhabit Big Pine Key. Conflict has inevitably arisen among conservationists, area developers and local residents who view the animals as foliage-consuming pests. The most pressing threat to Key deer, however, is highway traffic.

Bonefishing

The shallow, flat waters surrounding the Keys are home to several types of highly prized, and legendarily elusive, gamefish—including the famed bone-fish. Bonefishing is an arcane and demanding art. Success therein depends on skill, expertise, concentration and more than a little luck. The bonefish flats in Florida Bay, northwest of the Keys, range from 3ft to 8ft deep; thus, shallow-hull boats are necessary, and visitors must rely on knowledgeable guides to find their way through the maze of channels, flats and islands that, to an outsider, seem indistinguishable. The sun invariably blazes down, and afternoon winds prowl the waters; polarized sunglasses are needed to pick out the fish cruising the flats for prey. Anglers cast streamer flies (designed to look like small prey) ahead of the fish, and when hooked, memorable fights ensue on the light tackle typically used. Aside from bonefish, snook, tarpon and redfish are often caught; sea trout and sharks are secondary targets. The bonefish guiding community has begun to promote a catch-and-release conservation ethic, as the environmental problems besetting Florida Bay have curtailed the fishery somewhat. The area is also a waterfowl haven, and osprey and eagles are a common sight.

A full day of guided bonefishing starts at $600 (*rods and gear supplied by the guide*). It's essential to patronize guides whose principles include safeguarding the delicate environment of the Keys backcountry. Conservation-minded guides include Adam Redford who specializes in upper Florida Bay and the Everglades (℘800-632-0394), and Mike Collins in Islamorada (℘305-852-5837). In Key West, the Salt Water Angler (*243 Front St.;* ℘*305-294-3248; www.salt waterangler.com*) can arrange trips.

Bonefish

Key West ★★★

Pirates, wreckers, writers, US presidents and Cuban freedom fighters have all found a haven on this small island at the southernmost tip of the continent. Closer to Havana than Miami, Key West cultivates an atmosphere of sublime laissez-faire that encourages an eclectic mix of residents, from old-time "conch" families (descended from the island's original settlers) to a more recently arrived gay community. Well established is the lush landscape here, where banyan trees and palms shade older neighborhoods, while the scent of tropical flowers fills the evening air. Key West is undeniably commercial, yet it possesses a quirky charm and independent spirit that still appeal to writers and artists, as well as to the droves of tourists who come here each year.

- ▶ **Population**: 25,031.
- **Michelin Map**: p110.
- **Info:** ☏ 305-294-2587 or 800-527-8539; www.fla-keys.com/keywest.
- ▷ **Location:** The Mile Markers in the Keys end at 0, in Key West.
- **Parking:** Parking is rare and expensive in Key West. Some lodgings provide parking or discounts at municipal lots. Best advice if you're bringing a car is to park it, leave it, and walk or take taxis everywhere you want to go.
- **Don't Miss:** The sunset celebration at Mallory Square, a Key West tradition.
- **Timing:** Allow at least two days and two nights here.
- **Kids:** The touch tank at tiny Key West Aquarium is a hit with kids.

A BIT OF HISTORY

Early Prosperity – When **Ponce de León** arrived in 1513, he claimed the island for Spain and named it *Cayo Hueso* ("Island of Bones"), apparently for the abundance of Indian bones he found there. (The English later transformed *Cayo Hueso* into Key West.) Through the 18C the island remained largely the domain of the Calusa and Ais Indians. In 1822 Key West became permanently American and a customs house was established. In the late 1820s Key West served as headquarters for a lucrative enterprise called **wrecking**—salvaging goods from ships that ran aground on the Florida reef. By mid-century a new industry, **cigar making**, had begun. These industries thrived to the extent that, by 1889, the combined revenues from the fishing, sponging, wrecking and cigar-making industries had made Key West the wealthiest town per capita in the country.

During the Civil War the military used Key West to control ship traffic through the Florida Straits, but the island saw no serious action. After the war Cuban cigar barons, disaffected with Spanish control of Cuba, moved here and opened factories, attracting Cuban workers and revolutionaries. By 1890 the largest cigar-manufacturing city in the world was also a hotbed of Cuban revolutionary activity. Cuban liberator **José Martí** (1853–1895) soon head-quartered himself here. In 1898 the *USS Maine* departed Key West for Havana and exploded there, precipitating the short-lived **Spanish-American War**. In 1912 Henry Flagler's Overseas Railroad finally reached its terminus in Key West, connecting the island with the rest of the continent. Designed by the eminent New York firm Carrère and Hastings, the deluxe **Casa Marina** hotel (*see Address Book*) opened here nine years later, equipped with a hurricane-proof reinforced concrete exterior.

Chic Resort – Poor and rundown during the Depression, the town maintained its allure nonetheless, for in 1931 author **Ernest Hemingway**—destined to

The Conch Republic

The tradition of autonomy that pervades the Florida Keys dates back to the 18C, when pirates prowled the islands and salvagers first began to profit from the many reef wrecks along the Atlantic side of the Keys.

In 1980 the Mariel boatlift brought thousands of Cuban refugees to Key West. (Though most refugees dispersed, the town still maintains a palpable Cuban presence.) As a result of this influx US Border Patrol set up a roadblock on Highway 1 (US-1) north of town where all outbound vehicles were checked for guns, illegal aliens, guns and drugs. Key West residents did not take kindly to this

Flying the Conch Republic Flag

interference with their freedom and, on 23 April 1982, at high noon in Mallory Square, community activists declared their own country, the Conch Republic. The outraged Conchs, as native Key Westers call themselves (after the mollusk that once thrived in local waters and whose meat provided the mainstay of the settlers' diet), announced they were seceding from the US. A blue Key West flag was raised, speeches peppered the afternoon air, and a loaf of bread was pitched aloft as a declaration of war. It was, of course, completely tongue-in-cheek. Republic leaders quickly "surrendered" to seek foreign aid from the state of Florida!

The spirit of the Conch Republic lives on today, most conspicuously in the **Conch Independence Celebration** (www.conchrepublic.com) held in the last week of April: "Dedicated To The Fundamentally American Spirit Of A People Unafraid To Stand Up To 'Government Gone Mad With Power' That Embodied The Founding Of The Conch Republic In 1982. As The World's First Fifth World Nation, A Sovereign State Of Mind Seeking Only To Bring More Humor, Warmth, And Respect To A World In Sore Need Of All Three, The Conch Republic Remains The Country Who Seceded Where Others Failed."

During the festival hundreds of homes throughout the city fly the azure Conch Republic flag, asserting their cultural, if not political, perspective.

Conch Republic Red Ribbon Bed Race, during the Conch Independence Celebration

GETTING THERE

BY AIR – Key West Airport (EYW): serviced by most domestic airlines as well as charters (*☎ ☎ 305-296-5439; www.keywestinternationalairport. com*). Transportation to Old Town by **taxi** (*$7.50–$18*) and hotel courtesy shuttles. Major **rental car** agencies located here.

GETTING AROUND

Local **bus service** travels two routes (*Mon–Fri 6:30am–11:30pm, weekends 9:30am–5:30pm; $2; schedule and route information: ☎305-292-8160*). The best way to get around the Old Town is on foot, as most attractions are within walking distance of each other. The **Bone Island Shuttle** (*www. boneislandshuttle.com*) bus takes in Mallory Sq., Duval St. and the Seaport as well as major hotels. Beach cruiser or scooter rental from **Keys Moped & Scooter** (*$30, 1-4hrs; ☎305-294-0399*). Ride carefully along the narrow (and often one-way) streets. The **Bicycle Center** (*☎305-294-4556*) rents bikes for $15 a day and single-seater scooters for $40 a day. **Paradise Scooter Rentals** (*☎305-293-6063*) rents bikes for $13 a day and scooters from $54 a day/single, $65/double. Small electric cars are another option (*http://piratescooterrentals.com*). **Taxi service**: Friendly Cab (*☎305-292-0000*); Maxi Taxi (*☎305-296-2222*). **Parking** is limited in Old Town area; public parking lots average $1/hr.

VISITOR INFORMATION

Key West Chamber of Commerce provides information on lodging, shopping, entertainment, festivals and recreation (*510 Greene Street, First Floor, FL 33040; ◷open year-round Mon–Fri 8:30am–6pm, weekends 8:30am–5pm; ☎305-294-2587 or 800-527-8539; www.keywestchamber.org*).

SIGHTSEEING

Conch Train Tour (*departs from Mallory Square or Roosevelt Blvd. year-round daily 9am–4:30pm; round-trip 1hr 30min; commentary; $29; ♿ ☎305-294-5161; www.conchtourtrain.com*). **Old Town Trolley Tour** (*departs from various locations year-round daily 9am–4:30pm; round-trip 1hr 30min; commentary; $29; free re-boarding; ☎305-296-6688, www.trolleytours. com/Key-West*). Sharon Wells of **Island City Strolls** (*$27, four-person minimum; ☎305-294-8380; www.seekeywest.com*).

USEFUL NUMBERS

Police/Ambulance/Fire (*☎911*)
Police (non-emergency) Key West (*☎305-294-2511*)
Florida Highway Patrol (*☎305-289-2300*)
US Coast Guard Boating and Safety Hotline (*☎305-92-8700*)
Visitor Assistance Program (multilingual), (*Florida only*) (*☎800-771-KEYS*)

Conch Tour Train

© Bob Krist/Florida Keys News Bureau

Duval Street

Florida Keys and Key West Tourism

Key West Architecture

Diverse 19C and early 20C architectural styles found in Key West's
Old Town range from gracious
Neoclassical houses to gingerbread-
trimmed Victoriania and Caribbean-
influenced "Conch cottages."

Given the New England background
of many of the 19C seafarers who
settled here, much of Key West's
architecture follows the Classical
Revival style. Among the indigenous
features added to this style, the
"eyebrow" is unique. This West
Indian element consists of eaves
that partly overhang second-
story windows, thus resembling
a brow over squinting eyes. Like
an awning, the "eyebrow" blocks
out direct sunlight, thus keeping

Southernmost House

© Rob O'Neal/Florida Keys News Bureau

the house cool. Among the 50-some **eyebrow houses** in Key West are
401 and 525 Frances Street, 643 William Street and 1211 Southard Street.
Bahamian features, such as wide, breeze-catching verandas, also figure in the
architectural mix. Due to a lack of trees on the island, some early settlers from
the Bahamas actually dismantled their houses and floated them to Key West.
A couple of classic examples of imported **Bahama Houses** still stand.

The many vernacular buildings are known as **Conch houses,** built
1830s–1920s, and named for the 19C Bahamian settlers ("Conchs"). In general
these are simple wooden-framed structures, one or (maximum) two stories
high, with a porch across the front, running full-height on two-story houses,
and perhaps a widow's walk (a railed rooftop platform), possibly borrowed
from the New England houses seen by Key West seafarers. The narrow, single-
story **shotgun house** is a variation on this style. You'll also find a number of
elegant Queen Anne structures, notably the George Patterson House and the
Southernmost House.

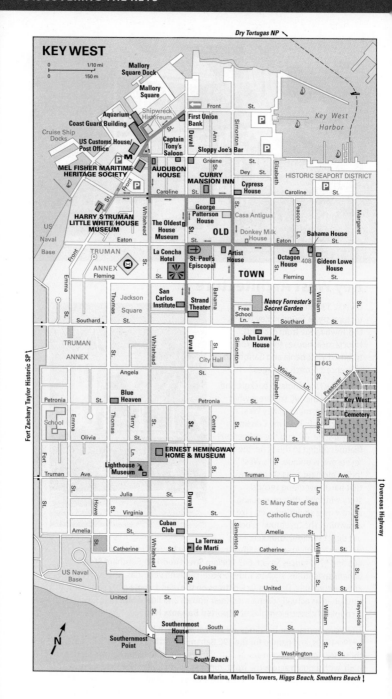

KEY WEST

Dry Tortugas NP

0   1/10 mi
0   150 m

Mallory Square Dock

Mallory Square

Aquarium

Coast Guard Building

Shipwreck Historeum

First Union Bank

Front St.

Simonton St.

Key West Harbor

Cruise Ship Docks

US Customs House/ Post Office

Captain Tony's Saloon

Duval

Ann St.

Sloppy Joe's Bar

MEL FISHER MARITIME HERITAGE SOCIETY

AUDUBON HOUSE

Greene St.

CURRY MANSION INN

Dey St.

Elizabeth St.

HISTORIC SEAPORT DISTRICT

Caroline St.

Cypress House

Caroline St.

Margaret St.

HARRY S TRUMAN LITTLE WHITE HOUSE MUSEUM

Whitehead St.

The Oldest House Museum

George Patterson House

Casa Antigua

OLD

Donkey Milk House

Eaton St.

Peacon Ln.

Bahama House St.

US Naval Base

Front St.

Eaton St.

TRUMAN ANNEX

Fleming St.

La Concha Hotel

St. Paul's Episcopal

Artist House

TOWN

Fleming St.

Octagon House

408

Gideon Lowe House St.

Emma St.

Thomas St.

Jackson Square

San Carlos Institute

Strand Theater

Bahama St.

Free School Ln.

Nancy Forrester's Secret Garden

Southard St.

William St.

Southard St.

TRUMAN ANNEX

Whitehead St.

Duval

John Lowe Jr. House

Simonton St.

City Hall

St.

Windsor Ln.

643

Passover Ln.

Angela St.

Petronia St.

Blue Heaven

Thomas

Terry St.

St.

Center St.

Petronia St.

Elizabeth St.

Key West Cemetery

School

Emma St.

Olivia St.

Fort

Truman Ave.

Lighthouse Museum

ERNEST HEMINGWAY HOME & MUSEUM

Olivia St.

Truman Ave.

Julia St.

Duval

St.

Virginia St.

St.

Truman Ave.

1

St. Mary Star of Sea Catholic Church

Margaret St.

Overseas Highway

Cuban Club

Amelia St.

Whitehead St.

La Terraza de Marti

Simonton St.

Amelia St.

Catherine St.

William St.

St.

Catherine St.

St.

Louisa St.

St.

United St.

US Naval Base

United St.

St.

St.

Reynolds St.

Fort Zachary Taylor Historic SP

N

Southernmost Point

Southernmost House

South St.

Washington St.

William St.

St.

South Beach

Casa Marina, Martello Towers, *Higgs Beach, Smathers Beach*

become Key West's most celebrated son—bought a house here, beginning a literary tradition that continues today. The town has been home to writers John Dos Passos, Tennessee Williams, Elizabeth Bishop, Robert Frost, Philip Caputo, John Ciardi, James Merrill, Thomas McGuane, Wallace Stevens,

Tightrope juggler during the sunset celebration, Mallory Square

© Bob Krist/Florida Keys News Bureau

Ralph Ellison and John Hersey, among others. *(Island City Strolls offers a Famous Writers and Artists of Key West tour; ♿ see Sightseeing below.)*

Using federal funds, local volunteers transformed the shabby town into an viable tourist destination. However, a violent hurricane in 1935 destroyed the railroad to Key West and the town languished for three years before the **Overseas Highway** was completed on the old rail bed, making Key West more accessible to travelers than ever before. In the 1950s President **Harry Truman** also fell under the charm of Key West, escaping to his Little White House on the Navy base there.

In the past several decades, the island has undergone a slow transformation from renegade outpost to fashionable resort. The town's overtly commercial main stem, 14-block-long **Duval Street,** is named for William Pope DuVal, the first governor of the Florida Territory. Amid the eateries, bars and boutiques that line the north end of Duval, Key West still cultivates its eccentricity. By night, live music fills the streets, spilling out of bars frequented over the years by such notables as authors Ernest Hemingway and Truman Capote, and singer-songwriter Jimmy Buffett.

🐾 WALKING TOUR
OLD TOWN
1.5mi. ♿ *See map p110.*

The 200-square-block area of the **Old Town**★★ was designated a National Historic District and ranks as one of the largest, boasting more than 3,000 significant historic structures. In addition there are a number of museums and attractions—some of which are housed in historic buildings—that draw Key West visitors.

Peppers of Key West

602 Greene St., ☏305-295-9333. www.peppersofkeywest.com.
Warm climates traditionally breed hot foods, and many of the fuels that feed the fire are featured at this small, engaging store and tasting shop. The hottest chiles on earth are native to the Caribbean (*habaneros* and Scotch bonnets) and are the key ingredient in the famous West Indies jerk meat marinades. At Peppers, you'll find a comprehensive array of hot sauces, salsas, marinades and spice mixes (many made in Florida). A session at the tasting bar (crackers and water are supplied) will bring tears to even the most seasoned chile-heads.

Key West Key Lime Pie Company

431 Front St. ☏305-2517-6720. www.keywestkeylimepieco.com.

This Old Town store devotes itself solely to the signature dessert of the Florida Keys, which was reputedly made for the first time at Curry Mansion in Key West. Since then, key lime pie has been the subject of much legend, amendment and competition. Most, if not all, restaurants in Key West (and far beyond) offer it for dessert; numerous delis and small grocery stores package their own versions; and an annual competition sponsored by a local radio station declares the city's best. Most versions are based on a graham-cracker crust, which holds a uniquely tart key-lime custard, topped with meringue or whipped cream. However many pies are over-sweetened, obliterating the bitter/tart tang that is unique to the limes. At the Key Lime Pie Company you can get not only the traditional pie and lime juice but several variations on the theme, including their exquisite Lime Pie Bar; a delicious slices of pie dipped in rich creamy chocolate, served on a stick.

▶ *Begin at the intersection of Duval and Front Sts. (northwest end of Duval St.).*

Ornate brickwork and balcony of the striking **First Union Bank** building on the far corner *(422 Front St.)* reflect the origins of the Cuban cigar manufacturers who financed its construction in 1891.

▶ *Continue west 2 blocks on Front St., turn right on David Wolkowsky St.*

Mallory Square

Behind Mallory Market on Front St. www.mallorysquare.com.

Overlooking Key West Harbor, this former warehouse area is named for Stephen Mallory, Florida's fourth US senator and son of one of the island's oldest families. It now harbors souvenir vendors, craft shops and eateries, and its adjacent dock provides a berth for the large cruise ships that call at Key West. Don't miss the sunset-watching ritual held every evening (weather permitting) on **Mallory Square Dock** *(behind Mallory Square; follow Fitzpatrick St. through parking lot to dock)*. Here, locals and visitors gather to view the spectacular Key West **sunset**★★, described by John James Audubon as "a blaze of refulgent glory (that) streams through the portals of the west." And each night the famous **Sunset Celebrations** *(www.sunsetcelebration.org)* are staged with street performers, jugglers, clowns, psychics, island musicians, artists and food vendors.

👪 Key West Aquarium

Wall St. ♿🕐Open year-round daily 10am–6pm. ⊜$12, child $5. ☏305-296-2051. www.keywestaquarium.com.

Founded in 1934, this was the Keys' first tourist attraction. Wall tanks here display a variety of denizens from local waters, such as pufferfish, grouper, angelfish and spiny lobsters. A touch tank allows tactile encounters with starfish, conchs, anemones and other sea creatures. At the rear of the building, a large **shark tank** harbors the gliding forms of a variety of sharks. Rays and barracudas occupy an outside pool.

▶ *Return to Front St. and continue west past the intersection with Whitehead St.*

Recognizable by its distinctive arched bays, the old Coast Guard Building (219 Front St.) served as the first naval storehouse in 1856. The town's oldest government edifice and the oldest masonry building in the Keys now holds the shops of **Clinton Square Market**. Adjacent to the building is the Key West Museum of Art and History.

Key West Museum of Art and History

281 Front St. 🕐Open year-round daily 9:30am–4:30pm. ⊜$10. ☏305-295-6616. www.kwahs.com.

The Custom House, built in 1891, served as a post office, courthouse and government center when wrecking made Key West the richest city, per capita, in the US. When Key West declined the building was boarded up and completely abandoned. Recently renovated, it now showcases the colorful history of the Keys while gallery space features the work of local artists.

Mel Fisher Maritime Heritage Society★

200 Greene St., opposite Custom House. ◕*Open year-round Mon–Fri 8:30am–5pm & Sat–Sun 9:30am–5pm.* ☜*$12.* ♿ 🅿 ✆*305-294-2633. www.melfisher.org.*

Housed in a former Navy building, the museum recounts the story of the discovery of the *Nuestra Señora de Atocha* and the *Santa Margarita,* two Spanish galleons that sank in the Florida Straits in 1622. The man behind the salvage and the museum, **Mel Fisher**, is the don of modern treasure hunters. Fisher, who died in 1998, spent 16 years and lost a son in his unswerving pursuit of the wreck. In 1985 his crew found their prize on the ocean floor; spoils included a 77.76-carat natural emerald crystal and a gold bar weighing over 6 troy pounds. Displays on the first floor feature some of the fabulous gold, silver, gems and other artifacts recovered from the dive site. The second floor is devoted to special exhibits and traveling shows.

◑ *Cross Whitehead St.*

Audubon House★

205 Whitehead St., across from Mel Fisher's museum. ◕*Open year-round daily 9:30am–5pm.* ☜*$10.* ♿ ✆*305-294-2116 or 877-294-2470. www.audubonhouse.com.*

Capt. John Huling Geiger built this gracious Neoclassical house in the 1840s. Its restoration by Key West native Mitchell Wolfson in 1960 sparked the island's preservation movement. Wolfson dedicated the house to America's premiere ornithologist, **John James Audubon,** who visited Key West in 1832 while working on his authoritative volume *Birds of America.* Decorated in 19C period furnishings, the house is notable for its fine collection of 28 original **Audubon engravings** and for its lovely tropical **garden.** Noteworthy also is a rare collection of porcelain birds by British artist Dorothy Doughty.

◑ *Continue one block south on Whitehead St. Cross Whitehead and enter the gates to the Truman Annex, a 44-acre private condominium development on the grounds of the former naval station. Continue for one block and turn left on Front St.*

Harry S Truman Little White House Museum★★

111 Front St. in Truman Annex. Entrance near Hilton Hotel at the presidential gates on Whitehead St. ◕*Open year-round daily 9am–5pm.* ☜*$15.* ♿ ✆*305-294-9911. www.trumanlittle whitehouse.com.*

This large, unpretentious white clapboard house, the favorite retreat of America's 33rd president, **Harry S. Truman** (1884–1972), gives a rare glimpse

---

Reef Relief

631 Greene Street. ✆*305-294-3100. www.reefrelief.org.*

This small store and information center is a treasure house of knowledge about the endangered tropical environment that surrounds the Keys and Key West. Numerous natural history books, pamphlets and broadsides explain the issues and challenges besetting the region—such as the effort to install sewage treatment systems in many of the Keys—and the unique landscapes and creatures that advocates are trying to preserve. The fact that visitors and residents alike must be reminded not to damage the reefs, bays and waters of south Florida is an unfortunate commentary on the state of affairs. Reef Relief pursues a friendly, low-key approach to the challenge.

Kayaking the Keys

The shallow waters, mangrove thickets and innumerable islands of the lower Keys are prime territory for sea kayakers. The **Great White Heron National Wildlife Refuge** northeast of Key West, for example, is a kayaker's delight. Here visitors can paddle for hours in quiet backwaters where fish splash, turtles lurk and herons, pelicans, osprey and dozens of other birds roost in the mangroves. Although afternoon breezes shuffle the open waters, they keep insects at bay. Narrow channels (called "creeks," though they are not) in the mangroves offer protection and solitude—and occasional deep holes where adventurous paddlers can slip from their kayaks for a plunge into warm waters sometimes sluiced by cool fresh water from deep springs.

Although experienced kayakers can find their way with the aid of detailed maps, local guides know the best routes. They can also provide commentary on the profusion of wildlife, including the shallow underwater community of sponges, fishes and sea grass, and on the environmental challenges that beset this fragile habitat. Visitors to the refuge must maintain a respectful distance from nesting birds, and not disturb any of the other rare animals found within, such as sea turtles. The rewards for a backwater trek are profound peace and solitude and an enhanced understanding of a unique tropical domain.

For guided kayak trips in the Keys, contact Big Pine Adventures Crystal Seas,
305 872-7474; www.keyskayaktours.com.

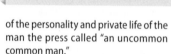

of the personality and private life of the man the press called "an uncommon common man."

Built in 1890 as a duplex for the paymaster of Key West's naval station, the unadorned dwelling, with wooden jalousies, was first visited by Truman in 1946 (his physician had persuaded him to take a respite from official duties). Prior to Truman, Thomas Edison had lived here while working on his depth charge for the Navy during World War I. Truman found the casual atmosphere and warm climate of Key West relaxing. Over his next seven years in office, he spent 175 days of "working vacations" at his "Little White House." He ran the country from the desk that still sits in a corner of the living room. Indeed, Truman came to relish his time in Key West, declaring it his favorite place in the world—aside from his boyhood home, a farm near Independence, Missouri.

Tours of the house begin with a 10min video detailing the time Truman spent here. The house is furnished much the way it was during the Truman era, with most of the pieces chosen by Miami decorator Haygood Lassiter in 1948. Truman's personal **desk** can be seen in his bedroom upstairs.

Return to Kelly's at the corner of Whitehead and Caroline Sts., and continue east on Caroline.

Curry Mansion Inn★

511 Caroline St. Open year-round daily 8:30am–5pm. $5. 305-294-5349 or 800-253-3466. www.currymansion.com.

William Curry, a self-made millionaire and mayor of Key West, built the rear of this rambling, white Victorian mansion before his death in 1896. His son Milton greatly expanded the house at the turn of the century, adding elaborate reception rooms and bedrooms to the front. Now an inn, the mansion retains its belle-epoque grandeur. Visitors can take a self-guided tour of the house, which offers the only publicly accessible **widow's walk** *(third floor)* in Key West. After your tour, relax on the wide, shady veranda.

Built around 1889, the elegant white frame **George Patterson House** *(across from Curry Mansion at 522 Caroline St.; not open to the public)* features gables, porches and galleries adorned by delicate spindlework—all characteristic elements of the Queen Anne style.

▶ *Continue to the corner of Caroline and Simonton Sts.*

Distinctive for its unpainted, weathered cypress exterior, the 1887 **Cypress House** *(601 Caroline St.)* was originally owned by the Kemp family, Bahamians who are credited with introducing the sponge industry to Key West. The low facade and simple lines of this private inn typify Bahamian architecture.

▶ *Turn right on Simonton St. and continue one block to Eaton St. Turn left on Eaton, then continue east on Eaton St. and cross Elizabeth St.*

One of Old Town's best-known homes, the unique **Octagon House** *(712 Eaton St.)*, was built in 1885 by Richard Peacon, who opened Key West's first supermarket. Renovated by acclaimed interior designer Angelo Donghia in the 1970s, the house was also briefly owned by clothing designer Calvin Klein.

▶ *Continue on Eaton St. to the corner of William St.*

Bahama House

730 Eaton St. ⚬➡*Not open to the public.* Originally constructed on the island of Abaco, this symmetrical white pine structure was disassembled and brought to Key West by schooner in 1847 as the home of Bahamian shipbuilder John Bartlum. Its wide airy verandas on both stories, louvered windows and doors, and low-ceilinged interior rooms typify Bahamian architecture. Exterior siding incorporates boards of different widths. Note these same features on the house next door *(408 William St.)*, which was transported from Green Turtle Cay.

▶ *Turn right on William St.*

Note the temple form of the **Gideon Lowe House** *(409 William St.)*, a fine mid-19C example of the Classical Revival style.

▶ *Walk two blocks south on William to Southard St. and turn right. Continue to*

Margaritaville Cafe

400 Duval St. ☎*305-292-1435. www.margaritavillekeywest.com.* This popular cafe and its adjacent souvenir shop is owned by Jimmy Buffett, who got his start playing in Key West bars. Enjoy a "cheeseburger in paradise" or go next door, where you can purchase items inspired by Buffett's song lyrics, including his famous "lost shaker of salt."

intersection of Simonton St. and turn right; walk one-half block north and turn right on Free School Ln. to a small gate at its end.

Nancy Forrester's Secret Garden

1 Free School Ln. 🕐*Open year-round daily 10am–5pm.* 🎟*$10.* ☎*305-294-0015. www.nfsgarden.com.*
Owner-artist Nancy Forrester has devoted more than 35 years to creating her personal one-acre tropical oasis amid the hubbub of downtown Key West, opening it to the public in 1994. Today the lush botanical garden enamors nature lovers who wander its winding paths among ferns, helicnias and orchids, beneath a canopy of century-old hardwood trees—Spanish

Flamingo Crossing

1107 Duval St. ☎*305-296-6124.* Take a refreshing break from sightseeing at this popular purveyor of warm-weather treats. All the ice cream and sorbet here is made by hand in the back. Naturally, the focus is on tropical flavors such as mango, key lime (tantalizingly and properly bitter) and coconut. Also on the menu is an array of frozen yogurt, fruit smoothies and tropical blended drinks. You can sit inside in the air-conditioned interior, but the elevated patio offers an excellent vantage on the Duval Street scene.

The Making of "Papa"

"Papa" Look-Alike contest, at Sloppy Joe's Bar, Hemingway Days festival

© Andy Newman/Florida Keys News Bureau/HO

Ernest Hemingway (1899–1961) first visited Key West in 1928 with his second wife, Pauline. He had already achieved literary fame with the 1926 publication of *The Sun Also Rises*, and was returning to the US after years of living in Europe. After a brief stay in Cuba, the couple arrived in Key West, where a new Ford was to have been waiting for them to drive north. However, shipment of the car was delayed, giving the Hemingways time to become acquainted with the island Ernest dubbed "the St. Tropez of the poor." They soon discovered that life in remote Key West was like living in a foreign country while still perched on the southernmost tip of America. Hemingway loved it. "It's the best place I've ever been anytime, anywhere, flowers, tamarind trees, guava trees, coconut palms … Got tight last night on absinthe and did knife tricks."

For three subsequent winters they returned here, then in 1931 purchased a large but run-down house, which Pauline described at the time as a "miserable wreck." They renovated the structure and Hemingway lived there until his marriage ended in 1939; Pauline remained in the house and continued to be a prominent member of Key West society until her death in 1951.

It was during his Key West years that Hemingway cultivated his machismo "Papa" image, spending his days writing, fishing and drinking with a coterie of locals he called the "Key West Mob." His legend continues to infuse many corners of the island and is the impetus behind the annual **Hemingway Days** festival. Held in conjunction with the writer's birthday (July 21), the week-long event features look-alike contests, arm wrestling, a bizarre Running of the Bulls, and several other "Papaesque" activities.

Other Hemingway landmarks include **Captain Tony's Saloon** (*428 Greene St.; www.capttonyssaloon.com*) who claim to be the original Sloppy Joe's Bar, frequented by Hemingway between 1933 and 1937; they still proudly display his favorite bar stool. Hemingway met his third wife, Martha Gellhorn, here in 1936. In fact the Johnny Come Lately on the block is, somewhat confusingly, **Sloppy Joe's Bar** (*201 Duval St.; www.sloppyjoes.com*), a cavernous local pub that has been here since 1937 and also claims to be "Papa's" favorite hangout. Have a beer or two in each and examine the evidence for yourself. Whatever the truth is, Hemingway also attended cockfights and boxing matches in the two-story, blue clapboard Conch cottage called **Rick's Blue Heaven** (*729 Thomas St.*). A former brothel, it now contains a cafe (see Address Book) and artists' studios.

Hemingway kept to a strict schedule while writing in Key West, waking at dawn and walking to his pool house, where he wrote at an old wooden desk. It was during this period that he penned *Death in the Afternoon, The Green Hills of Africa, To Have and Have Not* and *The Short, Happy Life of Francis Macombe*. Then, after work, at 3:30pm every afternoon he would meet his circle of friends at the bar. The rest, as they say, is the stuff of Key West folklore …

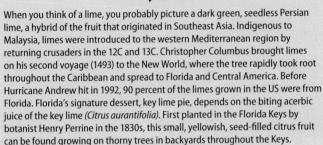

A Key to Limes

When you think of a lime, you probably picture a dark green, seedless Persian lime, a hybrid of the fruit that originated in Southeast Asia. Indigenous to Malaysia, limes were introduced to the western Mediterranean region by returning crusaders in the 12C and 13C. Christopher Columbus brought limes on his second voyage (1493) to the New World, where the tree rapidly took root throughout the Caribbean and spread to Florida and Central America. Before Hurricane Andrew hit in 1992, 90 percent of the limes grown in the US were from Florida. Florida's signature dessert, key lime pie, depends on the biting acerbic juice of the key lime *(Citrus aurantifolia)*. First planted in the Florida Keys by botanist Henry Perrine in the 1830s, this small, yellowish, seed-filled citrus fruit can be found growing on thorny trees in backyards throughout the Keys.

limes, sapodillas, gumbo-limbos—and a collection of rare palms. Adding to the ambience: a menagerie of tropical birds, cats and reptiles.

▷ *Return to Simonton St. and turn right. Continue 1.5 blocks north and turn left on Eaton St.*

Key West surgeon Thomas Osgood Otto built the lavender Queen Anne **Artist House** *(534 Eaton St.)*, which is distinguished by its octagonal turret. Now a guest house, the two-story 1887 structure features wraparound verandas ornamented with slender balusters and delicate corner brackets.

▷ *Continue west to corner of Eaton and Duval St.*

St. Paul's Episcopal Church

401 Duval St. ⊙*Open year-round Mon–Sat 9am–5pm, Sun 7am–5pm.* ♿🅿 ☏*305-296-5142 stpaulschurchkeywest.org.*
The oldest church in the Florida diocese, St. Paul's was established in 1832. The current white Spanish Colonial building (1919), with its imposing belltower, is the fourth church on the site. Vaulted wooden ceilings inside are designed to resemble inverted ships' hulls.

▷ *Turn left and walk south on Duval St.*

Since its opening in 1926, Duval Street's highest landmark building has been

La Concha Hotel *(no. 430; www.laconchakeywest.com)*. The six-story, pink concrete hotel (now a Crowne Plaza property) has housed such luminaries as Tennessee Williams, who wrote *Summer and Smoke* here in the mid-1940s. Late in the afternoon, stop by the hotel's rooftop bar, **The Top**, for a drink and a panoramic **view**★ of the island and its surrounding waters.

▷ *Cross Fleming St. to the 500 block of Duval St.*

San Carlos Institute

516 Duval St. ⊙*Open year-round Fri-Sun noon-6pm.* ⊙*Closed Jan 1, Easter Sunday, Dec 25.* ☞*$3 contribution requested.* ♿ ☏*305-294-3887. www.institutosancarlos.org.*
This imposing Spanish-Colonial structure was built in 1924, but its roots date back to 1871. Founded as a social club and school by Cuban exiles during the Ten Years' War, the nonprofit institute was named for Seminario San Carlos, a famed learning center in Cuba where Father Felix Varela planted the seeds of Cuba's independence movement (a bronze likeness of the priest stands in the lobby of the Key West site).
The present building, the third on this site, serves as school, museum, library, art gallery and theater. Two floors of exhibits relate to Cuba's fight for independence from Spain. Displays on the ground floor focus on **José Martí**, organizer of the second effort for Cuban independence, who often

117

Fort Jefferson

Florida Keys and Key West Tourism

From Prison to Park

Sixteen million bricks were used to form the perimeter walls of **Fort Jefferson** (*www.fortjefferson.com*), which measures 50ft high and 8ft thick. The weight of the structure eventually caused the walls of the ill-fated fort to sink into its unstable base of sand. By the time the Civil War broke out, the brick hexagon was only two-thirds completed.

Though soldiers never fired at an enemy from Fort Jefferson, it did serve as a prison for Union deserters during the Civil War. In 1865 **Dr. Samuel Mudd** was interned here as a co-conspirator in President Lincoln's assassination. (Mudd unwittingly set the broken leg of Lincoln's fleeing assassin, John Wilkes Booth, without realizing Booth's identity.) During a yellow fever epidemic in 1867, Mudd unstintingly treated the prison's victims of the disease. His efforts won him a pardon from President Andrew Johnson and he was released in early 1869. Yellow fever struck the citadel again in the early 1870s, and four years later it was finally abandoned. Proclaimed a national monument in 1935, the fort is protected as part of the Dry Tortugas National Park (see p121).

GETTING TO DRY TORTUGAS NATIONAL PARK

BY AIR - Departs from Key West International Airport year-round daily. One-way 40min; half-day excursion $249/person. Reservations required. Contact Key West Seaplane Adventures, *305-942-9777; www.keywestseaplanecharters.com.*
BY SEA - There is a choice of two ferry companies; both depart from the Historic Seaport, year-round daily

8am (check-in time: 7.30am), returning to Key West by 5pm or 5.30pm. Both include commentary. breakfast, lunch and snorkeling gear.
Yankee Freedom II takes around 2hr 15min each way (*$160; *305-294-7009 or 800-634-0939; www.yankeefreedom.com).*
The Sunny Days *Fast Cat* takes around 2 hrs each way: (*$145; *800-236-7937 or 305-292-6100; www.drytortugas.com).* Reservations recommended for both.

---

spoke here. Interior walls are lined with blue majolica tiles that were imported from Spain; floors incorporate checkered Cuban mosaics.

Ripley's Believe It or Not! Key West

108 Duval Street. Open daily 10am–late. $14.95, child (5–12 yrs) $11.95. 305-293-9939. www.ripleyskeywest.com.
Occupying the former **Strand Theater** 1930 movie palace, this curiously compelling collection, including a fabled white bufalo and a car made from 10,000 dimes, is a celebration of the odder things in life.

Continue up Duval St.

The **Cuban Club** *(1108 Duval)* is a two-story, white frame replica (1989) of the Key West headquarters of Sociedad Cuba, established in 1900 to offer education, medical care and social activities to the Cuban émigré community. Fire destroyed the original building in 1983; the present incarnation, which incorporates the original columns, turrets and facade pediment, houses shops and condominium units.
Nearby, at 1125 Duval St, the **La Te Da** (short for La Terraza de Martí) hotel, restaurant and bar complex occupies the former home (1892) of cigar manufacturer Teodoro Pérez. From its second-floor balcony, the leader of the Cuban Revolutionary Party, José Martí,

frequently exhorted his countrymen to action.

ADDITIONAL SIGHTS
Eco-Discovery Center★

35 East Quay Rd. at end of Southard St., Truman Annex. Open Tue–Sat 9am–4pm. 305-809-4750.
This state-of-the-art, 6,400sq ft underwater ocean laboratory allows visitors to view the Florida Reef without getting wet, thanks to underwater cameras and touch-screen computer displays. Journey through other Florida Keys habitats, including mangroves and pinelands, at this new (in 2007) attraction, modeled after Key Largo's Aquarius, the only underwater ocean lab in the world.

Pirate Soul Museum★

524 Front St. Open daily 10am–7pm. $15, child (under 10 yrs) $8.55. 305-292-1113. www.piratesoul.com.
Part kiddie attraction, part museum, this attraction features animatronics and a collection of nearly 500 pieces of booty. Don't miss a peek at the only authentic pirate treasure chest in America, and the 'sound show' that takes you into a faux prison cell. Scary, in a fun way.

Fort Zachary Taylor State Park

Enter through gatehouse to Truman Annex at the west end of Southard St. Open year-round daily 8am–dusk. $6/vehicle for 2 people plus 50¢/additional person. 305-292-6713. www.floridastateparks.org/forttaylor

Remains of the three-story trapezoidal 19C brick fort started in 1845 (but never completed) form the centerpiece of this 87-acre park overlooking the Atlantic Ocean. During the Civil War, some 800 Union soldiers were quartered here, although they saw no significant action. Today you can walk along vestiges of the fort's 5ft-thick battlements. Guided tours of the fort are available daily.

Nearby, a pleasant wooded grove edges a narrow, somewhat rocky Atlantic **beach**, suitable for swimming, fishing and snorkeling.

Ernest Hemingway Home and Museum★★

907 Whitehead St. ○*Open year-round daily 9am–5pm.* ✎*$11.* ✆*305-294-1136. www.hemingwayhome.com.*

Half-hidden amid lush vegetation, this gracious stucco house is where Key West's legendary resident novelist spent his most productive years.

Built by wealthy merchant Asa Tift in 1851, this one-of-a-kind house is made of coral rock mined on the property and covered with stucco. Tift brought the French Colonial-style cast-iron pillars, verandas and balusters from New Orleans. Full-length, double-paned arched windows open like doors to catch island breezes. Sparsely decorated rooms contain period pieces, some of which belonged to the family. In Hemingway's bedroom, notice the **ceramic cat** made for "Papa" by Pablo Picasso. In fact around the house there are more than 60 six- and seven-toed (real) cats, that are, dubiously, claimed to be descendants of Hemingway's own pets.

A wooden catwalk once connected the master bedroom to Hemingway's **studio**, a pleasant room above the carriage house where he wrote such classics as *Death in the Afternoon, For Whom the Bell Tolls* and *To Have and Have Not.* (The character of Freddy in the latter novel is modeled after Joe Russell, the late owner of Sloppy Joe's Bar.) The attractive grounds contain a large **swimming pool**—the first one built on the island. Commissioned by his second wife, Pau-

line, in the 1930s while Hemingway was off covering the Spanish Civil War, the $20,000 pool infuriated "Papa" when he returned. He reportedly railed at Pauline, declaring that she had spent his last cent, and threw a penny on the ground to emphasize his point. His wife had the coin embedded in the cement by the pool where it remains to this day.

Lighthouse Museum

938 Whitehead St., across from Hemingway House. ○*Open year-round daily 9:30am–4:30pm.* ○*Closed Dec 25.* ✎*$10.* ▣ ✆*305-295-6616. www.kwahs.com.*

Built in 1846 and decommissioned in 1969, this white-brick lighthouse now offers a sweeping **view** of the island from atop its 92ft tower. A **lightkeeper's quarters** on the grounds, paneled in gleaming Dade County pine, displays lighthouse lenses, military artifacts and period rooms, re-creating the lifestyle of early 20C lighthouse keepers.

City Cemetery

Margaret Street and Passover Lane. &○*Open daily 7am-7pm (winter 6pm).* Guided tours, Tue and Thu 9am, reservation required. ✎*$10.* ✆*305-292-6718. www.keywestcity.com.*

Monuments to Key West's past can be found among the 35,000-plus headstones, which date to 1847 when the earlier cemetery near the south coast was washed out by a hurricane. A bronze sailor surveys marble markers commemorating seamen lost in the 1898 sinking of the USS *Maine.* Wander on your own (a free comprehensive self-guided tour map is available inside the cemetery's front entrance) and read headstones with epitaphs that include "I told you I was sick" or take a guided tour.

East Martello Tower

3501 S. Roosevelt Blvd. ○*Open year-round daily 9:30am–4:30pm.* ○*Closed Dec 25.* ✎*$6.* ▣ ✆*305-296-3913. www.kwahs.com.*

The names of this brick tower and its counterpart, West Martello Tower, derive from a type of impregnable cylindrical tower first built in Corsica in the Middle Ages. Begun in 1862 as back-up fortifications to nearby Union stronghold Fort Zachary Taylor, the East Martello Tower was never completed. Yellow fever, labor strikes and wartime exigencies delayed the work, and in 1873 building ceased on the unfinished battlements.

Today, the remains of the tower house the **Key West Art & Historical Society**★. Historical exhibits range from ancient Indians to Ernest Hemingway and the **Ghosts of East Martello** (Robert the haunted doll is particularly creepy!), while the art gallery hosts special exhibits, notably, the "junkyard sculpture" of late Key West folk artist **Stanley Papio;** folk art by local Cuban painter **Mario Sanchez;** and the famous **portrait of Hemingway** by Erik Smith. Broad, man-made **Smathers Beach**— the largest on the island—stretches for 2mi along South Roosevelt Boulevard.

West Martello Tower

White St. and Atlantic Blvd., on Higgs Memorial Beach. ○*Open year-round Tue–Sat 9:30am–3:15pm (mid-Jan–mid-Apr 9:30am–5pm).* ○*Closed major holidays.* &.☐.✆*305-294-3210.*
Companion to the East Martello Tower, this Civil War citadel served as a lookout tower during the Spanish-American War. Its brick ruins are now edged in tropical plantings beautifully maintained by the **Key West Garden Club**.
Adjacent, **Higgs Beach** is popular with the gay community.

Southernmost House

1400 Duval St.
This rambling, cream-colored brick 1899 Queen Anne manse with pale green trim) is the southernmost house in the continental US. Now a hotel, the elegant structure exemplifies the Queen Anne style in Key West, modified to suit both local tastes and climate.
Small sandy shallow **South Beach** lies across from the house. Around the corner *(west end of South St.),* a much-

photographed red-black-and-yellow buoy marks what it claims is the **Southernmost Point** in the lower 48 states. (In fact, the true southernmost point extends from a restricted naval base just to the west.)

EXCURSION
⚓*See map p110.*
Dry Tortugas National Park★
69mi southwest of Key West. Accessible only by plane or boat (⚓see Box, p110). ○*Open year-round dawn–dusk.* ⏣*$5.* ⚠.✆*305-242-7700. www.nps.gov/drto.*
Encompassing 100sq mi in the Gulf of Mexico, the park protects the small cluster of reef islands called the Dry Tortugas. Spanish explorer Ponce de León named these islands *Las Tortugas* ("The Turtles") when he explored them in 1513. (The anglicized addition of the word "Dry" refers to the islands' lack of fresh water.) They remained Spanish possessions until Florida came under US control in 1821.

One of the islands, 10-acre Garden Key, is the site of **Fort Jefferson,** the largest coastal stronghold built by the US in the 19C (⚓*see p118).* Activities include wreck-diving, snorkeling and fishing *(information available at visitor center at fort).* A film details the fort's history inside the visitor orientation area. Parade grounds within the walls hold remnants of a cavernous magazine, soldiers' barracks and officers' quarters. A self-guided walk leads through the arched casemates and up onto the battlement wall, where a lighthouse (no longer functioning), still stands. From this vantage point, there's a **view**★★ of the fort and nearby Bush and Loggerhead keys. The top of the surrounding moat also serves as a walkway, and a palm-fringed white-sand **beach**, ideal for snorkeling, lies on the island's west side.

If you're into birding, plan your visit from March through September, when you'll see frigates, boobies and a large number of noddy and sooty terns (100,000 terns nest here).

ADDRESSES

🏠STAY

Most accommodations in Old Town Key West are **guest houses** and **bed-and-breakfast inns** ($85–$275). **Reservations** can be made through the Welcome Center of Florida Keys (℘305-296-4444). **Youth hostel** rooms ($28–$31; ℘305-296-5719; www.keywesthostel.com). **Camping and RV park**: Boyd's Key West Campground (℘305-294-1465; tent camping, $50–$60; RVs, $65-90).

$$$$ Gardens Hotel – 526 Angela St. ♿🅿🏊℘305-294-2661 or 800-526-2664. www.gardenshotel.com. 17 units. The luxurian gardens that fill much of this walled Old Town compound were once a private botanical preserve harboring tropical species collected around the world. Composed of three restored historic structures and two new additions, the complex has tastefully decorated rooms featuring wood floors and marble baths—many with jacuzzi tubs and steam showers. Rates include a buffet continental breakfast served in the sunlit garden room.

$$$$ Island City House Hotel – 411 William St. ♿🅿🏊℘305-294-5702 or 800-634-8230. www.islandcityhouse.com. 24 units. This small hotel encompasses three multistory late-19C clapboard buildings, with exterior stairs and balconies. Guest-room decor ranges from bright island fabrics and white wicker to Victorian antiques and lace curtains. Some of the cozy suites include kitchenettes. The family-friendly complex encloses a palm-shaded pool with a hot tub. Continental breakfast is served outside in the courtyard.

$$$$ Hotel Marquesa – 600 Fleming St. ✕♿🅿🏊℘305-292-1919 or 800-869-4631. www.marquesa.com. 27 rooms. Comprising four 1884 Conch houses encircling two pools and a palm-filled garden, this favored lodging in the historic district is listed on the National Historic Register. Breezy guest rooms mix soft tropical colors with Chippendale pieces and West Indies wicker; several of the poolside rooms have sitting areas and patios. The hotel's sleek **Cafe Marquesa** specializes in

Caribbean-inspired dishes with Asian and Central American influences.

$$$$ Simonton Court – 320 Simonton St. ♿🏊℘305-294-6386 or 800-944-2687. www.simontoncourt.com. 29 units. Although it's just two blocks from Duval Street, this secluded enclave of former cigar-makers' cottages is elegant and lush. Oleander, bougainvillea and hibiscus shade the two small pools—one placed within the foundation of a ruined brick house. Individually decorated rooms feature Florida pine furnishings and marble baths. Ask the knowledgeable staff anything at all about Key West.

$$$–$$$$ Casa Marina Resort – 1500 Reynolds St. ✕♿🅿🏊℘305-296-3535 or 866-397-6342. www.casamarinaresort.com. 311 rooms. Tile roofs, massive, hurricane-proof stucco walls and Spanish Renaissance styling mark the hotel that Henry Flagler envisioned as the endpoint resort for his Overseas Railroad. Darkly elegant black cypress encases the lobby; rooms are decorated in sunny pastels, light woods and rattan. On the expansive grounds you'll find almost every imaginable amenity, including two pools, a private beach, and numerous cabanas and bars. Shuttles run guests to Old Town.

$$–$$$$ Popular House/Key West Bed & Breakfast – 415 William St. 🏊℘305-296-7274 or 800-438-6155. www.keywestbandb.com. 8 rooms. Colorful handmade textiles by owner Jody Carlson and big, contemporary canvases add to a lively, artsy vibe at this stylish guesthouse. Four rooms have private baths, four share a bath, but all guests enjoy the tropical gardens, dip pool, Jacuzzi and dry sauna, lavish Continental breakfast. No kids under age 18; no TV in rooms.

$$$ Ambrosia House – 615, 618, 622 Fleming St. ♿🏊℘305-296-9838. www.ambrosiakeywest.com. 32 units. Rooms include twin inns, suites, townhouses and cottages. Each has a private entrance and a deck, porch or patio. Three swimming pools and spacious suites make Ambrosia House a hit with families, as does the poolside.

$$$ Pier House Resort – *One Duval St.* ✕ ⏣ 🅿 ⚓ ☎*305-296-4600 or 800-327-8340. www.pierhouse.com. 142 rooms.* One of Key West's original landmark resorts, the attractive white buildings house airy, comfortable and spacious, rooms, many, of which look out over the Harbor. A full-service spa and health club, located in a separate building, supplement the pool and private beach.

$$ Key West Hostel & Seashell Motel – *718 South St.* ⏣ 🅿 ☎*305-296-5719. www.keywesthostel.com. 92 beds. 10 rooms.* One of the best budget properties located near Old Town. Set in a residential area, it offers a peaceful stay, even during Spring Break. Rooms are dorm style, but private motel rooms are also available. Amenities include Wi-Fi *(free)*, lockers and bikes *(at a fee)*.

$$ Speakeasy Inn– *1117 Duval St.* ⏣ 🅿 ☎*305-296-2680 or 800-217-4884. www.speakeasyinn.com. 10 units.* Walk to the beach from your clean but no-frills room at this characterful historic speakeasy-turned-inn. Rooms include studios, suites and two-bedroom units. No pool, but a great location and value.

🍴/EAT

$$$$ Louie's Backyard – *Vernon and Waddell Sts.* ⏣ ☎*305-294-1061. www. louiesbackyard.com.* Louie's exquisite Continental cuisine is matched by the sensational setting, overlooking the Atlantic. The late-19C house containing the restaurant has been crisply refurbished, but the best spots are in the backyard. Outside tables are at a premium, though, so go early.

$$$ A&B Lobster House – *700 Front St.* ⏣ ☎*305-294-5880.* One of Key West's longest-established seafood restaurants, the A&B specializes in Maine and Caribbean lobster, as well as in traditional Keys favorites. Downstairs, **Alonzo's Oyster Bar** *(dinner only)*, offers a more economical seafood menu and a boisterous people-watching setting along the harbor walkway.

$$$ Mangoes – *700 Duval St.* ⏣ ☎*305-294-4606. www.mangoskeywest.com/ restaurant.* Nibble on wonderfully light tempura-fried ahi tuna and watch the passing parade from this inviting patio spot on Duval Street. Expertly prepared dishes on the Floribbean menu include mustard-rubbed rack of lamb.

$$$ Pepe's Café – *806 Caroline St.* ⏣ ☎*305-294-7192. www.pepescafe.net.* Check out the autographed celebrity photos, including a picture of Harry S. Truman playing the piano, at this low-key tavern, est. 1909. At midday the vine-covered patio becomes a cool retreat. The burgers, fried oyster plates and key lime pie are all good.

$$$ Seven Fish – *632 Olivia St.* ⏣ ☎*305-296-2777. www.7fish.com. Dinner only.* Crowds gather here almost every night, where rich seafood preparations—such as red snapper with a curry cream sauce—contrast markedly with the sparse decor. Culinary influences are global, from Japanese to Northern Italian. The key lime curd over shortbread is Seven Fish's estimable version of key lime pie.

$$ El Siboney – *900 Catherine St.* ⏣ ☎*305-296-4184. www.elsiboney restaurant.com.* Housed in a brick building on a back street, this traditional Cuban restaurant offers a down-home atmosphere, efficient service, and filling platters of shredded beef or pork, rice and beans and *plátanos*. Try the rich, flavorful conch chowder and be sure to order a cup of thick, sweet, strong Cuban coffee.

$$ Mangia Mangia– *900 Southard St.* ⏣ ☎*305-294-2469. www.mangia-mangia.com.* The largest wine list in the county is just a bonus here; Key West's best Italian place serves bountiful platters of homemade pasta with tasty sauces. The popular *bollito misto di mare* features fresh seafood sautéed with garlic, shallots and white wine. Dine on the bricked garden patio.

$$ Rick's Blue Heaven – *305 Petronia St.* ⏣ ☎*305-296-8666. http://blueheavenkw. homestead.com.* A former Hemingway hangout, Rick's menu is a West Indies hybrid—with dishes like jerk chicken with brown rice and black beans. Eat in the courtyard, where chickens peck under the tables and cats rub your legs.

The section of Gulf Coast stretching from the Suwannee River, near Florida's Panhandle, down to Hernando County, above Tampa, is often called "real Florida" because so much of the area has remained undeveloped. While ancient burial grounds indicate the region was inhabited as early as 500 BC, it remained a wilderness well into the 18C, when Spanish soldiers arrived.

Highlights

1 Swimming with manatees, **King's Bay** or **Crystal River** (p125)

2 Kicking back with a beer in down town **Cedar Key** (p125)

3 A boat trip and hike in the **Cedar Keys National Refuge** (p125)

4 Visiting the fishbowl observatory at **Homosassa Springs** (p126)

5 Watching the wacky mermaids at **Weeki Wachee** (p126)

A Bit of History

In the 1830s, the US government began forcing Seminoles out of Florida onto reservations in Oklahoma. White settlers then established plantations, growing sugar cane and Sea Island cotton. After the Civil War, commercial fishing and lumber industries thrived as fish caught in local waters were transported to wholesale dealers in Cedar Key by sailing sloop, and cedar trees were harvested and shipped to Crystal River and Cedar Key to be carved into pencils.

A few of the Gulf settlements began attracting northern visitors to large hotels and sportsmen's lodges. The area's quiet, natural beauty—which captivated landscape artists Winslow Homer and George Inness in the late 19C—was somewhat by-passed in the late 20C rush to commercialize southern and central Florida. Today it is being redisovered by visitors in search of a peaceful life.

The highlight of the region is Cedar Key, with the kind of

atmosphere and tumbledown shacks they re-create in Walt Disney World. Like WDW, this area is wonderful for young children: here they can commune with nature, face-to-face with countless species of fish and birds and, of course, Florida's most irresistible critter, the manatee.

Turning west off US-19/98 will lead to the unspoiled coastal hamlets of Suwannee, Yankeetown and Pine Island. An abundance of wildlife, including alligators, manatees, armadillos and bald eagles, makes its home in and around the region's wetlands, hammocks and crystal clear, spring-fed rivers.

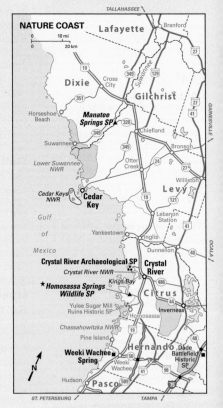

Cedar Key

This historic Gulf Coast town is located on Way Key, the largest in a cluster of low-lying islands 3mi off the mainland to which it linked by a bridge. It supports a mix of commercial fishermen, artists and weekenders, and hosts an annual Seafood Festival each October. The pace is slow in the down-home hamlet of tin-roofed porches and weathered piers with views of bayou and bay.

SIGHTS

Cedar Keys National Wildlife Refuge★

Boat trips depart from city marina year-round daily 11am–dusk; round-trip 1hr 30min. ➡$21. ⚑ ☏352-543-5904. www.cedarkeyislandhopper.com, www.fws.gov/cedarkeys.

These 13 pristine islands, 5mi off the coast of Cedar Key, range from one to 120 acres provide nesting areas for pelicans, ospreys, white ibis and hundreds of other species of birds. Atsena Otie Key has a dock, restrooms and hiking trail.

Manatee Springs State Park

34mi north, six miles west of Chiefland. ➡$6 per vehicle; diving $15. ⚑✕⚑⚑ ☏352-493-6072. Canoe and kayak rentals ☏352-490-9797. www. floridastateparks.org/manateesprings.

- ▶ **Population:** 790.
- ⚑ **Michelin Map:** p124
- ⚑ **Info:** 618 Second Street (mornings only, closed Thu); ☏352-543-5600; www.cedarkey.org.
- ⚑ **Location:** Cedar Key is 57mi northwest of Crystal River, and about one hour's drive from Gainesville.
- ⚑ **Don't Miss:** Gallery-hop and dine on fresh fish in Cedar Key's rustic downtown.
- ⚑ **Kids:** Looking for manatees at Manatee Springs.

Swimming, hiking (along an 8.4mi trail), biking and scuba diving (in open water and in caverns and caves) are among the attractions at this 2,000-acre nature preserve. Manatee Springs forms the centerpiece of the park; an area for swimming is roped off at the crystal-clear headwaters. Nearby, a boardwalk *(0.25mi)* zigzags alongside the run, passing through a swamp lush with cypress, gum, ash and maple trees. Among the residents here are bald eagles, alligators and various wading birds. During the fall and winter months, look for manatees, who find refuge in the constant 72-degree temperature of the springs. The boardwalk ends at an **observation deck** on the Suwannee River.

Florida's Gentle Giant

Although the manatee is a marine mammal, its closest relative is the elephant. The manatee's two front flippers contain the same bones as the human hand. Manatees use their undulating tails to propel themselves forward; flippers function as rudders. The manatee has earned the sobriquet "sea cow," given its habit of browsing on aquatic vegetation—consuming as much as 100 pounds per day. On such a diet, an adult manatee can measure up to 13ft long and weigh more than 3,000 pounds. Manatees have no natural enemies, but development of the state's coastal areas has diminished feeding grounds, forcing the slow-moving mammals into boating areas where they often become injured or killed in collisions. In 1973 manatees were listed as an endangered species and in 1978 the whole of Florida became a manatee sanctuary.

Visit Florida

Crystal River

Of the 30 natural springs feeding the Crystal River, 28 form headwaters at Kings Bay, considered one of the county's most important manatee sanctuaries. As the only area in Florida where people may swim and interact directly with manatees, Kings Bay is popular with nature lovers. Numerous local dive shops offer boat, snorkeling and scuba rentals, along with guided boat tours of the river and bay.

▶ **Population:** 3,600.
👣 **Michelin Map:** p124.
🚩 **Info:** 28 NW Hwy. 19, Crystal River; ℘352-795-3149; www. citruscountychamber.com.
📍 **Location:** Crystal River is in Citrus County, 57mi southeast of Cedar Key.
🕐 **Timing:** The best Manatee viewing time is Jan–Mar.
👁 **Don't Miss:** Snorkeling with manatees.
👪 **Kids:** The "fishbowl" at Homosassa Springs park; Buccaneer Bay.

SIGHTS

Among the best spots for viewing manatees in their natural habitat are Homosassa Springs State Wildlife Park and Kings Bay, which encompasses nine small, undeveloped bay islands *(accessible by boat only; for information check with local dive operators or refuge office, ℘352-563-2088; www.fws.gov/crystalriver).*

Crystal River State Park

3400 N. Museum Point Rd., 2mi north of town center. 💰*$3 per vehicle.* ♿🅿 *℘352-795-3817, www.floridastateparks.org/crystalriverarchaeological.*
It is believed that this 14-acre prehistoric ceremonial site was established by Indians of the Deptford culture (500 BC to AD 300). The **visitor center** *(🕐 open year-round daily 9am–5pm)* offers a display of ancient arrowheads and tools and an interpretive video. Outside, a path (0.5mi) leads past two midden mounds of discarded oyster shells, three burial mounds and two temple mounds. Eco-heritage boat trips run subject to weather conditions *(℘352-563-0450).*

👪 Ellie Schiller Homosassa Springs Wildlife State Park★

7mi south in Homosassa.
📍 *Take US-19/98 south to Rte. 490; turn right on Rte. 490 and follow signs to park at 9225 W. Fishbowl Dr. Alternatively, park at the main entrance and visitor centre on Rte. 19, and take an interpretive boat ride (included in admission fee; 20min; commentary) to*
the Wildlife Park. 🕐*Open year-round daily 9am–5:30pm.* 💰*$13, child (6–12 yrs) $5.* 🍴♿🅿 *℘352-628-2311 or 352-628-5343. www.homosassasprings.org.*
Homosassa Springs Wildlife State Park is a showcase for Florida wildlife. Visitors can walk underwater in a **"fishbowl" observatory** and view manatees and thousands of fish. The **wildlife walk**, an elevated boardwalk system, allows a close-up view of black bear, cougars, bobcats, gray fox, otters and birds of prey in spacious, natural habitats. Manatee, alligator and wildlife-encounter programs are offered daily. A Reptile House and Children's Education Center provide close-up viewing of native snakes and reptiles, plus hands-on activities.

👪 Weeki Wachee Springs State Park

21mi south Rte. 50 / US-19 in Weeki Wachee. 🕐*Open daily 10am–5:30pm. May be closed Mon-Wed off-season.* 💰*$13, child (6–12 yrs) $5.* 🍴♿🅿 *℘352-596-2062. www.weekiwachee.com.*
Designed around a freshwater spring, this "springs theme park" is famous for its underwater theater where local "mermaids" have performed (with the aid of air lines) in the crystal-clear water since 1946. You can cool off at adjoining **Buccaneer Bay** *(🕐open late Mar–May and Sept weekends only, daily Jun-Aug;* 💰*$26, child (6–12 yrs) $12),* the only natural-spring water theme park in the state.

NORTH CENTRAL FLORIDA

A magnet for biking, fishing and canoeing enthusiasts, the largely rural area of North Central Florida—running across the peninsula from Alachua, Marion and Lake counties in the west to Volusia and Seminole counties in the east—is one of remarkable natural beauty. A gently rolling terrain of open pasture and shady back roads distinguishes the region, which is perhaps best known for its darkly mysterious rivers, freshwater springs, complex strings of lakes (the Tsala Apopka chain alone contains seven) and the 430,000-acre **Ocala National Forest.**

A Bit of History

Timucuan and then Seminole Indians made their homes here before white settlers arrived in the mid-19C, and many of the lakes and rivers (Withlacoochee and Ocklawaha, for example) retain their Seminole names. During the period of British occupation (1763–83), the St. Johns River in the east was the site of sugar-cane and indigo plantations. After the Civil War, settlers arrived to take advantage of the Armed Occupation Act, which provided free 160-acre tracts of land to homesteaders in Florida. Most early settlers grew citrus and raised cattle and by the 1870s, commercial citrus cultivation accounted for

Highlights

1. Exploring the butterfly rainforest at the **Museum of Natural History**, Gainsville (p130)

2. Descending the bizarre **Devil's Millhopper** sinkhole (p130)

3. Discovering Marjorie Kinnan Rawlings' **Cracker Country** (p131)

4. Taking a glass-bottom boat at **Silver Springs** (p132)

5. Swimming at Juniper Springs in **Ocala National Forest** (p133)

Butterfly Rainforest, Florida Museum of Natural History

Visit Florida

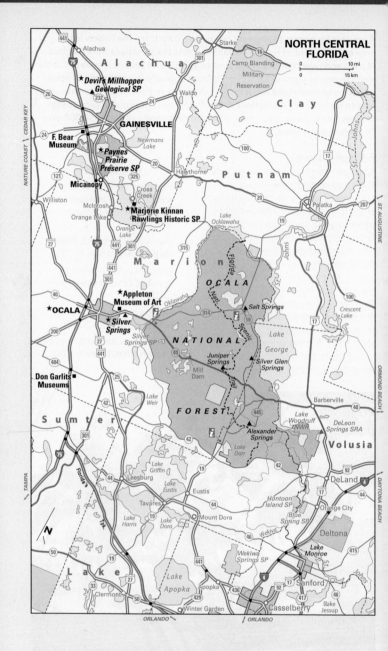

myriad small boomtowns that appeared across central Florida, shipping produce through Gainesville and Ocala. Well-preserved Victorian architecture in McIntosh, Windsor, Waldo and Mount Dora recalls the glory days.

While retirees and tourism now bolster the economy, central Florida continues to earn most of its revenue from agriculture, boosted by light manufacturing. Citrus remains an important local crop, and tiny Mom-and-Pop fruit stands abound on back roads.

Gainesville

*Paynes Prairie Preserve
State Parl*

A friendly college-town atmosphere pervades Gainesville, home to the University of Florida. The busy 2,000-acre campus lies primarily to the west of US-441, the main north-south thoroughfare. The historic downtown area, Courthouse Square and quiet residential streets lined with loblolly pines and live oaks occupy the east side of town.

A BIT OF HISTORY

In the late 19C, Gainesville thrived as a shipping center for citrus, strawberries, phosphate and lumber. Local revenues now depend largely on the university. Despite suburban sprawl, some 700 buildings are preserved in five historic districts.

Notable among the turn-of-the-last-century structures in the **Northeast Historic District** is the **Thomas Center** (*see below*). Built in 1910, the elegant Mediterranean Revival-style house was remodeled as a hotel in 1928 and is now a cultural center.

SIGHTS

Thomas Center Galleries

302 NE 6th Ave. Open Mon-Fri 8am–5pm (Tue 7pm), Sat 1–4pm. 352-334-5064. www.gvlculturalaffairs.org.

This is the cultural heart of Gainesville, with a dynamic exhibition and event schedule in its art galleries, plus 1920s rooms and local history exhibits.

Courthouse Square

S.E. 1st St. and University Ave.

Brick-paved streets, wide boulevards and early 20C commercial buildings—some housing pleasant outdoor cafes—help maintain the character of Gainesville's old downtown. A local landmark, the **clock tower** contains the original clock from the second (1885) Gainesville court-house. The grand Beaux-Arts style 1909 post office building fronted by a two-story Corinthian portico, is now home to the **Hippodrome State Theatre**.

▶ **Population:** 95,447

Info: 30 East University Ave. 352-374-5260; www.visitgainesville.net.

Location: Gainesville is between Atlanta and Miami—five hours from each.

Parking: Lots and parking spaces are generally easy to come by.

Don't Miss: The Devil's Millhopper is a real quirk of nature.

Timing: Come during college term time to experience the town at its best.

University of Florida

S.W. 13th St. between University Ave. and S.W. Archer Rd. Campus map and parking information available at Main Entrance information booth, US-441 (S.W. 13th St.) and S.W. 2nd Ave.

Located on 2,000 acres, this is Florida's oldest and largest university, consolidated in 1906 from several state educational facilities. The campus includes several early 20C Collegiate-Gothic-style buildings (now part of a historic district), a teaching hospital, an 84,000-seat foot-

Thomas Center Galleries

© gilg/iStockphoto.com

129

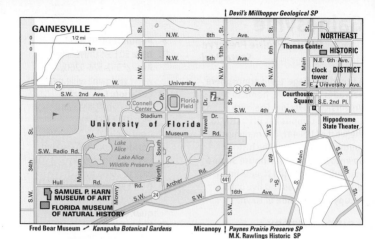

ball stadium (the Gators are a perennial national title contender), two museums and the Lake Alice Wildlife Preserve.

Samuel P. Harn Museum of Art

S.W. 34th St. and Hull Rd. ◎*Open year-round Tue–Fri 11am–5pm, Sat 10am–5pm, Sun 1pm–5pm.* ◎*Closed major holidays.* &🅿 ✆*352-392-9826. www.harn.ufl.edu.*

Opened in 1990, the Harn Museum is the state's first major art museum on a college campus. Nearly 40,000 objects—previously stored in attics and closets—are exhibited in the striking 62,000sq ft post-Modern building, distinguished by roof pyramids and a three-story glass atrium. Periodic shows draw on the permanent collection of 7,000 artefacts, which includes strong holdings in **early 20C American art;** the **tribal art** of West Africa and Papua New Guinea; and pre-Columbian pottery. Construction of a new Asian art wing, to house and conserve holdings of Asian sculpture and painting, will also incorporate an Asian garden.

Gallery talks, lectures and tours focusing on a particular collection area or aspect of a temporary exhibition help visitors to get the most out of their visit.

Florida Museum of Natural History★

S.W. 34th St. and Hull Rd. ◎*Open year-round Mon–Sat 10am–5pm, Sun & holidays 1pm–5pm.* 🕿*Permanent exhibits free, charge for traveling exhibitions (varies) and Butterfly Rainforest $9.50, child (4–12yrs) $5.* &🅿 ✆*352-846-2000. www.flmnh.ufl.edu.*

This museum houses the largest **research collection** of fossil and modern invertebrates, vertebrates and plants in the South.

Devoted to the natural history of Florida and the Caribbean, displays explore **Florida environments,** such as the ecosystems of a coral reef, a savanna, and temperate and tropical hammocks. The Northwest Florida exhibit features a limestone cave. Windows into Natural History lets you investigate the state's plants and insects using scientific equipment. Further galleries are devoted to fossils, flora and fauna, and a replica of a Mayan palace. Outside the museum is the 🏃🏻‍♂️**Butterfly Rainforest** where you can walk among the subtropical and tropical plants and trees which support 55 to 65 different species and hundreds of free-flying butterflies.

Devil's Millhopper Geological State Park★

4732 Millhopper Rd., off N.W. 53rd Ave./Rte. 232. ◎*Open daily 9am–5pm.* 🚶‍♂️*Ranger-led walks Sat 10am* 🚗*$4/vehicle.* ✆*386-462-7905. www.floridastateparks.org/devilsmillhopper.* ☺*Insect repellent recommended.*

Follow the winding staircase to the bottom of the dramatic , 500ft wide, 120ft deep **sinkhole** known as the Devil's

Millhopper, named for an Indian legend that told of the devil hurling human bodies into its depths. Here, watered by burbling falls and supported by cool, below-grade temperatures, thrives plant life similar to that of Appalachia. Mosses and liverworts hold moisture, allowing larger plants to grow. Needle palms—rare for northern Florida—grow here as the sinkhole rarely experiences freezing temperatures.

EXCURSIONS
Paynes Prairie Preserve State Park★

10mi south on US-441 in Micanopy.
🕐*Open daily 8am-sunset, visitor center 9am–4pm.* 👓*$6/vehicle.* ⛺♿🅿️✆*352-466-3397. www.floridastateparks.org/ paynesprairie.*

Named for King Payne, an 18C Seminole leader, this park ranks as one of Florida's most important natural sites. The irregularly shaped basin, measuring 8.5mi at its widest point, was formed as the terrain settled over a sinking limestone bed that periodically fills with water. A **visitor center** *(2mi from entrance at end of Park Dr.)* and nearby observation tower *(follow short path in front of visitor center)* both offer a sweeping **view** over **Paynes Prairie,** now a marsh where a wild herd of American bison roam. During the late 1600s, the prairie was the site of the largest cattle ranch in Spanish Florida. In the late 19C, the area became a lake with a busy steamboat route until the water drained abruptly, leaving one boat stranded. The 22,000-acre preserve today boasts a rich cross-section of Florida habitats, including swamps, ponds, pine flatwoods and hammocks woven with over 25mi of hiking trails. Sandhill cranes, bald eagles and other wildlife winter here.

Micanopy

10mi south on US-441. Most shops are open daily 10am–5pm.

An antiques center with a sleepy, unspoiled air, this tiny village was founded in 1821 as the first permanent white settlement in what is now Alachua County. Enormous live oaks shade the

Marjorie Kinnan Rawlings State Historic Site
Visit Florida

main street, Cholokka Boulevard; shops, housed in early 20C commercial buildings, overflow with vintage china, collectibles, clothing and books.

Marjorie Kinnan Rawlings State Historic Site★

17mi south in Cross Creek.
🕐*Grounds open year-round daily 9am–5pm.* ☞*Visit house by guided tour (45min) only, Oct–Jul Thu–Sun 10am–4pm (every hour).* 🕐*Closed Jan 1, Thanksgiving Day, Dec 25.* 👓*$3.* ♿🅿️✆*352-466-3672, www.floridastate parks.org/marjoriekinnanrawlings.*

Well known for her affectionate portrayals of life in backwoods Florida, author **Marjorie Kinnan Rawlings** (1896–1953) owned this rambling Cracker-style house and 72-acres of grounds from 1928 until her death.

Among the many original furnishings is the writing table, on the front porch, where Rawlings wrote her Pulitzer Prize-winner, *The Yearling* (1938), and a subsequent novel *Cross Creek* (1942). The house sits in a citrus grove dominated by a magnificent magnolia tree. Across the road, a leaf-carpeted path loops *(0.25mi)* through a hammock of wild palms, oaks, sweet gums, hickories and hollies.

Ocala★

Ocala National Forest

Centered in the rolling green countryside of Marion County, Ocala is synonymous with horses. The "Lexington of the South," as it has been dubbed, contains some 200 farms for Arabians, Clydesdales, thoroughbreds and quarter horses, and ranks high as a training and breeding center. For a view of the countryside farms, resplendent in rolling pasture and magnificent live oaks, drive south of the city on S.W. 27th Ave. (Rte. 475A) or S.E. 3rd Ave. (Rte. 475). The Chamber of Commerce can advise you on which farms are **open to the public for self-guided tours**.

SIGHTS
Appleton Museum of Art★

4333 N.E. Silver Springs Blvd.
Open Tues–Sat 10am–5pm, Sun noon–5pm Closed Jan 1 & Dec 25. May also close part of Aug for annual maintenance, see website. $6.
352-291-4455.
www.appletonmuseum.org.
A dramatic axial sculpture fountain welcomes visitors to this elegant two-story Neoclassical structure clad in travertine marble. First-floor galleries frame a central courtyard and feature Classical and Egyptian antiquities, West African sculpture, pre-Columbian pottery, and an extensive display of **Asian art,** including lovely jades, porcelains and Tibetan bronzes. The upper level is devoted primarily to traveling exhibits.

Don Garlits Museum of Drag Racing & Museum of Classic Automobiles

10 miles south, off I-75, 13700 SW 16th Ave. Open daily 9am–5pm. $15.
877-271-3278. www.garlits.com
Owned and curated by champion drag racer, Don Garlits, the museum of drag racing is the ultimate boy racers' fantasy collection, while all the family will enjoy the classic car collection.

▶ **Population:** 49,724.
Info: Chamber of Commerce, 409 SE Fort King St. 352-629-8051; www.ocalacc.com.
Location: Ocala is located 78mi west of Daytona Beach.
Parking: Finding a place to park your car, or your horse, isn't an issue here.
Don't Miss: The natural beauty of Silver Springs.
Timing: Plan your stay around how long you wish to hike, camp and explore the outdoors.
Kids: Kids love seeing the animals at Silver Springs.

Silver Springs★

5656 E. Silver Springs Blvd./Rte. 40 (1.5mi east of Appleton Museum). Open Mar-Sept daily 10am–5pm, (closed Mon-Tue late Aug onwards). $30, child (3–10yrs) €25. 352-236-2121.
www.silversprings.com.
A subtropical hammock surrounding 50 natural springs at the head of the Silver River sets the scene for this 350-acre natural theme nature park. Together the waters form the largest **artesian spring** in the world, producing about 5,000 gallons per second (which would fill an Olympic-size swimming pool in two minutes). Timucuan Indians worshipped the sparkling waters as the "shrine of the water gods." Visitors here began arriving by steamboat as early as the 1860s—making Silver Springs the oldest attraction in Florida.
Glass-Bottom Boat Rides *(25min)* provide a clear view of the underwater world of the main spring, including several caverns (the deepest is 81ft) that contain fossilized bones of Pleistocene animals. Waters here are so pure (98 percent) that they have been the setting for Tarzan movies and the James Bond film *Moonraker*.
The **Fort King River Cruise** carries you through Silver Springs' 10,000 year his-

tory. Interactive exhibits and displays include a working archaeological dig site, Seminole Indian village, the 1830s Fort King Army stockade, a late 1880s riverboat dock and train depot, and an authentic Florida pioneer "Cracker" homestead. There is even a third river cruise, the **Lost River Voyage**, exploring yet another aspect of Silver Springs. The popular **Jeep Safari** travels through a natural habitat site, where vultures, egrets, armadillos, rhesus monkeys and Amazonian two-toed sloths (which eat, sleep, mate and give birth while upside down) roam free.

Animal exhibits feature endangered Florida panthers and American alligators in natural habitats, including two very rare white alligators. **World of Bears** is the largest bear exhibit of its kind in the world.

Adjoining Silver Springs, **Wild Waters** (*Rte. 40; open Apr & May weekends, Jun–Aug daily, first weekend Sept 10am–5pm, later at peak times; over 4ft tall $29.99; 4ft and under $22.99, combi-ticket with Silver Springs $44.99 (valid 12 months); 352-236-2121; www.wildwaterspark.com*), is a nine-acre water park that features a 450,000-gallon wave pool, eight flumes with water slides up to three storys high.

EXCURSIONS
Ocala National Forest★
11mi east of Ocala. Enter at Highway 40 Visitor Center, 10863 E. Rte. 40; 2.5mi east of Silver Springs. Visitor center

Salt Springs, Ocala National Forest
Visit Florida

open year-round daily 9am–5pm. Closed Dec 25. 352-625-2520. www.stateparks.com. Two additional visitor centers serve the forest: Salt Springs to the north (14100 N. Rte. 19); and Pittman to the south (45621 Rte. 19) near Lake Dorr.

Locally known as "Big Scrub" for its predominance of scrub sand pine and oaks, the forest encompasses some 389,000 acres of wetlands, timber, scrub, hiking trails (including 67mi of the orange-blazed Florida National Scenic Trail, running north and south), freshwater lakes and some of central Florida's most beautiful natural springs grace the forest (*see Box below*).

Ocala National Forest Springs

Picturesque **Juniper Springs** (*17mi east of visitor center on Rte. 40; canoe rental*) features a palm-fringed swimming area and a short nature trail through subtropical foliage and past bubbling spring "boils." The 7mi trip down Juniper Creek through the Juniper Prairie Wilderness is a particularly popular canoe run, though best for experienced paddlers.

Clear waters draw boaters, snorkelers and scuba divers to **Alexander Springs** (*10mi southeast of Juniper Springs on Rte. 445*). The combination of fresh water and salt water flowing into the headspring at **Salt Springs** (*junction of Rte. 19 and Rte. 314; boat and canoe rentals*) creates differences in salinity at different depths, causing objects viewed underwater to appear unusually distorted.

Popular with snorkelers, **Silver Glen Springs** is surrounded by ancient Indian shell mounds (*8mi north of junction of Rte. 19 and Rte. 40*)

Motorists once raced through this corner on their way south, but more and more travelers are discovering the myriad charms of the 125-mile strand from Fernandina Beach to Daytona Beach. Long heralded for historic St. Augustine and boisterous Daytona Beach, northeast Florida also claims its own sea islands (the southern part of Georgia's famous chain). The city limits of Jacksonville take in the greatest area of any US city.

Highlights

1 Satisfying your need for speed at **Daytona 500** (p139)

3 Spending the day at the **Cummer Museum of Art** (p143)

4 Exploring Fort Clinch State Park, **Amelia Island** (p148)

2 Stepping back in time in **St. Augustine Old Town** (p154)

5 Uncovering oddities at the **Lightner Museum**, St. Augustine (p158)

The First Coast

The Spanish explorer Ponce de León claimed northeast Florida for Spain in 1513. A permanent settlement was founded, at **St. Augustine,** in 1565. Except for a brief British occupation, St. Augustine remained Spanish for the next 256 years, until Spain handed Florida over to the US in 1821. Soon afterward, 30mi north on the banks of the St. Johns River, **Jacksonville** was founded, rising to prominence as a port and tourist town. By the end of the 19C, Jacksonville's days as Florida's premier visitor destination were over, thanks largely to Henry Flagler's Florida East Coast Railway, which opened up St. Augustine and other sunny spots farther south. In recent times, Jacksonville has carried the banner of industry and commerce, and has reinvigorated its tourist offerings with art museums, a landscaped riverwalk and fine beaches. St. Augustine remains a bastion of history with its red-tile roofs, quaint courtyards, 17C coquina buildings, quiet tree-lined lanes and charming B&Bs. Another magnet for tourists in this region, particularly during Spring Break, is Daytona Beach, famous for its long sandy strip and fast cars. Less well known is **Amelia Island,** quiet, quaint and picturesque, with a colorful history—an ideal place for just kicking back.

Cummer Museum of Art and Gardens

Visit Florida

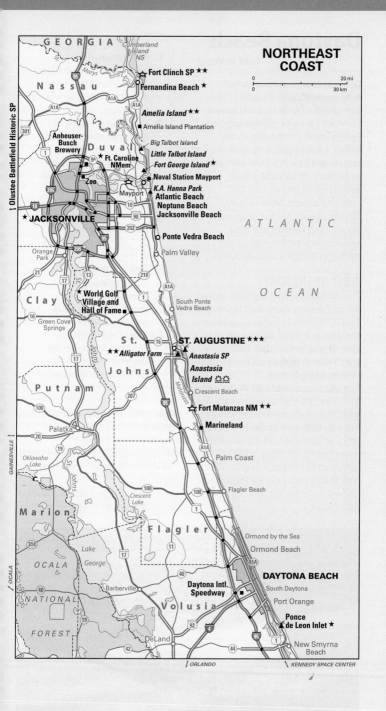

NORTHEAST COAST

0   20 mi
0   30 km

GEORGIA

Cumberland Island NS

N a s s a u

Marys

Fort Clinch SP ★★
Fernandina Beach ★

Amelia Island ★★
Amelia Island Plantation

Big Talbot Island
Little Talbot Island
Fort George Island ★

Anheuser-Busch Brewery

D u v a l

★ Ft. Caroline NMem

Zoo

Mayport

Naval Station Mayport
K.A. Hanna Park
Atlantic Beach
Neptune Beach
Jacksonville Beach

★ JACKSONVILLE

Ponte Vedra Beach

Orange Park

Palm Valley

C l a y

★ World Golf Village and Hall of Fame

Green Cove Springs

South Ponte Vedra Beach

S t .

★★ Alligator Farm

ST. AUGUSTINE ★★★

Anastasia SP

Anastasia Island ☼☼

J o h n s

Crescent Beach

P u t n a m

☆ Fort Matanzas NM ★★

■ Marineland

Palatka

Palm Coast

Oklawaha Lake

Flagler Beach

M a r i o n

Crescent Lake

Lake George

F l a g l e r

Ormond by the Sea
Ormond Beach

O C A L A

Barberville

Daytona Intl. Speedway

DAYTONA BEACH

South Daytona
Port Orange

N A T I O N A L

V o l u s i a

Ponce de Leon Inlet ★

F O R E S T

DeLand

New Smyrna Beach

↙ ORLANDO

KENNEDY SPACE CENTER

A T L A N T I C

O C E A N

← Olustee Battlefield Historic SP

GAINESVILLE ↑

OCALA ↙

135

Daytona Beach
and around

Gateway to a 26-mile stretch of hard-packed sandy **beach**⚑⚑, this sun-splashed resort town is known for stock-car races, college kids on Spring Break and driving on the beach. From February to April, the streets and beaches teem with an assortment of race-car drivers, motorcyclists, racing fans and college students. More recently, Daytona Beach has begun to court vacationing families and high-end leisure travelers with family packages and new upscale hotels.

A BIT OF HISTORY

The railroad's arrival in the 1880s and an influx of wealthy vacationers to Ormond Beach (12mi north) first put Daytona on the map as a travel destination. However, it was auto racing that altered the city's course and provided its most distinguishing feature.

The introduction of I-95 in the early 1970s pulled the town's commerce west. The downtown area deteriorated, but refurbishment began in 1982. The city's efforts paid off six years later when downtown Daytona Beach was placed on the National Register of Historic Places. Today eight million annual visitors make tourism the city's dominant industry.

▶ **Population:** 66,465.

🛈 **Info:** 126 East Orange Ave. ℘386-255-0415 or 800-854-1234; www.daytona beach.com.

◐ **Location:** Once you figure out where Atlantic Ave. (running north and south) and International Speedway Blvd. (east and west) are, you can easily find your way around town.

🅿 **Parking:** There's a big parking garage on Earl St. Traffic gets very heavy during race weeks.

◉ **Don't Miss:** The Daytona 500 Experience.

🕐 **Timing:** Even non-beach lovers can easily spend 2–3 days here.

👥 **Kids:** The Boardwalk and Main Street Pier; the Daytona 500 Experience for "junior-petrolheads."

While hotels along the strip still display "Welcome Spring Breakers" signs, Daytona Beach has become more family-friendly in recent years, offering special "Spring Family Break" promotions and discounts.

Local events range from Bike Week in March, drawing thousands of motorcy-

Daytona Beach

Visit Florida

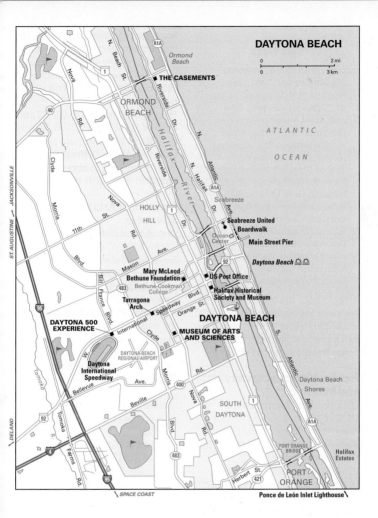

DAYTONA BEACH

clists, to the London Symphony Orchestra's summer concert series (July), when Daytona Beach becomes the LSO's "official American summer home."

SIGHTS

Surprisingly, to the many people who only know the city through its more lurid popular media images, Daytona has much to offer culturally and historically. To paraphrase the new tourist office slogan, there's way more here than just a beach.

The following sights start at the ocean and travel west:.

👥 Boardwalk and Main Street Pier

A 20ft-wide concrete walkway with benches and telescopes, Boardwalk extends three blocks north from Main St. to Ora St. The promenade and 4,500-seat coquina-rock bandshell was built in the 1930s; the 1,000ft-long pier dates from 1925, when it replaced the 1900 original, destroyed by fire. Tourists young and old gravitate to this area in all seasons, encountering a seaside bazaar of video arcades and fishing rentals, as well as the heart-stopping Sling-Shot (☜$25), which launches you 300ft into the air at 100mph (✆386-254-8626) and

Bike Week

Each year in early March some 350,000 bikers roll into Daytona Beach on their Harleys and Hondas for 10 days of races, swap meets and parties, known collectively as Bike Week. Festivities culminate with the **Daytona 200,** a superbike championship race first run in 1942 on Daytona's wide sands. Today the International Speedway hosts the event, which attracts motorcycle-racing fans from around the world.

For more information contact the Daytona Visitor Bureau office and/ or visit *www.daytonachamber.com/ bikeweek/ce* and *www.daytona internationalspeedway.com*.

the tame Sky Surfer gondolas(🚠$6; *𝒫352-23-1212)*. For the best view of the beach ascend to the the top of the 180ft **Space Needle** at the end of the pier.

Halifax Historical Society and Museum

252 S. Beach St. (3 blocks south of US-92). ◷*Open year-round Tue–Sat 10am–4pm.* ◷*Closed Thanksgiving weekend & Dec 25–Jan 1.* 🚠*$5. Free Thu. Children admitted free Sat.* ♿ *𝒫386-255-6976. www.halifaxhistorical.org.* Located in the Beaux-Arts Merchants Bank building (1910), this museum houses a 1938 model of the Boardwalk and murals of such landmarks as the

Ponce de León Inlet Lighthouse. The museum also keeps Native American artifacts and auto racing memorabilia, as well as an extensive collection of 19C postcards, plus traveling exhibitions.

The Spanish Renaissance-style **US post office** at 220 N. Beach St., built by Harry M. Griffin in 1932, features a terracotta roof and gargoyles. Griffin also designed the Mission-style **Seabreeze United Church** in 1930 *(501 N. Wild Olive Ave.)*.

Museum of Arts and Sciences★

1040 Museum Blvd. (off Nova Rd., .7mi south of US-92W). ◷*Open year-round Tue–Sat and hol Mons 9am–5pm, Sun 11am–5pm.* ◷*Closed major holidays.* 🚠*$13.* ♿🅿 *𝒫 386-255-0285. www.moas.org.*

An affilate of the Smithsonian Institute, this museum is located on Tuscawilla Preserve, where a raised boardwalk offers hiking trails. American popular culture stars in the **Root Family Museum,** including vintage automobiles, thousands of teddy bears, a restored apothecary store, and the largest collection of Coca-Cola memorabilia in Florida.

A pre-history wing showcases a 130,000-year-old giant ground sloth **skeleton,** found south of the museum. The **Cuban art** collection chronicles life in Cuba from 1759-1959, while the **African art** gallery presents masks, totems and objects from 30 different cultures.

Speed City

Auto racing began in Daytona on the beach, in 1902 and continued until the late 1950s, when a track was built. Early racers, including Barney Oldfield, Sir Malcolm Campbell and Sir Henry Seagrave, regularly set speed records on the beach, leaping exponentially from 57mph in 1902 to an incredible 275mph in 1935. Several major formula and stock-car races are now held at the **Daytona International Speedway,** including the famous **Daytona 500** in February. March brings thousands of rumbling motorcycles for **Bike Week**, followed by flocks of students for the annual rite of Spring Break. The tradition of driving on the beach continues to the present day. *For a $5 fee, motorists may cruise a designated stretch of the beach—driving no more than 10mph—or they may park, set up an umbrella and join the suntan set, which clusters around Main Street Pier and the Boardwalk amusement area. Be very careful as accidents do occur.*

The 👥**Charles and Linda Williams Children's Museum** is the only hands-on science center between Jacksonville and Orlando, and there are also free **Planetarium shows**.

Daytona 500 Experience★

1801 W. International Speedway Blvd. (1mi east of I-95). ◐*Open year-round daily 10am–6pm. Extended hours during peak seasons and event times* ◐*Closed Thanksgiving and Dec 25. $25.* ✕🅿️ *386-947-6800. www.daytonausa.com.*

Part auto-themed amusement park and part stock-car racing museum, this attraction is located at **Daytona International Speedway,** site of major car and motorcycle races including the famous Daytona 500. Begin your visit with a track tour, through the speedway's garage area, pit road, onto the infield area and around the 2.5mi track, with its 31° banked turns. Have your picture taken at Victory Lane. Inside the exhibit hall, test your racing skills in a NASCAR **simulator** that combines motion, video projection and sound. On this ride, you can experience the sensation of championship racing without the risk; you'll hop inside, buckle up and accelerate to more than 200mph. A 50min **IMAX movie, NASCAR 3D,** puts viewers in the midst of the 190mph action. If you want to ride it for real, the **Daytona Riding Experience** allows you to "ride shotgun" with a professional driver for three laps around the actual circuit at speeds over 160mph (👉*$135; must be 16 years of age or older*).

EXCURSIONS
The Casements★

5mi north in Ormond Beach at 25 Riverside Dr.
👉 *Take US-1 north to Granada Ave. Turn right (east) and cross Ormond Bridge. Turn right onto Riverside Dr.*
◐*Open year-round Mon–Fri 8:30am–5pm, Sat 8:30am–noon.* ◐*Closed major holidays.* ♿🅿️*386-676-3216.*

This gracious 1912 mansion was the winter home of oil tycoon **John D. Rockefeller** (1839–1937) from 1918 until his death. Rockefeller entertained various celebrities here, including Will Rogers, Harvey Firestone and racer Sir Malcolm Campbell. In the decades after Rockefeller's death, the house went through several incarnations, becoming a women's junior college, a retirement home and an apartment hotel.

Cracker Creek Canoeing★

1795 Taylor Rd., W. Port Orange.
👉 *From I-95 exit 256, head west on Taylor Rd (SR 421) approximately 1.5mi. At the Florida Historic Site marker, turn left. Call or check website for hours.* 👉*Canoes (2 persons) from $20/hr; kayaks from $15/hr.* *386-304-0788. www.oldfloridapioneer.com.*

Paddle down Spruce Creek, a meandering blackwater stream that reveals an unspoiled landscape of cypress swamp and hardwood forest, and, maybe, a sunbathing gator or two.
Narrated pontoon boat tours are also offered (*Thu–Sun, 11am and 2pm,* 👉*$10*); themed pirate cruises Sat and Sun 1pm, 👉*$8*).

Ponce de León Inlet Lighthouse★

👉*11mi south of US-92 in Ponce Inlet.*
👉 *Take A1A (which becomes Atlantic Ave.) south to Beach St. Turn right on Beach, continue .3mi to Peninsula Ave. and turn left, lighthouse is .2mi farther on left.* ◐*Open Memorial Day–Labor Day 10am–9pm, rest of year 10am–6pm.* ◐*Closed Dec 25 and Thanksgiving Day.* 👉*$5.* 🅿️*386-761-1821. www.ponceinlet.org.*

First lit in 1887, this 175ft tall red beacon never missed a night of operation until 1970, when expenses forced the government to move to a nearby Coast Guard station. Restoration began in 1972 and the light was relit 10 years later. Today this is one of the most complete restored light stations in Florida.
Several keepers' cottages and outbuildings display nautical memorabilia, maps, photographs and model ships. Climb the 203 steps of the original light tower for a breathtaking 360-degree **view**★★ of the ocean and inland waterway.

Jacksonville
The Sea Islands

This is the largest city in the US—in terms of area, at least—extending over 840 square miles of Florida's northeastern corner, anchored by the north-flowing St. Johns River. For visitors, however, the downtown and beaches area are the places to be, so the city never really feels that big. In recent decades, numerous revitalization projects, such as the transformation of the old Union Station into the **Prime F. Osborn Convention Center,** and the expansion of **Jacksonville Municipal Stadium** (now the Alltel Stadium) have helped offset urban blight. Broad beaches aside, other city offerings include museums of art and science, charming historic neighborhoods, a zoo and lively waterfront.

A BIT OF HISTORY

Jacksonville was founded in 1822, named in honor of Gen. Andrew Jackson, then provisional governor of Florida. During the Civil War, the city was sacked repeatedly. In 1867, noted author **Harriet Beecher Stowe** purchased a house just south of Jacksonville. In 1901 a devastating fire destroyed much of downtown. By 1910 the city had become the winter headquarters of the fledgling motion-picture industry; such popular

- ▶ **Population:** 790,689.
- **Info:** 550 Water Street. 904-798-9111 or 800-733-2668; www.jaxcvb.com.
- **Location:** Jacksonville is set on both sides of the St. Johns River.
- **Parking:** Lots on Monroe, Water, and Bay streets, and Riverside Dr.
- **Don't Miss:** Strolling Jacksonville Landing.
- **Timing:** Allow at least 3–4 days exploring Downtown, the museum and zoo, and don't overlook Jacksonville's excellent beaches.
- **Kids:** Kids love to hiss at the snakes at Jacksonville Zoo.

stars as comic actor Oliver Hardy began their careers here.

In the second half of the 20C, the **Port of Jacksonville,** extending along the St. Johns River between its main facilities at Talleyrand Docks and Blount Island, took its place among the Southeast's most important deepwater ports. Florida's three principal rail systems—CSX, Norfolk Southern and Florida East Coast—established headquarters here. Skyscrapers, notably Gulf Life Tower on the river's south bank (1967; now South

Jacksonville Landing

Gwen Cannon/MICHELIN

The Beaches
◔ *Map p144-145*

Kathryn Abbey Hanna Park – *500 Wonderwood Dr.; on A1A, south of Mayport Naval Station.* A distinctly sylvan atmosphere lures visitors to this 450-acre oceanfront park. Named in memory of Florida historian and educator Kathryn Abbey Hanna, the park boasts a splendid white-sand **beach**, minus the intrusive urban backdrop. Scenic hiking and biking trails lace the park.

Jacksonville Beaches – *East of downtown via Rte. 90/Beach Blvd. or Rte.10/ Atlantic Blvd.* Linked by Route A1A, three towns line the shore, north to south: Atlantic Beach, Neptune Beach and Jacksonville Beach, all from the turn of the 19C (as you head north, houses show more of the traditional Shingle style). **Atlantic Beach,** most affluent of the beach towns, contains a small but increasingly chic shopping district with several locally popular restaurant/bars. **Neptune Beach** is almost entirely residential. **Jacksonville Beach** is a blue-collar community turning upscale after almost a two-decade-long building moratorium. Its new downtown plaza is centered on a 7,000-seat amphitheater, the site, each spring, of one of America's largest blues festivals. The best beach restaurants are found at Jacksonville Beach (◔ *see Address Book*). A concrete boardwalk edges the beachfront between Fourth Avenue and the lifeguard station. At Fifth Avenue South, a long fishing pier juts into the ocean.

Ponte Vedra Beach – *From A1A south, bear left on Ponte Vedra Blvd.* Ranging along the coast south of Jacksonville Beach, this wealthy residential and resort community is home to some of the nation's most prestigious professional tennis organizations. From its headquarters in Ponte Vedra Beach, the Association of Tennis Professionals oversees nearly 70 tournaments in 31 countries; the Tournament Players Club is also located here.

Trust Bank) and Independent Square on the north bank, rose along the downtown skyline.

DOWNTOWN
Shopping, entertainment spots, offices and a hotel crowd the north side of the St. Johns River; the south bank offers strolls along a boardwalk and museum-browsing.

Two transportation services worth the ride link both sides of the river: the 2.5mi Skyway people mover and privately operated water taxis allow access to both banks without the annoyance of re-parking the car. Water taxis also provide transportation to the stadium on game weekends.

NORTH OF THE RIVER
Jacksonville Landing★
2 Independent Dr. ℘*904-353-1188. www.jacksonvillelanding.com.*
◷*Shops open Mon-Thu 10am-8pm, Fri-Sat 10am-9pm, Sun noon-5:30pm.*

This two-level, horseshoe-shaped building was completed in 1987 as an early part of the downtown's revitalization and has attracted many specialty shops and numerous eateries. After shopping, amble along the broad concrete walkways bordering the river for views of the opposite bank. It also hosts more than 300 events each year and is home to some of Jacksonville's hottest nightclubs.

Museum of Contemporary Art Jacksonville (MOCA)
333 N. Laura St. ◷*Open year-round Tue–Sat 10am–4pm (Thu 8pm), Sun noon–4pm. Artwalk daily (first Wed of month, only in winter) 5–9pm.* ◷*Closed major hols.* ⚌*$6. Free Wed 5–9pm; free to families Sun.* ℘*904-366-6911. www.mocajacksonville.org.*
The museum occupies five floors in the former Western Union building (1931) and is one of the southeast's largest contemporary art institutions, dedicated to presenting innovative

GETTING THERE

Jacksonville International Airport (JIA) – 15mi north of city *(information: ℘904-741-4902; www.jia.aero)*. Transportation to downtown: AirJTA bus (CT3) operates every day. A taxi will cost upwards of $35. Amtrak **train** station, 3570 Clifford Ln. *(℘800-872-7245; www.amtrak.com)*. **Greyhound bus** station, 10 N. Pearl St. *(℘800-231-2222; www.greyhound.com)*.

GETTING AROUND

Local **bus service** is provided by Jacksonville Transit Authority (JTA) *(year-round daily; shuttle service to Jacksonville Municipal Stadium, Kmart Plaza, Gateway Mall and Southside beaches; $6-$10. ℘904-630-3100; www.jtafla.com*.

The **Skyway Express monorail** travels between the Convention Center, Jefferson St., Hemming Plaza, Omni Hotel, San Marco and Florida Community College Jacksonville *(year-round Mon–Thu 6:30am–7:30pm, Fri 6:30am–10pm, Sat 10am–10pm; every 4min; 40c)*. **Water taxis** departs from the docks at Riverwalk and Jacksonville Landing *(year-round Sun–Thu 11am–9pm, Fri & Sat 11am–11pm; runs continuously; one-way 10min; $3-$5)*. **Bass Marine Taxi** *(℘904-730-8685)*.

Riverboat cruise, *(2hr 30min inc. lunch $30, or dinner $40)*.
For schedules and reservations, call **River Cruises Inc** ℘904-306-2200; www.jaxrivercruises.com.

VISITOR INFORMATION

Jacksonville and the Beaches Convention and Visitors Bureau, 550 Water St., Ste. 1000, Jacksonville 32202 *(open year-round Mon–Fri 8am–5pm. ℘904-798-9111 or 800-733-2668; www.jaxcvb.com)*. **Visitor center**, 2 Independent Dr. in Jacksonville Landing, *(open Mon–Sat 10am–7pm, Sun 12pm–5pm; ℘904-791-4305)* provides information on shopping, entertainment, festivals and recreation.

ACCOMMODATIONS – The *Area Visitors Guide* is available (free) from Jacksonville and the Beaches Convention and Visitors Bureau, or visit www.visitjacksonville.com/visitors/hotels. Campgrounds and RV parks are also available in the area.

SHOPPING – **Shops of Historic Avondale:** designer boutiques, antiques, restaurants (*www.historicavondale.com*); **Jacksonville Landing:** (💧*see above*); **Avenues Mall:** department stores, 110 specialty stores, eateries *(℘904-363-3060)*.

ENTERTAINMENT – Consult the arts and entertainment section of the *Times-Union* (Fridays, or visit *http://jacksonville.com*) and *Travelhost* publication for schedules of cultural events. **Jacksonville Symphony Orchestra** schedules Broadway shows and plays *(℘904-355-2787; www.jaxsymphony.org)*. **Theatre Jacksonville:** drama, comedy and musicals *(℘904-396-4425; www.theatrejax.com)*. **Times-Union Center for the Performing Arts** *(information: ℘904-633-6110; www.jaxevents.com)*. Free **concerts** at Jacksonville Landing, Center Courtyard *(℘904-353-1188)*. For arts and sporting events tickets contact **Ticketmaster** *(℘904-353-3309; www.ticketmaster.com)*.

SPORTS AND RECREATION – **Jacksonville Jaguars** (NFL) at Jacksonville Municipal Stadium, ℘904-633-2000, www.jaguars.com. **Jacksonville Suns,** AA affiliate of LA Dodgers at Wolfson Baseball Park, ℘904-358-2846; www.jaxsuns.com. **Golf** clubs that welcome visitors include: Champions Club at Julington Creek *(℘904-287-4653; www.championsclubgolf.com)*; Mill Cove Golf Club *(℘904-646-4653; www.millcovegolfcourse.com)*; Jacksonville Beach Golf Course *(℘904-247-6184; www.jacksonvillebeachgolfclub.com)*.
Fishing information is available in the Visitors Guide or visit www.jaxcvb.com.

The Great Fire

On the afternoon of 3 May 1901, a fire broke out at the Cleveland Fibre Factory near downtown. A deadly gusting wind carried sparks to the dry wood and pitch rooftops of nearby buildings; in the course of eight hours the fire destroyed over 2,300 buildings and left almost 10,000 people homeless. Miraculously there were only seven reported deaths. The worst disaster in Jacksonville's history, the fire nevertheless provided the city with an opportunity to transform itself. Architects and artisans flocked here, and a new downtown arose quickly from the ashes. In the decade following the fire, Jacksonville's population more than doubled.

exhibitions by the finest international, national and regional artists. Works by local and Florida artists, Pre-Columbian artifacts and artworks by Alexander Calder, Ellsworth Kelly and Helen Frankenthaler highlight the permanent collection.

Riverside/Avondale Historic District★

Bounded by the St. Johns River on the south and by I-10 and I-95 on the north. These two showcase neighborhoods feature a variety of architectural styles: Mediterranean Revival, Art Deco, Queen Anne, Colonial Revival, Georgian, Shingle, Tudor, Prairie and Bungalow. Developed after the Great Fire of 1901 (*see Box above*), both Riverside and Avondale enjoyed a long heyday as Jacksonville's most desirable addresses. Several houses in this district were designed by Henry John Klutho, who favored the Prairie style. The entire area was placed on the National Register of Historic Places in 1985.

Riverside Avenue between Memorial Park and Van Wert Street is the backbone of the historic area; streets between here and the river retain the most elegant, best-preserved houses. **Memorial Park** (*1600 block of Riverside Ave.*), recently rehabilitated and now a focal point for community events, was designed by Frederick Law Olmsted to commemorate Florida's World War I veterans. Nearby **Five Points** (*intersection of Park, Margaret and Lomax Sts.*) offers offbeat shopping and dining in an eclectic, historic setting, popular with youth. Drive down St. Johns Avenue for a pleasant passage beneath enormous live oak

trees. Some of the largest, most elaborate mansions survive along this broad thoroughfare. The avenue passes the Shops of Historic Avondale (St. Johns Ave. at Ingleside), an assemblage of upscale boutiques and restaurants established in the 1920s.

Well worth a look is the looming Riverside Baptist Church (intersection of Park and King Sts.), a massive Mediterranean Revival edifice conceived by celebrated Florida architect Addison Mizner.

Cummer Museum of Art and Gardens★★

829 Riverside Ave., at Post St. Open year-round Tue 10am–9pm, Wed–Fri 10am–4pm, Sat 10am–5pm, Sun noon–5pm. Closed major holidays. $10. Free Tue 4pm–9pm. 904-356-6857. www.cummer.org.

This elegant museum holds a broad collection of European and American art and decorative arts. With its remarkable **riverfront setting** and interactive arts education center, the Cummer boasts a reputation as one of Florida's best small art museums.

Jacksonville residents Arthur and Ninah Cummer constructed a grand residence on the Riverside estate that belonged to his father, the lumber baron Wellington W. Cummer. Ninah planted formal gardens and decorated the house with fine art. After her death the mansion and its art treasures were converted to a museum, as her will stipulated. In the 1960s the house was demolished and a new museum structure erected on the site, but the original Italian and English formal gardens were retained, as was the mahogany-paneled Tudor Room.

Through acquisitions and gifts, the collection has expanded to more than 6,000 works encompassing 8,000 years of art history. By proceeding clockwise through the galleries, which are set around an open courtyard, visitors can witness a progression of works from classical antiquity to the 21C.

Two galleries facing the garden are reserved for temporary exhibits. The museum is best known for the Wark collection of **early Meissen porcelain**. This is one of the three finest and most comprehensive collections of its kind in the world, featuring some 750 pieces of tableware dating from 1710-50, the first 40 years of European porcelain production. During this period, the factory in Meissen, Germany, was the first and only manufacturer of true, hard-paste white porcelain outside China. Don't miss the two complete 18C tea services, one owned by Marie, the last Queen of Hanover; and a dinner service owned by Elizabeth, Empress of Russia.

The concourse gallery leads to the interactive **Art Connections** (👥👤), where colorful, free-standing displays and hands-on activities interpret aspects of art. The formal Italian and English **gardens** behind the museum offer pergola-shaded paths among meticulously maintained greens and hedges, statuary and reflecting pools. Beyond the grounds rolls the St. Johns River.

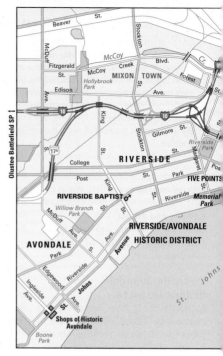

SOUTH OF THE RIVER
Riverwalk

The broad expanse of boardwalk extending a mile along the south bank across from downtown draws joggers, strollers and noontime lunchers by day, meanderers by evening, and fun-loving revelers during several annual festivals. The walk offers some of the best views of the river and the north bank, with Jacksonville Landing framed by gleaming office towers. Just west of the Main Street bridge lies Friendship Park, estab-

---

Heartworks Gallery & Cafe

🕯 *Map p144. 820 Lomax St. in Five Points.* ☏*904-355-6210.*

After a morning at the Cummer Museum, drive around the corner for lunch in colorful Five Points. The nondescript facade of this cafe belies its laid-back pace and funky interior, where a gallery of artistic concoctions leads to an equally eclectic eating space. Along with daily board specials, the carrot dog (organic carrot on Dijon bun) with twice-baked hazelnut potatoes, black bean chili salad, and other creations are offered with healthy tickers in mind. The hummus pita (with sunflower seeds, sprouts and feta) is especially heartwarming. A stroll along shop-lined Park Street should provide the requisite post-meal exercise.

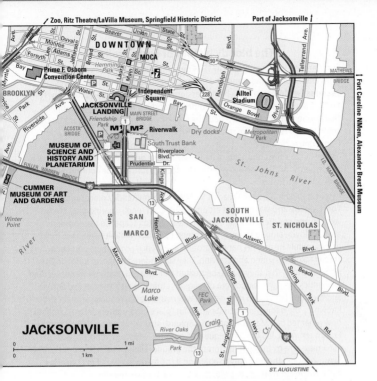

Zoo, Ritz Theatre/LaVilla Museum, Springfield Historic District — Port of Jacksonville

JACKSONVILLE

0   1 mi
0   1 km

ST. AUGUSTINE

lished in 1965; the geyser-like **fountain** at its center shoots jets of water high into the air.

🏛 Museum of Science and History and Planetarium★

1025 Museum Cir. ⏰*Open year-round Mon–Fri 10am–5pm, Sat 10am–6pm, Sun 1pm–6pm.* ⏰*Closed major holidays.* ∞*$11.* ♿🅿 ☏*904-396-6674 ext 210. www.themosh.org.*

History is adventure and science is fun at this hands-on museum near the foot of Main Street Bridge. Exhibits designed for all ages explore natural and physical sciences, regional natural history and north Florida's past. School-age children have the best time here, though, as they learn about northeast Florida wildlife, prehistoric beasts (including a life-size Allosaurus skeleton) and engage in interactive science demonstations.

The Alexander Brest Planetarium boasts a state-of-the-art sound system staging multimedia shows daily *(fee included in admission price; check at ticket office for show times).*

ADDITIONAL SIGHTS
🏛 Jacksonville Zoo

370 Zoo Pkwy, off Hecksher Dr. ⏰*Open year-round daily 9am–5pm (6pm Sat–Sun Mar–early Sept).* ⏰*Closed Thanksgiving Day and Dec 25.* ∞*$13–$17.50, child $8–$11.* ✕♿🅿 ☏*904-757-4463. www.jaxzoo.org.*

With a menagerie of thousands of exotic reptiles, birds and mammals thriving on its 120-acre site, this zoo ranks as a leader in botanical and zoological conservation; several endangered species have been successfully bred here.

A highlight is the **African veldt,** where a boardwalk crosses a 16-acre grassy enclosure, home to lions, ostriches and gazelles. **Seronera Overlook** puts visitors face-to-face with some of the most venomous snakes in the world.

On the **Range of the Jaguar,** the big cats roam on 40 acres. **Stingray Bay with Sharks** offers the chance to touch and feed some of the sea's most misunderstood creatures.

The bloody history of Fort Caroline

Fort Caroline was established in 1564 by some 300 Huguenots who arrived from France under the command of René de Laudonnière. On board was **Jacques Le Moyne,** a French artist assigned to document the expedition. They erected a triangular wooden fort some 5mi upriver. Starvation was rampant that spring of 1565. Disheartened, the French were preparing to abandon the colony when Huguenot mariner **Jean Ribault** arrived with fresh supply ships from France. He also brought disturbing news: the Spanish king was sending an armada under the command of Pedro Menéndez de Avilés to attack the French settlement. The Spanish arrived shortly after Ribault, but the confrontation proved inconclusive.

After establishing a beachhead at St. Augustine, Menéndez marched north to Fort Caroline and slaughtered around 150 of the French, sparing only 50–60 women and children. Around 50 men managed to escape, de Laudonnière and Le Moyne among them, and returned to France. Ribault was not so lucky as meanwhile he and his band of around 350 French protestants had been shipwrecked. Unarmed and starving, they surrendered to the Spanish, on the understanding that they would be treated well. Instead nearly all were executed as heretics. Even in a bloody era of religious strife this atrocity shocked Europe and the inlet, beach and river close to where the massacre took place are still known by the name *Matanzas* (Spanish for "place of slaughters"). Fort Caroline , now renamed San Matéo, remained a Spanish stronghold until 1568, when the French returned, led by Dominique de Gourgues who took vengeance for the 1565 massacre by burning the fort to the ground, killing all of its occupants. The Spanish rebuilt the fort, only to abandon it the following year. **Fort Caroline National Memorial** (*see p146) now commemorates the site.

Anheuser-Busch Brewery

150. 111. Busch Dr. ▷ *From downtown Jacksonville, drive north on I-95 to Busch Ave. east/Exit 125 and follow signs.* ◷*Open year-round Mon–Sat 10am–4pm.* ◷*Closed major holidays. If under 18 years of age, must be accompanied by an adult.* ♿ 🅿 ✆*904-696-8373. www.budweisertours.com.*

Fresh, yeasty aromas fill the air at this massive brewery north of downtown. Inside, self-guided and guided tours reveal the brewing and bottling processes and the long and colorful company history.

Alexander Brest Museum and Gallery

150. 2800 University Blvd. N., on Jacksonville University campus. Use north entrance to campus and bear left; follow signs. ◷*Open during college term time Mon–Fri 9am–4.30pm.* ◷*Closed weekends and university holidays.* ♿ 🅿 ✆*904-744-3950.*

A modest yet significant collection of decorative arts and pre-Columbian artifacts occupies four galleries of the Phillips Fine Arts Building. Most of the collection was acquired by Jacksonville engineer and businessman Alexander Brest, whose construction firm built much of the city's early road network. Be sure to see the **Tiffany and Steuben glass** and selected pieces of **Boehm porcelain** and intricately carved European and 17–19C oriental **ivories.**

Fort Caroline National Memorial★

150. 12713 Fort Caroline Rd. ▷ *13mi from downtown via Rte. 10A/ 115 east. Turn left (north) on Monument Rd. and follow signs to park.* ◷*Open year-round daily 9am–5pm.* ◷*Closed Dec 25.* ♿ 🅿 ✆*904-641-7155. www.nps. gov/foca.*
🐜*Insect repellent recommended.*

Begin at the visitor center, where displays recount the story of the original fort, built in the 1560s by French Huguenots, and of the French attempts to establish a stronghold in the New World (see p144). Artifacts on display include period weapons, tools, armor and Timucuan Indian artifacts.

From the visitor center, a short path leads to a replicated fort on the south bank of the St. Johns River.

Mayport and Mayport Ferry

On Mayport Rd.,
 15mi from downtown. Take Atlantic Blvd. (Rte. 10) east to Mayport Rd. (A1A).
The historic fishing village of **Mayport** *(west of naval base via A1A)* offers rough charm in its narrow streets, shrimping vessels and "shrimp shacks" that serve up generous portions of fresh crustaceans. The A1A crosses the St. Johns River via the car ferry from Mayport Landing to Fort George Island *(operates year-round daily 6:20am–10pm every half hour; one-way 10min; $3.25/car; St. Johns River Ferry Service. 904-241-9969. www.stjohnsriverferry.com).*

THE SEA ISLANDS
Fort George Island★

20mi northeast of Jacksonville.
 From downtown take I-95 7mi north to Exit 124 (Heckscher Dr. east). Continue east 15mi to Fort George Rd. and turn left.
Although this lush sea island, bordering St. Johns River to the north, holds stories from every phase of Florida's human history, it bears few marks of its long occupation. Timucuan Indians lived here for 3,500 years before the French—and later the Spanish—laid claim to Florida. The **Mission San Juan del Puerto** (for which the river was named) was founded here in 1587 by Spanish monks. It is thought that a fort established by the British General, James Oglethorpe, was located near the island's center, though no traces remain.

Today the land seems to be returning to wilderness. Ancient Timucuan shell middens lie concealed beneath dense overgrowth; elegant Sabal palms lining the avenue to Kingsley Plantation, an old cotton plantation, are nearly dwarfed by

surrounding evergreens. Tall stands of pampas grass flourish on the fairways of the deserted Ribault Club, once an exclusive golf resort. The plantation, along with Fort Caroline, lies on land protected by the 46,000-acre Timucuan Ecological and Historical Preserve.

Little Talbot Island

Just east of Fort George Island via A1A.
  904-251-2320. www.florida stateparks.org/littletalbotisland.
Sheltering Fort George Island from the Atlantic's force, this 2,500-acre barrier island has remained free of development and has been designated **Little Talbot Island State Park.** It includes over 5 miles of pristine, white-sand **beaches** , as well as a hiking trail *(4.1mi)* through live oaks and hollies in the hardwood hammock on the island's west side.

On neighboring **Big Talbot Island** *(just northwest of Little Talbot Island via A1A),* large sections of the hammock are developed as private residences.

Amelia Island★★

42mi northeast of Jacksonville via A1A.
Vacationers flock to this 13.5mi barrier island in Florida's northeast corner. Named by General James Oglethorpe after Princess Amelia (daughter of King George II of England), the island lies across St. Marys River from Georgia's Cumberland Island. Virgin beaches, salt marshes and hardwood forests attract nature lovers, while golf, tennis and the resorts of **Amelia Island Plantation** and **The Ritz-Carlton, Amelia**

Amelia Island

Visit Florida

Island lure luxury lovers. In the Centre Street Historic District of Fernandina Beach, you will find boutiques, specialty shops and impressive Victorian houses. Despite its popularity, the island is sparsely inhabited throughout the year.

Fernandina Beach★

On the north end of Amelia Island.
◐ *Follow A1A north and turn left on Atlantic Ave., which becomes Centre St.*
First inhabited by the Timucuan tribe, then named for Ferdinand, consort to Queen Isabella of Spain, the town was established in the late 18C, thriving as a port on the border between Spanish Florida and the US; smugglers routed clandestine goods through here when Thomas Jefferson's Embargo Act of 1807 closed US ports to foreign shipping.
As president of the Florida Railroad Co., Sen. **David Yulee** (1810–1886) persuaded residents to move the town south from its swampy site to its present location, where goods could easily be transferred from rail to cargo steamer. After the Civil War, Fernandina experienced a "Golden Age" of growth as shipping increased and tourists came to enjoy Florida's pleasing climate.
Fernandina Beach Depot (1899) now houses the Convention and Visitors Bureau, where walking-tour maps of the historic district are available *(102 Centre St.,* ◐*open year-round Mon–Fri 9am– 5pm, Sat 11am–4pm, Sun noon–4pm;* ♿ 🅿 ✆ *904 277-0717 or 800-2-AMELIA; www.islandchamber.com).*

Centre Street Historic District★

Between 11th St. and Front St., bounded on the north and south by Escambia and Elm Sts.
Fernandina's principal east-west artery ends at the waterfront overlooking the Amelia River. The street lies at the heart of a 50-square-block National Historic District filled with over 450 structures built between 1857 and 1910. The heaviest concentrations of historic buildings lie along North Sixth and South Seventh streets, and Centre Street itself. Most prominent is the brick **Nassau County Courthouse** *(Centre St. at 5th St.),* an eye-

catching Victorian structure (1891). Don't miss **Tabby House** *(northwest corner of 7th and Ash Sts.),* built in 1885 of tabby and Portland cement. The 1895 **Bailey House** *(opposite Tabby House)* sports the towers and fish-scale exterior paneling typical of Queen Anne style. **Fairbanks House** *(S. 7th and Cedar Sts.)* is a stunning Italianate pile (1885). Also worth seeing is eclectic **Villa las Palmas** *(315 Alachua St.),* a cedar-shingled residence dating from 1910.

Amelia Island Museum of History

233 S. 3rd St., 3 blocks south of Centre St. ◐*Open year-round Mon–Sat 10am & 4pm, Sun 1–4pm.* ✺*$7.* ◐*Closed major holidays.* 🅿 ✆*904-261-7378. www.ameliamuseum.org.*
The old county jail, lovingly refurbished, today guards local history. A departure from traditional museums, this "oral-history museum" features unlabeled artifacts and maps. Information is provided by docents (trained volunteer guides) who regale visitors with the story of Amelia Island.
🔊Tours proceed at a leisurely pace through display rooms; a reference room stocked with historical information, maps and architectural documents is open to visitors. The museum operates architectural and "8 Flags" historical walking tours of sections of Fernandina Beach and Centre Street *(11am and 2pm).*

Fort Clinch State Park★★

2601 Atlantic Ave. Park entrance just west of A1A. ◐*Fort open year-round daily 9am–5pm;* ✺*$6/vehicle.* △ 🅿 ✆*904-277-7274. www.floridastate parks.org/fortclinch*
This splendid expanse offers access to a wide beach, a fishing pier and nature trails; its centerpiece is a very well-preserved brick fort. Separated from Georgia by the St. Marys River, Fort Clinch was established in the late 1840s to protect Cumberland Sound, gateway to Fernandina Harbor, and named for General Duncan Lamont Clinch, a hero of the Seminole Wars. Fort construction was incomplete when the Civil War began in 1861 and Confederate troops took Fort

Fort Clinch State Park

Visit Florida

Clinch easily. The following year, the Georgia and South Carolina sea islands fell into Union hands, leaving Florida in isolation; the Confederates quickly withdrew. By the late 1860s however, the fort's brick and masonry walls were vulnerable to heavier shot from newly invented rifle-barreled cannons.

The federal government deactivated the obsolete fort in 1867, maintaining it without a garrison except briefly during the Spanish-American War. Fort Clinch opened in 1938 as one of Florida's first state parks. Displays in the visitor center outline US govern-ment defense systems prior to the 1840s and detail the construction of Fort Clinch. From the center, a short path leads to the fort, one of the best preserved in the country, its massive pentagonal walls interrupted only by a wooden drawbridge. Visitors are free to roam the impressive four-acre interior, exploring rooms, bomb-proof shelters and officers' quarters, or to climb the ramparts for a **view** of Cumberland Island across the river. Rangers in period dress offer daily living-history demon-strations, illustrating the life of soldiers billeted here.

ADDRESSES

🏠STAY

$$$$$ The Lodge & Club – *607 Ponte Vedra Blvd., Ponte Vedra Beach.* ✕⅋ 🅿🛥 ℘*904-273-9500 or 800-234-4304. www.pvresorts.com. 66 rooms.*
Pampering prevails at this sprawling Mediterranean-style seafront complex, complete with belvedere towers, red barrel-tile roofs and Palladian windows. Big, brightly tiled bathrooms house Jacuzzi or Roman tubs and separate showers. Attentive service and a full recreational menu are the order of the day. A multi-lane lap pool dominates the fitness center.

$$$-$$$$ Cabana Colony Cottages – *2435 S. Atlantic Ave., Daytona Beach Shores.* ⅋🅿🛥 ℘*386-252-1692 or 800-293-0653. www.daytonashoreline.com. 3 rooms.* These dwellings by the sea date from 1927. Outside and in, the cottages are painted in cool white and pastels and furnished in wicker, with seashell motifs and area rugs on tile. Each cottage has its own fully equipped kitchen and there's a guest laundry.

$$$ Amelia Island Williams House – *103 S. 9th St., Fernandina Beach.* ⅋🅿 ℘*904-277-2328 or 800-414-9258. www.williamshouse.com. 10 rooms.* Edging Fernandina's historic district, this 1856 mansion is the town's oldest. Its museum-like interiors show off furnishings that belonged to Napoleon III and the last emperor of China. Themed guest rooms (Italianate, Chinese, Victorian...) boast 17C Japanese block prints, brocaded bed linens, marble-topped tables or other lavish appointments. Generous bathrooms boast claw-foot or Jacuzzi tubs. Breakfasts are equally grand.

$$$ Casa Monica Hotel – *95 Cordova St., St. Augustine.* ✕ ♿ 🅿 ⌇ ☎*904-827-1888 or 800-648-1888. www.casamonica.com. 138 rooms.* This castle-like landmark was built in 1888 as a winter getaway for America's top-tier families. Its regal features—towers and arches, hand-painted tiles, iron poster beds—will make you think you've landed in Moorish Spain. Decorated with plush velvets and tapestry fabrics in jewel tones, rooms are fitted with amenities suitable for a modern-day king. Enjoy a martini and live music *(jazz Fri and Sat nights)* in the hotel's Cobalt Lounge.

$$$ The White Orchid – *1104 S. Oceanshore Blvd., Flagler Beach.* ♿ 🅿 ⌇ ☎*386-439-4944 or 800-423-1477. www.whiteorchidinn.com. 9 rooms.* Here, professional restaurateurs keen on accent and ambience operate an airy, Deco-styled B&B bordering the ocean. There's a cool, uncluttered look in guest rooms that highlight distinctive features and Oriental touches like a lacquer panel and orchid in the bathroom.

$$ House On Cherry Street – *1844 Cherry St., Jacksonville.* 🅿 ☎*904-384-1999. www.houseoncherry.com. 4 rooms.* ⊙*Jun–Sept.* Near downtown on historic Riverside, this two-story brick house dates from the early 20C. Most guest rooms enjoy river views, and all are furnished with solid antiques. Throughout are clocks, duck decoys, American coverlets, and Oriental rugs on oak and pine floors. A full breakfast is served; afternoon tea is a nice touch.

$$ Riverview Hotel – *103 Flagler Ave., New Smyrna Beach.* ✕ ♿ 🅿 ⌇ ☎*386-428-5858 or 800-945-7416. www.riverviewhotel.com. 18 rooms, 1 cottage.* This 1885 hotel, painted bright pink and accented with charming gingerbread, creates a tropical mood with lots of wicker, paddle fans and palms by the pool. Antique armoires and floral spreads on reproduction four-posters, feature in the guest rooms.

$$ St. Francis Inn – *279 Saint George, St., St. Augustine.* 🅿 ⌇ ☎*904-824-6068 or 800-824-6062. www.stfrancisinn.com.*

com. 17 rooms. In America's oldest city, no place exudes more warmth than this three-story, vine-covered inn (built 1791) on a cobblestone lane. An artesian fountain bubbles in the brick patio. Rough plastered ceilings, dark open beams and flickering fireplaces mark the public space, laid out with oriental rugs. Soft quilts, fringed lamps and vintage photos adorn the more modern guest rooms. Gourmet trencherman breakfasts are served.

🍴 EAT

$$$–$$$$ Clark's Fish Camp – *12903 Hood Landing Rd., Mandarin.* ♿ ☎*904-269-3474. www.clarksfishcamp.com.* If you feel you're being watched while you dine here, perhaps it's the glassy-eyed stares from the taxidermy mounts that serve as decor at this rather eccentric eatery on Julington Creek (near Jacksonville). If that doesn't put you off, head over to this former bait shop and see why there are often lines out the door. The menu seems to go on forever, featuring every kind of seafood imaginable. Stick to something simple, like grilled shrimp, and you can't go wrong. Carnivores rave about the prime rib.

$$$ Beech Street Grill – *801 Beech St., Fernandina Beach.* ♿ ☎*904-277-3662. www.beechstreetgrill.com.* Vacationers and locals alike can't resist this art-filled, two-story sea captain's house built in 1889. They're attracted by the refined interiors, the entertaining pianist, and, of course, the **Floridian** food. Chippendale-style balustrades, marble mantels and fireplace facades set the scene for signature dishes such as macadamia-nut-encrusted grouper with curried citrus glaze, and Parmesan-encased red snapper with mustard-basil cream. Many blackboard specials daily.

$$$ La Crepe en Haut – *142 E. Granada Blvd., Ormond Beach.* ☎*386-673-1999. www.lacrepeenhaut.net.* Graced with ornamental art, upholstered oval-back chairs and textured carpets, four warmly lit rooms, belle-époque style, ensconce patrons at this pricey, celebrity-favored haunt. The menu is rooted in French Nouvelle Cuisine (the appetizers alone are astounding), while nightly specials satisfy more contemporary tastes with offerings like mussels in pernod broth, filet mignon studded with green peppercorns, and lobster ravioli. The restaurant-cum-bistro/bar is housed upstairs within a tree-filled gallery of shops.

$$$ Matthew's – *2107 Hendricks Ave., Jacksonville.* ♿ ✆*904-396-9922. www. matthewsrestaurant.com. Dinner only.* South of the river in stylish San Marco, uber chef/owner Matthew Medure performs daring culinary moves within an open kitchen and a dining room that seats a mere 55. Walls of burnished blond wood rise high above Jacksonville's diehard foodies, who feast on Kobe beef carpaccio, yellowtail snapper, or seared duck breast with foie gras ordered from nightly changing menus. Alternatively, two chef's tasting menu are available. Patio dining depends on the weather.

$$ bb's – *1019 Hendricks Ave., San Marco, Jacksonville.* ♿ ✆*904-306-0100. www.bbsrestaurant.com. Closed Sun.* A stainless steel bar and concrete floors contrast smartly with the unabashed American comfort food dished up at this hip bistro. Diner classics get a modern twist—the pork chops are likely to be wrapped in prosciutto, for example, and a perfectly cooked filet is topped with boursin and hazelnuts with an onion reduction. Grilled pizzas and warm goat-cheese salad are popular lighter choices (portions are hearty).

$$ Columbia – *98 St. George St., St. Augustine.* ♿ ✆*904-824-3341. www. columbiarestaurant.com.* Hand-painted tiles, decorative arches and delicious aromas beckon diners into Columbia, a sister restaurant of the famous original Columbia in Tampa. The Cuban food is just as wonderful here (try the seafood paella and a glass of sangria) and the wait for a table, unfortunately, can be just as long. Folks at this land's-end locale have lived off the sea since 1846. The pace here is permanently slow, so you'll want to work on a beer and soak up the Old Florida atmosphere at a weathered plank table while waiting for your order of oysters, shrimp or crab. Long past its working days, the skiff *Genevieve* sails on as an inside bar. Of the quirky signs that decorate the restaurant's walls, perhaps the best reads: "Today's soup, cream of yesterday's special."

$$ Cortessés Bistro – *172 San Marco Ave., St. Augustine.* ♿ ✆*904-825-6775.* **Continental.** Intimate rooms with hardwood floors, clothed tables and fresh flowers exude Old World charm and romance at this bustling, Euro-style bistro. Blue Plate specials share menu space with pasta primavera, Minorcan fish stew (lobster, scallops and shrimp in stock, topped with romesco sauce) and veal Oscar. The baci fudge tart typifies Cortessés' tempting desserts. Dine outdoors in the greenery-garnished patio or sample late-night fare and live jazz in the Flamingo Room bar.

$$ Creekside Dinery – *160 Nix Boatyard Rd., St. Augustine.* ♿ ✆*904-829-6113. www.creeksidedinery.com. Dinner only.* It's hard to believe that a busy highway is only a quarter-mile away from this rustic floorboarded house, set beside a misty marsh and surrounded by tall oaks. Beer-battered shrimp, oak-planked grouper and broiled seafood platters spice up the spacious, informal setting. Sweet potatoes and cheese jazz up a humble side dish of grits. Tiki torches discourage the no-see-ums on the outdoor deck, but if you're not comfortable, retreat inside, or to the screened-in porch for a table over the water. A nice touch for families: Kids can make their own dessert, roasting marshmallows in the fire pit on the patio. "Dainty Diners" portions are available. Live music entertains patrons Wednesday through Sunday.

$$ Denoel French Pastry – *212 Charlotte St., St. Augustine.* ♿ ✆*904-829-3974.* Patrons come for mid-morning, made-on-the-premises French pastries to complement an espresso or cafe au lait. Otherwise they order sandwiches of Black Forest ham or Genoa salami on home-baked croissants or French bread. Soups du jour and tomatoes stuffed with shrimp or chicken salad are added attractions. A fixture among city merchants, the Denoels have been baking here in St. Augustine since 1966.

St. Augustine★★★
Anastasia Island

The oldest continuously occupied European settlement in the US, dating from 1565, lies on Florida's east coast, 33 miles south of Jacksonville. Situated on a finger of land extending south from the mainland, between the Matanzas River on the east and the San Sebastián River on the west, historic St. Augustine mingles humble, one-story 18C structures with architectural showpieces from the 19C. The city's time-burnished flavor is captured in narrow, cobbled lanes lined with red-roofed buildings of pale coquina, many of them survivors of the 18C. The historic district is home to more than 60 sites and attractions, and nearly 150 blocks are listed on the National Register of Historic Places.

No wonder St. Augustine draws so many day-trippers, eager to go back in time in the nation's oldest city.

▶ **Population:** 12,263.

Michelin Map: p153.

Info: Castillo Drive ✆904-825-1000. Also at: Riberia St. ✆904-824-0709; St. Augustine Beach. ✆904-471-1596; www.getaway4florida.com, www.augustine.com, www.oldcity.com.

Location: St. Augustine is 35mi south of Jacksonville.

Parking: Follow the signs to the Historic Downtown Parking Facility, rather than trying to snag a space on the street.

Don't Miss: Castillo de San Marcos National Monument and the Lightner Museum.

Timing: Allow at least three days.

Kids: Marineland, St. Augustine Alligator Farm Zoological Park, the beach at St Anastasia State Park.

A BIT OF HISTORY

European Tug of War – In 1565 Spanish ships commanded by **Pedro Menéndez de Avilés** dropped anchor near the present-day harbor. Menéndez' mission was to overpower "heretical" French Huguenots at Fort Caroline (*see Box, p144*) who claimed the territory as their own, and to establish two cities as footholds of the Spanish empire. Having ousted the French, about 600 settlers set about building a fort between the Matanzas and San Sebastián rivers. The new colony was named St. Augustine in honor of the patron saint of Avilés, the hometown of Menéndez. Ill-equipped to raise food, settlers plundered the stored harvests of the Indians. In retaliation, the natives drove the colonists from their homes back to their flimsy wooden fort. Worse was to follow when Sir Francis Drake, scourge of the Spanish, razed St Augustine in 1586.

In 1587 St. Augustine was rebuilt and became the capital of Spanish Florida. Subsequent years brought peace, in concert with the success of Franciscan missionary efforts among the Timucuans. Beginning in 1565, a chain of about 100 **missions** grew northward along the coast, but had disappeared by the early 18C, victims of British raids and the elements.

The English challenge to Spain's sovereignty grew in 1670 when England founded the Carolina colony, with its capital at Charles Town some 275mi north. In response St. Augustine's governor began construction of a massive stone fort, Castillo de San Marcos. using deposits of **coquina** that had been discovered on nearby Anastasia Island.

Created by sedimentation of seashells, the water-soaked stone proved an ideal material with which to build a permanent fortification (*see Box p157*). In 1702 British troops tried in vain to storm the fortress walls. In 1740 they tried again when British general **James Oglethorpe,** who had founded

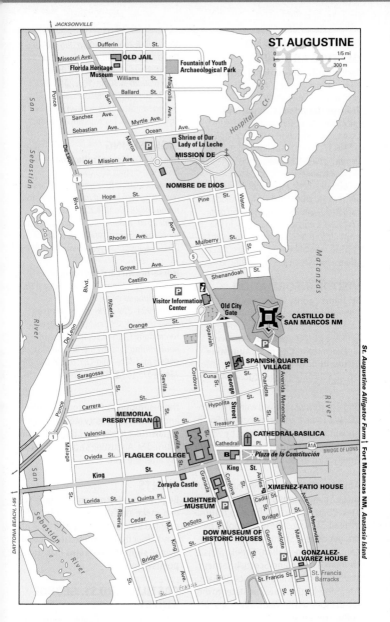

St. Augustine Alligator Farm ↑ Fort Matanzas NM, Anastasia Island

a settlement at the Savannah River in 1733, marched on St. Augustine; they were later forced to retreat when Spanish reinforcements arrived from Cuba. In fact, St. Augustine became British territory peacefully in 1763 when Spain relinquished Florida to England in exchange for Cuba, which had been captured by the British.

British St. Augustine – Following the transfer of land, nearly 3,000 Spanish citizens sailed from Florida to Cuba and the West Indies. The British settlers built roads, founded public schools and erected buildings in St. Augustine. During the American Revolution, the city became a training ground for forces preparing to defend Florida. In 1783 the

GETTING THERE AND GETTING AROUND

Jacksonville International Airport (JIA): 52mi north of St. Augustine via US-1 *(information: ℘904-741-4902)*.
Transportation to St. Augustine *(advance reservations required)*: East Coast Transportation *($70/1–3 people; ℘246-3741)*, or Dial-a-Ride *($55/1–2 people. ℘904-829-0880)*. Nearest Amtrak **train** station is in Palatka *(℘800-872-7245; www.amtrak.com)*. Greyhound **bus** station: 1000 Malaga St. *(℘800-231-2222; www.greyhound.com)*. Visitors are encouraged to park in the Visitor Information Center parking lot. Parking regulations are strictly enforced; yellow curbs indicate no-parking zones.

VISITOR INFORMATION

St. Johns County Visitors and Convention Bureau, 88 Riberia St., Suite 400, St. Augustine 32084 *(℘904-829-1711 or 800-653-2489; www.visitoldcity.com)*. **City of St. Augustine Visitor Information Center,** 10 Castillo Dr., near San Marco Ave. *(◷open Apr–May daily 8:30am–6:30pm, Jun–Labor Day daily 8am–7pm, early Sept–Oct daily 8:30am–6:30pm; rest of the year daily 8:30am–5:30pm; ✕⛐🅿 ($1.25hr): ℘904-825-1000)*. These organizations provide information on shopping, entertainment, festivals and recreation.

SIGHTSEEING

Narrated **Old Town Trolley tours** of historical district offer on-and-off privileges good for three consecutive days. *(Depart from Old Jail complex year-round daily 8:30am–4:30pm; every 15–20min; $20. ℘800-213-2474; wwwtrusted tours.com)*. Guided **walking tours** of Old St. Augustine *(year-round daily 8pm; $5)*, Ancient CityTours *(℘797-5604)*.
Horse-drawn carriage tours *(year-round daily 8:30am–11pm; round-trip 1hr; $55 minimum)* by St. Augustine Transfer Co. *(☎904- 829-2818)*. Scenic **cruises** leave from Municipal Marina *(◷year-round daily 11am–4:30pm, extended hours during summer months, additional cruises mid-May–mid-Oct; round-trip 1hr 15min; $15. ⛐🅿℘800-542-8316)*.

British governor received word that Florida was to be transferred back to Spain under the new Treaty of Paris, by which Great Britain formally acknowledged American independence.

Americanization – Only a handful of those Spanish settlers who had evacuated 20 years earlier chose to return. Instead, St. Augustine was peopled by a hodgepodge of Spanish, English, American, Minorcan, Italian, Greek, Swiss, German, French and Scottish settlers, slaves, free blacks and Seminole Indians. As trade with the American states to the north increased, St. Augustine's Spanish culture declined.

The American states to the north grew more populous and their residents became hungrier for territory. Upon ratification of the **Adams-Onís Treaty** in 1821, by which Spain ceded Florida to the US, the American flag rose over the Castillo.

The end of the Civil War brought an improved rail line to the city, but it was the resumption of the tourist trade—and the arrival of Henry Morrison Flagler in particular *(👈see Box opposite)*—that spurred St. Augustine's economic recovery after the war.

SIGHTS

Begin at the **visitor center,** where you can make reservations and buy discounted tickets to area attractions. A fun way to tour the city: aboard the privately owned **sightseeing trains** that stop at points of interest.

CASTILLO AND ST. GEORGE STREET

After a visit to the Castillo, a meander down **St. George Street** offers the best peek at St. Augustine's past and present. This backbone of the old city retains its historic flavor despite an abundance of gift and souvenir shops, restaurants and tourist haunts. Many of these businesses occupy restored 18C buildings. St. George Street is closed to vehicular traffic between the Old City Gate *(north*

Henry Morrison Flagler

The son of an itinerant Presbyterian minister, Flagler (1830–1913) was born in Hopewell, New York. At age 14, sick of school, he set out to Ohio to make his fortune. There he landed a job in a general store for $5 a month, and soon developed a knack for salesmanship. Eventually Henry entered into partnership with his friend, wealthy industrialist John D. Rockefeller. Their oil refinery, incorporated in 1870 as Standard Oil Co., established huge fortunes for the two influential men.

Flagler visited Florida in 1877 on the advice of doctors treating his invalid wife, Mary. Widowed by 1883, Flagler honeymooned in St. Augustine with his second wife—Mary's former nurse, Ida Alice Shourds. The businessman shrewdly observed that while its agreeable climate drew wealthy winter visitors, the city offered few amenities. Two years later, Flagler had hatched a plan to erect a luxury hotel and transform St. Augustine into a resort rivaling France's Riviera. His plan involved improving the railway to link the city with the populous centers of the Eastern seaboard.

Flagler's massive Ponce de Leon Hotel (*see Box p160*), its less elegant counterpart, the Hotel Alcazar (*see Box p159*), and the Casa Monica Hotel, a large property that he purchased, formed the basis of St. Augustine's heyday as Florida's premier resort destination. The oil magnate eventually acquired additional rail lines to found Florida East Coast Railway, extending south from Daytona to Miami via Palm Beach. Divorced and married a third time (his second wife had lapsed into incurable insanity), Flagler spent the rest of his life developing resorts in south Florida. Upon his death, his remains were interred at St. Augustine's Memorial Presbyterian Church, a lavishly appointed Renaissance-style edifice (1889, Carrère and Hastings) commissioned by Flagler to commemorate his daughter, who died from complications during childbirth.

St. Augustine's Memorial Presbyterian Church

Second Read Books

Cordova St. ℘*904-829-0334.* Forgot to bring a paperback along on your travels? Or just finished one and need new reading material? Then stop in at this small bookshop adjacent to Flagler College to peruse the selection of used hard- and softback fiction and nonfiction at bargain prices. Owned by two former teachers, Second Read stocks a variety of titles of contemporary interest. Mysteries, science fiction, novels and cookbooks share shelf space with books on self-help and spirituality, women's studies and religion. The bookstore's purchase of pre-owned books depends upon their quality and topical appeal; payment is made in the form of store credit or cash.

end of St. George St. at intersection with Orange St.) and the **Plaza de la Constitución** (bounded by St. George, King and Charlotte Sts. and Cathedral Pl.).

Castillo de San Marcos National Monument★★★

1 S. Castillo Dr. at Orange St. ⏱*Open year-round daily 8:45am–4:45pm (last admission).* ⏱*Closed Dec 25.* ⬤*$6. Cannon firings and reenactments, call for schedules:* ℘*904-829-6506. www.nps.gov/casa.*

Defender of St. Augustine since the beginning of the 18C, the oldest masonry fort in the US overlooks Matanzas Bay at the northern boundary of the old city.

The Castillo withstood every enemy attack that beset it and today ranks among the best-preserved examples of Spanish Colonial fortifications in the New World (⬤*see Box p157*).

Begin your visit with a ranger talk *(20–30min; daily from 10am every hour on the hour)* in the interior courtyard. Around here, rooms contain displays describing fort history.

Don't miss the presentation of ordnance used at the fort; from this display, you must stoop to enter a low passageway leading to the powder magazine deep in the northeast bastion. A long stairway ascends to the **gundeck,** outfitted with some of the Castillo's original cannons and mortars. The panoramic **view** from here demonstrates the ease with which sentries could monitor an intruder's approach.

Old City Gate

North end of St. George St. This handsome pair of coquina pillars supported a gate that served as the only entrance to the city through the Cubo Line, a wood-and-earthwork fortification erected after the English attacked it in 1702. The wall extended from the Castillo to the San Sebastián River. The present coquina structures were built in 1808.

Castillo de San Marcos

Brigitta L. House/MICHELIN

A Mighty Fortress of Shell Stone

The increasing threat from English, Dutch and French forces convinced Spanish officials in Madrid that St. Augustine needed a permanent stone fortification. By 1671 rafts had begun ferrying blocks of coquina to the site from quarry pits on Anastasia Island. Construction continued fitfully, but by 1695 the Castillo was largely complete. Four-sided, with pointed triangular bastions at each corner, the structure boasted 12ft-thick outer walls broken only by an iron portcullis. The outwardly sloping lower walls were designed to counter artillery fire. A wooden drawbridge traversed a broad moat. During the 18C, barrel-vaulted rooms were added. A coquina ravelin was erected beyond the drawbridge, and an earthen embankment, or glacis, rose outside the moat.

By 1702 the fort had proven its worth, sheltering St. Augustine's residents within its walls as English troops sacked the town. England saw the Spanish fort as a threat to land it claimed in Georgia. In 1740 English warships under Gen. James Oglethorpe bombarded the fort for 27 days. Their cannonballs sank into the soft coquina walls, however, and did little damage.

The Castillo was handed over to British authority in 1763, when Florida was transferred from Spain to Great Britain. Renamed Fort St. Mark and fortified during the American Revolution, the structure was recovered by Spain at the close of the war. In 1821 the Spanish flag was lowered here for the last time as Spain ceded Florida to the US. The Castillo, renamed Fort Marion for Revolutionary War commander Francis Marion (the legendary "Swamp Fox"), served as a military prison until the early 20C. In 1924 it was designated a national monument.

Colonial Spanish Quarter ★

33 St. George St. ○Open year-round daily 9am–4:45pm (last admission). ○Closed Dec 25. ✎*$6.95, $12.95 to include de Mesa House Museum and Government House Museum (* &*see p158). www.staugustinegovernment.com.*

Behind a low wall fronting St. George Street, this living-history museum re-creates the latter years of the city's first Spanish period. Within, eight structures have been rebuilt in accordance with research by the Historic St. Augustine Preservation Board.

After entering through Florencia House, visitors may walk the grassy "streets" of St. Augustine c.1740. The dwellings of a foot soldier, an artillery sergeant and a cavalryman emphasize variations in wealth, rank and status of soldiers based at the Castillo.

A smithy works in the restored **black-smith shop,** while costumed interpreters demonstrate activities of 18C life. One of the fine restored historic residences, **Mesa-Sanchez House (A)** began as a one-room coquina house built for the family of a shore guard stationed at the Castillo (☞ *visit by guided tour only*). Guides recount the house's history as a residence, boardinghouse, barbershop, store and restaurant. Of special interest is a large display of kitchen tools.

Cathedral-Basilica of St. Augustine★★

North side of Plaza de la Constitución. ○Open year-round daily 9am–4:30pm. & ✆*904-824-2806. www.thefirst parish.org.*

The scalloped facade and tower mark the home of the parish of St. Augustine, considered to have been founded in 1565, and therefore ranking as the oldest Catholic parish in the US. The parish church was abandoned and relocated numerous times throughout the 18C. Not until 1793 did diocesan authorities commission a permanent structure of coquina north of the plaza.

An 1887 fire destroyed all but the walls and facade. Architect James Renwick (visiting St. Augustine at the time of

Gators and Crocs

Still waiting to see a Florida gator? Some 2,500 crocodilians live at the **St. Augustine Alligator Farm Zoological Park★★** (*A1A, 1mi south of the Bridge of Lions;* ◷*open year-round daily 9am–5pm, (Jul and Aug–6pm);* ◌*$21.9;, child 3-11yrs $10.95;* ℘*904-824-3337; www.alligatorfarm.com*) in landscaped habitats and re-created swamps. Don't miss the shows in the reptile theater, where staff handle Florida snakes and an albino alligator. The granddaddy of the crocsand current star attraction—is Maximo, a 15ft, 1,250-pound saltwater crocodile, father of 18 little crocs. Don't miss the **Land of Crocodiles,** Alligator

Farm's outstanding, and rare, collection of all 23 species of crocodilians. The park also showcases komodo dragons, macaws and other exotic birds. The wading **bird rookery** is home to nesting egrets, herons and wood storks.

Gwen Cannon/MICHELIN

the fire) aided in the reconstruction. The cathedral was designated a Minor Basilica in 1976. Inside, massive decorated timbers support the ceiling above floors of colorful Cuban tile.

A large, ornamental reredos of gold and white wood, incorporating the marble altar table from the original church, highlights the sanctuary.

KING STREET
Government House Museum★ (B)

48 King St. ◷*Open year-round Mon–Fri 9am–4:30pm, Sat-Sun 10am–4:30pm.* ◷*Closed Dec 25.* ◌*$4 or $12.95, to include Colonial Spanish Quarter (*◉*see p160).* &*.* ℘*904-825-5079, www.staugustinegovernment.com*

The stately, two-story Government House retained its official purpose for nearly 400 years. The first construction on the site appeared in 1599 and included the governor's residence.

A crumbling hulk by 1687, it was rebuilt of more durable coquina but succumbed to fire during the British attack in 1702. Rebuilt by 1713, and twice renovated, the structure has been used as a courthouse, post office and civil services building.

Colorful displays feature five centuries of St. Augustine's history, along with artifacts from archeological digs and Spanish shipwrecks.

Flagler College★★

74 King St. ◉*Visit by guided tour only (30min).* ◷*May–Aug & Christmas school break daily 10am–4pm;* ◌*$6.* &*.* ℘*904-829-6481. www.flagler.edu.*

Formerly the Ponce de Leon Hotel (◉*see Box p158*), this grand edifice was the cornerstone of Henry Flagler's master plan to transform St. Augustine (and with it, much of Florida) into an American resort destination. The Spanish Renaissance building today houses the residence facilities, dining room and lecture halls of Flagler College. A handsome bronze statue of Henry Flagler stands before the arched main entrance leading into an arcaded courtyard. Tours begin in the Main Hall beneath an 84ft rotunda richly decorated with gold leaf and Maynard murals. The oak wainscoting, leaded-glass windows and whimsical lion's-head light fixtures in the **dining room** are all original. Some of the most prominent figures of the early 20C, including presidents Warren Harding, Theodore Roosevelt and William McKinley, sat on these dining-room chairs.

Lightner Museum★★

75 King St. ◷*Open year-round daily 9am–5pm.* ◷*Closed Dec 25.* ◌*$8.* ✕&🅿℘*904-824-2874. www.lightnermuseum.org.*

The massive bulk of Flagler's former Hotel Alcazar (◉*see Box p159*) echoes the

The Hotel Alcazar

Henry Flagler (*see Box p155*) commissioned the Hotel Alcazar in 1888, as a comfortable but less luxurious alternative to the Ponce de Leon Hotel (*see p160*). Designed by the same team of Carrère and Hastings, the poured-concrete structure boasted a ballroom, a bowling alley, a billiards room, a gymnasium and spa—including Russian (dry) and Turkish (steam) bathshops, plus a casino annex with what was then the world's largest indoor swimming pool. To Flagler's surprise, guests preferred the relaxed atmosphere of the Alcazar to the more formal Ponce de Leon, and the hotel soon outstripped its neighbor

Antiques Mall and Café Alcazar

© Pat Canova/Alamy

in popularity. However, the same economic factors that slowed business at the Ponce de Leon also proved the Alcazar's undoing. The hotel closed its doors for good in 1937.

In 1946, empty and forlorn, the building was purchased by Otto C. Lightner, a Chicago publisher. Following his own credo that "everyone can be a collector of something," Lightner had amassed a very ecelctic collection of objects and decorative arts, much of it from wealthy estates hard hit by the Depression. By 1947 his vast assemblage had been installed in the corridors of Hotel Alcazar. Financial difficulties plagued operations, but local citizens kept the museum alive and restored the building. The lobby casino and ballroom have been restored to their original condition and the Lightner Museum occupies three floors, including the former spa and gymnasium. In the Music Room demonstrations of mechanized musical instruments, dating from the 1870s through the 1920s, are scheduled daily. On the lower level of the museum there is an Antiques Mall and the Café Alcazar serving lunch and snacks in what was once the indoor swimming pool.

Gwen Cannon/MICHELIN

Tiffany Austrian crystal chandelier in the Grand Parlor, Ponce de Leon Hotel

© Pat Canova/Alamy

Florida's Ponce de León Hotel

Henry Morrison Flagler (see Box p155) determined that his flagship St. Augustine hotel would be a grand, permanent structure, reflecting the city's Spanish architectural heritage. The Villa Zorayda, built by Boston millionaire Franklin W. Smith in 1883, and based on the Alhambra Palace in Granada, was Flagler's inspiration. Flagler hired Thomas Hastings and John M. Carrère, an inexperienced team of young architects (Flagler's friendship with Hastings' father may have influenced his choice) who went on to an illustrious career, designing the New York Public Library. Working alongside were Bernard Maybeck (then in the early stages of his career) and Louis Comfort Tiffany. The interior decoration of the Ponce de Leon was Tiffany's first significant commission.

The architects produced the nation's first major building that employed poured-concrete construction. It was embellished with Medieval, Moorish, Mediterranean and Victorian elements; most prominent are its Renaissance overtones. The twin bell towers remain today a distinctive feature of St. Augustine's skyline. Terra-cotta ornamentation adorns the gray concrete walls, and palm trees flourish on the grounds. Decorated with Austrian crystal chandeliers crafted by Tiffany and dramatic murals painted by American artist George W. Maynard, the hotel opened for business in January 1888.

The Ponce de León fared well for only a few years; economic downturns and competition curtailed the flow of vacationers. During World War II, the building was leased to the US Coast Guard. It reopened after the war but its days as a resort hotel were numbered. In 1967 the hotel ceased operation and the building was converted into the private liberal-arts college it houses today.

Flagler College, formerly the Ponce de León Hotel

Visit Florida

Spanish flavor of Flagler College opposite. Today the corridors and rooms, where some of Florida's first tourists once trod, house a diverse assortment of decorative arts and collectibles, including art glass that belonged to the museum's namesake, Otto C. Lightner, a Chicago publisher who purchased the hotel building in 1946.

Some of the odder displays include collections of buttons, fruit crate labels, and objects made of human hair. Don't miss the steam engine created of blown glass, or the collection of antique music boxes. The main baths *(second level)* house Lightner's extensive collection of **art glass.** From Bohemian to Bristol to spatter and spangle, the handsomely displayed pieces are grouped largely by type, style and manufacturer. Works by Louis Comfort Tiffany, as well as Wedgwood, Meissen, majolica and lusterware glass and porcelain are featured.

Intricately carved 19C furniture from India, samplers stitched in the 18C, and an Art Nouveau parlor suite number among the pieces in Lightner's decorative arts collection *(third level)*.

SOUTH OF THE PLAZA
Ximenez-Fatio House★★

20 Aviles St. Visit by guided tour only, year-round Mon–Sat 11am–3:30pm. $6. 904-829-3575. www.ximenez fatiohouse.org.

This two-story coquina residence offers a look at the way early St. Augustine buildings were expanded and adapted for various uses. It was built in 1798 by Spanish merchant Andrés Ximenez as his residence and general store. Under a later owner, the establishment thrived as St. Augustine's most popular inn from the mid-19C to the late 19C, when competition from Henry Flagler's hotels slowed business.

Today the house is restored to reflect the period between 1830 and 1850; individual rooms are authentically appointed as if to accommodate various 19C boarders. Objects unearthed in archaeological digs at the site are displayed throughout the house.

Dow Museum of Historic Houses★

246 St. George St. (entrance on Bridge St.). Open year-round Tue–Sun 10am (Sun 11am)–4:30pm. Closed Thanksgiving Day, Dec 24–25. $8.95. 904-823-9722. www.moas.org/dowmuseum.html.

Nine historic houses (five are open to the public), dating from 1790 to 1910, occupy a full city block *(bounded by St. George, Bridge and Cordova Sts. and St. Joseph Convent)* that was part of the original 16C walled colonial town. Famous residents and visitors included Prince Achille Murat, nephew of Napoleon Bonaparte, John James Audubon and Mark Twain.

In 1988 a St. Augustine resident donated the properties to the Museum of Arts and Sciences of Daytona Beach.

The oldest is the pink **Prince Murat House** (1790), a Spanish Colonial constructed of coquina; contents include china that bears the Murat family cipher and Murat's father's bed from Château de Versailles near Paris. Under restoration is the Colonial Revival **William Dean Howells House** (1910), rented by the American novelist, who hosted writer Sinclair Lewis here.

Exhibits in the **Star General Store** and Dow and Canova houses pertain to the French in Florida's history and Cracker culture, among other topics. Several remnants are visible: the city's Rosario Defense Line (mid-1700s); footers of the bridge across Maria Sanchez Creek; and the oldest known Catholic burial ground in the US, dating to 1597. Throughout the village, interpreters provide entertainment and information.

Gonzalez-Alvarez House★★ (The Oldest House)

14 St. Francis St. (between Charlotte and Marine Sts.). Visit by guided tour (30min) only, year-round daily 9am–4:30pm (last tour). Closed Easter Sunday, Thanksgiving Day, Dec 25. $8. 904-824-2872. www.staugustinehistoricalsociety.org.

This museum complex includes Florida's Oldest House, two museums, a changing exhibition gallery, an ornamental garden, and a museum store. The handsome Gonzalez-Alvarez dwelling is thought to be St. Augustine's oldest extant residential structure. Initially a flat-roofed rectangular coquina building with tabby floors, the house was built in the early 18C for Tomás Gonzalez y Hernandez, a settler from the Canary Islands. A second story, fireplace and balcony were added when the structure housed a tavern. The Geronimo Alvarez family acquired the house in 1790 and it passed through generations before being sold in 1882. The gloomy lower level, with its rugged tabby floors and exposed coquina walls, depicts the spartan lifestyle of the Gonzalez family, while the upstairs reveals the relative comfort enjoyed by the Alvarez family. The mosquito-netted, four-poster bed and porcelain pitcher and washbowl in the upstairs bedroom date from Florida's Territorial Period.

Tour guides explain the history of the house and neighborhood, vividly evoking life in Colonial Florida.

Take a walk in the traditional ornamental **garden** where you can see plants grown by the Spanish, British and American colonists, and peek into the typical 18C-style kitchen, detached from the main house. The **Manucy Museum**, located in the 1924 Webb Building, was the first edifice in Florida designed and built as a museum. It presents over 400 years of Florida's history.

The **Page L. Edwards Gallery** presents changing exhibitions of materials drawn from the Historical Society's rich collections as well as traveling exhibits from other museums.

SAN MARCO AVENUE
Fountain of Youth
Archaeological Park

155 Magnolia Ave. ○*Open year-round daily 9am–5pm.* ○*Closed Dec 25.* ⌨*$9.* &♿*904-829-3168 or 800-356-8222. www.fountainofyouthflorida.com.*

While stories proclaiming this spot as the landing site of Ponce de León in his search for the mythical Fountain of Youth are the stuff of legend, the importance of the **archaeological site** here

is unquestioned. In recent decades, researchers have uncovered artifacts and building foundations that indicate the presence here of Pedro Menéndez de Avilés, as well as the probable location of the Timucuan village of Seloy, home to the Indians who welcomed Menéndez in 1565.

Visitors can drink from the small spring, although anyone expecting immortality, or even a pleasant taste, will be disappointed—the waters are sulfurous.

Mission de Nombre de Dios★

San Marco Ave. and Ocean Ave. ○*Open year-round Mon–Fri 8am–5pm, Sat 9am–5pm, Sun 9:30am–5pm.* ○*Closed major holidays.* 🅿♿*904-824 -2809. www.missionandshrine.org.*

A 208ft stainless-steel cross marks the approximate spot where Pedro Menéndez de Avilés and his men came ashore to take possession of Florida for Philip II of Spain in 1565 and establish the Mission de Nombre de Dios, the first Catholic mission in the US. Nothing remains today of the original structures. The gleaming cross, erected in 1966 to commemorate the 400th anniversary of the founding of St. Augustine, looms above the placid salt marsh bordering a forest of cypress and palm trees. Paths lead to an ivy-covered chapel housing the **Shrine of Our Lady of La Leche,** originally erected here in 1613 by Spanish settlers.

Old Jail

167 San Marco Ave. ○*Open year-round daily 8:30am–5pm.* ○*Closed Easter Sunday & Dec 25.* ⌨*$5.* 🅿♿*904-829-3800.*

This dark-red Victorian building has a somber history. Erected in 1892 to serve as the St. Johns County Jail and sheriff's residence, the edifice was largely funded by Henry Flagler, eager to see the previous jail relocated from near the entrance to his Ponce de Leon Hotel. Now smartly restored, the Old Jail depicts the extent to which the lives of the sheriff and his family revolved around the care of the prisoners. 🚶‍♂️ Guided tours explore the bedrooms, living room, office and kitchen of the sheriff's residence. The jailhouse itself is divided into separate sections for white, black and female prisoners and those requiring maximum security. The walls bear handcuffs, shackles and a collection of antique handguns used in crimes. Out back stand the gallows used to mete out punishment before the turn of the 19C.

ANASTASIA ISLAND
St. Augustine Lighthouse and Museum
81 Lighthouse Ave.

▶ *Take A1A south and turn left on Old Beach Rd., across from the Alligator Farm.* ⏲*Open year-round daily 9am–6pm (Jul and hols 7pm)* ⏲*Closed Easter Sunday, Thanksgiving Day, Dec 25.* ✆*$9.* 🅿 ✆*904-829-0745. www.staugustinelighthouse.com.*

This brick-and-iron lighthouse, painted with a black-and-white spiral, once guided ships to St. Augustine's shores. The current (1974) structure replaced an earlier wood-and-coquina tower that toppled into the ocean. A panoramic **view** awaits those who climb the 219 stairs to the top. The brick **lightkeeper's residence,** a Victorian structure gutted by fire in 1970, was rebuilt in 1988. Displays recount the lives of the keepers—who operated the light until its automation in 1955.

Anastasia State Park
A1A, just south of Lighthouse Museum. ⏲*Open daily 8am-sunset.* ✆*$8 per car.* ⚠ 🅿 ✆*904-461-2033. www.florida stateparks.org/anastasia.*

Devotees of sun and sand flock to the broad, lovely **beach**⚐⚐ edging this 1,492-acre state park for some of the area's finest fishing, swimming and sunning. A protected saltwater lagoon provides excellent canoeing and windsurfing.

EXCURSIONS
World Golf Village Hall of Fame★
12mi north via I-95, exit 95A. ⏲*Open year-round daily 10am–6pm, Sun noon-6pm.* ✆*$20.50 Hall of Fame; $7.50 IMAX;*

$17 combination ticket. ✕♿🅿 ✆*904-940-4123, 800-WGV-GOLF. www.wgv.com.*

This two-story, 75,000sq ft museum pays tribute to the greatest male and female golfers of past and present, both American and international. Crystal busts display the likenesses of top athletes while visitors watch video highlights of golfers' careers at computer stations. Elsewhere visitors can play an 1880s-style putting green with hickory-shafted putters; have their swings computer-analyzed; sink a final putt in front of a TV camera with a crowd watching; relive highlights of golf's greatest moments in a mini-theater; and play an 18-hole natural grass putting course.

The onsite 300-seat IMAX Theatre shows educational movies and regular feature films.

Fort Matanzas National Monument★★
15mi south via A1A, on Matanzas River south of Crescent Beach. ⏲ *Open year-round daily 9am–5:30pm.* ⏲*Closed Dec 25.* 🅿 ✆*904-471-0116. www.nps.gov/foma.*

A 300-acre park here preserves a coquina watchtower erected in 1742 to defend Matanzas Inlet. Matanza means slaughter, or killing, in Spanish, recalling how, in 1565 some 250 to 300 French Huguenot soldiers and settlers were massacred here by the forces of Pedro Menéndez de Avilés.

The 1740 siege of the Castillo de San Marcos made the Spanish realize the potential for British invasion, and the need for an armed fortification here at the "back door" to St. Augustine. Piers were sunk into the marshy soil of a small barrier island at the inlet's mouth, and the coquina structure soon arose.

In the visitor center, a short film describes the turbulent history and modern restoration of Fort Matanzas. From a nearby landing, board a ferry for the trip across the Matanzas River to the fort itself. Stairs and ladders lead up to the gun balcony, from which you can explore the soldiers' and officers' quarters and the upper balcony. Back

Fort Matanzas National Monument

Visit Florida

on the mainland, a nature trail leads among bayberry, live oak, saw palmetto, Spanish bayonet and red cedar trees to a plaque commemorating the site of the massacre.

🏛 Marineland

18mi south via A1A at 9507 Ocean Shore Blvd. ⏰Open year-round Wed–Mon 8:30am–4:30pm. ⏰Closed Dec 25. 🎫general admission $8.50, child under 13yrs $4. 🛑✕🅿 ☎904 471-1111 Ext. 116 or 877-933-3402 Ext. 116. www.marineland.net.

Marineland's focus is on marine science and dolphin research. Dolphins are the central attraction in the renovated **Dolphin Conservation Center** which recreates eight different dolphin habitats. You can simply visit and look at the dolphins or choose from a number of dolphin encounters. "Touch and feed" is the cheapest at $26, but if you want to get into the water with the dolphins, prices start at $149.

The six-hour "Trainer for a Day" program encompasses a variety of trainer responsibilities from preparing diets and feeding animals to learning about behavior, so that participants are well prepared for their hour-long encounter.

ADDRESSES

🏨 STAY

Visitors **lodging directory** available *(free)* from **St. Johns County Visitors and Convention Bureau.** Accommodations range from hotels *($110–$245)* to motels *($55–$125)* and B&B inns *($100–$225)*. KOA campground: St. Augustine Beach *(☎407-471-3113)*; RV and camping at Indian Forest Campground *(☎904-824-3574)*. 🐾*For St. Augustine lodgings and Where to Eat, see Jacksonville Address Book.*

🏃 SPORTS, RECREATION AND SHOPPING

St. Augustine Beach pier and the lighthouse pier offer excellent **fishing;** bait and tackle shop at 442 Ocean Vista Ave. Some area **golf clubs** welcome visitors: St. Augustine Shores Golf Club *(☎904- 794-GOLF)*; St. Johns County Golf Course *(☎904-825-4900; www. sjcgc.com)*. View St. Augtustine from the air, via parasail, at Municipal Marina. *(☎904-819-0980; www.smilehigh parasail.com)*.

Shopping: Walk along **St. George Street** in the historic district to check out the art galleries and specialtyshops; **Lightner Antique Mall** *(☎904-824-9948)* and **St. Augustine Premium Outlets** with 95 stores *(☎904-825-1555)*. **Belz Factory Outlet World** has 75 outlet stores *(☎904-826-1311)*.

The most popular tourist destination in the world, the Orlando area in central Florida attracts some 50 million visitors annually. Best known as the home of Walt Disney World, the region also boasts the other "super-theme parks" of Universal Studios and SeaWorld as well as many other major visitor attractions. The city of Orlando itself, now the state's largest inland city, serves as the region's hub and and hosts a number of major corporate headquarters. Though mega-highways, lined with chain hotels, resort complexes, eateries and discount shopping malls, now web the flat, lake-pocked subtropical landscape, historic neighborhoods still grace the older parts of its cities and towns. And in the outlying areas, bypassed by the gold rush of

Highlights

1   Gasping at the Gator Jumparoo at **Gatorland** (p167)

2   Viewing exquisite **Tiffany** masterpieces in Winter Park (p175)

3   Immersing yourself in **Sea World**'s watery wonderland (p180)

4   Screaming and laughing aboard **Universal Orlando**'s thrilling rides (p184)

5   Enjoying as much of **WDW** as time and budget allow (p189)

tourism, you can still find something of the old Florida: from spiritual to academic towns; from the sophisticated and artistic to rustic one-horse settlements.

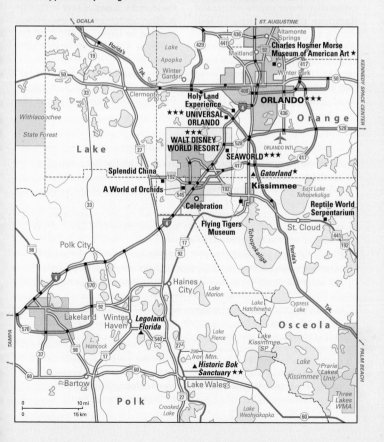

Kissimmee

and around

Two distinct personalities characterize Kissimmee [pronounced kiss-SIM-ee]. A placid residential community spreading along the shores of 29sq mi Lake Tohopekaliga quietly reflects the town's historic role as a center of Florida's cattle industry. Less than a mile away, visitors throng the glittering length of US-192, which extends from downtown to Walt Disney World, giving rise to the city's moniker, the "Gateway to Disney."

A BIT OF HISTORY

The area was not permanently occupied until American cowmen settled here in the 1840s. After the federal government ceded overflowed lands to the states for reclamation, Pennsylvania industrialist **Hamilton Disston** purchased four million acres in the swampy Kissimmee, Caloosahatchee and Peace river valleys. He established a land company at Allendale, a tiny settlement that he renamed Kissimmee and set about dredging canals linking lakes in the region. The South Florida Railway landed its terminus at Kissimmee and the town developed as a center for shipbuilding, agriculture and transportation. Demand for beef throughout the first half of the 20C fueled the region's cattle industry.

The opening of Disney World in 1971 foretold Kissimmee's metamorphosis from farm community to tourist cen-

- ▶ **Population:** 58,167.
- **Info:** 1925 E. Irlo Bronson Memorial Hwy. ℘407-742-8200; www.visit kissimmee.com
- **Location:** Kissimmee is located 10mi east of Walt Disney World on US-192, and south of downtown Orlando.
- **Don't Miss:** Gatorland is a quirky slice of Old Florida. The Saturday Night Classic Car parade at Old Town..
- **Timing:** Allow two to three days to see most of the sights below.

The Lay of the Land

As you move southwest, farther into the interior, the land becomes less developed and more devoted to agriculture. The towns of Lakeland and Lake Wales sit at the heart of the state's citrus-growing region and offer a quieter, more nostalgic atmosphere, as well as a subtle change in terrain. This area, at the southern end of the state's north–south-running Central Highlands, occupies a gently rolling landscape. Iron Mountain, just north of Lake Wales, is one of the peninsula's highest points at 298ft.

Central Florida experienced its first influx of settlers—largely north Florida cattlemen who were attracted to the area's lush grasslands—after the end of the Second Seminole War in 1842. Forty years later, towns mushroomed along the line of Henry Plant's **South Florida Railway.**

In contrast to the wealthy winter visitors who arrived by train in the early 1900s, mid-century tourists were middle-class families traveling by car. The ever-growing pace of tourism increased exponentially in the early 1970s with the opening of Walt Disney World 20mi southwest of Orlando. The corridor stretching between the two and south to Kissimmee quickly became a commercial mecca, while the area southwest of Kissimmee has managed to maintain its traditional base in the citrus economy. Today Orlando and its environs rank among the fastest-growing metropolitan areas in the US.

ter. US-192 became a lively corridor of amenities designed to accommodate the flood of Disney-bound visitors. As Kissimmee's population boomed, cattle ranchers retreated south to less populous areas. Today over 4 million tourists annually flock to the putt-putt golf courses, water parks, motels, shopping centers and amusement parks that line both sides of US-192. In the evening, crowds fill "dinner shows," where meals match the theme of the accompanying live entertainment; themes run the gamut from medieval England to Arabian nights to gangland Chicago.

Although development pushes eastward toward the town of St. Cloud, Kissimmee's old commercial area appears as it might have in the days before Disney. Placid Lakefront Park extends along the northern shore of **Lake Toho-pekaliga** a few blocks from downtown. A stroll along **Broadway Avenue** (south of US-192 via Main St.) reveals charming storefronts that are reminiscent of Kissimmee's late-19C days as a cattle town.

SIGHTS
👤👤 Gatorland★
6mi north of Kissimmee at 14501 S. Orange Blossom Tr. (US-17/92/441). 🕐Open year-round daily 9am–5pm. 👓$22.99., child 3–12yrs $14.99. 👥🅿 ☎407-855-5496 or 800-393-5297. www.gatorland.com.
What this park lacks in techno-magic, it makes up for with the charm common to 1950s-era theme parks. Gatorland was founded in 1949 as a combination amusement park and alligator farm selling alligators for their meat and skins. Gaping alligator jaws "swallow" visitors at the entrance to the gift shop. For a quick orientation, take a narrated chug around the park on the Gatorland Express. From the **observation tower,** views extend over the park and its 10-acre bird sanctuary. Plan to attend the live shows held throughout the day, most famously the **"Gator Jumparoo,"** during which alligators lunge 4ft out of the water at chicken pieces dangled by handlers. At the park's south end, a rope bridge leads to a boardwalk stroll through cypress swamp.

Gator Gully Splash Park is a new kids' area featuring a variety of ingenious themed ways for kids to soak themselves and their friends.

👤👤 Green Meadows Farm
1368 S. Poinciana Blvd. ▷ Follow US 192 for 3mi east of I-4 to S. Poinciana Blvd. Turn right. 🕐Open daily 9:30am–4pm (last tour). 👓$21. ☎407-846-0770. www.greenmeadowsfarm.com.
🐄If you prefer real cows, chickens, and geese, to Disney animatronics take a two-hour guided tour of this 40-acre farm and you'll encounter nearly 300 animals. What makes it special is that everyone can try their hand at milking a cow, feeding a goat and (hardest of all) catching a chicken. Pony rides for kids, and hayrides for all, add to the fun.

EXCURSIONS
👤👤 Legoland Florida and Splash Island Waterpark
34mi south of Kissimmee.
▷ From US-192 take I-4 west 10mi to US-27 south; continue 18mi. www.legolandfloridaresort.com
Opening in late 2011 on the site of the much-loved Cypress Gardens–Florida's original theme park, which closed after 73 years in 2009–this will be the biggest Legoland Park yet and will offer a mix of more than 50 rides, shows and attractions, including spectacular Lego models and other interactive elements.
The historic gardens that Cypress Gardens were so famous for will be maintained as part of the park, and Splash Island Waterpark will also be kept as a separately ticketed admission.

Boggy Creek Airboat Rides
2001 E. Southport Rd., Kissimmee.
▷ Take US 192 east to Poinciana Blvd. Go 19mi south until road deadends (road changes name to Southport). 🕐Open year-round daily 9am-5:30pm, every half-hour (no need to book). 👓$25.95. ☎407-344-9550. www.bcairboats.com.
Check out central Florida wildlife and wetlands on an airboat ride on Lake Tohopekaliga ("Lake Toho"). The 18-passenger airboats travel at some 45mph

Tower, Historic Bok Sanctuary

Visit Florida

and are noisy, so it won't be a mellow ride, but it will be scenic and fun. Night rides also go in search of the glinting red eyes of alligators.

Historic Bok Sanctuary★★

35mi south of Kissimmee. From US-192 take I-4 west 10mi to US-27 south.

◖ *Take US-27 south to Burns Ave. (Rte. 17A) and follow signs to the gardens at 1151 Tower Blvd.* ◷*Open year-round daily 8am–6pm.* ☎*$10, $16 inc. Pinewood Estate.* ✕♿🅿 ✆*863-676-1408. www.boksanctuary.org.*

Born in the Netherlands, **Edward William Bok** (1863–1930) worked in US publishing houses before founding his own publishing company in 1886. In 1920 his autobiography, *The Americanization of Edward Bok,* won a Pulitzer Prize. Bok decided to create a nature sanctuary as a gift to the American people. He invited Frederick Law Olmsted Jr., son of the famed creator of New York City's Central Park, to transform a sandy, pine-covered site atop Iron Mountain into a botanical haven. The 130-acre park was dedicated in 1929 at ceremonies led by President Calvin Coolidge.

Gardens and Tower – Begin at the **visitor center** *(follow signs from parking area)* to view displays on the gardens' history and an introductory film. From here, wander along bark-mulched paths amid lush stands of live oaks, conifers, palm trees and ferns. Ever-changing splashes of color are painted seasonally on this green canvas by flowering plants, among them azaleas *(in bloom Dec–Mar)* and camellias *(in bloom Nov–Mar).*

Window by the Pond, a small wooden hut fitted with a large plate-glass window, welcomes visitors to sit and watch the play of life unfolding in a freshwater pond. The marble **excedra,** a monumental semicircular conversation seat, marks the 298ft summit of Iron Mountain, considered the highest point in peninsular Florida. Encircled by a placid moat, the much-photographed 205ft Gothic Revival **tower** *(interior not open to the public),* of pink-and-gray-streaked Georgia marble and coquina, is the focal point of the gardens. Designed by Philadelphia architect Milton B. Medary, it is embellished with turquoise and brown earthenware tiles, sculptures, friezes and intricately wrought ironwork. Its famous **carillon** of 57 bronze bells ring out every half hour and give 45min concerts each day at 1pm and 3pm.

Warbird Adventures

Kissimmee Gateway Airport , 233 N. Hoagland Blvd. ◷*Open year-round daily 9am–5pm (closed Sun Jul–Oct).* ☎*museum $6; flight from $240.* ✆*407-870-7366. www.warbirdadventures. com, www.kissimmeeairmuseum.com. Reservation recommended for flights.*

This is arguably Florida's ultimate thrill. You are not here just for the ride and this ain't no Disney simulator! Under expert supervision (no previous flying experience necessary) guests get to actually take the front-seat controls of the premier fighter-trainer plane of Word War II, the North American T-6 TEXAN. The instructor handles the taxiing, take-off and landing but up in the air you get to take the controls for either 15min, 30min or 1 hour. Whether you want a thrilling aerobatic adventure or a smooth straight-and- level flight, the experience is completely tailored to your bravery, skills and, of course, budget.

There is also a museum on site with 16 actual planes, and helicopter rides are on offer.

Planning for the Theme Parks

Avoid the crowds. Research when the parks are least crowded (☞ see the theme parks own websites for help on this). Express passes are expensive but free timed rides systems are in operation on many rides at WDW.

Arrive early. You don't want to waste a single minute so if you want to be the first in line, arrive at least half an hour before official opening time and allow 20 minutes to get from the car park to the park entrance (by shuttle bus/tram/people-mover) and through the turnstile

Omaka Rocka, Aquatica

© SeaWorld Parks & Entertainment

Budgeting. If you intend visiting more than one park during your vacation (and most visitors do), research multiple park tickets. Always buy online for the best prices and never trust third parties offering cheap tickets (particularly if they are linked to time-share). Add car-parking charges (min. $12 per day), and food and drink, which is not cheap in the parks, plus of course souvenirs for the kids! Almost every park has splash ride attractions. Great if the weather is hot and sunny, not so great if it's cold and dull. Invest in ponchos—buying in advance is always much cheaper than in the theme parks.

Late Night Openings. Look out, in both senses, for these. Fireworks and lasers, Grand Parades, Sunset Celebrations and so on are a wonderful way to round off an unforgettable day, but it also makes what can be a tiring day even longer. Moreover, if you want to see what's going on, you'll need to stake out your spot at least 30 minutes to an hour before the event for Disney processions and the illuminations show at Epcot.

Special Events and Holidays. Unless you're a theme park veteran and know the ropes, avoid holiday periods such as Christmas and Halloween, as this is when the crowds are at their biggest.

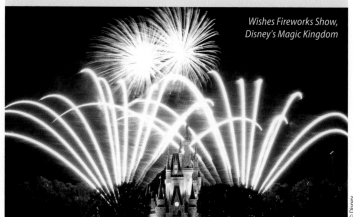

Wishes Fireworks Show, Disney's Magic Kingdom

© Disney

Orlando★★★

Once a sleepy orange-producing area, sprawling metropolitan Orlando now ranks as one of the nation's fastest-growing cities, as well as a tourist mecca attracting more than 50 million visitors annually. While the rapidly expanding southwestern corridor is filled with outlet malls, hotels, restaurants and entertainment complexes, the older, lake-dotted downtown, with its historic architecture, retains the charm of early 20C Florida.

▶ **Population:** 1.8 million.
 Michelin Map: p165, 171.
 Info: 8723 International Drive. ℘407-363-5872; www.orlandoinfo.com.
 Parking: Downtown has several parking lots.
 Don't Miss: Orlando Science Center.
 Timing: Allow at least a week here if you're visiting the theme parks.
 Kids: There's hardly an attraction in town that is not Kid friendly!

A BIT OF HISTORY

The US government established several forts in the area to protect pioneers during the Second Seminole War. The settlement that arose around **Fort Gatlin** (1838) formed the nucleus of the future city of Orlando. By the 1860s the embryonic town occupied part of a vast cotton plantation. Citrus intruded as a major crop in the 1880s when the new South Florida Railway gave local growers access to wider markets. Orlando's economy remained rooted in agriculture through the first half of the 20C until Disney forever changed the city's face.

The numbers today are mind-boggling. The city has nearly 500 hotels and 113,000 guest rooms, 26,000 vacation home rentals, more than 5,100 restaurants, 95 attractions, and nine shopping malls. Demographic and financial forecasters predict that, with Walt Disney World and Universal Orlando's continual expansion and the city's attraction as a convention center, Orlando will continue to be one of the fastest-growing areas in the US in the 21C.

DOWNTOWN

This area has been the city's administrative hub since Orlando's incorporation in 1875. Though it fell victim to the decay that afflicted most downtown areas in the mid-20C, the downtown has been revitalized, evolving into a lively night spot popular both with residents and visitors. An eight-square-block core, centered on Orange Avenue, is designated the **Orlando Downtown Historic District.**

Several residential historic districts surround downtown. The **Lake Cherokee District** (south edge of downtown) and the **Eola Heights District** (northeast of downtown), feature fine examples of Mediterranean, Colonial, Classical and Tudor Revival houses, as well as Art Deco structures, bungalows and substantial Victorian constructions built between 1875 and 1930.

Orange Avenue★

Old Orlando's main business thoroughfare holds an eclectic mix of architecture that reflects the city's past and present. Anchoring the south end of the avenue, the classically inspired, domed **City Hall** (1992), is fronted by an expansive fountain plaza. Off the interior lobby, the **Terrace Gallery** displays changing exhibits devoted to the works of regional artists. A block north, in the shadow of the SunTrust Center tower, is the old **First National Bank Building (A)** (corner of Orange and Church Sts.). Now part of Valencia Community College, the 1930 structure combines Classical Revival composition with Art Deco details. **McCrory Five & Dime** (corner of Orange and Pine Sts.) was once the largest McCrory store in the south, but now contains a game arcade. Its streamlined, horizontal lines exemplify the 1930s Art

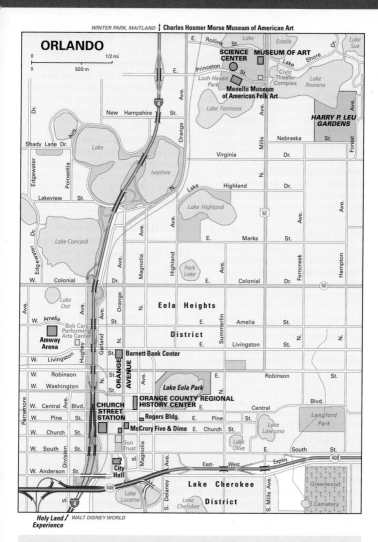

WINTER PARK, MAITLAND | Charles Hosmer Morse Museum of American Art

Holy Land / WALT DISNEY WORLD
Experience

The Dawn of Disney

In 1965, having secretly purchased almost 30,000 acres in Orange and Osceola counties, **Walt Disney,** the animated-film wizard and creator of California's Disneyland, announced plans to build a theme park outside Orlando. Overnight, land values in the area skyrocketed; throughout the rest of the decade, development engulfed the communities to the southwest along the I-4 corridor. Walt Disney World opened to great fanfare in 1971. SeaWorld followed two years later, and Universal Studios Florida joined the local theme-park ranks in 1990.

In the intervening years, metropolitan Orlando tripled its population and now boasts the largest concentration of hotel rooms in the US. The area ranks as one of the top commercial tourist destinations in the world. Service-oriented development has produced endless outlet malls, restaurants and entertainment facilities and, in turn, created more jobs: service sector employment has increased nearly 138 percent within the last decade.

GETTING THERE

Orlando International Airport (MCO): 7mi south of city; information booth *(open daily 6am–8pm; ✆407-825-2352)*. Transportation to downtown: **limo** *($125);* **taxi** *($30–$35);* 24hr-**shuttle** vans *($17 one way)* provided by Mears Transporation Group *(✆407-423-5566; www.mearstransportation.com);* **public transportation** *(bus #11: Mon–Sat 4:45am–10:45pm, Sun 5:45am–6:45pm; bus #51: Mon–Sat 5am–8:15pm, Sun 5:15am–7:15pm);* and hotel courtesy shuttles.
Amtrak **train** stations: 1400 Sligh Blvd., Orlando, and 150 W. Morse Blvd., Winter Park *(✆800-872-7245. www.amtrak.com).* Greyhound **bus** station: 555 N. John Young Pkwy. *(✆407-292-3424 or 800-231-2222; www.greyhound.com).*

GETTING AROUND

Local **bus service:** Lynx *(year-round daily; $1; transfers 10¢; schedule & route information: ✆841-8240).* The **Beeline** (Rte. 528), East-West Expressway and Central Florida GreeneWay are **toll roads.** Downtown **shuttle** service (free): Lymno *(Mon–Thu 7am–10:30pm, Fri 7am–midnight, Sat 10am–midnight, Sun 10am–10pm, every 5min; 407-841-5969; www.goLynx.com).* I-Ride **trolley system** services the International Drive area *(daily 7am–midnight; every 15 minutes; $1.25 each way; all-day ride $4; ✆866-243-7483; www.iridetrolley.com).* Metered downtown street parking 75¢/hr: average rate for parking garages $1/hr, $7/day. **Parking** information ✆407-246-2154.

VISITOR INFORMATION

Orlando/Orange County Convention and Visitors Bureau, 6700 Forum Dr., Suite 100, Orlando FL 32821; **Official Visitor Center,** 8723 International Dr., Suite 101 *(open year-round daily 8am–7pm, closed Dec 25; ✆ 407-363-5872; www.orlandoinfo.com).* The free **Orlando Magicard** *(www.orlandoinfo.com/magicard)* offers the holder savings on accommodations, attractions, dining and shopping.

Moderne style. Several blocks away *(nos. 37–39 Magnolia Ave)*, the Queen Anne-style **Rogers Building** (c.1906) boasts a rare facade of pressed zinc panels. At the north end of downtown rises the **Barnett Bank Center** *(formerly the Du Pont Center; Orange Ave. and Livingston St.)*, a lofty, three-towered high-rise topped by silver spires. Completed in 1987, the building displays works of art, including Renoir's *Washerwoman,* in its public courtyard and lobby areas.

👪 Orange County Regional History Center★

65 E. Central Blvd. in Heritage Sq.
🕐*Open year-round Mon–Sat 10am–5pm, Sun noon–5pm.* 🕐*Closed major holidays.* 👓*$9.* ♿ *✆407-836-8500. www.thehistorycenter.org.*
Housed in the former county courthouse (1927), this facility features four floors of engaging exhibits, many of them interactive, that highlight Central Florida's colorful history. Dominating the entry is the two-floor-tall orange **dome** with moving model icons from manatees to space shuttles. View the introductory video *(15min)* in a rocking chair in the Orientation Theater, then enter a re-created Timucuan village settle into a Florida cowboy's saddle, walk within a mock citrus grove and see how Disney's Cinderella's Castle was constructed. One of the original courtrooms is open for viewing *(third floor).*
Family Funshops offer families with young children the opportunity to engage in fun educational activities; adults can attend dinners with artists and authors.

Lake Eola Park

Central Blvd. and Rosalind Ave.
The city's most popular park offers a band shell for concerts, swan-shaped pedal boats, a playground and a cafe. This is the best place downtown for a pleasant stroll or quiet break. Attractive landscaping rims the lake, as does a pathway for walking, jogging and skating. Numerous benches provide good

Orlando Museum of Art

Visit Florida

spots to view the city skyline and the lake's fountain, which is illuminated at night.

ADDITIONAL SIGHTS

Orlando Museum of Art ★

2416 N. Mills Ave., in Loch Haven Park. ⏰*Open year-round Tue–Fri 10am–4pm, Sat & Sun noon–4pm.* ⏰*Closed major holidays.* ✒*$8.* ♿ 🅿 ✆*407-896-4231. www.omart.org.*

Formed as a local art center in 1924, the museum doubled its gallery space in 1997. The heart of the permanent collection is rotated in four contemporary galleries. More than 600 works of **19C and 20C American art** include paintings by John Singer Sargent, George Inness, Georgia O'Keeffe, Maurice Prendergast and Gene Davis. Pre-Columbian cultures are represented by Western Mexican, Peruvian and Costa Rican pottery, jade, stone and textile artifacts dating from 1200 BC to AD 1521.

An African collection features Yoruba beadwork, Asante statuary and Benin metalwork.

👥 Orlando Science Center ★

777 E. Princeton St., in Loch Haven Park. ⏰*Open Thu–Tue 10am–5pm.* ⏰*Closed Easter Sun, Thanksgiving Day & Dec 24–25.* ✒*$17, child 3–11yrs $12.* ✕♿ 🅿 ✆*407-514-2000. www.osc.org.*

This impressive cylindrical building with its four-story central atrium opened in 1997. On Level 1 *(ground floor),* Nature-Works features lifelike dioramas of Florida ecosystems, including cypress and mangrove swamps (with real turtles and baby alligators) and a coral reef. Level 2 is dominated by Science City, whose interactive displays relate to mathematics, physical sciences and engineering, among them a power station and a suspension bridge. On Level 3, Cosmic Tourist instructs visitors in geology and astronomy. Level 4 features human anatomy in BodyZone, and Tech Works emphasizes applied technologies, especially computer simulation and laser optics. New exhibits are added periodically.

The center's two theaters—one for large-format films and planetarium shows, and the other for live performances and science demonstrations—are complemented by the rooftop **Crosby Observatory** (⏰*open Fri & Sat, weather permitting),* which houses Florida's largest refractor telescope. With 207,000sq ft of floor space, the Science Center is among the first in the country to tailor its exhibits and programs to mandated public-school science and math curricula requirements.

Between the Science Center and Museum of Art in Loch Haven Park stands **Fire Station #3,** Orange County's oldest standing firehouse (1927). The brick structure holds Orlando's original fleet of American LaFrance fire trucks, as well as 19C and 20C fire-fighting equipment.

Lakeridge Winery & Vineyards

20mi west of Orlando. ▶ *Take the East-West Expressway west to the Florida Turnpike; head north on turnpike to Exit 285 (Rte. 50 west). Follow Rte. 50 west to US-27 and go north 5.5mi to vineyard.* ◑*Open year-round daily 10am (Sun 11am)–5pm.* ℗ *800-768-9463. www.lakeridgewinery.com*

Some 66 acres of native muscadine and Florida hybrid bunch grapes grow in the well-drained Lakeridge soil, where European varieties cannot survive. A guided tour includes a 12min introductory video and a view of the winery and bottling room from a second-story deck. At the end of the tour, visitors get to taste the vineyard's wines. Grapes are harvested in late June and early August.

Mennello Museum of American Folk Art

900 E. Princeton St., diagonally opposite the Science Center. ◑*Open year-round Tue–Sat 10:30am–4:30pm, Sun noon–4:30pm.* ◐*$4.* *407-246-4278. www.mennellomuseum.com.*

Installed in a restored mansion overlooking Lake Formosa, this museum is one of the country's few that showcase American folk art exclusively.

Most of the gallery space is reserved for Michael and Marilyn Mennello's definitive collection of works by Maine-born artist **Earl Cunningham** (1893–1977), who painted in St. Augustine for decades. Changing exhibits of other folk art, often whimsical and humorous, and a small well-stocked gift shop occupy remaining rooms. Be sure to stroll the lovely grounds at the rear of the mansion, where you may encounter Red and Fuzz, the museum's resident felines.

Harry P. Leu Gardens★

1920 N. Forest Ave. Purchase tickets in the Garden House. ◑*Open year-round daily 9am–5pm.* ◐*Closed Dec 25.* ◐*$7 (free first Mon of month).* ℗

407-246-2620. www.leugardens.org.

Orlando businessman and exotic-plant collector Harry P. Leu donated his house and 50-acre botanical reserve to the city in 1961. Situated along the southern shore of Lake Rowena, the gardens are renowned for their 2,000-plus **camellia collection** *(in peak bloom from Dec–mid-Feb).* Some 1,000 roses representing 250 varieties color the largest formal **rose garden** in the state *(in bloom from Mar–Jan).*

A small conservatory devoted to orchids, ferns and bromeliads stands near the southeast corner of the garden.

Built as a farmhouse in 1888, the two-story white frame **Leu House Museum** was enlarged by subsequent owners—including the Leu family, who lived here from 1936 to 1961 *(visit by 30min guided tour only, daily 10am–3:30pm; closed Jul).* The gracious Garden House holds a gift shop.

INTERNATIONAL DRIVE

Located approximately 8mi southwest of downtown Orlando, I-Drive, as it is locally known, runs for 7 miles from Route 417 north through SeaWorld, to the point where the Belz Outlet Mall meets Universal Orlando at the Florida Turnpike. This major thoroughfare is the focus of the city's tourism development, comprising hundreds of shops, dozens of restaurants and a variety of tourist haunts, including the following *(www.internationaldriveorlando.com).*

Wet 'N Wild

6200 International Dr. ◑*Open year-round from 9:30am/10am.* ◐*Closing times vary. See schedule online.* ◐*$47.95, child (3–9yrs) $41.95. Half-price admission in afternoon: see scehdule.* *407-351-1800 or 800-992-9453. www.wetnwildorlando.com.*

Watery thrill rides are the draw here. The Blast propels you down a 390ft stream with jets and gusts of water; meanwhile, riders on the Storm are washed down a towering chute, then swirled around in a bowl at high speeds, finally tumbling into a splash landing. Slightly tamer is the Disco

Wet 'n Wild

Visit Florida

H20, a retro raft ride through the 70s. Beyond all that, you can slide into pools from high towers, aim squirt cannons at your friends and boogie-board on artificial surf. On cool days, the action happens in the heated pools.

Ripley's Believe It or Not Orlando Odditorium

8201 International Dr. Open year-round daily 9am–1am. $18.95, child (4–12yrs) $11.95. 407-363-4418. www.ripleysorlando.com.

Housed in a structure that looks like it fell into one of Florida's sinkholes, this homage to the weirdly intriguing includes: a Rolls Royce made from toothpicks, a 13ft jade rickshaw, X-rays of a dog that swallowed a knife, P.T. Barnum's fake mermaid and many many other strange paraphernalia.

SkyVenture

6805 Visitors Circle. Open year-round daily 11.30am–9pm (Fri–Sat 10pm). from $44.95. 407-903-1150. www.skyventureorlando.com.

At this indoor skydiving wind tunnel, you can experience the sensation of freefall without needing a parachute, plane, or any previous skydiving experience. The IFLY experience is so similar to real skydiving that professional skydivers use the wind tunnel for training; yet it's also safe enough for kids aged 3 years and up to enjoy.

Wonder Works

9067 International Dr. Open daily 9am–midnight. $19.95, child (4–12yrs) $14.95. 407-351-8800. www.wonder worksonline.com.

This high-tech interactive amusement center is built to resemble a three-story mansion turned upside down, as if flipped by a Caribbean windstorm. The interior is filled with more than 100 interactive, high-tech games, where you can design and ride in your own rollercoaster, experience a virtual earthquake and much more. For an extra charge you can also play in the world's largest laser-tag arena (*$4.95*), go ape on a 3-story Indoor Ropes Course (*$9.95*), experience a 4-D Extreme Motion ride (*$9.95*), and more.

EXCURSIONS
Charles Hosmer Morse Museum of American Art★

445 N. Park Ave, Winter Park (5mi north of downtown Orlando). Take I-4 north to Exit 45 (Fairbanks Ave.) Go east on Fairbanks to Park Ave. Turn left onto Park Ave. Open year-round Tue–Sat 9:30am–4pm (Fri 8pm Nov–Apr), Sun 1pm–4pm. Closed Jan 1, Thanksgiving Day, Dec. 25. $3. Free Nov–Apr 4pm–8pm. 407-645-5311. www.morsemuseum.org.

The world's most comprehensive collection of works from the studios of artist **Louis Comfort Tiffany** (1848–1933) forms the centerpiece of this 4,000-piece collection of late 19C and early 20C American and European paintings, decorative and graphic arts, American art pottery, Art Nouveau jewelry and Arts and Crafts furniture. Founder Jeannette McKean named the museum after her industrialist grandfather, who retired in Winter Park. First shown at Winter Park's Rollins College in 1942, the Morse collection moved in 1995 to its present 10,000sq ft quarters, specifically designed to showcase large window panels and architectural elements.

Framed by two marble columns with capitals of Favrile glass daffodils from Tiffany's Long Island mansion, the 20ft-high Tiffany window gallery displays the exquisite **leaded windows** that he designed for the 1893 World's Columbian Exposition in Chicago. Another gallery is devoted to the **chapel interior** (1893) Tiffany created for the same exposition. Holdings include the stunning **Magnolia Window** from the Tiffany family's New York City mansion, as well as glass panels by William Morris, Frank Lloyd Wright and John Lafarge. Among the other beautifully preserved **Tiffany pieces** that occupy the major-

ity of the museum's 19 galleries (with more to come in 2011) are lamps, vases, jewelry, blown glass and pottery.

Wekiwa Springs State Park
1800 Wekiwa Cir, Apopka.
⊳ *Take I-4 exit 94 to Rte 434. Turn left on Rte 434, right on Weikwa Spgs Rd.* ⏱*Open daily, 8am-sunset.* ⊛*$6 per vehicle.* ⚠ ♿ ℘*407-884-2008. www. floridastateparks.org/wekiwasprings.*
This 6,400acre natural area is a great escape when you've had a bit too much of Orlando's concrete, crowds, and artificial everything, especially on weekdays, when you might have it all to yourself. Located at the headwaters of the tea-colored Wekiwa River, the park is a lovely place to paddle (canoe and kayak rentals are available: ℘*407-884-4311; www. canoewekiva.com*), especially along Rock Springs Run.

🚶 Thirteen miles of hiking trails take in some unspoiled Old Florida landscape, and give you a sense of what life was like before Disney. Watch for egrets and alligators.

ADDRESSES

🏠STAY

Area visitors' guide including **lodging directory** available *(free)* from **Orlando /Orange County Convention and Visitors Bureau,** or visit *www.orlando info.com/accommodations*.

All reputable hotels offer transportation to Disney and Universal attractions. For information on accommodations within the Disney parks, see Walt Disney World Resort section.

Hotel reservation service ℘800-950-0232. **Central Reservation Service** operates 24hr, courtesy phones at airport (℘*800-339-4116*). Accomodations range from luxury **hotels** *($150-$400)* to **motels** *($55-$125)* and condominiums **Youth Hostel:** Palm Lakefront Resort & Hostel *($15-$19/person)* ℘407-396-1759. *www.orlandohostels.com*.

Campgrounds and RV parks available in area.

$$$$ The Cabins at Disney's Fort Wilderness Resort – *4510 Fort Wilderness Tr., Lake Buena Vista.* ✕♿🅿🌊 ℘*407-939-6244. http://disney world.disney.go.com/resorts. 408 cabins. (Campsites also available $).*
The ultimate in resort self-catering, this collection of log houses and cabins is complemented by campsites designed for pitching tents or hooking up trailers and mobile homes. Outdoor grills are plentiful and activities range from hay- and pony rides to volleyball, biking, fishing and basketball; youngsters especially will enjoy the petting farm. Nightlife centers on a musical review *(nightly)*, where ticket holders enjoy an all-you-can-eat feast and sing-alongs.

$$$$ Disney's Grand Floridian Resort & Spa – *4401 Grand Floridian Way, Lake Buena Vista.* ✕♿🅿🌊 ℘*407-824-3000. http://disneyworld.disney.go.com/resort. 900 rooms.* Disney's most luxurious property is a Victorian-era waterside complex set on 40 acres along Magic

Kingdom's monorail route. The flagship resort's five-story lobby—with carved moldings, an aviary and an open-cage elevator—is topped by illuminated stained-glass domes. Elegant guest rooms feature late-19C-style woodwork and old-fashioned sink fittings. While parents are enjoying the full-service spa, kids can frolic at The Mouseketeer Clubhouse. The French-inspired menu at **Citricos** includes entrées such as the signature braised veal shank or bouillabaise.

$$$$ Loews Portofino Bay Hotel – 5601 Universal Blvd., Orlando. ✕🚗🅿 🏊 ☎407-503-1000 or 888-837-2273. www.loewshotels.com. 750 rooms. Operated by the Loews Corp. on Universal theme-park property, this colorful hotel edges a large body of water like the bayside Italian fishing village for which it is named. Tile roofs slant out over wrought-iron balconies and many rooms overlook a cobblestone piazza. Rooms are spacious, with four-poster beds, pillowtop mattresses, armoires and marble-accented bathrooms. There are even manicured, Italian-style bocce-ball courts. All guests are admitted to Universal parks an hour before the general public via water taxi across the lagoon.

$$$$ The Peabody Orlando – 9801 International Dr., Orlando. ✕🚗🅿🏊 ☎407-352-4000 or 800-PEABODY. www.peabodyorlando.com. 891 rooms. The eastern outpost of Memphis' original Peabody is in the Plaza International district. Potted palms, bamboo furnishings, and a two-story waterfall fill the lobby atrium. Twice a day the red carpet is rolled out for the resident ducks to march to the marble fountain. Light woods and pastels extend the hotel's tropical theme to the spacious bedrooms. The venerable **Dux** restaurant envelops diners in its signature motif—paintings of waterfowl on the walls and duck-shaped butter patties. The "haute global" cuisine includes such dishes as grilled veal chop with foie gras sauce and yellow tail snapper with artichoke and apricot chutney.

$$$ Disney's Animal Kingdom Lodge – 2901 Osceola Pkwy., Bay Lake. ✕🚗🅿🏊 ☎407-934-7639. http://disney world.disney.go.com/resorts/animal-kingdom-lodge. 1,293 rooms. When booking a reservation at this horseshoe-shaped lodge, ask for a Savannah View room, which offers vistas of Animal Kingdom's grazing animals from its private balcony. Bring binoculars and also a zoom camera, because some creatures come within 30ft. Other rooms overlook the parking lot or the 9,000sq ft swimming pool. Decorated with African spears and masks, the lobby has a stream running through it and a huge mud fireplace. Enjoy breakfast in Boma-Flavors of Africa, a family restaurant, and later stop for Kenyan coffee in Victoria Falls Lounge.

$$$ Eō Inn & Spa – 227 N. Eola Dr., Orlando. ✕🚗🅿 ☎407-481-8485 or 888-481-8488. www.eoinn.com. 17 rooms. Overlooking Lake Eola in Thornton Park and facing downtown Orlando's skyline, this upscale boutique hotel operates in a lavishly remodeled 1923 building. Luxurious guest quarters are electronically equipped to serve as a workplace around the clock. New Age music and soothing sounds of forests and seashores issue forth from each room's CD player. The third floor has a rooftop terrace where guests can soak up Florida sunshine and enjoy iced beverages; continental breakfasts are served here. Open to the public, the full-service day spa is up top along with a popular bakery-cafe, where locals and guests enjoy muffins and lattes.

$$$ Renaissance Orlando at Sea World – 6677 Sea Harbor Dr., Orlando. ✕🚗🅿 ☎407-351-5555 or 800-327-6677. www.renaissancehotels.com. 778 rooms. The exterior of the ten floor hotel at this massive, 27-acre complex, situated close to SeaWorld and other area attractions, is architecturally uninspiring, but its interior reveals a cavernous, sunlit atrium sheltering 13,000 plants, an aviary, a waterfall and a koi-filled fish pond. Guest quarters are large and attractively done in gold, green and teak. Facilities include basketball, volleyball and lighted tennis courts. From some rooms, guests have views of SeaWorld's roller coaster. Equated with excellent seafood and sterling service, **Atlantis** satisfies gourmets with offerings such as its signature lobster bisque and Florida grouper with honey bourbon sauce. A new spa adds to the extensive list of amenites here.

$$ The Courtyard at Lake Lucerne – *211 N. Lucerne Circle East, Orlando.* ♿⛶ *407-648-5188 or 800-444-5289. www. orlandohistoricinn.com. 30 rooms.* Arranged around a tropical courtyard, this complex of four historic residences (1893–1940) overlooks downtown's Lake Lucerne: each one reflects the period of its heyday, from Victorian jewel-tone fabrics and sleigh beds to offbeat Art Deco suites with kitchenettes. The Norment-Parry Inn, built in 1883, claims to be Orlando's oldest house; its six rooms are furnished with European and American antiques. Breakfast is served on the veranda of the antebellum manor that boasts three lavish Edwardian guest rooms as well as stately columns, stained-glass, and a marble fireplace.

♀/EAT

$$$$$ Victoria and Albert's – *Disney's Grand Floridian Hotel, Lake Buena Vista.* ⛶*407-939-3463. http://disneyworld. disney.go.com/resort.*
Disney's most luxurious restaurant (considered to be one of the top tables in Orlando) is decked out in Victorian finery, lavish decor, a harpist, personalized menus, and a seven-course tasting menu. Entrees feature elk, buffalo, Kobe beef, and quail. You'll pay extra for luxury touches like Iranian caviar. Surprisingly, they offer some delicious vegetarian choices as well. This may be your most expensive dinner out in Orlando, but it will definitely be memorable. *Dinner only.*

$$$$ Emeril's – *6000 Universal Blvd., Universal Studios CityWalk, Orlando.* ⛶*407-224-2424. www.emerils.com.* Famed New Orleans chef and TV star Emeril Lagasse arrived in Orlando with his signature "Bam!" in 1999. The place has been standing room only almost

ever since. Insiders sometimes take dinner at the bar because it beats the reservations backlog. Emeril is only in town once a month on average, so chef Barnard Carmouche holds the fort for him, serving up **Cajun-Creole** specialties like andouille-crusted redfish with shoestring fries and swoon-inducing sweets like chocolate soufflé with Grand Marnier, fresh berries and hot chocolate sauce. In the cellar some 12,000 bottles await uncorking.

$$$ Artist Point – *Wilderness Lodge, Walt Disney World, Lake Buena Vista.* ⛶*407-939-3463. http://disneyworld. disney.go.com/dining/artist-point.* Enter this **steakhouse** restaurant through the stunning lobby of Disneys' Wilderness Lodge and you're already wowed—the massive stone fireplace and totem poles recreate the rustic grandeur of national park lodges. The food doesn't disappoint. Themed as "northwestern cuisine," the restaurant's signature dish is cedar-plank salmon served with potato purée and roasted fennel. Another favorite is the grilled buffalo steak, low in fat and melt-in-your mouth tender. They will also do wine pairings with your meal from an extensive Pacific Coast wine list. *Reservations essential.*

$$$ Chatham's Place – *7575 Dr. Phillips Blvd., Orlando.* ♿ ⛶*407-345-2992. http:// chathamsplace.com.* This intimate, privately owned **Continental** restaurant is a comfortable change from all the city's theme-park hoopla. The smiling staff are friendly, and they do a fine job with the restaurant's signature dish, black Florida grouper slathered in pecan butter with a dash of cayenne. The rack of lamb *au jus* and filet mignon with peppercorn-cognac sauce also earn rave reviews.

$$$ Le Coq au Vin – *4800 S. Orange Ave., Orlando.* ⛶*407-851-6980, www.lecoqau vinrestaurant.com. Dinner only.* This small, unpretentious restaurant serves some of the best **French** food in central Florida. It's the place where rival chefs dine on their days off. Louis Perrotte supervises the kitchen, while his wife Magdalena welcomes the guests. The dining spot is named for its most popular, and least expensive, dish; more daring diners opt for the braised rabbit. The Grand Marnier souffle wins rave reviews.

$$$ White Wolf Cafe – *1829 N. Orange Ave, Orlando. ☎407-895-9911. www. whitewolfcafe.com.* Located in the heart of Orlando's Antique Row, this bistro is named for the owner's white German shepherd dog. The storefront started life as an antique shop, with a few snacks being served to bring in customers and give the local trade a place to relax. Gradually the food took over. Tables and chairs moved in, knick-knacks moved out., though a selection of antiques are for sale. The cuisine is mostly **American** plus pastas and pizzas.

$$$ Wolfgang Puck's Cafe – *Downtown Disney West Side, Lake Buena Vista.* �& ☎407-938-9653. *www.wolfgang puckorlando.com.* This isn't one restaurant, it's a quartet. There's a casual cafe (soups, salads) and a lively sushi bar downstairs, and a takeaway counter next door. Upstairs is Puck's famed **International** fine-dining establishment where few guests can resist one of the creative pasta dishes, studded with lobster, fish or chicken. Kitchens are open, so patrons can see Puck's signature pizzas being twirled and brick-oven-baked. Virtually every dish involves an imaginative fusion of American, Asian and European tastes and ingredients. *Dinner only in second-floor dining room.*

$$ San Angel Inn – *Epcot, Mexico, Walt Disney World, Lake Buena Vista* & ☎407-939-3463. *www.wdwinfo.com/wdwinfo/ dining.* Looking for a respite from the theme park heat and crowds? Duck into this ridiculously romantic spot in Epcot's Mexico (great for lunch, when prices are lower) and let Disney transport you to Mexico with a (fiber-optic) star-filled sky, smoking volcano and a lazy river. (Epcot's El River de Tiempo ride runs through the restaurant.) After the obligatory chips and salsa, you'll dine on authentic **Mexican** dishes that are a whole lot better than you might have expected given the surroundings: try the *mole poblano* or a salad spiked with cacti and a nice frosty margarita.

☺ ENTERTAINMENT

Read the arts and entertainment section in the *Orlando Sentinel* every Friday, or see its online content (*www.orlandosentinel.com*). See also *Travelhost* (*www.travelhost.com/orlando*) for schedules of cultural events, attractions and restaurant information. Top venues include the **Bob Carr Performing Arts Center:** Orlando Opera Company, ballet, Broadway performances (*☎407-849-2001; www. orlandovenues.net*); **Amway Arena:** sporting events, rock concerts, circus (*☎407-849-2001; www.orlandovenues. net*); **Florida Citrus Bowl Stadium:** rock concerts, sporting events (*☎407-849-2001; www.orlandovenues.net*).

⚐ SPORTS

SPECTATOR SPORTS
Orlando Magic basketball team play in the NBA (⚐*see p19*), Amway Arena (*☎407-896-2442; www.nba.com/magic*); **Orlando Jai-Alai** is the only Central Florida location for the world's fastest sport of jai-alai. (*Fern Park, ☎407-339-6221, www.orlandojaialai.com*).

GOLF
Many private golf clubs welcome non-members. Captain's Choice Golf Services, Inc (*☎407-352-1102; www.oflgolf.com*) books tee times and offers transportation to many local courses.

Public courses: Grand Pines Golf Club (*☎407-239-6909; golf.marriott-vacations.com*); Casselberry (*☎407-699-9310; www.casselberrygc.com*); Orange Lake Resorts offers golf and water sports (*☎407-239-0000, www.orangelake.com*).
Walt Disney World Resort offers five superb golf courses *(http://disney world.disney.go.com/golf)*, also open to non-resort guests.
For more golf courses and details of other sports: visit www.orlandoinfo. com/golf and www.orlandoinfo. com/recreation.

SeaWorld Orlando★★★

This 200-acre marine adventure park mixes entertainment and education in its many animal shows, theme rides, touch pools and aquariums. The park is one of three SeaWorlds nationwide. Together these parks, owned by Anheuser-Busch and accredited by the Association of Zoos and Aquariums, support the world's largest collection of marine life. In addition to its public attractions, SeaWorld actively pursues research and breeding programs, and has successfully bred killer whales (orcas). Its Animal Rescue and Rehabilitation Program has assisted hundreds of wild animals in distress, including manatees, dolphins and whales.

👥 SEAWORLD

7007 SeaWorld Dr. (International Dr.). ▷ *From downtown, follow I-4 west to Exit 28, then follow signs to SeaWorld.* 🕐*Open year-round daily 9am.* 🕐*Closing times vary, depending on events.* 🍴*$79, child (3–9yrs) $69.* ✕🅿️⌗ 🕾*407-351-3600 or 800-432-2424.www.seaworld.com.*

Enter through the park's six-acre gateway area with a 55ft lighthouse at its heart. If you want a bird's-eye **view** of SeaWorld, the **Sky Tower** lifts passengers 400ft into a rotating chamber.

Just beyond the gateway is the **Tropical Reef,** into which are set some three dozen small aquarium tanks representing a wide variety of marine habitats and sea creatures, such as moray eels and chambered nautiluses. Behind the building is a **Tidal Pool** where visitors may touch and examine sea anemones, sea cucumbers and other marine mammals while posing questions to a naturalist. To the right of the tropical reef, a short walkway leads to the **Dolphin Nursery,** where young marine mammals are nurtured.

The following are the main attractions and shows.

ℹ️ **Info:** 🕾407-351-3600 or 800-327-2424; www.seaworld.com.
▷ **Location:** The park is east of Disney World, off I-4.
🅿️ **Parking:** Available on site; just follow the signs.
👁 **Don't Miss:** A walk through Terrors of the Deep, tunneling through a 660,000 gallon aquarium.
🕐 **Timing:** Plan your visit around show times. Expect queues.
👥 **Kids:** The entire park! But, don't miss the famous Shamu show.

Animal Attractions
Key West at SeaWorld

This quirky village re-creates the spirit of Florida's farthest resort outpost. Attractions comprise the aquatic habitats of the denizens of warmer waters, and include **Stingray Lagoon,** where visitors can touch the broad flat fish as it swims by; **Turtle Point,** which introduces several endangered species; and **Dolphin Cove,** where staff members are on hand to stage playful interactions with the marine mammals. Visitors can take part in a nightly Sunset Celebration just like the ones in Key West.

Manatee Rescue

This exhibit immerses visitors in the underwater world of the famed Florida manatee. You can watch these marine giants, some weighing 1,000 pounds, from above the water and below. Narration explains how the gentle sea cow hears, sees and feels, and suggests ways that visitors can help to save the endangered species from extinction.

SeaWorld operates an ongoing manatee release program, in which orphaned or injured manatees are released into the wild (orphans are released at the age of five or six).

Penguin Encounter

Step on the moving walkway for a ride past a frosty 30°F setting where puffins, murres and several species of

Shark Encounter

© SeaWorld Parks & Entertainment

penguins—including chinstrap, gentoo, rockhopper and king—reside: through a glass-sided observation pool you can view the graceful swimming of these flightless birds.

Pacific Point Preserve

Rocky shoals of an open-air pool capture the atmosphere of the Pacific coast. Harbor and fur seals bob in the waters, sea lions lounge on rocks, and a symphony of sounds is always in progress. The best time to watch is when attendants are staging a feeding session.

Shark Encounter

At the entrance to this exhibit, a small outdoor pool houses several varieties of sharks and rays. Inside, visitors walk through an acrylic archway that tunnels through a 660,000gal aquarium.

The tank's B-shaped contours were specifically designed to accommodate the swimming patterns of sharks, five different species of which glide through these waters. Smaller tanks contain other deadly denizens of the deep.

Penguin Encounter

Six thousand pounds of snow fall daily inside this habitat, recreating the Antarctic's rocky cliffs and frigid waters. It is home to more than 200 penguins—king, gentoo, adelie, macaroni, chinstrap and rockhopper—(plus puffins), who enjoy a chilly 30 degrees and the water at an icy 45 degrees. Guests ride a 120-foot-long moving walkway through the frozen wonderland to watch the playful birds cavort both above and under the water.

Making the Most of Seaworld Orlando

As is the case with most Orlando attractions, the busiest periods are during summer, Christmas and spring vacations. Plan the core of your visit around scheduled show times, as the other attractions are relatively accessible throughout the day. The killer whale shows in Shamu Stadium are the most popular, so arrive early (30 mins before) to get a good seat. Speaking of which, bring a disposable waterproof camera: there's wet, and, if you're in the Soak Zone at Shamu stadium, there's Shamu wet (the front rows of Journey to Atlantic also guarantee a soaking). Whichever, you'll have a lot more fun if you don't have to watch out for an expensive camera. On a cool day pack a poncho, unless you want to walk around in cool weather when you're soaking wet! Eat off-peak to avoid restaurant lines; come back at night or late-afternoon. Be sure to check out online specials. Park characters usually gather at the front gate between 9am–noon for autographs and photos. When you enter the park, ask at the Information Center about the behind-the-scenes guided tours; a variety of tours are offered, ranging from $18 to $95.

Thrill Rides
Journey to Atlantis
You are guaranteed to get wet—very wet—at this thrill ride. As the story goes, the mythical lost city of Atlantis has mysteriously risen from the floor of the Aegean Sea, and you're one of the first explorers. Your eight-passenger Greek fishing boat is actually a high-speed roller coaster that carries you through dark passageways haunted by evil sirens, down a nearly vertical 60ft waterfall and around a pair of S-curves into another free-falling plunge.

Kraken
SeaWorld's wildest roller-coaster ride is floorless and billed as Orlando's "longest, fastest, tallest and steepest." Visitors who board this ride *(you must be at least 54in tall)* are whisked to the height of a 15-story building, plunged down at speeds of 65mph and turned upside-down seven times before the ride is concluded.

Manta
The newest ride is one of Orlando's finest, with a head-first, face-down twist, dipping in to the water. Themed to resemble a flying manta ray, It is said to be the first "flying" roller coaster of its kind in the world.

Wild Arctic
A virtual-reality helicopter ride takes passengers pitching and rolling over a crevassed landscape above caribou, polar bears and narwhals. After narrowly escaping an avalanche, you disembark at a mock-up of an Arctic research station, featuring above- and below-water views of beluga whales as well as polar bears, walruses and harbor seals.

Shows
Blue Horizons
This new "breakthrough theatrical spectacular" showcases dolphins and false killer whales, a rainbow of exotic birds and an entire cast of world-class divers and aerialists draped in elaborate costumes.

Clyde and Seamore Take Pirate Island
This very popular show stars the park's hilarious sea lions, otters and walrus in a swashbuckling mis-adventure on the high seas.

Shamu "Believe"
SeaWorld's signature attraction, staged in a five-million-gallon tank, stars the renowned five-ton killer whale Shamu, along with his protégés. Guided by their trainers, the trio leaps and twirls

Manta

© SeaWorld Parks & Entertainment

Aquatica

Next door to SeaWorld (separate entrance) this new waterpark features lots of exciting, and relaxing, themed water rides, slides and flumes, including a much-hyped one that goes through a lagoon of black-and-white Commerson's dolphins (though it's not easy to see them clearly with water spraying in your face!). There are beautiful white-sand beaches and animal shows, as well as a lagoon of exotic fish, birds such as spoonbills and kookaburras, and animals including tortoises and anteaters. Shaded loungers and private cabana rental *(additional charge)* is available; the latter includes a refrigerator stocked with juice, water and sodas, complimentary use of towels and lockers and a private island location.

Dolphin Plunge

© SeaWorld Parks & Entertainment

5800 Water Play Way, Orlando. Open year round; operating hours vary due to weather conditions; see website for up-to-date information. $48, child (3–9yrs) $42; $12. 866-787-4307. www.aquaticabyseaworld.com.

to music in a whalesome water ballet that is also projected on to an immense high-resolution video screen. Trainers enter the water to interact with the killer whale and to stage demonstrations.

DISCOVERY COVE★★

6000 Discovery Cove Way (International Dr.). Adjacent to SeaWorld. Open year-round daily 9am–5:30pm. $259-$279 with dolphin encounter, $159-$179 without dolphin encounter. Price includes lunch, parking and a seven-day SeaWorld or Busch Gardens Africa pass. Reservations required (4–6 weeks in advance advised); admission limited to 1,000 visitors/day. 877-434-7268. www.discovery cove.com.

This 30-acre marine park provides visitors a one-on-one encounter with a bottlenose dolphin as well as other sea and land creatures. Discovery Cove features a series of pools and lagoons amid sand beaches within a tropical landscape of towering palms and thatched huts. Pathways bordered by flowers and shrubs lead to the Coral Reef, the Ray Lagoon, Aviary, Tropical River and Dolphin Lagoon. Visitors may snorkel around the **coral reef** and several grottos, investigate a submerged shipwreck, and view thousands of exotic fish. Resembling the Caribbean's famed Stingray City, the watery habitat of the rays *(in which visitors may snorkel)* holds cownose and southern varieties up to 4ft in diameter. On shore, a large, net-enclosed **aviary** contains some 300 colorful birds in free flight; guests are permitted to feed and touch the birds. Winding through the aviary, as well as the rest of the park, is the river, where visitors can swim or float along on an inner tube. Guests may also enjoy the large swimming lagoon, bordered by a sandy beach.

For most visitors, the highlight is the 45min trainer-guided interaction with a bottlenose dolphin *(some weigh up to 600 pounds)* at Dolphin Lagoon, including a supervised and safe-for-all **ride** on the dolphin.

Universal Orlando★★★

At close to 840 acres, edgy and techno-savvy Universal Orlando gives Disney a real run for its money. Indeed, many people (late teens in particular) prefer this to the Mouse's offering. Initially a single theme park and working movie studio, it now includes a second theme park, **Islands of Adventure,** home to the wildest coasters in Orlando, plus **Universal CityWalk,** an upscale dining, entertainment and shopping complex. Also linked to the parks with walkways, shuttles and boats, are several resort hotels, including the first-ever Hard Rock Hotel, the Portofino Bay Hotel, and the Royal Pacific Resort.

1000 Universal Studios Plaza.
Follow I-4 west to Exit 29B. Turn right on Hollywood Way and follow signs to Universal Studios. Open year-round daily 9am. Closing times vary. $79, child (3–9yrs) $69 Universal Studios or Islands of Adventure; two-parks $109, child (3–9yrs) $99;. 407-363-8000. www.universalorlando.com.

UNIVERSAL STUDIOS FLORIDA

The original 444-acre theme park and working studio (with nine soundstages), Universal Studios Florida ranks as the largest motion picture and television facility outside Hollywood, California. Intended as a place where visitors can "ride the movies," the park bases its attractions on popular films and television shows, continuing the tradition begun in 1915 by the studio's California founder, **Carl Laemmle,** who encouraged paying visitors to stop by and watch movies being made. The Orlando site was chosen for its climate and established tourist base, and for its appeal to movie and television talent

Well-known film director-producer **Steven Spielberg** was consulted on the design of the Florida site as an "integrated production and entertain-

- **Info:** 407-363-8000 or 888-322-5537; www.universalorlando.com.
- **Location:** The complex is east of Disney World, off I-4.
- **Parking:** On-site parking garage ($11) is linked to the parks by escalators and moving sidewalks. Free parking after 6pm; valet parking ($18).
- **Don't Miss:** Harry Potter, The Simpsons and Hollywood RIp RIde Rockit, Earthquake, Terminator 2, the Hulk and Dueling Dragons coasters.
- **Timing:** Plan a full day at Universal Studios and another for Islands of Adventure. Return in the evenings to CityWalk, and/or head there for lunch one day.
- **Kids:** Seuss Landing and E.T. Adventure.

ment facility." Since streets frequently double as movie sets, you might see a film in progress as you tour the park. You may also visit soundstages such as the one used full-time by cable television's Nickelodeon Network.

Adjacent to the soundstages are thrill rides, shows (several in 3-D), animated characters and celebrity look-alikes, who pose for photos with visitors. A brass band and the Blues Brothers provide street theater.

Hollywood Rip Ride Rockit

Claiming to be the most technologically advanced roller coaster in the world, this rock music-themed coaster opened in 2009. Choose a song to ride along to before strapping in and the ride is recorded on video for you to take home. This is also Orlando's tallest coaster, rising to 17 storys, and features several heart-stopping "never been done" elements including the world's first non-inverting loop.

Shrek 4-D

Starring Shrek and Donkey and the voices of the original cast. this original 3-D film enter the 4th dimension with moving seats, water, wind, mist and other special effects that put you right in the middle of a fairytale adventure.

Revenge of the Mummy

Based on the 1999 blockbuster *The Mummy*, this thrilling indoor roller coaster plunges you into total darkness, interrupted by huge fireballs, swarms of scarab beetles and an army of warrior mummies!

The Simpsons Ride

The very latest in simulator technology motion rides will have you laughing and flying through the air on an amazing journey through the inimitable world of Homer, Bart, Marge, Lucy, Krusty and the rest of Springfield's loveable misfits.

Terminator 2: 3-D

Arny's back, with a vengeance, in a gripping 12min film-cum-live show that marries stunt work, state-of-the-art special effects and in-your-face 3-D to keep viewers on the edge of their seats. At $23 million, the action movie—directed by James Cameron—is said to be the most expensive footage ever shot, minute for minute.

🙂 A Bit of Advice 🙂

Arrive 30min to 1hr prior to opening time. As soon as the gates open head for Hollywood RIp Ride Rockit (at Universal Studios) or to Harry Potter (at Islands of Adventure). Visit less high-profile rides and shows in the middle of the day, when ride lines are likely to be longest; check the Preview of Today's Rides and Shows for scheduled times and waiting times. Alternatively you can bypass the lines by paying extra ($20–$60) for an Express Pass. Or you could stay the night as these are given free to residents of the resort's three hotels. For more details visit *www.universalorlando.com* and click on Express Pass.

E.T. Adventure

The magic of director Steven Spielberg's popular film is captured both in this ride and its waiting area, a long weave through a dark, dreamy Northwest forest, scented with evergreens. E.T. has returned to Earth to obtain our assistance in healing his Green Planet, which has fallen ill. Riders hop aboard bicycles that carry them and the unforgettable extraterrestrial on an airborne adventure above an American cityscape and on to E.T.'s beloved home.

Shrek 4-D

Universal elements and all related indicia TM & © 2010 Universal Studios. © 2010 Universal Orlando. All rights reserved.

Men in Black Alien Attack

This entertaining adventure, zapping over 100 aliens en route, was the first ride to allow two side-by-side vehicles to compete (the tabulated score is visible in each car).

Jaws

On a cruise through the waters around Amity, passengers find themselves virtually in the maw of the infamous near-indestructible great white shark.

Along the north edge of the Lagoon lies **San Francisco.** The old Ghirardelli chocolate factory and trolley tracks running through the street leave no doubt that you've entered that city's famous Fisherman's Wharf area.

Earthquake: The Big One

The attraction begins with a behind-the-scenes look at how Charlton Heston made the movie *Earthquake* in 1974. Visitors then board a San Francisco subway for a truly ground-breaking trip, in which the earth shakes and cataclysm follows.

Kongfrontation

After winding through a New York subway station complete with graffiti-splattered walls, passengers board cable cars for a trip above the city streets. But with the great Kong on the loose, they're guaranteed a primate confrontation.

Twister! Ride It Out

An adaptation of the 1996 movie of the same name, Twister! subjects visitors to the fury of a large tornado as it rages through a rural town on the Great Plains, right down to tanker fires, broken water mains and a flying cow, just 20ft away.

UNIVERSAL'S ISLANDS OF ADVENTURE

With producer-director Steven Spielberg as creative consultant, "Islands" is recognized as a triumph of imagination. Swooping roller-coaster loops tower over this 21C, high-tech amusement complex.

With its eclectic architecture representing a variety of world harbor cultures, **Port of Entry** serves as a shopping and dining area as well as a departure point for Universal Orlando's man-made archipelago around a large lagoon. One of the five islands, **Seuss Landing** features whimsical characters of children's literature favorite Theodor "Dr. Seuss" Geisel. Another island called **Toon Lagoon** brings to life classic cartoon characters. Realistic dinosaurs stalk visitors at **Jurassic Park,** while high-tech thrill rides are the main attractions of **The Lost Continent** and **Marvel Super Hero Island.** Shops and restaurants, themed to match the island whereon they stand, complement the attractions while offering visitors a calming break from the hair-raising, stomach-churning rides.

Port of Entry

The starting point begins here in this port town with its looming lighthouse and bustling arcade of food and beverage outlets, such as the Backwater Bar and chic shops like the Ocean Trader Market. Boats depart from here for the five themed islands that comprise the bulk of the park (though most visitors prefer to walk).

The Wizarding World of Harry Potter.

The latest mega-attraction to hit Orlando opened in June 2010. This Harry Potter "theme Park within a theme Park" occupies 20 acres and includes a magical Hogwarts school and an atmospheric snowy Hogsmeade.

There are three rides/experiences:

Dragon Challenge comprises two dueling high-speed roller coasters, while **Flight of the Hippogriff** is a beautifully themed, gentler "family roller coaster." **Harry Potter and the Forbidden Journey**, is an adventure through Dumbledore's office, the Defence Against the Dark Arts classroom, Gryffindor common room, the Room of Requirement, and more, before soaring above the castle grounds and coming face to face with magical creatures.

For a full preview visit *www.universal orlando.com/harrypotter*

Below are more highlights, in counter-clockwise order from the entrance.

Seuss Landing

On this island, all is linked to the famed series of children's books by Dr. Seuss. As his readers would expect, the architecture here lacks symmetry and straight lines. Mounts on the elaborate **Caro-Seuss-el** represent elephant-birds, the cowfish and other Seuss characters. For refreshments, visitors dine at the Green Eggs and Ham Cafe (where eggs are really green), or sip slurpies at the Moose Juice Goose Juice. Floppy headgear is available at the Cats, Hats & Things shop.

The Cat in the Hat

Visitors ride on 6-passenger "couches" through 18 scenes from Seuss books that include a 24ft perception-altering tunnel. Some 30 Seuss characters join the fun, among them The Cat in the Hat and Thing 1.

The Lost Continent

Dominated by the hills and valleys of the Dueling Dragons, this island, based on fantasy novels and movies, is of particular interest to older kids. Visitors can cool off at the Frozen Desert restaurant and browse at bazaars called Treasures of Poseidon and the Dragon's Keep.

Dueling Dragons

This thrill ride is a must if you're a roller-coaster enthusiast. The coaster, with two intertwined tracks, is inverted, so that passengers' legs dangle freely. Riders climb, four abreast, onto a dragon representing Fire or another representing Ice. As the two dragons zoom through a medieval forest, they climb 125ft side-by-side, then Fire shoots off to the left at 60mph and Ice dives right at 55mph to complete a series of upside-down flips that involve close misses with the other dragon.

Jurassic Park

Stephen Spielberg's technological savvy is much in evidence on this island, which is filled with dinosaur rides and scary experiences. Naturally, one of the snack spots is the Pizza Predatoria.

River Adventure

As you ride within the park, thunder and lightning split the stormy skies. The terrifying *Tyrannosaurus rex* is pursuing you closely, the beast's savage teeth coming at times within inches of your face. The only escape is down an 85ft water chute—reputedly, the longest, steepest and fastest built to date.

Pteranodon Flyers

Guests are invited to climb onto the backs of these replicated flying creatures from millions of years ago and take an aerial tour above **Camp Jurassic,** with its ancient volcano and amber mine. The flyers' wings extend 10ft on either side of the passengers.

Toon Lagoon

Here on this island comic books and film cartoons come to life, especially along **Comic Strip Lane,** home of the Pandemonium Cartoon Circus. If there's one place to eat an oversize sandwich, it has to be at Blondie's: Home of the Dagwood Sandwich, where patrons pay per the thickness of the sandwiches they make. Toon Toys and Gasoline Alley are two of the island's most visited stores.

Dudley Do-Right's Ripsaw Falls

Nell's in trouble, and the incompetent Canadian Mountie of "Rocky and Bullwinkle" fame must save her from the evil Snidely Whiplash. Visitors join the rescue, which ends with a 15ft plunge beneath a lagoon's surface, the first-ever ride below water level. Anticipate getting wet!

Popeye and Bluto's Bilge-Rat Barges

The 12 passengers on this rapid whitewater raft ride get squirted by water cannon from Popeye's boat and encounter an 18ft octopus, its 12ft tentacles bulging with water. On the last stop, a boat wash, passengers are sure to get drenched.

Marvel Super Hero Island

The highlight here is the Spider-Man ride. Eat *after* going on it or on **Doctor Doom's Fearfall**—Captain America's Diner is a popular choice for refreshments. The Comics Shop and the Marvel Alterniverse hold myriad memorabilia.

Amazing Adventures of Spider-Man

This ride was a theme-park first; an attraction that combines moving vehicles, filmed 3-D action and special effects. As they try to help Spider-Man retrieve the stolen Statue of Liberty, riders don 3-D night-sight goggles, take a 400ft "sensory drop" into darkness, and speed around a 1.5-acre set racked with fiery battles between good and evil.

Incredible Hulk Coaster

A series of chilling swoops and loops, this ride is a close competitor with the popular Dueling Dragons. Passengers are shot out of Dr. Banner's Gamma Force Accelerator with the same g-force of an F-16 jet. They zoom from 0–40mph in two seconds, roll over seven times and plunge underground twice, all within two minutes and 15 seconds.

UNIVERSAL CITYWALK

This 30-acre, two-tiered promenade of individually themed entertainment venues, hotels, restaurants and dance clubs, fronts a four-acre harbor. It is connected by bridges to the entrances of Universal Studios Florida and Universal's Islands of Adventure, which are accessible only through CityWalk.

Street performers are a common sight, and at Christmas time the streets throng with parades and carolers. An outdoor ice skating rink installed.

Famous names pop up everywhere in CityWalk. A paean to the Gulf Coast's vagabond minstrel, **Jimmy Buffett's Margaritaville** is a combination nightclub and restaurant featuring the requisite "cheeseburger in paradise." If you can hear the chef shouting "Bam," you're obviously in **Emeril's Restaurant Orlando,** dining on Chef Lagasse's famed Creole-style cuisine. Hoop fans tend to haunt the **NBA City** restaurant, autograph books in hand, while car buffs sip and sup at the NASCAR Cafe's bounteous buffet. CityWalk possesses the world's largest **Hard Rock Café** as well as a replica of New Orleans' celebrated watering hole, **Pat O'Brien's,** complete with dueling pianos and a "flaming fountain" patio.

As to music, there's plenty available in CityWalk night spots like Margaritaville and The Groove, Latin Quarter and others in addition to the 2,200-seat **Hard Rock Live,** where recognized artists from around the globe perform. At **Bob Marley's,** the Jamaican home and garden of the reggae messiah have been re-created.

The hip Red Coconut Club fuses decor and ambience from Cuba, Vegas and Polynesia across three bars, a balcony and at intimate tables—it's miles away from conventional theme park bars.

The hottest, and most expensive, ticket on City Walk, however, is for the **Blue Man Group**, whose music, comedy and multimedia shows are here on permanent residence.

Within CityWalk there's also a 20-screen, 5,000-seat Cineplex Odeon theater and a bounty of specialty shops sporting offbeat and colorful wares.

There are three luxury accommodations on the grounds of Universal Orlando, adjacent to CityWalk. The brightly colored **Portofino Bay Hotel** captures the look and feel of the Italian Riviera, with fishing boats in a harbor, like its namesake town in Italy. The first **Hard Rock Hotel** is adorned throughout with rock-music memorabilia. The **Royal Pacific Resort** is a lush oasis of waterfalls and tropical gardens, reminiscent of the South Seas. And each hotel offers its own entertainment (for guests and non-guests). The monthly Velvet Sessions at the Hard Rock Hotel feature rock legends performing live in the hotel lobby. There's the weekly Wantilan Luau at Loews Royal Pacific Resort. Each night at sundown you can listen to live Italian ballads during Musica della Notte on the Piazza of Loews Portofino Bay Hotel.

Walt Disney World® Resort★★★

This mega-sized theme park and resort playground is the top vacation destination resort on the planet. Truly a world unto itself, this immense 29,900-acre (47sq mi) complex—about twice the size of Manhattan Island—lies 20 miles southwest of downtown Orlando and encompasses four extensive theme parks (Magic Kingdom, Epcot, Disney's Animal Kingdom and Disney-MGM Studios), 24 resort hotels with nearly 30,000 rooms, eight nightclubs, two water parks, six 18-hole golf courses, a 200-acre sports complex, numerous lakes, a zoological park and much more.

MAGIC KINGDOM

▶ *Take I-4 west to Exit 25B (US-192 west). Turn right on World Dr. and follow signs to entrance of park.* ⏱*Open year-round daily 9am.* ⏱*Closing times vary.* The 107-acre park includes seven areas that radiate out from the Central Plaza in front of Cinderella Castle. This is the most child-friendly of all the theme parks, so if you have little ones in tow, start here.

MAIN STREET, U.S.A.

Tidy Victorian storefronts holding commercial shops re-create the milieu of an early 19C town. In designing Main Street, U.S.A., Walt Disney used a film device called forced perspective: upper

- ♿ **Michelin Map:** p190.
- 🛈 **Info:** ☏407-939-6244; www.disneyworld.com.
- ▶ **Location:** The resort is located southwest of Orlando, off I-4, west of the Florida Turnpike.
- 🅿 **Parking:** Available at all theme parks and resorts.
- 👁 **Don't Miss:** A stroll down Main Street, U.S.A. (Magic Kingdom); dining at one of the World Showcase (Epcot) restaurants; a close-up look at the Tree of Life (Animal Kingdom) and the Voyage of the LIttle Mermaid (MGM Studios).
- ⏱ **Timing:** Allow a full day each to explore the Magic Kingdom and Epcot. MGM Studios and Animal Kingdom are much smaller and easier to get around; though there's plenty to see and do, you can see most of the major attractions in half a day at each.
- 👥 **Kids:** Magic Kingdom and Animal Kingdom are tops with little kids; pre-teens and teens will enjoy the rides at MGM Studios.

Exploring Magic Kingdom

Magic Kingdom is the most popular—and thus most crowded—of the four parks, and the most time-consuming to access. After taking a shuttle across the parking lot to the **Ticket and Transportation Center,** you board either a monorail train or a replica paddlewheeler that crosses the Seven Seas Lagoon. Thrill rides—Space Mountain, Splash Mountain and Big Thunder Mountain Railroad—along with Pirates of the Caribbean tend to attract the greatest crowds, so head for them first.

🐾 A guided walking tour, Keys to the Kingdom, explains the park's history and technology and takes in several rides, as well as the Diamond Horseshoe Saloon Revue *(departs from City Hall daily 8:30am, 9:30am, 10am, 1:30pm, except holidays; 4.5-5hrs; 16 years or older; $60, including lunch; reservations required; theme park admission required;* ☏*407-939-8687).*

GETTING THERE

BY AIR – Orlando International Airport (MCO): 28mi northeast of Walt Disney World Resort; information booth *(open daily 7am–11pm; multilingual service; ℘407-939-1289)*.

Disney's Magical Express Shuttle service to Walt Disney World Resort *(departs from baggage claim area year-round daily, every 15–20min.* **Van, limo** and **taxi** service is also available. **Rental car** agencies are located at the airport. If **driving** from Orlando airport, take the Beeline Expressway, Route 528 west *(toll)*, then continue on I-4 west to parks.

BY CAR – Walt Disney World Resort is located 20mi southwest of downtown Orlando. Take I-4 west to Exit 26B for best access to Epcot, Typhoon Lagoon, Downtown Disney and River Country. For the most direct route to Disney's Animal Kingdom, Disney's Wide World of Sports, Disney-MGM Studios and the Magic Kingdom, take Exit 25B (Route 192 west) and follow signs to the various parks.

BY TRAIN OR BUS – Nearest Amtrak station: 1400 Sligh Blvd., Orlando *(24mi from park; ℘800-872-7245; www.amtrak. com)*. Greyhound station: 555 N. John Young Pwky., Orlando *(26mi from park; ℘407-292-3424)*, and 16 N. Orlando Ave., Kissimmee *(12mi from park; ℘800-231-2222; www.greyhound.com)*.

GETTING AROUND

Monorail trains, buses, ferry boats and water taxi *(all free)* link all attractions including hotels and resorts throughout the complex.

Buses operate approximately every 20min, 1hr prior to park opening until closing. Routes painted in RED are direct routes after 4pm. The only exceptions: service to Magic Kingdom, Epcot, Disney-MGM Studios from Disney's Old Key West Resort and the Disney Institute operate between noon and 6pm.

stories of buildings are not as high as lower ones, giving the buildings a taller appearance. Adding to the atmosphere, a horse-drawn trolley, antique fire engine, omnibus, "horseless carriages" and jitneys carry passengers between the Town Square and Central Plaza. Minstrels often stroll the street, and the cartoon-character-filled **Celebrate a Dream Come True Parade** wends its way down Main Street every afternoon, highlighting recent animated film successes *(check park brochure for show times)*. During evenings in peak periods (summer and Christmas holidays), special parades fill the street

Jungle Cruise Attraction, Magic Kingdom

© Disney

with a dazzling spectacle of Disney characters. The parade is often followed by **Fantasy in the Sky Fireworks,** featuring a flying Tinker Bell, or, on special nights, the magically illuminated **SpectroMagic Parade**. *(check brochure for show times)*.

TOMORROWLAND

Bowing to the age of technology, in the mid-1990s Walt Disney World Resort undertook a major overhaul of Tomorrowland attractions, many of which were outdated. Rather than attempt to predict the future, Disney opted to create a "fantasy future city," recapturing the futuristic visions of the 1920s and 1930s.

There's no doubting the favorite here, **Space Mountain** roller coaster enclosed in a futuristic mountain is one of Disney's all-time most popular rides.

Not for the faint of heart, a train hurtles passengers through near-darkness, plunging them into sudden, atmospheric comet showers and past faintly twinkling stars.

Buzz Lightyear's Space Ranger Spin is a brilliant "interactive space fantasy" which teams visitors with characters from *Toy Story* in defending the Earth's battery supply against the evil Emperor Zurg. Piloting your own XP-38 Space Cruiser equipped with twin laser cannons, you "shoot" and steer in an adventure "to infinity and beyond." As combatants fire the infrared lasers, targets spring to animated life.

Set high up, around Tomorrowland's colorful central spire, **Astro Orbitor** is one for younger kids, though adults will enjoy the views of the Magic Kingdom below.

At **Tomorrowland Speedway** young and old motorists alike take the wheel of mini-size sports cars and maneuver them along a gently curving raceway (inset with an iron track to

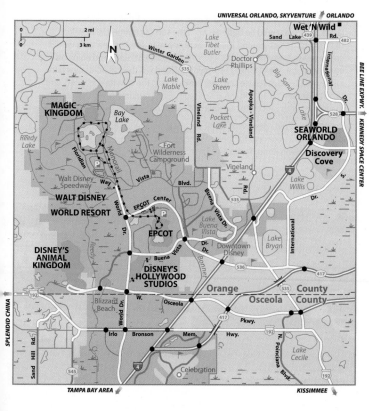

Disney's Dream

Born and raised in the Midwest, **Walter Elias Disney** (1901–1966) showed early signs of a keen imagination and an aptitude for drawing. By age 21 he had established an animation studio in Kansas City; when that failed, he headed for Hollywood, California.

© Moviestore collection Ltd/Alamy

The Disney Brothers Studios, established by Walt and his brother Roy in 1923, scored its first popular success in 1928 with *Steamboat Willie*. The film, starring a mouse named Mickey, combined animation and the new technology of sound. Disney's first full-length animated film, *Snow White and the Seven Dwarfs* (1937), met with instant success.

In the early 1950s, disillusioned with the tawdriness of amusement parks, Disney began planning his own. **Disneyland Park,** which opened in July 1955 in Anaheim, California, was destined to change the face of global amusement. Disney launched plans to open a second theme park. He wanted to acquire a far larger tract that could be buffered from the sort of commercial development that had sprung up around the 180-acre Anaheim site. His new park would create a Disney-styled world where visitors could eat, sleep and enjoy his entertainment. Walt Disney chose central Florida as the site of his new park in the mid-1960s, because land was inexpensive, the climate was good, and growth was anticipated in the area. Tragically, as building began, Walt was diagnosed with cancer; the 65-year-old cartoonist died in 1966.

In 1971 the Florida version of Magic Kingdom made its debut. The immensely popular Disney concept has been exported abroad. Today, there are Disneyland Resorts in Hong Kong, Tokyo and Paris.

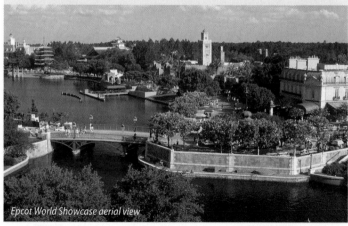

Epcot World Showcase aerial view

© Disney

keep things on course!). An overhead tram at the adjacent **Tomorrowland Transit Authority** offers a bird's-eye view of the "city of the future" as imagined by early science-fiction visionaries.

MICKEY'S TOONTOWN FAIR

Toontown Fair occupies a relatively quiet, three-acre corner of the Magic Kingdom. Scaled to visitors under age 10 the whimsical village is built of pastel-shaded, round-edged buildings with a sort of gingerbread appeal. For kids who want to meet their favorite Disney characters, this is the best place.

The **Toontown Hall of Fame** is in effect a big Disney store with the ambience of an old-fashioned country fair tent. The Hall of Fame boasts "character greeting locations" where Goofy and Pluto, among others, shake hands, scrawl their autographs and pose for photos.

If you've ever wondered wher the world's most famous mouse lives, it's here, in **Mickey's Country House**. Displayed in his cozy home are plaques and trophies of his years of success. A corridor leads to a soundstage and theater; Mickey himself (now in his 70s, but with a seemingly direct line to the Fountain of Youth) holds court backstage, signing autographs for admirers (except during parade times, when of course, he is on duty).

And opposite Mickey's house, of course, is **Minnie's Country House**, a quaint pink palace reflecting the traditional role for "the fairer sex" where even the appliances seem to smile and giggle. Across the lane is **Donald Duck's Boat,** the *Miss Daisy,* which lures youngsters to climb through its tunnels and up its stairs. Opposite, kids love riding **The Barnstormer at Goofy's Wiseacre Farm**, a mild, up-and-down coaster ride that's fun for little ones.

FANTASYLAND

With its fairy-tale atmosphere this is one of the most popular areas. Adults with a taste for whimsy are captivated by its old-fashioned magic, as are young children who have seen the Disney classics. Live shows are held periodically at the

Castle Forecourt Stage and at **Fantasyland Pavilion** *(check park brochure for show times).*

The icon of not only the park, but of the Disney empire, **Cinderella Castle** is a 189ft-high Gothic extravaganza, ornamented with turrets, towers, gold spires and leaded-glass windows . It was inspired by one of the 19C castles built in Bavaria by King Ludwig II. The interior is a restaurant, with the arched entrance through the castle gate inlaid with detailed mosaics depicting the rags-to-riches story of Cinderella.

The kids probably don't realise (or care) but many of the mounts on **Cinderella's Golden Carousel** are hand-painted antiques. A band organ plays Disney tunes as horses gallop beneath a canopy painted with scenes from the *Cinderella* movie.

The most famous, and most schmaltzy ride within the Magic Kingdom is **It's a Small World.** This cross-cultural fantasy was conceived for the 1964 World's Fair and embodies an idealized view of international brotherhood. Boarding small boats, visitors float past 500 Audio-Animatronics® children and animals representing nearly 100 nations, all singing the repetitive theme song.

🐭 A Bit of Advice 🐭

See popular attractions early, during a parade or late in the day.

Take a small pen light for young kids to use during dark and scary moments on some of the rides.

Eat lunch or dinner during non-peak hours (before 11:30am or after 2pm and from 4pm–6pm or after 8pm).

Choose a restaurant that takes priority-seating reservations.

See a show or browse in the shops in the afternoon when many rides have long lines.

In Epcot stake out your place by the lakeside at least 30 minutes ahead and (at busy times) up to 1 hour ahead, to see the fireworks and laser spectacular.

SHOPPING AND NIGHTLIFE
DOWNTOWN DISNEY

Take I-4 west to Exit 27. Turn north onto Rte. 535; left at first light on Hotel Plaza Blvd. Entrance to Marketplace at intersection of Hotel Plaza Blvd. and Buena Vista Dr.; Pleasure Island and West Side extend west along Buena Vista Dr. ✕ ♿ 🅿 📞*407-939-2648.*

Marketplace
🕐*Open 8:30am–11pm.* This complex boasts an overwhelming assemblage of Disney character collectibles, along with resort wear at the World of Disney. Restaurants cater to families on the go. At the LEGO Imagination Center, visitors of all ages are awed by gargantuan, detailed structures, built from the tiny plastic bricks.

Pleasure Island
🕐*Open 10:30am–2am.* The former nightclubs and theaters have gone, replaced by shopping and dining as this area is transformed through 2011. The Raglan Road Irish Pub & Bar, Fuego by Sosa Cigars, Paradiso 37, Curl by Sammy Duval, Orlando Harley-Davidson, and outdoor food and beverage locations remain open during the transition.

West Side
🕐*Open 10:30am–2am.* This includes; two restaurant-nightclubs – Bongos Cuban Cafe and the House of Blues; the hugely popular, though very expensive, Cirque du Soleil theater; a 24-screen cineplex; DisneyQuest (🕐*daily 11:30am–10pm, Fri–Sat until 11pm;* 💲*$35–$41*), a five-story interactive "virtual-reality" entertainment gaming center.

DISNEY BOARDWALK
Disney's BoardWalk contains more than 9,000 square feet of shops, restaurants and nightclubs. It encompasses Crescent Lake and is "a village on the water" near many Disney Resort hotels. Its sherbet-colored building facades, striped awnings, rising columns and archways, are designed after the boardwalks that were famous during the turn of the 20C along such coastal cities as Coney Island, New York and Atlantic City, New Jersey. When the sun cools down, the nightlife heats up with street performers, food vendors, midway games and lots of live entertainment. **Atlantic Dance Hall** showcases cool bands and hot DJs while **Jellyrolls** is a lively piano bar with dueling pianos and audience sing-alongs. Guests must be 21 years or older for both clubs.

A longtime favorite with small visitors, **Dumbo, the Flying Elephant** is a classic fairground ride that allows passengers to make their individual Dumbos soar up and down by manipulating a joystick in front of the seat. Similarly, the **Mad Tea Party** ride, aboard a giant teacup is a fairly tame tilt-a-whirl (waltzer) in which passengers control the amount of spin by turning a wheel in the center of each cup. In **Ariel's Grotto,** the Little Mermaid herself poses for photos in a sea cave as little ones line up with their parents to await their turns. The unpredictably spouting fountain outside the cave is a great place to cool off. Fantasyland lauds Disney's early celluloid successes with several enclosed or "dark" rides. Based on animated feature films, these rides whisk visitors past audio-animatronic figures and scenes. In **The Many Adventures of Winnie the Pooh,** passengers in "hunny pot" vehicles journey through a storybook page and into the Hundred Acre Wood to meet Pooh, Tigger and the other beloved characters. **Snow White's Scary Adventures** takes visitors from the Seven Dwarfs' cozy cottage to an encounter with the Wicked Queen and on to a happy ending. Riders aboard the pirate-ship gondolas of **Peter Pan's Flight** float out of the Darling children's bedroom above a charming, fiber-optic version of nighttime London. Soon after, passengers are plunged into Never Land, where Captain Hook, Smee and the Lost Boys await in their galleon.

LIBERTY SQUARE

A celebration of old-time America, Liberty Square re-creates a brick and clapboard colonial town set around a central square. Cast from the same mold as the revered original, a Liberty Bell sits in the center of the square. The 130-year-plus live oak designated as the site's "liberty tree" was discovered on the Disney property and carefully transplanted to this location.

Hosts of ghosts and ghouls spook the **Haunted Mansion** that looms ominously along the shore of the Rivers of America. From the "stretchroom," where heights and dimensions are not what they appear, visitors board small black "doom buggies" for a spine-tingling trip among holographic images and haunting, if humorous, special effects.

Moving on from haunted house to White House, the impressive **Hall of Presidents** multimedia production begins with an unabashedly patriotic film on the history of the Constitution, then blossoms into an Audio-Animatronics® tour de force in which every US Presidents appear on stage for a roll call and, of course, a few speeches.

You'll need a dose of fresh air after this and where better than aboard the **Liberty Belle Riverboat,** a three-decker, gingerbread-trimmed sternwheeler, plying the river, past audio-animatronic animals and an Indian village.

FRONTIERLAND

The Old West lives on in the wooden walkways, country stores and saloon of this frontier town. On many afternoons, gunslingers take to the rooftops for a shoot-out. At **Country Bear Jamboree,** a winsome troupe of audio-animatronic "Bear-itones" sing, tell jokes and generally delight crowds with their down-home performances (check park brochure for show times).

There are two excellent rides in this land. If you want to cool off, board a dugout for a languid float through swamps and bayous inside **Splash Mountain,** as Brer Rabbit, Brer Fox and other characters from the 1946 Disney classic Song of the South serenade passing boats.

At the mountaintop awaits a surprise: a 52ft flume that hurls dugouts down a 47-degree slope to a monstrous soaking splash.

The other ride is an old-fashioned roller coaster, in every sense. On **Big Thunder Mountain Railroad** the runaway train pulls out of an old mining town, then gathers steam as it roller-coasters through and around a red-rock mountain, negotiates a terrain of hoodoos, caves and canyons, and even plunges down through a dark, rickety mine shaft. En route, as usual, there's lot of visual interest and fun provided by audio-animatronic characters.

Log rafts carry energetic explorers across the Rivers of America to **Tom**

Big Thunder Mountain Railroad Attraction
© Disney

Sawyer Island, where they can wander through Injun Joe's cave, the stockaded Fort Langhorne, a swinging footbridge, a tree house and a quiet playground for young kids.

ADVENTURELAND

An eclectic mix of Polynesian, Moorish, French Colonial and Spanish Colonial architecture establishes an exotic atmosphere here.

An old favourite is **The Enchanted Tiki Room.** The 10min show presented here—"Under New Management"—introduces brash birds Iago (from Disney's *Aladdin*) and Zazu (from *The Lion King*) as the new landlords of the Tiki Room. When they offend the resident tiki gods, however, they find themselves in big trouble.

Little ones love the **Magic Carpets of Aladdin** ride that takes four passengers each on a ride around a mammoth genie lamp. Along the way, they try to avoid water "spit" from camels. On the ground, the **Agrabah Bazaar** and the Zanzibar Trading Company beckon visitors with a wealth of exotic merchandise.

An unexpected treat is the **Swiss Family Treehouse,** where visitors can climb through a sprawling, 80ft artificial (though very lifelike) banyan tree that re-creates the arboreal home of the indefatigable Swiss Family Robinson. This famous family originated in the

Spaceship Earth

© Disney

19C novel of Johann David Wyss, and was later immortalized in a Disney film. One of the most popular amusement park rides ever created (though nowadays looking rather old fashioned), **Pirates of the Caribbean** still embodies the spirit of Disney at its best. Boarding boats, visitors weave through a darkened swamp before entering a Caribbean village raided by pirates. There the crafts drift past a series of sets peopled by lifelike buccaneers, pigs, parrots and more.

There are more boats to board on the **Jungle Cruise**. Passengers on this nostalgic Disney favorite float down a jungle river that combines features of Africa, Asia and South America. Beware of mechanized crocodiles, hippos and elephants that pop up along the way past ruins overgrown with lush foliage. Boat pilots spice up the trip with punlaced dialogue.

EPCOT★★★

▶ *Take I-4 west to Exit 26B and follow signs.* ◑*Open year-round daily from 9am. Closing times vary. World Showcase open daily 11am (10pm during summer months).*

Over two and a half times the size of the Magic Kingdom at 260 acres, EPCOT is divided into two distinct areas: Future World, housing pavilions devoted to technology and innovation; and World Showcase, representing the culture and architecture of 11 nations.

Both The Land and The Seas pavilions function as working research centers as well as visitor attractions.

FUTURE WORLD

Eight large pavilions encircle the 180ft-high faceted geosphere "golf ball"—its proper name is **Spaceship Earth**—that has come to symbolize Epcot. (Visit here late in the day: it's very busy first thing). Each of the pavilions are sponsored by major American corporations and house rides, interactive display areas and movies Once inside Spaceship Earth, visitors spiral up 18 stories in a "time-machine" past animated scenes depicting the history of human communication from

Soarin' Lands

© Disney

prehistoric tribes to present-day technology. On the way down, you'll have a "satellite's view" of Earth. Back on the ground, take a film-simulated ride along the information superhighway and explore an ever-changing floorful of interactive simulations and video games that illustrate state-of-the-art communications technology.

The two buildings behind Spaceship Earth showcase some of the world's newest inventions and ideas with interactive workstations.

At **Innoventions West** *The Great Piggy Bank Adventure* teaches the importance of sound financial planning; *Smarter Planet* shows how new advances in computer design can significantly reduce our energy use; *Slapstick Studios* is a wacky game show to solve household problems...

Across the plaza at **Innoventions East** are *Storm Struck* – experience what it feels like to be in the perfect storm; *Don't Waste It!* – games that challenge you to recycle, reduce and reuse; and *Test the Limits Lab* – where you are invited to shatter, drop and impact some of the products you use at home every day. Innoventions even has its own website, http://innoventions.disney.com.

At **The Seas With Nemo and Friends Pavilion** you board a clam-mobile and ride beneath the sea to find Nemo and his friends. You'll travel through an acrylic cylinder in the world's largest (5.7-million-gallon) man-made saltwater aquarium, and after the gentle ride, have an interactive digital conversation with Crush, the turtle.

By contrast, **Test Track** is a 60mph thrill ride in which guests are automotive test subjects. Buckle up and ride the spirals and speeds that experimental cars endure, including road handling, impact-testing and suspension checks. Set in the futuristic **SPACE** pavilion, the Mars flight simulator ride, Mission: Space, sends trainee astronauts some 8,000 miles in less than 6 minutes on a journey to Mars, dodging meteors en route.

Back on terra firma, the earth as "a garden to be cultivated" (in an ecologically friendly way) is the theme of **The Land** pavilion which is effectively an enormous working greenhouse. A fascinating 14min boat ride transports visitors, accompanied by a live narrator, through a simulated rain forest, desert and prairie before emerging into the pavilion's greenhouse gardens. Here scientists experiment on a variety of herbs, vegetables and other plants to perfect growing methods and to develop new hybrids. Horticulture enthusiasts can take a further 45min **Behind the Seeds** guided walk through the greenhouses. The Land is also home to the popular **Soarin'** in which an IMAX projection dome wraps 180 degrees around you to simulate a peaceful hang-gliding flight over California floating above the Golden Gate Bridge, Malibu and LA.

Those lopsided landmark blue-glass pyramids are home to **Imagination!** The star of this pavilion is the **Honey, I Shrunk the Audience** show where you'll don 3-D glasses to watch a rollicking, multisensory experience packed with laughs and a few screams of fright too. Visitors are guided through the pavilion by an audio-animatronic chairman of the "Imagination Institute" on a fantastic journey through the potential of human imagination. At the journey's end, riders can exercise their own imaginations in **ImageWorks–The Kodak "What If" Labs,** an interactive treasure house of the latest high-tech hands-on gizmos.

At the **Universe of Energy** a pyramidal roof winks with 80,000 photovoltaic cells that capture solar energy to power the ride within. **Ellen's Energy Adventure,** starring comedienne Ellen DeGeneres, is a multi-dimensional journey that explores where energy has come from and where it may be going. Bill Nye, the Science Guy, takes Ellen on a trip all the way back to the Big Bang to explain the origin of fossil fuels; they get a fright in the Jurassic era when confronted by lifelike audio-animatronics dinosaurs. The ride aims to raise awareness of the world's current energy needs.

China Pavilion

© Disney

WORLD SHOWCASE

The 1.3mi promenade at World Showcase circles a 40-acre lagoon and passes the pavilions of 11 different countries. Each pavilion—staffed by nationals of the country it represents—reflects the authentic architecture, foods, crafts, costumes and traditions of that culture. Live performers are often on hand to play music or demonstrate other artistic endeavors specific to their native land. Some pavilions also feature rides or large-scale films and, most importantly, good quality restaurants.

A variety of live stage shows are held at **America Gardens Theatre** in front of the American Adventure pavilion. In the evenings, the World Showcase lagoon and pavilions become the setting for **Illuminations,** an unforgettable extravaganza of laser lights, music, fountains and fireworks.

Mexico is the most romantic of all the World Showcase pavilions, not least because of its permanent dusk setting, beneath artificial starlight. A lush tropical garden leads the way to a small-scale reproduction of a Mayan pyramid, housing a gallery of genuine pre-Columbian artifacts. Beyond lies a colorful colonial plaza where vendors sell Mexican wares. At the far edge of the plaza runs the **Gran Fiesta Tour Starring The Three Caballeros.** Passengers on this boat ride drift down the River of Time through a history of Mexico, from smoking volcanoes to the modern landscapes of Mexico City.

At **Norway** a small cobblestone plaza is lined with a mix of traditional and medieval architectural styles, including the tiny 12C Stave Church, which contains changing exhibits on Norwegian topics. **Maelstrom,** the pavilion's major attraction, plunges riders through treacherous northern seas aboard a Viking ship.

In flamboyant **China** the red and gold opulence of Beijing's Temple of Heaven (replicated at half size) overlooks a Chinese garden where koi shimmer through a pond crossed by elegant walkways. The interior houses an ornamental Hall of Prayer for Good Harvest, a **museum** that features changing exhibits of Chinese art, and a CircleVision 360 Theater, where the vastness of China wraps itself around the viewer in the film *Wonders of China: Land of Beauty, Land of Time.*

Germany of course means castles, and a facade modeled after the Eltz and Stahleck castles is the backdrop to the cobblestone St. Georgesplatz, named for its prominent statue of St. George and the Dragon. Small buildings reflecting the turreted structures of a German village surround the plaza, and a traditional glockenspiel chimes the hour. Buildings contain shops and the *biergarten*-style restaurant where a popular dinner show serves up oompah entertainment. East of the pavilion an outdoor model railway re-creates Germany's "Romantic Road" between Füssen and Würzburg.

Musicians, clowns and acting troupes provide lively entertainment in the piazza of **Italy**, alongside the elaborate Doge's Palace. There's also a brick campanile topped with a sculpted angel and Venice's Piazza San Marco. Antiqued facades, an open-air market, and a Bernini-inspired fountain *(rear of plaza)* add to the dolce vita atmosphere. Facing the pavilion on the lakefront is a Venetian gondola, though, alas, no gondolier.

A five-story brick building serves as the host pavilion for the **American Adventure** pavilion, prominently situated at the midpoint of World Showcase. Several major colonial landmarks inspire its architecture: Independence Hall in Philadelphia, Boston's Old State House, and Thomas Jefferson's Monticello in Charlottesville, Virginia. The highlight here is a state-of-the-art multimedia show *(25min)* narrated by startlingly lifelike audio-animatronic likenesses of Ben Franklin and Mark Twain. The pair comment sagaciously on the show's retrospective of great moments and figures in American history.

Landscaped with peaceful water and rock gardens and perfectly placed evergreens, the **Japan** pavilion captures the contemplative serenity of traditional Japan. Its prominent bright blue, five-story pagoda is based on the 8C Horyuji

Temple in Nara. At the rear, a re-creation of an 18C feudal castle houses changing exhibits of Japanese art. Visitors can purchase an array of Japanese items in Mitsukoshi Department Store, a venerable mercantile institution dating to the 17C, housed in a reproduction of Kyoto's 8C Gosho Imperial Palace. World Showcase Lagoon is perfectly framed by the pavilion's red torii, a Japanese gateway commonly built at the entrance to a Shinto shrine.

Elaborate tilework and carvings crafted by artisans under the patronage of the King of **Morocco** create a faithful and detailed representation of the sights, smells and sounds of this North African country. Fronted by a replica of Marrakech's landmark Koutoubia Minaret, the pavilion is divided into a new and old medina (city). Beyond the fountain of the new city's plaza lies the Royal Gallery, which houses changing displays of Moroccan art in its exquisitely ornamented interior. The narrow, exotic casbah opens onto a formal Moroccan restaurant and a bevy of shops.

Capturing the romantic atmosphere of turn-of-the-19C Paris, the main street of the **France** pavilion is lined with mansard-roofed buildings. Even the Eiffel Tower stands here, albeit at one-tenth its actual size.

A second street re-creates a provincial village scene, complete with shops and an authentic French restaurant. A 17C parterre garden is a nice place to sip a glass of imported wine. The whole of France fills five screens in the 200-degree widescreen film **Impressions de France** a compelling scenic tour of the country. Lest you forget this is Disney, however, the Hunchback of Nôtre Dame and Esmeralda, his love, occasionally sign autographs here.

Centuries of British architecture are represented in the **United Kingdom** pavilion here along a brick-paved street. You will find everything from a 15C brick home, to the 16C thatched-roof cottage of Anne Hathaway (Shakespeare's wife), to a 19C English garden. Specialty shops and a pub that serves British-brewed ales complete the scene. There's also a

Summit Plummet,
Blizzard Beach
Water Park
© Disney

Beatles tribute band regaling listeners in the pub courtyard.

The **Canada** pavilion features a model of a 19C French chateau-style hotel, totem poles and a longhouse, as well as a log trading post. Landscapes here vary from a replica of Victoria's famous Butchart Gardens to a re-created Rocky Mountain gorge. In the CircleVision 360 theater, the film O Canada! surrounds the audience in spectacular scenery.

DISNEY WATER PARKS

Both brilliantly themed, even by Disney standards, these two waterparks are the perfect way of cooling off in between theme park days. They do get hugely popular, however (particularly Blizzard Beach), so arrive early, and avoid peak times and major holidays, unless you want to wait an hour in line for a 20-second slide!

Both open daily 10am-5pm with extended hours in sumer *(visit http:// disneyworld.disney.go.com/parks)*. Towels and lockers are available for rent and, unusually for Disney, you are allowed to bring in your own food and drink (though no glass, nor alcohol). Both parks have the same admission charge *($45, child 3–9yrs $39)* though most guests buy a multi-park ticket to include one (or both) waterparks.

TYPHOON LAGOON

▶ *Take I-4 west to Exit 26B.*
Go west on Epcot Center Dr. and turn right on Buena Vista Dr. Follow signs.
🕐*Open year round.* 🕐*Closed Sun & Mon in winter.* 🎟*$39, children ages 3-9 $33.* ✆*407-939-7812.*

According to Disney legend, Typhoon Lagoon was created after the mother of all storms. Surfboards were hurled into palm trees and boats were tossed through thatched roofs of beach houses, and even onto the top of a volcanic mountain. And to this day the shrimp boat *Miss Tilly* still sits, impaled and precariously perched, atop Mount Mayday. Every half hour, the boat's whistle blows and the volcano attempts to dislodge its burden by shooting an enormous geyser of water skyward.

Water slides, rapids and a white-sand beach compete with the site's highlight: an immense wave pool pounded by the surf. Visitors can catch 6-foot waves in here. Or, more peacefully, they can float along the lazy river of Castaway Creek or snorkel Shark Reef—swimming freely with (benign) leopard and bonnethead sharks, stingrays and schools of colorful tropical fish in a fabulous coral reef environment.

BLIZZARD BEACH

Just west of World Dr., adjacent to Disney's All-Star Resorts.

◐ *Take I-4 west to Exit 25B. Turn right on World Dr.; then left on Buena Vista Dr. and follow signs.*

◐ *Open year round.* ◐ *Closed Fri & Sat in winter.* ◐ *$39.* ☎ *407-939-7812.*

Why "Blizzard Beach"? One day a freak snow storm blanketed Florida. Within the blink of a snowflake-tipped eye, a ski resort sprang up with slalom courses, toboggan slides and iceberg walkways. Then, just as quickly, the sun reappeared. The whole resort started to melt and became an exhilarating Water Park with a ski theme. Whatever... this is one of the stars in the constellation of Disney attractions, and entertains visitors with slides and rides in a tropical lagoon framed by snow-capped mountains. With rides for the whole family—from a kid-sized, snow-castle fountain play area to a twisting series of falls, an eight-lane race sluiceway, and a 120ft drop at 55mph on Summit Plummet, one of the world's tallest and fastest free-falling waterslides.

DISNEY'S ANIMAL KINGDOM

◐ *Take I-4 west to Exit 25B. Go west on US-192, right (north) on World Dr. and left (west) on Osceola Pkwy., then follow signs to parking plaza.*

◐ *Open year-round daily, usually 9am to 7pm.*

Disney's newest theme park is devoted mainly to creatures from the natural world, both living and extinct, but it also strays into creatures of the imagination. Geographically the largest park, Disney's Animal Kingdom has placed some 1,700 animals (of 250 species) and four million plants (of 3,000 species) on more than 500 acres of land. Whimsy meets stark reality here, as visitors move from colorful pageants to a re-created African savanna and villages, and can even watch veterinary surgeons at work. No matter that dinosaurs graze, dragons lurk and many animals and insects speak—this is Disney at its best.

Although animal-rights activists have expressed concern for the welfare of park denizens, Disney's Animal Kingdom delivers an unabashedly conservationist message. Visitors can meet with animal behavior experts, monitor animal-care facilities and learn about the depletion of world rain forests and grasslands. Mock research stations offer a glimpse of field observation procedures.

DISCOVERY ISLAND

Fashioned as a tropical artists' colony, Discovery Island is home to roving world musicians, puppeteers and storytellers as well as resident experts in fine arts and crafts.

Navigating the Animal Kingdom

Disney's Animal Kingdom extends in four directions from its hub, the **Tree of Life,** in the heart of Discovery Island. The two favorite attractions, Kilimanjaro Safaris and Dinosaur, are at opposite ends of the park; head first to one or the other to beat the crowds. Two popular live shows, "Festival of the Lion King" and "Tarzan Rocks!" are presented in large, open-air amphitheaters. You'll also find long lines for the 3-D film **It's Tough to Be a Bug** beneath the Tree of Life.

As you head toward Discovery Island from Animal Kingdom's main gateway, you'll first pass through **The Oasis,** a lush botanical garden whose grottoes are inhabited by brightly colored macaws, miniature deer, iguanas, tree kangaroos and other unusual animals. Discovery Island occupies a man-made riverine island; footbridges link it to the other segments of the park. If you think of The Oasis as being at 6 o'clock from this axis, you will find DinoLand U.S.A. at 4 o'clock, Camp Minnie-Mickey at 8 o'clock, Africa at 10 o'clock and Asia at 2 o'clock. Rafiki's Planet Watch is reached by train from Africa.

The park centerpiece is the giant **Tree of Life**. This man-made behemoth measures 145ft with a 50ft-wide trunk and 8,000 branches, intricately carved with 325 images of mammals, birds, reptiles, amphibians and insects. Birds and small animals revel in pools and meadow-like plots at its foot.

The highlight of this area is the show **It's Tough to Be a Bug!** in which a delightful cast of animated insects and arachnids—crickets, beetles, bees, ants, spiders and the like—express the harsh "reality" of their lives in a 430-seat theater beneath the "roots" of the Tree of Life. Meanwhile, the audience, wearing 3-D glasses, experiences such special effects as termite sneezes (you'll get wet), a cloud of pesticide (simulated fog), and even a gentle sting!

CAMP MINNIE-MICKEY

Resembling an Adirondack summer camp with its pine-and-oak buildings and picnic shelters, this is the perfect place for younger children to interact with favorite Disney characters. "Green rooms"—jungle and forest canopies—act as greeting areas where Mickey Mouse and friends, Winnie the Pooh, and characters from *The Lion King* and *The Jungle Book* sign autographs for their visitors. There are two live-per-

formance venues *(check park brochure for show times)*.

Festival of the Lion King is a splashy 30min show with 50 performers in bright African tribal garb or animal costumes, singing, dancing and doing aerial acrobatics on (or above) four giant rolling stages to melodies like "Hakuna Matata" and "The Circle of Life." Toward the end of the show, Simba (the Lion King) himself, assisted by Pumba (the warthog) and Timon (the meerkat), leads the audience in a chorus of "The Lion Sleeps Tonight."

AFRICA

While Disney excels at homogenizing and representing exotic cultures, real or imagined, the river port of **Harambe** may be its best effort yet. Shop owners peddle their wares from marketplace stalls in this authentic representation of a coastal Kenyan-style community. White-coral walls and reed-thatched roofs typify the Arab-influenced architecture.

Kilimanjaro Safaris "backcountry" journeys are the leading attraction of the Animal Kingdom. Open-sided all-terrain trucks carry 32 passengers at a time down a rutted and twisting dirt road, across river fords and through tropical forests, to the grasslands of the

Kilimanjaro Safaris

© Disney

Serengeti Plain. Assisted by a bush pilot-game warden (who flies ahead as a wild-life spotter), travelers look for rhinoceroses, elephants, lions, cheetahs, zebras, giraffes, baboons, various gazelles and antelopes, and other residents of the savanna. The animals are all real even if much of the journey is fantasy.

It's back to walking on the **Pangani Forest Exploration Trail.** This self-guided "safari" through a bamboo jungle affords close-up views (through crystal-clear acrylic windows) of two troops of lowland gorillas, some of whom seem to thrive on the attention. Several hippopotamuses are easily viewed swimming underwater from a bi-level viewing area, and nearly three dozen species of exotic birds may be seen beneath a canopy of trees in an enclosed aviary. A re-created wildlife research station includes maps and computerized exhibits, as well as a display of the cutaway burrows of rare naked mole rats, a creature that never sees the light of day.

Board the Wildlife Express—a 19C colonial-style, narrow-gauge steam train—from Harambe's East African Depot, then walk through a jungle of lush vegetation to the central building to **Rafiki's Planet Watch**. This off-the-beaten-path facility is Disney's best statement of eco-consciousness. In addition to animal-care facilities, which visitors can monitor through surveillance cameras, and the **Affection Section** petting zoo, there are interactive demonstrations and high-tech exhibits of animal behavior and of conservation work under way around the world.

Visitors are also able to look through a window on to an operating room where veterinarians perform surgical procedures on park animals.

ASIA

The fictional kingdom of Anadapus, a rural Asian village set within rain forest vegetation, is home to the **Maharajah Jungle Trek**. This walking tour winds past decaying temple ruins with glimpses of Bengal tigers, Komodo dragons and other animals that appear to roam freely without barriers from guests or from one another. **Kali River Rapids** is a whitewater thrill ride through the foaming rapids of the Clakrandi River. The most popular ride is the thrilling **Expedition Everest,** a high-speed coaster ride up the peak of the treacherous mountain—and back again!

Back down to earth make your way to the Caravan Stage to watch **Flights of Wonder,** featuring the avian talents of falcons, macaws, ibis and other birds featured in this free-flying show. The storyline features a treasure-seeking youth and a wise phoenix.

DINOLAND U.S.A.

Constructed to resemble a research camp from which a paleontological dig is taking place, the supposed discoveries of DinoLand's pseudo-paleontologists are shown at the **Fossil Preparation Lab** (now exhibiting the bones of a 50ft *Tyrannosaurus rex* as they are cleaned and studied by staff from the Field Museum in Chicago).

Meanwhile, research notes from the scientists accompany displays along the **Cretaceous Trail.** You'll find plants (cycads, palms, ferns) and animals (turtles, lizards, beetles) that survived the calamity, 65 million years ago, believed to have ended the age of dinosaurs. You may even spot a nest of fossilized dinosaur eggs.

Nearby is **The Boneyard,** a playground of slides, rope bridges, tunnels and caves that mimics a fossil park.

The highlight of this area is the **Dinosaur** thrill ride. Visitors board a 12-passenger "Time Rover," sent on a mission by a deranged scientist back to late-Cretaceous times to bring home a living dinosaur, just before an asteroid strikes the planet. Along the tilting, twisting, bumpy route, the ride dodges audio-animatronic dinosaurs and plunges through total darkness before narrowly escaping meteoric disaster.

Finally, it may have nothing to do with dinosaurs, but litle ones will probably love **Finding Nemo – The Musical,** at the Theater in the Wild. The show features live actors, larger-than-life puppets and original music and lyrics.

DISNEY'S HOLLYWOOD STUDIOS★★★

Take I-4 west to Exit 26B. Go west on Epcot Center Dr. and turn left on Buena Vista Dr. Follow signs to studio entrance on left. Alternate access via Exit 25B (US-192 west); turn right on World Dr. and follow signs to entrance on right.

Open year-round daily 9am.
Closing times vary. Expect long queues.

This theme park/studio celebrates the magic of filmmaking, from animation and stuntsmanship to adventure and romance. Art Deco architecture throughout the 154-acre site re-creates the look of Hollywood, California, in its heyday during the 1930s and 40s.

Sophisticated techniques coupled with a playful, fun-loving style characterize the attractions, which include rides, film performances and live shows (often with audience volunteers) that provide behind-the-scenes explanations of moviemaking. As a working studio, Disney's Hollywood produces scores of television shows and Disney animated films.

The park is compact, which makes visiting relatively easy. As always, get there before the official opening time and as soon as you get in, head for The Twilight Zone™ Tower of Terror, Rock 'n' Roller Coaster or the American Idol Experience.

Lined with palm trees and sleek, low-slung Art Deco-style buildings filled with commercial shops, **Hollywood Boulevard** opens onto a central plaza by a lush red-and-gold, pagoda-roofed replica of Mann's Chinese Theater in Los Angeles. The latter's forecourt is set with footprints of famous movie and Disney stars.

A 25min evening show, **Fantasmic!,** complete with Disney music, animation and special laser effects, is presented in a 6,900-seat amphitheater.

Studio Backlot Tour

Don't miss this thrilling and informative 35min, behind-the-scenes guided walk and tram ride that offers insight into how some of the most spectacular special effects in movies are made. You might like to follow this on with **The Magic of Disney Animation,** an inspirational and enlightening 20min show where guests of all ages discover the art that brings to life some favorite Disney characters. Then, under instructions from an expert it's time to show off your own drawing skills.

Rock 'n' Roller Coaster® Starring Aerosmith

The 360-degree twists and turns of the high-speed **Rock 'n' Roller Coaster** are amplified by a synchronized rock soundtrack by Aerosmith resonating from speakers in each vehicle.

The American Idol Experience

Get the experience of being on stage or in the audience —as if you're at an actual *American Idol* TV-show recording

The Great Movie Ride

Housed in the model of Mann's Chinese Theater, this 25-minute ride takes you on an unforgettable trip through the great movie classics. A tram with a live guide moves you through a multimedia show that includes everything from clips of classic Disney films to a western shoot-out where you're caught in the crossfire between the real and the imaginary.

Sunset Boulevard

For a glimpse of the glamorous Hollywood of the 1930s, walk down this palm-lined street set with its Mediterranean Revival facades, antique autos, fruit vendors in Depression-era garb, and the swing music of Glenn Miller playing from hidden speakers. At a neon-lit movie palace, Mickey and other Disney characters sign autographs and pose for photographs.

Beauty and the Beast – Live on Stage

A rousing live stage version *(25min)* of the Disney motion picture features lip-synching cups and pots as well as a costumed chorus singing and dancing their way through the film's highlights.

Lights, Motors, Action! Extreme Stunt Show

© Disney

The Twilight Zone™ Tower of Terror

At the end of Sunset Boulevard looms the wonderfully decayed Hollywood Tower Hotel, where guests enter a world of illusion. Incorporating part of an episode from the popular television series *The Twilight Zone* (1959–65), this 10min thrill ride transports visitors back in time to a stormy night when a group of guests mysteriously disappeared from the hotel. The ride culminates in a series of drops, including a 13-story plunge in the old service elevator.

Voyage of The Little Mermaid

17min. This musical stage show is based on the 1989 Disney animated hit *The Little Mermaid.* Special effects, such as the dark and misty undersea feel of the theater, enhance the experience.

Backlot Theater

32min. "Disney's The Hunchback of Notre Dame: A Musical Adventure" is featured in here. Lively gypsies give the hit movie a live-action spin with elaborate stage sets, puppetry and special effects.

"Honey, I Shrunk the Kids" Movie Set Adventure

Youngsters are dwarfed by enormous blades of grass and insects in this fantastical playground, where everything is made to be climbed on, slid through and touched.

Muppet Vision 3D

25min. After visiting a reproduction of the Muppet set, watch a comedy featuring the late Henson's winsome stars and some realistic 3-D and special effects.

Star Tours

10min. This popular thrill ride was jointly conceived by Walt Disney "Imagineers" and *Star Wars* creator George Lucas. Led by C-3PO and R2-D2, travelers board a StarSpeeder for a voyage to the Moon of Endor. Through the large "window" in their craft, space travelers are thrilled by special effects during a simulated, high-speed, out-of-this-world voyage.

Lights, Motors, Action! Extreme Stunt Show

30min. It's all about high speed, high-risk and high-tech maneuvers in this brilliantly revamped behind-the-scenes look at Hollywood's most daring stunts. Watch as a spy thriller movie is filmed in a European city, complete with racing sports cars, motorcycles, jet skies, explosions and jaw-dropping stunts.

Indiana Jones™ Epic Stunt Spectacular!

Watch in awe as scenes from *Raiders of the Lost Ark* are recreated in a large-scale outdoor 30min live show. Then discover the secrets behind the adventurous stunts that helped make the movie so memorable

VISITOR INFORMATION

For general information and to request a free Vacation Guide, contact **Walt Disney World Guest Information,** PO Box 10040, Lake Buena Vista FL 32830-0040 (*407-939-6244; www. disneyworld.com*). All Walt Disney World Resort attractions are accessible to visitors with disabilities. All attractions are free for children under three.

Parking – $14 (free to resort guests.) Same-day **re-entry** is permitted with a valid ticket and hand stamp. Proper dress is required at all times. **Baby strollers** and **wheelchair** rentals available in limited quantities (*$10*). For most visitor services (foreign language maps, information for guests with disabilities, baby facilities, lost and found, storage lockers, banking facilities, camera centers, Disney character greetings), contact **Guest Relations** at individual parks: City Hall, Main Street U.S.A. at Magic Kingdom; near gift stop at Epcot; Hollywood Boulevard at Disney-MGM Studios; next to Creature Comfort at Disney's Animal Kingdom. For **lost children,** check the lost children's logbooks at Baby Care Centers or contact Guest Relations. For **medical emergencies,** contact the First Aid Centers near Guest Relations.

Admission Fees – One-day/One park ticket – Adults $67. Children $56 (3–9 yrs). Free for children under 3 years of age. Also available are 4–7 day passes, as is an Annual Passport (unlimited admission to all 4 parks). Check www. disneyworld.com for most current fees. **FASTPASS** is a free, computerized system to avoid waiting in lines at the most popular attractions. Guests insert theme-park ticket into a turnstile and receive a FASTPASS with a time to return. Upon return they proceed directly to the attraction through a FASTPASS entrance, with little or no wait.

Park Hours – Each park has individual hours. In general Disney's Animal Kingdom opens at 8am, the other three theme parks open at 9am (Epcot's World Showcase opens at noon, however) and the water parks at 10am, while closing hours vary seasonally and depending upon the day's events.

☺ *It is strongly advised that you check http://.disneyworld.disney.go.com in advance of your trip to obtain the current hours for the month in which you intend to visit.*

WHEN TO GO

Walt Disney World is busiest during the summer, Christmas and spring holidays. The least crowded period falls between Thanksgiving and December 25, followed by September and October, then January. Mondays, Tuesdays and Wednesdays—except during holiday seasons—are the busiest days of the week at Magic Kingdom. Tuesdays and Wednesdays are more crowded at Epcot; attendance at Disney-MGM Studios is heaviest on Thursdays and Fridays. Sunday morning tends to be least crowded at all the parks. Due to constant updating and maintenance, some rides and facilities may be closed. During the summer months (*late May–late Sept*), temperatures range from 85°–95°F during the day, and from 68°–75°F at night. Humidity is high and afternoon thundershowers are frequent. The rest of the year, temperatures average from 75°-82°F during the day, and dip between 52°-65°F at night. Lightweight, comfortable clothing, a hat and sunscreen are suggested.

Your Visit – On the day of your visit, arrive at the park when ticket booths open, usually one hour before the scheduled opening time. With your ticket, you will receive a Walt Disney World Resort guide, detailed map and show schedule that lists times for performances, parades and all other entertainment (*for up-to-date schedules: 407-939-1289; www.disneyworld.com*). All **guided tours** are limited to 15–20 people; prices are in addition to park entrance fees; advance reservations are required (*407-939-6244*).

DISNEY BY NIGHT

During the summer months and on holidays, visitors are treated nightly to an extravaganza of lights, lasers and fireworks at the three original parks. **Wishes Nighttime Spectacular,** a stellar parade of lighted floats, makes its way down Main Street, U.S.A. each evening; **Illuminations** held around the lagoon at Epcot showcases a breathtaking display of lasers, fountains, music and fireworks. The **Fantasmic!** laser-and-water display at Disney-MGM Studios is also truly spectacular. Consult entertainment schedules for locations and times.

OTHER DISNEY PROJECTS

Walt Disney World Resort also includes the **ESPN Wide World of Sports** (*http://espnwwos.disney.go.com*)**,** a 200-acre complex with a baseball stadium and facilities for amateur and professional sports. This area is geared to visiting teams rather than individuals though baseball fans can watch Major League stars, Atlanta Braves, spring training in preparation for the regular season. The company has even launched a **Disney Cruise Line** (*http://disneycruise.disney.go.com*) based at Port Canaveral, on the Atlantic coast. Finally, there is an idyllic community called **Celebration,** located 15mi south of Magic Kingdom, which covers 4,900 acres and includes its own school, health-care facility and business district. It's worth a visit for its several fine restaurants.

USEFUL NUMBERS

Emergency ✆911
Guest Services ✆407-939-6244
Ticket information ✆407-939-1289
Walt Disney World Resort Information ✆407-939-7429
Resort Dining and Character Meals ✆407-939-3463

ADDRESSES

🏨STAY

The vast Walt Disney World Resort complex offers close to 30,000 rooms at 24 properties that include resort **hotels, villas, condominiums, cabins** and **campgrounds.**
Rates vary depending on location, type of hotel and season; rates are lower during early Jan–mid-Feb, mid-Apr–mid-Jun and Sept–mid-Dec. Children under 18 stay free in rooms with parents. In-room baby-sitting service is available. For full information and to make reservations: ✆407 939-7429; http://disneyworld.disney.go.com/resorts.
Outside the Disney Complex
Numerous lodgings lie within easy reach (*5–10min*) of the main entrances. Accommodations range from **luxury hotels** (*$220–$350 and up*) to moderate **hotels** (*$100–$220*) and budget **motels** (*$65–$100*). Many offer free shuttle service to Disney attractions. Make reservations three to five months in advance—especially for summer and holiday stays.
Information on area accommodations available from the **Orlando/Orange County Convention and Visitors Bureau,** ✆407-363-5872 or 800-972-3304; www.orlandoinfo.com.

🍽/EAT

A wide selection of eateries punctuates the complex. Sidewalk stalls sell fresh fruit, hot dogs, ice cream and snacks; cafeterias and carryout stands accommodate diners on the run; more expensive restaurants mirror the theme of the parks in which they are located. Make reservations online at **http://disneyworld.disney.go.com/reservations/dining**, or early in the day by contacting **Resort Dining** ✆*407-939-3463*. Crowds and lines are heaviest at peak dining hours (*11:30am–2pm and 6pm–8pm*).
Dining at any of the Disney Resort hotels and dinner shows is open to non-hotel guests. Breakfast and other meals with Disney characters are a great treat for little ones: visit **http://disneyworld.disney.go.com/dining** and click on Character Experiences.

🚴SPORTS AND RECREATION

Enjoy a round of **golf** on one of Disney's five manicured courses (*for tee times* ✆*407-939-4653*, http://disneyworld.disney.go.com/golf). Other recreational opportunities available to the general public and Disney Resort guests include tennis, boating, fishing, health club, swimming, waterskiing and horseback riding. For more details visit http://disneyworld.disney.go.com/recreation.

THE PANHANDLE

Squeezed between Georgia, Alabama and the Gulf of Mexico, the Panhandle extends 200 mi westward from the Florida peninsula in a band 30mi to 100mi wide. This region lies far enough north to trumpet a summer tourist season and far enough west to be in a different time zone from the rest of Florida (Central Time Zone begins at the Apalachicola River, 45mi west of Tallahassee). Rolling hills clad with pines and hardwoods mark the region. The state's highest point (345ft) is tucked up against Alabama. In personality, inland Panhandle resembles its Deep South neighbors, Georgia and Alabama, while the Gulf coast challenges any place in the state for rapid, upscale change.

Highlights

1 Going Underground at **Florida Caverns State Park** (p213)

2 Walking along white sands at **Grayton Beach State Park** (p215)

3 Experiencing aerial thrills at the **National Museum of Naval Aviation** (p220)

4 Dipping in to the natural world at **Walkulla Springs** (p230)

5 The Old South at **Pebble Hill Plantation** (p231)

A Bit of History

For 7,000 years mound-building tribes lived in the region and lived off the sea. Spanish explorers gained toeholds here in 1528 and 1539 at St. Marks and again in 1559, when Don **Tristán de Luna** established a short-lived settlement at Pensacola, six years before the founding of St. Augustine. Spain failed to rediscover northwest Florida until the late 17C and jockeyed with France for control of Pensacola Bay for nearly half a century. Settlement in the vicinity of Panama City began only in the late 19C, although France had established

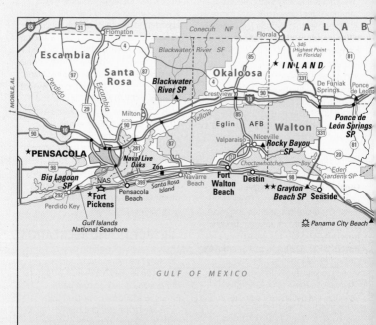

THE PANHANDLE

Gulf Islands National Seashore

Visit Florida

a fort in the area in 1717 and the British too attempted settlement during their possession. Spain again held the Florida Territories until 1819. In 1824 Tallahassee was chosen as state capital.

More recently, large military installations like Eglin Air Force Base and the Pensacola Naval Air Station have pumped money into the region, and a burgeoning tourist trade has lined the coast from Pensacola to Panama City with resorts and retirement homes. Fortunately, the **Gulf Islands National Seashore** protects large chunks of wild beach and dune environment.

Visitors to the Panhandle today are rewarded with gorgeous beaches, an emerald sea teeming with fish, well-preserved historic towns and true Southern hospitality.

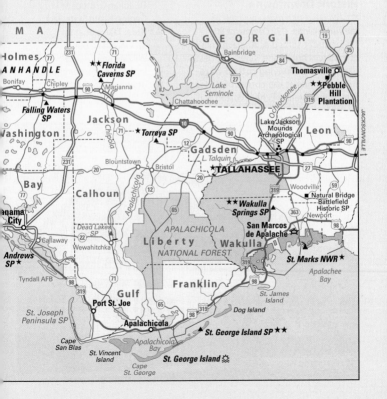

Apalachicola★
and around

Occupying the tip of a spit of land where the Apalachicola River empties into the Gulf of Mexico, Apalachicola (a Creek word meaning "land beyond") is a serene little fishing community. Within the last two decades, tourists have begun to discover the excellent deep-sea fishing and laid-back lifestyle in this formerly isolated section of Florida. The city's location on an estuary has long dictated its economy; fishing and oystering remain the town's major industries. The Apalachicola basin boasts one of the country's largest **oyster nurseries**, producing more than three-fourths of Florida's annual crop, about 1,500 tons of oyster meat, as well as more than half its shellfish.

SIGHTS
Historic Downtown★

Walking-tour maps available at the visitor center (122 Commerce St). Water Street served as Apalachicola's commercial hub in the 1830s. The best example of a surviving **cotton warehouse** stands at the corner of Water Street and Avenue E; here cotton was

▶ **Population:** 2,340.
⚅ **Michelin Map:** p208-209
▯ **Info:** 122 Commerce Street, ℘850-653-9419; www.apalachicolabay.org.
◖ **Location:** Head to the historic waterfront area, park the car, and stroll the cluster of avenues that branch out from Water Street.
🅿 **Parking:** Street parking is rarely a problem.
◉ **Don't Miss:** A meal at Boss Oyster (Apalachicola River Inn, 123 Water St.). You'll find some of the best sport fishing near Apalachicola; local charter trips are available.
◷ **Timing:** You can explore the town in an hour or so, then take a guided eco-tour of the nearby Dr. Julian G. Bruce St. George Island State Park.
👥 **Kids:** Take a boat to St. Vincent National Wildlife Refuge and look for sea turtles and gopher tortoises.

Gibson Inn

Visit Florida

compressed and readied for shipment. Just up the street *(corner of Ave. E and Commerce St.)* is the **Sponge Exchange** (c.1831), where harvested sponges were cleaned and sold; the industry employed over ten percent of the town's population at its zenith.

One of the city's best examples of Greek Revival antebellum architecture is the white porticoed **Raney House** *(128 Market St.)* built by merchant David Raney in 1838. The restored Victorian **Gibson Inn** *(corner of Ave. C and Market St.)*, whose wide wraparound veranda commands a view of the bay, has accommodated overnight guests for nearly 100 years. A number of early houses, like those along Avenue E, represent various styles, including Greek Revival and Victorian *(⊶ houses are not open to the public, but are indicated on the walking-tour map).*

Trinity Episcopal Church
6th St. and Ave. D, at Gorrie Square.
🕐 *Open year-round Mon–Fri 8am–noon, weekends 8am–5pm.* ♿ ✆ *850-653-9550.* Organized in 1835, Trinity is one of the oldest churches in North Florida. The white pine Greek Revival church was built in 1839 in upstate New York, then taken apart and shipped piece-by-piece to Apalachicola. Inside, note the original organ and pews (c.1840), as well as the unusual hand-stenciled ceiling.

Chestnut Street Cemetery
Between 6th and 8th St. on Ave. E.
Laden with moss-draped live oaks, the burial ground dates to before 1831 and contains the graves of yellow-fever victims; confederate soldiers, seven of whom fought at Gettysburg as part of the Florida Brigade; shipwrecked sailors and ordinary citizens. Noted botanist Alvin Wentworth Chapman, who moved to Apalachicola to study Southern flora, is also buried here.

Lafayette Park
West end of Ave. A.
This shaded park, replete with gnarled oaks and azaleas, is perched on a high bluff overlooking Apalachicola Bay. Brick walkways crisscross the landscape, lead-

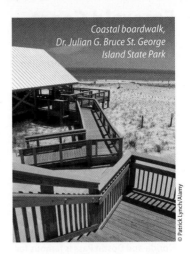

Coastal boardwalk, Dr. Julian G. Bruce St. George Island State Park

© Patrick Lynch/Alamy

ing to a replica gazebo in the center. Take the boardwalk on the south end to the overlook for an expansive **view** of the bay.

EXCURSION
St. Vincent Island ⛱
Accessible by boat only. Ferry service from Indian Pass: look for signs along Rte. 30 west of Apalachicola; St. Vincent Island Shuttle ✆ *850-229-1065.*
Now owned by the US Fish and Wildlife Service, the 12,358-acre St. Vincent National Wildlife Refuge provides sanctuary for endangered plants and animals, including bald eagles, loggerhead sea turtles, indigo snakes and gopher tortoises, as well as 180 species of birds. Red wolves are bred here for reintroduction into the wild.

Dr. Julian G. Bruce St. George Island State Park★★
East end of St. George Island. Follow Rte. 300 to park entrance.
🕐 *Open 8am–sunset.* ∞*$4.* ⚠♿🅿 ✆ *850-927-2111. www.floridastate parks.org/stgeorgeisland.*
High dunes dotted with sea oats and sparkling white **beaches** ⛱ characterize this 1,900-acre park. Its beaches consistently rank among the top in the US. Brackish salt marshes, pine forests and oak hammocks here are home to osprey, snowy plovers and diamondback terrapins.

Emerald Coast
and Inland Panhandle

This popular tourist area, including Fort Walton Beach, Destin, and Okaloosa Island, shimmers with miles of sugar-white beaches, towering condominiums and resorts, as well as boutiques, beach shops, seafood shacks and upscale eateries. Located on the Gulf coast, the area boasts nearly 25 miles of quartz sand beaches, ranked among the nation's best. You'll find a plethora of water sports, like sailing, snorkeling and deep-sea fishing. Destin claims the largest charter sportfishing fleet in Florida and Destin Pass is famous for its snorkeling. Or you could simply charter a cruise and watch pods of dolphins. Despite the building boom that has altered the face of Panama City Beach in recent decades, much natural beauty remains, particularly inland.

SIGHTS
Gulfarium

1010 Miracle Strip Pkwy, Fort Walton Beach (1mi east of town on US-98). Open mid-Mar–Aug daily 9am–6pm. Rest of the year daily 9am–4pm. Last admission 2hrs before closing. Closed Thanksgiving Day, Dec 24 & 25. $19.25, child (3–10 yrs) $11.50. 800-247-8575. www.gulfarium.com.

This marine life attraction has been running for more than 40 years. Trained dolphins leap 20ft into the air and perform other amazing stunts. Scuba divers handle sharks, stingrays and moray eels. Other exhibits showcase sea lions, tropical birds and fish. Gulfarium rescues stranded turtles and birds and conducts research using dolphins to coax responses from autistic children.

Big Kahunas Water Park

1007 Hwy 98, Destin. Open mid-June–mid-Aug daily 10am–6pm. Weekends only mid-May, mid-Aug–mid-Sept 10am–5pm. $36.99, child (under 48in) $29.99. 850-837-8319. www.bigkahunas.com.

▶ **Population:** 565.
Michelin Map: p208-209
Info: Emerald Coast Convention & Visitors Bureau. 1540 Miracle Strip Parkway. Fort Walton Beach. 800-322-3319; www.destin-fwb.com.
Don't Miss: Florida Caverns State Park.
Timing: Avoid driving the jammed streets.
Kids: Big Kahuna's Water Park.

This 25-acre water theme park in the heart of Destin features waterfalls, slides, pools, lagoons and coasters. It also features a mini golf, Super Speed Raceway and two thrill rides (*extra charges*).

EXCURSIONS
Fred Gannon Rocky Bayou State Park

16mi northeast in Niceville. From US-98, take Rte. 85 north 12mi to Rte. 20. Go east on Rte. 20 about 3mi to park. Open 8–sunset. $5/vehicle. 850-833-9144. www.floridastateparks.org/rockybayou. For a non-beach nature outing, try this secluded little park nestled against an arm of Choctawhatchee Bay. Rocky Bayou encompasses 357 acres of sand pine forest with hiking trails and campsites. Anglers can try their luck with both freshwater and saltwater fish. The former frequent Rocky Creek; the latter inhabit the bay.

INLAND PANHANDLE
Tourist information: 850-892-3191 www.waltoncountychamber.com.
This area of small, sparsely populated inland towns and the Apalachicola National Forest has changed little in decades. Farming and forestry still support the economy here.

Blackwater River State Park

7720 Bridge Rd., Holt. Take Exit 10 off I-10; follow Rte. 87 north to US-90. Take

US-90 east 5.6mi to sign, turn left and go 3mi to park. **Open 8–sunset.** *$4 per vehicle.* **850-983-5363. www.floridastateparks.org/blackwaterriver.**
This is a 590-acre oasis along a 2mi stretch of the Blackwater River, a tannin-stained, sandy-bottomed waterway with inviting white sandbars.

Ponce de León Springs State Park

On Rte. 181A, Ponce de León. **Take Exit 15 off I-10; follow Rte. 81 north and turn right on US-90. Park is half a mile south of US-90.** **Open 8am–sunset.** *$4 per vehicle.* **850-836-4281. www.floridastateparks.org/poncedeleonsprings.**
This park features a rock-and-concrete **pool**★ built around a spring flowing with emerald-green water. The refreshing 68°F water is just right for swimming on a hot day.

Falling Waters State Park

Off Rte. 77 south of Chipley. Take Exit 18 off I-10 and follow Rte. 77 south 1mi; turn left on Rte. 77A and continue 1mi to park. **Open 8am–sunset.** *$5 per vehicle.* **850-638-6130. www.floridastateparks.org/fallingwaters.**
The park takes its name for a **waterfall** which plunges into a 100ft-deep sink hole here. A wooden platform provides a good vantage point for peering into the abyss; where the water eventually flows to remains a mystery. Visitors can also see beautiful native and migrating butterflies in the butterfly garden, and take a dip in the lake

Florida Caverns State Park★★

On Rte. 166, 2.6mi north of Marianna. **Open 8am-sunset.** *$5 per vehicle.* **Caverns visit by guided tour (1hr) only, year-round Thu–Mon 9:30am–4:30pm. Call ahead (850 482-1228) to ensure that tours have not sold out for that day.** **Closed Thanksgiving Day & Dec 25.** *$8.* **850-482-9598; www.floridastateparks.org/floridacaverns.**
This is the only Florida state park to offer cave tours to the public. Its dazzling formations of limestone stalactites, stalagmites, soda straws, flowstones and draperies are comparable to some of the largest caves in the US.

Torreya State Park★

Off Rte. 12 in Rock Bluff, 13mi north of Bristol. **Take Exit 25 south off I-10; follow Rte. 12 south 11mi; turn right on Rte. 1641 and continue 7mi to park.** **Open 8am–sunset.** *$3 per vehicle.* **850-643-2674. www.floridastateparks.org/torreya.**
150ft-high **bluffs** afford views of the Apalachicola River and the thick forests beyond. A rare species of conifer *(Torreya taxifolia)* grows only on these bluffs. A seven-mile loop trail threads through the forest and then along the ridge. Forests of hardwood trees provide the best display of fall color in the state, and provide the habitat for more than 100 species of birds.

The White Beaches of the Panhandle

What makes the Panhandle coast beaches so white? According to Florida International University's Dr. Stephen Leatherman, director of the International Hurricane Center in Miami and popularly known as "Dr. Beach" for his ratings of America's leisure beaches, quartz is responsible for the color and texture of these sands. Whereas most beaches contain multiple minerals, the Panhandle's shores are composed of nearly pure quartz. Eons ago, sediments eroded from the Appalachian Mountains and washed down to the Gulf of Mexico.

Waves pummeled these sediments, grinding up the minerals and eventually washing most of them away, leaving quartz to color the sands. The Panhandle's beaches stay so sparkling white because the area's rivers flow over limestone on their way into the Gulf; since limestone does not produce sediment, no impurities are introduced into the pristine sand.

Panama City Beach

and Seaside

The 27mi stretch of sugar-white sand bordering turquoise Gulf waters is a hugely popular, and hugely commercialized, family vacation destination. Stretching along the main drag are high-rise condominiums, inexpensive motels, hot-dog and ice-cream stands, water parks and miniature golf courses.

SIGHTS

St. Andrews State Park★

4607 State Park Ln. (east end of Panama City Beach). ○*Open 8am–sunset.* ✇*$8 per vehicle.* △ ♿ 🅿 ℘*850-233-5140. www.floridastateparks.org/standrews.*
A lovely refuge of fine sand beaches and freshwater marsh, pine flatwoods and sand pine scrub, this park occupies land on either side of the entrance channel to St. Andrews Bay. Fishing piers and jetties extend into Grand Lagoon and the Gulf of Mexico, where flounder, trout, dolphin, bluefish, bonito, redfish and Spanish mackerel abound. Jetties form protected pools perfect for swimming and snorkeling; you'll find nature trails, camping, boat rentals, concessions and a visitor center, too.
A ferry (♿ *see Box, opposite*) carries passengers between St. Andrews State Park and uninhabited Shell Island, home to

▶ **Population:** 11,400.
♿ **Michelin Map:** p2008-209.
🖹 **Info:** Visitors' Information Center, 17001 Panama City Beach Parkway. ℘850-233-6503 or 800-722-3224; www.visitpanamacity beach.com.
▶ **Location:** Three streets traverse the city, east to west: Front, Middle, and Back (Hwy. 98). If you want to get somewhere fast, avoid tourist-packed Front St.
🅿 **Parking:** Public Beach accesses are plentiful, with small parking areas at each.
👁 **Don't Miss:** Grayton Beach State Park.
🕐 **Timing:** Beware, Panama City is a popular college spring-break destination
👪 **Kids:** Gulf World Marine Park.

one of the world's highest concentrations of bottle-nosed dolphins.

👪 Gulf World Marine Park

15412 Front Beach Rd. ○*Open last weekend May–first week Sept daily 9am–7:30pm. Rest of year daily 9am–5:30pm.* ○*Closed Dec 1–25.* ✇*$27, child (5–11yrs) $17.* ♿ 🅿 ℘*850-234-5271. www.gulfworldmarinepark.com.*

Panama City Beach

Visit Florida

This popular marine attraction features a 2,000-seat dolphin stadium and a tropical garden. Some 25 exhibits and shows throughout the day include performing parrots, scuba demonstrations and sea lion acrobatics. Visitors may interact with dolphins in the water and pet stingrays that have had their barbs removed. The park is part of a regional network established to rescue stranded sea animals.

Museum of Man in the Sea

17314 Panama City Beach Pkwy. (on US-98, 0.25mi west of Rte. 79). ◷*Open year-round Tue–Sun 10am–4pm.* ◷*Closed Jan 1, Thanksgiving Day, Dec 25.* ◉*$5.* ♿ 🅿 ℘*850-235-4101. http://maninthesea.org.*

This unusual museum is immedietelty recognizable by its outdoor display of large submersibles. Run by the Institute of Diving, it starts with dioramas of 17C divers who salvaged wrecked vessels using diving bells, and traces the progress of underwater scientific and technological endeavor right up to date. Among the various displays are diving suits, fish tanks, and artifacts from the Union transport ship, *Maple Leaf,* which sank near Jacksonville in 1864.

EXCURSIONS
Seaside

35mi west of Panama City off US-98A along Rte. 30A. Visitor Information Center, 25777 US Hwy 331 South (corner of U.S. Hwy 331 and Hwy 98). www.beachesofsouthwalton.com.

This tiny town is the nostalgic vision of developer **Robert S. Davis,** who remembered the area in simpler times. More than 400 cottages, shops and restaurants in pastel colors huddle together on 80 acres. Drawn from the East Coast's vernacular architecture, elements such as picket fences, widow's walks, latticework balconies, fanciful parapets, and steep-pitched roofs with deep overhangs were architectural guidelines. Although owners are free to hire their own architects, the community's building code requires they use only pre-World War II materials (i.e.

Shell Island ♨♨

Shuttle boat departs Jetty Dive Store at St. Andrews State Park Feb–Oct daily 9am–5pm (on the half-hour). One-way 5min. Commentary. ◉*$14.95 (with snorkeling gear $21.95).* 🅿 ℘*850-235-4004. http://shellislandshuttle.com.* ⊘*Shell Island has no facilities of any kind, nor any shade; plan accordingly.*

This unspoiled barrier island measures 7mi long and 0.5mi wide, with a gorgeous strand of aquamarine water and squeaky white sand, backed by a scrub-covered dune ridge. For best shell finds, walk away from the tip of the island, where visitors tend to cluster, and wade a few feet into the surf. There are two brackish water lakes on the island, where alligators can often be seen, and a small, protected lagoon for safe family swimming.

tin roofs and wood siding). The resulting variety of frame vernacular designs suggests a beach town of Key West ilk, but the newness of the place lends it the aura of a Hollywood set. Indeed, as "Seahaven," it was the focus of the popular 1998 movie, *The Truman Show.* Star Jim Carrey's Natchez Street "home" is known locally as the Truman House.

Grayton Beach State Park★★

1.5mi west of Seaside on Rte. 30A. ◷*Open year-round 8am–dusk.* ◉*$5/ vehicle.* ⚠♿ ℘*850-267-8300. www. floridastateparks.org/graytonbeach.*

This small park harbors a gorgeous 1mi strand of shoreline that has been rated one of the country's top 10 beaches by the University of Maryland's Laboratory for Coastal Research. Though not as wide as some area beaches, Grayton offers plenty of room for exploring or just swimming and sunning. A lovely nature loop *(1mi)* penetrates a tunnel of dwarf live oaks and emerges out past the dunes and pine flats on a trail lined with wild daisies, goldenrod and saw palmetto.

Pensacola★

Coastal Panhandle Drive

Hugging the western shore of Pensacola Bay and well protected by Santa Rosa Island and Perdido Key, Pensacola remains the Panhandle's leading port. To the southwest, **Pensacola Naval Air Station** has become a major contributor to the city's economy. At the other end of town, the University of West Florida lends a youthful vibrancy. Vacationers come for the delightful mix of history, culture and outdoor activities. **Pensacola Beach** and nearby Gulf Islands National Seashore are major draws.

▶ **Population:** 54,055.
⦿ **Michelin Map:** p217
▤ **Info:** 1401 E. Gregory St. ☏850-434-1234 or 800-874-1234; www.visit pensacola.com.
◔ **Location:** Several major highways provide easy access to the city, including east-west I-90, I-98 and I-10 and north-south I-110.
🅿 **Parking:** Plenty in the downtown area.
☻ **Don't Miss:** Tours of the Seville, Palafox and North Hill historic districts and a walk in the leafy, moss-draped trails at the Naval Live Oaks Reserve.
🕓 **Timing:** Spend a day touring Pensacola's downtown historic districts, then head out to the beach or nearby Gulf Islands National Seashore.
👫 **Kids:** Gulf Breeze Zoo and the National Museum of Naval Aviation.

A BIT OF HISTORY

Spanish conquistadors visited Pensacola Bay as early as 1516 but permanent settlement did not occur until 1698. For decades thereafter, the Spanish, French and British played tug of war with Pensacola. In 1781, Spain recaptured the town from the British, rechristening English streets with Spanish names like Salamanca and Tarragona.

When the British and Americans warred in 1812, Spain allowed the British use of Pensacola as a base from which to incite Indian resistance against the Americans. Andrew Jackson stormed into town in 1814 and routed the British. In 1821 Spain ceded Pensacola to the US as part of the Florida purchase, ending the ports' turbulent ownership issues.

SIGHTS

⦿ *Map p217*

Seville Historic District★

Concentrated between Tarragona St., Florida Blanca St. and Garden and Main, Seville is the oldest of the three contiguous historic districts, brimming with frame vernacular, Victorian and Creole houses, many converted to offices, restaurants and shops. Streets here were plotted by the British in 1765 and renamed by the Spanish.

Within this district is Historic Pensacola Village which consists of 27 properties, 11 of which are museums and homes with interpreted facilities that are open to the public.

Purchase tickets for Historic Pensacola Village at the the visitor center (which is the first of the 11 properties). Tivoli House, 205 E. Zaragoza St.
🕓*Historic Village properties open year-round Mon–Sat 10am–4pm.* 🕓*Closed major holidays.* ⬤*$6.*
☚*Guided tours Tue–Sat 11am, 1pm and 2.30pm; call for prices.* ☏ 850-595-5988. www.historicpensacola.org.

Museum of Commerce

Tarragona and Zaragoza Sts.
Contained in this masonry warehouse is a turn-of-the-19C streetscape, complete with wooden sidewalks, dim street lamps, walk-in barbershop, leather and harness shop, music store and others.

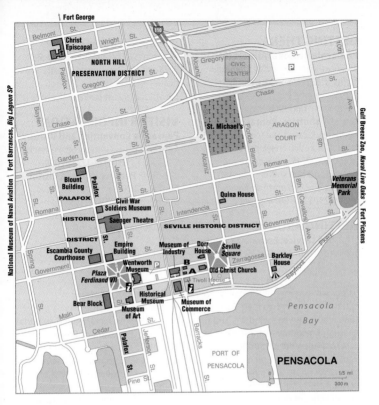

Museum of Industry

200 E. Zaragoza St. (opposite Museum of Commerce).

A late 19C warehouse showcases the industries that fueled Pensacola's early growth—brick making, forestry, shipping and fishing. Among the informative exhibits are a replica brick kiln, lumber machinery and an old fishing boat.

Julee Cottage (A)

210 E. Zaragoza St.

Completed in 1808, this saltbox dwelling is one of the oldest extant houses in the city. Owned by Julee Panton, a free black woman, the house originally sat five blocks to the west. In the recreated interior, the lives of free blacks in colonial Florida are traced.

Lavalle House (B)

205 E. Church St. (across courtyard from Julee Cottage).

The 1805 French Creole home was built by brick-maker and builder Charles Lavalle. Bright interior and exterior color schemes typify the Creole style. Inside, where four rooms display 1820s furnishings, the ochre and yellow walls mimic the colors of local clays.

Old Christ Church

Adams and Zaragoza Sts.

This white-washed brick church, built in 1832, was used by the Union army as a barracks and hospital; it later served as a public library and home to the Pensacola Historical Museum. The church sits opposite **Seville Square,** a pleasant park with overhanging live oaks, where the Spanish built a fortified outpost in the 1750s.

Dorr House

Church and Adams Sts.

An example of 19C gracious living, this 1871 Greek Revival house was built by Clara Barkley Dorr, widow of lumber tycoon Eben Dorr and daughter of merchant George Barkley. The

GETTING THERE

Pensacola Regional Airport (PNS):
3mi northeast of the city (*domestic
flights* ℘*850-436-5000; www.fly
pensacola.com*). Transportation to
downtown: **taxi** (*$15*) and hotel
courtesy **shuttles. Rental car
agencies** located at airport. Amtrak
train station: 980 E. Heinberg St.
℘*800-872-7245. www.amtrak.com.*
Greyhound **bus** station: 505 W.
Burgess Rd. (*7 mi north of downtown.*
℘*800-231-2222; www.greyhound.com.*)

GETTING AROUND

Local **bus service:** Escambia County
Transit System (℘*850-595-3228*). The

city's trackless **trolley** runs every
7–15min (*$1. For schedule* ℘*850-595-
3228 ext. 30*). Downtown historic
district is best explored on foot.
Downtown street parking available.

VISITOR INFORMATION

**Pensacola Convention and Visitors
Center,** 1401 E. Gregory St., Pensacola
FL 32502 (℘*850-434-1234 or 800-
874-1234*); **Pensacola Beach Visitor
Center,** 735 Pensacola Beach Blvd.
(*open year-round daily 9am–5pm;*
℘*850-932-1500 or 800-635-4803;
www.visitpensacola.com*).

restrained elegance of the pale yellow
exterior gives way to a more luxurious
style within. Big bay windows and the
unusual **jib windows**—the lower halves
of which open out like doors—lend a
light, airy feel. Heart-pine floors, slid-
ing pocket doors, and a roomy kitchen
bespeak the residents' refined lifestyle.
Period antiques grace the rooms.

Quina House
204 S. Alcaniz St.
This simple wood-frame cottage was
built in the early 1800s by Italian native
Desiderio Quina in the Creole style.
Slaves constructed the 1.5-story house
on brick piers using native pine, cypress
and oak. Furnishings include an 1840
mahogany-laminated buffet, a maple
wood bed, finger-pine kitchen floors,
and a mid-19C Chippendale cabinet.

Barkley House
Florida Blanca and Zaragoza Sts.
Wealthy Pensacola merchant George
Barkley erected this grand bayfront
house in the 1820s. The wide gallery
porch and dormer windows represent
Creole architectural influences, while
the central-hall floor plan borrows from
American tradition. Sometimes called a
"high house" because of its elevated first
floor, the home commands a splendid
view of Pensacola Bay.

St. Michael's Cemetery
Alcaniz and Chase Sts.
Established on land deeded as burial
ground by the King of Spain in 1806,
this plot contains many noteworthy
examples of monumental sculpture.
Early town settlers, as well as priests,
political leaders and slaves are all buried here. Among the 3,000 or so graves
are many raised tombs, similar to those
found in New Orleans.

👥 T.T. Wentworth Jr. Florida State Museum
330 S. Jefferson St. 🕐*Open year-round
Tue–Sat 10am–4pm.* 🕐*Closed major
holidays.* ♿ ℘*850-595-5990.
www.historicpensacola.org.*
Part of both Palafox Historic District
(�GOsee below) and Historic Pensacola Village, this eclectic museum is housed in
the former City Hall, a substantial Renaissance Revival structure built in 1908. It
features a triple-arched entrance, four
red-tiled towers and a second-story
arcade. Among the grab bag of items
found here are mounted animals,
antlers, license plates, old radios and
antique Coke machines. A hands-on
Discovery Gallery for children occupies
the third floor.
In the plaza behind the museum, visitors
may view the **Colonial Archaeological
Trail** an in-progress excavation that has

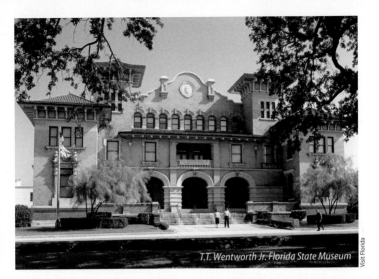

T.T. Wentworth Jr. Florida State Museum

Visit Florida

unearthed evidence of Spanish, British and American forts built between 1752 and 1821 *(visit during daylight hours; site is not lit at night).*

Palafox Historic District★

Just west of the Seville Historic District (along Palafox St. from Garden St. to Pine St.).

Palafox Street, the commercial spine of Pensacola since the late 19C, retains the look of earlier days. Though fires and hurricanes have destroyed some of the old buildings, many remain intact and others have been restored.

Stroll the streets leading down to the water to see the 1907 Beaux-Arts **Blount Building,** the Spanish Baroque **Saenger Theatre** (1925), the massive 1887 **Escambia County Courthouse**, and the 10-story **Empire Building** (1909).

On the other side of Government Street lies a peaceful park of live oaks and magnolias; **Plaza Ferdinand VII** is where Spanish Governor Callava handed over West Florida to Andrew Jackson in 1821.

Pensacola Museum of Art

407 S. Jefferson St., 1 block south of T.T. Wentworth Museum. Open year-round Tue–Fri 10am–5pm, Sat–Sun noon–5pm. Closed major holidays. $5. 850-432-6247. www.pensacolamuseumofart.org.

This yellow stucco Mediterranean Revival structure (1908) served as the city jail until the 1950s. The museum's permanent collection of Steuben and Tiffany glass pieces and 20C American works on paper is augmented by annual traveling exhibits.

Veterans Memorial Park

9th Ave. and Bayfront Pkwy. Open daily year-round. See www.pensacolawallsouth.org for contact details.

Set between the Aragon neighborhood and beautiful Pensacola Bay, this manicured little park possesses a 256ft black granite wall with the engraved names of all 58,217 Americans who died in the Vietnam War. A small-scale replica of the Vietnam Veterans' Memorial in Washington, DC, the memorial is accompanied by a computer that provides data about the veterans and helps friends and relatives locate their loved ones' names on the wall.

North Hill Preservation District

Bordered by Blount, Wright, Palafox and A Sts. 850-438-2156. www.historicnorthhill.com

Just northwest of the Palafox Historic District lies the 50-block North Hill neighborhood, a gathering of Victorian

219

National Museum of Naval Aviation

© Danny Hooks/Dreamstime.com

houses built at the turn of the 19C for Pensacola's upper middle class. Architectural styles represent Queen Anne, Neoclassical, Mediterranean Revival and Tudor Revival. Massive Spanish Colonial-style **Christ Episcopal Church** (1902) squats at Palafox and Wright streets, with a copper dome rising 64ft and stained glass taken from the Old Christ Church on Seville Square.

👥 National Museum of Naval Aviation★★

Located at the US Naval Air Station, 8.5mi from downtown. ⊳ *Take Garden St./US-98 west (which becomes Navy Blvd./Rte. 295). Stay on Rte. 295 south and follow signs to museum.* 🕒*Open year-round daily 9am–5pm.* 🕒*Closed Jan 1, Thanksgiving Day, Dec 25.* 🚹 🅿 ✆*850-453-2389 or 800-327-5002; flight deck:* ✆*850-453-2025. www.navalaviationmuseum.org.*

This hands-on museum is one of only two places in the US that features four F-14 military flight-training simulators. More than 150 aircraft and nearly 300,000sq ft of exhibit space make this one of the largest air and space museums in the world. Among the many aerial highlights are a sleek fleet of the Blue Angels' A-4 Skyhawks, a replica World War II aircraft carrier, a replica World War II airship, hands-on trainer cockpits, and a Stearman biplane flown by former president George H. Bush.

A new 9,000sq ft **Flight Adventure Deck** features simulators (✆*$5–$25*) and interactive displays, including several wind tunnels. The IMAX theater (✆*$8–$8.50*) presents a variety of films, some in startling 3D, backed by an enormous soundsystem, including the museum's signature film *The Magic of Flight*.

🚗 DRIVING TOUR

Coastal Panhandle drive

15mi. Route 399 from Pensacola Beach east to Navarre Beach.

Traversing an undeveloped section of **Santa Rosa Island,** this lovely route offers unspoiled views of the Gulf of Mexico on one side and the Intracoastal Waterway on the other. Though the first few miles pass the shops and condos of Pensacola Beach, the road soon enters a quiet strand with vistas of a pale green sea broken by rolling dunes of sea oats and wildflowers. Along this stretch you'll find many public beach access points. After 6.5mi you enter the Santa Rosa area of the Gulf Islands National Seashore. The drive ends at the low-key hamlet of Navarre Beach.

EXCURSIONS
Naval Live Oaks Reserve

1801 Gulf Breeze Pkwy. 8mi southeast via US-98. ⊳ *Cross Three-Mile Bridge into Gulf Breeze (6mi from downtown) and*

head east 2mi. ○Open year-round daily 8.30am–4:30pm. ○Closed Dec 25. ♿🅿 ☎850-934-2600. www.nps.gov/guis.
Headquarters for the **Gulf Islands National Seashore,** this 1,300-acre preserve encompasses land set aside by President John Quincy Adams in 1829 as a federal tree farm to supply timber for warships. Dense, disease-resistant live oaks that thrived in coastal areas were ideal for building ships. Displays in the visitor center demonstrate methods and materials of early shipbuilding, and interpretive trails meander to Pensacola Bay and Santa Rosa Sound through a peaceful forest of pines and majestic live oaks bearded with Spanish moss. The national seashore, which stretches sporadically westward 150mi from Fort Walton Beach, Florida, to Gulfport, Mississippi, includes several beach parks— among them Rosamond Johnson Beach on Perdido Key, southwest of Pensacola, and Santa Rosa Island Beach to the southeast—as well as Fort Pickens (see below) and Fort Barrancas.

Big Lagoon State Park
13mi southwest at intersection of Rtes. 293 and 292A. Take US-98 west to Gulf Beach Hwy. (Rte. 292). Turn south on Rte. 293 and follow signs. ○Open 8am–sunset. ☎$6 per vehicle. ♿🅿☎850-492-1595 or 800-326-3521. www.florida stateparks.org/biglagoon.
Spreading across 698 acres alongside Big Lagoon, this aromatic haven of pines and evergreen oaks, saw palmetto and rosemary harbors a wealth of mammals and waterbirds. Trails lead back along a tidal marsh and out to the lagoon. The park road curves through a pine forest open to views of the water and ends 2.5mi later at a boardwalk punctuated by picnic pavilions. A short walk takes you to a 40ft observation tower that affords excellent **views** of Perdido Key, the Gulf and lagoon, and herons wading in the sun-dappled shallows.

Fort Pickens★
17.6mi southwest on Santa Rosa Island. Cross Three-Mile Bridge into Gulf Breeze and continue on Rte. 399 to Santa

Rosa Island. Turn right (west) on Fort Pickens Rd. and follow it 9mi to fort on western tip of island. ○Open Mar–Oct 9:30am–5pm, Nov– Feb 8:30am–4pm. Tours 2pm daily. ○Closed Dec 25. ☎$8/vehicle. ♿🅿☎850-934-2600 or 800-365-2267. www.nps.gov/guis.
Located on the Gulf Islands National Seashore, this is the largest of the forts, erected by slave labor in 1834, to defend Pensacola Bay and the navy yard.
The colossal bastion was acclaimed as a triumph of coastal military defense engineering. Visitors can see both the original fort and the changes it underwent during its 118 years of service. These include the quarters where in 1886–88 the famous Apache warrior **Geronimo** was imprisoned and "exhibited" as a tourist attraction.
The area also includes a visitor center, trails, fishing pier and small museum.

Gulf Breeze Zoo
17mi east in Gulf Breeze. Take US 98 east 11mi to 5701 Gulf Breeze Pkwy (entrance on sough side). ○Open year-round daily summer 9am–5pm, winter 9am–4pm. ☎$12, child (2–12yrs) $8. ♿🅿☎850-932-2229. www.gulfbreeze zoo.org.
Among over 900 animals on show here are several endangered species, including gibbons, ring-tailed lemurs and scimitar-horned oryx. The lowland gorilla enclosure and the petting zoo are hits with kids, as well as the 20min train ride (☎$3) through a 30-acre open range, home to more than 100 animals, such as the pygmy hippopotamus and the alligator.

ADDRESSES

STAY
Area visitors' guide including **lodging directory** available (free) from Pensacola Convention and Visitor Center. Accommodations offered include **hotels** ($65–$190), **motels** ($40–$90) and **condominiums** (rates lower in winter). **Campgrounds** and RV parks are also available. Coastal

camping: Big Lagoon State Park (*℘800-326-3521; www.floridastateparks.org/biglagoon*); Fort Pickens, Gulf Islands National Seashore (*℘800-365-2267; www.nps.gov/guis*).

ENTERTAINMENT

Consult the arts and entertainment section of the *Pensacola News Journal* (Fridays) for schedules of cultural events.
Pensacola Civic Center: concerts, shows, public ice skating, and sporting events (*℘850-432-0800; www.pensacola civiccenter.com*).
Saenger Theatre: Broadway shows, plays and symphony concerts (*℘850-595-3880; www.pensacolasaenger.com*).
Pensacola Little Theatre (*Pensacola Cultural Center, 400 S. Jefferson St. ℘850-434-0257; www.pensacolalittletheatre. com*) is one of the oldest, continually producing community theatres in the Southeastern U.S.

The **Pensacola Symphony Orchestra** (*205 E. Zaragoza St. ℘850-435-2533 www.pensacolasymphony.com*) is one of the largest performing arts organizations in the Florida Panhandle.

SHOPPING

Palafox Historic District and Seville Historic District.

SPORTS AND RECREATION

Lost Key Golf Club (*℘850-549-2161; www.lostkey.com*).
Pensacola Greyhound Track (*open year-round; ℘850-455-8595; www.pensacolagreyhoundpark.com*).

A variety of local outfitters offer guided **canoe, kayak and nature excursions**.

Tallahassee ★
and around

Set amid rolling hills some 12mi from the Georgia state line and 20mi from the Gulf of Mexico, Florida's capital city was considered a sleepy southern town—despite the presence of Florida State University (FSU) and Florida Agricultural and Mechanical University (Florida A&M)—until its explosive development in the 1970s and 1980s. Today Tallahassee is primarily a center of government. Despite the city's recent growth, its moss-draped live oaks, abundant azaleas, and the gracious old houses at its historic core evoke the charm of the Old South.

A BIT OF HISTORY

From Mounds to Missions – Members of the Mississippian culture peopled the shores of Lake Jackson as early as AD 1000. Evidence of their existence survives in three earth temple mounds at **Lake Jackson Mounds Archaeological State Park**. By the time European explorers arrived in the 16C, the area

- ▶ **Population:** 243,870.
- **Michelin Map:** p224
- **Info:** 106 E. Jefferson Street ℘ 850-606-2305 or 800-628-2866; www.visit tallahassee.com.
- **Location:** I-10 and US 90 run east-west and US 27 and US 319 run north-south for easy access to the city.
- **Parking:** There are public lots and street parking throughout the downtown area.
- **Don't Miss:** A self-guided walking tour of the Park Avenue Historic District, including a visit to the Old City Cemetery.
- **Timing:** Spend a day downtown, the rest of your time exploring nearby nature parks and on a Canopy Road driving tour.
- **Kids:** Take a glass-bottom river boat ride (watch for alligators and turtles!) at Wakulla Springs State Park.

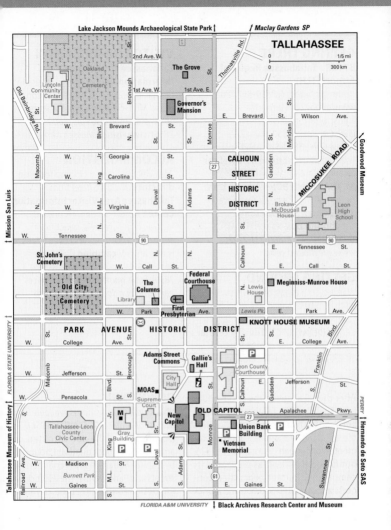

was dominated by the Apalachee, an agricultural Mississippian tribe with established villages throughout northwest Florida.

In 1528 Spaniard Pánfilo de Narváez led an unsuccessful gold-seeking expedition to Apalachee country. De Soto and his men camped in the area during the winter of 1539–40; a historical marker recalls the event at the **Hernando de Soto State Archaeological Site** *(1022 DeSoto Park Dr.).* By 1675 Franciscan friars had constructed seven missions near the modern capital; **San Luis de Talimali** eventually served as the provincial seat for more than 40 Apalachee villages. Missions endured until the 18C, when most were destroyed by British soldiers and Seminoles during Queen Anne's War (1702–13).

Apalachees who were not killed in the conflict fled to other areas, opening the way for Seminoles to migrate into the region from Georgia. (Tallahassee is a Seminole Indian word meaning "old fields.")

Birth of a Capital – Under Spanish rule, Florida was divided into two provinces, East and West Florida, with capitals at St. Augustine and Pensacola, 400mi apart and connected only by rough trails.

GETTING THERE

BY AIR – **Tallahassee Regional Airport (TLH)**: 5mi southwest of city; domestic flights (*850-891-7802; www.talgov.com/airport*). Transportation to downtown: taxi (*$20: City Taxi 850-562-4222; Yellow Cab 850-575-1022*) and hotel courtesy **shuttles. Rental car agencies** are located at the airport.
BY TRAIN AND BUS – Amtrak **train** station: 9181/2 Railroad Ave. (*800-872-7245; www.amtrak.com*). Greyhound **bus** station: 112 W. Tennessee St. (*800-231-2222; www.greyhound.com*).

GETTING AROUND

Walking-tour maps of downtown historic districts available *(free)* from Tallahassee Area Visitor Information Center *(below)*. Local **bus** service: Star Metro*(www.talgov.com/starmetro)*. Street parking available downtown.

VISITOR INFORMATION

Tallahassee Area Visitor Information Center, 106 E. Jefferson St., Tallahassee FL 32301 *(open year-round Mon–Fri 8am–5pm, Sat 9am–1pm; 850 606-2305 or 800-628-2866; www.visittallahassee.com)*.

ACCOMMODATION

Area visitors' guide including **lodging directory** available *(free)* from **Tallahassee Area Visitor Information Center.** Accommodations offered include hotels, motels, beachfront homes and cottages and cozy B & Bs. Rustic and RV **camping**: Tallahassee East KOA Kampground (*850-997-3890*). *Rates quoted are average prices per night for a double room and are subject to seasonal variations.*

After the US acquired the two Floridas from Spain in 1821, Tallahassee, halfway between the two capitals, was chosen as the site of the permanent seat of government. Work began on a capitol in 1826, but financial difficulties prevented its completion. Thirteen years later, Congress appropriated $20,000 and a brick and mortar edifice was erected in 1845, the year Florida gained statehood.

As early settlers usurped the land, hostilities with the Seminoles continued until most of the Indians were relocated after 1858. When the Civil War broke out, Tallahassee was the largest town in northcentral Florida, with much of its success attributable to the cotton industry. It became the only Confederate capital east of the Mississippi to remain uncaptured.

Today a monument at **Natural Bridge Battlefield Historic State Park** commemorates the battle *(re-enacted every March)* in which Union troops were repulsed *(Natural Bridge Rd., off Rte. 363, 6mi east of Woodville)*.

DOWNTOWN

A walking-tour map is available from the visitor center (106 E. Jefferson St.).
Downtown Tallahassee sprouted up around a four-block quadrant bounded by Capitol Square, Adams and Monroe streets and Park Avenue. The 200ft clearing designed to protect the city from Indian attack now contains a seven-block-long linear park.

Although most of the major commercial activity has moved to suburban malls, a focal point of the modern downtown is **Adams Street Commons,** a block-long, brick-paved section *(between Pensacola St. and College Ave.)*. This serpentine thoroughfare, lined with restaurants and offices, creates a pleasant lunchtime retreat for local business people. The two-story brick building with ornamental ironwork on the northeast corner of Pensacola and Adams Streets was formerly **Gallie's Hall** (c.1874), the city's first opera house.

On the other side of City Hall sits the modern ♟♟ **Mary Brogan Museum of**

Art and Science (MOAS), with three floors of interactive exhibits as well as permanent and rotating works of art *(350 S. Duval St.; ℘850-513-0700; www. thebrogan.org).*

Capitol Complex★

400 S. Monroe St., at Apalachee Pkwy.
Crowning Tallahassee's downtown is the Capitol Complex. The restored 1845 Capitol and the modern 1978 Capitol juxtaposed here symbolize Florida's evolution.

Old Capitol★

🕐*Open year-round Mon–Fri 9am–4:30pm, Sat 10am–4:30pm, Sun & holidays noon–4:30pm.* 🕐*Closed Thanksgiving Day & Dec 25.* ♿🅿
℘*850-487-1902. www.flhistoric capitol.gov.*
This white stucco Neoclassical building, with its elegant columned portico and gray-trimmed pediment, ornaments the plain concrete structure that rises behind it. Constructed near the site of a log cabin that held the Florida's first legislative meeting in 1824, the original Capitol has undergone major transformations such as the doubling of usable space. Its 1970s restoration required demolishing 80 percent of the structure. Frank P. Milburn's 1902 design features a handsome lantern-crowned dome and bas-reliefs of the state seal on the front and back pediments.
Since 1982 the Old Capitol has served as a museum. A self-guided tour directs visitors to the **Old Supreme Court Chamber** and to early-20C governor William Jennings' office suite on the first floor. The second floor features the former **House and Senate Chambers.** Historical exhibits, including a collection of reproductions of the state's constitutions, fill the rooms between the chambers.
Directly across Monroe Street from the Old Capitol, the twin marble columns of the **Vietnam Memorial** *(corner of Apalachee Pkwy. and S. Monroe St.)* honor more than 300,000 Floridians who served in the Vietnam War.

Capitol Complex

Visit Florida

New Capitol

🕐*Open year-round Mon–Fri 8am–5pm.* 🕐*Closed major holidays.* 🍴♿
℘*850-488-6167.* ☛*Guided tours: call for hours.*
This 22-story concrete tower, flanked by two domed, four-storey wings, looms 307ft above the original Capitol. Built by Edward Durell Stone (architect of the Kennedy Center in Washington, DC) in 1978, the New Capitol ranks as Tallahassee's tallest building. Guided tours take in the Heritage Chapel, the **House of Representatives and Senate chambers** (🕐*open to the public when Legislature is in session, each Feb and Mar)*, and the rotunda containing the marble and bronze Great Seal of Florida. An observation deck affords sweeping **views★** of the city and its surroundings atop the skyscraper's 22nd floor. Original works of art and a permanent collection of paintings by Florida artists are displayed throughout the building.

Challenger Learning Center of Tallahassee

Kleman Plaza. 🕐*Open: see website for schedule.* 🎫*$8 IMAX, $5.50 Dome, combiticket $12.50.* ℘*850-644-IMAX (4629) for schedule; 850-645-7796 for Box Office. www.challengertlh.com*
The city's newewst attraction is a 32,000 square-foot University outreach facility

which uses aerospace as a theme to foster interest in math, science, engineering and technology, and to motivate students to pursue higher education and careers in these fields. If that sounds a little worthy, don't worry, it's great fun too! It features an IMAX theatre, a domed high-definition planetarium and a state-of-the-art Space Mission Simulator (*simulator only open to the public on second Sat of the month*).

Union Bank Building

219 Apalachee Pkwy., at Calhoun St. ○*Open year-round Mon–Fri 9am–4pm.* ♿ *℘850-561-2603. www.museumof floridahistory.com/sites/unionbank.* Built c.1841, this is the oldest surviving bank building in Florida. It housed one of Tallahassee's first banks, but lasted just two years before its failure. The building has been restored to its original appearance, furnished with period antiques.

Park Avenue Historic District★

District runs along a seven-block section of Park Ave. bounded by Macomb St., Meridian Rd. and Call St. 🅿 *℘850-4413-9200. www.taltrust.org.* In 1830 this mixed-use neighborhood, now composed of commercial, residential and religious buildings and bisected by parks, formed the northern boundary of Tallahassee. Adjoining downtown, Park Avenue became a prestigious address. Although the Greek Revival style predominates, other styles of architecture are represented, including Victorian and Classical Revival. Anchored on the west by the city's two oldest cemeteries, the district spreads eastward to the vernacular 1854 **Meginniss-Munroe House** (*125 N. Gadsden St.*), now the **LeMoyne Art Foundation**, a local gallery that hosts traveling art exhibits. Self-guided maps are available at the visitor center.

Knott House Museum★

301 E. Park Ave. 👣*Visit by guided tour (1hr) only, year-round Wed–Fri 1pm, 2pm, 3pm. Sat on the hour 10am–3pm.* ○*Closed Jan 1, Thanksgiving Day,* *Dec 24–25.* ♿ *℘850-922-2459. www.taltrust.org.* In the waning months of the Civil War, this two-story wood Classical Revival residence (c.1843) served as the headquarters of Union general Edward McCook, who read the **Emancipation Proclamation** from its front steps on May 20, 1865. A mahogany staircase leads to the second floor, where a bedroom has been converted into a gallery for local history exhibits.

Federal Courthouse

110 W. Park Ave., at corner of Monroe St. ○*Open year-round Mon–Fri 8:30am–5pm.* ○*Closed major holidays.* ♿ Dedicated in 1939 by US Treasury Secretary Henry Morganthau, the imposing Georgia marble Classical Revival courthouse (1936, Eric Kebbon) is notable as Tallahassee's most significant Works Progress Administration (WPA) project. The building, which once served as the city's post office, contains murals depicting milestones in Florida history. A $20 million annex of glass and marble was completed in 1998.

First Presbyterian Church

110 N. Adams St. To view the sanctuary, inquire at church office next door. This prim, white Greek Revival church (1838) reigns as the oldest sanctuary in continuous use in Florida. The structure, which provided early settlers refuge from Indian attacks, has undergone four renovations over the years. White paneling and wainscoting and a simple wooden communion table decorate the austere interior. The building contains its original slave gallery, where, sitting apart from their masters, slaves were admitted to membership.

The Columns

100 N. Duval St. ○*Open to the public only as offices of the Tallahassee Chamber of Commerce.* Tallahassee's oldest house within the original city limits was built by banker William "Money" Williams in 1830. This stately brick Greek Revival structure, with its two-story pedimented entrance portico, served as Williams' Bank of Florida office as well as his home. Moved from its original site across the street in 1975, The Columns now houses the Chamber of Commerce.

Old City Cemetery
Entrance on M.L. King Jr. Blvd. between Park Ave. and Call Sts. Walking-tour brochure available online, or at entrance. 850-222-7100.

Live oaks, azaleas and camellias dot the landscape of Tallahassee's oldest public cemetery. Markers ranging from flat marble slabs to elaborate carved monuments in the 11-acre plot bear witness to the city's earliest history. Among those buried here are slaves, free men, Confederate and Union soldiers, and victims of the 1841 yellow fever epidemic.

St. John's Cemetery
Entrance on Call St. between Macomb and M.L. King Jr. Blvd. 850-222-2636.

Adjacent to the Old City Cemetery and graced by native flowers, palmettos and oaks, this graveyard was established in 1840 to serve parishioners of St. John's Episcopal Church.

Twin stone obelisks mark the graves of Prince Achille Murat, nephew of Napoleon Bonaparte, and his wife, Princess Catherine. Former Florida governors David S. Walker (1865–68) and William Bloxham (1881–85; 1897–1901) are also interred here.

Calhoun Street Historic District
District lies along and adjacent to Calhoun St., bounded by Tennessee, Georgia and Meridian Sts.

This area was laid out in 1827 as the "North Addition" to the city. Called "Gold Dust Street" in the mid-19C because it counted so many prominent Tallahassee citizens among its residents, Calhoun Street still boasts a number of elegant town homes, Antebellum mansions and cottages.

Take a self-guided walking tour of the district, which includes 14 historic sites; maps are available at the visitor information center.

Florida Governor's Mansion
700 N. Adams St., 1mi north of Capitol Complex. Visit by guided tour (30min) only, early Mar–mid-May, Mon, Wed & Fri 10am–noon. Call for Dec holidays. 850-922-4991. www.floridagovernorsmansion.com

Patterned after Andrew Jackson's antebellum home near Nashville, Tennessee, this Neoclassical residence has housed Florida's governors since 1957, when it was built on the site of the preceding 1907 mansion. A beveled-glass window inscribed with the state seal crowns the front door; six Corinthian columns flank the entrance.

Tours include the state dining room, reception room, guest bedroom, Florida Room and garden. Guests exit by way of a formal brick-walled English garden. Next door, you can glimpse **The Grove,** a brick antebellum house built for the Territorial Governor Richard Keith Call in 1825.

ADDITIONAL SIGHTS
Museum of Florida History★ (M)
500 S. Bronough St. In the R.A. Gray building, two blocks west of Capitol Complex; entrance on basement level. Open year-round Mon–Fri 9am–4:30pm, Sat 10am–4:30pm, Sun & holidays noon–4:30pm. Closed Thanksgiving Day & Dec 25. 850-245-6400. www.museumof floridahistory.com.

Occupying the ground floor of the state archives building, museum exhibits such as a re-created Confederate campsite and a 1926 Florida farmhouse kitchen recount the state's history from prehistoric times to the 20C. Of particular interest is a 12,000-year-old **mastodon skeleton** discovered in Wakulla Springs in 1930.

A replica citrus packing house (c.1920) illustrates the importance of the citrus industry to the state's economy, while panels of early photographs detail the contribution of the lumber industry. Highlighting the waterways display is a reproduction of the forward portion of the steamboat *Hiawatha,* which plied the Oklawaha River in the early 1900s.

Mastodon skeleton, Museum of Florida History

Visit Tallahassee

Black Archives Research Center and Museum

On the campus of Florida A&M University. ◯*Open year-round Mon–Fri, 9am–5pm.* ◯*Closed major holidays.* &P *℘850-599-3020. www.famu.edu.*
Housed in the Greek Revival Carnegie Library (1907), the eclectic group of artifacts and papers held here tell the story of the black presence in southern, national and international history. Several small rooms, opened to the public in 1977, display a collection of items ranging from Zairean ivory carvings to a Ku Klux Klan robe.

Among the museum archives are the original copy of the 1864 National Anti-Slavery Standard and a collection of rare recordings of famous black musicians.

Maclay Gardens State Park★

3540 Thomasville Rd. Gardens on left, 5mi north of Capitol Circle. ◯*Open park: 8am–sunset. Gardens: 9am–5pm* ⊜*$6 per vehicle, plus $6 per person Jan–Apr.* & *℘850-487-4556. www.florida stateparks.org/maclaygardens.*
This 28-acre garden was created by New York financier Alfred B. Maclay in 1923 and donated to the state of Florida by his widow 30 years later. Maclay planned his garden around winter and spring—the seasons he stayed here.

From January through April over 100 varieties of **camellias** burst into bloom, and azaleas, dogwood, wisteria, mountain laurel and magnolias festoon the grounds.

Mission San Luis★

2020 W. Mission Rd. ▷ *From downtown, take Tennessee St. west past Florida State University; turn right on White Dr. and right again on Mission Rd.*
◯*Open year-round Tue–Sun 10am–4pm.* ◯*Closed Thanksgiving Day & Dec 25.* ⊜*$5.* &P *℘850-245-6406. www.missionsanluis.org.*
This Spanish mission village (c.1656) and fort (c.1696) was the largest Florida mission established by the Franciscan friars. Here the Spaniards and Apalachee Indians lived together for 50 years. In its heyday, San Luis boasted a population of 1,500 and comprised a fort, an Apalachee council house, a church, Spanish-style residences and a large central plaza. Today, visitors wander around a reconstructed colonist's home (known as the Spanish House), the mission church (c.1680), the friary and Apalachee chief's house and council house (c.1660). The site of the fort is still undergoing excavation. Throughout the site, costumed interpreters demonstrate period crafts and activities.

♟♟Tallahassee Museum of History and Natural Science★

3945 Museum Dr. ▷ *Take Capitol Circle S.W. to Orange Ave., turn right on Rankin Ave.; continue 3mi to where*

Rankin dead-ends into Museum Dr.
🕐*Open year-round Mon–Sat 9am–5pm,
Sun 12:30pm–5pm.* 🕐*Closed major
holidays.* 🌐*$9, child (4–15yrs) $6.*
✕🏷🅿️✆*850-576--1636.*
www.tallahasseemuseum.org.
This museum, set on 52 wooded acres
interprets North Florida history, nature
and wildlife. Follow the boardwalk
through a cypress swamp to a natural-
habitat **zoo** featuring indigenous animals such as river otters, white-tailed
deer and Florida panthers. A butterfly
garden provides food and shelter for
butterflies at each stage of their life
cycle, while the .5mi nature trail is
perfectly suited for a leisurely stroll or
nature study. **Big Bend Farm** comprises
a 19C Cracker farmhouse, church and
schoolhouse, which were relocated
to this site. Near the visitor center sits
Bellevue, the modest log house (1841)
of Catherine Murat, widow of Prince
Achille Murat. This nephew of Napoleon Bonaparte came to America in the
early 19C and established a plantation
near Tallahassee, where he met and
married Catherine Daingerfield Willis,
great-grandniece of George Washington. The residence was moved to the
museum in 1967.

Canopy Roads★

Driving guide available from visitor center.
Shaded by an airy vault of moss-draped
live oak branches, five specially designated historic roads—Old St. Augustine,
Old Bainbridge, Meridian, Centerville
and Miccosukee—fan out from Tallahassee. Although most of the roads still
maintain their rural Old South character,
part of the bordering landholdings have
been sold off to developers, and local
traffic has increased.

Old St. Augustine Road
The oldest of the canopy roads dates
to the 1600s when, known as the Royal
Road, it linked St. Augustine with the
missions in Leon County. During the British occupation, it was called King's Highway. Later it was renamed Bellamy Road,
because Leon County landholder John
Bellamy's slaves were used in the 1820s

to extend the highway to Pensacola.
Today Old St. Augustine contains cool
stretches of dense canopy from Capitol
Circle to Williams Road.

Old Bainbridge Road (Route 361)
Originally a Native American trail, Old Bainbridge served as a major route for Leon
County's early Spanish inhabitants. A mission once occupied the plot that now forms
the right-of-way where Old Bainbridge
crosses I-10; several Spanish *rancheros* were
located along this stretch of road.

Meridian Road (Route 155)
This route runs due north from its
starting point at the prime meridian
line from which all land surveys in the
state of Florida were conducted (*corner
of Meridian Rd. and Bloxham St.*) beginning in 1824. Although the road starts
in the city, the canopied portion doesn't
begin until the route crosses I-10. From
there, Meridian leads to US-319 in Grady
County, Georgia, terminating near Pebble Hill Plantation.

Centerville Road (Route 151)
Thought to have been established in the
1820s as an avenue linking area plantations to the capital city, Centerville
Road also begins in Tallahassee, but
the canopied portion is limited to the
section east of Capitol Circle. From there
it winds along a shaded 17mi course,
passing through the tiny community of
Chemonie Crossing and ending at Miccosukee. On the way, the **Old Pisgah
United Methodist Church** (*Old Pisgah
Church Rd., 7.6mi north of Capitol Circle*),
a simple wooden structure built in 1858,
exemplifies early frontier church design.

Miccosukee Road (Route 146)
In the 1700s this former footpath led to
Miccosukee, an Indian village located in
the same spot as its modern namesake.
In the 1850s plantation owners carted
bales of cotton on this road to markets
in Tallahassee. Today vast acres of plantation woodland still line picturesque
Miccosukee Road. The remains of one
of these plantations can be visited at
Goodwood Museum & Gardens (*below*).

Southern-Style Cooking

Bradley's country sausage *(10655 Centerville Rd. ℘850-893-1647; www.bradleyscountrystore.com)* has been a local favorite for more than 70 years. Stop by the old-fashioned country store for one of Grandma Mary's seasoned sausage biscuits, then pick up hardwood smoked sausages, cracklings and country milled grits to go.

For low-country Cajun cuisine, check out **Po' Boys** *(224 E. College Ave. ℘850-224-5400; www.poboys. com).* Try one of the juicy voodoo burgers or pressed sandwiches, served with red beans and rice. Fried crawfish tails and catfish fingers are favorites, too.

Goodwood Museum & Gardens★

1600 Miccosukee Rd. ⌇Visit the museum by guided tour (45 min) only, summer Tue–Fri 10am–3pm, Sat 10am–2pm. Winter, see website for schedule. ⏰Gardens open Mon–Fri 9am-5pm, Sat 10am–2pm.≋$6. ℗℘850-877-4202. www.goodwood museum.org.

The buildings and grounds that remain from the original 2,400-acre plantation offer respite from bustling suburbia. Restored as a house museum, it is now owned by a private foundation and serves as a setting for luncheons, concerts and community events.

Fronted by a columned portico, the two-story stucco **Main House** is topped by an eight-sided, windowed cupola. The interior of the house boasts the first frescoes in Florida. The Old Kitchen serves as a visitor center and gift shop.

A five-room cottage, Rough House, now a tearoom, was built to function as the pool cabana. The c.1911 swimming pool has been renovated as a reflecting pool and the 19-acre grounds have been restored to approximate features of the estate's gardens in the 1920s.

EXCURSIONS
⏰*See map p208-209*

⛲ Wakulla Springs State Park★★

16mi south in Wakulla Springs.
▶ *Take Rte. 61/319 south from Capitol Circle; follow left fork and continue 8mi on Rte. 61; turn left on Rte. 267. ⏰Open 8am–sunset. River Cruise Wildlife Tour: daily 9:45am–4:30pm; round-trip 45min; commentary; ≋$6 per vehicle. glass-bottom boat cruise (water conditions permitting): daily 11am–3pm; round-trip 45min; commentary. ≋$8, child (12yrs and under) $5. ✕℗℘850-224-5950. www.floridastateparks.org/ wakullasprings.*

Set amid lush vegetation in rural Wakulla County, one of the world's largest and deepest springs forms the centerpiece

Wakulla Springs State Park

Visit Tallahassee

of this 2,900-acre park. Reputed to have been discovered by Spanish explorer Ponce de León c.1521, the spring was home to paleo-Indians over 10,000 years ago. Known by indigenous peoples as "mysterious water," this underground spring pumps some 400,000 gallons of crystal-clear water per minute into the Wakulla River. The source of the spring's waters is a secret. Although divers have plumbed to depths of 360ft, the spring's source has never been reached.

Longleaf pine, beech and cypress trees dripping with Spanish moss surround the river; alligators, turtles and a wealth of waterbirds call its shores home. This primeval atmosphere provided the jungle setting for a number of films, including various *Tarzan* movies (late 1930s–early 1940s), and *Creature from the Black Lagoon* (1954).

Nature trails within the park wind through a variety of plant communities, including old-growth floodplain swamps and longleaf pine forests.

St. Marks Lighthouse and National Wildlife Refuge★

23mi south in Newport. ⭕ *Take Rte. 363 south to Wakulla and turn left on Rte. 267; continue to US-98 and turn left. Travel 3mi on US-98 and turn right on Rte. 59 to park entrance.* ⭕*Open May–Sept daily 6am–9pm, Oct–Apr daily 6am–7pm.* ⭘*$5.* ⭑ 🅿 ✆*850-925-6121. www.fws.gov/saintmarks.*

This 40mi, 67,000-acre parcel covers one of Florida's oldest lighthouses, a nature museum, wildlife preserve and recreation area. The **visitor center** (⭕*open year-round Mon–Fri 8am–4pm, weekends 10am–5pm;* ⭘*closed major holidays)* introduces the refuge via a video *(15min)* and several shadowbox exhibits detailing area history and wildlife.

Constructed in 1829 of limestone bricks taken from the ruins of nearby San Marcos de Apalache, the **lighthouse** *(7mi south of nature center)* remains in use today. A wooden observation tower offers an opportunity to watch some of the park's 300 species of birds and the Monarch butterflies who migrate here in late October.

EXCURSION TO THOMASVILLE, GA
25mi northeast via US-319 (Thomasville Rd.). ⭑*Map p208-209*

The area around the Florida/Georgia border between Tallahassee and Thomasville is host to the greatest concentration of original plantations in the US. The majority of these sites are now private estates. Pebble Hill Plantation, in Thomasville, is one of only three 71 existing antebellum estates open to the public Goodwood and Melhana are the other two. Vast acres of pine forests join the two cities along Route 319.

Thomasville is a thriving Main Street City, with a revitalized downtown, several parks, and a variety of accommodations and attractions.

Downtown

Colorful Broad Street is flanked by spruced-up storefronts housing restaurants, home furnishings and gift shops. Stop by the city's **visitors center** (*Corner of Jackson St. and Crawford St.;* ✆*229-228-7977; www.thomasvillega.com)* for information, then stroll Dawson St., home to several handsome dwellings, including the 1885 **Lapham-Patterson House** (*626 Dawson St.; call or see website for schedule and admission charge;* ✆*229-226-7664, www.gastateparks.org/LaphamPattersonHouse).*

Pebble Hill Plantation★★

5mi south of downtown on US-319; entrance on right. ✎*Visit by guided tour (2hr) only, Oct–Aug Tue–Sat 10am–5pm, Sun 1pm–5pm.* ⭘*Closed Jan 1, Thanksgiving Day & Dec 24–25.* ⭘*Grounds $5, house $10.* ⭑ 🅿 ✆*229-226-2344. www.pebblehill.com.*

Venerable live oaks shade the lane winding up to the graceful white-brick manor house. For many years this 3,000-acre plantation was a private retreat for wealthy northerners who came south during the winter to hunt quail; the site was opened to the public in 1983. Virtually all the furnishings are original.

A free-standing mahogany staircase dominates the foyer of this 42-room mansion. English wallpaper, antiques

Coalson Plantation's Garden

Gwen Cannon/MICHELIN

Historic Coalson Plantation & Inn

The Coalson Plantation began in 1825 when Paul Coalson purchased 750 acres of land for one dollar an acre. It is believed that Mr. Coalson built the original antebellum mansion—the core of the main house and inn—at today's Coalson Plantation Resort, which offers a rare opportunity to stay overnight in a genuine Southern plantation house.

Housed in the antebellum manor and in converted outbuildings, the Inn's 33 suites and rooms are lavishly appointed, and combine modern amenities such as Wi-Fi with traditional fixtures and fittings: most accommodations have floral bedspreads and draperies, antique furnishings and four-poster or iron beds. Generous bathrooms feature mirror-paneled walls, showers and Jacuzzi tubs.

Abounding with tropical plants, the terrarium-style **pool house** holds a large swimming pool, dressing cabanas, fireplace and sitting area.

The Peacock Restaurant boasts a monthly menu of **New American Cuisine** with a Southern influence and a gourmet menu is served Thursday to Saturday 6pm—9pm.

Located 4mi south of Thomasville off US-319 at 301 Showboat Lane, the resort is open year-round for guests. For tours (90 min; ⮑$15) ✆229-226-2290. http://stopstayrelax.com. Rooms range from $125 to $600 per night, with breakfast included in the room rate.

Pool House

Historic Coalson Plantation & Inn

Pebble Hill Plantation

© Cyrille Gibot/Alamy

and early **Audubon prints** number among the treasures found here. Outside, a formal garden with brick walkways connects beds of azaleas, camellias and annuals.

All of the barns and stables are modeled after designs by Thomas Jefferson. Among the 17 outbuildings are a bathhouse built to resemble Noah's ark, a log cabin school where plantation children were tutored, and a guest cottage. Returning to Tallahassee, the most scenic route is via Meridian Road *(Rte. 155; exit Pebble Hill and turn right on US-319; go 4.7mi. south and turn right on Meridian Rd.)*, one of Leon County's designated Canopy Roads.

ADDRESSES

🛏️STAY

$$$$ Henderson Park Inn – *2700 Scenic Hwy. (Rte. 98E), Destin.* ✕♿🅿🏊 ℘*866-398-4432. www.Hendersonparkinn.com. 36 rooms.* Set apart by its namesake park from the hurly-burly of high-rise Destin, the inn sports a shingled exterior that evokes cottages at Cape May, NJ, or Newport, RI. The two three-story buildings front either the pool or beach. Most rooms are luxuriously large, done in soft seashell tones, with ceiling fan, three-way lamps and French doors to a balcony or porch; amenities include Jacuzzi, microwave and small refrigerator. Complimentary buffet breakfast is served in the stylish lobby restaurant that features contemporary American fare.

$$$$ WaterColor – *34 Goldenrod Circle, Santa Rosa Beach.* ✕♿🅿🏊 ℘*866-426-2656 or 850-534-5000. www.watercolor vacations.com. 60 rooms, plus cottages and homes.* This very chic seaside resort village, spread across 499 acres boasts a 1,000ft, a Town Center with boutiques and shops, beach club, tennis center, spa, children's camp, five restaurants, nature trails through a pie forest, and lots of family-friendly activities.

$$$ Coombs House Inn – *80 6th St., Apalachicola.* ♿🅿 ℘*850-653-9199. www.coombshouseinn.com. 18 rooms.* The two houses that make up the inn date from early 1900 and feature cypress-beamed interiors with hand-carved antiques, rich chintzes and hand-colored prints. Innkeeping is warm, yet thoroughly professional; breakfasts are extravagant and fun amid fellow boarders. Porches are equipped with ceiling fans and rocking chairs.

$$$ Governors Inn – *209 S. Adams St., Tallahassee.* 🅿 ℘*850-681-6855 or 800-342-7717. www.thegovinn.com. 41 rooms.* Arched and understated, the exterior of this hotel (just a briefcase-toss from the capitol) resembles a high-end jewelry store. In fact, two 19C shops were gutted to house the hotel, skylights installed and rooms furnished with plantation-style reproductions, including finial-topped four-poster beds. Filled by lobbyists during the spring legislative session, Governors offers expanded continental breakfasts, evening cocktails and snacks in the clubby lounge. The weekend package for two is good value.

$$$ Sterling Beach – *6627 Thomas Dr., Panama City Beach* P *850-236-9595 or 8066-573-7678. www.sterlingresorts. com. 92 units.* This deluxe resort condominium complex sits on five acres, fronting a wide swath of sugar-white sands in the heart of Panama City Beach action. Super spacious units are luxuriously furnished, with private balconies overlooking the water. Sterling has a variety of other top choices in Panama City Beach and throughout the Panhandle, including the recently opened Splash (a family favorite) and the Sterling Club at Bay Point on St. Andrews Bay.

$$ By The Sea Legacy Resort – *15325 Front Beach Rd. Panama City Beach.* P *850-249-8601 or 888-886-8917. www.bytheseaersorts.com. 139 rooms.* You can't beat this condo beachfront high-rise for value and convenience. Rooms are basic but all have full kitchens, sitting areas and private balconies. As an added bonus there ia a free airpot shuttle service, free local calls, continental breakfast and high speed internet access. There's a heated pool and hot tub, and restaurants and shops within walking distance.

$$ New World Inn– *600 S. Palafox St., Pensacola.* P *850-432-4111 or 800-258-1103. www.newworldlanding.com. 15 rooms.* Pride of Pensacola, this inn celebrates the port city's nearly 450 years of European settlement. An old warehouse in the seaport district— close to Seville Square shops and restaurants—was converted to house the low-scaled, two-story structure some 15 years ago. It is so solidly built that even street-facing corner rooms admit no sound. All guest quarters are large and distinctively furnished with art and artifacts. Complimentary continental breakfast.

⍨ EAT

$$$$ Marina Cafe – *404 Hwy. 98E.,Destin.* ℰ*850-837-7960. www.marinacafe.com. Dinner only.* **New American.** Upscale Marina Cafe is one of Destin's best eateries with high ceilings tiered for great views of the yachts right outside the restaurant. Moet & Chandon can be ordered by the glass, to accompany sushi appetizers and entrees like pan-seared redfish, rotisserie duck or prime filet mignon. If the weather's good, dine on a dockside table.

$$$ Bud & Alley's – *2236 E. Hwy. 30A, Seaside.* ℰ*850-231-5900. www.bud andalleys.com.* **Mediterranean.** South Walton's oldest restaurant, est 1987, and one of Seaside's popular gathering places, is a favorite for tapas and drinks. Below are beamed dining rooms where tee shirts and shorts are accepted despite white-linen service. Favored dishes include crawfish and andouille gumbo, grilled Georgia quail and grouper with spicy steak fries. This is a fun, lively place, with water views and fine fare. Music is provided nightly in summer.

$$$ Capt. Anderson's Restaurant – *5551 N. Lagoon Dr., Panama City.* ℰ*850-234-2225. www.captandersons.com. Dinner only.* **Seafood.** This pride of the Panhandle can serve 2,000 diners a night without a single bad meal. Since 1967 the restaurant has grown to accommodate 725 seats; located dockside, guests start arriving at 4pm to see the fleet come in. Its rooms are festooned with nets, upside-down dories and dive suits. Another option is the Dockside Bar. Top menu items are the Gulf shrimp and crabmeat casserole au gratin, whole fresh Gulf flounder, and churrasco steak.

$$$ Chez Pierre – *1215 Thomasville Rd., Tallahassee.* ℰ*850-222-0936. www. chezpierre.com.* **French.** This big, two-story, rose-colored house, full of whimsical French art and provincial furniture, dishes up worldly cuisine amid the "y'all" style of regional politics. Pierre's is a magnet for both high-rolling lobbyists and vacationers indulging in a small splurge. Tournedos of beef, roasted duckling, and slow-cooked lamb chops epitomize the classic

French fare. Diners who want to enjoy a full sit-down lunch in under an hour should let their server know of this when they are seated and then choose from the specific one-hour lunch items on the menu.

$$$ McGuire's Irish Pub – *600 E. Gregory St., Pensacola.* &. *℘850-433-6789. www.mcguiresirishpub.com.* **Irish/American.** This award-winning restaurant, known for its quality steaks, blends a friendly, fun ambiance with good grub. Housed in the 1927 Old Firehouse, the dining area includes five themed rooms. Look up—you're in the money! At last count, there are more than 700,000 dollar bills hanging from the ceilings. The menu is huge, too, from simple pasta dishes to wasabi-dabbed yellowfin tuna, to gourmet burgers and salads. You can't go wrong with the fried mashed potato appetizer, followed by one of the hefty signature steaks. There's a McGuire's in Destin too.

$$$ Saltwater Grill – *900 N. Spring St., Panama Beach City.* &. *℘850-230-2739. www.saltwatergrillpcb.com.* **Continental.** When you've tired of beach bars and seafood shacks, head to this lively, upscale eatery and martini bar. Seafood specialities like macadamia- crusted grouper and coconut gulf shrimp are popular, as well as the slow-roasted prime rib. The restaurant, complete with a wrap-around bar and 25,000-gallon aquarium, can get a bit noisy; ask for a tiny table in the corner if you're looking for intimate conversation or romance.

$$ Boss Oyster – *123 Water St. Apalachicola.* &. *℘850-653-9364. www.apalachicolariverinn.com.* **Seafood.** If you're an oyster lover, you must try this long-standing and much-beloved riverfront eatery, with old Florida, ramshackle style and just off-the-boat bivalves. At last count, Boss served up more than 20 ways to have your oyster. There's shrimp, scallops, even steak on the menu but, really, you have to try the famous Appalachicola oysters!

🛒 SHOPPING

Historic downtown (*E. Park Ave. and the Capitol*); the town of Havana (*on US-27, 12mi north of city*) was once a center for the production of shade tobacco and is now known for its antique shops and galleries showcasing local and regional artists.

🎭 ENTERTAINMENT

Consult the arts and entertainment section of the *Tallahassee Democrat* (Fridays) for its schedule of cultural events (also available online at *www.tallahassee.com*).

Florida State University stages year-round theatre, concerts, recitals and opera; for schedules and ticket information *℘850-644-4774; www.tickets.fsu.edu.*

For more classical music see the **Tallahassee Symphony Orchestra** schedule *℘850-224-0461; www.tallahasseesymphony.org.* For the best in blues music visit the **Bradfordville Blues Club** *℘850- 906-0766; www.bradfordvilleblues.com.* Every Saturday March–November **Downtown Marketplace** (*Ponce de Leon Park.* *℘850-224-3252; www.tallahasseedowntown.com*) is a stage for local musicians, authors and poets to present readings, and regional artists to show their arts and crafts. For more information visit www.visittallahassee.com/things-to-do/visual-and-performing-arts.

🏃 SPORTS AND RECREATION

There are four public and two semi-private courses open to visitors with veryaffordable rates.

Hilaman Golf Course (*℘850 -891-3935; www.hilamangolfcourse.com*) is a par 72, 18-hole municipal course located on Blair Stone Road in the heart of Tallahassee.

Whippoorwill Sportsman's Lodge, at Quincy, offers fishing, boating and camping (*℘850-875-2605*).

There's hiking, fishing, crabbing and bird-watching at **St. Marks National Wildlife Refuge** (*℘850-925-6121; www.fws.gov/saintmarks*), and **Wakulla Springs State Park** features nature trails and river cruises (*℘850-224-5950; www.floridastateparks.org/wakullasprings*).

The Gulf beaches are located about 70mi south of Tallahassee. For more information visit www.visittallahassee.com/things-to-do/sports/

SOUTH FLORIDA

Florida's most heavily developed strip extends along the Atlantic in a 70mi-long megalopolis from Miami to West Palm Beach. Called the Gold Coast, this region packs in some of the state's most valuable real estate, from the multi-million dollar compounds of Palm Beach to the high-rise condos of Miami Beach. Here in the urban backdrop to America's sandbox, many people live in the fast lane, work hard, play hard, and take the big business of tourism seriously. The sea is never too far away and the majority of South Florida's residents live on a slice of land some five to ten miles wide.

Highlights

1 Attending a tea ceremony at the **Morikami Museum** (p241)

2 Strolling the Riverwalk in **Fort Lauderdale**, "the Venice of America" (p242)

3 Relaxing in **John U. Lloyd Beach State Park** (p246)

4 Walking through idyllic **Butterfly World** (p246)

5 Exploring **Miami**'s Art Deco district on foot (p277)

A Bit of History

Before the arrival of the first European explorers, South Florida was inhabited by Tequesta Indians. These hunter-gatherers subsisted on a diet of fish, clams, manatee and turtle meat, and flour made from the roots of the coontie, a palm-like tropical plant that grew wild throughout the region.

During his initial explorations in 1513, Ponce de León sailed into Biscayne Bay, but there was no real effort to colonize Indian territory until Pedro Menéndez de Avilés turned his sights to South Florida—ideally situated to control the Florida Straits—after founding St. Augustine in 1565. After failing to establish a permanent settlement and mission here in 1567, the Europeans retreated.

Tourism first came to the area in the 1890s as a result of **Henry Flagler** taming the mosquito-bitten frontier with his famous **Florida East Coast Railway**, which began at St. Augustine and finally reached Key West in 1812. Legend has it that he was inspired by frost-free orange blossom sent to him from Miami during a particularly bitter winter up north.

As it was to the earliest tourists, 21C southeast Florida is synonymous with warm sunshine and fresh oranges, and attracts millions of visitors each year to its white-sand beaches, clear blue water and elegant resorts.

Compared to child-friendly Orlando this is much more of an adult playground, with the upmarket shops of Palm Beach's Worth Avenue, the art museums of West Palm Beach, Miami Beach's bright parade of world-class Art Deco architecture, Fort Lauderdale's famous beach, and Miami's cultural melting pot of eateries, festivals and languages. Now the star of the region, Miami has transformed itself from a sleazy, even dangerous, metropolis (during the 1980s) into one of the world's sexiest cities. The city of decaying hotels, where Snowbirds once gathered to escape the harsh north winter is now the stamping ground of music stars, fashionistas and movie celebrities.

CityPlace, West Palm Beach

©Palm Beach County CVB

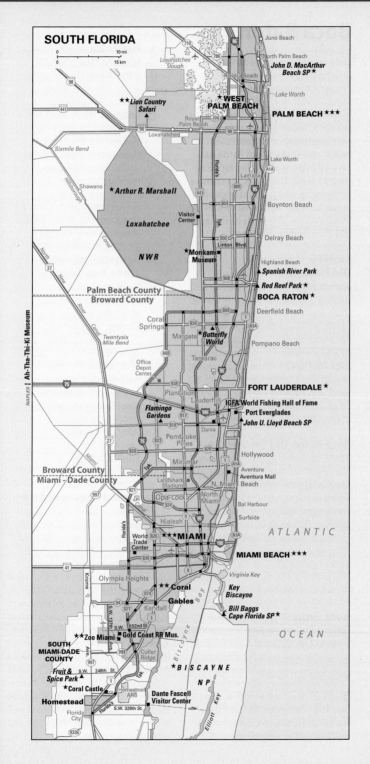

SOUTH FLORIDA

0   10 mi

0   15 km

Juno Beach

North Palm Beach

John D. MacArthur Beach SP ★

Loxahatchee Slough

Riviera Beach

Lake Worth

★★ Lion Country Safari

★ **WEST PALM BEACH**

PALM BEACH ★★★

Royal Palm Beach

Loxahatchee

Sixmile Bend

Lake Worth

Shawano

Lantana

Hillsborough

Boynton Beach

★ Arthur R. Marshall

Delray Beach

Loxahatchee

Visitor Center

Linton Blvd.

Highland Beach

Morikami Museum

▲ Spanish River Park ★

N W R

▲ Red Reef Park ★

BOCA RATON ★

Palm Beach County

Broward County

Deerfield Beach

Coral Springs

★ *Butterfly World*

Margate

Pompano Beach

Twentysix Mile Bend

Tamarac

Office Depot Center

Plantation

FORT LAUDERDALE ★

Lauderhill

Lauderdale

Flamingo Gardens

IGFA World Fishing Hall of Fame

■ Port Everglades

John U. Lloyd Beach SP ★

Dania

Pembroke Pines

Hollywood

Broward County

Miami–Dade County

Miramar

Aventura

Aventura Mall

Landshark Stadium

N. Miami Beach

Opa-Locka

North Miami

Bal Harbour

Hialeah

Surfside

World Trade Center

★★★ MIAMI

ATLANTIC

MIAMI BEACH ★★★

Olympia Heights

Virginia Key

★★ **Coral Gables**

Key Biscayne

Kendall

Bill Baggs Cape Florida SP ★

152nd St.

★★ Zoo Miami

Gold Coast RR Mus.

OCEAN

SOUTH MIAMI-DADE COUNTY

Cutler Ridge

★ *B I S C A Y N E*

Fruit & Spice Park ▲

S.W. 248th St.

N P

★ Coral Castle

Homestead ARB

Homestead

Dante Fascell Visitor Center

Florida City

S.W. 328th St.

Elliott Key

B I S C A Y N E   *Bay*

Boca Raton★

Early mapmakers mistook the area for a similar site near Miami's Biscayne Bay and called it by the same Spanish name, *Boca Ratone* (popularly translated as "mouth of the rat"). Situated halfway between Fort Lauderdale and West Palm Beach, sun-soaked Boca Raton has catered to the well-heeled for more than 70 years. This clean, prosperous community, whose 2mi stretch of public beaches is warmed by Gulf Stream waters 200 yards offshore, still attracts monied visitors.

SIGHTS
Old Floresta

Bounded by W. Palmetto Park Rd., Periwinkle St., N.W. 9th Ave. and N.W. 7th Ave. Drive down Aurelia, Azalea, Hibiscus or Oleander Street for a glimpse of one of Boca's oldest neighborhoods. Designed by Addison Mizner for his executives in 1925, Old Floresta still boasts 29 original houses characterized by red barrel-tile roofs and light-colored stucco walls. Large palm and banyan trees shade these quiet, pleasant avenues.

Boca Raton Old Town Hall★

71 N. Federal Hwy. ○*Open year-round Mon–Fri 10am–4pm.* ○*Closed Dec 25– Jan 2.* ♿ P ☏*561-395-6766. www.bocahistory.org.*
This elegant building was designed by Addison Mizner as Boca Raton's first municipal edifice. The finished building, fashioned with beams and paneling of pecky cypress and pine floors, housed city officials and the fire and police departments until 1983.

Boca Express Train Museum

○*Open mid Jan–mid Apr first and third Fri 1pm–4pm.* ○*Closed Good Fri.* ⊚*$5.* ☏*561-395-6766. www.bocahistory.org*
Close to the town hall, the historic F. E. C. Railway Station (also known as the Count de Hoernle Pavilion) is home to two 1947 Seaboard Air Line streamlined (Budd dining and lounge) rail cars, restored to their original splendor.

▸ **Population:** 86,600.
⌚ **Michelin Map:** p237, 239
ℹ **Info:** 1800 N. Dixie Highway ☏561-395-4433; www.bocaratonchamber.com.
▶ **Location:** North-south I-95 to US 808 is the quickest way into the city; Rte. 1 travels north-south, parallel to the ocean shoreline.
P **Parking:** There are several garages in the city, including the Quality Garage on 13th St. just west of N. Dixie Hwy. Another is just off E. Palmetto Park Rd.
⊚ **Don't Miss:** Mizner Park and the Boca Raton Museum of Art area with restaurants, shops, museums, and more.
○ **Timing:** A day or two to explore Boca Raton sights is plenty, then head to the beach or check out top attractions in nearby Fort Lauderdale.
👪 **Kids:** Take an airboat ride through the northern tip of the Everglades at Loxahatchee National Wildlife Refuge.

Boca Raton Museum of Art★

501 Plaza Real, in Mizner Park. ○*Open year-round Tue–Fri 10am–5pm (Wed 9pm), Sat & Sun noon–5pm.* ○*Closed major holidays.* ⊚*$8.* ✗♿ P ☏*561-392-2500. www.bocamuseum.org.*
One of South Florida's finest cultural attractions, the Boca Raton Museum of Art presents changing exhibitions of national and international importance. The pink pastel, two-story structure, a modern take on the Mediterranean Revival style, includes a sculpture garden. The museum's permanent collection includes late-19C and early-20C works by such modern masters as Matisse, Degas, Picasso and Klee as well as pre-Columbian and African art and contemporary works.

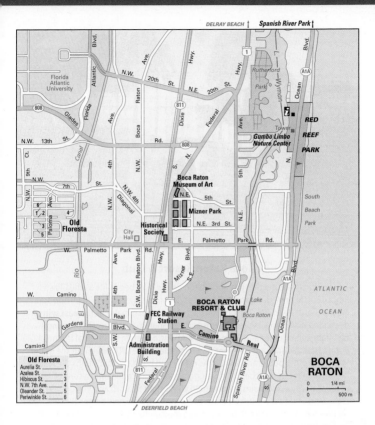

DELRAY BEACH ↑   **Spanish River Park** ↑

/ DEERFIELD BEACH

Mizner's Magic

In 1925 Addison Mizner's corporation began construction of a hotel that would draw hundreds of rich and famous visitors. The open arcades and pastel pink walls of the Mediterranean Revival-style Cloister Inn (now Boca Raton Resort & Club, ⓒ see Box p240) rose from the coastal swampland in just six months. The flamboyant architect envisioned an entire city with landscaped gardens and promenades, world-class theaters and a huge cathedral. Work on his grandiose plan was well underway when the Florida real-estate bubble burst. Even so, by the end of 1925 Mizner had sold $11 million worth of lots.

The Boca Raton Resort & Club remains a testament to Mizner's vision, as does **Camino Real,** a 160ft-wide avenue once divided by a canal on which gondolas ferried the Cloister's guests from the inn to the beach. Another surviving Mizner structure, the **Administration Building** *(2 E. Camino Real, at intersection of Dixie Hwy.),* modeled after El Greco's home in Toledo, Spain, now houses a popular restaurant. After decades of uninspired building, the Mediterranean style has returned with **Mizner Park** *(400 N. Federal Hwy., between Palmetto Park Rd. and Glades Rd.),* a pink stucco shopping/office/apartment complex (1991) distinguished by its airy arcades, fountains and courtyards.

For a fascinating look at the many projects that Mizner planned but never realised (and a few more that he did finish) visit www.bocahistory.org/exhibits/exhibits_mizner.asp.

Boca Raton Resort & Club

Boca Raton Resort & Club

The world-class hotel that put Boca Raton on the map began life as the Cloister Inn, a 100-room Mediterranean Revival-style inn completed in 1926 by Addison Mizner (💿 see Box p239). The original part of the hotel remains as the **east wing**, decorated with pecky cypress beams and 15C Spanish furniture. On the wing's first floor, gilt columns and a soaring ceiling distinguish the Cathedral Dining Room. Note the scrupulous attention to ornamental detail throughout the grand lobby and other public areas. Outside, espaliered bougainvillea climbs the wall beside Romanesque arches, while a loggia and cloister open onto a central courtyard whose fountains are accented with bright Spanish and Portuguese tiles. A 1929 addition—300 rooms in two wings—by the new owner, Indiana utilities millionaire Clarence Geist, created the hotel's present horseshoe shape. Arthur Vining Davis, founder of the Arvida Company, bought the hotel in 1969 and added the 300ft pink tower.

501 E. Camino Real. ♿ ✆561-395-3000. www.bocaresort.com. ⚓Visit by guided tour (1hr 30min) only, year-round Tue 2pm–3:30pm, Sat in Aug. ⚐$15 plus $10 car valet fee; reservations with Boca Raton Historical Society. ✆561-395-6766. www.bocahistory.org

BEACHES
Red Reef Park★
1400 N. Ocean Blvd. (A1A), 1 mi north of Palmetto Park Rd. ⚐$16/vehicle 🅿 *✆561-393-7974. www.ci.boca-raton.fl.us.*

A densely vegetated dune, a boardwalk and a pleasant beach for swimming, fishing and snorkeling over an artificial reef occupy the east side of this 67-acre park. The west side contains the **Gumbo Limbo Nature Center** 👥, a 20-acre swatch of tropical hammock preserved in its natural state.

A **visitor center** (🕐 *open year-round Mon–Sat 9am–4pm, Sun noon–4pm;* 🕐*closed major holidays;* ⚐*suggested*

$5.00 donation per person; ♿ *✆561-338-1473; www.gumbolimbo.org) displays* live snakes, tanks of living corals and crustaceans, and a shell collection. Large outdoor saltwater tanks allow visitors an up-close look at anemones, urchins, loggerhead turtles and other marine life. An informative short boardwalk trail winds through a tropical hammock and mangrove wetland, past strangler fig trees, paradise trees and the red-bark gumbo-limbo. A 40ft observation tower clears the forest canopy, providing ocean views.

A comprehensive activities schedule gives visitors the opportunity to get closer to nature (guided hammock walks; daily feeding of lobster, turtles and sharks; beachcombing), and make their own souvenirs (kites; fish prints).

Spanish River Park

3001 N. Ocean Blvd./A1A.
Entrance on west side, just north of Gumbo Limbo Nature Center.
🕐*Open year-round daily 8am–dusk.*
🎫*$16 per vehicle.* ♿🅿 ☎*561-393-7815.*
www.ci.boca-raton.fl.us.

Taking its name from a shallow freshwater stream that coursed along its western edge before the creation of the Intracoastal Waterway, the park provides oceanfront as well as coastal woodlands recreation. A nature trail beside the lagoon provides a pleasant short stroll through the forest. The picnic area is equipped with grills and tables.

EXCURSIONS
Morikami Museum and Japanese Gardens★

4000 Morikami Park Rd. 12mi northwest of Boca Raton in Delray Beach.
▶ *Take I-95 north to Linton Blvd. and go west 3.5mi; turn south on Jog Rd. and continue 1.5mi.* 🕐*Open year-round Tue–Sun 10am–5pm.* 🎫*$12.* ✕♿🅿
☎*561-495-0233. www.morikami.org.*

Built on a 200-acre parcel donated to Palm Beach County by prosperous pineapple farmer George Sukeji Morikami, this complex pays homage to Japanese culture. Changing exhibits showcase art objects and artefacts from the collection, and range from vintage toys to laquerware, woodblock prints and textiles.

In the Seishin-an Tea House adjacent to the lobby, visitors can watch an authentic Japanese **tea ceremony** *(second or third Sat of every month, see website, at noon, 1pm, 2pm & 3pm; $5).* A lakeside walk away lies **Yamato-kan**★, inspired by a Japanese imperial villa.

Some 16 acres of gardens typifying traditional Japanese styles from the 9C to the 20C feature traditional koi ponds, waterfalls and a **bonsai garden.**

♟♟ Arthur R. Marshall Loxahatchee National Wildlife Refuge★

8mi west of Boca Raton, on US-441.
▶ *Take I-95 to Rte. 806/Atlantic Ave. west to US-441; go north on US-441 3mi to refuge entrance.*
🕐*Open year-round daily sunrise– sunset.* 🎫*$5 per vehicle.* 🅿 ☎*561-734-8303. www.fws.gov/loxahatchee.*

This huge refuge *(221sq mi)* at the northernmost tip of the Everglades, is home to more than 18,000 alligators and numerous species of birds and other wildlife, including the endangered snail kite and wood stork. The visitor center *(*🕐*open daily 9am–4pm;* 🕐*closed Dec 25)* contains dioramas and exhibits on local ecology. Behind the center a boardwalk *(0.4 mi)* snakes back into a bald cypress swamp. Reptiles flourish here, as do a variety of ferns and colorful bromeliads and trees, some streaked with the red baton rouge lichen. Another trail *(0.8 mi)* marked with interpretive signs circles a freshwater impoundment past an observation tower. Canoeists can take a 5.5mi-loop trail into the refuge, which is surrounded by a 57mi long canal and levee that stores water for area residents. Saturday morning kids programs range from reading and craft activities to bird watching.

Ibis, Arthur R. Marshall Loxahatchee National Wildlife Refuge

© FloridaStock/iStockphoto.com

Fort Lauderdale★

Fort Lauderdale is the largest city of sprawling Broward County. Straddling 300mi of natural and artificial waterways, this "Venice of America" is a boater's paradise with 40,000-plus registered yachts, many of which are moored at the Radisson **Bahia Mar Yacht Basin** on the Atlantic Intracoastal Waterway. Ranked second among Florida's busiest ports (behind Miami), **Port Everglades** handles some 23 million tons of cargo each year and is the world's third largest cruise port with close to three million people departing annually for Caribbean ports of call.

A BIT OF HISTORY

The area's first residents were Tequesta natives, followed by the Spanish in the 16C and, by the early 1800s, the Semi-noles, who cohabited peacefully with area settlers until the Second Seminole War. Major William Lauderdale and his detachment built an army fort atop a series of Tequesta Indian mounds here in 1838; the city that grew up around it inherited the name of the fort's com-manding officer. In 1896 Henry Flagler's Florida East Coast Railway entered Fort Lauderdale en route to Miami, catalyzing the development of a busy agricultural community. Like Miami to the south, Fort Lauderdale continues to boom.

SIGHTS

Fort Lauderdale's lively downtown **Arts and Sciences District**—bounded by E. Broward Boulevard on the north, the New River on the south, and S.E. Third and S.W. Seventh avenues on the east and west, respectively—encompasses the Museum of Art, the Museum of Dis-covery and Science and the Broward Center for the Performing Arts. The latter, a contemporary complex on the river's north bank, brings world-class performances to the city. The Broward Center sits at the western terminus of

▶ **Population:** 152,397.
◉ **Michelin Map:** p237, p244
▣ **Info:** 100 E. Broward Blvd. ℘954-765-4466 or 800-227-8669; www.sunny.org.
▷ **Location:** Fort Lauderdale lies between Miami, 23 miles to the south and Boca Raton to the north. I-95 runs north-south, just west of downtown.
🅿 **Parking:** Parking garages along SW 2nd St. are the best spots for exploring the downtown and Riverwalk area.
◉ **Don't Miss:** Stroll the Arts and Sciences District, including Riverwalk.
◷ **Timing:** Go with the flow: allow plenty of time to browse, waterfront shops and galleries and take in a free outdoor concert or event. In downtown Hollywood you can walk the beach boardwalk, flanked by galleries, boutiques and restaurants. Bike rentals are available, too.
👥 **Kids:** Kids won't want to miss the Museum of Discovery and Science, which is fun for all ages.

Riverwalk, a tree-lined bricked espla-nade that stretches along the north and south banks of the New River. Just east of downtown, trendy **Las Olas Boule-vard** boasts a wide variety of shops, galleries and outdoor cafes (between S.E. 6th and 11th Aves.).

Stranahan House★

335 S.E. 6th Ave., 0.2mi south of Las Olas Blvd. just above New River Tunnel. ◷Open year-round daily, ⟿by guided tour (45–60min) only 1pm, 2pm, 3pm. ◷Closed major holidays. ⬤$12. 🅿 ℘954-524-4736. http://stranahanhouse.org.

Visit Florida

The Strip

Lauderdale's famed **Strip**★ of beach, which stretches for 2mi along Atlantic Boulevard *(on A1A, from Sunrise Blvd. to Bahia Mar Yacht Basin)* had become known in the 1950s not only for its beauty but as the destination for thousands of college students from all over the US who flocked there each year during Spring Break. Fort Lauderdale reigned for some 30 years as the mecca of Spring Break bacchanalia—celebrated in the film *Where the Boys Are* (1960). In the mid-1980s, city officials began actively discouraging the legions of collegiate visitors from adopting local beaches as a springtime playground. As a result Fort Lauderdale Beach is now relatively quiet, with families and older visitors making up its predominant elements.

The Strip, which fell into a state of seediness in recent decades, has been enlivened by an ambitious beach redevelopment program that has attracted new businesses and added a $26 million beachfront promenade. Having shed its image as the capital of springtime frivolty, Fort Lauderdale, with its diversified economy—tourism generates billions of dollars annually—and growing cultural offerings, now ranks among America's most attractive and liveable mid-size cities.

Airy and elegant, the two-story frame house skirted by wide verandas is Broward County's oldest building, and its most popular historical site. It was built on the banks of the New River in 1901 by **Frank Stranahan,** the area's first permanent white settler, who came to the area in 1893 from Ohio to operate a ferry on the New River.

This graceful example of Florida pioneer architecture is located on the site of the trading post Stranahan originally set up to serve settlers and Seminoles. The interior boasts double-beaded wall paneling expertly crafted from Dade County pine.

Museum of Art, Fort Lauderdale★ (MoA)

1 E. Las Olas Blvd. ◷*Open year-round Tue–Sat 11am–5pm (Thu 8pm), Sun noon–5pm.* ◷*Closed major holidays.* ☙*$10.* ✕&🅿 ☏*954-525-5500. www.moafl.org.*

Edward Larrabee Barnes designed this three-story white structure (1986) on a prominent corner near the New River, as part of the city's downtown revitalization. A two-story wing designed by Oscar Vago recently added 10,000sq ft of exhibit space. The museum comprises over 5,000 pieces ranging from a sizable collection of paintings by Ameri-

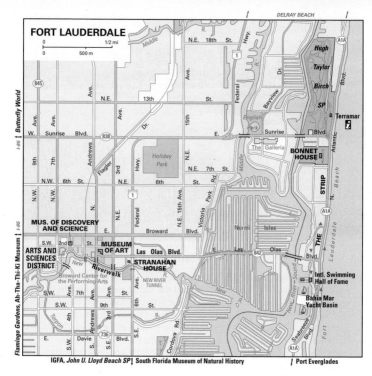

FORT LAUDERDALE

IGFA, *John U. Lloyd Beach SP* | South Florida Museum of Natural History | Port Everglades

can Impressionist **William Glackens** to works by Pop artist Andy Warhol.

However, the MoA is best known for its collection of **CoBrA art**★★ — the largest assemblage in the US. Born in Paris in 1948, the CoBrA movement consisted of Expressionists from **C**open-hagen, **B**russels and **A**msterdam who drew their inspiration from folk art and children's drawings. Pierre Alechinsky, Christian Dotremont, Karel Appel and Carl-Henning Pedersen are among the movement's best-known artists. Pan-African, pre-Columbian, Native American and a growing collection of contemporary Cuban art round out the museum's holdings.

Old Fort Lauderdale Village & Museum

219 S.W. 2nd Ave. ⏰*Open year-round Tue–Sun noon–4pm.* ⏰*Closed Jan 1, Jul 4, Dec 25.* 🎫*$10.* ♿ 📞*954-463-4431. www.oldfortlauderdale.org.*

Housed in the 1905 **New River Inn,** this facility chronicles the city's past from its founding to the present day.

Changing exhibits focus on specific aspects of local history. The museum is operated by the Fort Lauderdale Historical Society, which also maintains a research library nearby *(219 S.W. 2nd Ave.).*

The building housing the research library forms part of the **Historic Village Complex** *(bounded by S.W. 2nd St., N.W. 1st Ave., Broward Blvd. and the New River),* containing several vernacular early-20C structures. The 1904 **Bryan Homes** *(301 and 303 N.W. New River Dr.)* have been connected and converted into the River House restaurant and the New River Inn. All three properties were owned by the Bryan family, who were among the city's first settlers. Broward County's oldest hotel, the inn was constructed using hollow concrete blocks made with local sand by Fort Lauderdale's first builder, Edwin King. The Dade County pine **King-Cromartie House** *(229 S.W. 2nd Ave.),* built in 1907 on New River Drive, was moved via river barge to its present site in 1971 *(Guided tour available 1pm, 2pm, 3pm).*

GETTING THERE

Fort Lauderdale/Hollywood International Airport (FLL): 4mi south of city *(information: ℘ 954-359-1200)*. A commuter line links Broward, Palm Beach and Miami-Dade counties, with free shuttles to the airport (℘800-874-7245); **taxi** service *($15–$20)* and hotel courtesy shuttles are also available. **Rental car agencies** located at airport. Train service to Palm Beach and Miami by **Tri-Rail** *(℘800-874-7245)*. **Amtrak train** station: 200 S.W. 21st Terr. *(℘800-872-7245; www.amtrak.com)*. Greyhound **bus** station: 515 N.E. 3rd St. *(℘800-231-2222; www.greyhound.com)*.

GETTING AROUND

Local **bus service:** Broward County Mass Transit (BCT) *($1; information: ℘954-357-8400)*. **Downtown shuttle** between Courthouse and BCT Terminal *(year-round Mon–Fri 7:30am–6pm, every 10min)* and the TMAX Express *(year-round Fri–Sat 6pm–1pm; ℘954-761-3543)*. If you are driving there is metered **parking** *(25¢/30 minutes)* along Andrews Ave. by the hospital and along Las Olas Blvd.

Water taxi: You haven't visited Fort Lauderdale until you've seen it from the water, along the Intracoastal Waterway and New River *(year-round daily 10am–1:30am; ℘954-467-6677; www.watertaxi.com)*.

Anticipation Yachts offer daily narrated **riverfront cruises** *(℘954-463-3220 or ℘800-499-2248; www.anticipation.com)*.

VISITOR INFORMATION

Greater Fort Lauderdale Convention and Visitors Bureau, 100 E. Broward Blvd., Fort Lauderdale FL 33316 *(open year-round Mon–Fri 8:30am–5pm; ℘954-765-4466 or 800-227-8669; www.sunny.org)*.

Greater Fort Lauderdale Chamber of Commerce, 512 N.E. 3rd Ave., Fort Lauderdale FL 33301 *(open year-round Mon–Fri 8:30am–5pm; ℘954-462-6000; www.ftlchamber.com)*.

A free iPhone visitor information **app**, iVisitLauderdale, can be downloaded at itunes.apple.com.

♣♣ Museum of Discovery and Science★★

401 S.W. 2nd St., one block south of Broward Blvd. ◷*Open year-round Mon–Sat 10am–5pm, Sun noon–6pm.* ☜*$11, child (2–12yrs) $9; IMAX theater $9, child $7; combo ticket for museum and IMAX $16, child $12.* ♿ 🅿 *(☜$3)* ℘*954-467-6637. www.mods.org.*

This slick mega-size, hands-on museum attracts people of all ages. The three-story facility boasts more than 200 interactive exhibits—beginning with the fantastic **gravity clock** in the atrium. **Florida EcoScapes** dominates the first floor: live trees and native plants form the setting for examples of local flora and fauna, including a colorful coral reef, an underground cave and a walk-in beehive. A children's **discovery center** features interactive exhibits and a play area.

On the second floor the exhibit **Gizmo City** gives visitors an opportunity to play

Museum of Discovery and Science

Visit Florida

virtual volleyball and surf the Internet. Other highlights include **Runways to Rockets: Our place in Aerospace,** where you can transform yourself into a bird by putting on wings and stepping into a giant wind tunnel so you can see what it feels like to fly, and of course there is the giant IMAX theater.

Hugh Taylor Birch State Park

3109 E. Sunrise Blvd. and A1A.
🕐 *Open 8 am–sunset* 🚗 *$6 per vehicle.*
♿ 🅿 📞 *954-564-4521. www.florida stateparks.org/hughtaylorbirch.*
Canoe, hike, bike, and picnic at this 180-acre site, resting on a barrier island between the Atlantic Ocean and the Intracoastal Waterway. Ringed today by urban development, the park extends along 1.5mi of beachfront and includes a lagoon system, mangrove swamps and hardwood hammocks. Birch's former home, Terramar (c.1940), now houses the **Terramar Visitor Center**.

Bonnet House★

900 N. Birch Rd. 🕐 *Open year-round,* 👣 *house by guided tour only, Tue–Sat 10am–4pm, Sun noon–4pm.* 🚗 *$20; grounds only, $10.* 🅿 📞 *954-563-5393. www.bonnethouse.org.*
Nestled on a 35-acre wooded oasis, this two-story coral rock and Dade County pine house reflects the talent of its architect, Chicago muralist and art collector **Frederic Clay Bartlett** (1873–1953).
A lagoon rimmed with stately Royal palms fronts Bartlett's 1920 interpretation of a plantation house. Named for the yellow Bonnet lilies that still bloom at the south end of the lagoon, the 30-room structure contains the family's eclectic furnishings and objets d'art. The first building on the estate, Bartlett's **studio,** with its high-beamed ceiling and two-story north window, displays his works as well as those he collected. Also on the grounds is an orchid house.

EXCURSIONS
John U. Lloyd Beach State Park

4mi south in Dania Beach. 1mi north of intersection of Dania Beach Blvd. and A1A at 6503 N. Ocean Dr. 🕐 *Open 8am–sunset* 🚗 *$6 per vehicle.* ✕ ♿ 🅿 📞 *954-923-2833. www.floridastateparks.org/lloydbeach*
This 251-acre park at the northern end of a narrow, elongated barrier island offers great views, uncrowded beaches and quiet forests. The 11,500ft-long **beach** is dotted with shaded picnic sites and sea turtle nesting areas, and extends northward to a paved fishing jetty. Whiskey Creek, a mangrove-lined tidal waterway, divides the park along its length and harbors manatees and abundant bird life. A hardwood forest and man-made wetland fill the park's interior. A self-guided walk traverses the hammock.

👥 IGFA World Fishing Hall of Fame & Museum★

12mi south in Dania Beach. 🚗 *From Las Olas Blvd., take I-95 south to Griffin Rd., then west to Anglers Ave. Turn left and continue to center's entrance at 300 Gulf Stream Way in Sportsman's Park.*
🕐 *Open year-round Mon–Sat 10am–6pm, Sun noon–6pm.* 🕐 *Closed Thanksgiving Day & Dec 25.* 🚗 *$8, child (3–16yrs) $5.* ✕ ♿ 🅿 📞 *954-922-4212. www.igfa.org/About.*
The large metallic fish anchoring this three-story 60,000sq ft facility clearly identifies the headquarters of the **International Game Fish Association.** Six museum galleries, a children's discovery room, library, museum store, cafe, the hall of fame, an outdoor marina and 3.5-acre wetlands make up this complex. In the Fishing Hall of Fame, life-size mounts of record catches dangle from the ceiling. Museum highlights include the **Catch Gallery,** where visitors can reel in a fish via virtual reality.

👥 Butterfly World★

10mi north in Coconut Creek.
🚗 *Take I-95 north to Sample Rd.; continue west 4mi to 3600 W. Sample Rd.; enter at Tradewinds Park, on left.*
🕐 *Open year-round Mon–Sat 9am–5pm, Sun 11am–5pm.* 🕐 *Closed Thanksgiving Day & Dec 25.* 🚗 *$24.95, child (3–11yrs) $19.95.* ✕ ♿ 🅿 📞 *954-977-4400. www.butterflyworld.com.*

Butterfly World offers a lovely walk through a screened-in aviary, landscaped with waterfalls and bright blooms to resemble a tropical rainforest. Inside, some 10,000 rainbow-colored butterflies and hundreds of birds flit around, vying with the flowers in beauty. Outside the aviary, a rose garden and vine-covered arbor surround a small pond, attracting local species of the order *Lepidoptera*. A small pavilion here contains mounted specimens of exotic insects and butterflies from around the world.

👥 Flamingo Gardens

16.5mi west in Davie. ❯ *Take I-595 west to Flamingo Rd.; continue 3mi south to entrance on left at 3750 Flamingo Rd.* ◷ *Open year-round Oct–May daily 9:30am–5pm. Closed Mon Jun–Nov.* ⬟*$17, child (4–11yrs) $8.50.* ✖&🅿 🕿 *954-473-2955. www.flamingo gardens.org.*

Lush tropical plantings grace the grounds of the former citrus plantation owned by Floyd and Jane Wray. Paved paths traverse a mosaic of tropical plants and a narrated tram tour *(25min; ⬟$4)* takes visitors through a wetlands area and part of the original citrus grove. Displays of alligators, crocodiles and birds of prey, a walk-through aviary "free-flight" facility housing one of the largest collections of wading birds in America, and daily wildlife encounters add to the fun.

Ah-Tha-Thi-Ki Museum

65mi west of Fort Lauderdale via I-75. ❯ *Take I-75 west to Rte. 833 (Exit 14); turn north 17mi to Big Cypress Seminole Indian Reservation.* ◷*Open year-round daily 9am–5pm.* ⬟*$9.* &🅿 🕿*863-902-1113. www.seminoletribe.com/museum.* Run by the Seminole Indians this multi-million dollar facility illustrates tribal customs and beliefs, including traditional jewelry, clothing, weapons and instruments, and also tells of the Seminoles struggles to remain in Florida. A 1.5mi boardwalk points out native medicinal and other plants. About halfway along its route stands a "living

village" of chickee homes where members of the Seminole tribe can be seen cooking and creating traditional crafts, like wood carvings, handmade dolls and basketry. Ritual ceremonies and dancing may be performed on special occasions *(call ahead for information)*.

ADDRESSES

🛏 STAY

Area vacation planner including lodging directory available *(free)* from **Greater Fort Lauderdale Convention and Visitors Bureau.** Accommodations range from luxury **hotels** and **spa resorts** *($175 and up)* to moderate **inns** and **motels** *($100–$175)* and superior small **lodgings** *($50–$100)*. Youth **hostel** rooms *($20; 🕿954-567-7275)*, campgrounds and RV parks available.

🎭 ENTERTAINMENT

Consult the arts and entertainment section of the *Sun Sentinel* either in the paper (Fridays) or online at www.sun-sentinel.com and *Travelhost* online magazine at www.travelhost.com/fortlauderdale. Or visit the official website: www.sunny.org. The top theater in town is the **Broward Center for the Performing Arts** *(🕿954-462-0222; www.browardcenter.org)*.

🏃 SPORTS AND RECREATION

For information on recreation and area parks: 🕿954-563-PARK or visit www.sunny.org.

Cruise ships depart from Port Everglades. Carolina **Golf Club** *(🕿954-753-4000; www.carolinagolfclub.com)*, Jacaranda **Golf Club** *(🕿954-472-5836; www.golfjacaranda.com)* and Diplomat Country Club *(🕿866-716-8107; www.starwoodhotels.com/diplomat_country_club)* welcome non-members.

Shopping: if you want upscale, head to Las Olas Blvd downtown. **Galleria Mall**, Sunrise Blvd. *(🕿954-564-1015)*; Swap Shop, 3291 W. Sunrise Blvd. (shopping and entertainment 🕿954-791-7927); Sawgrass Mills, 12801 W. Sunrise Blvd. (outlet mall 🕿954-846-2350).

Miami★★★
and around

Renowned for its tantalizing tropical landscape of blue sky, aqua waters and fabulous white beaches, Miami is one of the most popular resort destinations in the US. Each year some ten million visitors from around the world pour into Greater Miami. Star-studded South Beach—dubbed SoBe—is a magnet for the see-and-be-seen crowd. There's plenty to do in this vibrant, sun-drenched playground, including golf, tennis, yachting, deep-sea fishing, scuba diving, arts and culture, a lively nightlife— and sunbathing! Because of its key position on the Florida Straits near the southeastern tip of the state, Miami also boasts the world's largest cruise port, accommodating passengers to and from the Caribbean and South America.

A BIT OF HISTORY

Early Explorers – **Pedro Menéndez de Avilés** came ashore here in 1566. In 1567 additional Spanish colonists, led by a Jesuit priest, arrived to found a short-lived Catholic mission. The native Tequesta population depleted during the next century and a half, struck by disease and wars with the Creek Indians. When Florida became a British Colony in 1763 at the end of the French and Indian War, the remaining Tequestas accompanied the retreating Spanish to Cuba.

The US Government established **Fort Dallas** on the north side of the Miami River in 1838. When the Second Seminole War ended in 1842, William English, nephew of the plantation's owner, platted a town on the south side of the river. His name for the new town, Miami, is thought to derive from an Indian word meaning "sweet water."

The Mother of Miami – By the late 19C, **William and Mary Brickell** and **Julia Tuttle** were the two major landholders in the area. Brickell, a native of Steubenville, Ohio, bought part of the

▶ **Population:** 391,355.
🌀 **Michelin Map:** p249, 252, 256-257.
ℹ **Info:** 1920 Meridian Ave.; ☎305-672-1270; www.miamibeachchamber.com.fl.us.
▶ **Location:** Flagler Street divides the city north-south; Miami Avenue runs east-west. The major north-south access routes are A1A, US 1, I-95, US 441 and the Florida Turnpike.
🅿 **Parking:** There are parking lots and garages,but street metered parking is hard to find. Take a cab.
🐾 **Don't Miss:** A tour of the Art Deco Historic District in South Beach.
🕐 **Timing:** This is a sprawling city; allow time to travel from one attraction to the next. Plan on a day to explore Downtown Miami sites, another to explore sizzling Miami Beach.
👫 **Kids:** The cageless Zoo Miami has nearly 1,000 animals roaming in natural habitats. Young kids will also enjoy the exotic animals at Jungle Island.

William English tract on the south side of the Miami River in 1870 and opened a store. By 1880 the Brickell family owned all of the prime bayfront land south to Coconut Grove.

Meanwhile, Julia Tuttle's campaign to put the fledgling town on the map earned the widow from Cleveland the title "Mother of Miami." She sought the help of **Henry Flagler** and his Florida East Coast Railway (FEC). In exchange for riparian rights and half of Tuttle's land, the entrepreneur laid out streets, supplied the town with water and electricity, financed a channel across the bay and donated land for community buildings.

BISCAYNE NATL. PARK ⟍ MIAMI METROZOO, EVERGLADES NATL. PARK

In April 1896, the first train chugged into the village of 300 citizens, which was incorporated three months later. The following year the grand **Royal Palm Hotel** opened on the old Fort Dallas site, complete with swimming pool, elevators and a park with coconut palms.

Boom, Bust and Recovery – While growth corresponded directly to the development of the FEC and the federal highway system, a number of developers lured buyers with the promise of something new and different: Carl Fisher's Miami Beach; George Merrick's planned Mediterranean paradise, Coral Gables (complete with man-made canals and costumed gondoliers imported from Italy); and the North Miami-Dade developments of Hialeah and Miami Springs (created by James Bright and Glen Curtiss at the beginning in the early 1920s).

GETTING THERE

BY AIR – Miami International Airport (MIA): 7mi northwest of downtown; international and domestic flights (*305-876-7000; www.miami-airport.com*). Tourist Information Service, Central Terminal E, Level 2 *(open daily year-round)*. Transportation to downtown: **SuperShuttle** (*$20; 305-871-2000; www.supershuttle.com*), taxi *($25-$30)*, **Metrobus** and hotel courtesy **shuttles**. **Rental car agencies** located near the airport.

BY TRAIN AND BUS – Amtrak **train** station: 8303 N.W. 37th Ave. (*800-872-7245; www.amtrak.com*). Greyhound **bus**: Miami International Airport: 4111 N.W. 27th St. and 700 Biscayne Blvd.; Miami Beach: 7101 Harding Ave. *(reservations: 800-231-2222; www.greyhound.com)*.

GETTING AROUND

BY PUBLIC TRANSPORTATION – Miami-Dade Transit Agency (*305-770-3131; www.miamidade.gov/transit*) operates a public transit system connecting Greater Miami and beaches via Metrorail, Metromover and buses. **Metrorail** trains serve downtown Miami extending northwest to Hialeah and south to Kendall. **Metromover** elevated rail system links the Brickell Ave. and Omni areas, and loops around downtown. Metrorail connections at Government Center and Brickell stations, with limited nearby public parking. **Metrobus** operates county-wide. Schedules and route information, www.miamidade.gov/transit. Disabled visitors: 305-770-3131. **Tri-Rail** (*800-TRI-RAIL, www.tri-rail.com*) provides **commuter rail** service between West Palm Beach and Greater Miami connecting to Metrorail. **BY CAR** – Miami is laid out on a grid: the intersection of Flagler St. and Miami Ave. divides the city into four quadrants: southwest, northwest, southeast and northeast. Avenues and courts run north-south; streets and terraces run east-west. **Speed limit** within city: 25mph unless otherwise posted. Signs with the orange "Follow the Sun" symbol direct visitors to major tourist destinations (maps available at airport and from car rental agencies). Downtown metered **parking**: $1.50/hr. Parking lots $1.50–$3.25/1/2hr.

BY TAXI – Metro Taxi (*305-888-8888*); Yellow Cab (*305-444-4444; www.ycab.com*).

VISITOR INFORMATION

Downtown Miami Welcome Center, Olympic Theater, 174 E. Flagler St., Miami, FL 33131. 305 379-7070.
Miami Beach Latin Chamber of Commerce Visitor Information Center, 510 Lincoln Rd. Miami Beach, FL 33139 (Art Deco District/South Beach). 305-674-1414. http://www.miamibeach.org.
Miami Beach Visitor Information Center, 1920 Meridian Ave., Miami Beach FL 33139 305-672-1270; www.miamibeachchamber.com.fl.us. For general information online visit www.miamiandbeaches.com/visitors.

SIGHTSEEING

For sightseeing tours go online (*see above*), or consult the *Greater Miami & the Beaches Vacation Planner* available from the Greater Miami Convention and Visitors Bureau. Daily **cruises** around Greater Miami and Fort Lauderdale operate from Bayside Marina and the docks at 24th St. and Collins Ave. Miami Beach Art Deco Historic District **walking and bike tours** (*305-672-2014; www.mdpl.org*). Dr. Paul George's Historic Tours—including Little Havana—are organised through the Historical Museum of Southern Florida *(Oct–Jun; boat tours, coach tours, gallery tours and walking tours; 305-375-1621; www.hmsf.org)*.

LOCAL PRESS

Daily news: *Miami Herald;* entertainment section *Weekend* (Friday), online at *www.miamiherald.com*.
Spanish editions: *El Nuevo Herald* and *Diario Las Americas*. Periodicals: *Miami New Times (www.miaminewtimes.com), Travelhost (www.travelhost.com/miami)*.

The mid-1920s marked the beginning of the end. Anti-Florida propaganda and tax investigations had already put a damper on investment by 1925, when a Miami cargo embargo, forced by a backlog of unloaded steamship and railroad freight, severely affected the state's economy. A deadly hurricane in 1926 dealt the final blow.

While Florida's troubles may have preceded the 1929 crash, the state's economy was also among the first in the country to revive. Ironically, Prohibition helped. Eager for tourists, officials generally turned a blind eye to illegal gambling and to rumrunners who smuggled liquor in from the Bahamas.

In 1931 the state legalized pari-mutuel betting and tourists from the North poured in. Joining them were thousands of Latin American travelers arriving by sea plane.

Growing Pains – By the mid-1980s, the national recession hit Miami hard. Banks foreclosed on unfinished condos, shopping malls stood half-rented and the new billion-dollar Metrorail ran virtually empty. For a time it appeared the only people profiting in the faded resort were the "Cocaine Cowboys"—from illegal drug smuggling.

Modern Multicultural Metropolis – The popular television show, *Miami Vice* (1984–89), helped Miami's comeback, giving an allure to the city's pink stucco and palm trees, and even to its seamy side. A more tangible economic boost came from a new free trade center (now **World Trade Center** Miami) established in the early 1980s.

Today the city has once again re-invented itself into a booming, diverse center for avant garde arts and culture, fashion and design (and frequent celebrity sightings). It's also one of the country's top vacation hot spots.

GEOGRAPHY

Greater Miami embraces all of Miami-Dade County along with numerous islands, including Miami Beach, a long, narrow barrier island located 2.5mi off the mainland between Biscayne Bay and the Atlantic Ocean.

To the east of downtown lies 39mi-long Biscayne Bay. Seven causeways link the mainland to Miami Beach, while an eighth, Rickenbacker Causeway, brings auto traffic to Virginia Key and Key Biscayne, situated to the south.

The bustling city has a diverse mix of Latinos, Caucasians and African Americans. As a result, distinct ethnic communities exist, most notably Little Havana, just west of downtown; Little Haiti, west of Biscayne Boulevard below 79th Street; and the African-American neighborhoods of Overtown, Liberty City and Brownsville. The mix is one of the things that makes Miami so interesting and culturally vibrant.

DOWNTOWN

A vibrant 1.5sq mi quarter surrounded on three sides by the warm waters of Biscayne Bay and the Miami River, Miami's downtown exudes the bustling atmosphere of a Latin city. The opening of the **Carnival Center for the Performing Arts** and the revitalization of **Bicentennial Park** has brought new energy and vitality to the downtown area.

The site of the city's first wooden commercial structures now features a dense array of government and office buildings in a host of architectural styles including Neoclassical, Art Deco, Mediterranean Revival and the stark contemporary design of the skyscrapers that illuminate Miami's night skyline.

The commercial area built by **Henry Flagler** was incorporated as the City of Miami in July 1896. On Christmas night of that year, a fire devoured most of the small downtown. Vulnerable frontier buildings were quickly replaced with new masonry structures that adhered to a vernacular style of architecture. The downtown's best example of vernacular storefront architecture is the 1914 **Chaille Block** (Miami Ave. between N.W. 4th and N.W. 5th Sts.), which was recently incorporated into the facade of the new federal prison. By World War I, new hotels and stores incorporated open walkways beneath a second-floor veranda, an architectural style clearly suited to the subtropics.

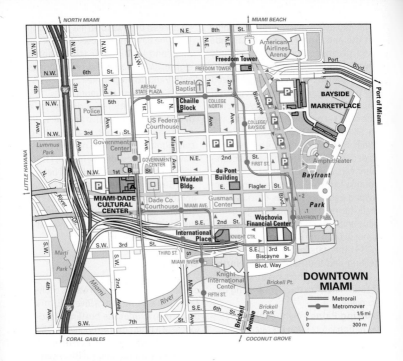

DOWNTOWN MIAMI

Metrorail
Metromover
0   1/5 mi
0   300 m

Metromover at International Place

© Greater Miami CVB

Several such structures remain, notably the 1912 **Waddell Building** (24–36 N. Miami Ave.).

In recent years, this revived quarter has welcomed a large cluster of contemporary high-rise hotels and office buildings, including **International Place** (1985, I.M. Pei & Partners), a 47-story tiered tower *(100 S.E. 1st St.)* lit nightly by colored lights, and the 55-story **Wachovia Financial Center** (1984, Edward Bassett, Skidmore, Owings & Merrill), the tallest building in South Florida *(200 S. Biscayne Blvd.).* The spread of downtown south of the Miami River along Brickell Avenue has resulted in the emergence of that area—once lined with the homes of Miami's richest citizens—as an international financial district.

Bicentenial Park★

1075 Biscayne Blvd. ✆*305-358-7550.*
The 30-acre park, located on Biscayne Bay, seven blocks north of Bayfront Park, is undergoing major renovation and is expected to become a new cultural hub of downtown by 2013. Re-named Museum Park, it will be anchored by the Miami Art Museum, the Miami Museum of Science (scheduled to be completed 2014), and a branch of the Historical Museum of Southern Florida.

Miami Art Museum★ (A)

🕐 *Open year-round Tue–Fri 10am–5pm, weekends noon–5pm.* 🕐 *Closed Jan 1, Thanksgiving Day, Dec 25.* ✎ *$8, second Sat each month free.* ♿ 🅿 ✆ *305-375-3000. www.miamiartmuseum.org.*

Dedicated to presenting international art of the post-World War II era—with an emphasis on art of the Americas—the museum stages several major shows a year in its two levels of gallery spaces and auditorium.

The permanent collection, a small selection of which is displayed on a rotating basis, includes 50 works by such noted contemporary artists as Christo, Alexander Calder, Jasper Johns, Robert Rauschenberg, Marcel Duchamp and Rufino Tamayo. Exhibits of new work change four times a year.

Plans for a new museum building, to be designed by Herzog & de Meuron, are underway. It is expected to be completed in 2013 (⌚see above).

Miami Science Museum (A)

⌚*See p262.*

Historical Museum of Southern Florida★★(B)

🕐 *101 West Flagler Street. Open year-round Mon–Sat 10am–5pm (third Thu each month 9pm), Sun noon–5pm.* 🕐 *Closed Jan 1, Thanksgiving Day, Dec 25.* ✎ *$8.* ♿ 🅿 ✆ *305-375-1492. www.hmsf.org.*

This is the region's most important historical museum. Housed on the museum's second floor, the permanent exhibit "Tropical Dreams: A People's History of South Florida" recounts the area's colorful past. The wealth of artifacts and mixed-media presentations include an early Tequesta Indian settlement, treasures from sunken Spanish galleons, a Conch house from the heyday of Key West's sponge trade and a 1923 trolley car. The first floor contains a gallery for temporary exhibits focusing on Miami history and folklife, and a research library with an extensive collection of books, maps and historical photographs.

Bayfront Park

Biscayne Blvd. between N.E. 4th and S.E. 2nd Sts. 🕐 *Open daily year-round.* ✆ *305-358-7550. www.bayfrontpark miami.com.*

This 32-acre green space recently underwent a multi-million dollar renovation and reopened in 2009. In addition to its 6,500-seater amphitheater, which draws music megastars, other activities include free classes in self-defense for women and yoga, a trapeze school, Tiki Beach Cruises, Xtreme Parasail and a kids' playground.

Look for sculptures by Isamu Noguchi, the famed Japanese landscape architect—the *Challenger Memorial* (1) and *Slide Mantra* (2) for children—as well as a prominent fountain and a laser light tower (3).

Bayside Marketplace★

401 Biscayne Blvd. 🕐 *Open year-round Mon–Fri 10am–10pm Sat 10am–11pm, Sun 11am–9pm.* ✆ *305-577-3344. www.baysidemarketplace.com.*

Linked to the north side of Bayfront Park via sidewalk, this hugely popular complex, composed of several buildings connected by plazas and open-air walkways, sits on the northeastern edge of downtown Miami overlooking the turquoise waters of Biscayne Bay. Its profusion of boutiques, retail outlets, eateries and entertainment sprawls over 235,000sq ft of space and lures visitors with its beguiling ambience and vibrant nightlife. The lower level teems with vendors hawking ethnic wares and local souvenirs; the upper level is devoted to mainstream chain stores.

Freedom Tower

600 Biscayne Blvd.

One of Miami-Dade County's most striking buildings, the tower sits on the northern edge of downtown. Designed by the famed New York architectural firm of Schultze and Weaver, whose credits also include the Biltmore in Coral Gables and The Breakers in Palm Beach, the Spanish Renaissance Revival building consists of a three-storey base that buttresses a slim 12-storey tower. At the top is a cupola inspired by the 16C Giralda Tower in Seville, Spain.

Brickell Avenue

Named for a wealthy pioneering family who owned bayfront land south of the Miami River, Brickell Avenue is a broad, four-lane street—divided by a tree-shaded median—that parallels the contours of nearby Biscayne Bay for its entire 2mi length south of downtown. By the early 1900s, elegant estates began to spring up along the street, leading to its sobriquet **"Millionaires' Row."** Signature residential high rises include **The Palace** (no. 1541), recognizable by the striking stepped wing emanating from its east side; **The Imperial** (no. 1627), with its red veneer, square windows and sloping roof; and **The Atlantis** (no. 2025), whose much-photographed "skycourt" consists of a 37ft square-shaped hole punched out of its central massing. Sitting between The Palace and The Imperial is the 28-story **Villa Regina** (no. 1581), a condominium notable for its vivid color scheme, a product of the imaginative palette of Israeli artist Yacov Agam.

LITTLE HAVANA

See map p256-257.

Immediately east of downtown, a 3.3sq mi section of Miami bounded by the Miami River (east), S.W. 37th Avenue (west), N.W. Seventh Street (north) and Coral Way (south) represents one of the city's most lively and exotic neighborhoods. Along **Calle Ocho,** or Eighth Street—Little Havana's main thoroughfare—sidewalk vendors hawk a variety of wares and ubiquitous stand-up *cafeterias* dispense tiny cups of dense black *café Cubano.*

A bewildering array of small businesses, including the diminutive *botanicas* that sell religious paraphernalia for practitioners of *Santería,* a form of voodoo, cater to a Latin clientele. English is rarely spoken.

Cuban history is remembered in places such as **José Martí Park** (351 S.W. 4th St.). Named for the apostle of Cuban independence (José Martí, 1853–1895),

the park overlooks the western bank of the Miami River.

Visit the following sights beginning at S.W. 32nd Ave. and S.W. 8th St., and work your way east. Note that at S.W. 26th Ave., Calle Ocho becomes a one-way thoroughfare heading east. Metered parking is available on both sides of S.W. 8th St.

Woodlawn Park Cemetery

3260 S.W. 8th St.

Miami's largest and one of its oldest (1913) burial spots, Woodlawn Park is the final resting place for thousands of Cuban refugees. Two former exiled Cuban presidents, as well as Anastasio Somoza, longtime dictator of Nicaragua, are interred here. Gothic statuary, crypts and a mausoleum with stained glass windows make for a somber atmosphere.

Latin Quarter

This quarter stretches along Calle Ocho between S.W. 17th and S.W. 12th avenues. (The north-south portion of the quarter reaches from N.W. First to S.W. Ninth streets.) Here quaint street lamps rise above brick sidewalks set with stars bearing the names of an international array of prominent Hispanic entertainers, including Julio Iglesias and Gloria Estefan.

Máximo Gómez Park

Southeast corner of S.W. 15th Ave.

For a glimpse of local color drop by this tiny plaza, named for the Dominican Republic-born Chief of the Cuban Liberating Army and known locally as Domino Park. As they have been doing since the early 1960s, Cubans, primarily elderly men, assemble here daily for spirited games of dominoes (introduced to the hemisphere by the Spanish), chess, cards and checkers.

Cuban Memorial Plaza (A)

In the median of S.W. 13th Ave./Cuban Memorial Blvd. and S.W. 8th St.

A hexagonal marble monument topped by a flickering eternal torch decorates this small square.

A Haven for Refugees

Ever since Cubans fleeing the Castro regime began pouring into the area in 1959, Little Havana has remained a magnet for refugees from a variety of Spanish-speaking nations. By the late 1920s, Eastern Europeans had moved into the quarter, reaching their peak population in the early 1950s. Thereafter many residents relocated and the old neighborhood declined. By the mid-1950s, Hispanics occupied the quarter, paving the way for the subsequent Cuban influx that reached flood proportions after the US commenced its "Freedom Flights" in 1965.

The large concentration of Cubans in the quarter prompted its sobriquet, "Little Havana." Southwest Eighth Street, alternately known as Highway 41 and Tamiami Trail, became the district's most important commercial thoroughfare. Densely populated Little Havana is largely an immigrant community with a preponderance of young Latin American families and elderly residents. Although Nicaraguans count among the thousands of Hispanics who call Little Havana home, the sector remains the political nerve center of the influential Cuban exile colony. Refugees still seek sanctuary here, where virtually everyone speaks Spanish, and housing—although limited—is inexpensive.

Created in 1971 to honor those members of Brigade 2506 who lost their lives in the aborted invasion of Cuba in April 1961, the plaza now serves as a rallying point for political demonstrations.

Teatro Martí
420 S.W. 8th Ave., at southwest corner of S.W. 4th St.
This is one of Little Havana's oldest, (founded in 1963) and most important, of the quarter's four theaters for film and live presentations. The theater is housed in the Riverside Commercial Building, built by the Ku Klux Klan as its headquarters in 1926.

Templo Adventista del Septimo Dia (B)
862 S.W. 4th St. at corner of 9th Ave.
Built in 1925 by the Seventh Day Adventist Church, this stucco structure exemplifies Mission-style architecture erected by the Spanish in many parts of their colonial empire.

Warner House
111 S.W. 5th Ave. www.historic preservationmiami.com.
A Neoclassical mansion built in 1912 by the Warner family, who lived here and used it as a venue for a floral business. Fully restored, it now houses the Archae-

ological and Historical Conservancy. One block east of Warner House, the **Miami River Inn (C)** *(118 S.W. South River Dr.)*, comprises several restored early 20C buildings that now function as a bed-and-breakfast inn.

CORAL GABLES★★
See map p256-257.
Grandest and most successful of South Florida's boomtime developments, Coral Gables covers a 12.5sq mi area just southwest of downtown Miami.
The area is bounded roughly by S.W. 57th Avenue (Red Road) on the west,

El Crédito Cigar Factory

1100 S.W. 8th St. ℘305-858-4162. http://elcreditocigars.com.

In 1969 the El Crédito company, which began in Havana in 1907, opened in Miami. Descendants of the founding Carillo family owned and operated the business until only recently; it remains one of the top hand-rolled cigar producers in Miami-Dade County. Visitors can watch the cigar-making process through glass windows looking into the factory before visiting the on-site store.

S.W. 37th Avenue (Douglas Road) on the east, S.W. Eighth Street (US-41) on the north, and S.W. 72nd Street (Sunset Drive) on the south, and embraces a 6mi bayside stretch running south along Old Cutler Road. While largely residential, this city within a city also boasts the **University** and some of the area's finest Mediterranean Revival architecture and mature tropical landscaping.

Entrances – Designed to set Coral Gables apart from surrounding areas, grand drive-through entrances welcomed visitors with suitable pomp—much in the spirit of the triumphal arches of Spanish cities like Seville and Toledo. The 1922 **Granada Entrance** (Granada Blvd. and Tamiami Tr.) is made of rough-cut coral rock; the 300ft-long gateway boasts a 40ft-high arch and flanking pergolas. **Commercial Entrance** (Alhambra Circle, Madeira Ave. and Douglas Rd.) is dominated by a 600ft curved coral-rock wall and archway marking the approach to the business section of the Gables. Costing nearly $1 million, the 1925 **Douglas Entrance** (Tamiami Tr. and Douglas Rd.), called La Puerta del Sol (Gate of the Sun), was designed with a series of arcades and complexes to suggest a Spanish town square. Smaller than originally planned, it nevertheless included a 90ft clock tower, grand arch, shops, galleries, apartments and a lavish ballroom. (Renovated, it now houses offices.) Equally elaborate is the **Country Club Prado Entrance** (Country Club Prado and Tamiami Tr.). This 1927 gateway of stuccoed concrete occupies a 240ft length of grassy median at the end of a tree-shaded boulevard. Recalling an Italian Renaissance garden, the symmetrical layout incorporates 20 masonry

Fairchild Tropical Garden /

pillars topped with classical urns and pedestal fountains at both ends of a reflecting pool.

Plazas – Intended to break the predictable grid of house lots, 14 plazas were also created for Coral Gables. Many served as European-style traffic circles, highlighted by fountains, such as the elaborate tiered pedestal supporting an obelisk at **DeSoto Plaza** (Sevilla Ave. and Granada and DeSoto Blvds.).

To visit downtown, park on Miracle Mile (Coral Way) or Ponce de Leon Blvd. (metered parking) and walk. Giralda Ave. between Ponce de Leon Blvd. and

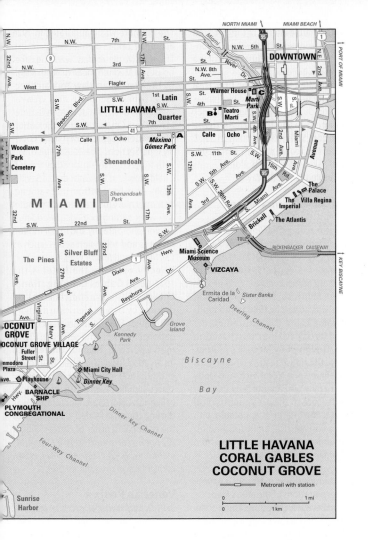

LITTLE HAVANA
CORAL GABLES
COCONUT GROVE

Metrorail with station

0   1 mi

0   1 km

Galiano St. is notable for its trendy restaurants, and Aragon Ave. for its specialty shops. Other sights in Coral Gables are best reached by car. Street names in residential sections of Coral Gables are painted on whitewashed concrete markers and placed at corners, low to the ground.

A free Coral Gables driving-tour map is available at the City Hall (see below) information desk. Coral Gables Chamber of Commerce is another source of information (224 Catalonia Ave.; ℘305-446-1657; www.gableschamber.org).

Coral Way

This busy thoroughfare is the main east-west artery in downtown Coral Gables. The four-block (half-mile) section between Douglas and LeJeune roads is known as **Miracle Mile**. Shops range from discount stores to chic boutiques. Fronted by Corinthian columns, the two-story, coral-colored 1926 **Colonnade Building** (no. 169) features a baroque, Spanish-inspired arched entrance topped by spires. Used as a training center for World War II pilots and as real-estate offices, the building now holds a restaurant. Walk inside to

257

view the marble interior of the 75ft-high **rotunda,** connected to the Omni Colonnade Hotel tower built just north of the Colonnade Building in 1985.

Miracle Mile terminates at **City Hall** *(405 Biltmore Way).* Designed by Phineas Paist and Denman Fink, this coral-rock monument topped by a three-tiered tower cost $200,000 to build in 1927. The curved, colonnaded front bay is slightly skewed so the building aligns with angled Biltmore Way.

Coral Gables Merrick House

907 Coral Way. ⊙*Grounds open daily year-round.* ✎*Visit by guided tour (45min) only, year-round Wed & Sun 1pm, 2pm & 3pm.* ⊙*Closed major holidays.* ⊚*$5.* ♿ 🅿 ☏*305-460-5361. www.coralgables.com.*

George Merrick's two-story boyhood home was added in 1906 to the modest frame cabin that existed on the land Merrick's father purchased in 1899. Designed by Merrick's mother, Althea, the house features indigenous oolite limestone (coral rock) and Dade County pine and adapts New England architecture to the area's subtropical climate. The interior is appointed with period and Merrick family furnishings; surrounding gardens contain trees from the family's original plantation.

Houses along Coral Way between Toledo and Madrid streets represent a variety of interpretations of the area's Mediterranean Revival architecture. Three doors west of Coral Gables Merrick House is **Poinciana Place** *(937 Coral Way),* the home George Merrick built in 1916 for his new wife. Coral Gables' first mayor, Edward "Doc" Dammers, originally lived at 1141 Coral Way. Architect H. George Fink designed the one-story, rock **Casa Azul** *(1254 Coral Way),* distinguishable by its blue glazed-tile roof, for himself in 1924.

Biltmore Hotel★★

1200 Anastasia Ave. ✎*Guided tour (30min), year-round Sun 1:30pm, 2:30pm & 3:30pm.* ✖♿🅿 ☏*305-445-1926 or 800-915-1926. www.biltmorehotel.com.*

The Biltmore was inaugurated in 1926 as South Florida's premier winter resort. This massive tile-roofed "wedding cake" boasted a Mediterranean Revival design by the prestigious New York architectural firm of Schultze and Weaver (designers of the Waldorf-Astoria Hotel in New York City) and formed the centerpiece of Coral Gables' 1,600-acre "Country Club Section." The 300ft-high tower with triple cupola—inspired by the 16C Giralda tower of the Cathedral of Seville, Spain—can be seen from miles around. Its former glory fully reclaimed, the hotel is now the setting for elegant weddings, fashion photography and major motion pictures and television series (such as *CSI: Miami* and *Miami VIce).*

Directly opposite the hotel is the 1924 **Coral Gables Congregational Church** *(3010 DeSoto Blvd.),* built on land donated by George Merrick in memory of his father, Solomon Merrick, a Congregational minister who served at Plymouth Church in Coconut Grove. With its arcaded loggias, arched bell tower and ornate baroque entry, the yellow stucco building is an excellent example of Spanish Colonial architecture and was the first church in Florida to be named to the National Register of Historic Places (⊙*open year-round daily by appointment only;* ♿🅿 ☏*305-448-7421; www. coralgablescongregational.org).*

Venetian Pool★★

2701 DeSoto Blvd. ⊙*Open late-May/ Jun–mid-Aug/early Sept Mon–Fri 11am–7:30pm, weekends & holidays 10am–4:30pm. Rest of the year Tue–Fri 11am–5:30pm, weekends & holidays 10am–4:30pm.* ⊚*$10.50.* ✖♿🅿. *Children must be a minimum of 38 inches tall and 3 years old.* ☏*305-460-5306. www.venetianpool.com.*

A limestone quarry that supplied building materials for the area's early homes formed the base of this whimsical municipal pool. Working in tandem in 1922, artist Denman Fink and architect Phineas Paist concocted a fanciful design incorporating a casino, towers, striped light poles (inspired by those lining Venice's Grand Canal) and

The City Beautiful

Inspired by the Garden City and City Beautiful movements of the 19C and early 20C (particularly the 1893 Columbian Exposition in Chicago), **George Merrick** (1886-1942) purchased 3,000 acres of undeveloped scrubland just outside Miami to form a comprehensively planned community in which buildings, streets, public plazas and utilities—discreetly out of sight— were conceived as a unified whole. Broad boulevards, formal entrances, sculpture and parklike landscaping associated with European cities were important components. Merrick

Venetian Pool

© Greater Miami CVB

assembled a team of top engineers, planners and designers. Among them were landscape architect **Frank Button,** artist **Denman Fink** (Merrick's uncle), and architects **H. George Fink, Phineas Paist** and **Walter DeGarmo,** the first registered architect in Florida. The prevailing style was **Mediterranean Revival,** a popular early 20C design featuring elements such as clay roof tiles, small towers, wrought ironwork, breezy courtyards and loggias.

George Merrick ca. 1926

© Bettmann/Corbis

Beginning in 1925, several small thematic villages designed to reflect the architecture of China, Italy, South Africa, France and the antebellum South added a theatrical touch to Merrick's fantasy city. Years in advance of zoning laws, Merrick segregated business, manufacturing and public services into specific areas. Street lighting and fire alarms ensured safety. Luxury hotels, an exotic swimming pool, a country club and playing fields offered recreation. Churches and schools— including the first buildings of the University of Miami—met religious and educational needs. In 1925 Merrick's development received its charter, becoming the City of Coral Gables and prompting Merrick to make the statement: "The building of Coral Gables has not been a thing of the moment, but a wonderful monument that will as solidly endure as does the everlasting coral upon which it is founded."

George Merrick's real genius however lay in promotion. He opened sales offices in Atlanta and Chicago, operated 86 buses to haul in prospective buyers, and managed a sales force of 3,000, including **Edward "Doc" Dammers,** the city's first mayor, who sold lots from a horse-drawn wagon. A series of canals (linking the landlocked community to Biscayne Bay) enabled Merrick to advertise waterfront property—the "Miami Riviera"—in his development. By 1924 $7 million worth of lots in the new community had been sold. Today it is as popular as it ever was, and still one of Miami's most desirable addresses.

footbridges that crossed the free-form swimming area. The pool is drained each night and refilled with water from underground artesian wells.

Today the renovated Venetian Pool, ornamented with waterfalls and pocked with rock caves, provides a unique recreational venue for Coral Gables residents and visitors.

Lowe Art Museum★

1301 Stanford Dr., on University of Miami campus. ❯ *Take US-1 (S. Dixie Hwy.) south to Stanford Dr.; turn right on Stanford and pass under Metrorail; museum is second building on right.* ◔ *Open year-round Tue–Sat 10am–4pm, Sun noon–4pm.* ◔ *Closed Jan 1 & Dec 25.* ☞*$10.* ♿ 🅿 ✆ *305-284-3535. www.lowemuseum.org.*

The museum, housed in a high-ceilinged, 38,600sq ft, one-story structure, showcases a permanent collection of some 8,000 works. Highlights include objects from the pre-Columbian and Greco-Roman periods, Renaissance and Baroque paintings, European masters and 19C–20C American paintings, Native American textiles and jewelry, and African and Asian art.

The new **Myrna and Sheldon Palley Pavilion for Contemporary Glass and Studio Arts** features a stunning $3.5 million glass collection with masterpieces by Dale Chihuly, Richard Jolley, William Carlson and others, as well as 3-D art by some of the most talented contemporary artists.

Off a central garden, several smaller galleries include masks, sculpture, ceramics and beadwork from Africa, Asia and the Americas. A fine **Native American collection** of textiles, baskets and pottery from the southeast, southwest and northwest cultural areas occupies the Barton Gallery. The Green galleries and halls at the rear of the museum showcase contemporary art and changing exhibits.

Fairchild Tropical Garden★★

♿ *See map p249. 10901 Old Cutler Rd., 10mi south of downtown.* ◔ *Open year-round daily 9:30am–4:30pm. Tram tours* (40min) Mon–Fri 10am–3pm on the hr, weekends 10am–4pm on the hr. ◔*Closed Dec 25.* ☞*$20.* ✕♿🅿 ✆*305-667-1651. www.fairchildgarden.org.*

Set on 83 well-tended acres studded with a series of 12 man-made lakes, the largest botanical garden in the continental US boasts more than 2,500 species of plants and trees from around the world. The gardens, named for plant explorer David Fairchild, opened in 1938. Plants here are grouped by families and arranged in spaces that vary from narrow allées to open beds.

A tram tour takes visitors past a sampling of the garden's flora, including 500 species of **palms** and a group of rare **cycads,** a species that dates from the Cretaceous period some 100 million years ago. Tropical vegetation is maintained in a steamy greenhouse; a separate garden nurtures endangered botanical species.

COCONUT GROVE★★

♿ *See map p256-257.*

Lush foliage and banyan trees enhance the tropical feeling of this picturesque village stretching 4mi south of Rickenbacker Causeway along Biscayne Bay. The oldest community in the Miami area, Coconut Grove retains a strong sense of history in its quiet residential neighborhoods, where many of the vine-covered bungalows and Mediterranean-style estates date to the early 20C. By contrast, trendy bars and cafes make the downtown one of Miami's liveliest entertainment spots. Pulsing with activity at night and on weekends, the Grove is also widely known for its Saturday farmers' market and colorful fairs held throughout the year.

To fully enjoy this area, reserve a day to see the Miami Museum of Science and Space Transit Planetarium, and a second day to explore Coconut Grove proper; to shop in the village and tour The Barnacle, park on Grand Ave. or Main Hwy. (metered parking) and walk. Other sights are best visited by car.

Tourist information: Coconut Grove BID (✆*305-461-5506; www.coconut grove.com*).

Vizcaya, overlooking Biscayne Bay

© Richard Goldberg/Dreamstime.com

The Men Behind Vizcaya

The second son of William Deering, developer of the Deering harvester machine, James joined the family's Illinois-based farm machinery business after graduating from Northwestern University and Massachusetts Institute of Technology. When his company merged with McCormick Harvester Co. in 1902, Deering became vice president of the newly formed International Harvester Co. Like many of the Sunshine State's illustrious snowbirds, Deering came to Florida for health reasons.

In 1912 Deering purchased 180 acres of Miami shoreline. Craving privacy, Deering envisioned a "homey" cottage on the banks of Biscayne Bay. His decorator and art advisor, Paul Chalfin, had grander ideas. A graduate of the École des Beaux-Arts in Paris and former curator at the Boston Museum of Fine Arts, Chalfin accompanied Deering to Europe, where the two men combed old European castles and Italian villas for treasures to fill the house, which had yet to be built. By the time they returned, Deering had amassed such a collection that he realized his house would have to be designed to fit its furnishings instead of the other way around. For this job, Chalfin hired New York architect F. Burrall Hoffman Jr. Inspired by 15C and 16C villas in the Venetian countryside, Hoffman's design resulted in a triumphal merging of Italian Renaissance style with Florida's tropical landscape. Two floors of rooms surround a central courtyard (now roofed to protect the priceless art within from heat and humidity). An airy loggia follows three sides of the ground floor; second-floor rooms open onto galleries overlooking the courtyard.

Vizcaya★★★

3251 S. Miami Ave. ○Open year-round daily 9:30am–4:30pm. Free guided tour of house available. ○Closed Dec 25. $15. ✕⚌🅿 ☏305-250-9133. www.vizcayamuseum.com.
Overlooking the calm, blue waters of Biscayne Bay, this ornate Italian Renaissance-style villa and formal gardens embody the fantasy winter retreat of their builder, **James Deering** (1859–1925). The 35-acre estate was raised

from a Florida hardwood hammock in 1916. Deering's Vizcaya (a Basque word meaning "elevated place") required 1,000 workers, $15 million and over two years to complete.

On Christmas Day 1916, Deering moved into his new 70-room mansion. Deering, who never married, lived at Vizcaya until his death in 1925. The following year, the house and gardens were badly ravaged by the legendary 1926 hurricane. The Deering family hired Paul Chalfin in 1934 to renovate the house and replant the gardens in preparation for opening the house as a museum. But public interest in Vizcaya waned, and in 1945 the family sold 130 acres to the Catholic Church to build a hospital complex. Deering's estate remained in the hands of his heirs—his brother's children—until 1952, when Dade County purchased the villa and its remaining 35 acres for $1 million.

The 34 rooms open to the public incorporate elements of four major styles: Renaissance, Baroque, Rococo and Neoclassical. The Neoclassical **entrance** hall contains hand-blocked c.1814 wallpaper from the Paris workshop of Joseph Dufour. Three pairs of 1C Roman marble columns adorn the **Renaissance Hall.** The walls and ceiling of the Italian Rococo **Music Room** are covered with canvas panels hand-painted with a fanciful marine theme. Overlooking the gardens, the **Tea Room** is actually an enclosed loggia, featuring a 17C Nubian marble mantelpiece and a modeled ceiling with Neoclassical motifs. The room's stained-glass wall

displays Vizcaya's emblematic sea horse and caravel.

The **East Loggia,** with its striking colored-marble floor, opens onto the terrace that fronts the bay. Just off the terrace sits the **Stone Barge,** an ornamental Venetian-style breakwater where Deering once tied his luxurious 80ft yacht, Nepenthe. The barge is embellished with sculpture by A. Stirling Calder (father of renowned 20C sculptor Alexander Calder) and bordered by striped replicas of Venetian gondola poles.

More than 10 acres of formal gardens flank the south side of the house. The garden's central axis draws the eye up a water stairway to a two-room baroque casino, or garden house, set atop a hill. Semicircular pools and domed gazebos define the garden's east-west axis.

Miami Science Museum

3280 S. Miami Ave., across from Vizcaya. ⏱*Open year-round daily 10am–5pm.* ⏱*Closed Thanksgiving Day & Dec 25.* 🎟*$10.* ♿🅿 ✆*305-646-4200. www.miamisci.org.*

Housed in a Mediterranean-style building decorated with arches and barrel tiles, the museum features over 150 exhibits that allow visitors to touch objects, climb a rock wall and dig for fossils while learning about everything from gravity to mastodon teeth. Out back, the Wildlife Center—which doubles as a rehabilitation facility for birds of prey—displays wood storks, tortoises, pythons and boa constrictors. The adjacent planetarium offers astronomy and laser shows. Special events have ranged from experiencing hurricane force winds (to appreciate the benefit of being prepared) to discovering the physics behind yo-yos.

Streets of Mayfair

Located on Grand Avenue between Virginia Street and Mary Street is this fascinating mix of high-end shops, art galleries and restaurants. Its large trademark concrete building was designed in 1979 by Grove architect Kenneth Treister (whose work includes the Holocaust Memorial in Miami Beach) and originally housed boutiques reportedly used to launder South American drug money. Be sure to explore the interior courtyard (enter from Virginia St.), reminiscent of the style of architect Antonio Gaudí in Barcelona. Treister adorned this courtyard with lush greenery, multilevel walkways, tiled fountains and striking copper bird sculptures. For livelier crowds and nightlife, head across the street to CocoWalk (👣 *see opposite*).

Miami City Hall

3500 Pan American Dr. (off S. Bayshore Dr.). Located on **Dinner Key,** a small island attached to the mainland by landfill, this two-story Streamline Moderne gem with a flat roof and glass-block windows was designed in 1933 as the seaplane terminal for Pan American Airways. (Note the roofline frieze of winged globes, rising suns and eagles.) In the peak years of the late 1930s, flights left for 32 foreign countries and some 50,000 passengers per year passed through making this the largest international port of entry in the US. (Charles Lindbergh was one of the early pilots.) The terminal originally featured a second-story restaurant and promenade deck. Watching the spectacle of large flying clipper ships taking off and landing in Biscayne Bay—tended by ground crews clad in bathing suits—was a popular weekend pastime. The last flight left Dinner Key in 1945 and the building has served as the city hall since 1954.

Coconut Grove Village★

Centered on the intersection of Grand Ave. and Main Hwy.

The heart of the Grove, the downtown has undergone several transformations in recent decades. Today sidewalk cafes and clothing shops cater to the under-40 crowd, attracting local students, professionals and tourists alike.

A mélange of high-end shops and boutiques fill **Streets of Mayfair** and **CocoWalk.** Cafes line **Commodore Plaza** and the north end of Main Highway, while interesting boutiques are tucked into **Fuller Street.**

CocoWalk

3015 Grand Ave. on the west side of Virginia St. Sun–Thu 10am–10pm, Fri–Sat 10am–11pm. Nightclubs close at 3am. ℘305-444-0777. www.cocowalk.net.

This upscale retail, dining and entertainment center of bars, chain stores, clubs and movie theaters embraces an open plaza with a central cupola-topped pavilion. Pink stucco and three levels of loggias and balconies give the mall a cheerful tropical air.

Barnacle State Historic Park★★

3485 Main Hwy. ⊙Park open year-round Wed–Mon dawn–dusk. House open year-round Fri–Mon 9am–5pm. ⟶Guided tours (1hr) 10am, 11:30am, 1pm, 2:30pm. ⊙Closed Jan 1, Thanksgiving Day & Dec 25. ⊕Park $2, house $3. ℘305-442-6866. www.floridastateparks. org/thebarnacle.

This five-acre bayfront site preserves one of the last patches of tropical hardwood hammock in Coconut Grove, along with the 1891 home of **Ralph Middleton Munroe**, an accomplished

© Greater Miami CVB

The Grove

Cocoanut Grove (spelled with an "a" until 1919) owes its name to Horace Porter, a Connecticut doctor who started a short-lived coconut plantation here in 1873. In 1882 Charles and Isabella Peacock opened a hotel called Bay View House (later Peacock Inn); the fashionable hostelry established a sense of social cachet and attracted many winter visitors who returned to build houses of their own.

By 1890 Cocoanut Grove had become the largest town on the south Florida mainland, boasting the first school, library and yacht club in the region. A sizable black Bahamian community took root on the west side of town. These settlers supported themselves by salvaging shipwrecks, manufacturing coontie starch, and working in the local construction and service industries. By the early 20C, estates on the eastern and southern bayfront had become a prime winter address for society figures and affluent industrialists like James Deering. Artists, academics and writers—including Robert Frost—affiliated with the Winter Institute of Literature at the University of Miami were drawn to the town's intellectual community. Alexander Graham Bell and Charles Lindbergh were frequent visitors.

Although Coconut Grove was annexed by the City of Miami in the summer of 1925, the village has not lost its independent character and bohemian flair.

sailor and yacht designer. Nicknamed "The Barnacle," for its octagonal center that tapers to a small open-air vent, the five-room, hip-roofed structure features a Bahamian design well-suited to the Grove's tropical climate. Virtually unchanged since Munroe's day, the house remained in the family until the 1970s and still contains the original furnishings. The 1926 **boathouse,** showcasing Munroe's shipbuilding tools, is also open to visitors.

Charles Avenue

Once called Evangelist Street for its many churches, this quiet road runs west through the oldest black community on mainland Florida. Known as Kebo, the area was settled in the 1880s by Bahamians who came north by way of Key West. These pioneers helped northern settlers cultivate tropical greenery in the village and brought many of the seeds for the soursops, sugar apples and Barbados cherries that thrive here today. The avenue is notable for its early 20C **shotgun houses.** A drive west to the corner of Douglas Road brings you to one of the first cemeteries in South Florida, used since 1906.

Farther down Douglas Road, just south of Main Highway, is **The Kampong,** part of the **National Tropical Botanical Garden** (4013 Douglas Rd.; ⏰open year-round Tue–Thu 9am–2pm; ⊜$15; ✆305-442-7169; www.ntbg.org), formerly the private estate and garden of the great botanist David Fairchild, who first introduced soybeans and many exotic fruits to North American soil. His original plantings are still here.

Plymouth Congregational Church★

3400 Devon Rd. Visit by appointment only. ⏰Open Sun for church service only. ♿🅿✆305-4446521. www.plymouthmiami.com.

This 1917 Spanish Colonial-style church was modeled after a 16C mission in Mexico, recalled by the broad facade with symmetrical bell towers flanking a curving roof parapet. Of local oolitic limestone, the building and massive cloister walls were reportedly built by a single Spanish mason using nothing more than a hatchet and a plumb line. The walnut door (c.1600) is thought to be from a monastery in the Pyrenees mountains.

Tucked into the charming banyan-shaded grounds are a small meditation garden, a rose garden and a tropical cloister garden.

Moved from its original site near the Peacock Inn, the one-room **schoolhouse** at the north end of the property dates-back to 1887 (🕐*open by appointment only*). Built of lumber from a salvaged shipwreck, it initially housed a Sunday school run by Isabella Peacock. In 1889 it became the first public school in what is now Miami-Dade County. The bell is original.

KEY BISCAYNE

Tourist information: Key Biscayne Chamber of Commerce. 📞*305-361-5207. www.keybiscaynechamber.org.*

Located 2mi south of downtown Miami, this 7mi-long barrier island is a haven for water sports and cycling as well as being a very desirable residential neighborhood. First named Santa Marta by Ponce de León in 1513, Key Biscayne caught the public's attention when President Richard Nixon bought a vacation home here in the 1970s. It is now an affluent community boasting luxury accommodations, fine restaurants and some of the state's prettiest beaches.

In 1825 the Cape Florida Lighthouse was erected at the tip of the key to guide ships safely through the Florida Channel. In the early 1900s, Dr. William J. Matheson dredged a yacht basin and planted thousands of coconut trees here. The Rickenbacker Causeway opened in 1947 linking Miami to the island across Biscayne Bay. Key Biscayne experienced a construction surge in the 1960s and high rises sprang up next to working-class residential neighborhoods.

Today residents of Key Biscayne—now its own incorporated city—enjoy a slow pace bolstered by a small but thriving commercial center. The southern end is home to two popular beachfront parks, Crandon Park and Bill Baggs Cape Florida State Park. Head west on the causeway toward Miami for spectacular **views**★ of downtown and its commercial artery, Brickell Avenue.

👥 **Miami Seaquarium**★

4400 Rickenbacker Causeway, 5mi east of the Key Biscayne tollbooth. 🕐*Open year-round daily 9:30am–6pm (last series of shows 2:30pm).* 🎫*$37.95, child (3–9yrs) $27.95.* ♿🅿 📞*305-361-5705. www.miamiseaquarium.com.*

In its late 1950s heyday, this 38-acre marine-life park served as the set for the TV series *Flipper* and was home to its star, the eponymous dolphin. Today, visitors can swim with dolphins (*additional charge*), watch killer whale shows, and fish and sharks being hand-fed by divers in a reef tank. Crocodile Flats houses some two-dozen Nile crocodiles. The main building provides two levels to view some 10,000 varieties of aquatic life. At the back of the park, sharks swim in an open-air channel that is crossed by several bridges. The world's first controlled manatee breeding program—a joint effort with the University of Miami marine lab next door—also takes place here.

Bill Baggs Cape Florida State Park★

1200 S. Crandon Blvd., 7mi from Key Biscayne tollbooth. 🕐*Open 8am-sunset.* 🎫*$8 per vehicle.* ⚠🍴🅿 📞*305-361-5811. www.floridastateparks.org/capeflorida.*

A mile of Biscayne Bay beachfront and a 74-acre wetlands area attract locals to this secluded 412-acre park on the south end of Key Biscayne. The park owes its name to the newspaper editor of the now-defunct *Miami News,* who encouraged the land's preservation. The original 95ft-high brick **Cape Florida Lighthouse** was constructed in 1825. Tours of the keeper's quarters and kitchen follow presentation of a 14min video (📹*visit by 1hr guided tour only—arrive 30min early; Thu–Mon 10am & 1pm*). During the Seminole War in 1836, Indians set fire to the structure. In 1846, engineers rebuilt the tower and, in 1855, raised it 30ft. The light was destroyed again in 1861—this time by Confederate sympathizers. Relit after the war, the beacon operated until 1878 when it was replaced by the iron Fowey Rock Lighthouse set in the reef some 7mi southeast of Cape Florida. The light is operational again, serving as a navigational aid. The hardwood hammock bordering the beach has been replanted with such native species as sea grape trees and wax myrtle. A bicycle trail loops through the park, and a 1.5mi nature trail weaves through an adjacent 63-acre resurrected wetland.

GREATER MIAMI NORTH

During the boom years of the 1920s, planned subdivisions, including Morningside, El Portal and Miami Shores, were developed as theme communities, often featuring Spanish or Mediterranean Revival-style architecture. Many of the other new North Miami communities stood unfinished after the bottom fell out of the real-estate market in 1926.

Today Greater Miami North is largely residential, a mix of luxury apartment houses, modern suburban developments and remnants of the older, established neighborhoods. The fashionable district of Aventura, just north of Lehman Causeway, comprises luxury resorts and the upscale **Aventura Mall** (*www.aventuramall.com*), containing fine shops and department stores.

Museum of Contemporary Art★

770 N.E. 125th St., North Miami. ○*Open year-round Tue & Thu–Sat 11am–5pm, Wed 1pm–9pm, Sun noon–5pm. Last Fri each month 7pm–10pm Jazz at MOCA.* ○*Closed major holidays.* ∞*$5.* ♿🅿 ☏*305-893-6211. www.mocanomi.org.*

Architect Charles Gwathmey combined cubes and cylinders in designing the simple but elegant building on palm-studded grounds. MOCA's permanent collection reflects significant artistic developments in contemporary art by emerging and established artists from the US and abroad.

Ancient Spanish Monastery★★

16711 W. Dixie Hwy., North Miami Beach. ◐ *Take Biscayne Blvd. (US-1) north to N. Miami Beach Blvd. Turn left, then right on W. Dixie Hwy.* ○*Open year-round Mon–Sat 9am–5pm, Sun 1:30pm–5pm.* ○*Closed major holidays.* ∞*$5.* ♿🅿 ☏*305-945-1461.*

Nestled on a woodsy site, the Cloisters of St. Bernard of Clairvaux provides an in-depth look at a 12C monastery. This superb example of early Gothic architecture, named for the influential leader of the Cistercian Monks, was completed in the Spanish province of Segovia in 1141. Nearly eight centuries later it was disassembled and moved to the US (♿ *see box below*) by **William Randolph Hearst**. A wealthy American newspaperman and collector extraordinaire, Hearst purchased the monastery in 1925, planning to reconstruct his "greatest art treasure" on the grounds of San Simeon, his lavish California estate, but his plans went awry.

Visitors enter the Ancient Spanish Monastery, as it is locally known, through a 200-pound wrought-iron gate crowned with the Latin inscription meaning "These Sacred Cistercian Walls." On the

---

A Giant Jigsaw Puzzle

Packed in hay and shipped from Spain in numbered boxes, the stones of the monastery were quarantined by US officials (hoof-and-mouth disease had broken out in Segovia). The hay was destroyed and the haphazardly repacked stones were left in crates for over 25 years. After Hearst's death in 1951, two South Florida developers bought the stones, hoping to reconstruct the cloisters as a tourist attraction.

All 36,000 stones—some weighing 3,000 pounds—were spread over the 20-acre site. Allan Carswell, a renowned stone mason, was hired to supervise the process of fitting the stones together, using photographs that Hearst had taken of the intact monastery. Nineteen months and $1.5 million later, the reconstructed cloisters opened in 1954, only to be sold in 1964. The complex now houses an Episcopal church.

southern perimeter of the lush side garden stands the entrance to a long cloister. The top of its portal is adorned with the figure of Mary, the mother of Christ, encircled by angels. A series of ribbed arches form the cloister's vault; tile now covers the floors that once consisted of small stones.

The **Chapel of St. Bernard de Clairvaux,** which served as the monks' refectory, occupies the first corridor; the small iron bell at the entrance once called the brothers to meals. Above the altar, two circular stained-glass windows, depicting scenes from the Book of Revelation written by St. John, are as old as the monastery: they represent two of only three known **telescopic windows** in existence (so-named for the three rings of receding frames that encase the windows, creating a telescopic effect). In the middle of the complex stands a **prayer well** composed of elements of an AD 1C Roman temple.

A life-size statue of King Alfonso VIII stands at the end of the first corridor; diagonally across the courtyard is a statue of his grandfather, King Alfonso VII of Castile and Leon, under whose auspices the monastery was initially built. Located midway along the second corridor, the **Chapter House** formed part of the original monastery. The medieval pink-limestone, Gothic-style altar (at the corner past the Chapter House) was carved in Cannes, France. Ten corbels along the cloister walls—part of Hearst's art collection—portray shields of 12C Segovia noble and royal families who pledged their allegiance to both the Catholic Church and the Spanish king.

SOUTH MIAMI-DADE COUNTY

Isolated by the marshy fringes of the Everglades, the southern portion of Miami-Dade County (below Coral Reef Drive) was among the last parts of Florida to be settled, and remains a separate community in both spirit and appearance. While the fast-growing region has its share of tract housing and new shopping malls, its rural western section is still dominated by produce farms, lime groves and tropical plant nurseries,

preserving a distinctive small-town feel virtually nonexistent elsewhere in the Miami area.

Development came with the southern expansion of the Florida East Coast Railway from Miami in the early 1900s. Homestead, now the largest city in South Miami-Dade, was named in 1904 when flat railcars full of building materials labeled "homestead country" arrived at the end of the line. The region's fertile soil, produced by draining the swampy Glades, proved ideal for beans, tomatoes, avocados and other cash crops. By the 1950s South Miami-Dade was one of the top vegetable-producing areas in the US.

Its agricultural economy was devastated in 1992, when Hurricane Andrew spent its full fury in and around Homestead. Recovery was aided by the $7.9 billion Hurricane Relief Bill. Funds provided a face-lift to **Homestead's Old Downtown** (38mi southwest of downtown Miami), the historic business district where recently restored early-20C storefronts lining Krome Avenue recapture the original character of this former railroad town.

👥 Zoo Miami ★★

12400 S.W. 152nd St. 18mi from downtown Miami. ▶ *Take Florida's Turnpike south to Exit 16. Go west on S.W. 152nd St. and follow signs to zoo.* 🕐 *Open year-round daily 9:30am–5:30pm (admission gates close at 4pm). Narrated tram ride (⌖$5) tours the zoo and offers behind-the-scenes glimpse of hatcheries and breeding pens.* ⌖$15.95, *child (3–12yrs) $11.95.* 🍴♿🅿✆*305-251-0400. www.miamimetrozoo.com.* Occupying 290 acres of landscaped park, this popular cageless zoo, one of the finest in the US, specializes in tropical species adaptable to South Florida's hot climate. Some 900 reptiles, birds and mammals, primarily from Asia, Africa and Australia, are showcased. Camouflaged moats and other inconspicuous barriers separate zoo visitors from the animals, which appear to roam completely free in their natural habitats. Simply wander at your own pace along

White tiger, Zoo Miami

© Greater Miami CVB

Gold Coast Railroad Museum

12450 S.W. 152nd St., across the road from Metrozoo. ◷*Open year-round Mon–Fri 10am–4pm (Thu 7pm), Sat–Sun 11am–4pm.* ◷*Closed major holidays.* ⊗*$6. Free first Sat of month. Caboose rides $6.* 🅿 ℰ*305-253-0063. www.gcrm.org.*

A self-guided tour of this museum's grounds reveals numerous historic, renovated railroad cars, including the California Zephyr. A highlight is the Pullman car Ferdinand Magellan, used by presidents Franklin Roosevelt, Harry Truman, Dwight Eisenhower and Ronald Reagan. A collection of train parts and related memorabilia are also on display.

Coral Castle★

28655 S. Dixie Hwy., 30mi south of Miami (2mi north of Homestead). ◷*Open year-round Sun–Thu 8am–6pm Fri–Sat 8am–9pm.* ◷*Closed Dec 25. $9.75.* ♿🅿 ℰ*305-248-6345. www.coralcastle.com.*

This three-acre mansion and mono-lithic sculpture garden is Florida's most intriguing sight. It was crafted of more than 1,100 tons of coral rock (oolitic limestone) from 1918 onwards by Ed Leedskalnin, a slight 5ft-tall, 110-pound Latvian immigrant. Built under the cover of night and in secret, no-one knows how Ed created his Coral Castle. He didn't use machinery and, when questioned, would only say that he knew "the secret of the pyramids." When he died, his secrets died with him, and to this day scientists (and talk shows) still debate Ed's methods and his reasons for building Coral Castle. Whatever, it has been listed on the National Register of Historic Places since 1984.

Most remarkable are the movable **Nine-Ton Gate;** the **Polaris Telescope**, a 25ft-high, 30-ton rock telescope aimed toward the North Star; the 20ft-long **Florida Table**, carved in the shape of the state and surrounded by 10,000-pound coral rock chairs; and the two-story tower where Leedskalnin lived in spartan quarters upstairs and labored with crude tools in the room below.

the 3mi loop trail that winds through the park. An elevated monorail also makes regular runs around the grounds, offering its riders a bird's-eye view of the animal habitats.

Among the highlights are an affectionate band of **lowland gorillas** (a walk-in viewing cave permits a close-up look) and a group of stunning **Bengal tigers,** whose habitat features a replica of Cambodia's 13C Angkor Wat ruins. Animal feedings and wildlife shows occur throughout the day *(check brochure for times)*. At the **Samburu Giraffe Feeding Station** visitors can feed the giraffes treats and get a really close-up view.

Amazon and Beyond, is dedicated to the flora and fauna of tropical America, home to species like the anaconda, giant river otters, golden lion tamarins and harpy eagles. The zoo also has a children's playground and exhibit area, complete with frogs, snakes and spiders and a tropical free-flight aviary housing some 300 Asian birds. The Field Research Center highlights the link between birds and their ancestors, the dinosaurs.

Biscayne National Park★

East end of N. Canal Dr. (S.W. 328th St.) in Homestead. 38mi south of downtown Miami. ⊙Visitor Center open year-round daily 9am–5pm; park grounds open year-round daily 7am–5:30pm ⊙Closed Dec 25. ⚠⬇P ℘305-230-7275. www.nps.gov/bisc.

This is the largest marine park in the US, established in 1980 to help protect a 275sq mi area of coastal wetlands, mangrove shorelines, coral reefs and 32 small keys/barrier islands. The protected waters stretch 26mi south from Key Biscayne to Card Sound near Key Largo, running between the coastline and the underwater continental shelf.

Star attractions are the **reefs★★★**, located about 10mi offshore. Here warm Gulf Stream currents nurture some 50 species of living coral that create a hospitable environment for loggerhead turtles, spiny lobsters, sponges and flamboyant tropical fish, including the brilliant rock beauty and parrot fish.

Begin your visit at the **Dante Fascell Visitor Center** at Convoy Point (located at the park headquarters and entrance), which features life-size dioramas of the park's habitat areas. Three videos—an overview, a park history and the effects of 1992's Hurricane Andrew—are shown in a theater. Interpretive exhibits are displayed along a short bayside walking trail from which fishing is permitted. To bird-watch or explore estuaries along the main coast, you can rent a canoe from the Visitor Center.

The park's concessionaire offers canoe and kayak rentals, snorkeling the bay (*$40*) and the reef (*$45*), and cruises (*$35*) to Boca Chita Island (*℘305-230-1100; www.BiscayneUnderwater.com*).

In winter (when mosquitoes are less numerous), boat transportation is offered with reservations to Elliott Key, 7mi offshore. The park's largest island was once a thriving community of pioneers engaged in pineapple farming, sponging, wrecking and other pursuits. Today the island offers camping, picnicking, swimming, wildlife watching and the park's only hiking trail.

♟♟Jungle Island★

1111 Parrot Jungle Trail ⊙Open year-round daily 10am–5pm (weekends 6pm). ⬡$32.95, child (3–10yrs) $24.95. ✕⬇P$8. ℘305-400-7275. www.parrotjungle.com.

This popular attraction, set on Biscayne Bay, is home to more than 1,100 exotic birds, including some 80 pink flamingos. Paths wind through lush tropical gardens and through major exhibits, including a serpentarium, tortoise and crocodile ponds, aviary, penguinarium and petting barn. There are three shows: **Winged Wonders** is a conventional bird show while **Tale of the Tiger** is a more unusual treat, featuring a rotating cast of big cats (from tigers to Black Panthers, Lynx to Spotted Leopards, Cougars to Ligers). Other animals including orangutans, chimpanzees and gibbons may also join the show. Jungle Island also has its own beach where you can relax under an umbrella and have a swim.

Fruit & Spice Park

24801 S.W. 187th Ave. at S.W. 248th St. in Homestead. 27mi southwest of downtown Miami. ⊙Open year-round daily 9am–5pm. ☞Guided tours 11.30am, 1pm, 3pm. ⊙Closed Dec 25. ⬡$8. ⬇P ℘305-247-5727. www.fruitandspicepark.org.

Opened in 1944, this unusual tropical park rebounded from Hurricane Andrew with a flourish. Hundreds of varieties of exotic fruit and nut trees, vegetables, herbs and spices have been replanted in geographical theme areas across its 35 acres, with mango and avocado orchards among the most interesting groves. The Park showcases 125 varieties of mango, 75 varieties of bananas, 70 bamboo varieties, and numerous other exotic edibles. There also are such striking specimens as the Panama candle tree, named for its long yellow fruit. An interesting gift shop offers an array of delicacies, including canned jackfruit, lychee, sugarcane and palm nuts (plus free samples to try!). Workshops on tropical plants and edible oddities are offered weekly.

ADDRESSES

🏨 STAY

Area visitors guide including **lodging directory** available *(free)* from the **Greater Miami Convention and Visitors Bureau.** Reservation service: Greater Miami & Beaches Hotel Assn. (*℘305-531-3553 or 800-531-3553; www.gmbha.org*). Accommodations range from downtown **hotels** *($125–$300)* and luxury beachfront hotels *($250 and up)* to economy **motels** *($99–$150)*. The three main Miami Beach **hostels** are the Tropics (*305-531-0361; www.tropicshotel.com*); the Clay Hostel (☾ *see below*) and the South Beach Hostel (*℘305-672-2137; www.thesouthbeachhostel.com*). Shared room rates range from $20–$36.

$$$$$ Biltmore Hotel – *1200 Anastasia Ave., Coral Gables.* 🛋⚹🅿 *℘305-445-1926 or 800-915-1926. www.biltmore hotel.com. 276 rooms.* This massive National Historic Landmark in Coral Gables looks like a misplaced Spanish palace. Its wedding-cake shape is topped by a 300ft tower modeled after the Cathedral of Seville's Giralda tower. Vaulted hand-painted ceilings, palm-filled courtyards and balustraded balconies are just some of the features that have attracted presidents, royalty and movie stars here since 1926. Then there's the 1.25-million-gallon pool and personalized service. Well-appointed guest rooms include feather beds, easy chairs and private safes. The hotel is famed for its lavish Sunday champagne brunch served outdoors in a tropical setting and also has an immaculate 18-hole golf course.

$$$$$ The Breakers – *1 S. County Rd., Palm Beach.* 🛋⚹🅿 *℘561-655-6611 or 888-273-2537. www.thebreakers.com. 560 rooms.* A Palm Beach icon, this 1926 mega-resort takes its cue from Italy's Renaissance palazzos. Twin belvedere towers recall Rome's Villa Medici and the nymph fountain at the entrance resembles the one at Florence's Boboli Gardens. The regal lobby's hand-painted, vaulted ceiling recalls the Palazzo Carega in Genoa. Luxurious guest rooms are done in light woods,

seaside colors and tobacco-leaf prints. The half-mile private beach includes a new Mediterranean-style Beach Club with three oceanside pools. Set on 140 acres, the resort also has two 18-hole golf courses, tennis courts, restaurants, a spa, and shopping arcade.

$$$$$ The Chesterfield – *363 Cocoanut Row, Palm Beach.* 🛋⚹ 🅿 *℘561-659-5800.www.chesterfield pb.com. 60 rooms.* Located around the corner from Worth Avenue, this posh, white stucco property, accented with red-and-white striped awnings, embodies quiet elegance. The intimate boutique hotel counts Oscar de la Renta, Catherine Deneuve and Margaret Thatcher among its guest list. It continues to cater to an upscale clientele with amenities like fresh fruit in the lobby, terry robes and sachets in rooms and a gourmet basket upon arrival. Guest quarters sport a singular decor, spacious closets and marble bathrooms.

$$$$$ Delano – *1685 Collins Ave., Miami Beach.* 🛋⚹🅿 *℘305-672-2000. www.delano-hotel.com. 208 rooms.* South Beach's minimalist trend started with Philippe Starck's redo of New York hotelier Ian Schrager's 1947 beachside oasis named for Franklin Delano Roosevelt. Billowing white curtains—not doors—give access to the lobby, where large, overstuffed Alice-in-Wonderland chairs are installed. More curtains separate lounge areas sparsely clad with antiques, bric-a-brac, and artworks by Dalí and Man Ray. Plush, white-on-white guest quarters boast top amenities and fresh flowers. Delano's "simple-chic" decor and rooftop spa are magnets for celebrities. The Delano's **Blue Door** restaurant, formerly co-owned by Madonna, is also a favored celebrity haunt.

$$$$ Boca Raton Resort & Club – *501 E. Camino Real.* 🛋⚹🅿 *℘561-35-3000 or 888-491-2622. www.bocaresort.com. 1,070 rooms.* Grand dame of Boca Raton, this exclusive property was designed by Addison Mizner in 1926 as the Cloister Inn. Successive additions retained the graceful blend of Spanish, Italian and Moorish styles, helping to create a well-landscaped, self-contained paradise, to which entry is rigidly guarded. The height of luxury, lodgings can be reserved in the Cloisters (the original building), the modern 27-story tower, the oceanfront beach club, the Yacht Club, or at a spacious one or two-bedroom golf villa. Nine dining spots, several lounges, two golf courses, six pools, a spa, tennis courts, a private beach, and a wide spectrum of sybaritic pamperings round out the offerings.

$$$$ The Hotel – *801 Collins Ave., Miami Beach.* 🏊♿🅿 ☏*305-531-2222 or 877-843-4683. www.thehotelof southbeach.com. 53 rooms.* Todd Oldham designed nearly everything in this renovated Art-Deco gem (1936) off South Beach's famous Ocean Drive. A huge mirror-shaped tile mosaic and velveteen couches—block-patterned in rose, green, and gold—pick up flecks of color from the lobby's original terrazzo floor. Blue and neon-green cottons and pale wood furniture brighten the bedrooms. Bask in the sun at the neo-Mediterranean-style rooftop pool and Spire bar, and reserve a table at **Wish,** the indoor-outdoor restaurant, where celebrity sightings are probable.

$$$$ Sea View Hotel – *9909 Collins Ave. Bal Harbour.* 🏊♿🅿 ☏*305-866-4441 or 800-447-1010. www.seaview-hotel.com. 100 rooms.* A beachfront jewel, this upscale Euro-styled boutique hotel was built in 1947 as one of Bal Harbour's first high rises. Remarkably spacious, designer-appointed guest quarters show off rich fabrics, wicker chairs, glass-topped metal tables and solid pine armoires. Walk-in closets, mini-refrigerators and marble-floored bathrooms are added amenities. Cozy cabanas rim the Olympic-size pool that overlooks the Atlantic. On-site services include a beauty salon, fitness center and restaurant.

$$$ The Pillars – *111 N. Birch Rd., Fort Lauderdale.* 🅿🏊 ☏*954-467-9639. www.pillarshotel.com. 22 rooms.* Bordering the busy Intracoastal Waterway, this upscale urban oasis cultivates British Colonial cachet in decor and personal attention. The front door opens onto hardwood floors and an intimate sitting area. Adjoining is a small library, complete with grand piano and shelves of books. Carpeted in leopard print, a curved staircase leads to upper-level guest quarters. Rooms are smartly appointed with floral bedspreads, armoires and plantation shutters. Pool and patio overlook the water, with its continuous parade of yachts.

$$$ Hotel Place St. Michel – *162 Alcazar Ave. Coral Gables.* 🏊♿ ☏*305-444-1666 or 800-848-hotel. www.hotelstmichel.com. 27 rooms.* Nestled within Coral Gables' pedestrian-friendly downtown, this two-story European-style bed-and-breakfast inn appeals especially to those from abroad and those with a passion for antiques. The parquet-floored reception area and adjoining sitting room are reminiscent of homey Continental inns. The subdued, Old World-style decor of each guest room typically features floral bedspreads and matching curtains. Amenities include fresh fruit upon arrival, evening turn-down with French chocolates, complimentary continental breakfast and morning newspaper. **Gaetano's Ristorante** serves authentic Italian cuisine in style.

$$ A Little Inn By The Sea – *4546 El Mar Dr., Lauderdale-By-The-Sea.* 🏊 ☏*954-772-2450 or 800-492-0311. 29 units.* Fronting 300ft of private beach, this Mediterranean-style bed-and-breakfast inn is centrally located in a seaside village just north of Fort Lauderdale. Family-run, it's reminiscent of Old Florida in the 1950s. Furnished in wicker, the breezy, three-floor lobby includes a 10ft fountain. A tropical, brick-covered courtyard overlooks the pool, barbecue area and beach. There's even an adults-only rooftop patio for sunning au naturel. Rooms and suites are done in floral patterns. A continental breakfast buffet is served in the lobby. Beach chaises and bikes are complimentary to guests.

$$ Miami River Inn – *118 S.W. South River Dr. Miami.* 🏊 ☏*305-325-0045 or 800-468-3589. www.miamiriverinn.com. 40 rooms.* Listed on the National Register of Historic Places, this downtown bed-and-breakfast inn was completed in 1910. Located just steps from Mlami's Little Havana, the gated compound is also within walking distance of Brickell Avenue. Painted pale yellow with olive trim, the inn serves as a tropical oasis of soaring palms and native plants amid Miami's bustling downtown. Refurbished rooms, most with hardwood floors, are appointed with period antiques and feature spacious baths. Two cottages have a living room and fireplace. Complimentary continental breakfast, with homemade muffins, can be savored outdoors.

$ The Clay Hostel (Hostelling International Miami Beach) – *1438 Washington Ave., South Beach.* 🏊 *305-534-2988 or 800-379-2529. www.clayhotel.com/clay-hostel.htm. 120 private rooms; 220 dorm beds.* Located on a bustling commercial corner just steps from colorful Espanola Way, this high-occupancy hostel offers good value for your lodging budget. Sporting a strawberry-hued exterior with striped awnings, the three-story Art Deco building is rich in history: it was home to Al Capone's gambling ring in the 1930s, Desi Arnaz' rumba craze in the 1950s, and the filming of the pilot for *Miami Vice.* Rooms with private baths offer air conditioning, mini-refrigerators, TV, and phones with voice mail. Luggage storage, laundry facilities, kitchen, patio dining area, and fax and computer services are available on-site.

♀/EAT

$$$$ Café L'Europe – *331 S. County Rd., Palm Beach.* ♿ *561-655-4020. www.cafeleurope.com.* **Continental.** French doors, beveled brick, mahogany paneling and gleaming brass lend an air of refinement to this venue. Fresh floral bouquets and colorful place settings add panache. Epitomizing la belle vie Palm Beach style, L'Europe serves more than 5,000 ounces of caviar each year. The menu chages seasonally but you might expect dishes like Peruvian shrimp ceviche, seafood linguini, potato-wrapped red snapper, and roasted rack of lamb. The traditional Wiener schnitzel is a Cafe L'Europe classic.

$$$$ The Forge – *432 Arthur Godfrey Rd. (41st St. & Royal Palm Ave.), Miami Beach.* ♿ *305-538-8533. www.theforge.com.* **Continental.** There's no sign on the exterior of this ornate building, but the beefy valets and sleek cars curbside are clues to the clientele. Thick carpet, plush sofas, stained glass, tapestries and art adorn the restaurant's brick-walled interior. Soft piano music and candlelight add a romantic air. Considered one of the best steakhouses in America, you can't go wrong with the signature oak-grilled prime rib. Wednesday is party night at the restaurant, noted for frequent sightings of celebrities, politicos and athletes.

$$$ Cap's Place – *2765 N.E. 28th Court in Lighthouse Point, north of Pompano Beach. Turn east at US-1 & N.E. 24th St. and follow signs to Cap's Place Dock, adjacent to Lighthouse Point Yacht Basin & Marina. From there it's a 10min boat ride.* ✆ *954-941-0418. www.capsplace.com.* **Seafood.** Listed on the National Register of Historic Places, this restaurant/bar is rustic, rich in history, and fun, especially for families. In the 1920s founder Cap Knight relocated several wooden shacks, floating them on a barge up the Intracoastal Waterway from Miami to Cap's Island, north of Pompano Beach. Back then, the place was a gambling casino and rum-running joint. Celebrity diners have included Winston Churchill, the Vanderbilts and the Rockefellers, Errol Flynn and George Harrison. Memorable dishes include the house-smoked fish dip, the hearts of palm salad, homemade rolls and key lime pie.

$$$ Joe's Stone Crab – *11 Washington Ave., Miami Beach.* ♿ *305-673-0365. www.joesstonecrab.com.* **Seafood.** Located at the southern end of Miami Beach, this high-energy eatery has been a legend since 1913, when founder Joe Weiss began serving the succulent rust-colored crustaceans. Caught mainly off Florida's Gulf Coast between October and May, stone crabs possess the ability to grow new claws within 12 to 18 months (fishermen take just the claws, since they contain the crab's only edible meat). Medium to jumbo-size stone crab claws are conveniently cracked open and served chilled with the house mustard sauce. Sides—coleslaw and creamed spinach—are big enough for two. Expect to line up for dinner, but if you're too hungry to wait, order from Joe's adjacent take-out counter and have a surfside picnic.

$$$ Mai-Kai – *3599 N. Federal Hwy., Fort Lauderdale.* &♿ ☎*954-563-3272. www.maikai.com.* **Polynesian.** Popular for its dinner show, Mai-Kai has been attracting tourists and locals since 1956. Its South Seas appearance—thatched roofs, tiki torches, tropical palms and cascading waterfalls—seems out of place alongside a six-lane thoroughfare. Entering the fenced "village" via a wood-plank bridge, patrons can order one of 50 specialty drinks in a dimly-lit saloon that resembles a wrecked ship. Served in intimate dining rooms or on the garden patio, exotic dishes include lobster Bora Bora, roast duck Mai-Kai, filet mignon Madagascar and coconut curry bouillabaisse. Standard American fare is also available. What most people come for are the Tahitian dances performed by the curvy dancers and muscular musicians of the Islander Revue troupe *(nightly; extra cost).*

$$ El Rancho Grande – *1626 Pennsylvania Ave., Miami Beach.* ☎*305-673-0480. www.elranchogrande mexicanrestaurant.com.* **Mexican.** Located just off lively Lincoln Road Mall, this family-owned dining spot feels like a roomy cantina. The extensive menu offers standard Mexican dishes and sides, presented in a variety of combinations. For a sampling of several flavors, try the *plato Mexicano,* a hearty assemblage of marinated pork, chicken enchilada, *chile relleno* (green pepper stuffed with cheese), beef burrito, refried beans and rice. (*Second location at North Beach, 314 72nd St.; 305-864-7404.*)

$$ Cafe Versailles – *3555 S.W. 8th St., Little Havana.* &♿ ☎*305-444-0240.* **Cuban.** Near the western perimeter of Little Havana lies one of the quarter's most prominent attractions. Local transplants get their fix of home cooking at Versailles. In this large dining spot you can enjoy ultra-sweet café Cubano from a stand-up counter inside or outside.

Hearty Cuban sandwiches and heaping plates of food from a magazine-size menu are served inside the main dining room. Most rib-sticking dishes, such as roast pork and grilled *palomilla* steak with garlic and onions, come with generous portions of black beans and white rice. Specialties include *ropa vieja* (shredded beef in a tomato-based sauce) and *plátanos verdes* (fried green plantains).

$ The Floridian Restaurant – *1410 E. Las Olas Blvd., Fort Lauderdale.* ☎*954-463-4041.* **American.** Inexpensive, tasty food and generous portions are what make "the Flo" popular among Las Olas insiders. It's always busy at this 24/7 diner-style eatery, where dining rooms are cheery with poster-lined red, green or blue walls. Allow 5min to read the encyclopedic menu that includes peanut-butter-chip muffins; 17 types of burgers; Mexican meatloaf; and a "Fat Cat" breakfast of strip steak, eggs, grits, toast and Dom Perignon for two. Another caloric dish ("the mess!") is heavenly hash, topped off with chocolate cake. No one leaves hungry.

$ Hamburger Heaven – *314 S. County Rd., Palm Beach.* ☎*561-655-5277.* **American.** A Palm Beach institution since 1945, this old-fashioned diner boasts the "world's greatest hamburgers" and more. At the counter of the always-packed place, diamond- and Gucci-clad millionaires are often seated next to construction workers. Red fabric booths along the wall offer more space for dining. Breakfast fare, soups, salads, cold or grilled sandwiches, and burgers, fill the straightforward menu. Take your pick of hamburger toppers from jalapeño peppers, onions, smoked bacon and cheese to sauerkraut, avocado, mushrooms or homemade chili.

$ News Cafe – *800 Ocean Dr., Miami Beach, FL.* ☎*305-538-6397.* **American.** People-watching is a 24-hour activity at this sidewalk cafe that opened in the 1980s to give production crews and models a casual place for a quick bite. Everything from French toast to salads is listed on the extensive menu.

$ Tobacco Road – *626 S. Miami Ave., Miami. ℘305-374-1198. www.tobacco-road.com.* **American.** This neighborhood bar, one block west of Brickell Avenue in downtown Miami, holds the oldest liquor license in the county. During Prohibition, "The Road" was a speakeasy, frequented by the likes of Al Capone. During World War II, its licenses were revoked on charges of indecent behavior. Regentrified today, Tobacco Road attracts a mix of downtown yuppies, lawyers, students and bikers. It's known for offering some of Miami's best live music nightly; Blues singers B.B. King and Koko Taylor have played here. Sandwiches, burgers and steaks are the mainstay menu items; the place stays open until 5am, the kitchen until 4am.

🛒 SHOPPING

Downtown: Downtown Miami Shopping District, Omni International Mall and shopping district, Bayside Marketplace. **Coconut Grove:** CocoWalk. **Miami Beach:** Lincoln Road Mall. **North Miami Beach:** Bal Harbour Shops. **Aventura:** Aventura Mall. **South Miami-Dade:** The Shops at Sunset Place.

⊛ ENTERTAINMENT

Consult the arts and entertainment section of local newspapers for schedules of cultural events and addresses of theaters and concert halls. To purchase tickets, contact the box office or **Ticketmaster** (*℘305-533-1361; www.ticketmaster.com*).

American Airlines Arena – Touring shows and sporting events in Miami (*℘786- 777-1000; www.aaarena.com*).

Miami-Dade County Auditorium – Greater Miami's premier performing arts center for grand opera, symphony, theater, concerts, ballets (*℘305-547-5414; www.miamidade.gov*).

Colony Theater – Miami Beach's Art Deco theater: music, dance, theater, opera, comedy, performance art and film (*℘305-674-1040; www.colonyandbyrontheaters.com*).

Jackie Gleason Theater – Miami City Ballet, prestigious Broadway shows, and electric concerts (⚅*see p282*): (*℘305-673-7300; www.gleasontheater.com*).

Olympia Theater at the Gusman Center for the Performing Arts – This magnificently restored 1926 theater is home to live performances, films and community events (*℘305-374-2444; www.gusmancenter.org*).

🏃 SPORTS AND RECREATION

Tennis courts are plentiful; some area hotels offer tennis instruction and clinics. For further information contact Miami-Dade Parks and Recreation Department (*℘305-755-7800; www.miamidade.gov/parks*).

Public **golf** courses: Miami Springs Golf and Country Club (*℘305-805-5180; www.miamispringsgolfcourse.com*); Normandy Shores Golf Course, Miami Beach (*℘305-868-6502; www.normandyshoresgolfclub.com*); Crandon Park Golf Course (*℘305-361-9120; www.crandongolfclub.com*).

SPECTATOR SPORTS

Thoroughbred racing at Calder Race Course, 21001 N.W. 27th Ave. *(year-round Thu–Mon 12:30pm; ℘305-625-1311; www.calderracecourse.com)*; Gulfstream Park, 901 S. Federal Hwy., Hallandale *(Jan–mid-Mar Wed–Mon; ℘954-454-7000 or 800-771-TURF; www.gulfstreampark.com)*.

Greyhound racing at Flagler Greyhound Track, 401 N.W. 38th Court *(year-round daily; ℘305-649-3000; www.flaglerdogs.com)*.

Miami Dolphins (NFL) (*℘1-888-FINS-TIX; www.miamidolphins.com*).

University of Miami Hurricanes sporting events (*℘800-GO-CANES; http://hurricanesports.cstv.com/*).

Miami Heat (NBA) (*℘786-777-HOOP; www.nba.com/heat*).

Florida Marlins (MLB) (*℘877-MARLINS; http://florida.marlins.mlb.com*).

Miami Beach★★★
and around

One of the country's great tropical paradises, Miami Beach is justifiably famed for its fabulous palm-studded shoreline, Art Deco architecture and colorful local residents. Built on dreams and speculation, this is an island in perpetual transition, where the atmosphere can shift from shabby to chic in a single block. Today, Miami Beach and particularly its SoBe (South Beach) quarter are hotter than ever, with a sizzling nightlife and celebrity-studded cafes, clubs and beaches.

GEOGRAPHICAL NOTES

A separate community from Miami, the City of Miami Beach occupies a narrow barrier island (7mi long and 1.5mi wide) 2.5mi off the mainland, along with 16 islets scattered in Biscayne Bay.

Dredging and land-fill have recon-figured the main island, where mangrove swamps once covered the entire area west of present-day Washington Avenue. Fisher Island, located at the southern tip, was created in 1905 when the Government Cut shipping channel sliced through to link Biscayne Bay with the Atlantic.

The famous **South Beach** area *(below 23rd St.)* and **Art Deco District** are reached directly by MacArthur Causeway, which passes the exclusive residential neighborhoods on man-made Star, Palm and Hibiscus islands, and offers a great view of the enormous cruise ships that dock in the Port of Miami.

A BIT OF HISTORY

In 1912 New Jersey horticulturist **John C. Collins** formed the Miami Beach Improvement Co. to raise capital for a trans-bay bridge. When funds ran short, **Carl Fisher** (an Indiana automobile magnate who built the Indianapolis Speedway in 1909) stepped in with a loan. In return Fisher received 200 acres from the ocean

▷ **Population:** 87,933.
⊙ **Michelin Map:** pp 249, 280.
▯ **Info:** 1920 Meridian Ave., Miami Beach FL 33139; ℘305-672-1270; www.miamibeachchamber.com.fl.us.
▷ **Location:** Hwy. 195 over the Julia Tuttle Causeway and Hwy. 395 over the MacArthur Causeway provide access to Miami Beach.
ℙ **Parking:** There's on-street parking spaces, six parking garages and more than 60 surface parking lots—and you'll still have trouble finding a space! The 13th Street and Collins Avenue Garage is most convenient to the Art Deco Historic District.
⊚ **Don't Miss:** A tour of the Art Deco Historic District.
◔ **Timing:** Allow at least a day to explore South Beach, including a tour of the Art Deco District and time to browse shops and people-watch.

to the bay south of the 2.5mi Collins Bridge (now the Venetian Causeway). Two Miami bank presidents, brothers **John and James Lummus,** laid out their first subdivision, offering small lots and modest bungalows. Fisher founded his own realty company and ensured a steady stream of sunseekers to his higher-priced tropical paradise by financing a paved road from Chicago to Miami; his famed **Dixie Highway** opened to great fanfare in 1915. That same year, Collins, Fisher and the Lummuses merged their companies and soon afterwards incorporated their land as the City of Miami Beach.

By 1921 five luxury hotels provided lodging for those who could afford it. By day polo grounds, golf courses and tennis courts offered diversion. At night

Miami Beach

Miami's beaches

Immortalised by the TV series *Miami Vice*, and dozens of movies, the 12-mile stretch of sugar-white sands that make up Miami Beach is one of the world's most famous playgrounds.

Moving from south to north the island beaches begin at South Pointe Park. This and First Street Beach are very popular with families, busy at the weekends, and a great place to watch cruise ships sailing out to sea. Next is the most glamorous and buzzing of all the beaches, South Beach (SoBe), which starts at 5th Steet and is patronised by the young, rich—the Miami Beach Polo World Cup (*www.miamipolo.com*) is held here every March/April—beautiful and trendy of every persuasion. If you want to see and be seen, this is the place. Lummus Park, whose sands were shipped in from the Bahamas, is the heart of the SoBe scene. The rainbow flag at 12th Street marks an unofficial gay section. Between 21st Street, where South Beach ends, and 46th Street, is family-oriented Central Beach. North Beach, from 46th Street to 78th Street, is community centered, with an old-fashioned bandshell. Moving further north, upscale Bal Harbour beach offers a palm-shaded jogging path, and Haulover Beach, between Sunny Isles Beach and Bal Harbour Beach, is Miami's only legal "clothing optional" beach. That said, many sunbathers decline to bare all and the nudist section is clearly marked to avoid potential embarrassment. Haulover is also a good spot for surfing. Opposite here, on "the mainland," Oleta River State Park beach offers many recreational activities and is a popular spot for boating and kayaking along nearby Snake River.

Visitors in search of watersports should head south to Key Biscayne, to Hobie Beach/Windsurfer Beach. Key Biscayne is also home to the lovely beaches of Bill Baggs State Park (⊙ *see p265*), Virginia Key Beach and Crandon Park. For more information visit www.miamiandbeaches.com/visitors/beaches.asp.

South Beach

locals flocked to the gambling and bootleg liquor operations hidden in the back rooms of nightclubs, hoping to catch a glimpse of **Al Capone,** the notorious Chicago gangster who bought a house on Palm Island in 1928.

The end followed the crash. The area boomed again in the late 1930s due to a resurgence of tourism. In 1936 alone, some 36 hotels and 110 apartment houses were built in the new Art Deco style in South Miami Beach.

Around 1947, gangsters began buying up estates north of 23rd Street, breaking the zoning code in order to build big hotels. Miami's "Gold Coast" strip enjoyed its heyday in the 1950s and 60s, when hotels like the famous Fontainebleau flourished, then slipped into an economic decline that left many faded resorts in its wake.

ART DECO HISTORIC DISTRICT★★★

Listed on the National Register of Historic Places in 1979, this enclave of small-scale Art Deco hotels and apartment houses dating from the late 1920s to the early 1940s amounts to the largest concentration of architecture of its kind in the world. The official district measures about one square mile and is roughly bounded by the Atlantic Ocean on the east, Lenox Avenue on the west, Sixth Street on the south and Dade Boulevard along the Collins Canal to the north. People-watching is a prime pastime here in SoBe (local slang for South Beach), now a magnet for fashion models, designers and assorted glitterati. The real stars, however, are the buildings themselves.

Architectural Heritage – As new investment focused on north Miami Beach after World War II, the south grew increasingly shabby and economic decline was firmly entrenched by the 1960s. In 1966, however, a retrospective of the International Exposition of Modern Decorative and Industrial Arts held in Paris in 1925 sparked a renewed interest in the Art Deco style. (The term "Art Deco" was coined at this time.) A decade later, **Barbara Baer Capitman** and **Leonard Horowitz,** two local design professionals, formed the Miami Design Preservation League to identify significant architecture in Miami Beach. The area's ensuing 1979 designation as a National Register Historic District was remarkable in that the roughly 800 Art Deco buildings included were only about 40 years old—and not of an age typically considered historic. Following the 1980 Mariel boatlift, when hundreds of Cuban prisoners were shunted off to South Beach, much of the established population fled and the Art Deco buildings—regarded as tacky and outdated—began to crumble.

Fueled by the efforts of Capitman and Horowitz, preservation of the Deco District began in earnest in the 1980s and continues to this day. Because National Register listing does not prevent demolition, several exceptional buildings have been lost to new development. Exterior changes and paint colors of new construction are, however, subject to approval by a local review board. The current trend for bright tropical hues is somewhat controversial, as the original Art Deco buildings were painted white and trimmed in primary colors.

Many Art Deco buildings here, exemplified by **1244 Ocean Drive** (originally the Leslie hotel, 1937, Albert Anis; currently under renovation) and **650 Ocean Drive** (formerly the Imperial hotel, 1939, L. Murray Dixon; now part of the Park Central Hotel), tend to have an angular look, with symmetrical, stepped-back facades and strong vertical banding and bas-relief decoration. The 11-story St. Moritz (1565 Collins Ave.), designed by Roy France in 1939, stretches upward with a soaring tower housing elevators and mechanical works.

In contrast to the angularity of these Deco structures, the later **Streamline Moderne style** featured aerodynamic imagery, horizontal racing stripes and wraparound corners, reflecting a fascination with speed and motion fostered by contemporary advances in transportation and industrial design. In an unabashed imitation of an ocean liner, for example, a building might gain

South Beach

© Greater Miami CVB

Art Deco Style Defined

The Art Deco Historic District is especially remarkable for its continuity of architectural scale and style. This continuity occurred because South Beach of the 1930s was redeveloped rapidly over a short period by a relatively small group of like-minded designers—most notably architects **L. Murray Dixon, Henry Hohauser, Albert Anis, Robert Swartburg** and **Roy France.**

Although the majority of structures in the district illustrate Art Deco designs, about a third were built in the Mediterranean Revival style. The 1930 **Casa Casuarina** *(1114 Ocean Dr.)*—renovated as the grand palazzo-style home of the late clothing designer Gianni Versace—is one of the best remaining examples. Derived from the minimalist **International Style** that originated in post-World War I Europe, Art Deco used decorative stylized elements to embellish simple, massive forms.

Reveling in its own sun-washed locale, Miami Deco went a step further, incorporating flamingos, herons, palm trees and other evocative tropical motifs into exuberant door grills, bas-relief plaques, murals and etched windows of frosted glass. The timing of these joyful designs—accented with neon and brightly colored trim—was ideal. Concrete-block buildings were relatively cheap to construct and allowed the new South Beach designers (many of whom were trained as engineers) to experiment with machine-age design.

portholes, periscope-like air ducts and tubular railings, as seen in the 1930s **Beach Patrol Station** *(1001 Ocean Dr.)* designed by Robert Taylor. The patrol station now forms the rear facade of the **Oceanfront Auditorium,** which was added in the 1950s.

South Beach is best navigated by foot. Parking is by meter (quarters only) with a strictly enforced 2hr limit. The Miami Design Preservation League (MDPL) offers walking tours that depart from the Art Deco Welcome Center (near Oceanfront Auditorium), 1001 Ocean Dr. (year-round Thu 6:30pm & Wed, Fri– Sat & Sun

10:30am; 1hr 30min; $20; 305-672-2014; www. mdpl.org). MDPL bike tours depart from Miami Beach Bicycle Center, 6015th St. (daily 10am; 4hrs. $50; 305-673-2002). An annual Art Deco Weekend, featuring special programs and lectures, is held in South Beach in January.

Ocean Drive★★

Along this lively north-south boulevard bordering the Atlantic Ocean beats the heart of the SoBe scene. By day locals and tourists have snacks at shaded side-walk cafes, while scantily clad youths streak by on in-line skates and willowy models pose for fashion shoots. At night vivid neon signs beckon revelers to some of Miami's hottest bars and dance clubs. Across the street lies fabulous **Ocean Beach**⬜⬜, refurbished and widened as part of a multimillion-dollar city project in 1982. **Lummus Park,** a magnet for teenage skaters and elderly dog-walkers alike, runs along the beach from 1st to 15th Streets. Located in the park is the nautically inspired Oceanfront Auditorium, which houses the **Art Deco Welcome Center,** an information center (1001 Ocean Dr.; ℘305-672-2014) stocked with books and souvenirs.

The park offers a great **view**★ of Ocean Drive and its pastel parade of Art Deco hotels. The seven-story, blue-tinted **Park Central** (no. 640), designed by Henry Hohauser in 1937, displays the characteristic symmetrical facade with vertical banding, steel corner windows (designed to maximize breezes in pre-air-conditioning days) and shaded central entrance. Notable for its horizontal racing stripes and futuristic double-faced tower, the yellow-and-blue-painted **Breakwater** (no. 940) shares a pool with the 1935 **Edison.** This Hohauser building (no. 960) designed with a ground-floor arcade, arched windows and three-story twisted colonnette, recalls the area's earlier Mediterranean Revival architecture.

Among the first hotels to be restored were a now-famous quartet: the former **Leslie** (1937, Albert Anis) at **no. 1244;** the **Carlyle** (1941, Kiehnel and Elliott) at **no. 1250;** the **Cardozo** (1939, Henry Hohauser) at **no. 1300**, now owned by singer Gloria Estefan; and the **Cavalier** (1936, Roy France) next door at **no. 1320**. Among the latest to be renovated is **The Tides** (1936, L. Murray Dixon) at **no. 1220**, owned by music-industry impresario Chris Blackwell. This 11-story hotel is the tallest on Ocean Drive.

Sanford L. Ziff Jewish Museum of Florida

301 Washington Ave. ⏰*Open year-round Tue–Sun 10am–5pm.* ⏰*Closed Jewish holidays.* 🎫*$6.* ♿✕*(Closed Sat).* ℘*305-672-5044. www.jewishmuseum.com.*

Art Deco Memorabilia

If you're fond of all things Deco, or if you simply want to support a worthy cause, stop in at the beachfront shop run by the Miami Design Preservation League *(1001 Ocean Dr. at 10th St;* ℘*305-672-2014; www.mdpl. org).* Inside you'll find a bounty of arty souvenirs promoting the historic district as well as Miami Beach: hotel-shaped mugs with palm-tree handles, fake flamingoes, Art Deco posters, photo postcards, picture frames, coffee-table books, model cars and toys, bakelite jewelry, journals and notecards, writing pens and logo-laden ball caps and T-shirts. There's a sizable stock of books, too.

🦐The store also serves as a welcome center and departure point for the League's guided tours of the area. The volunteer staff can answer most questions about the district, so don't be hesitant to pose a question.

Housed in the restored, copper-domed Beth Jacob Orthodox Synagogue (1936, Henry Hohauser), this cultural institution opened in 1995 to display art and artifacts relating to more than 230 years of Jewish history in the Sunshine State. A ten-year study of Jews in Florida led to some 10,000 artifacts, photographs and mementos being combined in the MOSAIC exhibit, which became the museum's core collection in 1996. In addition, related temporary exhibits rotate three times a year.

Light streams into the large, domed room through eight colorful stained-glass windows. At the eastern end stands a marble ark, crowned by a carved Torah supported by lions.

A continuously running video illustrates the struggles and achievements encountered by Jews since they first landed on the Florida coast with Ponce de León to escape persecution in Spain.

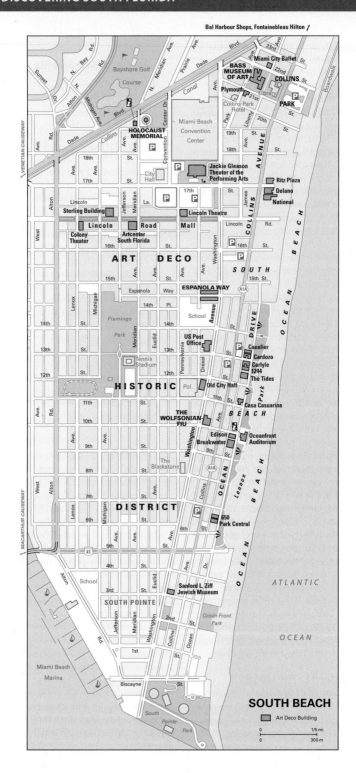

Bal Harbour Shops, Fontainebleau Hilton

SOUTH BEACH

Art Deco Building

0   1/5 mi
0   300 m

The Wolfsonian-FIU★★

1001 Washington Ave. ⏰*Open year-round Thu-Sun noon–6pm (Fri 9pm).* ⏰*Closed major holidays.* 🎟*$7. Free Fri 6–9pm.* ♿ 📞*305-531-1001. www.wolfsonian.org.*

The seven-story Washington Storage Co. building (1927, Robertson and Patterson)—distinguished by an elaborate gold-colored Moorish relief facade of cast concrete—once stored clothing and furniture during summer months, when most apartments were vacant. Now owned and operated by Florida International University, it houses a museum and research center that oversees the Mitchell Wolfson Collection: more than 70,000 pieces of American and European (mainly British, German, Italian and Dutch) decorative arts and crafts dating from 1885 to 1945. Rare books, graphics, political and propaganda artworks, architectural models, sculpture, glass, ceramics and furniture are included in the collection.

A **fountain** made from a glazed terracotta window grille from a 1929 movie theater dominates the lobby. The fifth floor is devoted to the permanent collection; about 300 works are displayed at any one time, illustrating how design has been used to help people adjust to the modern world. Focal points include design reform movements, urbanism, industrial design, transportation, world's fairs, advertising and political propaganda. Temporary exhibits occupy the sixth and seventh floors. The lower floors house museum administration and student study areas.

Washington Avenue

A busy commercial thoroughfare encompassing chic restaurants and trendy dance clubs as well as ethnic markets and Cuban coffee shops, Washington Avenue features several public buildings of note. The grand, eight-story, Mediterranean-inspired **Old City Hall** *(no. 1130)* was designed by Martin Luther Hampton in 1927, before the Deco wave swept Miami Beach.

A newcomer is the **World Erotic Art Museum** at no. 1205 (⏰*open year-round Mon–Thu 11am–10pm, Fri–Sun 11am–midnight;* 🎟*$15;* 📞*866-969-WEAM; www.weam.com. Both the website and museum contains adult content and material, so you must be 18 or over to enter),* housing the largest collection of erotic art in America.

The **US Post Office** *(no. 1300)* dates from 1939. Stripped of exterior ornament, the building displays the angular lines, glass-block window treatment and somewhat harsh overall modernist look widely adopted for Works Project Administration (WPA) structures of the 1930s—a style sometimes called Depression Moderne. Lined with cast brass lockboxes, the central **rotunda** features a 1940 mural by Charles Hardman depicting vignettes from Florida history.

Planned as an artists' colony in the 1920s, **Espanola Way**★ *(between Washington and Drexel Aves.)* breathes fresh air into an otherwise shabby area. This gas-lit enclave, with its movie backdrop ensemble of Mediterranean Revival buildings decorated in coral-colored stucco and hand-painted tiles, features cozy courtyards, pink sidewalks and chic boutiques offering such apparel as sequined bikinis.

Lincoln Road Mall

On Lincoln Rd. between Washington Ave. and Alton Rd. 📞*305-534-9857.*

This lively, lengthy pedestrian mall abounds with trendy shops, galleries and restaurants that border a central planted thoroughfare of tiled fountains and coral rock pools. Lincoln Road is the oldest commercial street on the island, laid out in 1915 by Carl Fisher. The area staged a second comeback after it was relandscaped and closed to traffic by Morris Lapidus (a set designer-turned-architect, who designed the Fontainebleau Hotel) in the 1960s, only to be deserted in the 1970s. After a recent $16-million face-lift, its latest transition is complete. The shops *(most don't open until 11am),* specializing in antiques, jewelry, books and designer clothes—as well as the galleries—improve in quality as you go west of Drexel Avenue. There are plenty of restaurants, serving a wide variety of cuisine; several offer alfresco dining and an opportunity for serious people-watching.

Originally a cinema, the 1935 Deco **Lincoln Theatre** *(nos 555–541)* was until very recently the home of the city's renowned New World Symphony academy. Regular public exhibitions are on show at the **Artcenter South Florida** *(nos 800–810 and 924; www.artcentersf. org)*, a warren of exhibit areas and studio space for photographers, ceramic artists, painters, jewelry designers and printmakers. Across the street the two-story **Sterling Building** *(no. 927)* dominates the streetfront with an undulating wall of tile-studded stucco and glass block.

Jackie Gleason Theater of the Performing Arts

1700 Washington Ave.
For performance information: ✆ *305-673-7300. www.gleasontheater.com.*
This confection of peach-colored concrete and glass block (1951, Pancoast, Hohauser and Dixon) was remodeled by Morris Lapidus in 1976, and originally hosted comedian Jackie Gleason's popular television series from 1964 to 1970. The 3,000-seat theater now stages Broadway shows and ballets. Look for Roy Lichtenstein's red-and-white-striped **Mermaid (1)** on the south lawn *(fronting 17th St.)*. Set into plaques on the adjacent yard, cement footprints of such celebrities as Julie Andrews and Don Johnson form the Walk of the Stars.

Holocaust Memorial★

Nos. 1933-1945 Meridian Ave. ◷*Open daily 9am–9pm.* ♿ 🅿 ✆ *305-538-1663. www.holocaustmmb.org.*
Set in and around a tranquil lily pond, this memorial leads visitors through a circular plaza of pale pink Jerusalem stone designed as a series of outdoor passages. Names inscribed on the walls are a simple but poignant reminder of lives lost to the Nazis during World War II. The centerpiece is Miami artist and architect Kenneth Treister's *Sculpture*

of Love and Anguish, which comprises several bronze vignettes and a giant 42ft-high outstretched arm symbolizing the last reach of a dying person. (Treister also designed the Streets of Mayfair shopping complex in Coconut Grove).

Collins Park

Between 21st and 22nd Aves. next to the ocean.
The area around Collins Park is the site of the first lots sold by John Collins to finance his bridge project in 1912. Modernist hotels replaced older buildings in the 1930s. The futuristic tower fin on the restored **Plymouth** *(3362 1st St.),* designed by Anton Skislewicz in 1940, characterizes designs inspired by the space-age pylon featured at the 1939 World's Fair. The lobby mural by Ramon Chatov shows scantily clothed figures cavorting on the beach.

Collins Park is being ex panded to include a cultural campus, under the development of noted architect Robert A.M. Stern. Part of the campus is the three-story administrative building/ballet school, designed by Arquitectonica for the **Miami City Ballet** *(2200 Liberty Ave.; www.miamicityballet.org).* At weekends between 10am and 6pm passersby can watch the dancers practice their pliés and pas-de-deuxs behind huge glass windows.

Bass Museum of Art★

2121 Park Ave. ◷*Open year-round Wed-Sun noon–5pm.* ◉$8. ♿✆ *305-673-7530. www.bassmuseum.org.*
This important and acclaimed regional museum maintains a permanent collection of more than 3,000 works, encompassing European, American, Asian and contemporary art. Its European holdings are particularly rich in religious artifacts and French and Flemish tapestries.

The original landmark Art Deco structure (1930, Russell Pancoast) of oolitic limestone decorated with Mayan motifs was designed as the centerpiece of a nine-acre park given to the city in 1920 by developer John Collins, who had moved to Florida from New Jersey to establish a farming venture but found success

Bass Museum of Art

© Greater Miami CVB

financing real estate development. First used as both a library and art center, the building was renamed in 1964 when Austrian-born New York entrepreneur John Bass donated his art collection to the city of Miami Beach. A recently completed expansion by Japanese architect **Arata Isozaki (**who designed the Team Disney offices near Orlando), increased the museum's size to 37,000sq ft, adding new gallery space, an enlarged museum shop, a courtyard and cafe. Surrounded by a reflecting pool, an outdoor sculpture terrace is tucked amid the exposed columns of the raised main gallery. The latter, a white-stucco rectangular block, admits natural light through a panel of clerestory windows.

The Bass displays European paintings, furnishings, altarpieces, sculpture and other works spanning the 15 to 21C. Highlights include art by such masters as Peter Paul Rubens and Sandro Botticelli as well as 19C tapestries by Louis-Marie Baader. The main upstairs gallery will be devoted to temporary displays.

Collins Avenue★

Although Collins Avenue is now one of the main traffic arteries in Miami Beach, it originally knew a more affluent lifestyle, catering to pedestrians with juice bars and small boutiques. Between 16th and 23rd Streets, hotels climb to 10 stories, the maximum height allowed; below 16th they may rise higher. Among the stars from the 1940s are the **National** *(no. 1677)* by Roy France; Robert Swartburg's **Delano** *(no. 1685)*, renovated in 1995 but still recognizable by its finned spaceship tower; and the **Ritz Plaza** *(no. 1701)* by L. Murray Dixon. With their squared, stepped-back facades and quirky central towers, these local landmarks resemble a trio of oversized party-goers dressed in giant overcoats and jaunty hats. For the best view, walk west two blocks on 17th Street and look east.

Driving north on Collins you will encounter a 13,000sq ft **mural** *(at 44th St.)* bearing the trompe l'œil image of a triumphal arch framing the **Fontainebleau Hilton** Resort and Towers, by noted muralist Richard Haas. The real Fontainebleau is just around the corner *(no. 4441)* on the 20-acre site of the former Harvey Firestone estate. This 1,200-room extravaganza (1954) is the work of Morris Lapidus, who dubbed it "modern French Château Style." The hotel fronts a beachside boardwalk (monitored by beach-patrol joggers) stretching 24 blocks from 23rd to 47th Streets.

To the north and west lie the exclusive residential areas of Middle Beach and Bal Harbour Village, a complex of high-rise condos and resorts.

Bal Harbour Shops (no. 9700; www. balharbourshops.com) is a mecca of high-fashion stores and boutiques including Tiffany & Co., Louis Vuitton, Cartier and Neiman Marcus, as well as cafes and coffee shops.

Palm Beach★★★
and around

Occupying the northern part of a 16 mile-long subtropical barrier island, this strip of real estate harbors one of the highest concentrations of multimillion-dollar mansions in the world. Though it has been a refuge for the rich for more than a century, Palm Beach attracts streams of tourists—particularly in winter—who venture across one of the bridges from the mainland to sample fine restaurants, stay in world-class hotels, shop along Worth Avenue and ogle the elegant estates bordering the ocean.

A BIT OF HISTORY

When a Spanish schooner, aptly named *La Providencia*, wrecked off this coast in 1879, the area's few settlers happily inherited a windfall cargo of coconuts. They planted the spoils and met with surprising success: a flourishing grove of around 20,000 coconut palms.

This lush, tropical-looking shoreline caught the eye of **Henry M. Flagler** as he was scouting out a site for a new resort town. In Palm Beach Flagler claimed to have found "a veritable paradise."

In the 1890s, Palm Beach had its first taste of the kind of development that would characterize the area for decades to come. Flagler's Royal Poinciana Hotel, now gone, opened in 1894 (the year his railroad came to town) with 540 rooms and the claim that it was the world's largest wooden structure. Flagler's indelible mark on the town is most apparent in two remaining buildings: The Breakers hotel and Whitehall, his former Palm Beach home (now the Flagler Museum).

The spectacular building boom of the late 1910s and early 20s left the town utterly changed. Early wooden seaside cottages and hotels were replaced by baronial mansions, giving Palm Beach an affluent image that lives on today. Known as the "winter Newport" (for the Rhode Island retreat of the rich

- ▸ **Population:** 10,468.
- ⑥ **Michelin Map:** p285.
- 🗐 **Info:** 400 Royal Palm Way; ☎561-655-3282; www.palmbeachfl.com or www.palmbeach chamber.com.
- ▷ **Location:** Southern Blvd., Royal Palm and Flagler Memorial bridges run west-east providing access to Palm Beach.
- 🅿 **Parking:** There are several public parking garages (follow signs) off A1A.
- ⊘ **Don't Miss:** A driving tour along the Atlantic to see how and where the rich and famous live.
- ⊘ **Timing:** Allow a half-day or more for the driving tour, including a stop at the Flagler Museum.
- 👫 **Kids:** DivaDuck Amphibious Tours (☎561-844-4188 or 877-844-4188; *www.divaduck.com; ⊜$25, child aged 5–15 $15)* offers fun-filled tours of the area.

and famous), Palm Beach had restaurants, shops, clubs, hotels and villas, all tailored to the tastes of the wealthiest people on both sides of the Atlantic—the Vanderbilts, the Rockefellers, the Duke and Duchess of Windsor. When Florida real-estate speculation caved in on itself and the Depression gripped the country in the late 1920s, Palm Beach society continued to enjoy a luxurious lifestyle; the rich merely became less ostentatious.

Bastion of Elegance – Today Palm Beach remains a picture-perfect island of palm-lined thoroughfares, immaculately clean streets and opulent houses where the only signs of activity are the perpetually busy gardeners. Visitors to this small, well-to-do city will find shopkeepers and restaurateurs congenial, prices high and architectural beauty widespread.

High Society Architecture

The growth of Palm Beach owes much to the aquaintance of two men: Paris Singer, son of the sewing-machine magnate, and architect Addison Mizner (1872–1933). They met in Palm Beach, where both men had come in 1918 to convalesce. Singer's interest in architecture and Mizner's wit and bonhomie made for a quick friendship, and soon Singer was financing Mizner's bold ideas. Born into a prominent California family, Mizner at age 16 had traveled to Central America, where his father was serving as a diplomat. He later attended classes at the University of Salamanca in Spain and, though he never earned a degree, he began trading on his big talent and personality. His early exposure to Spanish culture showed in the country homes he designed in New York, where he practiced for 14 years before coming to Palm Beach.

By the time Mizner and Singer went to work, Palm Beach was already a posh resort for the wealthy. Thus when their first project, a veteran's hospital, failed to attract enough patients, they simply converted the building into the exclusive Everglades Club, of which Singer was the sole owner. Mizner was then hired by the reigning social queen, Eva Stotesbury (wife of Philadelphia banker Edward Stotesbury), to build a lavish 32-room mansion. This and similar commissions for palatial homes occupied Mizner—now Florida's foremost society architect—throughout the early 1920s, until he began his projects in Boca Raton.

Mizner and other Palm Beach architects took their inspiration from Spanish colonial manor houses and Italian Renaissance villas and palaces, developing or importing the necessary craftsmen, ceramic kilns and materials. To create an antique feeling, Mizner purposely chipped stone carvings, blackened ceilings with soot, and punctured furniture with fake wormholes. His style—broadly known as Mediterranean Revival and characterized by pastel pink stucco walls, red-tile roofs and breezy loggias with fanciful embellishments—is now considered authentic Palm Beach style and is still imitated by modern architects.

🚗 DRIVING TOUR

▶ *7.5mi. Start at Southern Blvd. and Ocean Blvd. (A1A) and head north. The speed limit is 35mph, though most people drive at a lower speed.*

This drive begins along the Atlantic, offering expansive **views**★★ of the ocean on the right and large, elegant houses on the left. The first mansion, partially hidden by walls and a massive gate, is **Mar-a-Lago** (1927, Joseph Urban and Marion Syms Wyeth), so-named ("sea to lake") because it extends from the Atlantic to Lake Worth. Widely considered the grandest residence in Palm Beach, this 188-room Moorish fantasy, built for cereal heiress Marjorie Merriweather Post, has been owned in recent years by Donald Trump; it is now a private country club.

▶ *Drive north 2.6mi on Ocean Blvd. and turn left at dead end on Barton Ave. Park beside church on Barton Ave. or on Via Bethesda, one street to the north.*

Episcopal Church of Bethesda-by-the-Sea★★

141 S. County Rd. 🕐*Open year-round daily 8am–5pm.* 🚶*Tours following 11am serivce on second and fourth Sun of each month.* 🕐*Closed major holidays.* ♿🅿 📞*561-655-4554.*

This graceful structure of cast stone, built in the Gothic Revival style in 1927, was designed by Hiss and Weeks of New York.

The church features a prominent bell tower and notable ornamentations, including sculptures of the four Evangelists standing in niches in the main entrance archway.

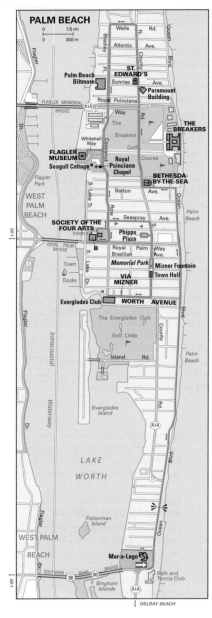

In the south transept hangs a 17C **Madonna and Child** by Spanish painter Esteban Murillo and a suspended model ship.

A cloister to the left of the entrance leads to a courtyard and then to the **Cluett Memorial Gardens,** a small formal garden with fountains, a gazebo and cruciform parterres.

Continue 0.3mi north on County Rd.

The Breakers★★

1 S. County Rd. Visit by guided tour (1hr) only, year-round Tue 2pm; meet in main lobby. *$15. Reservations suggested. 561-655-6611 or 888-273-2537. www.thebreakers.com.*

When Henry Flagler's famous hotel burned down for the second time in 1925, his heirs put up $6 million, hired the best architects, imported 75 artisans from Italy, and employed 1,200 craftsmen to construct a palatial hotel. Eleven and a half months later, the new Breakers was complete.

Fast forward 85 years and $250 million has been spent on improvements in the last decade! The hotel roughly follows an H-shaped layout and features twin two-tiered belvedere towers with open arches, a colonnaded porte cochere and exterior relief panels. The lobby runs the entire 200ft length of the center section (the cross in the "H") with an 18ft vaulted ceiling. From the lobby extends a lush courtyard with fountains and a sunken garden.

Continue 0.3mi north to the southeast corner of Sunrise Ave.

Paramount Building

139 N. County Rd.

This yellow building with green awnings, distinguished by its central entranceway and tall pointed arch, dates from 1927 when it opened as a 1,028-seat movie

Inside, the nave sweeps upward to wooden rafters and forward to a blue stained-glass window above the altar. Called the **Te Deum Window,** the three lancets depict the apostles St. Peter and St. Paul, the risen Christ, and martyred saints Stephen and Catherine.

The Breakers

Courtesy of The Breakers Palm Beach

palace. Joseph Urban, set designer for the *Ziegfeld Follies* and architect to Austrian Emperor Franz Josef, designed the theater, reportedly drawing the plans on a tablecloth in a Manhattan restaurant. Live performers included Charlie Chaplin, W.C. Fields and Glenn Miller. Women patrons wore so much jewelry that the semicircle of box seats was dubbed the "diamond horseshoe," and season tickets sold for as much as $1,000 apiece. The theater has been replaced by galleries, shops and offices.

▷ *Cross N. County Rd.*

Saint Edward's Church★

144 N. County Rd. ◷*Open year-round Mon–Fri 7am–4pm, Sat 7am–7pm, Sun 6:30am–1pm.* ♿🅿 ✆*561-832-0400.* Distinguished by elaborate decoration inside and out, this Roman Catholic church (1926) features a baroque entrance of cast stone, a belfry and a red-tile roof. In the narthex, spiral marble pillars and wooden gates lead into a vast sanctuary vaulted with a 65ft hand-painted coffered ceiling. The main altar was carved from a single piece of Carrara marble and measures 28ft by 15ft.

▷ *Continue north 0.6mi on County Rd. and turn left onto Wells Rd. and left again on Bradley Pl.*

Seven blocks down on the right stands the **Palm Beach Biltmore** *(Bradley Pl. and Sunrise Ave.),* a 1927 resort hotel that closed in 1970. The building now houses luxury condominiums.

▷ *Proceed two blocks farther south and cross Royal Poinciana Way. Continue south on Cocoanut Row (the continuation of Bradley Pl.); take the first right onto Whitehall Way.*

Flagler Museum★★

Whitehall Way. ◷*Open year-round Tue–Sat 10am–5pm, Sun noon–5pm.* ◷*Closed Jan 1, Thanksgiving Day, Dec 25.* ⬤$18. ✕🅿 ✆*561-655-2833. www.flaglermuseum.us.* Florida railroad magnate and Standard Oil partner **Henry Morrison Flagler** built Whitehall, this 55-room Gilded Age mansion overlooking Lake Worth, in 1901 as a wedding gift for his third wife, Mary Lily Kenan.
The mansion has been restored to its Flagler-era appearance with many of the original furnishings. **Marble Hall** is a 110ft-by-40ft imitation of a Roman villa's atrium, decorated in seven different shades of polished marble.
The **Louis XIV Music Room** is hung with Baccarat chandeliers and paintings by such 18C masters as Gainsborough and Romney.

The **ballroom** features gilt mirrors, crystal chandeliers, damask draperies and bronze fixtures hung with crystal grapes, pears and Florida bananas. The **Francis I Dining Room,** with its carved walnut woodwork and coffered plaster ceiling, saw a procession of royalty, wealth and fame with names such as Rockefeller, Astor and Vanderbilt. Flagler's private railroad car, "Rambler," stands on the south lawn. Visitors may walk through the car to see its sumptuous sleeping berths and kitchen area.

On the lawn, the gray-wood **Royal Poinciana Chapel** (60 Cocoanut Row, just south of the museum) was built by Flagler in 1896 for use by guests at his Royal Poinciana Hotel. Behind the chapel stands the oldest extant house in Palm Beach, **Seagull Cottage** (⌒ not open to the public).

▶ *Drive south 0.7mi and turn right on Royal Palm Way; take first right into Four Arts Plaza.*

Society of the Four Arts★

Four Arts Plaza. ◷*See below for opening times.* ♿🅿 ✆*561-655-7226. www.fourarts.org.*

The Society of the Four Arts was established in 1936 to foster an appreciation for art, music, literature and drama. The **Gioconda and Joseph King Library** contains more than 60,000

volumes for community use (◷*open Nov–May Mon–Fri 10am–5pm, Sat 10am–3pm).*

The **Esther B. O'Keeffe Gallery Building** (◷*open Dec–Apr Mon–Sat 10am–5pm, Sun 2–5pm*) provides space for exhibits, films, lectures and concerts. Near the library, intimate **gardens** feature a Chinese rock garden, a rose garden and fern-rimmed pools. At the entrance is the adjoining **Philip Hulitar Sculpture Garden**.

▶ *Cross Four Arts Plaza (north), turn right on Seaview Ave. Take first left on Cocoanut Row, then right on Seaspray and right on N. County Rd. Take second right into Phipps Plaza.*

Phipps Plaza

On N. County Rd. between Seaview Ave. and Royal Palm Way.

Planned by affluent resident socialite John S. Phipps, this peaceful Old-World cul-de-sac is a mix of residential and commercial properties. Distinctive features include belfries and walls covered with tiles taken from old buildings in Cuba, ornate iron gates, winding staircases and a densely planted central park of ficus yucca, frangipani and golden shower trees.

▶ *Turn right on County Rd. and continue 3 blocks south.*

Town Hall

©Palm Beach County CVB

Town Hall

360 S. County Rd., between Australian and Chilian Aves.

Designed by Harvey and Clarke in 1924, this attractive building features beige stucco walls rising to a barrel-tile roof crowned by an enclosed bell tower.

On the north side of Town Hall, **Mizner Fountain** splashes into three basins upheld by rearing horses. Addison Mizner designed the fountain and surrounding **Memorial Park,** an oasis in the middle of busy County Road, which features cut coral-stone pavement and plantings that flank the narrow pool leading from the fountain.

◐ *Continue two blocks south of Town Hall and turn right on Worth Ave.*

Worth Avenue★★

Between Ocean Blvd. and Cocoanut Row.

The East Coast's answer to Rodeo Drive in Beverly Hills, California, this upscale street acts as a magnet for well-heeled tourists and residents, as well as the merely curious, who come to eat and browse at the shops. Worth Avenue's mélange of styles succeeds in creating a picturesque street with a decidedly European flair.

Addison Mizner designed many of the connecting two-story villas along the street in 1924, as well as the delightful vias, or alleyways, that thread off the main road into charming little courtyards of tile-work fountains and hanging flower baskets. Among these, **Via Mizner★** stands out for its labyrinthine passages and pastel walls of yellow, pink and aqua. Mizner's own four-story apartment dominates the skyline here. At the west end of the street sits his first Florida commission, the three-story **Everglades Club** *(no. 356),* which embodies the ebullient, expansive spirit of pre-Depression Florida and secured his reputation as the architect of the wealthy in Palm Beach.

West Palm Beach★

and around

This center of commerce and industry remains, to some degree, in the shadow of its glamorous parent, Palm Beach. Although it has outstripped the resort island in size, population and skyline, West Palm Beach is still viewed as a commercial suburb. Nevertheless, the city offers its own attractions, including one of Florida's finest art museums.

A BIT OF HISTORY

West Palm first attracted workers who came to build the grand hotels on Palm Beach. By 1909 West Palm Beach attained the county seat and propelled itself into a booming era of construction that lasted through the 1980s.

Today, West Palm Beach is again experiencing a resurgence in construction. Bustling **CityPlace,** an entertainment

▸ **Population:** 89,905.

⚲ **Michelin Map:** p290.

▤ **Info:** 400 Royal Palm Way; ☏ 561-655-3282; www.palmbeachfl.com or www.palmbeach chamber.com.

◐ **Location:** Two major thoroughfares (US-1 and I-95) cut through West Palm Beach, and Florida's Turnpike runs just west.

🅿 **Parking:** Public garages throughout downtown. Street metered parking.

⊘ **Don't Miss:** Norton Museum of Art.

◕ **Timing:** Allow a full day to explore the Norton Museum of Art and Ann Norton Sculpture Gardens.

👪 **Kids:** Take a safari through the wild 500-acre Lion Country preserve.

For Golf Lovers

Sports lovers will have a field day at **PGA National Resort and Spa** *(400 Ave of the Champions in Palm Beach Gardens; 561-627-2000 or 800-863-2819; www.pga-resorts. com)*, the national HQ for the Professional Golfers of America. Billed as the "largest complex in the Western Hemisphere," it features five 18-hole tournament courses on 2,300 acres of manicured fairways, as well as a croquet complex. There are 339 guest rooms, 65 cottages, eight restaurants and lounges, 19 tennis courts and a 26-acre lake. For nonsporting types or weary athletes, the spa includes an outdoor mineral pool with Dead Sea healing waters.

and business complex, is linked to downtown's thriving Clematis Street, filled with trendy shops and eateries.Along **Flagler Drive** high-rise banks and office buildings contrast with such Palm Beach landmarks as The Breakers and Whitehall visible across Lake Worth. The **Old Northwood** neighborhood *(bounded by Flagler Dr. and Broadway Ave., 25th and 36th Sts.)* contains a number of Spanish-style homes dating from the 1920s.

Norton Museum of Art

©Palm Beach County CVB

SIGHTS

Norton Museum of Art★★

1451 S. Olive Ave. *Open year-round Tue–Sat 10am–5pm (second Thu of month 9pm) , Sun 1pm–5pm.* *Closed major holidays.* *$12.* 561-832-5196. www.norton.org.
Founded in 1941 by steel tycoon **Ralph H. Norton** (1875–1953), the collection consists of over 7,000 works concentrated in European, American, Chinese, Contemporary art, and photography. In its permanent holdings, special emphasis is placed on 19–20C American and European works and Chinese art from 1700 BC to the early 1900s. Highlights include its **French Impressionist** and **post-Impressionist** paintings by such notables as Cézanne, Matisse, Monet, Renoir, Gauguin and Picasso. Twentieth-century **American art** includes works by Hopper, O'Keeffe, Rauschenberg, Warhol and Pollock.
The museum's renowned **Chinese collection** comprises archaic jade tomb carvings from as early as the third millennium BC and ritual bronzes from the Shang (c.1450–1100 BC) and Western Zhou (c.1100–771 BC) dynasties. Ceramics and Buddhist sculpture, some from the Tang period (AD 618–906), round out this collection.

Ann Norton Sculpture Gardens

253 Barcelona Rd., north corner of Flagler Dr. *Open Sept–Jul Wed–Sun 10am–4pm.* *Closed major holidays.* *$5.* 561-832-5328. www.ansg.org.
This former residence of Museum of Art founder Ralph Norton *(see above)* has been converted to a display grounds for his second wife's sculpture. **Ann Weaver Norton** (1905–1982) came to the area in 1942 as the Norton School of Art's first instructor in sculpture. The house now contains more than 100 of Ann Norton's sculptures. In the garden, a walking trail leads past nine of Norton's monumental brick and granite **abstract megaliths,** designed to suggest Tibetan shrines, mythical beasts and totemic figures. An outstanding collection of palms—representing over 300 varieties—graces the property.

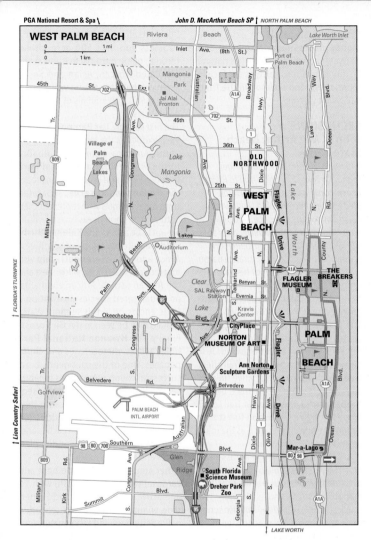

PGA National Resort & Spa \   *John D. MacArthur Beach SP* | NORTH PALM BEACH

👥 Palm Beach Zoo at Dreher Park

1301 Summit Blvd., just east of I-95, accessible from Southern Blvd. or Forest Hill Blvd. exits. 🕐*Open year-round daily 9am–5pm.* 🕐*Closed Thanksgiving Day and Dec. 25.* 💰*$14.95, child (3–12 yrs) $9.95.* 🍴⛽🅿️ 📞*561-533-0887. www.palmbeachzoo.org.*

Set on 23 acres, this small zoo is home to more than 1,500 animals representing 275 different species. None of the animals displayed here were captured in the wild—some were borrowed from other zoos, some were donated, and oth-

ers were placed here by wildlife officials. A short boardwalk nature trail *(0.25mi)* leads through lush tropical foliage.

👥 South Florida Science Museum

4801 Dreher Trail North, just north of the zoo. 🕐*Open year-round Mon–Fri 10am–5pm, Sat 10am–6pm, Sun noon –6pm.* 🕐*Closed Thanksgiving Day & Dec. 25.* 💰*$9, child (3–12yrs) $6; additional $4 (child $2) for planetarium shows. Laser concerts take place second Sat of month, 7pm and 8:30pm, $8.* ♿🅿️ 📞*561-832-1988. www.sfsm.org.*

More than 50 hands-on exhibits, a digital planetarium, freshwater and saltwater aquariums, as well as natural history exhibitions, such as the locally found mastodon skeleton in the front hall, await visitors.

EXCURSIONS
John D. MacArthur Beach State Park★

9mi north of Palm Beach, on Singer Island. ◗ *Take US-1 north 4mi to Riviera Beach; turn right on Rte. 708 (Heron Blvd.), which becomes A1A. Follow A1A north 5mi to park entrance.* ⏱*Open 8am–sunset.* ◉*$5 per vehicle.* ♿ ✆*561-624-6952. http://macarthurbeach.org*

Named for the eccentric insurance baron who donated a portion of his valuable property on Singer Island, this natural haven encompasses 760 acres of mangrove estuary and pristine beach.

The weathered wood **nature center** contains exhibits and a video explains the ecosystem of a barrier island. Just outside, the Butterfly Garden Trail offers a peaceful stroll among native flowers and the butterflies they attract; beside the parking lot, the Satinleaf Trail *(.5mi)* loops through a hardwood forest that supports tropical trees such as the mastic and strangler fig.

A 1,600ft wooden bridge across Lake Worth Cove (accessible by foot or tram) provides wonderful **views★** of the mangrove estuary and its birdlife—150 species, mainly waterfowl but also songbirds and raptors, have been identified here. A dense coastal hammock anchors the east end of the bridge, where vistors may continue on to a wide beach littered only with brown sargassum.

👥 Lion Country Safari★★

16mi west of I-95 on Southern Blvd. (Exit 50). ◗ *Turn right at sign and continue 2mi to entrance. Pets and convertibles not allowed (air-conditioned sedans available for rent). Visitors drive an 8mi road through the park and must remain in their cars with windows closed.* ⏱*Open year-round daily 9:30am–4:30pm.* ◉*$25.50, child (3–9 yrs) $18.50.* ⛺✖♿🅿 ✆*561-793-1084. wwwlioncountrysafari.com.*

Billing itself as North America's first cageless zoo, this 500-acre, drive-through game preserve features seven simulated African, Asian and South American habitats, taking visitors past more than 1,300 animals of 131 different species.

The first section, **Las Pampas,** features such exotics as the lowland tapir from South America, llamas and albabra tortoises. The **Ruaha National Park** includes kudu and impalas. Lions roam the **Gorongosa Reserve,** separated from other animals who represent their natural prey. Though easily visible, lions are apt to be asleep. The **Kalahari Bushveldt** features antelope of southwest Africa, and on the **Serengeti Plain** visitors can spot waterbuck, wildebeest and the African ostrich. African elephants, an endangered species, live within a large enclosure in this section. Water buffalo may be seen in the **Gir Forest.** Finally, the **Hwange National Park** holds zebras, rhinoceroses and chimpanzees. One of the continent's most successful chimp populations inhabits several little islands, each family segregated from the others because they cannot swim. Several generations, led by a dominant male, live on each island, which is furnished with wooden platforms and vine-like ropes.

Other amusements include boat and carousel rides, Safari Splash, with 23 interactive water functions and a waterslide, animal demonstrations, miniature golf, a petting zoo and a short nature trail.

Lion Country Safari

Visit Florida

From the cultural enticements of Sarasota and the sparkling beaches and excellent resorts of the barrier islands, to the fossilized sharks' teeth buried in Venice's sands and the fashionable shops and restaurants in Naples, this diverse region offers visitors a corner of paradise.

A Bit of History

Though Ponce de León and other 16C Spanish explorers sailed along this shore, they concentrated their attentions on Tampa Bay, leaving the southwest coast to the Calusa Indians. White settlement, which commenced in the mid-1800s, proceeded in fits and starts until the turn of the 19C, when development happened at a leisurely pace. While Tampa and the east coast were booming with railroads and buildings, the southwest remained agricultural. Fishing villages and a handful of scattered tourist hotels attracted those with a taste for adventure and the resources to make an excursion by boat. By the late 1920s the area was coming into its own: in 1927 **John Ringling,** who had begun developing some of the islands near Sarasota, started wintering his famous circus here. This was also the same year that the Seaboard Air Line Railway finally reached Naples.

Southwest Florida is less built up than other parts of the state, yet it now faces many of the same dilemmas looming elsewhere. Most of its coast is already developed, though a largely sophisticated and environmentally aware population is working to control the rampant growth of past decades. Large tracts of land on Sanibel and other barrier islands have been preserved for shorebirds and other wildlife; residents realize the need for long-term planning in an area where tourism ranks as the top industry and the silky white sand beaches of the area are the jewel in its crown.

Today's holiday playground stretches 120 miles along the Gulf of Mexico, from Bradenton down to Naples. It has much to offer, from the high-end culture and fine dining of Sarasota to canoe and kayak tours among mangrove and cypress swamps. Naples is the Palm

Highlights

1 Marveling at the history in the **Edison/Ford homes** (p296)

2 The Wildlife Drive at **J. N. Ding Darling Refuge**, Sanibel (p303)

3 Rolling up to see the fabulous **Ringling Museum**, Sarasota (p307)

4 Feeling the talcum-soft sands underfoot at **Siesta Key** (p314)

5 Taking an airboat tour at **Myakka River State Park** (p315)

Cà d'Zan, Sarasota Bay

Visit Florida

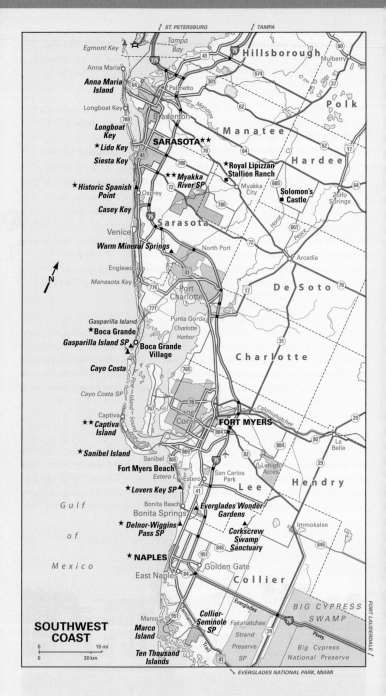

SOUTHWEST
COAST

0   15 mi
0   20 km

Beach of the Gulf Coast; Fort Myers is worth a visit for its extraordinary Edison/Ford homes; Sanibel and Captiva islands are America's Tahiti. Wherever you go along the coast you'll find the most wonderfu beaches, boardwalks, exhibits and guided nature programs.

Fort Myers

A city of royal palms and tropical flowers, Fort Myers curves along the shore of the gentle Caloosahatchee River. Though development in recent decades has sprawled the urban area out past I-75 and into the jam-packed adjoining communities of North Fort Myers and Cape Coral, a renewed downtown offers historic houses and a scenic waterfront. Just south on Estero Island, **Fort Myers Beach** is the center of the local sun-and-fun scene.

▶ **Population:** 50,575.

Info: 2310 Edwards Drive; ☎800-366-3622 or 239-332-3624; www.fortmyers.org.

Location: I-75 and Hwy. 41 provide north-south access. Hwy 867 crosses the bay to Sanibel and Captiva islands.

Don't Miss: Edison Ford Winter Estates and Edison Museum.

Kids: Look for gators and manatees at Lovers Key State Park.

A BIT OF HISTORY

Fort Myers was established when relations between settlers and Native Americans flared up after the Second Seminole War. In 1885 Fort Myers incorporated, elected a mayor and received a visitor who would become the town's most important citizen.

Newly widowed and in poor health, inventor **Thomas Alva Edison** traveled from New Jersey to Florida to look for a winter home in which to recuperate. He bought a 14-acre estate in Fort Myers and set up shop, developing some of the world's earliest lighting, phonographic, cinematic and telegraphic equipment (in addition to the humble toaster, electric fans, eater softener and more!). An active member of the community, Edison imported royal palms from Cuba to line his property along **McGregor Boulevard.** The city took up where Edison left off, and now some 14mi of the city's signature avenue are edged with stately palms. The publicity that followed America's most famous inventor gave a tangential boost to Fort Myers; by the 1920s building boom, the city was off and running. Like most of southwest Florida, the economy of Fort Myers is dependent on tourism, construction and agriculture.

SIGHTS
Edison & Ford Winter Estates★★

2350 McGregor Blvd. ♿*(Edison's Home).* 🕐*Open year-round daily 9am–5:30pm.* 🕐*Closed Thanksgiving Day & Dec 25.* 🍴*Homes & Gardens Tour $20. Botanical Tour $24. Laboratory & Museum only $12.* 🅿✕ ☎*239-334-7418. www.efwefla.org.*

Situated on the Caloosahatchee River, this complex holds the winter homes and tropical gardens of inventor **Thomas Edison** (1847–1931) and automaker **Henry Ford** (1863–1947). Edison bought his property in 1885 and designed two connecting cottages, some of the first

---

Paddling the back waters

Canoe or kayak the backbay estuaries on a naturalist-guided tour departing from **Lovers Key State Park** (ⓒ*see p298*) to discover the rich ecosystems of the area, or sign up for a guided paddle trip to Mound Key and hike to native American shell mounds. Pontoon cruises for novice anglers *(equipment provided)* or for leisurely viewing of the backbay are also offered along with overnight paddling excursions. The park also rents canoes and kayaks (including sea kayaks), as well as rod and reels on an hourly, half-day or full-day basis. Call for fees, schedules and reservations, ☎*239-463-4588.*

The Shell Factory

2787 US-41, north of Littleton Rd. in North Fort Myers. (🕐open winter daily 10am-6pm, summer Wed-Sun 10am-6pm. ☎239-995-2141 or 800-282-5805. www.shellfactory.com.

If you're tired of sifting through broken shells, this store gives you the easy way out. Shells from many countries fill the huge warehouse space, along with shell jewelry, shell lamps and a multitude of other souvenirs. There's a Nature Park here too.

prefabricated houses in the country. In his laboratory and botanical gardens, he perfected the light bulb, the phonograph, the moving-picture camera and projector, and the storage battery.

In 1896 Edison met Henry Ford. Edison encouraged Ford, who was then working in the Edison Illuminating Co. in Detroit, to follow his dream of building cars. The men became friends, and in 1916 Ford bought an adjacent house to spend winters near his mentor. After Edison died, Ford never again wintered in Fort Myers, saying he could not bear to be there without his friend.

Edison's Home – The star attraction of the estate, Edison's spacious house, "Seminole Lodge," nestles in an Eden of tropical flowers and trees, odd hybrids and towering bamboo—all part of the botanical gardens the inventor used for his experiments. Tours wend along garden paths and enter the "double house," as the two connected structures are called.

Ford's Home – Ford bought the "Mangoes" (1911), a relatively modest cottage, for $20,000 in 1916. Tours take in the pantry, kitchen, dining room, living room and guest and employee bedrooms. Outside, a garage houses vintage Ford automobiles. A paved path

connects the properties, curving by the river where Ford and Edison used to fish.

The Botanic Research Laboratory – Outfitted with the original apparatus and equipment this is one of the most absorbing features of the estate. When the price of rubber soared in the late 1920s, Thomas Edison, Henry Ford and Harvey Firestone combined their efforts, talents and finances in search of a natural source for rubber. Together they established the Edison Botanic Research Company. Extensive research proved Goldenrod, a common weed growing to an average height of 3–4ft, produced 5 percent yield of latex. Through hybridization, Edison produced Goldenrod in excess of 12ft, yielding 12 percent latex.

FORT MYERS
SANIBEL AND CAPTIVA

0 ——— 5mi
0 ——— 7km

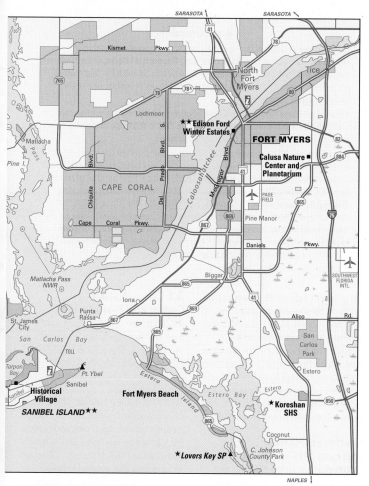

Model T in front of Ford's Home

Lee County VCB/www.FortMyersSanibel.com/Visit Florida

Boca Grande★

This charming village of sun-splashed houses and pastel-colored shops perches at the southern end of 7 mile-long **Gasparilla Island,** separated from the mainland by a 2 mile toll bridge and causeway. Spanish for "big mouth," Boca Grande refers to the pass that opens to Charlotte Harbor, one of the state's deepest natural inlets.

Vacationers come for the island's lovely peaceful beaches, while fishermen cast their lines in the waters of Boca Grande Pass in the hope of netting tarpons which can weigh as much as 300 pounds.

Boca Grande Village (*south end of Gasparilla Island; follow Gasparilla Rd. south to Park St.*) is a charming hamlet meriting a couple of hours to wander through its quaint shops, sample its restaurants, and stroll past the handful of restored early 20C buildings that make up its center. Don't leave without exploring **Gasparilla Island State Park** (*on the southern end of the island; follow Gulf Blvd. south of village; www.floridastateparks.org/gasparillaisland*). Relax on the sparkling white beach, and visit the two-story, white-frame **Boca Grande Lighthouse** (*open daily Nov–Apr 10am–4pm, May–Jul & Sept Wed–Sun 10am–4pm; www.barrierislandparkssociety.org*).

The adjacent **Edison Museum** houses six rooms filled with thousands of items, including more than 200 Edison phonographs—his favorite invention. Outside the laboratory, the **banyan tree**, which tire magnate Harvey Firestone brought back from India for Edison in 1925, has grown to measure some 400ft around its myriad trunks, and ranks as the world's third largest banyan.

Southwest Florida Museum of History

2300 Peck St., at Jackson St. Open *year-round Tue–Sat 10am–5pm, Sun noon–5pm.* Closed major holidays. $9.50. 239-321-7430. *www.swflmuseumofhistory.com.*
Housed in a 1924 railroad depot, the museum features exhibits on the Calusa and Seminole Indians, Spanish explorers and white settlers. Among the indoor displays is a saber-toothed cat skeleton found in central Florida. The museum hosts special events such as Night at the Museum author evenings. Outside is the **Esperanza,** an 84ft private railcar—the longest and one of the last built by George Pullman. On the other side of the museum is a replica of a vernacular Cracker house.

Calusa Nature Center and Planetarium

3450 Ortiz Ave. Open *year-round Mon–Sat 9am–5pm, Sun 11am–5pm.* $9, child (3–12 yrs) $6. 239-275-3435. www.calusanature.com.
Live turtles, fish and snakes occupy the indoor exhibits; outside there's an aviary for injured raptors. Three miles of interpretive boardwalk trails weave through hammocks of pine and cypress frequented by raccoons, otters, lizards and other animals. At the end of one trail sits a replica of a Seminole village.

EXCURSIONS
Lovers Key State Park★

30mi south on Lovers Key. Take I-75 *south to Exit 18 and turn right on Bonita Beach Rd., which becomes Estero Blvd.; continue 11mi to park entrance.* Open *8am–sunset.* $5. 239-463-4588. *www.floridastateparks.org/loverskey.*
Occupying a gorgeous stretch of undeveloped barrier island, Lovers Key encompasses 712 acres of tidal lagoons, mangrove estuary and white-sand beach. Wildlife includes roseate spoonbills, egrets, alligators and endangered West Indian manatees. A boardwalk to the beach crosses two peaceful lagoons, where fishermen cast for trout, redfish and snook (see p297).

Naples★

and around

Just west of Big Cypress Swamp and north of the Everglades, Naples marks the edge of civilization at the southwest end of Florida. Like a small-scale Palm Beach, it is characterized by fine restaurants and hotels, upscale shops, the 1,200-seat Philharmonic Center for the Arts, more than 40 golf courses and 9 miles of sun-drenched beaches. Many vacationers sample the archipelago to the south known as the **Ten Thousand Islands;** at the chain's northern extreme, **Marco Island** offers modern resort life on one end and the old maritime village of Goodland on the other.

A BIT OF HISTORY

Impressed by the area's dazzling beaches and subtropical foliage, Walter S. Haldeman, owner of the *Louisville Courier-Journal,* created the Naples Town Improvement Co. in 1887. The city's name probably derives from early comparisons with Naples, Italy. The company built the Naples Hotel and the Pier, but overextended itself and went out of business.

Accessible only by boat or ox cart, the town attracted well-to-do families and reclusive millionaires who erected impressive estates along the beach. Real prosperity for Naples had to wait until the 1920s, with the arrival of the railroad and the completion of the Tamiami Trail in 1928—the latter financed largely by local landowner **Barron G. Collier** (1873–1939), a wealthy Memphis businessman who owned 1 million acres of royal palm hammock in the area. Today his namesake Collier County remains the one of the richest and fastest-growing counties in Florida.

SIGHTS
Scenic Drive★

6mi. ◗ *Follow Mooring Line Dr. (north of downtown, off US-41) south as it becomes Gulf Shore Blvd.; turn left on 19th Ave. and travel 1 block to Gordon*

▶ **Population:** 21,709.
Ġ **Michelin Map:** p294, 300.
🛈 **Info:** 2800 Horseshoe Drive; ℘239-403-2384 or 800-688-3600; www.paradisecoast.com.
◗ **Location:** Hwy 41 runs north-south through the city; Gulf Shore Blvd. skirts the waterfront.
⊛ **Don't Miss:** Browsing shops and dining in historic Old Naples.
🕐 **Timing:** A day in downtown plus a day on the island beaches. Return for shopping and dining in the city.
👥 **Kids:** Take a boat ride past alligators, monkeys, lemurs, and apes at the Naples Zoo.

Dr.; turn right and follow to dead end at Gordon Pass.

Driving south on Gulf Shore Boulevard, you pass some of the finest houses in Naples, with the larger, more modern houses situated along the last 2.5mi of Gordon Drive. Built in 1888, the 600ft wooden **Naples Pier** *(at 12th Ave. S.)* harkens to the days when vacationers disembarked at this point. On the opposite side of the boulevard on 12th Ave-

Bayfront Place Along Naples Bay

Gwen Cannon/MICHELIN

299

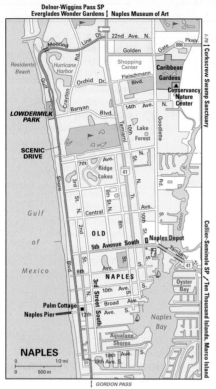

Delnor-Wiggins Pass SP
Everglades Wonder Gardens | Naples Museum of Art

NAPLES

GORDON PASS

5th Ave. S.), built in 1927 as the southern terminus of Seaboard Air Line Railway's west coast line. It is now an office and shops complex and **museum** (🕐 *open Mon–Fri 9am–5pm, Sat 9am–4pm*; ☎*239-262-6525*). Seminole dugout canoes, a mule wagon, antique swamp buggy, restored rail cars and exciting interactive exhibits tell the story of how trade and travel transformed Naples. There is an extensive model railroad layout and miniature train rides for kids.

🧍🧒 Naples Zoo and Caribbean Gardens
1590 Goodlette-Frank Rd. (just south of Golden Gate Pkwy.). 🕐*Open year-round daily 9am–5pm.* 🕐*Closed Thanksgiving Day, Dec 25.* 🎫*$19.95, child (3–12 yrs) $11.95.* ✕🅿 ☎*239-262-5409. www.napleszoo.com.*

Exotic trees and animals fill this 52-acre garden park that began as a botanical collection in 1919. Visitors stroll among trees like the gumbo-limbo, jacaranda and Hong Kong orchid while viewing alligators, zebras, tigers and birds. The high point is a **boat ride** on an island-dotted lake that gives visitors a close look at agile primates, including the white-handed gibbon. Animal lectures and shows add to the fun.

Conservancy Nature Center
1450 Merrihue Dr., off 14th Ave. N. (adjacent to Naples Zoo and Caribbean Gardens). 🕐*Open year-round Mon–Sat 9am–4:30pm, Sun noon–4pm.* 🕐*Closed major holidays.* 🎫*$9.* 🅿 ☎*239-262-0304. www.conservancy.org.*

A modern educational facility, this 15-acre preserve boasts hands-on displays, live snakes and other exhibits on southwest Florida's various ecosystems. Outside, a boardwalk trail loops through a mangrove swamp and past a wildlife

nue is **Palm Cottage** *(no. 137;* 🚶*visit by guided tour only;* 🕐 *open May–Oct Wed & Sat 1pm–4pm; Nov–Apr Tue-Sat 1pm-4pm;* 🕐*closed major holidays;* 🎫*$8;* ♿☎*239-261-8164).*Constructed of tabby mortar (burnt seashells), this is the oldest residence in Naples and serves as headquarters for the Naples Historical Society.

Old Naples★
5th Ave. S. and 3rd St. S.
The historic downtown offers chic shops and restaurants that open onto palm-lined streets, as well as shaded courtyards perfect for sipping tea or coffee. Galleries along **Third Street South**, particularly near Broad Avenue, sell original paintings, sculpture, prints and glass objects. For other shops, stroll down **Fifth Avenue South** between Third and Ninth streets.

Across Fifth Avenue stands the Mediterranean-style **Naples Depot** *(1051*

rehabilitation center, where injured pelicans and other birds take therapeutic swims. A boat ride on the Gordon River is included in the admission fee; canoes and kayaks are for rent.

Naples Museum of Art★

5833 Pelican Bay Blvd., adjacent to Philharmonic Center for the Arts. ○*Open Oct–Jun Tue–Sat 10am–4pm, Sun noon–4pm.* ○*Closed major holidays.* ⊛*$12.* ⮭🅿️☎*239-597-1900. www.thephil.org.*

Art and architecture are suitably matched in this striking three-story showpiece adorning the Philharmonic campus. The 15-gallery museum showcases temporary exhibits and a permanent collection of ancient Chinese and 20C American art. Visitors enter a massive granite portico via 16ft metal gates designed by Albert Paley and step into an outdoor sculpture court. Inside the domed conservatory, a stunning 30ft red glass chandelier by **Dale Chihuly** serves as an eye-catching centerpiece. Permanently displayed on the first floor is the Gow Collection of Ancient Chinese Art spanning 450BC to the 19C.

On the second floor, selections of American art from 1900 to 1955 include works by Jackson Pollock and Marsden Hartley.

EXCURSIONS
Delnor-Wiggins Pass State Park★

West end of Bluebill Ave., off US-41. ○*Open 8am–sunset.* ⊛*$6 per vehicle.* ⮭🅿️☎*239-597-6196. www.floridastate parks.org/delnorwiggins.*

Punctuating the heavily developed shoreline north of Naples, this delightful park offers more than a mile of unspoiled white sugar sand, backed by sea grapes, sea oats, cabbage palms and mangroves, rated as one of the best beaches in the nation.

Through Wiggins Pass, at the park's north end, the Cocohatchee River spills to the sea. Also at this end, a 30ft observation tower clears the jungle canopy to provide glimpses of the Gulf of Mexico and its backwaters.

⚱ Everglades Wonder Gardens

14mi north in Bonita Springs.
▶ *Take US-41 north turn right (east) on Business US-41; entrance 1mi north of Bonita Beach Rd.* ○*Open daily 9am–5pm.* ○*Closed Dec 25.* ⊛*$15, child (3–10 yrs) $8.* ⮭🅿️☎*239-992-2591.*

Established in 1936 and redolent of bygone Florida tourism, this old-fashioned attraction exhibits some 2,000 species of plants and animals from Florida, Asia, and Central and South America. Included are crocodiles, alligators, panthers and flamingoes housed in animal enclosures set amid lush gardens. Shows and tours are included, too.

Corkscrew Swamp Sanctuary

30mi northeast of Naples.
▶ *Take US-41 north 9mi to Rte. 846/ Immokalee Rd.; turn right (east) on Rte. 846 and continue 18mi. Turn left on Sanctuary Rd.* ○*Open mid-Apr–Sept daily 7am–7:30pm; rest of the year daily 7am–5:30pm.* ⊛*$10.* ⮭🅿️☎*239-348-9151. www.corkscrew.audubon.org.*

The country's largest stand of virgin cypress occupies this 11,000-acre tract owned by the National Audubon Society. A 2.25mi boardwalk trail begins in pine flatwoods and snakes through dense saw palmetto to a cypress swamp marked by soaring 500-year-old bald cypress trees. Visitors may see alligators, endangered wood storks, tropical orchids and swamp lilies.

Collier-Seminole State Park

17mi southeast on US-41. ○*Open 8am–sunset.* ⊛*$5 per vehicle.* △⮭🅿️☎*239-394-3397. www.floridastateparks.org. collierseminole.*

This 6,400-acre preserve boasts a wide diversity of plants and wildlife. Rare royal palms flourish in this tropical hammock, and mangrove and cypress swamps, salt marshes and pine flatwoods create an unusually variegated landscape.

A 6.5mi trail offers the promise of wood storks, bald eagles, black bears and Florida panthers; the boardwalk trail *(0.9mi)* loops to a viewing platform. Canoe rentals are available.

Sanibel and Captiva Islands★★

Long known as a paradise for shelling, these popular barrier islands, connected by causeways to each other and to the mainland, form a 20-mile arc into the Gulf of Mexico 23 miles southwest of downtown Fort Myers. Though the winter season brings a steady stream of traffic, the pockets of tranquillity and beauty that exist on these islands merit the drive over.

- ▶ **Population:** 6,102.
- ⌚ **Michelin Map:** pp294–296.
- ▤ **Info:** 1159 Causeway Road, Sanibel Island; ℘239-472-1080; www.sanibel-captiva.org.
- ▷ **Location:** Periwinkle Way and Sanibel-Captiva Road traverse the islands.
- ⊘ **Don't Miss:** J.N. Ding Darling National Wildlife Refuge; take a guided tram or kayak tour.
- ⊙ **Timing:** Allow at least a couple of nights here.
- ⚎ **Kids:** Take a boat trip over to Cayo Costa beach.

A BIT OF HISTORY

Spanish navigators who first discovered Sanibel and Captiva in the 16C never settled here, leaving the islands to the Calusa Indians. Pioneers attempted to settle Sanibel as early as 1833. Development proceeded slowly up to 1963 when the causeway was built, at which time the floodgates opened to tourism. Conservation groups rallied to protect their island from unchecked development. One noteworthy result of their efforts, the J.N. "Ding" Darling National Wildlife Refuge, preserves more than one-third of Sanibel's total acreage.

Naming the Islands

Sometime between the 16C and the 18C, the Spanish labeled the islands *Puerto de Nivel del Sur* ("port of the south plain") and *Boca del Cautivo* ("captives' entrance"). Over the years these names became corrupted to Sanibel and Captiva. Pirate lore maintains that buccaneers kept the most beautiful women prisoners on the smaller northern isle, hence its name. However, since many of these legends are inextricably tangled with early 20C real-estate hype, the more likely original captive was a Spaniard named Juan Ortiz, kidnapped by the Calusa in 1528.

The main thoroughfare today passes boutique-and-restaurant complexes on Sanibel's south end, then traverses a long stretch of bayside wilderness before crossing to Captiva for the 3.5mi drive to the end. Traffic moves at a leisurely pace. Though occasionally affording a view of the sea, the road mostly tunnels through the dense greenery shielding tasteful resorts and expensive houses.

SIGHTS
Bailey-Matthews Shell Museum

3075 Sanibel–Captiva Rd. ⊙*Open year-round daily 10am–5pm.* ⊙*Closed major holidays.* ⬤*$7.* ♿ ℗ ℘*239-395-2233 or 888-679-6450. www.shellmuseum.org.*
A must for conchologists, this attractive stucco building houses a reference collection of some two million shells. In the main exhibit hall, displays range from the geographic location of shells worldwide to the variety of mollusks that can be found on Sanibel and Captiva Islands. The museum explores, among other things, the role of shells in tribal art, medicine and as a food source, as well as the 19C phenomenon of sailors' valentines, the pointillist-style art form made for seamen plying the New England-Caribbean route.

Observation tower along Wildlife Drive,
J.N. "Ding" Darling National Wildlife Refuge

© James Schwabel/Alamy

Sanibel Historical Village and Museum

950 Dunlop Rd., off Periwinkle Way in the government complex.

Visit by guided tour (1hr) only, Nov–Apr Wed–Sat 10am–4pm, May–mid-Aug Wed–Sat 10am–1pm. $5. 239-472-4648. www.sanibelmuseum.org.

Set up as a pioneer village, this local history museum-village is comprised of eight buildings. All were brought from elsewhere on the island. In the 1913 Cracker house there is a dining room, parlor and kitchen furnished to depict early island life. Additional rooms contain fossil and shell displays, Spanish shipwreck artifacts and 2,000-year-old remains of the Calusa Indian culture. Other buildings on-site include the old tea room, the 1926 Sanibel post office and Bailey's General Store.

Sanibel-Captiva Conservation Foundation

3333 Sanibel-Captiva Rd. (1mi southeast of J.N. "Ding" Darling Refuge entrance).

Nature Center open year-round Mon–Fri 8:30am–4pm (Jun–Sept 3pm), also Dec–Apr Sat 10am–3pm. Closed major holidays. $3. 239-472-2329. www.sccf.org.

This 247-acre site surrounds a nature center containing a touch tank and informative displays on wetlands ecology. Out front is a native plant nursery; behind the center, nearly 5mi of boardwalk trails wind through wetland and upland habitats. One walk (*0.3mi*) leads to a 30ft observation tower that provides fine **views** of the Sanibel River and forest canopy.

J.N. "Ding" Darling National Wildlife Refuge★★

1 Wildlife Dr., off Sanibel-Captiva Rd.

Education Center open Nov–Apr daily 9am–5pm. Rest of the year daily 9am–4pm. Wildlife Drive open Sat-Thu 7am/7:30am to half- hour before sunset. Closed major holidays.

Wildlife Drive $5 (exact change required). 239-472-1100. www.fws.gov/dingdarling.

A showcase of barrier island wildlife abounds here in canals, inlets, mangrove swamps and upland forests. Begin at the **Education Center** to learn about the 6,300-acre refuge and its natural history through displays and videos. Then take the (one-way, unpaved) 4mi-long **Wildlife Drive**, which offers virtually guaranteed sightings of water birds and other animals, including the alligator. A 20ft observation tower along the drive offers **views** of herons, egrets, roseate spoonbills, ospreys and others.

For best bird-watching, visit near dawn, at sunset or at low tide, when the mud flats are exposed.

Near the end of the drive, the **Shell Mound Trail** (*.3mi; parking on left*) loops through lush vegetation over an ancient Calusa shell mound.

Visitors who want to take a closer look at the local flora and fauna can hike the refuge's 4mi of interpretive trails, or paddle the 6mi of marked canoe courses.

GETTING THERE

Southwest Florida International Airport (RSW): in Fort Myers, 26mi east of islands; international and domestic flights *(information: ℘239-590-4800; www.flylcpa.com)*. Transportation to Sanibel/Captiva: airport **shuttle** *($56; reservations: ℘239-472-0007 or 800-395-9524)*; **taxi** *($56–$75)*. Visitor booth in baggage claim area *(open daily; hrs. vary seasonally, ℘239-338-3500 or 800-237-6444)*. **Rental car agencies** located at airport and in Fort Myers. Nearest Amtrak **train** station is in Tampa, with Greyhound/Trailways **bus** connection to Fort Myers *(℘800-231-2222; www.greyhound.com)*. **Major access roads:** I-75, US-41 and Route 869 south to Sanibel Causeway; toll in-bound.

GETTING AROUND

Sanibel **Taxi** *(℘239-472-4160 or 888-527-7806; www.sanibeltaxi.com)* is the only taxi on the island. The best way to get around is by bicycle. Captiva is less attractive to cyclists because of its narrow winding roads. **Bicycle rental shops:** Finnimore's Cycle Shop, The Winds Center, 2353 Periwinkle Way *(℘239-472-5577; www.finnimores.com)*; Billy's Rentals *(1470 Periwinkle Way; ℘239-472-5248 or 800-575-8717; www.billysrentals.com)* offer all kinds of bike, motor scooters and even **Segway** tours *(www.segwaysanibel.com)*. Yolo Watersports *(℘239-472-1296; www.yolo-jims.com)* offer Scoot Coupes (small 3-wheeler automobiles) , golf carts, motor scooters and bikes.

VISITOR INFORMATION

Lee County Visitor and Convention Bureau, 2180 W. First St., Fort Myers FL 33901 *(open Mon–Fri 8am–5pm; ℘239-338-3500 or 800-237-6444; www.fortmyers-sanibel.com)*.

Sanibel-Captiva Islands Chamber of Commerce, 1159 Causeway Rd., Sanibel FL 33957 *(open Mon–Sat 9am–7pm, Sun 10am–5pm; www.sanibel-captiva.org; ℘239-472-1080)*.

Canoes, bicycles and fishing equipment are available for rent. Guided kayak and canoe tours from Canoe Adventures along the Drive (℘239-472-5218) and in Tarpon Bay with Tarpon Bay Explorers (http://tarponbayexplorers.com), the refuge concessionaire, who also offer guided tram tours along Wildlife Drive.

EXCURSIONS
Cayo Costa

Accessible by boat only. Reservations required. ⊜*Full day $45, half-day $35.* 🅿*Captiva Cruise, ℘239-472-5300. www.captivacruises.com.*

Cayo Costa (Spanish for "key by the coast") is owned by the state park department and protected from development. The 1,600-acre island maintains its pre-European appearance, dense with palmetto brush and pine. **Cayo Costa State Park** occupies the north part of the island *(🕓open 8am-sunset; ⚠⊜$2; ℘239-964-0375; www.floridastateparks.org/cayocosta)*. Visitors may hike or bike the 5mi of developed inland trails, or stroll the deserted shell-strewn beach and watch pelicans and dolphins at play. In summer, loggerhead turtles come to the island's shores to lay their eggs.

Cabbage Key

Accessible by boat only. Reservations required. ⊜*Full-day $35.* 🅿*. Captiva Cruises. ℘239-472-5300. www.captivacruises.com. www.cabbagekey.com.*

To visit this tiny island in Pine Island Sound is to travel back to the earliest days of Florida tourism. Its dominant building is the weathered **Cabbage Key Inn** (1938), built on a Calusa Indian shell mound as a winter residence for the son of mystery writer Mary Roberts Rinehart. In the early 1940s a subsequent owner turned the house into an inn. Some 25,000 dollar bills, signed by patrons, hang from the ceiling of the restaurant, which serves good, simple fare. After lunch, you can take a half-mile nature trail through a dense understory of mangroves, strangler figs and sea grapes. A 30ft water tower provides a **view** of the surrounding islands.

The Sanibel Stoop

Dubbed *Costa de Carocles* ("Coast of Seashells") by 16C Spanish explorers, Sanibel and Captiva beaches continue to harvest a staggering number and variety of colorful shells. The islands' unusual east-west orientation intersects with the junction of gulf currents, acting as a natural catchment for the more than 200 species of mollusks that inhabit the Gulf of Mexico's shallow continental shelf. A common "afflction" here is the Sanibel Stoop, the bent-over posture assumed by serious conchologists, or shell collectors.

Visit Florida

For best finds, arrive an hour before low tide; tides are especially low at new and full moons. Two days after a northwesterly wind is the optimum time to discover the largest assortment churned up on the beach from deep waters. Common among the myriad shells found here are calico scallops, kitten's paws, turkey wings, lightning whelks, fighting conchs and tiny coquina clams. Rare finds include the prized brown-speckled junonia, lion's paw and Scotch bonnet. Lovely Bowman's Beach *(3mi north of "Ding" Darling Refuge entrance; turn left on Bowman's Beach Rd.)* and Turner Beach *(at Blind Pass between the islands)* are popular starting places for beginner shell collectors.

ADDRESSES

🏨 STAY

Area visitors' guide including lodging directory available free from **Lee County Visitor and Convention Bureau.**

Advance reservations are strongly recommended in season *(Dec–Apr)* and during Jul–Aug. Weekly and monthly rentals of condominiums and **apartments** available through local rental and real-estate agencies.

Camping: Periwinkle Park *(tents and RVs; ℘239-472-1433; www.sanibel camping.com)*. Camping is permitted only in specified campgrounds. Cayo Costa State Park is accessible by boat only: **hiking, shelling, camping, bicycle rental** *(for cabin reservations contact Cayo Costa State Park; ℘239-964-0375; www.floridastateparks.org)*.

🚶 SPORTS AND RECREATION

Most **beaches** have public access and restrooms. Parking *(7am–7pm; $2/hr)*. Water sports include boating, sailing, canoeing, saltwater and freshwater fishing. A **bike** path runs from Lighthouse Point to Blind Pass at the western end of the island.

Golf and Tennis: Beachview Golf & Tennis Club *(℘239-472-2626; www. beachviewgolfclub.com)* and Dunes Golf & Tennis Club *(℘239-472-2535; www. dunesgolfsanibel.com)* both allow non-members.

🎭 ENTERTAINMENT

Consult the *Sunny Day Guide* and *Sanibel-Captiva Islands Chamber of Commerce* publication, available free locally for schedules of activities, dining and local events.

J. Howard Wood Theatre: comedies, musicals and Broadway favorites *(Nov–May; ℘239-472-0006)*; **Old Schoolhouse Theater:** Sanibel Island's only professional musical theater offers Broadway caliber talent in an intimate atmosphere *(Nov–May; ℘239-472-6862; www.theschoolhousetheater.com)*.

Sarasota★★

Lying on the Gulf Coast just south of Bradenton, Sarasota offers one of Florida's best-balanced menus of attractions. Here you'll find the official art museum of Florida, a host of cultural and sports activities, two shopping districts that rival the swankiest in Palm Beach, restaurants catering to all palates and budgets, and a 35-mile stretch of superb beach. In addition to tourism, Sarasota's economy rides on information technology, health care and financial services to provide for the area's many monied retirees.

A BIT OF HISTORY

The bulk of the area's pioneers began arriving in the late 1860s, enticed by free land offered by the federal government. In 1885 a boatload of Scottish settlers quickly set about building a community. The town elected as its first mayor, in 1902, the son of a Scottish nobleman, and the builder of one of the country's first golf courses in Sarasota.

Another influential city father, **John Ringling**, bought a house in Sarasota in 1912. For several years Ringling traveled with his famous **Ringling Bros. and Barnum & Bailey Circus.** Involved in local real estate in 1917, he poured much of his time and money into the area, even serving as chamber of commerce president. Thanks to Ringling, the barrier islands—once his personal property—are now linked by causeway to the mainland. In 1927 he moved the circus' winter headquarters to Sarasota, providing a much-needed injection to the local economy. Visitors paid 25 cents to watch rehearsals, with proceeds going to charity. That same year, Ringling and his wife began construction of a grand Italian Renaissance-style residence to house their growing collection of paintings.

In the late 1940s Arthur Vining Davis' Arvida Corp. changed Lido, St. Armands, Longboat and other keys into bastions of high-toned houses, shops and resorts.

▶ **Population:** 54,349.
⏲ **Michelin Map:** pp294, 231.
ℹ **Info:** 701 North Tamiami Trail Sarasota; ✆800-800-3906; www.sarasotafl.org.
◐ **Location:** Highways 41 and 301 travel north-south through the city. East-west Hwy. 789 crosses Sarasota Bay to Longboat Key. Once over the bridge, Gulf of Mexico Blvd. runs north-south from Anna Maria Island to Lido Key.
🅿 **Parking:** Street parking in downtown Sarasota can be a hassle. Avoid Main St.; look for parking garages and lots.
◉ **Don't Miss:** The Ringling museums, including the Museum of Art and Circus Museum.
◔ **Timing:** Allow a day to explore the Ringling Museum complex and visit the Art District.
👥 **Kids:** An airboat ride at Myakka River State Park.

Neighborhoods like **Indian Beach,** just south of the Ringling Museum, showcase older houses in styles ranging from Mediterranean Revival to simple Craftsman bungalows; some are on the National Register of Historic Places. The Ringling complex, the adjacent **Florida State University Center for the Performing Arts** and the purple shell-shaped **Van Wezel Performing Arts Hall** cover the cultural spectrum, presenting art, music, dance and theater. Other options include the Sarasota Ballet, Sarasota Opera Association, Florida West Coast Symphony, and a number of small theaters and annual film festivals. Baseball enthusiasts can watch the Cincinnati Reds and Pittsburgh Pirates play spring exhibition games in the area (◔see Spectator Sports).

GETTING THERE AND AROUND

BY AIR – **Sarasota Bradenton International Airport (SRQ)**: 3mi north of city *(information: ℘359-5200; www.srq-airport.com)*. Transportation to downtown: **Regal Limo** *(℘941-351-2547 or 800-600-2547; www.regal-limousine.com)* and **Diplomat Taxi/ West Coast Executive Sedan** *(℘941-359-8600; www.diplomattaxi.com)*, 24hr reservations suggested *($40)*; and taxi *($15–$40)*. **Amtrak bus** connection to Tampa leaves from 1995 Main St. (next to movie complex) *(℘800-872-7245; www.amtrak.com)*. **Greyhound bus** station: 575 N. Washington Blvd. *(℘800-231-2222; www.greyhound.com)*.

BY BUS – Local **bus service**: Sarasota County Area Transit *(Mon–Sat 5:30am–7pm; 50¢)*; for bus schedule and route information, ℘941-861-1234; www.scgov.net.

BY CAR – **Rental car agencies** are located at airport. Downtown metered **parking** *(50¢/hr)* garages and lots are available.

BY TAXI – Yellow Cab *(℘941-366-3333 or 888-459-7827; www.yellowcabflorida. com/westcoast)*; Diplomat *(℘941-365-8294 or 877-859-8933; www.diplomat taxi.com)*.

VISITOR INFORMATION

Sarasota Convention and Visitors Bureau, 701 North Tamiami Trail (US 41) Sarasota FL 34236 *(open year-round Mon–Sat 10am–5pm; ℘800-800-3906; www.sarasotafl.org)*.
This organization provides information on shopping, entertainment, festivals and recreation.

Accommodations
Area visitors' guide including lodging directory available free from Sarasota Convention and Visitors Bureau. Accommodations range from luxury **hotels** and resorts *($150–$800)* to moderate *motels ($125–$200)* and **bed-and-breakfast inns** *($150–$250)*. *Rates quoted are average prices per night for a double room and are subject to seasonal variations.*

THE MAINLAND

Sarasota's museums and many of its other sights are concentrated along US-41 north of downtown. Begin your exploration with the Ringling Museum and work your way south to the Downtown Art District.

John and Mable Ringling Museum of Art★★

5401 Bayshore Rd. Tickets include admission to Ringling Museum, Cà d'Zan, and Circus Museum. ⊙Open year-round daily 10am–5pm. Museum of Art and Circus Museum: Open until 8pm on Wed. ⊙Closed Jan 1, Thanksgiving Day, Dec 25. ⊛$25. ☜Docent-led tours of the art museum, mansion and circus museum (free, 30min)are offered throughout the day. ✕🚻🅿 ℘941-359-5700. www.ringling.org.
After decades of underfunding, in 2007 a massive $76-million expansion and renovation, including the opening of

the Arthur F. and Ulla R. Searing Wing, catapulted this museum into the ranks of the greats, making it the 16th largest in the country. More than 150,000sq ft were added to the original site which includes the art museum, the newly renovated circus museum, the Ringlings' mansion, the historic Asolo Theater, and Mrs. Ringling's rose garden. Later, a Visitors Pavilion was also added to the 66-acre landscaped complex, along with an Education and Conservation Complex, Learning Center and Miniature Circus.

A treasury of European culture, this museum stands as the artistic triumph of southwest Florida. Complemented by magnificent architecture, the Ringling concentrates on paintings of the late Renaissance and Baroque periods (1550–1750), including significant works by Rubens, Van Dyck, Velázquez and Poussin. The **Baroque Collection** is considered one of the finest in the US.

The Triumph of the Eucharist, series of five cartoons at The Rubens Galleries, John and Mable Ringling Museum of Art

A gift of John Ringling to the State in 1936, the site was designated in 1946 as the official art museum of Florida. Ringling's museum is the Greatest Show on Earth in formal attire. Where the man was quiet, his museum is flamboyant. The majestic entrance shouts its Italian-villa influence with three soaring arches crowned by a balustrade upon which stand four larger-than-life figures representing music, sculpture, architecture and painting.

Galleries

More than 10,000 objects (the majority acquired after Ringling's death), including 1,000 paintings, 2,500 prints and drawings, and 1,500 decorative art objects are exhibited here. Inside and out, the building displays an abundance of architectural flourishes: friezes, medallions, cartouches, wall fountains, inlaid marble mosaics and other ornamentations that Ringling found in his travels. These elements accentuate—and sometimes overshadow—the paintings.

The Showman's Art

John Ringling (1866–1936), one of the founding partners of the Ringling Bros. and Barnum & Bailey Circus, first visited Sarasota in 1911, lured by reports from land speculators. The following year, he bought property north of Sarasota and built a winter home. He and his beloved wife, Mable, lived primarily in New York City at that time, and traveled abroad several times a year looking for new acts for the show. During these trips they began buying paintings, turning their passion for fine art into a dedicated connoisseurship. By the 1920s they had amassed hundreds of objets d'art, including the world's largest private collection of works by Baroque master **Peter Paul Rubens** (1577–1640).

The Ringlings soon envisioned plans for a palatial repository for their holdings. They hired architect **John H. Phillips**, previously known for his design work, and construction of the art museum began in 1927. Two years later, just before the museum's opening, Mable died. Ringling's fortunes declined from then until his own death, seven years later. The museum complex is his gift to Sarasota, a legacy to his adopted state.

A wing of 11 rooms, the **North Galleries** *(galleries 1-11)* offer a broad survey of late Medieval through early Baroque art of Italy and northern Europe, with emphasis on 16C and 17C Italian works. The **Rubens Galleries** center on four huge paintings (each about 15ft tall) executed by Rubens and his assistants around 1625. Part of a series called *The Triumph of the Eucharist,* the paintings were commissioned by Hapsburg Archduchess Isabella Clara Eugenia as patterns for tapestries, which to this day hang in a Carmelite convent in Madrid. The series originally included 11 paintings, although four of them were destroyed in a 1731 fire in the Archduchess' palace in Brussels. Ringling bought four in 1925; the museum acquired a fifth in 1980. These paintings, with their brilliant colors, their dramatic scenes and their breathtaking size, manifest the appeal that the Baroque period had for Ringling. The second Rubens gallery occupies a vast chamber with clerestory windows more than 30ft above the ground; the floor is of teak bought by Ringling in South America.

Continuing through this wing, you'll find numerous other Baroque masterpieces, as well as fine examples from the Middle Ages and Renaissance. Among the many outstanding pieces are: Rubens' *Portrait of the Archduke Ferdinand* (1635), Lucas Cranach the Elder's visually sumptuous *Cardinal Albrecht of Brandenburg as St. Jerome* (1526), Piero di Cosimo's *Building of a Palace* (1515–20) and Francesco del Cairo's mysterious *Judith with the Head of Holofernes* (c.1630).

A graceful central **courtyard** extends 350ft out from a marble-paved bridge linking the two wings. From the bridge you can behold the formal plantings and sculpture in the elegant garden, which is lined by parallel vaulted loggias. More than 90 columns support the loggias, some of which date back to the 11C. On the other side of the bridge stretches a lovely view of Sarasota Bay.

The **South Galleries** *(galleries 12–21)* present a survey of 17C–19C European and 18C–19C American art. Found here are major works by Poussin, Vouet, Van Dyck, Jordaens and Tiepolo. The **West Galleries** *(off gallery 12)* display changing exhibits of contemporary art and house an educational area called "inner space." A nod to the museum's circus background may be seen in two American works acquired in the mid-1970s. Reginald Marsh's playful *Wonderland Circus: Sideshow, Coney Island* (1930) and Robert Henri's sensuous *Salomé* (1909) both depict early 20C performers in costume, the latter bearing the same name as Ringling's mother. Galleries 19 and 20 showcase the **decorative arts.** Furnished in the styles of Louis XV and Louis XIV, respectively, these rooms were purchased from the New York City mansion of Mrs. William Backhouse Astor. Such painted panels, gilt moldings, Chinese fans and Rococo medallions are typical of the interiors favored by American aristocrats in the late 19C.

More than 20,000-square feet of the **Arthur F. and Ulla R. Searing Wing** will be devoted to traveling exhibitions.

Cà d'Zan

Same hours as museum.

Guided tours (☞$5) are offered daily, on the hour 11am-4pm.

A paved pathway leads from the museum to Ringling's sprawling, extravagant Venetian-style palace overlooking Sarasota Bay. Ringling built the Cà d'Zan (Venetian dialect meaning "House of John") as a winter residence in 1926. The mansion, with its terra-cotta walls and red-tiled roof, its balconies and grand turret, incorporates Italian and French Renaissance, Venetian Gothic, Baroque and modern architectural elements. The west side, facing the water, glows amber in late afternoon as the sun lights up its terra-cotta walls. Inside, note the 30ft-high **court room** with painted cypress beams, the stained glass in the **tap room,** Ringling's eight-piece mahogany bedroom suite and his Siena marble bathtub. Ceiling panels in the **ballroom,** depicting dance costumes from various nations, were painted by Willy Pogany, set designer for the New

York *Ziegfeld Follies*. Be sure to walk out on the **marble terrace** for a sweeping **view** of Sarasota Bay.

👥 Circus Museum

Same hours as museum. ••○*Guided tours (free) are offered daily at noon, 1pm, 2pm & 3pm.*

The newly renovated museum boasts the largest miniature circus in the world. Located in the Circus Museum's Tibbals Learning Center, The Howard Bros. Circus model is a replica of Ringling Bros. and Barnum & Bailey Circus from 1919–1938. Complete with eight main tents, 152 wagons, 1,300 circus performers and workers, more than 800 animals and a 59-car train, the model occupies 3,800 square feet. The miniature circus was created over a period of more than 50 years by master model builder Howard Tibbals. The scope and detail of the exhibit, which traces the circus from beginning to end, are impressive. Though not part of Ringling's original plan, the circus museum was added as a tribute to the circus king in 1948. Ringling himself did not collect circus artifacts, but the gallery exhibits items from his era. Circus posters and photographs, antique circus wagons and calliopes, and a hodgepodge of other memorabilia depict the old days of the big top.

Sarasota Classic Car Museum

5500 N. US-41; across from Ringling Museum. ○*Open year-round daily 9am–6pm.* ○*Closed Dec 25.* ⊜*$8.50.* ♿🅿 ☎*941-355-6228. www.sarasota carmuseum.org.*

This more-than-50-year-old attraction boasts antique cars, musical instruments and arcade games. Over 100 classic and antique automobiles occupy one wing, including such makes as Rolls-Royce,

Restored circus wagon in the Circus Museum

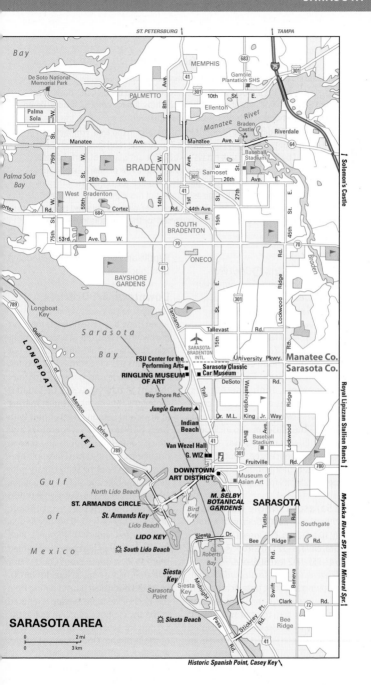

SARASOTA AREA

```
0          2 mi
0          3 km
```

Mercedes and Pierce Arrow. Highlighting the collection are four cars owned by circus magnate John Ringling, John Lennon's psychedelic-painted 1956 Bentley and Paul McCartney's Mini Cooper. Classic and muscle cars are on display side by side, including Don Garlits' *Dragster Number Two*.

Bring dimes and quarters for the old-fashioned arcade and pinball games.

The Gator Club

1490 Main St. ☏941-366-5969. www.thegatorclub.com.

Opened in 1913 as a grocery store and later housing a brothel, this downtown nightspot is one of Sarasota's favorite nightclubs. It has a colorful history, When Prohibition ended, it debuted as Gator Bar and Grill.

In the 1930s Gator was the hangout for circus folks in the area. Fun seekers still arrive nightly, nowadays to dance to Top 40 tunes and Rythm and Blues performed by live bands seven days a week. The antique mahogany bar sports a brass footrest, and the original tin ceiling holds a row of heart-shaped straw fans. Upstairs, an upscale pub occupies the second floor, complete with pool tables, sofas, antiques and a large assortment of more than 125 single-malt scotch's from around the world. The club's name? Well, it's believed that when the place was turned into a bar, it was named for the alligators in the area.

G.WIZ

1001 Blvd. of the Arts. ⏱Open year-round Mon–Sat 10am–5pm, Sun noon –5pm. ⏱Closed major holidays. ☞$10, child (3–16 yrs) $7. ♿🅿 ☏941-309-4949. www.gwiz.org.

The initials stand for Gulfcoast Wonder and Imagination Zone, and this hands-on facility offers good educational fun for young children. Equipped with bubblemakers, funhouse mirrors, touchable reptiles, a beehive and lots of other gear—over 100 hands-on exhibits in all—the museum also includes a butterfly-filled habitat, a kids' lab and an outdoor science area. Annually, San Francisco's Exploratorium lends G.WIZ some 35 exhibits for display here.

Sarasota Jungle Gardens

3701 Bay Shore Rd. ⏱Open year-round daily 10am–5pm. ⏱Closed Dec 25. ☞$15, child (3–12 yrs) $10. ✕♿🅿 ☏941-355-1112 (ext 306) or 877-861-6547. www.sarasotajunglegardens.com.

Envisioning an exotic botanical garden, local newspaperman David Lindsay bought a ten-acre tract of swampland in the early 1930s, drained it and planted tropical trees and flowers imported from around the world. Brick paths wind through a dense jungle of coconut palms, viburnum, rubber trees and other fauna. Bridges cross lakes and lagoons loud with the calls of flamingos and the rush of waterfalls. An enchanting wonderland for children, the gardens also include a petting zoo and playground.

Reptile and bird shows are scheduled throughout the day.

Downtown Art District★

Palm & Pineapple Aves. & Main St.

Along these three streets beats the heart of downtown Sarasota. Main Street maintains the charm of old-time Sarasota, but these days it is lined with sidewalk cafes, French bakeries, art galleries, gourmet markets and chic boutiques. On Saturday mornings *(7am–noon)* a **farmers'market** at Main and Lemon streets brims with fresh flowers, herbs, vegetables and fruits, home-baked goods and garden ornaments. A stroll down Pineapple Avenue encompasses the Selby Library, with its artful mobiles and archway aquarium. One notable building, the red-tiled 1926 **Sarasota Opera House** *(one block north of Main St.)*, once hosted vaudeville acts and minstrel shows; Will Rogers, Elvis Presley and other big names performed there. Walk south to Burns Court, a tiny sidestreet with a popular foreign film cinema, and bungalow houses dating from the 1920s. Pineapple Avenue is reputed as the city's antique center as well as the setting for several favored cafes with outdoor dining. One street over, Palm Avenue is lined with art galleries.

At the northern end of downtown, framed by Morrill Street and US 301, Towles Court is a full block of Caribbean-colored old Sarasota houses, transformed into galleries and artists' studios that welcome the public; its centerpiece is an imaginative sculpture garden. South of downtown lies **Sarasota Quay** *(on US-41 at Fruitville Rd.),* an attractive bayfront park heralded by pine arches and planted with oleander and palms. For a quiet diversion from the bustle of downtown, investigate the quay's boat docks and watch the shorebirds. At night restaurants and nightclubs pick up the pace.

Marie Selby Botanical Gardens★

811 S. Palm Ave. ⏰*Open year-round daily 10am–5pm.* ⏰*Closed Dec 25.* ⚲*$17.* ♿🅿 ☎*941-366-5731.* *www.selby.org.*

Occupying a nine-acre peninsula on the downtown waterfront, these lovely gardens display more than 20,000 tropical plants, including 6,000 orchids. The **Tropical Display House**, just beyond the entrance, is widely known for its **epiphytes** (plants that grow on other plants and take their nourishment from the air and rainfall), which include a large collection of colorful orchids and bromeliads. A paved path outside circles 20 garden areas, including the cycad collection (a class of plants that date from the age of dinosaurs), the cactus and succulent garden, the shady banyan grove and a native plant community. Here an elevated walkway takes visitors along a lush grove of palms and bamboo, past a mangrove swamp, to an idyllic **view** of Sarasota Bay, framed by a spreading pipal fig tree, known to Buddhists as the *bodhi* tree, or tree of enlightenment. The **Mansion,** at the north end of the garden, was built as a private residence in 1935 and now hosts changing exhibits of art and photography with a botanical theme. Nearby you'll find the tropical food and medicinal plant gardens, as well as the butterfly garden, and the Tree Lab with creatures of the rainforest.

BARRIER ISLANDS

Flung out north and south along Sarasota's Gulf Coast lie several idyllic barrier islands, connected to the mainland by causeways. To the north, **Longboat Key** is a resort island, offering vacation condos and a wide variety of hotel accommodations along its 10mi of glittering sand. Directly across the causeway from downtown Sarasota lie fashionable St. Armands Key and the pleasant beach parks of Lido Key. To the south stretch the white high rises of Siesta Key and, finally, tiny residential **Casey Key,** its pastel houses tucked amid lush foliage, where fishermen cast their lines from Venice Jetty and watch dolphins cavort in the channel.

Anna Maria Island

Northwest of Sarasota.
▶ *From Longboat Key, follow Gulf of Mexico Dr. north to Anna Maria Island.*
This "Margaritaville" of the Gulf Coast barrier islands is coveted for its laid-back lifestyle, cottage-style residences and three fishing piers laden with water-view restaurants. Though heavily developed like most of the large barrier islands in the area, Anna Maria is worth the drive, especially for the parks on its north and south ends. Starting at the island's southwest end, attractive **Coquina Beach**⚐ provides picnic tables, ample free parking, a beach cafe, playground and a wide expanse of white sand and inviting gulf water. Just south of the Route 684 causeway, **Bradenton Beach** is a quaint but energized seaside town with low-rise motels, shops and ice-cream parlors.

For a look at one of Florida's few remaining early fishing villages, drive east across the causeway to **Cortez** *(south of Cortez Rd./Rte. 684 at 119th St.).* This Manatee County Historic District contains a good sampling of vernacular structures built with local materials, one of the last working fish houses in Florida and casual waterfront restaurants.

The hub of Anna Maria Island is Holmes Beach, known for its antique shops, pancake breakfasts on the beach (⚲*see Cafe on the Beach),* uncrowded stretches of sand and modest houses. At the northern end of the island, **Anna Maria Bayfront Park** *(northeast end of Pine Ave. at Bay Blvd.)* holds a 1,000ft expanse of shoreline running just north of City Pier. Built in 1911, the pier extends 678ft into

Tampa Bay and tempts visitors with a no-frills oyster bar.

St. Armands Key

Located across the John Ringling Causeway from downtown Sarasota.

Named after its first homesteader, French farmer Charles St. Armand, this key began as a mangrove island rumored to have been won by John Ringling in a poker game. The majority of its 132 acres is covered by Sarasota's most famous shopping district, **St. Armands Circle**★, which owes its existence to John Ringling's vision and devotion to his wife. As Ringling explained it: "Now Mable won't have to go to Palm Beach to shop." Strategically positioned at the end of the John Ringling Causeway, the circle and the streets that radiate from it encompass more than 150 specialty shops, galleries, restaurants and businesses. The circle's hub is an oasis of palms, bougainvillea and hibiscus; around its edge, bronze plaques honor great circus performers of the past. Peak-season traffic is often bumper-to-bumper, however.

Mixon Fruit Farms

2712 26th Ave. E. in Bradenton. ⏱ *Open year-round Mon–Sat 10am-3pm.* ☎ *941-748-5829. www.mixon.com.*

Set amid 350 acres of lush groves, this popular citrus outlet began life in 1939 as a roadside fruit stand. Visitors may stand on an observation platform and enjoy the hustle and bustle of the plant: 600 oranges per minute ride the conveyor belts toward a quality-control room where workers separate the good fruit from the bad. Select oranges continue on into crates for shipping or end up in the juicing room. Free samples of juice and sections of grapefruit, orange and tangerine are available in the sizable gift shop. Tram tours of the groves ($8) are also offered.

 Mote Marine Laboratory

1600 Ken Thompson Pkwy., 2.2mi north of St. Armands Circle. ⏱ *Open year-round daily 10am–5pm.* ☜ *$17, child 4–12 yrs $12.* ✕ ♿ 🅿 ☎ *941-388-4441 or 800-691-6683. www.mote.org.*

Mote is one of the few organizations in the world that combines marine research with public outreach through a full-fledged aquarium that features sea turtles, skates, moray eels and other denizens of Sarasota Bay and the Gulf of Mexico. One perennial favorite, the huge shark tank, offers both above- and below-water viewing areas. A 30ft touch tank allows visitors an opportunity to handle living sea creatures. Another exhibit, a preserved 25ft giant squid, is the centerpiece of the mollusk section. At the Sharktracker exhibit, you can learn how researchers track sharks in the wild using high-tech sensing equipment and underwater microphones. Known for its research efforts with sharks and environmental pollutants, the Mote also operates a visitor center adjacent to its research lab and a marine mammal center across the street.

Lido Key★

Just west of St. Armands Key via Ringling Causeway.

Some of the area's most prestigious real estate lies on this J-shaped barrier island, developed by John Ringling in the late 1920s. Ringling built roads and canals with the help of his circus elephants who transported timber for the causeways. A year after the key opened to the public, the Depression slowed business and the barrier islands lay quiet until the 1950s. Now posh hotels, condominiums and homes share the narrow island with popular Lido Beach, pine-fringed North Lido Beach and lovely **South Lido Beach**⌂, flanked by an expanse of mangroves on its bay side *(1.8mi south of St. Armands Circle).*

Siesta Key

6mi southwest of Sarasota.

▶ *From downtown, take US-41 south to Siesta Dr. (Rte. 758); go west on Siesta Dr. 1mi to Siesta Key.*

This popular barrier island, with its clutch of white high-rise condominiums, is much regarded for its soft white-sand beaches. Analyzed by Harvard geologists, the fine-grained sand is millions of years old and 99 percent pure quartz (with no shell or coral content), resulting in a talcum-soft texture. **Siesta Beach** sports 2,400ft of sparkling shoreline and a seaside pavilion with a snack bar, souvenir shop and rental stand (*Beach Rd., 1mi southeast of Ocean Blvd.*).

EXCURSIONS

Historic Spanish Point★

8mi south in Osprey, via US-41.
Open year-round Mon–Sat 9am–5pm, Sun noon–5pm. Closed Jan 1, Easter Sunday, Thanksgiving Day, Dec 25. $10. 941-966-5214. *www.historicspanishpoint.org.*
Jutting into scenic Little Sarasota Bay, this peaceful 30-acre site illuminates the lives of prehistoric Indians and early pioneers. Tours follow a gravel path through a landscape varying from mangrove estuary to live oak forest to formal gardens (after the tour, visitors are free to stroll the grounds on their own). The path winds past a burial mound, a packing house, a chapel, graveyard, and an archaeology dig within a 15ft-high shell midden, one of the largest intact prehistoric villages in southwest Florida. Called **Window to the Past,** the exhibit allows visitors to actually see the shells, bones and shards in the midden, while

Cafe on the Beach

4000 Gulf Dr. in Holmes Beach on Anna Maria Island. 941-778-0784 or 800-608-2525.

A great way to start the day is right here on the patio at a table topped by a red and white umbrella. The cafe sits, as its name states, on the beach, and attracts volleyball players, sun worshippers and the like at all three mealtimes. The all-you-can-eat pancake breakfast, served up with sausages and hot coffee, is the biggest draw. Folks come to watch the cooks flip flapjacks in the special screened "pancake cage"—and then enjoy the results of their culinary dexterity.

video footage and other displays explain the sleuth work of archaeologists. The grounds also hold the largest butterfly garden on the Gulf Coast, while the restored gardens of former Chicago socialite Bertha Honoré Palmer, Sarasota County's leading lady in the early 1900s, are another highlight.

Myakka River State Park★★

14mi east in Myakka via Rte. 72 (Clark Rd.). Open 8am-sunset. $6 per vehicle. 941-361-6511. *www.floridastateparks.org/myakkariver.*

Myakka River State Park

Visit Florida

DISCOVERING SOUTHWEST COAST

Solomon's Castle

4533 Solomon Rd. ◷*Open Oct–
Jun Tue–Sun 11am–4pm; $10
(cash only).* ✆*863-494-6077.
www.solomonscastle.com.*

Local artist and sculptor, Howard
Solomon, built his 12,000sq ft
home in the 1970s to resemble
a medieval castle, complete
with turrets, stained glass
and a drawbridge. Wacky and
impressive, the castle and its 300
pieces of original sculpture were
made entirely from discarded
materials. The castle's siding,
for example, incorporates shiny
aluminum printing plates from
a local newspaper. Visitors take
a pun-filled 30min tour of the
interior. A 60ft replica Spanish
galleon, handmade by Solomon,
contains a restaurant. Also on
location are picnic tables, a
gift shop and a nature trail that
meanders along Horse Creek.

One of the oldest and largest of Florida's
parks, this 28,875-acre parcel stretches
along the primeval Myakka River—protected by the State as a designated Wild
and Scenic River—for 12mi and encompasses a wide variety of animal and plant
communities. Deer and bobcat favor the
palm hammocks, pine flatwoods and dry
prairies, while alligators and numerous
species of wading birds inhabit Upper
Myakka Lake and its grassy marshes.
Hiking trails traverse the park, as does
a flat road suitable for bicycling. The
new Canopy Walk, an 85ft-long suspension bridge, sways some 25ft high
among the treetops. Popular **tram and
airboat tours** give visitors a close-up
look at native flora and fauna (◷*Mid-
Dec–May: airboats 10am, 11.30am, 1pm,
2:30pm; tram 1pm, 2:30pm. Jun–mid Dec
airboats 10am, 11.30am, 1pm; no tram
tours.*✆*$12;* ♿🅿 *Myakka Wildlife Tours,
Inc.* ✆*941-365-0100).* Concessionaire at
the boat basin sells fishing, camping
and picnicking supplies and rents boats,
bicycles and canoes.

South Florida Museum/ Parker Manatee Aquarium/ Bishop Planetarium

▷ *Take US 301 north to Manatee Ave.
W (Hwy 64 W). Turn left, continue .5mi.
Turn right on 10th St West.*
◷*Open Jan–Apr & Jul Mon–Sat 10am–
5pm Sun noon to 5pm. Rest of year Tue–
Sat 10am–5pm. Sun noon–5pm.*
◷*Closed Thanksgiving, Dec 25 & Jan 1.*
✆*$15.95.* ♿🅿 ✆*941-366-5731.
www.southfloridamuseum.org.*

Located on the banks of the Manatee
River, this newly expanded and renovated museum and aquarium complex
traces the cultural and natural history
of the Florida Gulf Coast. Life-size dioramas, casts of Ice Age mammals, and an
impressive collection of artifacts and
fossils are showcased, but the biggest
draw is **Snooty**, arguably the world's
most recognized manatee. You can
watch Snooty frolicking and feeding in
a 60,000-gallon pool.

The **Bishop Planetarium** is a multipur-
pose state-of-the-art domed theater,
boasting one of the most advanced all-
digital projection systems in the world.

👥 Herrmanns' Royal Lipizzan Stallions★

23mi east in Myakka City. ▷ *Take
Fruitville Rd. (Rte. 780) east 17.5mi to
Verna Rd. Turn left and continue 1.1mi to
Singletary Rd. Turn right and go 4.3mi to
ranch (entrance on left) at 32755.*
◷*Training sessions (90min) open to
the public Jan–Apr Thu & Fri 3pm, Sat
10am. Check website for times and
dates. Arrive early to get choice seats.*
✆*Contribution requested.* ♿🅿✆*941-
322-1501. www.hlipizzans.com.*

Bred from strains of Arabian and Anda-
lusian stallions, the so-called "aristocrats
of the horse world" perform amazing
feats that originated more than 300
years ago as battle maneuvers, including the famous capriole, in which the
horse jumps up and kicks his hind legs
out parallel to the ground.

These spectacular leaps and plunges
were originally meant for use by
mounted riders to inspire terror in the
hearts of foot soldiers. These winter ses-

sions, staged free of charge, prepare the troupe for a rigorous annual US tour.

The Springs at Warm Mineral Springs

30mi southeast in Warm Mineral Springs. ▶ *Take I-75 south to Exit 34; go 5mi south to US-41. Turn left on US-41 and continue 2.5mi to Ortiz Blvd.; turn left on Ortiz and follow 1mi to springs' entrance on right.* ⏰*Open year-round daily 9am –5pm.* ⏰*Closed Thanksgiving, Dec 25 & Jan1.* 🎫*$20, includes free classes.* ✕ 🚫 🅿 ☎*941-426-1692. www.warmmineral springs.com.*

Indians knew of the warm mineral springs here for perhaps 10,000 years before an English hunter discovered the area in 1874. The springs were not developed for tourists until the 1930s. Billed today as a resort, Warm Mineral Springs retains the flavor of a latter-day Florida spa.

Palms and lawn chairs fringe the 1.5-acre, spring-fed lake, set in a trim carpet of grass. The clientele takes to the soothing 87°F waters and enjoys massage, whirlpool and acupuncture.

ADDRESSES

🛏 STAY

$$$$$ Ritz Carlton – *1111 Ritz-Carlton Drive, Sarasota.* ✕ 🚫 🅿 ⚓ ☎*941-309-2000. www.ritzcarlton.com. 266 rooms.* If money is no object, pamper yourself at this top-notch resort, set on 11 acres in the heart of Sarasota. Rooms are spacious and decked out with modern amenties, plush linens and private balconies, some with bay or marina views. You'll find it tough to leave the grounds with a full-service spa, fitness center, 18-hole award-winning golf course, tennis courts and more. A private beach club is located 3mi away at pretty Likdo Key, with a swath of sugar-white sand and oceanfront swimming pools.

$$$$$ Sanibel Harbour Resort & Spa – *17260 Harbour Pointe Dr., Fort Myers.* ✕ 🚫 🅿 ⚓ ☎*941-466-4000 or 800-767-7777. www.sanibel-resort.com. 347 rooms, 70 condos.* Anchoring the western edge of a private peninsula along San Carlos Bay, this modern Marriott mega-resort includes three hotel/condominium high rises, a 40,000sq ft spa/fitness center, fishing pier and marina, six swimming pools, three restaurants and a berth for its private yacht. The state-of-the-art tennis facilities have hosted two Davis Cup tournaments. Rooms boast a private balcony, bathrobes and Internet access. Dining choices range from spa

cuisine to dinner cruises and Sunday brunch aboard a 100ft private yacht.

$$$$ Bokeelia Tarpon Inn – *8241 Main St., Bokeelia.* 🚫 🅿 ☎*239-283-8961 or 866-827-7662. www.tarponinn.com. 5 rooms.* It's worth heading off the beaten path to this ultra-luxury B&B, reminiscent of the days when millionaire Barron Collier came to the area to fish. Built on the shore of Charlotte Harbor, the 1914 house still lures renowned anglers and those seeking seclusion. The handsome living room has hardwood floors, an original fireplace, Indonesian furnishings and a rack of wines, from which guests help themselves. The Chart Room sports a fly-tying bench and rod-and-reel adorned walls. Overlooking the water, the second-story screened porch is a coveted spot. Guests can tour the island in the inn's golf cart or bicycles (kayaks available, too) and fish from the private pier (fishing guides can be reserved in advance).

$$$$ Hotel Escalante – *290 Fifth Ave. S., Naples.* 🚫 🅿 ⚓ ☎*239-659-3466 or 877-485-3466. www.hotelescalante.com. 10 rooms.* Encased in lush foliage, this Mediterranean-style complex seems more a sprawling private villa than a public hotel. Yet this sumptuous escape sits just around the corner from the trendy shops of fashionable Fifth Avenue, and only a block from the beach. Generous, ground-level guest quarters include mahogany armoires, ceiling fans, sizable closets, spacious bathrooms, and French doors opening onto a garden or poolside patio. Complimentary continental breakfasts, a well-stocked library and a frangipani-filled footpath encircling the retreat make for a special stay.

$$$$ Longboat Key Club & Resort – *301 Gulf of Mexico Dr., Longboat Key.* ✕♿🅿🏊 *☎941-383-8821 or 888-237-8821. www.longboatkeyclub.com. 215 rooms.* Hidden from public view behind a guard gate, this exclusive recently renovated 410-acre Gulf Coast resort sits on a private beach of sugary white sand. Long a choice for refuge-seeking celebrities, this hotel is also a golfer's delight—45 holes are divided between two courses. Tennis is served up on 38 courts in two tennis centers. Extra-spacious rooms and suites with kitchens are have large balconies with views of the beach, sea or golf course. Yoga and massage are offered in the expansive fitness center, and bicycles, aqua cycles, sea kayaks and snorkeling equipment are on hand for guests.

$$$$ 'Tween Waters Inn – *15951 Captiva Rd., Captiva Island.* ✕♿🅿🏊 *☎239-472-5161 or 800-223-5865. www.tween-waters.com. 138 rooms.* Framed by the gentle gulf surf and calming waters of Pine Island Sound, this timeless, self-contained resort keeps customers coming back for its recreational options and relaxed Old Florida feel. The original beach cottages harbored the likes of Anne Morrow Lindbergh and conservationist "Ding" Darling. Those seeking contemporary space may settle into newer quarters built on stilts for great water views. Tennis clinics, an Olympic-size pool, a spa, fitness center and marina keep guests well occupied. Bicycles, kayaks and canoes can be rented (a popular short paddle crosses the sound to Buck Island).

$$$ The Cypress – *621 Gulfstream Ave. S., Sarasota.* ♿🅿 *☎941-955-4683. www.cypressbb.com. 5 rooms.* This B&B is a surprising downtown find, nestled as it is within an oasis of green across from the city sailboat anchorage. Built of cypress wood in 1940, the two-story house is compact, its Intimate interiors

dressed in art and antiques. Common rooms brim with seashells, old books and musical instruments. Themed guest rooms, furnished with French mansion beds, plantation armoires and hardwood floors, overlook the bay or garden. Served in a sunny, bayside space, breakfasts are extravaganzas of fresh squeezed orange juice, granola and French toast. Main Street shops and the marina are a short walk away.

$$$ Jensen's Twin Palms Cottages – *15107 Captiva Dr., Captiva Island.* ♿🅿🏊 *☎239-472-5800. www.jensen-captiva.com. 14 units.* Perhaps the most laid-back place this side of Key West, Jensen's counts cottages, coconut palms (more than 50) and beach proximity among its most alluring assets. The resort sits right on the waters of Pine Island Sound, where lucky observers might spot manatees, dolphins and otters. The modest Old Florida cottages (and apartments) come with screened porches and kitchen facilities. Guests can hop aboard Jensen's water taxi to explore the outer islands or rent a boat at the marina.

$$$ Sunshine Island Inn – *642 East Gulf Dr., Sanibel Island.* ♿🅿🏊 *☎239-395-2500. www.sunshineislandinn.com. 6 rooms.* This small, pastel-shaded inn is known for its enduring hospitality and comfort. Guest rooms are light and cheery, each with an efficiency or full kitchen and sliding door to the pool area. The on-site laundry facilities and barbecue grill for guests are extra amenities that appeal especially to families. The inn is located in a quiet neighborhood across the street from the beach and a short bicycle ride away from the fishing pier and lighthouse.

$ Cedar Cove Resort & Cottages – *12710 Gulf Dr., Anna Maria Island.* ♿🅿🏊 *☎941-778-1010 or 800-206-6293. www.cedarcoveresort.com. 19 units.* Location, location, location. This cozy, comfy beach resort sits on a swath of pretty Holmes Beach on Anna Maria Island. One and two-bedroom suites are bright and simply furnished; most have views of the Gulf from private decks or patios. The atmosphere is friendly and casual; guests gather at the Tiki Hut on the beach and around the convenient barbecue grills.

$ Tides Inn Motel – *1800 Stickney Point Rd., Sarasota.* ♿🅿🏊 ☏*941-924-7541 or 800-823-8594. www.myplanet.net/tidesinn. 12 rooms.* Ultra-clean and simply appointed, this mom-and-pop motel offers rare value. The spacious rooms are sparsely but comfortably furnished and there's a large grassy backyard that's perfect for pitching horseshoes, playing shuffleboard, picnicking or plucking oranges from the trees (juicers provided). The pool area is a private, fenced-in oasis, and the famous beaches of Siesta Key lie eight blocks away, with shops, restaurants, boat rentals and a bait shop en route.

♈ EAT

$$$$ Beach Bistro – *6600 Gulf Dr., Holmes Beach, Anna Maria Island.* ♿ ☏*941-778-6444. www. beachbistro.com. Dinner only.* **American/ Continental.** This tiny bistro sits right on a white, sandy beach. The best seating faces the green waters of the Gulf of Mexico and the setting sun. Signature salads include the warm Bella Roma tomato salad and duckling spinach salad. "Lobstercargots" is a popular small plate, while Bistro bouillabaisse and "Floribbean" grouper (encrusted in toasted coconut and cashews, topped with a red pepper papaya jam) are winning entrées.

$$$ Bistro 821 – *821 Fifth Ave. S., Naples.* ♿ ☏*239-261-5821. www.bistro821.com. Dinner only.* **Continental.** The interior dining space of this chic restaurant spills out onto sidewalk seating, creating a casual, open-air feeling. Facing the bar and open kitchen, one long fabric-bedecked wall booth promotes easy conversation with neighboring diners. Start with a small plate of jumbo prawns served with sweet chili-Thai basil butter or rock lobster satay. Entrees include a large selection of pasta and risotto dishes, and chef specialties like miso-sake roasted seabass and Chef Jess's "Pot Roast."

$$$ Cafe on the Bay – *2630 Harbourside Dr., Longboat Key.* ♿ ☏*941-383-0440.* **American.** Drive through the guard gate or dock your boat (Marker 15) at Longboat Key Moorings when you come to dine in this exclusive Mediterranean-styled setting of coconut palms and countless impatiens. The marina-hugging haunt hauls in the resort-casual crowd with a chic-nautique interior, awash in ocean blues and assuasive aquariums. For outdoor dining, try the shady veranda, cooled by sea breezes. Cafe's creative menu means appetizers like tuna carpaccio and entrées such as vegetarian napoleon (warm polenta rounds layered with grilled vegetables in smoked tomato sauce), or a mixed grill of veal and ostrich medallions.

$$$ The Veranda – *2122 Second St. (at Broadway), Fort Myers.* ♿☏*239-332-2065. www.verandarestaurant.com.* **Continental.** Gracious Southern hospitality awaits at this "dressy casual" restaurant, where vintage photos adorn the walls. The century-old, side-by-side houses possess a history that mixes cattlemen, a military captain, and a member of the Pulitzer publishing family. Tastes of Dixie flavor the chef's take on old favorites—Cajun grilled sea scallops, or Southern grit cakes with pepper jack cheese and andouille sausage. Try the Southern Sampler mixed grill of fresh fish or the Bourbon Street filet medallions in a smoky sour-mash whisky sauce.

$$ Bangkok – *4791 Swift Rd., Sarasota.* ♿ ☏*941-922-0703. www.bangkok sarasota.com.* **Thai.** Fresh fruits and vegetables intricately carved into bird and flower shapes, waitstaff costumed in native dress, and hand-carved teak furnishings all translate into a serene setting for enjoying authentic Thai cuisine. Favored by locals and visitors who come for the exotic flavors, beautiful presentation and pleasing prices, Bangkok excels in stir fries and spicy curries, crispy duckling and a variety of tofu dishes. The most-ordered appetizer is the chicken *satay* with thick peanut sauce; the much-in-demand dessert is fried bananas. Take-outs make great beach picnics.

$$ The Dock – *845 12th Ave. S. (next to City Dock), Naples.* ♿ ☏*941-263-9940. www.dockcrayoncove.com.* **Caribbean.**

Join the hullabaloo at this hive of open-air dining on the waterfront at Crayton Cove. The Old Naples institution (est. 1976) has them waiting in line, especially on weekends, for great seafood, specialty sandwiches and "docktails." Order Bahamian conch fritters or rock shrimp nachos to start and move on to the pineapple-glazed sea bass or banana macadamia nut-crusted grouper. Jamaican Red stripe baby back ribs and veal pot pie are other temptations on the menu.

$$ Moore's Stone Crab Restaurant – *800 Broadway, Longboat Key.* & *941-383-1748 or 888-968-2722. www.home. earthlink.net/~mooresrest.* **Seafood.** A Longboat Key institution since 1967, this unpretentious, family-owned restaurant at the north end of the island offers stunning views of Sarasota Bay. Gathering stone crabs by hand in 1927 on the flats of the bay, Papa Jack Moore began the restaurant's reputation for serving the freshest stone crabs around. The family now harvests the crustacean with its own sizeable fleet. Presented as combination platters, single plates or sandwiches, the restaurant's variety of catches, from grouper to pompano, are year-round attractions.

$$ RC Otters – *11506 Andy Rosse Lane, Captiva Island.* & *239-395-1142.* **American.** It's easy to feel the island spirit here in this shiplap-constructed cottage. The casual restaurant it now houses offers alfresco dining on the front porch or brick patio, and inside in intimate rooms decked with paintings by area artists. An affordable menu offers more than 200 items ranging from large, crispy salads, and sandwiches of all kinds, to lobster, ribs, steak and fish and a children's menu. Nightly entertainment byshowcases bands well-versed in Jimmy Buffett.

$$ Sharky's on the Pier – *1600 S. Harbor Dr., Venice.* & *941-488-1456. www.sharkysonthepier.com.* **American.** Thatched-roofed shelters and sturdy palms sprout from the spacious deck of this popular eatery, positioned to oversee all the comings and goings of anglers, surfers and sunbathers. The enclosed dining area sports dark woods, a nautical look and tables crammed with convivial crowds of seafood lovers, who come for the conch fritters, fired fish and chip baskets, Macadamia grouper, gulf shrimp, steaks and baby back ribs. It's a great spot to watch the setting sun.

$ Old Salty Dog – *1601 Ken Thompson Pkwy., City Island, Sarasota.* & *941-388-4311. www.theoldsaltydog.com.* **American.** This fun spot combines an Old Florida nautical look with the ultra-casual atmosphere of boater hang-outs, while offering great views of bay traffic along New Pass. Cold beer from around the world keeps locals at the hull-shaped bar, but the real magnet is the Salty Dog: a quarter-pound hot dog dipped in beer batter, deep fried and topped with sauerkraut, sautéed onions or cheese. Traditional fish and chips, and grouper or golden snapper sandwiches can be relished inside or out on the shady wooden deck built above the water. There's a second location on Siesta Key.

⊙ ENTERTAINMENT

Consult the arts and entertainment section of the *Sarasota Herald-Tribune* (Fridays) or **INFOline** (*941-953-4636; www.heraldtribune.com)* for schedules of cultural events.

Van Wezel Performing Arts Hall (*941-955-7676 or 800-826-9303; www.vanwezel.org);* **Ringling Museum of Arts** (*941-351-8000; www.ringling. org/Performances.aspx);* **Sarasota Opera House** (*941-366-8450 or 888-673-7212; www.sarasotaopera.org).*

SPORTS AND RECREATION

Golf: Forest Lake Country Club (*941-922-1312; http://sarasota.golfersguide. com);* Bobby Jones Golf Club (*941-365-4653; www.bobbyjonesgolfclub.com).*

Sailing charters and sunset cruises (*$40–$70/person);* Enterprise (*941-951-1833 or 888-232-7768; www.sarasota sailing.com).*

This region, stretching some 40 miles from Titusville to Melbourne along the Atlantic coast, experienced phenomenal growth after the birth of the space program in the late 1950s. The edge of Brevard County and its overlapping barrier islands, separated by lagoons known as the Indian and the Banana rivers, have been home to thousands of people employed in the space industry for over 60 years, or in electronics and computer companies. The north part of the Space Coast holds one of the state's largest wilderness areas.

A Bit of History

During the late 19C Mosquito County (as the region was known) was famous for the quality of its Indian River Oranges (see Box p326), which it sent all over the world. By the end of the following century it was world famous as the home of Cape Canaveral (and then Cape Kennedy), and had sent men to the moon, and beyond.

Today, although the great days of space exploration may be past (or at least on hold), it is still the nerve center of America's space race and a pioneer of cutting-edge technology.

Highlights

1 Taking in impressive space hardware at the **Kennedy Space Center** (p322)

2 Experiencing old-time Florida at **Cocoa Village** (p327)

3 Riding the simulators at the **US Astronaut Hall of Fame** (p328)

4 Getting back to nature at **Merritt Island Wildlife Refuge** (p329)

5 Relaxing on **Playalinda Beach**, with or without costume (p329)

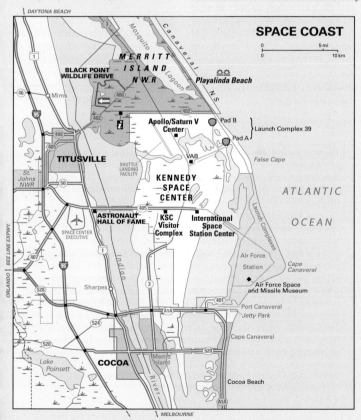

Kennedy Space Center ★★★

Protruding from Florida's Atlantic coast, this barrier island of orange groves, tidal flats and pristine beaches is home to the nation's space program. Here the world's most sophisticated technology emerges from Florida's largest east-coast wilderness. Every US rocket—from the one that carried the Explorer I satellite in 1958 to the space shuttles launched to visit the International Space Station and missions beyond—has blasted off from Merritt Island or adjoining Cape Canaveral.

- **Michelin Map:** p321.
- **Info:** ℘321-449-4444; www.kennedyspace center.com.
- **Location:** Follow the signs from north-south I-95 or east-west Hwy. 528. The center is about 45 minutes from Orlando.
- **Parking:** Free parking is available at the center.
- **Don't Miss:** The bus tour for the best overview of the center. The IMAX 3-D presentations with authentic space footage are stunning.
- **Timing:** Allow a full day for tours, shows and exhibits.
- **Kids:** The Children's Play Dome.

A BIT OF HISTORY

Rocket launches from the beginning of the American space program up to 1964 took place exclusively at Cape Canaveral Air Force Station (called Cape Kennedy from 1963–73), located on the spit of land extending southeast from Merritt Island. In October 1958, the National Aeronautics and Space Administration (NASA) was created; its mission was the exploration of space.

Since the late 1990s NASA has concentrated on the **International Space Station**, a combined effort of the US, Russia, Canada, Japan and the 14 member nations of the European Space Agency. Proposed budget cuts foresee the development and operation of new

To Boldly Go...

The Mercury and Gemini missions (1961–66) captured the attention of the world in general and the nation in particular. **Alan Shepard**'s 15min ride in the cramped nose of a Redstone rocket in 1961 made him the first American in space. Early in 1962 **John Glenn** became the first US astronaut to orbit the earth. In 1965 Edward White was the first American to walk in space.

The new Apollo program stalled after White and fellow astronauts Gus Grissom and Roger Chaffee died in a fire on the launchpad in 1967. Following this first NASA disaster, manned missions were halted until *Apollo 7* was launched in October 1968. On July 20, 1969, **Neil Armstrong** and **Buzz Aldrin** walked on the moon, a mere eight years after Kennedy's challenge. After launching Skylab, the first US space station, the Apollo series concluded in a joint mission with a Soviet Soyuz spacecraft in 1975. NASA's answer to a reduction in funding in the late 1970s was a fleet of reusable space shuttles, which have been the centerpiece of the space program since the maiden voyage of *Columbia* in 1981. The 1986 explosion of *Challenger,* killing the entire crew of seven, concentrated national attention again on NASA. Though the flawed Hubble Space Telescope unleashed a storm of criticism, NASA regained its prestige with the spectacular in-space repair job of the telescope in December 1993. Ongoing NASA investigations include in-depth Mars and Saturn surveys, as well as studies of the Earth, Sun and missions to Mercury and Pluto.

April 12, 1981: Columbia, the first reusable spacecraft to launch from Cape Canaveral

NASA/courtesy of nasaimages.org

American Space Firsts

◆ 31 January 1958: The US launched its first earth satellite, *Explorer 1.*

◆ 5 May 1961: The first American in space was Alan B. Shepard Jr., who completed a 15-minute suborbital flight aboard *Freedom 7.*

◆ 20 February 1962: John Glenn Jr., aboard *Mercury,* became the first American to orbit the earth.

◆ 3 June 1965: Edward White was the first American to walk in space when he took a 21-minute stroll outside his *Gemini 4* craft.

◆ 11 October 1968: Frank Borman, James Lovell and William Anders completed the first manned orbits of the moon during the *Apollo 8* mission.

◆ 20 July 1969: During the *Apollo 11* mission—the first manned moon launch— Neil Armstrong became the first man to walk on the moon.

◆ 15 July 1975: *Apollo 18* initiated the first cooperative international space flight; crew members Vance Brand, Thomas Stafford and Donald Slayton linked their spacecraft with the USSR's *Soyuz 19.*

◆ 12 April 1981: The era of reusable spacecraft was inaugurated with the first space shuttle launch from Cape Canaveral.

June 3, 1965: Edward White, the first American to walk in space

NASA/courtesy of nasaimages.org

GETTING THERE

BY AIR – Melbourne International Airport (MLB): 35mi south of Kennedy Space Center; international, domestic and commuter flights *(information: ☎321- 723-6227; www.mlb.air)*. Transportation to Kennedy Space Center: **Airport Shuttle** (☎321-724-1600 or 800- 826-4544). **Beach Buggy Taxi** (☎321-427-7560; *beachbuggytaxi.com*). **Rental car agencies** located at airport and on US-1. Space Coast visitor information booth adjacent to baggage claim area (☎321-952-4589).

Orlando International Airport (MCO): 37mi west of Kennedy Space Center; international, domestic and commuter flights *(information: ☎407-825-2001)*. Regularly scheduled shuttle to Cocoa Beach leaves from ground level *(every two hours daily 9am–7pm; $30 one-way; reservations required)*; Cocoa Beach **Shuttle** (☎321-631-4144, *www.cbshuttle.com*).

BY CAR – Kennedy Space Center is located roughly in the middle of Florida's east coast, in a region often referred to as the Space Coast. The area can be reached in about an hour's drive from most central Florida locations via **Route 528** *(Beeline Expressway)*. Sample distances from Cocoa Beach: Orlando 51mi; Jacksonville 156mi; Miami 187mi. From Interstate I-95, **exit on Route 407** East; take **Route 405** *(NASA Parkway)* east across causeway and follow signs. Kennedy Space Center is located 6mi east of US-1 on NASA Parkway.

BY TRAIN OR BUS – Nearest **Amtrak train** station is in Sanford, which is 48mi northwest of Kennedy Space Center (☎321-323-4800 or 800-872-7245). Greyhound/Trailways **bus** station: 302 Main St., Cocoa and at Melbourne International Airport (☎800-231-2222). Local bus service: Space Coast Area Transit (☎321-633-1878).

WHEN TO GO

The Space Coast region enjoys a mild climate with an average annual temperature of 73°F. Highs during the summer months reach into the mid-80s with frequent afternoon thunderstorms. The main tourist season for the area is *October through May*, and **Kennedy Space Center** is busiest *between June and August* and on holidays. Weekends at the KSC are less crowded.

rockets and capsules shifting from the government to private industry.

VISIT

🕐*Visitor Complex open year-round daily 9am–dusk. Tours begin 10am, last tour 2:45 pm.* 🕐*Closed Dec 25 and some launch days.* 👓*$38 includes all exhibits, IMAX films, KSC bus tour, and Astronaut Hall of Fame (🕐 see p328). Special interest tours ("Cape Canaveral: Then and Now" and "NASA Up Close") additional $21 each.* ✕👤🅿 ☎321-449-4444. www.kennedyspacecenter.com.

Visitor Complex

The main visitor complex is divided into themed areas, exhibits, rides and live shows, including the opportunity to meet and talk with a real-life astronaut at the **Astronaut Encounter**, and **Mad Mission to Mars**, complete with special effects. The **Shuttle Launch Experience** invites you to board a space shuttle for a virtual tour and enjoy live-action theatrical shows like "Mad Mission to Mars."

Eye on the Universe: The Hubble Space Telescope showcases the most powerful telescope in history, which is orbiting the earth 350mi above. Set in an ultra-dark environment, beautiful images showcase deep space, unlocking some of the mysteries of our universe. The **IMAX 1 & 2** theaters present compelling films in 70mm format throughout the day. Projected on screens more than five stories high, two films—*Magnificent Desolation: Walking on the Moon 3D* and the new *Hubble 3D*—include

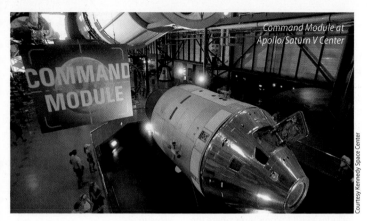

Command Module at
Apollo/Saturn V Center

Courtesy Kennedy Space Center

stunning footage shot from space. Seat-rumbling, six-channel digital stereo adds to the realistic effect.

At the **International Space Station Center,** visitors learn about the venture that is driving the space industry in the 21C. Exhibits include a movie about the station and mock-ups of its various elements, including living quarters and working space. An enclosed catwalk offers a bird's-eye view of the factory floor where module components are being processed. Outside, the **Rocket Garden** displays rockets and other impressive interstellar hardware.

KSC Bus Tour

Departs every 15min. 2hrs. Video-supplemented commentary. Special operations or imminent shuttle launches may alter tour itineraries.

The gigantic cubical 525ft-high **Vehicle Assembly Building**, where the shuttle is assembled (and where the *Apollo* and many other craft were built), is the second largest building in the world; it could hold nearly four Empire State Buildings laid end-to-end.

Once ready, the space shuttle inches to the pad at 1mph on the six-million-pound Crawler Transporter. At **Launch Complex 39,** visitors can climb a 60ft observation gantry and, perhaps, see a shuttle awaiting launch from another nearby complex. Presented here are a short film and an exhibit on the launch procedure that, commendably, is not afraid to include NASA's disasters.

Rocket Launches

Although the government-funded Space Shuttle program ended in 2010, launches were scheduled for beyond the retirement date to Jupiter; the Moon and Mars *(for more details visit www.nasa.gov/missions/highlights/schedule.html).*

Kennedy Space Center isn't the only place to watch a launch.

Try the following alternative sites *(arrive early and make sure you have an unobstructed view to the east):* Canaveral National Seashore; Route 402, north of Complex 39 in Merritt Island National Wildlife Refuge (parts of refuge may be closed due to launch activities); along the Indian River on US-1 in Titusville between Route 528 and Route 402 (the city permits roadside parking up to 24hrs before launch time).

However don't be overly disappointed if you find these spaces full, or restricted. So awesome is the blast-off that anywhere within a 40mi radius of the launch pad is spectacular.

An excellent movie about the *Apollo 11* mission and a close-up inspection of a 363ft Saturn V moon rocket highlight a stop at the **Apollo/Saturn V Center.** Built of stages destined for canceled Apollo missions, the Saturn V is one of three such rockets in the world. Tours of the **Launch Control Center** include a stirring multimedia review of the Apollo series and displays of original lunar-excursion and command-service modules.

Special Interest Bus Tours

Additional charge ⊚$21 per tour.
Both special tours sell out daily. Buying tickets online in advance is recommended. Concentrating on space-flight history, **Cape Canaveral: Then and Now** begins with a scenic 11mi drive out to Cape Canaveral. En route, visitors can glimpse shuttle facilities and the ships that salvage rocket boosters. The tour includes a visit to complexes where the

first manned space flights, and more recent probes, were launched. Launch site of the first US satellite, the **Air Force Space and Missile Museum,** a 30min stop, offers an impressive array of rockets and historical artifacts—you may be surprised to learn of the debt that the early space program owes to the Nazi V2 rockets—displayed on the grounds and in two indoor exhibit spaces (ℰ321-853-3246).

The highlight of the **Discover KSC: Today & Tomorrow Tour** is the camera stop, where guests can access the closest possible Space Shuttle Launch Pad viewing site.

ADDRESSES

🏨STAY

A wide range of hotels, motels, condominiums and campgrounds are available in Titusville, Cocoa Beach, Cocoa and Melbourne.

For information, contact:
Florida's Space Coast Office of Tourism, 430 Brevard Avenue, Suite 150, Cocoa Village (ℰ877- 572-3224 or 321-433-4470; www.space-coast.com);
Titusville Area Chamber of Commerce, 2000 S. Washington Ave., Titusville FL 32780 (ℰ321-267-3036; www.titusville.org) or **Cocoa Beach Area Chamber of Commerce,** 400 Fortenberry Rd., Merritt Island FL 32952 (ℰ321-459-2200; www.cocoabeach chamber.com).

These organizations provide information on shopping, entertainment, festivals and recreation. Daily room rates range from $85–$175 and up. Numerous campgrounds and RV parks offer full-service amenities, fishing and other recreational facilities.

🍴 EAT

$$$ Atlantic Ocean Grille – *Cocoa Beach Pier. ℰ321-783-7549. Dinner only, plus Sunday champagne brunch*. When you're named "Best Restaurant With A View" by Florida *Today* newspaper readers for seven consecutive years you must be doing something right. Fresh seafood is their thing—Thursday

Lobster Night is a bargain—but they also do succulent steak. Do reserve a window table and before coming here start the night off with a sunset cocktail at the Mai Tiki Bar at the end of the pier, 800ft above the ocean).

$$$ The Fat Snook – *2464 South Atlantic Ave. Cocoa Beach. ℰ321- 784-1190. http:// thefatsnook.com. Dinner only.*

This beachside restaurant is rated as one of the best seafood places in Brevard County. Expect creative seafood and fish dishes, such as herb encrusted wild Coho salmon, with vodka cranberry jelly, served in a tropically themed SoBe-style interior.

$$ Sunset Waterfront Cafe and Bar – *500 W Cocoa Beach Causeway, Cocoa Beach. ℰ321-783-8485. www.sunset waterfrontcafeandbar.com.* This hugely popular informal waterfront eaterie is the perfect place for a sundowner then dinner. Classic fish and seafood dishes are what locals and vacationers flock here for, with lots of choice on shrimps and tasty oysters.

🏃SPORTS AND RECREATION

Melbourne Greyhound Park (*Mon–Sat noon & 6:30pm, Sun noon; ℰ321-259-9800; www.mgpark.com*). **Airboat rides** on St. Johns River at **Lone Cabbage Fish Camp** (*depart year-round daily 10am–6pm; round-trip 30min; ⊚$22; ♿ ℰ321-632-4199; www.twisterairboatrides.com*). For information on other recreational activities, guided eco-tours and more, call tourism offices or chambers.

Cocoa

and Cocoa Beach

This small coastal town might have grown faster if developer Henry Flagler, angry that he could not purchase the Plaza Hotel, had not torn out the railroad spur line serving that grand Cocoa establishment. Today the town, boosted over the last few decades by the space industry, sprawls along the Indian River, with a modest population.

SIGHTS

Historic Cocoa Village is the principal sightseeing interest here. Cocoa Beach is known for being the nearest seaside resort to Orlando and is a favorite surfers' destination.

Cocoa Beach

Due east of Cocoa , 8 mi across the Merritt Island Causeway (Route 520).
Unpretentious **Cocoa Beach**, is a place where water sports more than holds their own against spaceflight. Several surfing competitions are held here, and informal beach activity abounds, particularly near the 800ft **Cocoa Beach Pier** *(Meade Ave., off A1A; www.cocoabeachpier.com)*, which offers open-air bars and live music.

Cocoa Village★

South of Rte. 520 at Brevard Ave.
℘*321-632-1830. www.cocoavillage.com.*
For a relaxing afternoon, walk through this charming four-block, brick-paved historic district of cafes and boutiques shaded by old trees.
Here, the three-story 1924 **Cocoa Village Playhouse** *(300 Brevard Ave.; www.cocoavillageplayhouse.com)*, once a venue for vaudeville acts, continues to stage a wide range of performances. The **Porcher House** *(434 Delannoy Ave.;* ⏱ *open year-round Mon–Fri 9am–5pm;* ♿🅿℘*321-639-3500; www.cocoavillage.com/porcherhouse)* was built in 1916 of local coquina rock. The first floor is furnished with period pieces.

▶ **Population:** 16,898.
⏱ **Michelin Map:** p321.
ℹ **Info:** 8501 Astronaut Blvd., St., Cape Canaveral; ℘877-321-8474 or 321-454-2022; www.visitcocoabeach.com.
◑ **Location:** Rte. 1 runs north-south through the city; Rte. 520 crosses the bridge to Cocoa Beach.
🅿 **Parking:** Street parking, public lots, and beach access parking is available.
⊗ **Don't Miss:** A stop at one of the open-air bars on Cocoa Beach Pier, or the manatees, alligators and sea turtles on a guided eco-tour.
⏱ **Timing:** Allow a day here, more if you're a beach lover.
👪 **Kids:** Jungle Adventures.

BCC Planetarium & Observatory

1519 Clearlake Rd. ⏱*Open: see website for schedule of shows and prices.* ℘*321-433-7373. www.brevardcc.edu/planet.*
The Brevard Community College Observatory is home to the largest public telescope in Florida *(open Fri & Sat dusk–10pm)*. It also boasts a world-class planetarium seating 210 under a 70ft dome projection screen.

EXCURSION
Jungle Adventures

8mi west of I-95. 26205 E. Hwy. 50, Christmas. ⏱*Open daily 9:30am–5:30pm.* ⊛*$19.95.* ♿🅿℘*407-568-2885. www.jungleadventures.com.*
You'll find a bit of old Florida-style fun at this quaintly old-fashioned animal theme park. Take a guided riverboat cruise around Wild Animal Island amid some 200 alligators and myriad tropical birds, and back on dry land enjoy encounters with (captive) Florida panthers, black bears and gray wolves. There are also live animal–animal demonstrations and alligator wrangling.

Titusville

Once a shipping point for oranges, Titusville now ties its fortunes primarily to Kennedy Space Center, which lies across the Indian River and employs some 60 percent of the local work force. The vital artery from Merritt Island to the mainland, Highway 405, is often congested with commuter and visitor traffic.

SIGHTS
US Astronaut Hall of Fame★
Intersection of US-1 and Rte. 405.
Open year-round daily 9am–5pm (extended summer hrs). Closed Dec 25. $17 or free with Kennedy Space Center ticket (see p322).
321-449-4444.
www.kennedyspacecenter.com.
This priceless collection of space-related artifacts celebrates the accomplishments of astronauts everywhere. The latest attaction here is **Science On a Sphere**, which provides a 3-D representation of a view of the Earth and planets as viewed from space.

The real attraction for younger visitors, however, is its many hands-on activities and simulators, where you can suit up, strap in and blast off into an interactive experience that gives you a true taste of space: from the G-Force Trainer that lets you feel the pressure of four times the force of gravity, to the space shuttle landing simulator and riding a rover across the rocky Martian terrain.

▶ **Population:** 43,767.
Michelin Map: p321.
Info: 321-267-3036; www.titusville.org.
Location: Located on Rte. 1 along Florida's Atlantic Coast, 46mi south of Daytona Beach and 40mi east of Orlando, it's easily accessible from north-south I-95 and east-west Hwy. 406.
Parking: Free parking at the center with a shuttle service to the Astronaut Hall of Fame; street parking and public lots downtown and by the beach.
Don't Miss: Take the 7mi wildlife driving tour at Merritt Island National Wildlife Refuge; fishing charters, bird watching and guided eco-tours.
Timing: Spend a full day combining a visit to the Astronaut Hall of Fame and the Kennedy Space Center plus a half-day for a walk or tour of Merritt Island National Wildlife Refuge.
Kids: Discover what it's like to blast into space on one of the flight simulators at the Astronaut Hall of Fame.

Indian River Oranges

One of the earliest settlers here, Capt. Douglas Dummitt, acquired land on Merritt Island in 1843. In this period just after the Second Seminole War, the Armed Occupation Act offered 160 acres to anyone who would stay for at least five years. In a jungle landscape known as Mosquito County, Dummitt began a commercial orange grove that would blossom into Florida's largest in just 25 years' time. Here he developed his famous Indian River Oranges, which he would wrap in Spanish moss and pack in barrels for shipment by dugout canoe to St. Augustine.

Schooners relayed the delicious cargo to ports as far north as Boston. And so widespread grew the fame of the fruit that the czars of Russia sent ships here for them. Today about six million bushels are still shipped worldwide annually.

EXCURSION
Merritt Island National Wildlife Refuge★★

4mi east on Rte. 402. ◑Open year-round daily dawn–dusk (subject to space shuttle launches). ♿ ᴘ ☎321-861-0667. www.fws.gov/merrittisland.

Set on 140,000 acres owned by NASA, this refuge provides habitat to more than 500 animal species, including such endangered and threatened animals as the southern bald eagle, the manatee and the loggerhead sea turtle. Areas open to the public include the **visitor center** (on Rte. 402, 3mi east of Rte. 406), with informative displays on wildlife, nature trails, a 7mi wildlife driving tour, and manatee observation deck.

Playalinda Beach⚏⚏

6mi east of visitor center, accessible from A1A. ◑Open May–Oct daily 6am–8pm; rest of the year daily 6am–6pm. ◑Closed Jan 1 & Dec 25. ◉$3. ♿ ᴘ ☻No drinking water, showers or lifeguards. ☎321-267-1110. www.nps.gov/cana.

This four miles of gorgeous unspoiled beach is part of **Canaveral National Seashore;** there's not a high-rise in sight—except for the Vehicle Assembly Building and the two shuttle launchpads on the southern horizon. Watch pelicans skim the surf and sea oats bend in gentle breezes. Anglers gather along the south shoreline; nude bathers congregate along the north end.

Ron Jon Surf Shop

4151 N. Atlantic Ave. ♿ ☎321-799-8888. www.ronjons.com.

You can't miss the many signs advertising Ron Jon's—this is their flagship branch and the world's largest surfshop—and once you're in Cocoa Beach, it's even harder to miss this gaudy two-story Art Deco surfwear palace, which has been here since 1963. If it's related to the beach or water sports, you'll find it in this two-acre emporium: surfboards, in-line skates, boogie boards, beachwear, bathing suits, sunglasses, surfboard wax, flip-flops and a plethora of T-shirts.

Black Point Wildlife Drive★

Entrance 2mi west of visitor center, off Rte. 406. Stop at visitor center for self-guided driving-tour brochure. Bring binoculars.

This 7mi one-lane dirt road traverses a dike built in the 1950s to control mosquitoes. Here you'll be treated to close-up views of waterbirds and an opportunity to compare the different habitats associated with a shallow-water impoundment and a natural marsh.

A short trail leads to an observation tower about halfway along, and several turn-outs provide places to study wildlife.

Canaveral National Seashore

Visit Florida

Highlights

1 Chillin' out on **Caldesi Island**'s white sand beach (p332)

2 Surveying the genius of Salvador Dalí in **St. Petersburg** (p336)

3 Lapping up the Latin flavors of **Ybor City**, day and night (p342)

4 African-themed fun and thrills at **Busch Gardens** (p343)

5 Going Greek at the small town of **Tarpon Springs** (p349)

Blessed with perennially fine weather and a resplendent waterfront setting, Florida's second-largest metropolitan area has carved a niche for itself as the state's west-coast capital. It is a destination not only for vacationers—who come for the sugar-white beaches, the fabulous Salvador Dalí Museum and the world-class rides and animals of Busch Gardens—but also for business travelers. On the east side of the bay sits Tampa and its soaring skyscrapers, while to the west lies the Pinellas Peninsula, site of St. Petersburg ("St. Pete's") and such easygoing beach towns as Treasure Island and Clearwater. Just north, Tarpon Springs adds international flair, supporting a community of Greek sponge divers. South of St. Petersburg, one can see the stunning **Sunshine Skyway** bridge— its mastlike yellow suspension cables pointing skyward—straddling the bay.

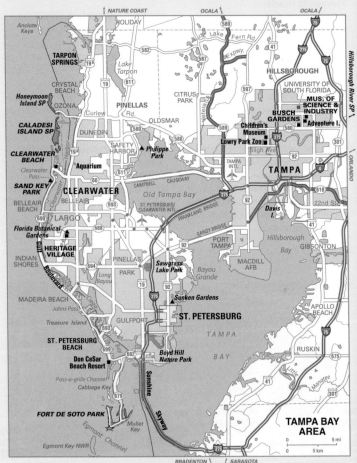

Clearwater

and around

Consisting primarily of a 4-mile stretch of Gulf Coast barrier island, Clearwater is Tampa's beach. This popular resort, located 22 miles west of Tampa, attracts more than a million visitors each year, who contribute the largest amount of revenue to the city. Vacationers cavort on the powdery sands and in the calm, sparkling waters of **Clearwater Beach**☆, which is connected to downtown by Memorial Causeway. Although you pass through a dense commercial strip to get to the shore, once you reach it you'll find a low-key resort town that appeals to families, couples and seniors alike.

SIGHTS

The commercial center began to develop in the late 19C after Henry Plant extended his railroad through the city and built the elegant Belleview Hotel, now the Belleview Biltmore, nearby (see p346). The c.1898 pink frame **Louis Ducros House** *(1324 S. Ft. Harrison Ave.)*, ornamented with Gothic Revival fretwork, survives as one of the few remaining structures from that period. Down the street, the Neoclassical **Pinellas County Courthouse** *(324 S. Ft. Harrison Ave.)* was hastily built in 1917 in an attempt to steal the county seat from neighboring St. Petersburg. The hefty, brick **South Ward School** *(610 S. Ft. Harrison Ave.)*, which dates back to 1906, is the county's oldest school to operate continually in one building.

Sand Key Park★

1060 Gulf Blvd. ⏰*Open daily 7am–sunset.* ♿☎*727-588-4852. www.pinellascounty.org/park.*
Located on 65 pristine acres on a spit jutting into the Gulf of Mexico, Sand Key has been voted among the top 10 parks in the whole of the US and provides a respite from the development that crowds Clearwater Beach. Edged with sea oats and sea grape trees, a wide,

▶ **Population:** 112,033.
⏲ **Michelin Map:** p330.
🛈 **Info:** 333 C South Gulfview Blvd. Clearwater Beach; ☎888-799-3199 or 727-447-7600; www.visitclearwaterflorida.com or www.floridasbeach.com.
▶ **Location:** St. Petersburg/Clearwater is easily accessible from north-south I-75 and I-95, and east-west I-4. The Memorial Causeway leads to the shoreline.
🅿 **Parking:** Metered lots and street parking are approx $1.5/hr; cashier-operated lots slightly more.
👐 **Don't Miss:** A visit to pristine Caladesi State Park, or sunsets at Pier 60, a nightly celebration.
⏰ **Timing:** Allow several days here.
👪 **Kids:** The Clearwater Marine Aquarium, with Winter the dolphin, and touch tanks.

sugary sand beach forms the centerpiece of the park.

👪 Clearwater Marine Aquarium

249 Windward Passage, Clearwater Beach. ⏰*Open year-round Mon–Thu 9am–5pm, Fri–Sat 9am–7pm, Sun 10am–5pm.* ⏰*Closed major holidays.* 💰*$14.95, child (3–12 yrs) $9.95. Sea Safari $22.95, child $14.95.* ♿🅿 ☎*727-441-1790. www.seewinter.com*
The CMA is a private, nonprofit research facility, dedicated to public education and the rescue, rehabilitation and release of injured or sick marine mammals, otters and sea turtles. A 55,000-gallon mangrove seagrass pool offers visitors a close-up view of the estuary environment. A variety of sea turtles, dolphins, sharks and stingrays are on display and feature in various shows

and exhibits. The star here is **Winter the dolphin**. Rescued in Clearwater in 2006 after being badly injured in a crab trap, she was rushed to the CMA and subsequently become famous worldwide as the world's first bionic sea creature after being fitted with an artificial tail.

The CMA's **Sea Life Safari** is a two-hour trip into the intracoastal waterway, looking for dolphins, sea birds and other marine life.

EXCURSIONS
Philippe Park

8mi east in Safety Harbor. 2525 Philippe Pkwy. ◯Open daily 7am–sunset. ♿ 🅿 ✆727-669-1947. www.pinellas county.org.

This county park occupies 122 acres of huge oak trees and sweeping green lawns that afford water views along its mile-long shoreline. The Tocobaga Indians, the last aboriginal culture to exist on Florida's central west coast, left a legacy of massive ceremonial mounds in the park. The **temple mound** *(turn left into the first parking area; mound is by the water, marked with a sign)* was the seat of the principal village of Tocobaga.

👥 Heritage Village★

8mi south in Largo. ◯ US-19A south to Ulmerton Rd; turn right and proceed to 125th St.; turn left; follow signs to village at 11909 125th St. N. ◯Open year-round Wed–Sat 10am–4pm, Sun 1pm–4pm. ◯Closed major holidays. 🅿 ✆727-582-2123. www.pinellascounty.org/Heritage.

More than 28 of the county's earliest structures and building features are displayed at this 21-acre re-created pioneer community, complete with a replica one-room schoolhouse, an early church, train depot and private homes.

Florida Botanical Gardens

8mi south in Largo. ◯ Take US-19A south to Ulmerton Rd. Turn right on Ulmerton and proceed to 125th St. Turn left; follow signs to Pinewood Cultural Park at 12175 125th St. N. ◯Open year-round daily 7am–7pm. 🅿 ✆727-582-2200. www.flbg.org.

Located across the bridge from Heritage Village, this 162-acre development features colorful plants arranged thematically, including serene woods, a sculpture garden and an art museum. Fountains, bridges and benches highlight paths that wind past exotic and native flowers; oak, palm and fruit-bearing trees; and herb-filled courtyards and creek banks.

Caladesi Island State Park★

9mi north on Caladesi Island. Accessible only by boat from Honeymoon Island. ♿◯Open daily 8am–sunset. 🚗$8 per vehicle entrance to Honeymoon Island. Ferry year-round daily every hour 10am–4:30pm. 🚗$12. ✆727-469-5918. www.floridastate parks.org /caladesiisland.

Situated in the Gulf of Mexico off the coast of Dunedin, Caladesi Island's white-sand **beach**⬜⬜ is framed by undulating grasses and is often ranked among the nation's top five beaches (in 2008 it was ranked first).

Benefiting from an inaccessible location that failed to attract developers, the 600-acre island survives with its native flora and fauna intact. Along the 2mi beach, visitors swim, fish, picnic, shell, stroll or explore the nature trail *(2.5mi)* through the island's interior.

Honeymoon Island State Park

9mi north in Dunedin. ◯ Take US-19A north to Dunedin. Turn left on Dunedin Causeway Blvd./Rte. 586 and follow causeway to park. ◯Open daily 8am–sunset. 🚗$8 per vehicle. 🅿 ✆727-469-5942. www.floridastateparks.org.

A causeway from Dunedin connects the mainland to the 385-acre park, which features a rocky beach (shelling is particularly good here) and 208 species of plants. One of the last virgin slash-pine forests still standing in south Florida lies along the island's northern loop trail.

Tarpon Springs★

13mi north via US-19A. ✆727-937-6109. www.tarponsprings.com. (◑See p349).

History of Tampa Bay

Tampa Bay was a favorite landing site for gold-seeking Spanish explorers in the early 1500s. **Juan Ponce de León, Hernando de Soto** and **Pánfilo de Narváez** all sought glory and wealth in their expeditions around this wide natural harbor. After encountering hostile natives and equally inhospitable territory, the Europeans abandoned the area for nearly three centuries.

In the early 1880s, financier Henry Plant assured Tampa's future importance by connecting it via railroad to the east coast and building luxury hotels along the line. Tampa soon established a reputation as the world's cigar-manufacturing center and a significant port for the shipment of cattle, phosphate and citrus. In the meantime, St. Petersburg and other towns across the bay became known for their healthy climate, good fishing and fine beach resorts.

Henry Plant

© Hulton Archive/Stringer/Getty Images

Today, despite the growing pains associated with urbansim, increasing numbers of retirees and young professionals continue to bolster the population of Hillsborough and Pinellas counties. Tampa Port is the state's largest, accommodating half of Florida's cargo and providing employment for thousands in the ship repair and building industry, as well as services at the recently expanded cruise facilities. Nearby, the resort-laden beach strand from St. Petersburg Beach up to Clearwater, rates as west Florida's most popular. Away from the intensively developed shore, fringes of mangrove swamp and mudflats are home to more than 200 species of fish. The warm water outfalls of coastal power plants raise sea temperatures, which draws one out of every six endangered manatees to spend the winter.

From the modern cityscape of downtown Tampa, to the timeless allure of the Gulf's white-sand beaches, the Tampa Bay area epitomizes Florida on the move.

Downtown Tampa

© Judy Kennamer/iStockphoto.com

St. Petersburg ★★

Linked to its sister city's fast-paced commerce by three bridges, sunny St. Petersburg is Tampa's seaside resort and Florida's fourth most populous city. A thriving mix of young professionals, university students retirees and sun-seeking vacationers enjoy St. Pete's relaxed lifestyle, first-rate museums, sparkling Gulf beaches, blue skies and sunshine.

A BIT OF HISTORY

In the 1840s fishermen and settlers arrived in the area, some lured by tales of the Espirito Santo springs at Safety Harbor, discovered in the 16C by de Soto. By the beginning of World War I, a second railroad connected St. Pete to Tampa, and development of the beaches had started. The Florida land boom of the 1920s elevated St. Petersburg to resort status, with 3,000 hotel rooms and a population of 60,000. Two world-class resorts were built during this decade: the Vinoy Park (now the **Renaissance Vinoy Resort**) and the **Don CeSar**. Two sizable wildlife preserves lie outside the downtown core: Boyd Hill Nature Park *(1101 Country Club Way S.; entrance just west of 9th St. S.)* and **Sawgrass Lake Park** *(7400 25th St. N.),* both excellent spots for bird-watching.

BayWalk

Gail Baxter/MICHELIN

▶ **Population:** 248,000.

◔ **Michelin Map:** pp330, 335.

▤ **Info:** ℘727-464-7200; www.floridasbeach.com.

◖ **Location:** Hwy. 275 crosses Tampa Bay, linking the city of Tampa with St. Petersburg. The beaches lie 10mi west of downtown.

🅿 **Parking:** There are several downtown parking lots, including Central Parking garage on 2nd St. N and South Core garage on 1st Ave. S. Parking along Gulf beaches can be a challenge.

⊙ **Don't Miss:** The Salvador Dalí Museum; the Florida International Museum, with top-notch traveling exhibits from the Smithsonian Institution.

◔ **Timing:** Allow a full day to explore downtown and visit top museums.

🐣 **Kids:** The beaches; the Pier aquarium for younger ones.

DOWNTOWN

Downtown smoothly blends old and new styles of architecture; Art Deco and Mediterranean harmonize with contemporary styles. Seven miles of landscaped waterfront parks attract visitors to the bayside to stroll the Pier, take in art museums and nearby galleries, and bask in the sun at the expansive municipal marina. The St. Petersburg Yacht Club, established more than 90 years ago, has hosted numerous international regattas. **BayWalk** *(2nd & 3rd Aves. N. and 1st & 2nd Sts.)* is a multilevel shopping/entertainment complex packed with shops, restaurants and a movie theater around a tile-paved courtyard.

Immediately west of downtown is **Tropicana Field** *(1 Tropicana Dr.; entrance off 10th St. S. at 3rd Ave. S.; http://tampabay.rays.mlb.com)*, a 45,360-seat, covered baseball stadium where the Tampa Bay Devil Rays play their home games. To

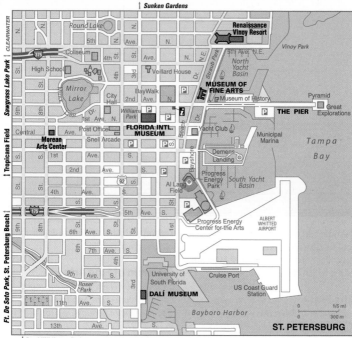

Sunken Gardens

Boyd Hill Nature Park

guarantee a constant 72° temperature inside the stadium, the Yale University professor who designed the field took into account such factors as humidity, air flow and atmospheric pressure within the dome.

Florida International Museum at St. Petersburg College

244 Second Ave N. 🕐*Open Mon–Sat 10am–5pm, Sun noon–5pm.*

🕐*Closed Easter Sun.* 🎫*$12.* ✕♿🅿*727-341-7900. www.floridamuseum.org.*

The Florida International Museum opened in 1995 and helped spark the resurgence of downtown St. Petersburg, by staging a series of blockbuster traveling exhibitions over the next several years, including exhibits from the Smithsonian Institution, with which it is affiliated (as well as from other museums). It has recently changed its status to

---

The Healthy Option

One of those who moved to the area for his health in the late 1870s was Detroit native **John C. Williams,** a retired Union general who purchased 1,600 waterfront acres. In 1885 an American Medical Assn. journal proposed that a "health city" be founded on the Pinellas Peninsula. The combination of warm climate, fresh air and good beaches made the Tampa/St. Petersburg area a leading candidate. Although the spa city never came into being, the peninsula's fame caught the attention of Russian speculator **Peter Demens,** who in 1888 brought his Orange Belt Railroad to John Williams' farm. Legend has it that Demens beat Williams on the flip of a coin to earn the right to name the new city, which he did for his hometown in Russia.

The original downtown laid out by Williams and Demens that year extended from Seventh Avenue South to Fifth Avenue North, and from about Ninth Street to the bay. Population lagged until 1900, when word of St. Pete's healthy climate and good fishing began to spread.

335

The Pier

Visit Florida

become part of St. Petersburg University and has also acquired the contemporary art collection of the Gulf Coast Museum of Art which closed in 2009.

The Pier★

East end of 2nd Ave. N.E.
Open year-round Mon–Thu 10am–8pm, Fri & Sat 10am–9pm, Sun 11am–7pm. 727-821-6164.
www.stpete-pier.com. Valet parking; pay parking lots and some free parking along the Pier. Free trolley rides from Pier to parking lots and to local museums.
The Pier, with its modernistic upside-down pyramid, juts a quarter of a mile into Tampa Bay. The five-story structure contains an **information desk** (*open Mon–Sat 10am–8pm, Sun 11am–6pm*) restaurants and shops, an aquarium (*$5, Sun $2.50*) aimed mostly at younger children, and an observation deck on the top.

Morean Arts Center (Chihuly Collection)

719 Central Avenue. Open year-round Mon–Sat 9am–5pm. $8. 727-822-7872. http://moreanartscenter.org.
Providing art exhibitions and classes for over 90 years, this local arts center has become the latest major artistic attraction in town by securing a permanent Dale Chihuly studio glass collection. This is to be exhibited in a new 10,000sq ft space on Beach Drive, scheduled to open July 2010, which will also house a working space for glass artists, with

seating and viewing areas to watch glass blowing in action.

Museum of Fine Arts★★

255 Beach Dr. N.E. Open year-round Tue–Sat 10am–5pm, Sun 1pm–5pm. Closed major holidays. $16. 727-896-2667.
www.fine-arts.org.
Housed in an attractive Palladian-style building designed by John Volk, this museum features a wide-ranging collection of art, from antiquities and world masterpieces to contemporary works. The Acheson Gallery displays some of the museum's most notable paintings by French artists—works by Cézanne, Renoir, Monet and others. The adjacent Poynter Gallery holds a remarkable trove of early **Asian** art, including an intricate Jaina shrine (c.1600) from India. Other collections include pre-Columbian art, 20C American paintings, fine examples of art from ancient Greece and Rome, the Renaissance, 18C Europe and 19C America.
A recently added two-story building sits adjacent to the original gallery, on Beach Drive, and houses the Special Exhibition Galleries.

Salvador Dalí Museum★★★

1000 Third St. S. Open year-round Mon–Sat 10am–5:30pm (Thu 8pm), Sun noon–5:30pm. Closed Thanksgiving Day & Dec 25. $17 ($5 after 5pm Thu). 727-823-3767.
www.salvadordalimuseum.org.

The Surreal Sr Dalí

Born and raised in a Catalonian farming village near Barcelona, **Salvador Dalí** (1904–1989) began painting at a young age. He attended the San Fernando Academy of Fine Arts in Madrid and held his first one-man show in Barcelona in 1925 at age 21. In 1929 he moved to France, where he joined the Paris Surrealist Group led by writer André Breton. Also in that year, he met Gala Eluard, his future wife and inspiration for much of his work. Surrealists eschewed convention and believed instead in the omnipotence of dreams and the suspension of conscious thought. Dalí soon became one of the movement's brash leaders, painting fantastic subjects in obsessive detail and declaring, "The difference between me and the Surrealists is that I am Surrealism." By 1940, however, Dalí had broken with the group and announced his intention to return to "Classical" painting, as embodied in the High Renaissance works of Raphael. Dalí continued executing his detailed symbolic and trompe l'œil effects in 18 masterworks—huge canvases dealing with historical, scientific or religious themes. By the time of his death he had become as famous for his trademark handlebar mustache and publicity stunts, which often involved wild animals, as for his artistry.

So, how did many of Dalí's greatest works end up here in Florida? Cleveland industrialist Reynolds Morse and his wife Eleanor enjoyed a 45-year friendship with Dalí and his wife, Gala, and avidly collected his works. When they finally sought a space to exhibit them, the enlightened leaders of St. Petersburg council persuaded them to move the collection here. The Salvador Dalí Museum opened in March 1982 and welcomes over 200,000 visitors each year.

Detail of Still Life - Fast Moving (1956) by Salvador Dalí, Salvador Dalí Museum

This is one of Florida's most popular art museums and the world's most comprehensive collection of works by the late Spanish Surrealist. It is housed in a modern airy single-story building located on Bayboro Harbor. Work is currently underway on a new multi-million dollar gallery that will be over double the present size. It will be located a few blocks north of the current museum, adjacent to the Mahaffey Theater within the Progress Energy Center for the Arts and is scheduled to open winter 2011

Six galleries display pieces from the museum's collection of 95 oil paintings, more than 100 watercolors and drawings, and 1,300 graphics, sculptures, photographs and objets d'art. There are four of Dalí's masterworks exhibited, each of which took at least

The Tampa Bay Hotel

Henry B. Plant Museum

During the 1880s, Henry Bradley Plant was building an empire of railroads, steamships and hotels. The Tampa Bay Hotel, however, was financed by Plant personally, not by investors, at a cost of $2,500,000 plus another $500,000 on furnishings. It took two years to build, covered six acres and was one-quarter mile long. The 511 rooms were the first in Florida to be electrified. The building featured all of the latest luxuries including a billiard room, barbershop, shoeshine service, beauty shop, flower shop, telegraph office, formal dining room, Grand Salon, Music Room with orchestra and telephones in all guest rooms. The grounds of the Hotel covered 150 acres. The amenities included an 9-hole golf course, tennis courts, croquet courts, boathouse, hunting and fishing grounds, stables, racetrack, kennels, casino with 2,000-seat auditorium, heated indoor swimming pool, bowling alley, spa facilities and card rooms, totaling 21 buildings in all. After the death of Henry Plant, the building was bought by the city of Tampa in 1904. However, by 1932 the boom years were long gone and it ceased to be a hotel. Today it is, fittingly, home to the Henry B. Plant Museum.

a year to complete. These tremendous canvases, measuring about 13ft by 10ft, were painted between 1948 and 1970. Hour-long free tours run throughout the day and, given that many of Dalí's works involve amazing *trompe l'oeils,* are an essential part of the gallery experience.

OTHER SIGHTS
Sunken Gardens

1825 4th St. N. ○*Open year-round Mon–Sat 10am–4:30pm, Sun noon– 4:30pm.* ≈$8. ♿🅿 𝒫727-551-3102. *www.stpete.org/sunken.*
Dating back to 1935, Sunken Gardens ranks as one of the area's oldest attractions. Footpaths wind 15ft below street level past tropical foliage and flowering shrubs. Wildlife displays and presentations feature tropical birds and reptiles.

🏖 St. Petersburg Beach

St. Pete Beach ⌂, stretching 18mi north to Clearwater, offers clean white sand and gentle Gulf waters. It is the setting for the historic **Don CeSar Beach Resort and Spa** (♿see p346).

🏖 Fort De Soto Park★

8mi south of St. Petersburg Beach on Mullet Key. ○*Open daily 8am–sunset.* ⚠♿🅿 𝒫727-582-2267. *www.pinellascounty.org/park.*
Construction of the fort here began during the Spanish-American War in 1898. A reconstructed storehouse houses exhibits and a presentation of the fort's history. Other activities in this 1,100-acre park include hiking, fishing, kayaking and swimming. Its pristine quiet white sands were named America's top **beach** for 2009 .

Tampa★★

Florida's third-largest city is both port and resort. Visitors can choose from attractions ranging from the Latin accents of Ybor City to the thrill rides of Busch Gardens. The bustling city attracts young professionals, retirees and vacationers with its major sports venues, historic architecture, modern hotels and resorts, and a thriving culinary and arts scene, all within a short drive of the famed sugar-white beaches of Florida's sunset coast.

A BIT OF HISTORY

Exploration and Settlement – By the 16C the area was occupied by the Calusa and Timucua tribes, who subsisted on shellfish and game. Pánfilo de Narváez is credited with being the first Spanish explorer, in 1528, to see Tampa Bay. De Soto also landed briefly but continued west, never to return. When Florida became a US Territory in 1821, the government established an army post near Spanishtown Creek, a small village built by Cuban and Spanish fishermen in an area that now defines the Hyde Park neighborhood west of downtown.

Railroad transportation and a flourishing port assured Tampa's growth by attracting new businesses and commercial developers who would forever change the face of the city. One such entrepreneur was **Vicente Martínez Ybor,** who relocated his cigar business to Tampa from Key West in 1886. Ybor bought land east of downtown, where he built a factory that, after a year, produced 900,000 cigars a month.

Other cigar makers soon relocated to Tampa and Spanish, Italian and Cuban workers flocked to the factories. Their community is now Tampa's historic Spanish neighborhood, Ybor City.

Today, Tampa's many amenities and varied economy continue to attract new businesses, residents and visitors; city leaders are banking on these factors to propel the city into a new chapter of prosperity in the 21C.

▶ **Population:** 326,593.
◔ **Michelin Map:** pp330, 340.
▤ **Info:** 615 Channelside Drive; ☏813-223-2752 or 800-448-2672; www.visittampabay.com. Ybor City Visitor Information Center, 1600 E. 8th Avenue; ☏877-9-FIESTA or 813-241-8838.
▶ **Location:** East-west I-4 and north-south I-75 provide direct access to the city. I-275 and Hwy. 19 cross Tampa Bay to oceanfront beaches.
⌖ **Don't Miss:** Busch Gardens, historic Ybor City or the Museum of Science and Industry.
◷ **Timing:** Allow a full day at Busch Gardens, and another to explore downtown attractions and museums.
♟ **Kids:** Busch Gardens is a must.

DOWNTOWN

The best of early Tampa's architecture survived the wrecking ball and stands today in the shadow of 30–40-story skyscrapers; the elegant 1915 Beaux-Arts **City Hall** (Kennedy Blvd. and Florida Ave.) nestles among the city's tallest buildings. The development boom of the mid-1980s included improvements like the Franklin Street Mall—a pedestrians-only brick avenue with plantings, fountains and stores extending from Cass Street to Washington—and the many sculptures and artworks that grace public spaces.

Downtown Tampa has added major entertainment centers, such as the Ice Palace arena for the city's hockey team and the $300 million **Garrison Seaport Center,** which includes the Florida Aquarium and two cruise terminals, from where liners sail to the western Caribbean and Mexico's Yucatán Peninsular.

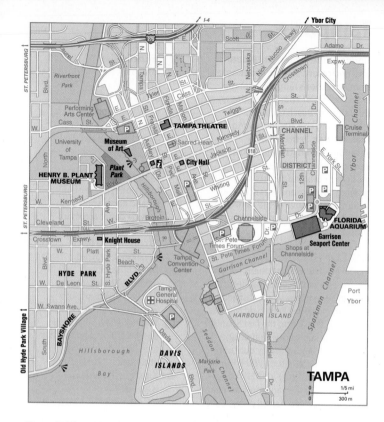

TAMPA

0   1/5 mi
0   300 m

Henry B. Plant Museum★

401 W. Kennedy Blvd. ⏱*Open Tue–Sat 10am–4pm, Sun noon–4pm. Also open Mon during Dec.* ⏱*Closed major holidays.* ⏱*$10 (additional charge during Dec).* ♿🅿 ✆*813-254-1891. www.plantmuseum.com.*

The silver minarets and gold crescents atop the former **Tampa Bay Hotel**★★ (*see Box p338*) have been synonymous with Tampa since the hotel's lavish opening in 1891. Although the architecture is spectacular, the interior has not been restored. Note the domed Fletcher Lounge, which served as the hotel's main dining room, and the Grand Salon, where guests socialized.

Inside the museum, visitors glimpse what life was like for Plant's fortunate guests, luminaries such as Thomas Edison, Theodore Roosevelt and Babe Ruth.

Hyde Park★

North and south of Swann Ave. between South Crosstown Expressway (Rte. 618) and Bayshore Blvd.

Tampa's wealthiest families built homes here in a wide range of architectural styles. Today Queen Annes and Colonial Revivals elbow Mediterranean Revivals and eclectic bungalows. Some of the finest houses lie south of Swann between Rome Avenue and South Boulevard. Tampa's most fashionable shopping district, **Old Hyde Park Village,** lines South Dakota and Snow avenues south of Swann Avenue.

Peter O. Knight House

245 S. Hyde Park Ave. ⏱*Open year-round by appointment.* ⏱*Closed major holidays.* 🅿 ✆*813-259-1111.*

Constructed in 1890 as a honeymoon cottage by Colonel Knight, one of Tampa's early business leaders, the house is currently headquarters for the Tampa

GETTING THERE

BY AIR – **Tampa International Airport (TPA)**: 5mi west of city center (*℘813-870-8700; www.tampa airport.com*). Transportation to downtown: The **Bay Shuttle** (*⊜$13; ℘813-259-9998; www.tampabay shuttle.com*), **taxi** (*$25*) and hotel courtesy **shuttles. Rental car agencies** located at airport.
BY TRAIN AND BUS – Amtrak **train** station; 601 N. Nebraska Ave. (*℘800-872-7245; www.amtrak.com*). Greyhound **bus** station; 610 E. Polk St. (*℘813-229-2174 or 800-231-2222; www.greyhound.com*).

GETTING AROUND

BY PUBLIC TRANSPORTATION – Local **bus service:** HARTline Transit System (*⊜$1.50-$2.50; ℘813-254-4278; www.hartline.org*). **Suncoast Beach Trolley** from Clearwater to Pass-A-Grille (*daily 5:45am–10pm, every 30min; $1.75; ℘727-540-1900; www.psta.net/beachtrolley.html*).
BY CAR – Limited on-street parking; public parking garages.

BY TAXI – TPA (*℘877-288-2672; www. unitedtaxi.net*); Yellow Cab (*℘813-253-0121; www.yellowcaboftampabay.com*).

VISITOR INFORMATION

Tampa Bay Convention and Visitors Bureau, 615 Channelside Drive, Suite 108A, Tampa, FL 33602. *℘*800- 44-TAMPA or 813-223-2752 (*open Mon–Sat 9.30am–5:30pm, Sun 11am–5pm; ℘813-223-1111; www.visittampabay.com*).
Tampa Convention Center, 333 South Franklin St., Tampa, FL 33602. *℘*800-44-TAMPA or 813-223-2752. Hours vary, please call. (*These centers provide information on shopping, entertainment, festivals and recreation.*)
Local Press and websites – *The Tampa Tribune* (*www.tampatrib.com*); *TBO Extra.* (*http://tboextra.com*); *The Weekly Planet* and *See Tampa* (available free at hotels and restaurants) are handy guides to arts, entertainment and sports.
Foreign Exchange Office – American Express Travel Services, One Tampa City Center, at Franklin Street Mall and Jackson Street (*℘813-273-0310 or 800-221-7282*).

Historical Society. Exhibits explain the city's cigar industry, Tampa Bay's Victorian era, the role of women in Tampa, and area shipbuilding. The Historical Society maintains a photo archive and library here.

Bayshore Boulevard★

Skirting the shore from the Hillsborough River to MacDill Air Force Base, this 7.2mi signature roadway provides fine **views**★ of Hillsborough Bay and the downtown skyline, and sweeps past Hyde Park, one of Tampa's oldest neighborhoods.
At the north end, Bayshore passes the three-masted schooner *José Gasparilla.* Continuing south, the road swerves inland at Ballast Point and ends at Mac-Dill, which served as the command center for Operation Desert Storm in 1991.

Tampa Theatre★

711 Franklin St. 🔊🔍*For tours ℘813-274-8981. www.tampatheatre.org.*
This grand 1926 movie palace boasts iron entrance gates, a glazed-tile lobby and a fanciful interior holding 1,446 seats. Today it presents classic and art-house films, concerts and special events.

Tampa Museum of Art

120 W. Gasparilla Plaza. ◷*Open year-round Mon–Fri 11am–7pm (Thu 9pm), Sat–Sun 11am–5pm.* ◷*Closed Jan 1, Thanksgiving Day, Dec 25.* ⊜*$10.* ♿ *℘813-274-8130. www.tampamuseum.org.*
This spectacular 66,000-square-foot building was designed by San Francisco architect Stanley Saitowitz, and features a shimmering pierced aluminum exterior, and state-of-the-art gallery spaces with innovative translucent ceilings and polished concrete floors.

Tampa Theatre

Visit Florida

Highlights from the permanent collection of this museum include the **Classical World Gallery,** which features more than 400 Greek and Roman works. Marble sculptures, grave altars, bronze figurines and an outstanding collection of painted **Greek vases**★ offer insight into the origins of Western civilization. By contrast the museum also has a rich collection of contemporary US art and is famed for its world-class traveling exhibitions.

🏊‍♂️ Florida Aquarium★

701 Channelside Dr. at Garrison Seaport Center. ◷*Open year-round daily 9:30am –5pm.* ◷*Closed Thanksgiving Day, Dec 25.* ⊜*$19.95, child (2–12 yrs) $14.95.* ✖⛐🄿(⊜*$5)* ✆*813-273-4000. www.flaquarium.org.*

Beneath a signature green glass dome, Tampa's aquatic-life facility harbors more than a million gallons of fresh and salt water. Viewing galleries are laid out in different aquatic communities. In **Wetlands,** a humid zone of cypress swamps, mangrove forests and saw grass marshes, habitats display freshwater bass, white ibis, great horned owls and other animals. The ecosystems of **Bays and Beaches** include bay bottoms, with graceful stingrays and floordwelling guitarfish. In the popular **Coral Reef,** colorful butterfly fish dart through forests of staghorn coral and sharks lurk in dark grottoes. One room contains a tri-panel transparent wall 14ft high and 43ft wide for the display of 60 species of tropical fish. **Sea Hunt** presents scorpion fish, the giant Pacific octopus and other residents of the deep sea. At the newest gallery, **Ocean Commotion**, visitors walk through a fog screen and enter an interactive gallery celebrating the energy of our oceans. **Explore A Shore** is a water fun zone.

YBOR CITY★

1.6mi from downtown Tampa. ⛐*See map below. Ybor City Chamber of Commerce operates a visitor center at the **Centro Ybor**, 1800 E. 9th Ave.* ✆*813-241-8838. www.ybor.org.*

This mile-square historic district is Tampa's Latin Quarter and was once the the cigar capital of the world. For many years seedy and rundown, it is now an upcoming neighborhood with a buzzing nightlife. In 1990 it was designated as a National Historic Landmark District.

Seventh Avenue★

A walk along this avenue reveals some of the district's more interesting architecture. A landmark since 1905, **Columbia Restaurant** *(no. 2117;* ⛐*see p347)* is justly praised for its colorful exterior **tilework.** The three-story Neoclassical **Italian Club** *(at 18th St.),* distinguished by its tripartite facade, has served as a center of cultural enrichment, education and financial aid to local Italians since

1894; the present structure dates from 1918. **Centro Ybor** (*www.centrobor. com*) includes restaurants, retailers, a comedy club, a high-tech entertainment center and a multi-screen movie theater set around an open air plaza.

The avenue takes on a Mardi Gras atmosphere on Thursday, Friday and Saturday nights throughout the year, when Seventh becomes a pedestrian promenade between 13th and 20th streets.

Two blocks off Seventh Avenue sits the yellow brick **Cuban Club** (*2010 Avenida Republica de Cuba*), which dates from 1917. The nearby two-story brick **Cafe Creole** (*1320–1330 E. 9th Ave.*), with its graceful arches, gained fame as El Pasaje, or the Cherokee Club, a rowdy hotel and restaurant that opened in 1888. In its heyday, the hotel welcomed Cuban revolutionary José Martí, presidents Teddy Roosevelt and Grover Cleveland, Sir Winston Churchill and many Florida governors.

Ybor City State Museum

1818 9th Ave. ⏱*Open year-round daily 9am–5pm.* ⏱*Closed Thanksgiving Day & Dec 25.* ⏺*$3.* 👣*Museum staff lead walking tours through the historic district from the museum ($5 extra charge).* ♿ 🖉*813-247-6323. www.ybormuseum.org.* Housed in the 1923 yellow-brick Ferlita Bakery building, with a lush Mediterranean-style garden and the "**casita**" representative of a typical cigar-worker's family home, this museum outlines the development of Ybor City from frontier village to its recent renaissance. Watch a demonstration of hand rolling cigars on Fridays and Saturdays (*10am–1pm*).

Ybor Square

1911 N. 13th St.
Built in 1886 by Vicente Martínez Ybor, this three-story, red-brick building once contained Ybor City's oldest and largest hand-rolling cigar factory.
From the front steps of the building, José Martí, hero of the Cuban revolution, rallied his countrymen.

🏛👤 BUSCH GARDENS★★

3000 E. Busch Blvd. ⏱*Open year-round daily 9:30am–6pm; longer hours during holidays and special events.* ⏺*$74.95, child (3–9 yrs) $64.95.* ✕♿🅿 (⏺*$12*). 🖉*813-987-5090 or 888-800-5447. www.buschgardens.com.*
This internationally famous zoo-amusement park with an African theme is the home of around 3,000 animals, 300 acres of tropical gardens; some of the state's best roller coasters and many fine shows, plus themed dining and shops.
The first area visitors encounter is **Morocco** where a mosaic-tiled palace and bustling marketplace recall the romance and mystery of North Africa.
Nairobi features a variety of animals, including those in **Myombe Reserve,** a three-acre gorilla and chimpanzee habitat, where guests can observe primates up-close through a glass win-

Sheikra at Busch Gardens

© SeaWorld Parks & Entertainment

dow. Asian elephants, tortoises, a petting zoo and an animal nursery are also located here.

In **Timbuktu**, a replica of a desert trading center, you'll find the **Scorpion** roller coaster that drops 62ft into a 360-degree loop; and the Dolphin Theatre, starring leaping dolphins and a comical California sea lion.

The **Congo** is home to some of the Southeast's most gut-wrenching roller coasters, including **Kumba,** one of the largest and fastest (60mph), which zooms riders through seven inversions. **Congo River Rapids** is a very popular water ride. **Gwazi,** billed as Florida's first dueling, or double, wooden roller coaster, sends guests spiraling along 7,000ft of track in two simultaneously operating trains at speeds in excess of 50mph. There are different thrills at **Jungala**, four acres of fun filled with up-close animal interactions, a three-story maze of rope bridges and nets for kids to climb, two rides and live entertainment.

Bird Gardens were Busch's original interest, and showcase some 500 tropical birds from around the world as they paint the sky with a rainbow of brilliant colors in this free-flight aviary. **Lory Landing** is another freeflight aviary where a cupful of nectar will soon bring you an armload of feathered friends.

Stanleyville, built to resemble an African village, includes the **Stanley Falls Log Flume** and the **Tanganyika Tidal Wave**, a ride that creates a huge splash as it careens down a 55ft drop. Even scarier is **SheiKra**. Riders on this floorless coaster are hauled up to 200ft over the edge of a true 90-degree drop, then tipped face down, to begin a 70mph descent into an underground tunnel! Afterwards, view the orangutans and warthogs, an orchid garden and hands-on reptile exhibit.

Edge of Africa, a short trek past baboons, hippos, lions, hyenas and meerkats, is an introduction to the park's largest area, **Serengeti Plain.** From antelopes to zebras (ostriches, rhinos, giraffes and more), over 700 large African animals roam in herds on the grassy savanna.

You can take the skyride or train, but the flatbed trucks of the **Serengeti Safari** (⊜additional charge $33.99) tours provide a closer vantage point. **Rhino Rally** takes passengers off-road through

☺ Busch Gardens Tips ☺

As with any major theme park, a little planning goes a long way at Busch Gardens. The owners, Anheuser Busch, also own SeaWorld and Adventure Island so if you plan on visiting either (or both) of these too save money with a combi-ticket and always buy online. Unfortunately, unlike at the other major theme parks, there is no fast-pass or queue-beating scheme here so you will just have to arrive early (see website for opening times, then come 30 minutes before that), and make a beeline first for the coasters or water rides. After that it's a case of looking at the notice boards for ride times.

Finally, if the kids are old enough, then why not let them get on with it while you enjoy a complimentary glass or two of Budweiser (or soft drink) in the Hospitality House.

remote terrain and ends with a river ride aboard a washed-out pontoon bridge. Finally, **Egypt** holds nearly seven acres of rides, including **Montu**, a spine-tingling inverted roller coaster, as well as a replica of **King Tut's tomb**.

Adventure Island

⏰*Open late Mar–early Sept daily; weekends mid-Mar, Sept, Oct 9am/ 10am–5pm/6pm (later in high season).* ✕&P*$12.* ◉*$41.95; child (3–9 yrs) $37.95* 📞*888-800-5447. www.adventureisland.com.*

Located across the street from Busch Gardens (and under the same management) this 30-acres waterpark features a combination of high-speed thrills and tropical, tranquil surroundings for guests of all ages. Within a soothing Key West atmosphere await slides, corkscrews, water falls, a wave pool, a children's water playground and other family attractions

NORTH TAMPA
Museum of Science & Industry (MOSI) ★★

4801 E. Fowler Ave. ⏰*Open Mon–Fri 9am–5pm, Sat–Sun 9am–6pm.* ◉*$20.95 (incl. IMAX and planetarium), child (2– 12 yrs) $16.95.* ✕&P 📞*813-987-6000. www.mosi.org.*

This superlative hands-on science museum, designed primarily for children 12 and under, comprises some 450 interactive exhibits which make it the largest Science Center in the southeast. Its two top exhibit areas are: **Disasterville**, featuring WeatherQuest, an exhibition on the science behind tornados, hurricanes, wildfires and much more; and **The Amazing You**, which is about the human body and features a **High Wire Bike** where guests harness themselves onto a bicycle along a 98-foot-long steel cable, suspended 30 feet above ground. When little hands begin to tire, try an **IMAX** 3-D film in a domed theater, or a planetarium show. Alternatively, get back to nature in the museum's 47-acre backwoods which include a **butterfly garden**, a gopher and tortoise habitat and several acres of wetlands.

Family favourite zoo

Lowry Park Zoo – *7530 N. Blvd.* ⏰*Open year-round daily 9.30am– 5pm.* ◉*$20.95, child $15.95.* 📞*813- 935-8552. www.lowryparkzoo.com.* Rated best zoo in the US by *Parents* magazine, the near natural habitats here are home to 1,600 animals, including endangered species such as the Florida panther, Sumatran tiger and West Indian manatees.

EXCURSION
Hillsborough River State Park

20mi northeast in Thonotosassa.

▶ *From downtown, take I-4 east 6mi to US-301 north (Exit 6); follow this 14mi to park entrance on left at 15402 US- 301 N.* ⏰*Open year-round daily 8am– dusk.* ◉*$3.25/vehicle.* ⚠P 📞*813-987- 6771. www.dep.state.fl.us.*

Tampa's largest park covers nearly 4,000 acres of marshes, cypress swamps and pine flatwoods. Centerpiece of the park, the Hillsborough River cuts through outcroppings of Suwannee limestone and creates a series of Class II rapids *(contact Canoe Escape for 2hrs or full-day canoe/ kayak trips:* 📞*813-986-2067; www.canoe-escape.com).* Eight miles of marked trails, some with interpretive plaques, course along the river and through hammocks of magnolia, Sabal palm, hickory and live oak. Bring mosquito repellent in summer months.

Across US-301 sits a reconstruction of **Fort Foster,** which served as a supply depot from 1837–38 during the Second Seminole War *(🚶visit by 1hr guided tour only;* ⏰*open Dec–Mar daily on the hour 10am–2pm; rest of the year weekends only on the hour 10am–2pm;* ◉*$2;* P 📞*813-987-6771).* Gen. Zachary Taylor commanded the fort briefly in 1838. During the annual Rendezvous celebration (early Feb), soldiers in period uniforms interpret life in the rustic wooden fort. Tours begin just north of the ranger station at a small museum that displays Seminole War artifacts.

ADDRESSES

🏨 STAY

GENERAL INFORMATION

Area visitors' guide including **lodging directory** available *(free)* from **Tampa Bay Convention and Visitors Bureau. Reservation service:** ☎800-44-TAMPA. Accommodations range from luxury **hotels** and resorts *($120–$350)* to budget **motels** *($65–$120)* and **bed-and-breakfast inns** *($95–$150). Rates quoted are average prices per night for a double room and are subject to seasonal variations.*

$$$$ Don CeSar Beach Resort and Spa – *3400 Gulf Blvd., St. Petersburg Beach.* ✗&🅿🛏 ☎727-360-1881 *or* 800-282-1116. *www.doncesar.com. 277 rooms.* This flamingo-pink sand castle—complete with turrets and bell towers—is a St. Petersburg area landmark. Carrara marble fountains and Cuban tile floors evoke the ten-story Moorish-Mediterranean-style hotel's jazz-age heyday when F. Scott Fitzgerald was a regular; FDR and the New York Yankees baseball team also patronized the place in the 1920s and 30s. Elegantly designed in breezy Florida pastels and light woods, guest rooms overlook the Gulf of Mexico or Boca Ciega Bay.

$$$$ Renaissance Vinoy Resort – *501 Fifth Ave. N.E., St. Petersburg.* ✗& 🅿🛏 ☎727-894-1000 *or* 888-303-4430. *www.renaissancehotels.com. 360 rooms.* Babe Ruth was among the celebrities who wintered at this opulent Mediterranean Revival 1925 landmark, considered one of St. Pete's architectural jewels. The resort features a salmon-colored exterior facade, and restored lobby quarry-tile floors, stenciled cypress beams and frescoed ceilings. Bedrooms are done in contemporary furnishings and muted colors. Golf, tennis and tropical gardens enhance the site. The resort's downtown location is a plus.

$$$ Don Vicente de Ybor Historic Inn – *1915 Republica de Cuba (9th Ave. at 14th St.), Ybor City.* ✗&🅿 ☎813-241-4545. *http://donvicenteinn.com. 16 rooms.* Crystal chandeliers, Persian rugs, gilded furnishings and velvet draperies decorate this glitzy boutique hotel within Ybor City's lively Latin Quarter. Spacious suites feature draped beds, guest robes and slippers plus a private balcony—perfect for toasting the sunset. First owned by cigar-manufacturing entrepreneur Vicente Martinez Ybor, the two-story 1895 structure now includes a 100-seat restaurant and cigar and martini bar. The shops and restaurants of Seventh Avenue are a short walk away.

$$$ Mansion House B&B and the Courtyard on Fifth – *105 Fifth Ave. N.E., St. Petersburg.* &🅿🛏 ☎727-821-9391 *or* 800-274-7520. *www.mansionbandb. com. 13 rooms.* Cozy and casual, these two historic homes and carriage house create a comfortable oasis. Fresh flowers and hand-painted furniture add flair to guest rooms, while common areas and an outdoor pool make for pleasant places to mingle.

$$$ Saddlebrook Resort – *5700 Saddlebrook Way, Wesley Chapel.* ✗&🅿🛏 ☎813-973-1111 *or* 800-729-8383. *www.saddlebrook.com. 800 rooms.* Nestled among 480 acres of cypress-shaded countryside, this luxury retreat combines fine dining and spa pampering with two 18-hole Arnold Palmer-designed golf courses and 45 clay, grass and concrete tennis courts, plus a fitness center and 7,000sq ft spa. All rooms and suites feature a balcony or patio with views of the greens, the courts or the scenic surroundings.

$$ Belleview Biltmore Resort & Spa – *25 Belleview Blvd., Clearwater.* ✗& 🅿🛏 ☎727-373-3000 *or* 800-237-8947. *www.belleviewbiltmore.com. 246 rooms.* Perched on a bluff overlooking Clearwater Bay, this sprawling, Victorian structure (1897) was once a retreat for the elite, and sports indoor and outdoor swimming pools, tennis courts, a fitness center, spa and 18-hole golf course on its 21 acres. It is closed until sometime in 2012 for a $100-million-plus restoration and renovation.

$$ Safety Harbor Resort and Spa – *105 N. Bayshore Dr., Safety Harbor.* ✗& 🅿🛏 ☎727-726-1161 *or* 888-237-8772. *www.safetyharborspa.com. 193 rooms.* Built on springs sighted by Pánfilo de Narváez in 1528, this historic landmark, is one of the oldest US spas, and the only one in Florida with natural spring waters. Its 22-acre setting on Tampa Bay permits views of egrets, manatees and other wildlife. Indoor and outdoor pools brim with mineral water, while the 50,000sq ft spa and fitness center offers feet-to-face rejuvenation. Super-size guest rooms boast walk-through closets and large bathrooms.

$$ Seahorse Cottages and Apartments – *10356 Gulf Blvd., Treasure Island.* 🅿 *☏727-367-2291 or 800-741-2291. www.seahorse-cottages.com. 11 rooms.*
Tucked among the conventional motels and high-rise hotels lining Treasure Island's beachfront, these cottages offer vacationers a quaint accommodations alternative. Choices range from stand-alone cottages, some with decks and views of the beach, to second-floor apartments. The cabinlike quarters have a cozy feel and feature dark wood paneling and fully equipped kitchens. Picnic shelters, swings and beach chairs, flowering plants and palm trees enhance the common area.

$ Behind the Fence B&B – *1400 Viola Dr., Brandon.* 🅿 🛁 *☏813-685-8201. www.floridasecrets.com/fence.htm. 3 rooms, 2 cottages.* More country than cosmopolitan in its appearance and ambience, this Cracker-style house overflows with early-American antiques, authentic Amish quilts and hand-dipped candles. The one-bedroom cottages border a large tree-shaded backyard and swimming pool, while rooms in the two-story house overlook a quiet neighborhood.

♀/EAT

$$$ Bern's Steak House – *1208 Howard Ave., Tampa.* ♿*Dinner only.* ☏*813-251-2421. www.bernssteakhouse.com.* **American.** Hyde Park's 40-year-old landmark, and a Tampa tradition, offers more than 95 choices, including 21 types of caviar. Meat connoisseurs can pick from six different cuts of aged US prime beef, from chateaubriand to T-bone, served with garlic butter, soup, salad, baked potato, onion rings and home-grown, organic vegetables. The encyclopedic **wine list** has nearly 8,000 entries.

$$$ Chateau France – *136 4th Ave. N.E., St. Petersburg.* ♿ *Dinner only.* ☏*727-894-7163. www.chateaufranceonline.com.* **French.** This early-1900s house-turned-restaurant features intimate dining on two floors and a wraparound veranda for cocktails. Bright floral wallpaper, lace curtains, wood floors and fresh roses fashion an elegant interior, where red-vested servers dote on diners' every need.

$$ Columbia – *2117 E. 7th Ave., Ybor City.* ♿ ☏*813-248-4961. www.columbiarestaurant.com.* **Spanish.** Encompassing an entire block within Tampa's historic district, Florida's oldest operating restaurant (1905), still family-owned, is a bastion of Old World charm and Spanish-Cuban cuisine. Linen tablecloths, gracious service and hand-painted tiles throughout set the scene for tapas, gazpacho and Columbia's signature paella "A la Valenciana," the national dish of Spain. Choose a vintage label from the house cellar or try the freshly made fruit-filled sangria. Guests can also enjoy a flamenco dancing show (*Mon–Sat, charge*). Other locations in Clearwater Beach and St. Petersburg.

$$ Hurricane Seafood Restaurant – *807 Gulf Way, St. Petersburg Beach.* ♿ ☏*727-360-9558. www.thehurricane.com.* **Seafood.** For nearly four decades this popular, large beachfront bar, restaurant and nightclub has been the spot to watch the area's signature sunsets. From the rooftop deck of the third floor, beachgoers and business types alike enjoy drinks and 360 degrees of gulf, mainland and bay. The seafood matches the view, especially the local favorite—grouper, a flaky saltwater fish served grilled, broiled, blackened or fried.

$$ Mise en Place – *442 W. Kennedy Blvd., Tampa.* ♿ ☏*813-254-5373. www.miseonline.com.* **New American.** This acclaimed bistro is a trendy two-tier dining room within a 1920s building downtown, across the street from the Plant Museum. Arches and half walls separate the sprawling setting into intimate nooks where locals feast on ever-changing creative dishes, like Mediterranean tapas, Yucatán seared venison loin or LA pizza with figs.

$$ Salt Rock Grill – *19325 Gulf Blvd., Indian Shores.* &. ℘727-593-7625. *www.saltrockgrill.com.* **American.** Oversize glass and metallic fish dangle from the ceiling, while oversize fresh fish, packed in ice and on display, await tossing on the fire at this popular waterfront eatery. Named for the local limestone used in the restaurant's flooring, Salt Rock is famed for its wood-grilled steaks, chicken, Alaskan King Crab legs and lobster tail, served with fire-roasted vegetable kabobs. Diners overlook the intracoastal waterway from the Tiki Deck or from the main room's floor-to-ceiling windows. *Dinner only.*

$$ SideBern's – *2208 W. Morrison Ave., Tampa.* &. ℘813-258-2233. *www.sideberns.com.* **Modern Mediterranean.** Bern's less ornate, less sedate sister restaurant buzzes and bustles as diners fill the lounge, dim sum bar and main room. Sheer drapes soften the industrial-strength interior, which includes a back-lit stainless steel bar. Food here is inventive and edgy with entrées like hog snapper with ginger crab mojo.

$ Mykonos – *628 Dodecanese Blvd., Tarpon Springs.* &. ℘727-934-4306. **Greek.** White walls and blue accents brighten this modest, family-owned dining spot, where locals and visitors have flocked for almost a decade to enjoy authentic Greek cuisine. Baskets bulge with daily baked breads and plates overflow with Greek salad, lamb gyros and crispy *spanakotiropita* pastries. Fluent in the language, waitstaff are ready to help with tongue-twisting pronunciations of *soutzoukakia* and other specialties that issue from the open kitchen. After your meal, stroll the shops and sponge docks of this quaint riverside community.

$ Skipper's Smokehouse Restaurant – *910 Skipper Rd., Tampa.* ℘813-971-0666. *www.skipperssmokehouse.com.* **Seafood.** The weather-beaten walkways and overturned boats fronting this landmark restaurant belie its offshore location. Inside, the atmosphere is definitely beach style: laid back and low key. Seating is limited and the tiny **oyster bar** fills up fast, but overflow crowds can dine on alligator chili, garlic crab,

and steamed mud bugs (crawfish) under the stars at outside picnic tables. Nightly, reggae, blues and zydeco musicians perform beneath the Skipperdome's thatched awning, while patrons (some shoeless) head for the outdoor dance floor.

🛒 SHOPPING
Old Hyde Park Village, W. Swann Ave. at Dakota St. (℘813-251-3500; *www.hydeparkvillage.net*); **Centro Ybor,** between 7th and 9th Aves. at 16th St., Ybor City (℘813-242-4660; *www.centroybor.com*); **The Shops at Channelside,** 615 Channelside Dr. (℘813-254-3636; *www.channelside.com*); **International Plaza,** West Shore Blvd. at Spruce St. (south of the airport) (℘813-342-3790; *www.shopinternationalplaza.com*).

🎭 ENTERTAINMENT
Consult the arts and entertainment section in the local newspaper for a schedule of cultural events and addresses of principal theaters and concert halls.
Tampa Bay Performing Arts Center (℘813-229-7827; *www.tbpac.com*). For arts and sporting events tickets: **Ticketmaster** (℘813-287-8844; *www.ticketmaster.com*).

🏃 SPORTS AND RECREATION
Football: Tampa Bay Buccaneers (℘813-879-BUCS or 800-795-2827; *www.buccaneers.com*).

Baseball: Tampa Bay Devil Rays (St. Petersburg) (℘727-825-3120; *www.devilraysmlb.com*).

Hockey: Tampa Bay Lightning (℘813-301-6600; *www.tampabaylightning.com*).

Thoroughbred racing: Tampa Bay Downs (℘813-855-4401; *www.tampadowns.com*).

Greyhound racing: Tampa Greyhound Track (℘813-932-4313; *www.tampadogs.com*).

Public **golf courses:** Babe Zaharias (℘631-4374; *www.babezahariasgc.com*); Rocky Point Golf (℘813-673-4316; *www.rockypointgc.com*).

Tarpon Springs★

A taste of the Mediterranean flavors this small town on Florida's west coast. Best known as a commercial sponging center, Tarpon Springs derives much of its character from a close-knit Greek community, which fans out from the sponge docks on the Anclote River, an estuary of the Gulf of Mexico.

A BIT OF HISTORY

Arriving in 1876, the first settlers supposedly named the area Tarpon Springs for what they thought were tarpon in the mineral spring at the head of the bayou (in fact they were mullet). Sponge beds were discovered in the area in the 1870s, and soon thereafter the Key West commercial market moved its hub to Tarpon Springs. By the next decade, the town had developed as a winter resort and health spa. Wealthy 19C "snowbirds" built Victorian houses and bungalows around the graceful Golden Crescent that surrounds **Spring Bayou.** Beginning in 1905, expert sponge divers (most of whom hailed from the Dodecanese Islands near Crete) immigrated from Greece. Surpassing Key West, the Tarpon Springs sponge business peaked in the 1930s. By the late 1940s, a local blight, America's preference for synthetic sponges, and growing Mediterranean competition decimated the Florida market. In 1986, however, the Soviet nuclear-reactor disaster in Chernobyl wiped out Mediterranean beds, and Tarpon Springs became the largest natural sponge market in the world—with annual revenues of $7 million.

▶ **Population:** 22,651.
◔ **Michelin Map:** p330.
🛈 **Info:** 100 Dodecanese Blvd; ℘727-937-8028. Also at 11, E. Orange St.; ℘727-937-6109; www.tarpon springschamber.org.
▶ **Location:** Tarpon Springs is located approximately 15 miles north of Clearwater off US Hwy. 19.
🅿 **Parking:** Street parking and spaces in surface lots are easy to come by.
◉ **Don't Miss:** Visit the working shrimp and sponge boat docks, or take a cruise down the Anclote River on an authentic sponge boat.
🕐 **Timing:** Allow a half-day to explore the city, docks, and browse shops. Plan lunch at a Greek restaurant.
👥 **Kids:** Touch sting rays and sharks at the Tarpon Springs Aquarium.

Sponge Docks

© Richard Nowitz/Apa Publications

SIGHTS

Dodecanese Boulevard North★

North of Tarpon Ave., off N. Pinellas Ave./US-19A.

Running parallel to the Anclote River, this lively waterfront thoroughfare forms the commercial spine of the Greek community. While sidewalk vendors cater primarily to tourists who busily poke through bins of sponges and curios from the sea, the colorful family-run cafes and bakeries draw as many locals as out-of-towners to sample honey-soaked baklava and other Greek specialties that scent the air.

Near the east end of the boulevard, working shrimp and sponge boats are tied up at the main dock.

Here a **cruise**★ aboard one of the **St. Nicholas Boat Line** traditional sponging vessels *(departs from sponge docks year-round daily 10am–4pm; round-trip 30min; commentary; ☞$8; P ($2); ☎727-942-6425)* offers a demonstration of sponge harvesting. **Sun Line Cruises** also run tours, including to **Anclote Key**, which has a beautiful beach *(☞$20; ☎727-944-4468 www.sunlinecruises.com)*.

Across the street, the former **Sponge Exchange** *(no. 735; www.thespongeexchange.com)* now houses over 30 specialty shops and displays an early-20C sponge-diving boat in the plaza.

Sponge Diver
Visit Florida

The **Tarpon Springs Aquarium** *(no. 850; ☻open year-round Mon–Sat 10am–5pm, Sun noon–5pm; ☺closed Dec 25; ☞$7.75; ♿P ☎727-938-5378; www.tarponspringsaquarium.com)* features a 120,000-gallon aquarium full of 30 species of exotic fish and a touch tank filled with stingrays and baby sand sharks. Four times daily, a trained diver enters the tank and hand-feeds all of its inhabitants. There are also shark-feeding and alligator-feeding demonstrations.

St. Nicholas Greek Orthodox Cathedral

36 N. Pinellas Ave. ☻Open year-round Mon–Sat 9am–4pm, Sun 12:30pm–4pm. ♿P ☎727-937-3540. www.epiphanycity.org.

Crowned by a three-story central **rotunda** and soaring corner bell tower, this Byzantine Revival-style church of buff-colored brick was built in 1943 to accommodate the town's rapidly growing Greek Orthodox population. Site of one of the most elaborate Epiphany rituals in the US, the cathedral also draws thousands of pilgrims each year to view the glass-framed icon of St. Nicholas.

Unitarian Universalist Church

57 Read St. at Grand Blvd. ☞Visit by guided tour (25min) only, Nov–Apr Tue–Sun 2pm–5pm. ☺Closed major holidays. Contribution requested. P ☎727-937-4682. www.uutarpon.org.

The 1909 masonry edifice dominated by a crenellated tower has 11 **paintings**★ by **George Inness Jr.** (1854–1926), a Tarpon Springs seasonal resident.

Fred Howard Park

1700 Sunset Dr., 2mi west of downtown. ♿P ☎727-943-4081. www.pinellascounty.org/park.

A palm-shaded causeway leads out to this lovely island park, which features a pristine crescent of white-sand beach and an expansive view of the Gulf of Mexico. A favorite for fishing, sunning, swimming and jogging, nesting ospreys and eagles may sometimes be viewed as they fish for food. Dolphins and manatees are also seen in the area.

The stretch of Florida's east coast between Jupiter in north Palm Beach County and the city of Melbourne, 100 miles further north, has earned the moniker "Treasure Coast" in memory of the millions of dollars worth of sunken booty that has been recovered from its offshore waters.

A Bit of History

During the early 18C treasure fleets were sent every year by Spain on a sweep of the silver and gold mines in Mexico and South America. The return route threaded the Caribbean islands, then followed the Gulf Stream up to the Florida coastline. In July 1715 a fleet of Spanish galleons, laden with treasure, was driven by a hurricane onto the reefs off Florida's east coast. Eleven of the 12 ships went down beyond the barrier islands extending from St. Lucie Inlet to Sebastian Inlet. Around 700 people perished, but of more concern to the Spanish government was the loss of freight, valued at 17 million pesos. In fact, so dependent was Spain, and to a lesser extent, the rest of Europe, on these regular injections of precious metals and gems, that an economic depression resulted from their loss. The 1,500 or so shipwreck survivors set up camp on the shore opposite Sebastian and, with the help of local Ais Indians, began salvaging the sunken treasure. Though most was eventually recovered, much of the booty was looted by British pirates and spirited away to Jamaica.

Modern treasure hunters have determined, much to their delight, that the wrecked galleons carried treasure not even reported on ship manifests and a great deal of such undeclared cargo has been found off this coast in recent decades. And pieces of eight (17C Spanish pesos) and other artifacts still occasionally wash ashore after storms churn up the ocean waters.

By contrast with the neighboring Palm Beach area, the rate of expansion here has been slow. If you are traveling north-south you will be struck by the emergence of wide open natural spaces and quiet uncommercialized barrier-island beaches.

Highlights

1 Joining the US elite forces at the **UDT-SEAL Museum** (p353)

2 Tracing the past at St. Lucie **County Regional History Center** (p353)

3 Exploring the wilderness by boat at **Jonathan Dickinson SP** (p355)

4 Watching the water blow high at **Blowing Rocks Preserve** (p355)

Blowing Rocks Preserve

© Rich & Galina Leighton/Dreamstime.com

MELBOURNE, KENNEDY SPACE CENTER

Sebastian Inlet SP

TREASURE COAST

| 0 | | 10 mi |
| 0 | | 15 km |

Sebastian

Pelican Island NWR
Wabasso Beach

Wabasso

Indian River

Indian River Shores

A T L A N T I C

Vero Beach

O C E A N

ORLANDO

Harbor Branch
Oceanographic Institution

Jack Island
SPres

Urca de Lima

FORT PIERCE

■ **UDT-SEAL Museum** ★
▲ *Fort Pierce Inlet SP*
**St. Lucie Regional
History Center** ★

Florida Cracker Trail

St. Lucie

Hutchinson Island

■ **Energy Encounter**

Port St. Lucie

Indian River Drive

Jensen Beach

■ **Elliott Museum** ★
■ *Florida Oceanographic Coastal Center*
■ **Gilbert's Bar House of Refuge** ★
▲ **Bathtub Reef Beach**

Stuart

St. Lucie Inlet SP

OKEECHOBEE

ALLAPATTAH

▲ **Hobe Sound NWR**

Martin

Hobe Sound

Jupiter Island

St. Lucie Canal

Indiantown

★ *Jonathan
Dickinson
SP*

Florida's Tpk

FLATS

■ **Blowing Rocks Preserve** ★

Dupuis
Reserve
SF

↓ Jupiter Inlet

JUPITER

Palm Beach

■ **Marinelife Center**
Juno Beach

Loxahatchee
Slough

John D. MacArthur SP

North Palm Beach

MIAMI ↓ WEST PALM BEACH

Fort Pierce
and Hutchinson Island

This mid-sized coastal town exists on two shores: the cluttered business district that lies along the west side of the Intracoastal Waterway, and the tranquil beaches on nearby Hutchinson Island. Barrier-island beaches and 21 miles of inviting shoreline attract vacationers and second-home owners.

From the old downtown, Indian River Drive travels 16 miles south to Jensen Beach, offering fine views of the river and the hulking twin containers of the St. Lucie nuclear power station.

SIGHTS
UDT-SEAL Museum★
3300 N. A1A, in Pepper Park (1mi north of Fort Pierce Inlet State Park). ○*Open Jan–Apr Mon–Sat 10am–4pm, Sun noon–4pm. Rest of the year Tue–Sat 10am–4pm, Sun noon–4pm.* ○*Closed major holidays.* ⊕*$6.* ⏴🅿 ℰ*772-595-5845. www.navyseaalmuseum.com.*

Exhibits here vividly outline the history of the Navy SEALs (Sea, Air and Land)— the elite commando units—including life-size dioramas and films on SEAL operations. In the grounds are boats from World War II and the Vietnam War, and an *Apollo* space capsule.

Fort Pierce Inlet State Park
905 Shorewinds Dr. off A1A, south tip of North Hutchinson Island. ○*Open 8am–sunset.* ⊕*$6 per vehicle.* ⏴🅿 ℰ*772-468-3985. www.floridastate parks.org/fortpierceinlet.*

On the north of the Inlet, a scenic park preserves 340 acres of beachfront and maritime hammock. This is a peaceful place to surf and swim, or picnic and watch pleasure craft ply the waters.

St. Lucie County Regional History Center★
414 Seaway Dr. ○*Open year-round Tue–Sat 10am–4pm.* ○*Closed major holidays.* ⊕*$4.* 🅿 ℰ*772-462-1795. www.stlucieco.gov/history.*

▸ **Population:** 37,841.

◔ **Michelin Map:** p352.

ℹ **Info:** ℰ772-462-1535 or 800-344-8443; www.visitstluciefla.com.

▶ **Location:** 55mi north of West Palm Beach. Rte. 1 snakes through downtown and along the shoreline. Causeways provide access to north-south A1A, traveling along Hutchinson Island.

🅿 **Parking:** Garage and surface lots available downtown; free parking at most beaches (metered parking at Dollman Beach and Fort Pierce Inlet).

◉ **Don't Miss:** Take a scenic drive along A1A, stopping at beaches and parks along the way.

◔ **Timing:** Allow 2hrs plus beach time.

👫 **Kids:** The Florida Oceanographic Society Coastal Centeron Hutchinson Island has touch tanks and nature trails.

Housed in a replica of the town's Florida East Coast Railway station, this museum tells the story of Treasure Coast history. Exhibits include artifacts from the Ais Indians, who occupied the area more than 2,000 years ago, a 1715 treasure fleet, and early 19C storefronts and offices depicting pioneer life.

👫FP&L Energy Encounter
6501 S. A1A at Florida Power & Light Co., Jensen Beach. Entrance at Gate B on north side of plant. ○*Open year-round Mon–Fri 10am–4pm.* ○*Closed major holidays.* ⏴🅿 ℰ*772-468-4111 or 877-375-4386. www.fpl.com.*

A perfect rainy-day activity for children, the facility offers hands-on displays that explore the worlds of electricity, nuclear power, energy conservation and envi-

© Jurie Maree/Dreamstime.com

Sea Turtles

Large air-breathing reptiles of the families *Dermochelyidae* and *Cheloniidae*, sea turtles inhabit all but the coldest of the earth's oceans. Five of the world's eight species of sea turtles frequent Florida waters; all are endangered, except the loggerhead (*Caretta caretta*), which is threatened. Atlantic green turtles (*Chelonia mydas*), leatherbacks and an occasional hawksbill (*Eretmochelys imbricata*) nest along the Atlantic coast of Florida between Cape Canaveral and Palm Beach. Loggerheads nest along both the Atlantic and Gulf coasts; the Kemps Ridley turtle is predominantly found in Gulf of Mexico waters.

During June and July, a variety of local organizations offer guided "turtle walks" to known nesting sites along the coast. Lucky groups may see nesting females or even tiny hatchlings. Led by a naturalist or park ranger, the walks take place after dark and can last several hours. Contact local visitor centers for a list of organizations offering walks and make reservations well in advance of your trip, as these popular walks tend to fill up quickly.

ronmental protection. Manatees are occasionally spotted in the warm waters outside the plant. A boardwalk nature trail *(1mi)* traverses Turtle Beach.

HUTCHINSON ISLAND

This 22mi-long spit of land is home to condominiums, golf courses, high-rise hotels and beach cottages, covering much of the island's south end. Despite this development, long, unhurried beaches remain, enticing visitors.

Take a leisurely drive, stopping at sights along the way.

The Florida Oceanographic Society Coastal Center (*890 N.E. Ocean Blvd.; 772-225-0505; http://floridashutchinsonisland.com*) includes a marine-education center, two trails *(1mi and 0.75mi)*, aquariums, touch tanks and computer games. The site provides excellent opportunities for education and research aimed at increasing the general knowledge of these unique environments. **Gilbert's Bar House of Refuge** (*301 S.E. MacArthur Blvd.; 772-225-1875; www.elliottmuseumfl.org*) at the **Elliott Museum**★ was erected in 1875 to aid shipwrecked sailors. The boathouse displays antique lifesaving equipment and other marine artifacts, while the main museum features a historical gallery, antique cars and vintage vehicles, and a collection of local social reformer Sterling Elliott's most notable inventions.

Bathtub Reef Beach (*on MacArthur Blvd., 2.3mi south of A1A*) is a favorite with families: it has a shallow wading area created by an 85-acre offshore reef.

Jupiter

Jupiter is a thriving blend of businesses, upscale resorts, and golf and yachting communities. The area's wide public beaches and numerous reefs attract snorkelers and surfers, as well as thousands of sea turtles that nest on the shores.

SIGHTS

Loggerhead Marinelife Center

Juno Beach Park. Open year-round Mon–Sat 10am–5pm, Sun noon–4pm. Closed major holidays. Contributions requested. Turtle walks in summer. &P 561-627-8280. www.marine life.org.

Dedicated to rehabilitation and research of the area's sea turtles, the Center has scores of turtle mounts and skeletons, including a giant prehistoric sea turtle skeleton, along with four aquariums and hands-on displays. Staff explain how injured turtles are cared for until they can be released back into the sea.

Jupiter Inlet Lighthouse & Museum

Jupiter Lighthouse Park. Visit by guided tour (1hr) only. Open year-round Tue–Sat 10am–5pm. Closed major holidays. $7. P 561-747-6639. www.lrhs.org.

George Meade, commander of the Union forces at Gettysburg, designed this bright red beacon, which reigns as the county's oldest surviving structure. Visitors may climb the 105 steps to the top of the lighthouse tower for a birds-eye **view** of the surrounding area.

Jonathan Dickinson State Park★

7mi north of Rte. 706 on US-1. Open 8am–sunset. $6 /vehicle. ▲ P 772-546-2771. www.floridastateparks.org.

This 11,500-acre tract of land and river contains the largest piece of sand-pine scrub in southeast Florida and shelters alligators, manatees, gopher tortoises and bald eagles. Visitors can walk the **Hobe Mountain Trail** *(0.5mi)* to a high

- ▶ **Population:** 45,100.
- **Michelin Map:** p352.
- **Info:** 800 North US Highway One; 561-746-7111; www.jupiterfl.org.
- **Location:** North end of the Palm Beach County coast.
- **P Parking:** Parking is free along Jupiter Beach.
- **Don't Miss:** A boat tour on the Loxahatchee River at Jonathan Dickinson State Park.
- **Timing:** Allow at least a day.
- **Kids:** Loggerhead Marinelife Center to see recovering sea turtles.

sand ridge topped by a 26ft wooden observation tower that provides a **panorama** of the flatlands and beyond to the Atlantic. A tour boat plies the scenic Loxahatchee River, through primeval wilderness (*departs from boat dock in park year-round Wed–Sun 9am, 11am, 1pm & 3pm; round-trip 2hrs; commentary; $14.50; P 561-746-1466*).

Blowing Rocks Preserve★

S. Beach Rd., 1.8mi north of Jupiter Inlet. Guided walks year-round Sun 11am. Open year-round daily 9am–4:30pm. $2. P 561-744-6668. www.nature.org/wherewework.

Extending for nearly a mile along the beach, this large limestone outcropping contains fissures that become waterspouts during very high tides, creating dramatic plumes up to 50ft high.

Hobe Sound National Wildlife Refuge

2.5mi north of Bridge Rd. (entrance at dead-end of Beach Rd.). Open year-round daily dawn–dusk. $5/vehicle. P 772-546-6141 or 772-546-2067. www.fws.gov/hobesound.

At the north end of Jupiter Island, 735 acres of wild coastal habitat provide a refuge for the area's diverse animal and plant life. Guided turtle walks begin at **Hobe Sound Nature Center**.

THE BAHAMAS

This archipelago of coral islands, surrounded by what are said to be the clearest waters in the world, are located just 55 miles off the southeast coast of Florida, easily accessible by cruise ship from Miami or Port Everglades, which sail mostly to Nassau (the capital) and Freeport. The name Bahama derives from the Spanish *baha mar*, meaning "shallow sea," an apt description of the reef-strewn turquoise waters.

Highlights

1 Haggling in the **Staw Market** at Nassau (p361)
2 Big-game fishing or looking for Atlantis off **Bimini** (p364)
3 Chilling by day and partying by night at **Cable Beach** (p365)
4 A day at **Aquaventure water park** at Atlantis Resort (p366)
5 Swimming with dolphins off **Grand Bahama** (p368)

A Bit of History

The Bahamas were the site of Columbus' first landfall in the New World in 1492. The Spanish never colonised the islands though they did ship the natives into slavery in Hispaniola (today's Haiti/Dominican Republic). British colonists arrived in 1650 and have stayed on in some form or another until the present day. The Bahamas are now an independent member of the British Commonwealth.

Today more than 3.5 million visitors annually—many of whom arrive via cruise ship—are drawn to this tropical Caribbean island group. In total there are 29 islands (though definitions of "island" and "cay" can vary), and a further 661 small, mostly uninhabited rocky cays.

The principal islands are New Providence, Paradise Island and Grand Bahama; the less-developed Out Islands (also called the Family Islands) include Acklins, Bimini, Cat, Crooked, Eleuthera, Long, Mayaguana, Ragged and San Salvador islands; the Abacos, Berry, Exuma and Inagua groups; and Rum Cay. The largest island is Andros, famous for one of the longest coral reefs★★★ in the world, which extends 140 miles along its eastern edge.

Serviced by commercial airlines and inter-island boats, the Out Islands are gaining popularity, particularly among sailing, fishing, snorkeling, diving and birding enthusiasts. They boast pristine beaches and residents who are even more easygoing and friendly than those on the main islands.

Harbour Island

© Bahamas Tourist Office

Resort roofs of Paradise Island

© Ramunas Bruzas/Dreamstime.com

New Providence Island★

As the governmental and commercial center of the Bahamas, New Providence teems with activity. Despite being one of the smaller islands in the Bahamas, it claims more than 60 percent of the country's total population. The island's historic heart, Nassau, still retains a traditional British flavor, while modern American resorts rise nearby, particularly on Paradise Island to which New Providence is now connected.

A BIT OF HISTORY

A Providential Place – Lucayan Indians had occupied the Bahamas for more than 500 years before when **Christopher Columbus** arrived in the Caribbean in 1492. The **Lucayans**, enslaved by the Spanish to work mines on Hispaniola, were victims of disease and poor treatment. They were virtually extinct within 25 years of Columbus' arrival.

The Age of Empire – At the end of the 17C, the British began to exercise control over the island when Proprietary Governor Nicholas Trott arrived. The settlement and its harbor soon became a center for British privateers involved in plundering Spanish and French ships

▸ **Population:** 330,000.
◔ **Michelin Map:** pp362–363.
▤ **Info:** Market Plaza, Bay Street, Nassau; ℘242-322-7500; www.bahamas.com.
◖ **Location:** 180mi off the coast of southern Florida, New Providence is 22mi long and 7mi wide at its widest point.
👥 **Kids:** Aquaventure waterpark at Atlantis resort.

in the Caribbean and for wreckers salvaging vessels that had gone down on the treacherous offshore reefs. In the early 18C the island's first Royal Governor, **Woodes Rogers,** transformed the rundown, garbage-strewn town of Nassau into a "civilized place." In the 1780s the modestly prospering island witnessed a new influx of refugees as American Loyalists to the British Crown fled the Revolution.

American events continued to affect Bahamian prospects throughout the 19C and 20C. In the 1920s American Prohibition brought further prosperity as local **rum runners** became involved in smuggling liquor to mainland bootleggers, and American gangsters and gamblers flocked to Nassau. Interest in tourism outlasted the end of Prohibition in the

WHEN TO GO

Weather in the Bahamas is pleasant all year. High season is mid-Dec through mid-Apr: hotel reservations should be made well in advance. During the winter months *(Nov–Feb)* temperatures average 72°F/22°C, while southern trade winds keep the islands comfortable during the summer months when temperatures average 80°F/27°C. From Jun through Oct showers are frequent but brief.
Planning your Trip – Citizens of the US, Canada, Mexico, Central and South America, the Caribbean and Bermuda must present a passport or similar document. **Bahamas Tourist Office in Florida:** 19495 Biscayne Blvd., Suite 809, Aventura FL 33180, *℘305-932-0051 or 800-327-7678 (US).*

GETTING THERE

BY AIR – Major US and international airlines fly into **Nassau International Airport** and **Freeport International Airport. Bahamasair** (*℘242-377-8451; www.bahamasair.com)* provides regular service from Nassau to most of the Out Islands.
BY SEA – The following **cruise lines** operate from Port Everglades: **Discovery** (*www.discoverycruiseline.com*) offer one-day all-inclusive fun cruises and vacation packages staying for one or more nights on Gran Bahama; **Disney** (*http://disneycruise.disney.go.com*) offer 3, 4, and 5 nights;

Carnival (*www.carnival.com*) offer 2, 3 and 4 nights; **Royal Caribbean** (*www.royalcaribbean.com)* offer 3 or 4 nights; NCL (*www2.ncl.com*) offer 3 or 4 nights, sailing from Miami.

GETTING AROUND

BY CAR AND TAXI – **Scooters** *($50/day)* and **bicycles** *($10/day)* can be rented throughout the islands. **Taxis:** Four Seasons Executive Service (*℘242-423-3777; www.bahamas.com/vendor/four-seasons-executive-service)* and Godfrey Simms Taxi Service (*℘242-324 5050; www.taxi516.com).* Small buses called **"jitneys"** are the most economical way to get around the islands *(daily dawn–dusk; $1-$2; exact change required).*
If you want to **island-hop** and have time to spare, the best option is to use the mail-boat network. The hub of this is Nassau so for the latest scehdule contact the Dock Master's Office in Nassau, under the Paradise Island Bridge on Potter's Cay (*℘242-393-1064)*

VISITOR INFORMATION

Bahamas Ministry of Tourism, PO Box N 3701, Market Plaza, Bay Street, Nassau (*℘242-322-7500; www.bahamas.com)* provides information regarding accommodations, shopping, entertainment and recreation.

Foreign Exchange – The Bahamian dollar is equivalent to the US dollar.

1930s, resulting in the development of Cable Beach as a resort area.
Today – Over half of all visitors to the Bahamas spend time here. Nassau also ranks as a regular port-of-call for some 30 cruise ships, which deliver about a million visitors to its shores annually.

NASSAU★★

Long the center of the island's tourism, Nassau's historic heart beats along 25 blocks of the harbor front bordered by Bay Street on the north, Hill Street on the south, Elizabeth Avenue to the east, and West Street to the west. Along Bay Street, countless duty-free shops cater to cruise-ship passengers, while quieter side streets shade classic pink-and-white Bahamian Colonial structures.

St. Matthew's Anglican Church

Shirley St. west of Mackey St. ⓞ*Open year-round daily 9am–5pm.* ♿ *℘242-323-8220. www.stmatthews.org.bs.*
The oldest extant church structure (1802) in the Bahamas, the simple rectangular stone edifice with its Neoclassical detailing was originally referred to

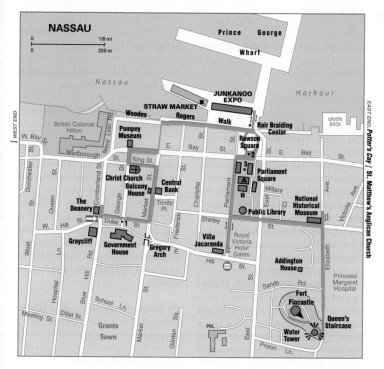

as the "eastern church," since it served parishioners on that side of town. A chancel, organ chamber and vestry room were added in 1887. The extensive cemetery surrounding the church contains headstones covering two centuries.

Potter's Cay

Just north of the intersection of E. Bay and Mackey Sts. ⊙*Open year-round daily 7am–8pm.* ♿🅿.

Located beneath the Paradise Island bridge, the stalls of this colorful marketplace feature an array of fresh fruits, vegetables and seafood. Island fishermen tie up at the dockside market to sell conch, lobster, grouper and other local specialties.

🐾 OLD TOWN WALK

Begin at the intersection of West Hill St. and Cumberland St., which becomes Blue Hill Rd.

Graycliff

10 W. Hill St. (on corner of Cumberland St./ Blue Hill Rd.).

One of the oldest hotels in the Bahamas, this dignified Georgian Colonial structure with its foot-thick limestone walls and two-story veranda is attributed by legend to Capt. John Howard Graysmith. The daring privateer of the schooner *Graywolf*, Graysmith is said to have built the house in the mid-18C on the site of Nassau's first Anglican church. By 1844 the building had become Nassau's first inn, and today Graycliff still operates as a fine inn and restaurant (*www.graycliff. com*). The interior is furnished with early 20C pieces, including a Baccarat chandelier that graces the entrance hall.

A half-block north on Cumberland Street stands **The Deanery** *(west side).*

Built at the turn of the 19C as a parsonage for Christ Church, this three-story stone building with its lattice timber gallery is considered the oldest extant residence in Nassau.

▶ *Cross Cumberland St. and walk briefly south; turn left (east) on Duke St.*

Broad stone steps on the street's south side lead to Government House. A statue of **Christopher Columbus (1)**, situated about halfway up the staircase, looks out over the town.

Government House
Corner of Blue Hill Rd. and Duke St.
Not open for public tours.
The stately white-columned, pink mansion now crowning Mount Fitzwilliam was built in 1932, one in a succession of official residences of Governors General dating from the 1730s. In the 1940s the **Duke and Duchess of Windsor** occupied the building during the Duke's tenure as Governor General of the Bahamas. (The Duke had reigned briefly as Edward VIII before abdicating to marry American divorcee Wallis Simpson.)
On alternate Saturdays, a public **Changing of the Guard** ceremony is held here, accompanied by music provided by the Royal Bahamas Police Force Band (*open year-round every other Sat 10am*). The Governor General also hosts a **public tea party** at Government House on the last Friday of every month (*open Jan–Aug 4pm–5pm; reservations and proper attire required; 242-326-5371*).

▷ *Continue east on Duke St. to the intersection with Market St.*

Note the stone archway on the south end of the street: known as **Gregory Arch,** it0 was built in the 1850s and served as an access point to Grant's Town, one of the traditionally black "over the hill" neighborhoods.

▷ *Turn left on Market St. and continue one block.*

Balcony House (*Market St. and Trinity Pl.; closed to the public*) is distinctive for its cantilevered balcony. Built of American cedar and over 200 years old, the house also features a staircase believed to have been part of a ship. Directly across Market Street, the **Central Bank of the Bahamas** devotes its public lobby area to changing exhibits of works by Bahamian and foreign artists.

▷ *Continue one block north on Market to King St. Turn left on King and walk west one block to George St.*

Christ Church Cathedral
George and King Sts.
Established in 1670, Christ Church was the first Anglican church in the Bahamas. The current Gothic Revival edifice with its stone buttresses and timbered, trussed interior roof was constructed in 1840 and is the fifth church on the site;

Government House

© Lena Bernatsky/Dreamstime.com

Straw Market

© Ray Wadia/The Bahamas Ministry of Tourism

the two east bays were added subsequently. It was designated the cathedral of the diocese in 1861.

▷ *Turn right on George St. and walk one block north to Bay St.*

The historical **British Colonial Beach Resort** (now a Hilton property) anchors the north end of East Bay Street, former site of Fort Nassau (1695–1899). At the turn of the 19C the railroad and hotel magnate Henry Flagler built the spacious Hotel Colonial on this spot. When fire destroyed it in 1922, the government purchased the land and constructed a new hotel, later bought by Sir Harry Oakes and renamed the British Colonial.

▷ *Cross Bay St. to north side.*

Pompey Museum
Bay St., at George St. ◷*Open year-round Mon–Fri 9am–5pm.* ◷*Closed major holidays.* ✑*$1.* ℘*242-326-2566; www.bahamasgo.com/treasures/pompey.htm.*
This museum devoted to the history and culture of the Bahamas occupies historic Vendue House, a well-proportioned two-story stone structure with arched bay windows. Built as a public market in the mid-18C, it served as the site of slave auctions. Exhibits trace the hardships and brutality of slave life, and the coming of emancipation. A second-story gallery features a display of the **paintings★** of local folk artist **Amos Ferguson**.

▷ *Continue 1 block east on Bay Street.*

As you walk east on Bay Street, you'll pass numerous shops selling duty-free liquors, European crystals, gems, perfumes and other merchandise.

Straw Market★
Bay St. across from Market St. ◷*Open year-round Mon–Sat 7am–6pm.* ♿ ℘*242-363-6000.*
Famous throughout the Caribbean, Nassau's labyrinthine Straw Market consists of a warren of small stalls where vendors, most of them women by tradition, hawk a plethora of inexpensive straw goods, T-shirts, local wood carvings and other items designed to tempt tourists. Straw-plaiting and straw work have long been done by Bahamian women, particularly on the Out Islands. Haggling with the market's vendors over the price of goods is part of the fun here.
The adjacent **Junkanoo Expo** is dedicated to the Bahamian equivalent of Mardi Gras that takes place on 26 Dec.

▷ *Walk through the market to its north, waterfront side.*

Woodes Rogers Walk
Named for the Bahamas first Royal Governor, this walk leads along the dock area to shady **Rawson Square**, in the center of which is a statue (**2**) of Sir Milo Butler, first Bahamian Governor-General. Across from the north side of the square, an open-air plaza serves as the popular

hair-braiding center, where Bahamian women negotiate with tourists to plait their hair into tiny braids, or cornrows. Behind lies the capacious dock area of **Prince George Wharf**. Large commercial cruise ships on tour through the Caribbean dock here—some only overnight—to allow their passengers to visit Nassau.

▶ *Walk north to Rawson Square and cross to south side of Bay Street.*

Parliament Square

Governmental hub of the Bahamas, the square is centered on a **statue (3)** of a serenely young Queen Victoria. Three pink-and-white public buildings, built in the early 19C and modeled on the Tryon Palace in New Bern, North Carolina, flank the statue. The columned Southern Colonial structure in the middle serves as the **House of Assembly (A)**. Behind this edifice, more pink official buildings, including the stately, colonnaded **Supreme Court (B)** (1921), overlook the Garden of Remembrance, a palm-shaded greensward commemorating Bahamians who lost their lives while fighting beside the British in World Wars I and II.

▶ *Walk south up Parliament Street and cross Shirley Street.*

Two gateposts on the east side of Parliament Street bear the insignia of the **Royal Victoria Hotel,** once the Bahamas' most fashionable hostelry. Built in the mid-19C, the elegant building played host to Confederate blockade runners and Prohibition-era rumrunners. Fire ravaged it in 1990 and Hurricane Andrew further devastated the ruins.

Across Parliament Street, just below the intersection with East Hill Street, stands gracious **Villa Jacaranda** (⚍ *not open to the public*), whose double galleries, shutters and stone exterior exemplify

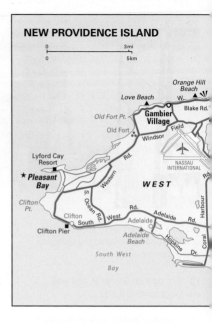

the Loyalist architectural tradition prevalent in Nassau in the mid-19C.

▶ *Walk one block north to Shirley St. and turn right (east).*

The octagonal **Nassau Public Library,** on the south edge of Parliament Square *(corner of Parliament and Shirley Sts.)*, is topped by a third-floor wraparound gallery and belfry, whose bell once summoned members to openings of the House of Assembly. Originally constructed as a prison at the turn of the 18C, it became a public library in 1873.

▶ *From the library, continue east on Shirley Street.*

After passing the intersection *(left side)* of Millars Court, note the expansive lawn that sweeps upward to the mid-19C **Addington House,** formerly the official residence of the Anglican Bishop of Nassau and the Bahamas.

▶ *Walk east on Shirley St. to the intersection with Elizabeth St. and turn left.*

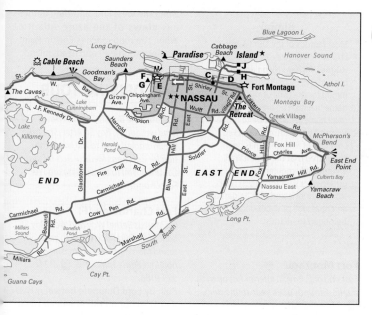

National Historical Museum/ Bahamas Historical Society

Northwest corner of Shirley and Elizabeth Sts. Open Sept–Jun Mon, Tue, Thu, Fri 10am–4pm, Sat 10am– noon. Closed major holidays. $1. 242-322-4231. http://bahamas historicalsociety.com.

Since 1976 this former hall of the Daughters of the Empire has been used by the Bahamas Historical Society to display Lucayan Indian stone tools, crockery and artifacts from the Loyalist period, old photographs and personal memorabilia.

Walk south one block along Elizabeth Street.

Hewn into the rock of Bennet's Hill, the steep, 66-step **Queen's Staircase** occupies a surprisingly sylvan setting, next to a pleasant waterfall spilling over fern-draped rocks. The stairs were purportedly built by slaves in the 1790s to allow access to Fort Fincastle.

Located at the top of the Queen's Staircase.

Fort Fincastle

Open year-round daily 8am–5pm.
This small fort, atop the town's highest point (74ft) and shaped like a paddle wheeler, was built by Lord Dunmore in the 1790s. Today the ramparts command a fine view of the waterfront and much of the island's interior.

The 126ft **water tower** adjacent to the fort was built in 1928 and is topped by a beacon light. No longer used as a water tower, it now houses an elevator that whisks visitors to an open-air observation deck with 360-degree **views**★ of the island's interior and its eastern shoreline (50¢).

EAST END

Threaded by Eastern Road and more densely populated than the West End, the island's East End is devoted to pleasant waterfront homes and the local community of Fox Hill.

Rocky **Yamacraw Beach** curves below McPherson's Bend at the eastern tip of the island. The drive along Eastern Road skirts the shoreline framed by elegant homes and ends at **East End Point**, where a panoramic **view** encompasses cerulean waters and offshore cays.

Bimini

Most famous of the Out Islands, Ernest Hemingway, Howard Hughes, Richard Nixon and many others have all been lured to Bimini for the thrill of the big-game fishing. The biggest catch of all however would be to prove that this is the site of the fabled Lost City of Atlantis. It has been suggested that the Bimini Wall, an unusually regular-shaped underwater rock formation near North Bimini island may be part of an entire wall or water dock that belonged to Atlantis.

Fort Montagu

East end of E. Bay St. Interior not open to public. Grounds open year-round daily. 🅿 ✆242-325-2212.
Commanding the east entrance to the harbor, the small stone battlement (1742) is the oldest extant fort on the island. It was the second fort to be constructed after Fort Nassau and was intended to ward off possible attack by Spanish forces. A roadside beach on Montagu Bay stretches south from the fort.

The Retreat

Village Rd., south of the intersection with Shirley St. and Eastern Rd. 🕐*Open year-round Mon–Fri 9am–5pm.* 🕐*Closed holidays & Dec 25–Jan 1.* ⊚*$2.* 🅿 ✆242-393-1317. www.bnt.bs/parks_retreat.php.
This 11-acre botanical preserve features 92 genera of rare and exotic **palms**★, including species from Asia, Africa, Australia, and North and South America. Shaded paths weave past mahogany and cedar trees and orchids.

WEST END

This sparsely settled part of the island is home to two large lakes (Killarney and Cunningham), the airport, several private resort complexes, and a number of commercial sites.
After West Bay Street leaves the historic district, it hugs the coastline along the West End, affording numerous **views** of the azure Atlantic. When the road reaches Clifton Point, it swings southeast and heads inland.

🚗 DRIVING TOUR

▷ *From the British Colonial Hotel, head west on W. Bay St. After .5mi take the unmarked road to the left at the sign for Bahamas Medical Arts Institute. Continue .3mi to the parking area for Fort Charlotte.*

Fort Charlotte★ (F)

On Marcus Bethel Way and West Bay St. behind Clifford Park. 🕐*Open year-round Mon–Sat 8am–4pm, Sun & holidays 8am–3pm.* ⊚*$5.* 🅿 ✆242-325-9186.
Built by Lord Dunmore between 1787 and 1796 during the American Loyalist period, the island's largest fortress complex actually comprises three forts: the original eastern portion, Fort Charlotte, named for George III's queen; the middle section, Fort Stanley; and the western works, Fort D'Arcy. Occupying a hill overlooking the town and harbor, the fortress was constructed of stone and armed with some 40 guns. Fort Charlotte never saw battle and ceased to function in a military capacity in 1891; an enormously expensive construction it is known as "Dunmore's Folly."
Today various casemates, living quarters and parapets are open to the public, as is a loosely re-created "pirate's torture chamber." The battlements of Fort Stanley offer a panoramic **view** of the island and western harbor.

▷ *Return to W. Bay St. and continue west. Turn left on Chippingham Ave. and continue .3mi. Turn right at sign for zoo.*

Ardastra Gardens and Zoo (G)

Off Chippingham Ave., just west of Botanic Gardens. 🕐*Open year-round daily 9am–5pm.* 🕐*Closed Dec 25, 26, Jan 1.* ⊚*$15.* ✖& ✆242-323-5806. www.ardastra.com.

A 5.5-acre commercial animal park, Ardastra comprises a series of small cages set amid lush vegetation. Around 60 species are represented, including tropical birds, monkeys and reptiles. A troupe of marching Caribbean flamingos (the national bird) performs several times daily.

▷ *Return to W. Bay St., turn left and continue west .5 mi.*

Following the curve of the shoreline, you will pass **Saunders Beach,** a narrow but popular roadside beach with views out to Crystal and Long cays. After rounding Brown's Point, the road bends south along **Goodman's Bay,** another roadside beach. A sweeping view here scans the high rises of Cable Beach.

Cable Beach ⚓

Sometimes called the Bahamian Riviera, Cable Beach rises in a gleam of towering hotels and casinos that virtually wall off the beach itself. In 1892 a telegraph cable was laid between this point and Jupiter, Florida, providing the first such communication between the Bahamas and the North American mainland and giving the beach its name. Pineapples were cultivated along this stretch of the island until the 1920s, when Americans began building fine vacation homes here. Sir Harry Oakes, a Canadian entrepreneur, began developing Cable Beach as a major resort—complete with casino—in the 1930s. The area remains a mix of tourist facilities along its eastern half and upscale private homes to the north. A lovely stand of casuarina trees overarches portions of the road through the residential section.

▷ *Continue west on W. Bay Street.*

After crossing the Sandyport Bridge, the road returns to the water's edge. A pink house *(private)* hugging a point *(.8mi beyond the bridge)* was used as one of the settings from the James Bond movie *Thunderball*. After .6mi, look to the left for **The Caves,** a limestone labyrinth once used by Lucayan Indians and now home to a colony of bats. Beyond this, the road curves past long, narrow **Orange Hill Beach.** At the intersection of West Bay Street and Blake Road *(.2mi farther on)*, notice the *Ficus benjamina* tree in the intersection's grassy triangle. US President John F. Kennedy planted the tree in 1962 in commemoration of his meeting on the island with the prime ministers of Canada and Britain.

▷ *Continue west 2mi past Blake Rd.*

Gambier Village

This hamlet is one of the oldest settlements on the island. Liberated Africans, freed from Caribbean slave ships by the Royal Navy, established Gambier Village

Cable Beach Resort

© Bahamas Tourist Office

Aquaventure, Atlantis Resort

© Kerzner International Holdings Limited

Paradise Island★

Now a mega-resort complex, the 826-acre island (5.5mi long and .6mi at its widest) on the north side of Nassau Harbour was for centuries called Hog Island—reportedly so-named by Nicholas Trott after his father's estate in Hog Bay, Bermuda. Early in the 20C wealthy Americans established a winter colony of vacation homes here. The island's quiet tenor remained unchanged until 1959, when American grocery-store heir and philanthropist Huntington Hartford bought a large parcel on the island: determined to develop its resort potential, Hartford successfully petitioned the government to change the name from Hog to Paradise. Though his endeavors failed financially, they did succeed in establishing the tourist potential of Paradise Island. In 1967 the current arcing bridge—1,500ft long and 70ft at its pinnacle—was built, linking it to Nassau.

Today, the island is famous for pristine beaches and luxury resorts, including the mega-size **Atlantis** resort (*☎888-528-7155 or 954-809-2100; www.atlantis. com*). The lavish resort includes **Aquaventure**, one of the largest waterparks in the Eastern Hemisphere which includes aquariums featuring some of the largest sealife tanks in the world. Aquaventure is open to non-guests (*$110 per adult, $80 per child; includes, towels, deck chairs and access to grounds*).

as a farming community shortly after 1807. Recently it has become a tourist destination with the development of Compass Point, a resort identifiable by its small but vividly colored oceanfront cottages. Beyond Compass Point, the road passes the fine houses of **Love Beach** for 3.5mi, before reaching the entrance gates to exclusive **Lyford Cay**, a private gated community (*not open to the public*) frequented by film stars and royalty.

▶ *From Lyford Cay continue south 2.5mi. Go right at turnoff for Pleasant Bay, marked by a sign for Atlantis Submarines.*

Pleasant Bay★

A crescent beach with public access edges the southern half of the small protected bay here, culminating in Clifton Point. The bay's northern half fronts the exclusive homes of Lyford Cay. The dock was used as a set in one of the *Jaws* movies and now serves as a starting point for submarine excursions to the offshore reef.

▶ *Return to the main road and continue south 1mi. Freighters exporting rum and importing commodities dock at Clifton Pier at the tip of the island.*

Grand Bahama Island

The second-most-visited island in the archipelago and fourth-largest in the chain (measuring 96 miles by 17 miles at its widest), Grand Bahama lies a mere 55 miles east of Florida. The bustling towns of Freeport and Lucaya, established in the mid-20C, were specifically developed for tourism and commerce.

A BIT OF HISTORY

Covered in pines for much of its history, Grand Bahama was first home to Lucayan Indians who inhabited the land prior to the Spanish arrival in the Caribbean. After their decimation, the island supported few inhabitants until the 1870s, when sponge fishermen settled here. The West End of the island became a major hub for rum runners until the repeal of Prohibition in the 1930s. The island economy was soon to receive another blow when a blight destroyed Bahamian sponges.

A new boom began in 1944 when the Abaco Lumber Co. relocated here, having exhausted the pine forests on Abaco Island. Four years later, **Wallace Groves,** an American entrepreneur living in the Bahamas, purchased the failing company and made it profitable. In 1955 he entered into the **Hawksbill Agreement** with the Bahamian government, which allowed him to develop a free port on the island, where goods could be imported without heavy duty taxes. Infrastructure for residential and resort areas was eventually laid out around the inland administrative area that was to become Freeport and the oceanside resort area of Lucaya. The island never developed as Groves had hoped. To bolster his failing investment, he opened a casino at the Lucayan Beach Hotel in 1963. Gambling rather than commerce became the lifeblood of the island. Groves' infrastructure was developed to support half a million people, but only about 46,000 now live on Grand Bahama. The network of roads, intended

for residential areas, lead only into the pine barrens. Activity revolves around resorts and the shopping complexes of Freeport and Lucaya. A harbor on the island's southwest edge accommodates a host of cruise and cargo ships.

FREEPORT

Built as the administrative and commercial core of the island, the inland town of Freeport revolves around the business and governmental activities of **Churchill Square** (intersection of E. Mall Dr. and Pioneers Way), the tourist activities at **International Square** (intersection of W. Sunrise Hwy. and E. Mall Dr.) and the extensive Bahamas Princess Resort and Casino complex that adjoins it. **Xanadu Beach,** adjacent to the Xanadu Hotel on the south shore of Freeport, offers a lovely stretch of white sand.

Along the island's west end, a string of small towns remains largely the domain of Bahamians, though the hamlet of West End itself, on the far tip of the island, holds a modest marina that attracts boaters and visitors.

- **Population:** 46,954.
- **Michelin Map:** p369.
- **Info:** 242-352-6909 or 800-448-3386 (US); www.grandbahama.bahamas.com.
- **Location:** The main resorts, shopping, casinos, and other commericial businesses and activities are clustered in the Freeport/Lucaya area.
- **Parking:** Street parking available but Freeport is packed.
- **Don't Miss:** The International Bazaar.
- **Timing:** Spend a half-day in Freeport to browse shops, then head to the beach.
- **Kids:** Sign up for a dolphin encounter program with the Underwater Explorers Society in Port Lucaya.

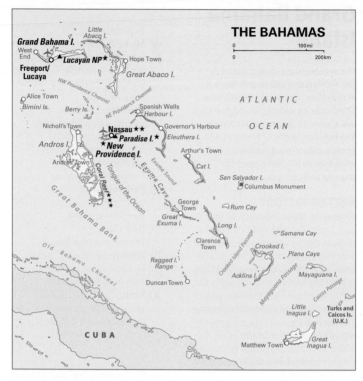

THE BAHAMAS

International Bazaar
Intersection of W. Sunrise Hwy. and E. Mall Dr. ⏰*Open year-round Mon–Sat 9:30am–5:30pm, Sun hours vary.* *www.grand-bahama.com/bazaar.htm.* This ten-acre maze of shops, fronted by a landmark *torii* (a Japanese ceremonial gate), was designed by American special-effects artist Charles Perrin. The architecture of some-90 shops and eateries, as well as their themes and merchandise, reflect the motifs of 25 different countries. Peek behind the scenes at the **Perfume Factory**, where you can tour the facilities and mix your own personal fragrance, or watch jewelers at work at Paris in the Bahamas. A local **straw market** behind the bazaar sells African-inspired textile items and other souvenirs.

Rand Nature Centre★
E. Settlers Way. ⏰*Open year-round Mon–Fri 9am–4:30pm.* ⏰*Closed major holidays.* ☎$5. 🅿 ☎242-352-5438. *www.bnt.bs/parks_rand.php.*

This 100-acre nature preserve was established in 1969 by Dorothy Rand in memory of her husband, James Henry Rand, an American inventor and founder of the Remington Rand Corp. A half-mile trail rambles through the varied native and introduced flora, with a rich display of orchids, pines and palms. At the trail's end a large pond provides habitat for flamingos, herons, egrets and other waterbirds.

LUCAYA AND EAST END
Comprising a small open-air mall of souvenir shops and restaurants overlooking Bell Channel Bay, **Port Lucaya** *(south end of Seahorse Rd.)* is the base for the **Underwater Explorers Society (UNEXSO)** which runs scuba-diving and **dolphin interaction** programs. The open-ocean dolphin swim is very popular (⏰*departs year-round daily;* ☎*$169, observers $75;* ☎*242-373-1244 or 800-992-3483; www.unexso.com; reservations required; swimmers must be at least 55in/140cm tall).* Participants take a

20min boat ride east along the coast to sheltered Sanctuary Bay, home of more than a dozen Atlantic bottlenose dolphins. After an introduction to dolphin behavior, guests are allowed to swim and also interact in certain ways with the dolphins, spending around 20–25min in the water.

Across Seahorse Road, several large hotels rise along popular **Lucayan Beach**, which is great for watersports, from snorkeling to parasailing.

Port Lucaya Marketplace, is a picturesque 12-acre waterfront complex of shopping—the Straw Market here is one of the largest in the Caribbean — restaurants and bars, and is also home to Count Basie Square, featuring dancing and live entertainment by local bands nightly.

East of Port Lucaya, **Taino Beach** is an idyllic strand of soft white sand, generally quiet and uncrowded, despite the presence of resorts and clubs *(from Port Lucaya, take Midshipman Rd. east to W. Beach Rd.).*

The virtually undeveloped 60mi stretch of island between Lucaya and McLean's Town on the far eastern tip is blessed with spectacular, deserted beaches along its southern edge.

Grand Bahama Highway follows the coastline here, cutting through Lucayan National Park and through scrub pine forests that obstruct views of the ocean. The isolation of this area is broken only momentarily by the tiny hamlets of Free Town, High Rock, Pelican Point, Rocky Creek and, finally, McLean's Town.

Lucayan National Park★

On Grand Bahama Hwy., 26mi east of Freeport. ○*Open year-round daily 9am–4pm.* $3. 242-352-5438.

Watered by Gold Rock Creek, this park has one of the longest underwater cave systems in the world (diving in the caves is allowed in specified areas only and by special permission from UNEXSO; *see p368*). and also one of the best beaches on the island. On the north side of the road, a park trail *(.3mi)* leads past two limestone caverns. In 1986 explorers found the skeletal remains of Lucayan Indians in **Burial Mound Cave.**

On the south side of the park *(across the street from parking lot)* a half-mile trail loops through a lush mangrove marsh and leads to the oceanfront. Here the island's second-highest coastal dunes—13ft—are dotted by palms, casuarinas, sea grapes and other tropical vegetation. Beyond the dunes lies **Gold Rock Beach**; named for the limestone formation that juts out of the sea offshore and takes on a golden hue at sunset.

Port Lucaya Market Place Grand Bahama,

© Bahamas Tourist Office

INDEX

A

Accidents and Emergencies...........34
Accommodations 34
Adams-Onís Treaty 59, 154
Adams Street Commons 224
Adventureland 196
Ah-Tha-Thi-Ki Museum 247
Air Travel..........................31
Alexander Springs...................133
Allen, Hervey.......................71
Alligators 92
Amelia Island 147
   Centre Street Historic District........... 148
   Museum of History.....................148
   Plantation 147
American Alligator 88
American Crocodile 88
Anastasia Island 163
Anastasia SP 163
Ancient Spanish Monastery......... 266
Anheuser-Busch Brewery 146
Anhinga 88
Animals............................77
Anna Maria Island 313
Ann Norton Sculpture Gardens...... 290
Antiques...........................24
Apalachicola 210
Apalachicola River Bluffs.............73
Appleton Museum of Art 132
Ardastra Gardens and Zoo 364
Art 64
Art Deco 69, 278, 279
Art Deco Historic District,
   Miami Beach 277
Arthur R. Marshall Loxahatchee
   National Wildlife Refuge 241
Astronaut Hall of Fame 328
Atlantic Beach......................141
Atlantis, The 254
Audubon House....................113
Audubon, John James 113
Avilés, Pedro Menéndez de 52, 59,
   146, 152

B

Baer Capitman, Barbara............. 277
Bahama House 115
Bahama Houses 109
Bahamas, The 7, 356
Bahia Honda State Park 104
Bailey-Matthews Shell Museum..... 302
Barkley House......................218
Barnacle State HP 263

Barnum & Bailey Circus 306, 308
Barrier Islands, Sarasota 313
Barron Collier 92
Bartlett, Frederic Clay............... 246
Bartram, John.......................70
Basic Information 38
Bass Museum of Art 282
Bathtub Reef Beach 354
Bayshore Boulevard 341
Bayside Marketplace 253
Bicentenial Park, Miami............. 252
Big Cypress
   National Preserve 93
   Swamp 93
Big Cypress Bend....................93
Big Lagoon State Park 221
Big Talbot Island.....................147
Bike Week..........................138
Biking 11
Bill Baggs Cape Florida State Park ... 265
Biltmore Hotel 258, 287
Biscayne Aquifer 77
Biscayne NP...................... 269
Bishop, Elizabeth....................71
Black Archives Research Center
   and Museum 228
Black Point Wildlife Drive 329
Blue Hole 104
Boating 15
Boca Grande 298
Boca Raton........................ 238
Boca Raton Historical Society 238
Boca Raton Resort & Club........... 240
Boggy Creek Airboat Park...........167
Bok, Edward William............... 168
Bonefishing........................ 105
Bonnet House..................... 246
Books.............................26
Breakers, The...................... 286
Brevard Museum of History and
   Natural Science................... 327
Brickell Avenue 254
Brickell, William and Mary 248
British Period, The 53
Broward, Napoleon..................82
Buffett, Jimmy 65
Bureau de Change...................39
Burrall Hoffman Jr., F. 261
Burroughs Home 298
Busch Gardens Tampa Bay 343
Business Hours......................38
Bus Travel 32, 34
Butterfly World.................246, 247

C

Cabbage Key............................ 304
Cable Beach............................ 365
Caboto, Giovanni........................52
Cà d'Zan............................... 309
Caladesi Island State Park........... 332
Calendar of Events 27
Calhoun Street Historic District...... 227
Calusa Indians..........................82
Calusa Nature Center and
     Planetarium....................... 298
Camp Minnie-Mickey................ 202
Canoeing 21
Canopy Roads......................... 229
Capitol Complex 225
Capone, Al 277
Captiva Island........................ 302
Car Rental.............................33
Car Travel 32
Casa Casuarina 278
Casa Marina Hotel 106
Casements, The 139
Castillo de San Marcos NM 156
Cathedral-Basilica of St. Augustine ...157
Cayo Costa............................ 304
Cayo Hueso 106
Cayo Largo............................101
Cedar Key.............................125
Cedar Keys NWR.......................125
Centerville Road 229
Central Highlands 74
Chalfin, Paul 261
Challenger Learning Center of
     Tallahassee....................... 225
Chapel of St. Bernard de Clairvaux... 267
Charles Hosmer Morse Museum of
     American Art, Orlando 175
Chestnut Street Cemetery,
     Apalachicola 211
Children 23
Chokoloskee Bay 92
Christ Church Cathedral,
     New Providence Island........... 360
Circus Museum........................310
CityPlace, W. Palm Beach 289
Cleveland Fibre Factory..............143
Climate 75
Coalson Plantation 232
Coastal Lowlands......................74
Cocoa................................. 326
Coconut Grove 260
CocoWalk, Miami..................... 263
Collier, Barron G. 299

Collier-Seminole SP................. 301
Collins Avenue 283
Collins, John C........................275
Collins Park 282
Columbus, Christopher 357
Columns, The 226
Conch Houses.................. 67, 109
Conch Republic, The.................107
Conservancy Nature Center, Naples . 300
Consulates............................30
Cooper, James Fenimore...............70
Coral Castle 268
Coral Gables 255
Coral Way............................ 257
Corkscrew Swamp Sanctuary 301
Courthouse Square...................129
Cracker Cooking.......................49
Cracker Creek Canoeing 139
Cracker house.........................67
Crafts.................................24
Crane, Stephen........................70
Credit Cards..........................39
Cruises...............................17
Crystal River.........................126
Crystal River Archaeological SP 126
Cuban Memorial Plaza............... 254
Cummer Museum of Art and Gardens .143
Cunningham, Earl 174
Currency Exchange....................39
Curry Mansion Inn....................114
Customs Regulations 30

D

Dade County Pine 90
Dalí, Salvador 337
Davis, Robert S. 215
Daytona 200 138
Daytona 500 138
Daytona Beach 136
     Boardwalk and Main Street Pier......... 137
Daytona International Speedway.....138
Daytona USA.........................139
Deering, James.......................261
Delnor-Wiggins Pass SP............. 301
Demens, Peter 335
Destin 212
Devil's Millhopper Geological SP 130
DinoLand USA 203
Discovery Cove.......................183
Discovery Island..................... 201
Disney MGM Studios................ 204
Disney's Animal Kingdom........... 201
Disney, Walt................... 171, 192

INDEX

Disston, Hamilton 56, 60, 166
Dixie Highway. 275
Dodecanese Boulevard North 350
Dorr House, Pensacola. 217
Douglas, Marjory Stoneman . . .63, 71, 83
Downtown Disney. 194
Driving 38
Driving Tours. .10
 Bahamas
  New Providence Island 364
 Everglades National Park
  Southern Everglades Driving Tour 86
 Naples. 299
Dr. Samuel Mudd. 118
Dry Tortugas National Park 119, 121
Duval Street. 111

E

East Everglades Expansion Act 83
East Martello Museum. 120
Eating Out 37
Economy. 44
Edison Ford Winter Estates. 295
Edison's Home 296
Edison, Thomas Alva. 295
El Crédito Cigar Factory 255
Electricity. 39
Embassies 30
Emerald Coast. 212
Emergencies 39
Energy Encounter 353
Entertainment .22
Entry Requirements 29
EPCOT Center 196
Episcopal Church of Bethesda-by-
 the-Sea 285
Ernest F. Coe Visitor Center,
 Everglades 86
Ernest Hemingway Home and
 Museum, Key West. 120
Estefan, Gloria 65
Everglades City. .92
Everglades Forever Act 63, 83
Everglades National Park 61
Everglades, The 6, 75
Expeditions 17
Eyebrow Houses 109

F

Fairchild Tropical Garden 260
Fakahatchee Strand Preserve
 State Park 93
Falling Waters State Park. 213

Fantasyland. 193
Fauna. 77
Federal Courthouse 226
Ferguson, Amos. .361
Fernandina Beach 148
Films 26
Fire, The Great, Jacksonville. 143
First Presbyterian Church,
 Tallahassee. 226
Fisher, Carl 275
Fisher, Mel 113
Fishing 12
Flagler College 158
Flagler, Henry Morrison. . . 56, 60, 94, 155
  159, 236, 248, 284, 287
Flagler Museum 287
Flagler's Folly 94
Flamingo 90
Flamingo Crossing. 115
Flamingo Gardens. 247
Flatwoods 77
Flights 31
Flora and Fauna 77
Florida Aquarium. 342
Florida Botanical Gardens. 332
Florida East Coast Railway . . 56, 236, 248
Florida Governor's Mansion 227
Florida International Museum. 335
Florida Keys NMS. 96
Florida Museum of Natural History . . .130
Floridan Aquifer. .77
Florida National Scenic Trail. 93
Florida Oceanographic Society
 Coastal Center. 354
Florida Panther. 89
Florida Plateau 72
Florida Reef 96
Florida Slash Pine 90
Food and Wine. 49
Ford's Home 296
Fort Caroline. 146
Fort Caroline National Memorial 146
Fort Charlotte. 364
Fort Clinch State Park. 148
Fort Dallas 248
Fort De Soto Park. 338
Fort Fincastle 363
Fort Foster 345
Fort George Island. 147
Fort Jefferson 118, 121
Fort Lauderdale .242
Fort Lauderdale Museum of Art 243
Fort Lauderdale Strip 243

Fort Matanzas National Monument ..163
Fort Montagu 364
Fort Myers 295
Fort Pickens......................... 221
Fort Pierce 353
Fort Pierce Inlet State Park 353
Fort Zachary Taylor HSP 119
Foster, Stephen Collins 65
Fountain of Youth
    Archaeological Park...............162
Freedom Tower, Miami 253
Frontierland 195
Frost, Robert.........................71
Fruit 50
Fruit & Spice Park, Homestead 269
Future World........................ 196

G

Gainesville.....................129
    Northeast Historic District 129
Gambier Village 365
Gasparilla Island SP 298
Gator Club, The.....................312
Gator Farm..........................158
Gator Jumping 167
Gatorland...........................167
Geology 72
Getting There and Getting Around. 32, 34
Gilbert's Bar House of Refuge 354
Glackens, William 244
Gold Coast Railroad Museum 268
Golf 13
Gonzalez-Alvarez House.............161
Goodwood Museum & Gardens 230
Government House, Nassau......... 360
Government House Museum,
    St. Augustine 158
Grand Bahama Island
    Freeport 367
    Lucaya and East End.................... 368
Graycliff............................359
Grayton Beach State Park 215
Greater Miami North 266
Great White Heron NWR 114
Greek Revival style 67
Green Meadows Farm 167
Groves, Wallace 367
Gulfarium..........................212
Gulf Islands National Seashore .. 209, 221
Gulf World Marine Park 214
Gumbo Limbo Nature Center 240
Gumbo Limbo Trail 87
G. Wiz 312

H

Halifax Historical Society
    and Museum 138
Hardwood hammocks................77
Harry P. Leu Gardens...............174
Harry S. Truman Little White
    House Museum...................113
Hawksbill Agreement, The.......... 367
Heade, Martin Johnson 64
Health 30
Heartworks Gallery................. 144
Hemingway, Ernest..........71, 106, 116
Henry B. Plant Museum............. 340
Hiking 13
Hillsborough River State Park 345
Historical Museum of
    Southern Florida................. 253
Historic Smallwood Store 93
Historic Spanish Point, Sarasota 315
History
    20C 57
    British Period 1763-1783 53
    Civil War and Reconstruction 56
    Early Settlement and the Seminole Wars . 55
    First Spanish Period 1513-1763 52
    Florida Today 58
    Prehistoric and Native Floridians......... 51
    Second Spanish Period 1784-1821........ 54
Hobe Sound National
    Wildlife Refuge 355
Holocaust Memorial, Miami Beach .. 282
Homosassa Springs Wildlife SP.......126
Honeymoon Island State Park....... 332
Horowitz, Leonard 277
Horseback Riding 16
Hotel Alcazar, The 159
Hotel and motel chains 35
Hugh Taylor Birch State Park 246
Hunting............................16
Hunt, William Morris................64
Hurricanes 14, 76
Hurston, Zora Neale 71
Hutchinson Island 354
Hyde Park.......................... 340

I

IGFA World Fishing Hall 246
Imperial, The....................... 254
Indian Removal Act, The 60
Indian River Drive 353
Industry 44
Inland Panhandle 212
Inness, George Jr..................... 350

INDEX

International Bazaar 368
International Drive 174
International Museum of Cartoon Art 238
International Style. 69
International Visitors 29
Irving, Washington 70
Islamorada 102, 103

J

Jack C. Watson Wildlife Trail 104
Jackie Gleason Theater of the
     Performing Arts 282
Jacksonville 140
     Beaches 141
     Jacksonville Landing 141
     Museum of Modern Art. 141
     North. 141
     Riverside/Avondale Historic District. . . 143
     Riverwalk. 144
     South. 144
     Zoo. 145
J.N. Darling NWR 303
John and Mable Ringling Museum
     of Art 307
John D. MacArthur Beach SP 292
John Pennekamp Coral Reef SP 101
Johnson, James Weldon 71
John U. Lloyd Beach State Park 246
Jonathan Dickinson State Park 355
Julee Cottage 217
Juniper Springs .133
Jupiter. 355
Jupiter Inlet Lighthouse 355

K

Kampong, The 264
Kathryn Abbey Hanna Park 141
Kennedy Space Center. 322
Key Biscayne 265
Key Deer 105
Key Largo 101
Key Largo NMS 96
Key Lime Pie 50
Key Lime Products. 98
Key Limes 117
Keys, The 6
Key West 106
     Aquarium. 112
     Cemetery 120
     Lighthouse Museum 120
     Museum of Art and History 112
Key West Key Lime Pie Co. 112
Kids 23

Kissimmee 166
Knott House Museum 226
Koreshan State HS 298

L

Lafayette Park. 211
Lake Eola Park. 172
Lake Okeechobee 77
Lakeridge Winery 174
Lake Tohopekaliga 167
Lanier, Sydney 70
Lapham-Patterson House. 231
Lapidus, Morris. .69
Latin Quarter. 254
Laudonnière, René de 146
Lavalle House 217
León, Juan Ponce de. 52, 59, 106, 333
Liberty Square 195
Lido Key, Sarasota 314
Lightner Museum 158
Lightner, Otto C.. 159
Lincoln Road Mall 281
Lion Country Safari 292
Liquor Laws. 39
Literature 70
Little Havana. 254
Loggerhead Marinelife Center,
     Juno Beach. 355
Long Key SP 103
     Dolphin Research Center 103
Lovers Key SP 298
Lowe Art Museum. 260
Lower Keys. 104
Loxahatchee National
     Wildlife Refuge 241
Lucayans, The. 357
Lummus, John and James. 275
Luna, Tristán de 52, 59, 208

M

MacDonald, John D. 71
Maclay Gardens State Park 228
Magic Kingdom 189
Mahogany Hammock. 90
Mail 39
Main Street USA, Walt Disney
     World® Resort 189
Mallory Square 112
Manatee 125
Mangroves. 78
Marathon 102, 103
Margaritaville Cafe 115
Marianna Lowlands 73

Marie Selby Botanical Gardens 313
Marjorie Kinnan Rawlings
    Historic SP. 127, 131
Martí, José 106, 117
Mary Brogan Museum of Art
    and Science, Tallahassee 224
Mary McLeod Bethune Foundation. . .139
Máximo Gómez Park 254
McGregor Boulevard 295
Measurements 40
Mediterranean Revival Style 67
Mel Fisher Maritime Heritage Society. 113
Menéndez de Avilés, Pedro 248
Mennello Museum of American
    Folk Art, Orlando 174
Meridian Road 229
Merrick, George 259
Merrick House. 258
Merritt Island National
    Wildlife Refuge 329
Miami 248
Miami Art Museum 253
Miami Beach 275
Miami City Hall. 262
Miami Metrozoo. 267
Miami Museum of Science & Space
    Transit Planetarium 262
Miami Seaquarium 265
Micanopy 131
Miccosukee Indian Village 91
Miccosukee Road. 229
Mickey's Toontown Fair. 193
Middle Keys. 102, 103
Middleton Munroe, Ralph. 263
Mile-Marker (MM) System, Miami 95
Millionaires' Row, Miami 254
Miracle Mile, Miami. 257
Mission de Nombre de Dios 162
Missions 53
Mission San Luis. 228
Mizner, Addison. 239, 285
Money. 39
Moran, Thomas .64
Morikami Museum and
    Japanese Gardens 241
Motels 35
Motor Sports. 17
Moyne, Jacques Le 52, 146
Mrazek Pond. 90
Museum of Art, Fort Lauderdale. 243
Museum of Arts and Sciences,
    Daytona Beach 138
Museum of Commerce, Pensacola. . . .216

Museum of Contemporary Art, Miami 266
Museum of Discovery and Science,
    Fort Lauderdale 245
Museum of Florida History,
    Tallahassee. 227
Museum of Industry, Pensacola 217
Museum of Man in the Sea,
    Panama City Beach 215

N

Nancy Forrester's Secret Garden 115
Naples. 299
Naples Museum of Art 301
Narváez, Pánfilo de. 52, 59
NASA missions 322
Nassau. 358
Nassau Public Library. 362
National Historical Museum,
    New Providence Island. 363
National Key Deer Refuge. 104
National Monuments. 11
National Parks. 11
Natural Bridge, Battle of 60
Nature. 72
Nature and Safety 14
Nature Coast 6
Naval Live Oaks Reserve 220
Naval Station Mayport. 147
Neptune Beach. .141
New Capitol. 225
New Providence Island
    East End 363
    West End 364
New Urbanist Movement 69
North Central Florida 6
Northeast Coast. 6
Northern Everglades 91
Northern Highlands 73
North Hill Preservation District. 219
North Tampa. 345
Norton, Ann. 290
Norton Museum of Art,
    West Palm Beach 290
Norton, Ralph H. 290

O

Ocala 132
Ocala National Forest. 127, 133
Ocean Drive. 277, 278
Oglethorpe, James 152
Old Bainbridge Road 229
Old Capitol. 225
Old Christ Church, Pensacola. 217

INDEX

Old City Cemetery, Tallahassee...... 227
Old Floresta, Boca Raton........... 238
Old Fort Lauderdale Museum
   of History 244
Old Naples........................... 300
Old St. Augustine Road, Tallahassee . 229
Olustee, Battle of......................60
Opening Hours.......................38
Orange Avenue, Orlando 170
Orlando....................... 6, 170
Orlando Museum of Art..............173
Orlando Science Center..............173
Osceola..............................60
Outdoor Fun 11
Overseas Highway.............. 94, 111
Overseas Railroad 94

P

Pa-hay-okee Overlook................90
Palafox Historic District..............219
Palm Beach 284
Palm Beach Zoo 291
Palm Trees...........................78
Panama City Beach 214
Panhandle, The 7
Papio, Stanley........................121
Paradise Island 366
Paradise Key Hammock...............87
Paramount Building, Palm Beach.... 286
Park Avenue Historic District,
   Tallahassee.................... 226
Parker Manatee Aquarium 316
Parks 11
Parliament Square................... 362
Parrot Jungle and Gardens.......... 269
Paynes Prairie Preserve SP 131
Pebble Hill Plantation 231
Pensacola............................216
Pensacola Museum of Art............219
Peppers of Key West.................111
Peter O. Knight House 340
Philippe Park........................ 332
Phipps Plaza 288
Pinelands Trail 90
Places to Stay 34
Plantation houses 67
Plantations...........................55
Plant, Henry Bradley.............56, 60
Plants................................77
Playalinda Beach 329
Pleasant Bay 366
Plymouth Congregational Church... 264

Pompey Museum,
   New Providence Island............361
Ponce de León Hotel 160
Ponce de León Inlet Lighthouse......139
Ponce de León Springs State Park 213
Ponte Vedra Beach 141
Population...........................47
Porcher House 327
Potter's Cay 359
Providencia, La...................... 284

Q

Queen Anne 67
Quina House 218

R

Racing 18
Railroad Boom, The...................56
Rand Nature Centre 368
Rauschenberg, Robert................64
Rawlings, Marjorie Kinnan 71, 131
Recreation...........................48
Recreational Vehicle (RV) Rentals......33
Red Reef Park 240
Reef 96
Reef Relief 113
Refugees 255
Regions..............................6
Rental Cars...........................33
Reptiles.............................92
Restaurants..........................37
Retreat, The........................ 364
Ribault, Jean 52, 59, 146
Ringling Bros....................306, 308
Ringling, John.......... 293, 306, 308
Ritz-Carlton, The 147
Road Regulations 33
Rod and Gun Club 92
Rogers, Woodes..................... 357
Royal Palm Hotel 249
Royal Palm SP 82, 87
Royal Victoria Hotel 362
Rubens, Peter Paul 308

S

Safety 14
Safety, Storm........................11
Sailing 15
Salt Springs 133
Salvador Dalí Museum.............. 336
Samuel P. Harn Museum of Art,
   Gainsville 130
San Carlos Institute..................117

Sanchez, Mario........................121
Sand Key Park........................331
Sanford L. Ziff Jewish Museum
      of Florida........................ 279
Sanibel Island 302
Sanibel Stoop 305
San Marcos, Castillo de 59
Sawgrass Lake Park................. 334
Scuba Diving..........................22
Seabreeze United Church...........138
Sea Islands, The 147
Seaside 215
Sea Turtles 354
SeaWorld Orlando................. 180
Seminole Wars, The 55, 59
Senior Citizens 31
Seven-Mile Bridge...................103
Seville Historic District..............216
Shark Valley...........................91
Shell Factory 296
Shell Island 215
Shopping............................24
Siesta Key...........................314
Sinkholes 73
Smoking...............................39
Snail Kite............................89
Snakes................................92
Snorkeling 22
Society of the Four Arts............. 288
Solomon's Castle, Sarasota...........316
Soto, Hernando de 52, 59
South Beach 275
Southernmost House, Key West 121
Southern-Style Cooking 230
South Florida 7
South Florida Museum 316
South Florida Railway, The 166
South Florida Rockland..............75
South Florida Science Museum...... 291
South Miami-Dade County.......... 267
Southwest Coast 7, 293
Southwest Florida Museum
      of History 298
Souvenirs............................24
Space Coast......................7, 321
Spanish-American War, The........57, 61
Spanish Military Hospital 161
Spanish Period, The 54
Spanish River Park...................241
Springfield Historic District 143
Springs 349
St. Andrews State Park...............214
St. Armands Key.....................314

State and Local Parks 11
St. Augustine....................152
   Castillo and St. George Street 154
   Colonial Spanish Quarter 157
   King Street................................ 158
   Lighthouse and Museum 163
   Old City Gate............................. 156
   Old Jail 162
   San Marco Avenue 162
Steamboat Age, The 56
Stevens, Wallace 71
St. George Island State Park.........211
St. John's Cemetery................. 227
St. Lucie County Regional
      History Cente.................... 353
St. Marks Lighthouse and
      National Wildlife Refuge 231
St. Michael's Cemetery, Pensacola 218
Stowe, Harriet Beecher 70, 140
St. Paul's Episcopal Church...........117
St. Petersburg 334
St. Petersburg Beach 338
Straw Market........................361
Streamline Moderne style 277
St. Vincent Island 211
Sunken Gardens.................... 338

T

Tallahassee 222
Tallahassee Hills......................73
Tallahassee Museum of History
      and Natural Science.............. 228
Tamiami Trail..........................82
Tampa 339
Tampa Bay 7
Tampa Bay Hotel 338, 340
Tarpon.............................. 349
Tarpon Springs 332
Taxes and Tips.......................39
Teatro Martí, Miami................. 255
Telephones 40
Temperature 10, 40
Templo Adventista del Septimo Dia,
      Miami............................ 255
Theater of the Sea, Windley Key......102
The Strip, Fort Lauderdale 243
Thunderstorms and Lightning 15
Tiffany, Louis Comfort 175
Time Line 59
Time Zone 40
Tips..................................39
Titusville............................ 328
Tomorrowland 191

INDEX

Topography............................72
Torreya State Park 213
Tourism Offices.......................29
Tranahan House....................242
Traveler's Checks 39
Treasure Coast 7
Treaty of Payne's Landing, The 60
Trinity Episcopal Church,
    Apalachicola 211
Tropical Crane Point Hammock......103
Truman, Harry S 113
T.T. Wentworth Jr. Florida State
    Museum, Pensacola..............218
Tuttle, Julia 248
Twentieth Century, The 57
Typhoon Lagoon 194

U

UDT-SEAL Museum 353
Uelsmann, Jerry 64
Union Bank Building, Tallahassee.... 226
Universal Citywalk 188
Universal Orlando 184
Universal's Islands of Adventure..... 186
Universal Studios Florida 184
University of Florida 129

V

Venetian Pool, Miami 258
Veterans Memorial Park, Pensacola...219
Villa Jacaranda, New Providence
    Island 362
Villa Regina, Miami 254
Visitor Impact 14
Vizcaya 261

W

Wakulla Springs State Park.......... 230
Walking Tours
    Bahamas
        Old Town 359
    Key West
        Old Town 111

Walt Disney World® Resort.......... 189
Warm Mineral Springs 317
Warner House, Miami................ 255
Washington Avenue, Miami Beach .. 281
Water Resources 77
Water Sports 21
Way Key 125
Websites.............................10
Weeki Wachee Spring 126
Wekiwa Springs SP 176
Western Highlands 73
West Lake Trail 90
West Martello Tower..................121
West Palm Beach 289
When and Where to Go...............10
Wilderness Waterway 93
Wild Waters.........................133
Williams, Hiram 64
Williams, John C. 335
Williams, Tennessee 71
Wolfsonian-FIU, The 281
Woodes Rogers Walk 361
Woodlawn Park Cemetery 254
World Golf Village and Hall of Fame ..163
World Showcase 198
World War II......................57, 61
Worth Avenue...................... 289

X
Ximenez-Fatio House................161

Y
Ybor City............................ 342
Ybor, Vicente Martínez 339
Yulee, David........................ 148

🏨 STAY

Anna Maria Island
Cedar Cove Resort & Cottages 318
Bal Harbour
Sea View Hotel 271
Bay Lake
Disney's Animal Kingdom Lodge 177
Bokeelia
Bokeelia Tarpon Inn 317
Camino Real
Boca Raton Resort & Club 270
Captiva Island
Jensen's Twin Palms Cottages 318
'Tween Waters Inn 318
Coral Gables
Biltmore Hotel 270
Hotel Place St. Michel 271
Duck Key
Hawk's Cay Resort 98
Everglade City
Ivey House and Everglades Spa
& Lodge 85
Fort Lauderdale
Pillars, The 271
Fort Myers
Sanibel Harbour Resort & Spa 317
Homestead
Redland Hotel 85
Islamorada
Casa Morada 98
Cheeca Lodge 97
Jacksonville
Daytona Beach
Cabana Colony Cottages 149
Fernandina Beach
Amelia Island Williams House 149
Flagler Beach
White Orchid, The 150
House On Cherry Street 150
New Smyrna Beach
Riverview Hotel 150
Ponte Vedra Beach
Lodge & Club, The 149
Key Largo
Jules' Undersea Lodge 98
Kona Kai Resort 98
Largo Lodge 98
Key West
Ambrosia House 122
Casa Marina Resort 122
Gardens Hotel 122
Hotel Marquesa 122
Island City House Hotel 122

Key West Hostel & Seashell Motel 123
Popular House/Key West B&B 122
Simonton Court 122
Speakeasy Inn 123
Lake Buena Vista
Disney's Grand Floridian Resort & Spa . 176
Lauderdale-By-The-Sea
A Little Inn By The Sea 271
Longboat Key
Resort at Longboat Key Club 318
Miami
Miami River Inn 271
Miami Beach
Delano 270
Hotel, The 271
Naples
Hotel Escalante 317
New Providence Island
Graycliff 359
Orlando
Courtyard at Lake Lucerne, The 178
Peabody Orlando, The 177
Portofino Bay Hotel 177
Renaissance Orlando Resort 177
Palm Beach
Breakers, The 270
Chesterfield, The 270
Pompano Beach
Cap's Place 272
Sanibel Island
Sunshine Island Inn 318
Sarasota
Ritz Carlton 317
The Cypress 318
Tides Inn Motel 319
South Beach
Clay Hotel, The 272
St. Augustine
Casa Monica Hotel 150
St. Francis Inn 150
Tampa
Behind the Fence B&B 347
Belleview Biltmore Resort & Spa 346
Don CeSar Beach Resort and Spa 346
Don Vicente de Ybor Historic Inn 346
Mansion House B&B and the
Courtyard on Fifth 346
Renaissance Vinoy Resort 346
Saddlebrook Resort 346
Safety Harbor Resort and Spa 346
Seahorse Cottages and Apts. 347

INDEX

⍭ EAT

Anna Maria Island
Beach Bistro 319

Captiva Island
RC Otters 320

Fort Lauderdale
Floridian Restaurant, The 273
Mai-Kai 273

Fort Myers
The Dock 319, 320
The Veranda 319

Jacksonville
Fernandina Beach
Beech Street Grill. 150
Matthew's 151
Ormond Beach
La Crepe en Haut. 150

Key West
A&B Lobster House. 123
Alonzo's Oyster Bar. 123
El Siboney 123
Louie's Backyard 123
Mangia Mangia 123
Mangoes 123
Pepe's Café 123
Rick's Blue Heaven 123
Seven Fish 123

Lake Buena Vista
Artist Point 178
San Angel Inn 179
Victoria and Albert's 178
Wolfgang Puck's Cafe 179

Little Havana
Versailles Restaurant 273

Longboat Key
Café on the Bay 319
Moore's Stone Crab Restaurant 320

Mandarin
Clark's Fish Camp 150

Miami
Tobacco Road. 274

Miami Beach
Blue Door Restaurant. 270
El Rancho Grande 273
Forge, The 272
Joe's Stone Crab. 272
Wish. 271

Naples
Bistro 821 319

Orlando
Chatham's Place. 178
Emeril's. 178
Le Coq au Vin 178
White Wolf Cafe. 179

Palm Beach
Café L'Europe 272
Hamburger Heaven 273

San Marco
bb's 151

Sarasota
Bangkok. 319
Old Salty Dog 320

St. Augustine
Columbia 151
Cortessés Bistro 151
Creekside Dinery. 151

Tampa
Bern's Steak House 347
Chateau France 347
Columbia 347
Hurricane Seafood Restaurant 347
Mise en Place 347
Mykonos. 348
Salt Rock Grill 348
SideBern's 348
Skipper's Smokehouse Restaurant 348

Venice
Sharky's on the Pier 320

MAPS AND PLANS

THEMATIC MAPS

Principal Sights........ Inside front cover
Driving Tours.......... Inside back cover

MAPS

The Everglades
Southern Everglades 87
Florida Keys....................... 96-97
Key West.............................110
Nature Coast
Nature Coast.........................124
North Central Florida
North Central Florida 128
Gainesville..........................130
Northeast Coast
Northeast Coast......................135
Daytona Beach.......................137
Jacksonville...................... 144-45
St. Augustine........................153
Orlando Area
Orlando Area........................165
Orlando.............................171
Walt Disney World® Resort 191
The Panhandle
The Panhandle 208-209
Pensacola...........................217
Tallahassee 223
South Florida
South Florida 237

Boca Raton......................... 239
Fort Lauderdale 244
Miami 249
Downtown Miami 252
Little Havana, Coral Gables,
    Coconut Grove................ 256-257
South Beach 280
Palm Beach 286
West Palm Beach 291
Southwest Coast
Southwest Coast 294
Fort Myers, Sanibel and Captiva. 296-297
Naples............................. 300
Sanibel and Captiva Islands 302
Sarasota 310-311
Space Coast
Space Coast.........................321
Tampa Bay Area
Tampa Bay Area 330
St. Petersburg 335
Tampa 340
Ybor City........................... 343
Treasure Coast
Treasure Coast 352
The Bahamas
Nassau..............................359
New Providence Island 362-363
The Bahamas........................ 368

COMPANION PUBLICATIONS

MAP 492 EASTERN USA AND EASTERN CANADA

Large-format map providing detailed road systems; includes driving distances, interstate rest stops, border crossings and interchanges.

◆ Comprehensive city and town index
◆ Scale: 1:2,400,000 (1 inch = approx. 38 miles)

MAP 930 USA ROAD MAP

Covers principal US road network while also presenting shaded relief detail of overall physiography of the land.

◆ State flags with statistical data and state tourism office telephone numbers
◆ Scale: 1:3,450,000 (1 inch = approx. 55 miles)

MAP LEGEND

	Sights	Beaches
Highly recommended	★★★	≋≋≋
Recommended	★★	≋≋
Interesting	★	≋

Sight symbols

▭─◉───────	Recommended itineraries with departure point			
⌂ ⁀	Church, chapel		▭	Building described
o	Town described		▭	Other building
B	Letter locating a sight		▪	Small building, statue
▪ ▲	Other points of interest		⊚ ⁂	Fountain – Ruins
⚒ ⌒	Mine – Cave		🛈	Visitor information
🗼 ⚓	Windmill – Lighthouse		⬌ ⚓	Ship – Shipwreck
☆ ⛪	Fort – Mission		☀ ⚐	Panorama – View

Other symbols

🛡 Interstate highway		🛡 US highway		🛡 Other route
Highway, bridge			Major city thoroughfare	
Toll highway, interchange			City street with median	
Divided highway			One-way street	
Major, minor route			Tunnel – Pedestrian street	
18 Distance in miles			Steps – Gate	
2149 Pass (elevation in feet)			P ✉ Parking – Main post office	
△ 6288 Mtn. peak (elevation in feet)			🚉 🚌 Train station – Bus station	
✈ ✈ Airport – Airfield			Cemetery	
⛴ Ferry: Cars and passengers			Swamp	
⛴ Ferry: Passengers only			International boundary	
⇤ ⇠ Waterfall – Lock – Dam			State boundary	
🍷 Winery			● Subway station	

Recreation

▪-o-o-o-o-▪ Gondola, chairlift			Park, garden, wooded area
⛵ ⚓ Harbor, lake cruise – Marina		🌐	Wildlife reserve
⚑ Golf Course		🐾	Zoo
⬭ Stadium		– – – – –	Walking path, trail

Abbreviations

NP	National Park	SP	State Park	NS	National Seashore		
NF	National Forest	SF	State Forest	SRA	State Recreational Area		
NM	National Monument	SHS	State Historic Site	NWR	National Wildlife Reserve		
NMem	National Memorial	SPres	State Preserve	NMS	National Marine Sanctuary		
		SAS	State Archaeological Site				

Symbols specific to this guide

··········· Intracoastal Waterway

All maps are oriented north, unless otherwise indicated by a directional arrow.

You know
the Green Guide

...Do you really
know MICHELIN?

• Data 31/12/2009

MICHELIN
A better way forward

The world No.1 in tires with 16.3% of the market

A business presence in over **170 countries**

A manufacturing footprint
at the heart of markets

In 2009 **72** industrial sites in **19** countries produced:

- **150** million tires
- **10** million maps and guides

Highly international **teams**

Over **109 200** employees* from all cultures on all continents

including **6 000** people employed in R&D centers

in Europe, the US and Asia.

*102 692 full-time equivalent staff

The Michelin Group
at a glance

Michelin competes

At the end of 2009

- **Le Mans 24-hour race**
  12 consecutive years of victories

- **Endurance 2009**
  - 6 victories on 6 stages
  in Le Mans Series
  - 12 victories on 12 stages
  in American Le Mans Series

- **Paris-Dakar**
  Since the beginning of the event,
  the Michelin group has won
  in all categories

- **Moto endurance**
  2009 World Champion

- **Trial**
  Every World Champion title
  since 1981 (except 1992)

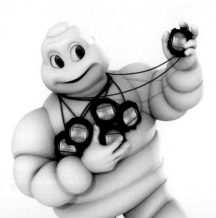

Michelin, established close to its customers

72 plants in 19 countries

- Algeria
- Brazil
- Canada
- China
- Colombia
- France
- Germany
- Hungary
- Italy
- Japan
- Mexico
- Poland
- Romania
- Russia
- Serbia
- Spain
- Thailand
- UK
- USA

A Technology Center spread over 3 continents

- Asia
- Europe
- North America

Natural rubber plantations

- Brazil

Our mission

To make a sustainable contribution to progress in the mobility of goods and people by enhancing freedom of movement, safety, efficiency and the pleasure of travelling.

Michelin committed to environmental-friendliness

Michelin, world leader in low rolling resistance tires, actively reduces fuel consumption and vehicle gas emission.

For its products, Michelin develops state-of-the-art technologies in order to:
- Reduce fuel consumption, while improving overall tire performance.
- Increase life cycle to reduce the number of tires to be processed at the end of their useful lives;
- Use raw materials which have a low impact on the environment.

Furthermore, at the end of 2008, 99.5% of tire production in volume was carried out in ISO 14001* certified plants.

Michelin is committed to implementing recycling channels for end-of-life tires.

*environmental certification

**Passenger Car
Light Truck**

Truck

**Michelin
a key mobility enabler**

Earthmover

Aircraft

Agricultural

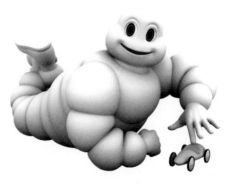

Two-wheel   **Distribution**

Partnered with vehicle manufacturers, in tune with users,
active in competition and in all the distribution channels,
Michelinis continually innovating to promote mobility today
and to invent that of tomorrow.

Maps and   **ViaMichelin,**   **Michelin**
Guides   travel   **Lifestyle,**
                    assistance   for your travel
                    services   accessories

MICHELIN
plays on balanced performance

- ● **Long tire life**
- ● **Fuel savings**
- ○ **Safety on the road**

... MICHELIN tires provide you with the best performance, without making a single sacrifice.

The MICHELIN tire pure technology

1 Tread
A thick layer of rubber provides contact with the ground. It has to channel water away and last as long as possible.

2 Crown plies
This double or triple reinforced belt has both vertical flexibility and high lateral rigidity. It provides the steering capacity.

3 Sidewalls
These cover and protect the textile casing whose role is to attach the tire tread to the wheel rim.

4 Bead area for attachment to the rim
Its internal bead wire clamps the tire firmly against the wheel rim.

5 Inner liner
This makes the tire almost totally impermeable and maintains the correct inflation pressure.

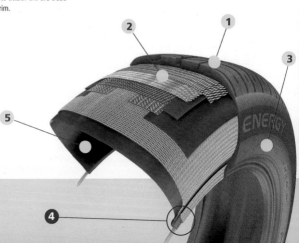

Heed
the MICHELIN Man's advice

To improve safety:
- I drive with the correct tire pressure
- I check the tire pressure every month
- I have my car regularly serviced
- I regularly check the appearance

  of my tires (wear, deformation)
- I am responsive behind the wheel
- I change my tires according to the season

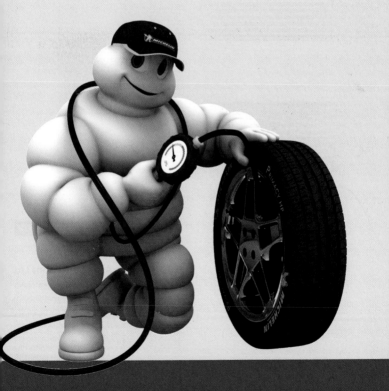

www.michelin.com
www.michelin.(your country extension – e.g. .fr for France)

Michelin Apa Publications Ltd

A joint venture between Michelin and Langenscheidt

58 Borough High Street, London SE1 1XF, United Kingdom

No part of this publication may be reproduced in any form
without the prior permission of the publisher.

© 2011 Michelin Apa Publications Ltd
ISBN 978-1-907099-19-9
Printed: November 2010
Printed and bound in Germany

Although the information in this guide was believed by the authors and publisher to be accurate
and current at the time of publication, they cannot accept responsibility for any inconvenience,
loss, or injury sustained by any person relying on information or advice contained in this guide.
Things change over time and travellers should take steps to verify and confirm information,
especially time-sensitive information related to prices, hours of operation, and availability.